WORLD WAR II

WORLD WAR II

A MILITARY HISTORY

ALAN WARREN

TEMPUS

First published 2008

Tempus Publishing
Cirencester Road, Chalford
Stroud, Gloucestershire, GL6 8PE
www.thehistorypress.co.uk
Tempus Publishing is an imprint of The History Press Limited

British Library Cataloguing in Publication Data.
A catalogue record for this book is available from the British Library.

ISBN 978 0 7524 4597 7

Typesetting and origination by The History Press Limited
Printed and bound in Great Britain by Ashford Colour Press Ltd,
Gosport, Hants.

Contents

Preface

On 22 June 1940 a delegation representing the French government signed an armistice with Nazi Germany conceding military defeat on the field of battle. Adolf Hitler was now at the height of his power. Soon after the end of the campaign in France, Hitler made his first and only visit to Paris, accompanied by the architect Albert Speer. A cinema photographer was present to record the event. Speer, who was thirty-five years old in 1940, had been commissioned by Hitler to rebuild Berlin. Speer had belonged to Hitler's inner circle during the heady period of the mid to late 1930s. The two men had enthusiastically studied architectural drawings for a futuristic Berlin, sometimes into the early hours of the morning. To inspire their dreaming, a model city populated by monumental ministerial buildings and great boulevards had been set up in the former exhibition rooms of the Berlin Academy of Arts.[1] Speer had been summoned to Hitler's field headquarters near Sedan for the visit to Paris, a city that had fascinated Hitler since his youth.

The aircraft carrying the party landed at Le Bourget airfield near the French capital at 5.30 a.m. on 23 June. Three large Mercedes sedans awaited them. The civilians had been dressed in field-grey uniforms to match their military colleagues. Hitler later regaled his dinner guests with the story of his time in Paris:

> I paid my visit very early in the morning, between six and nine. I wanted to refrain from exciting the population by my presence. The first newspaper-seller who recognised me stood there and gaped. I still have before me the mental picture of that woman in Lille who saw me from the window and exclaimed: 'The Devil!'[2]

The motorcade drove through the suburbs of Paris to the neo-baroque opera house, a long-time favourite of Hitler's. Speer noted his reaction. 'He seemed fascinated by the Opera, went into ecstasies about its beauty, his eyes glittering with an excitement that struck me as uncanny.'[3] The party proceeded to see the sights of Paris, driving past the Madeleine, down the Champs-Elysees, stopping at the Eiffel Tower and Hotel des Invalides. The Pantheon and church of Sacre Coeur in Montmarte were among the final sights. Hitler told Speer: 'It was the dream of my life to be permitted to see Paris. I cannot say how happy I am to have that dream fulfilled today.'[4] Hitler wanted the remodelled National Socialist Berlin to be even more beautiful than the French capital.

At the Invalides Hitler had stood and gazed at the tomb of Napoleon for a considerable time. He later remarked: 'That was the greatest and finest moment in my life.'[5] Hitler and Napoleon are the two great conquerors of modern European history. It should not be a surprise that Hitler drew inspiration from the life of Napoleon. From the end of the eighteenth century, revolutionary France and Napoleon had for a generation inflicted warfare and misery upon Europe and beyond in a bid to establish and maintain French hegemony. As a military commander, Napoleon had aggressively manoeuvred his forces to fight decisive, war-winning battles and campaigns.[6] A decisive brand of warfare has been favoured by the great tyrants of history since Alexander the Great and Julius Caesar. The armies of National Socialism were marching the same roads of Europe once taken by Napoleon's *Grande Armee*.

The art of warfare in the Napoleonic period was to be a major influence on the German military. In June 1815 a Prussian army joined with a British-led coalition force at Waterloo to turn possible defeat into one of the greatest decisive victories in history. In a series of wars from 1864 to 1871 Prussian military efficiency unified the German states under Prussia's leadership. Paris was besieged and the King of Prussia was proclaimed German Emperor in the Hall of Mirrors at Versailles. The sword had helped to build a united Germany.

By the end of the nineteenth century, the new German state was among the strongest in Europe and had a crucial role to play in the harmony of the Continent given its central geographic position.[7] Kaiser Wilhelm II and his advisers, however, had grand and disruptive ambitions. They wanted to establish Germany as a world power. Supporters of this policy spoke vaguely of 'a place in the sun' for Germany and 'Weltpolitik' or 'world policy'.[8] When war broke out in 1914, German planning was unequivocally offensive and based on an acceptance of the need for pre-emption.

The German Army overran Belgium and parts of northern France in 1914, but a costly stalemate had followed. An armistice came into force on 11 November 1918 with the German Army in retreat, though still in possession of most of its conquests in western Europe. Unlike the vanquished Tsarist, Ottoman and Austro-Hungarian empires, however, Germany emerged from the First World War as a united nation. Shortly after the 1919 Treaty of Versailles was negotiated, the French Marshal Ferdinand Foch commented that it was no more than a twenty-year truce.

When the next European war began in 1939 many of the same nations were involved in another conflict to determine Germany's role in Europe and the world, a problem that the First World War had failed to solve. In the interwar period there had been a revolution in political ideology brought about by the advent of fascism and Nazism. The Nazi leadership understood that another stalemated war would inevitably end in Germany's defeat. Nazi Germany's political and military leaders aimed for rapid and decisive victories in battle in a revival of the old Napoleonic style.

By the 1940s military science had recreated the possibility of a decisive battle, something that had been missing on the western front during the glacial campaigns of national attrition of 1914–18. Motorised vehicles and aircraft restored an annihilating form of combat to Western warfare. During the Second World War new ideologies and new machines of war would carry destruction across the globe. The armies and commanders of the major participants would determine the course and shape of the conflict through the battles they won and lost. Military technique and strategy can change the course of history.

I would like to express my thanks to all those who have helped me during the preparation of this book, in particular Martin Sheppard, Tony Morris, David Cuthbert and Eleanor Hancock. I am grateful to the State Library of Victoria for a Creative Fellowship in 2004. The State Library of Victoria's world-class collection of published material has been an invaluable support throughout the research and writing of all my work. Lastly, my publisher, Jonathan Reeve, and editor, Robin Harries, came to the rescue at just the right moment to summon this book into existence.

1
The Invasion of Poland

The military provisions of the 1919 Treaty of Versailles were designed to destroy Germany's ability to strike against her neighbours. The vast army of Wilhelmine Germany was disbanded. Next to the French border, the Rhineland was demilitarised and occupied by Allied forces. The *Reichswehr*, the new German military, was restricted to 100,000 men for border and internal policing duties. The Versailles treaty denied Germany tanks, military aircraft, a general staff, and other sophisticated weapons, including poison gas and heavy artillery. The *Reichswehr's* men were long-service regulars to avoid the creation of a large, trained reserve. Indeed the growth and toleration of paramilitary bodies in Weimar Germany was partly caused by the lack of any other organised reservist force.[1]

Germany in the 1920s was characterised by a democratically elected civilian government that sought to revise some of the provisions of the Versailles treaty by diplomacy. The *Reichswehr* had no chance of successfully opposing the French Army, especially with Allied occupation forces in the Rhineland until 1930. In eastern Germany there was also the possibility of war against the new Polish state, to which both Germany and the Soviet Union had lost a lot of territory. Geography meant that Germans could never cease to take the threat of land warfare seriously. Germany's open borders and potential enemies on either side continued to encourage thinking about military affairs. In secret the Germans bought arms from the Soviets during the 1920s, and operated air force and tank training facilities on Soviet soil. The Kazan tank school in Russia continued until 1933. Arms control had only increased interest in new weaponry in Germany, and created a need for theoretical understanding in light of the limited availability of certain types of equipment. The *Reichswehr* was a hothouse of skilled and motivated veterans, unburdened by obsolete equipment and the need to train annual classes of conscripts. There was time available to devote to the study of warfare, a contributory factor to German weapons development throughout the Weimar and Nazi periods.[2]

The economic crisis of the Great Depression helped to bring Adolf Hitler's Nazi Party to power by electoral means in January 1933. A very different strategic environment was quickly established in Europe. Hitler had a distinguished record of trench service in the 1914–18 war. He had been wounded and had won the Iron Cross First Class, but had not advanced beyond the rank of lance-corporal. Nonetheless, Hitler's close political association with General

Ludendorff during the 1920s had helped to round out his military education. Ludendorff had been one of the German Army's most important commanders during the First World War. After 1933, Hitler rapidly expanded the German military to the great approval of professional officers. The nature of the Nazi Party's rise to power had given Hitler a strong understanding that surprise, risk and decisiveness were vital to making gains in public life. Those principles were just as relevant to warfare, and provided him with a personal military creed that guided his actions in the years ahead.

In March 1935 Hitler announced the reintroduction of conscription and the creation of a new air force. The military provisions of the Versailles treaty had become a dead letter. (By the end of 1936 the international naval limitation treaties of 1922 and 1930 had also collapsed due to Japanese non-compliance.) A huge process of expansion and Nazification enveloped the German military, which had never lost its high status within German society. The 1920s had seen the proliferation of motor vehicles across the civilian economies of the Western world. In consequence, motorisation and new machinery would play central roles in the reformed German armed forces.

The 1920s German Army had been strong in horsed cavalry but, unlike in Britain, the temptation to use the cavalry as a framework for new mechanised formations was resisted. The motor transport troops of the infantry divisions were the principal founders of the panzer (tank) arm. A signals specialist named Heinz Guderian became Chief of Staff to the Inspector of Transport Troops. Guderian had given a great deal of thought to mechanised warfare.

Born in 1888 in East Prussia and the son of an army officer, Guderian had attended the War Academy in Berlin on the eve of the First World War. He had served mainly in staff postings from 1914–18. Guderian was well read in French and English. He had carefully studied the use of Allied tank forces in the later part of the First World War.[3] By 1918 armoured vehicles had begun to make an impact on Western Front battlefields, but they were slow-moving and prone to breakdown.[4] During the 1920s more mechanically reliable and faster tanks had replaced the monsters the British had used in 1916–18 against German troops. Tank formations could now attempt cross-country manoeuvres over longer distances. Guderian wanted to concentrate all tanks in mobile divisions that included large bodies of motorised infantry and artillery. Many senior panzer commanders and staff officers were not tank specialists, but former infantrymen and artillerymen. This contributed mightily to the development of the combined-arms panzer division.[5] With all arms able to travel at the same speed, the impact of tanks would be much greater.

In 1934 the Panzer Mark I was introduced, a fast vehicle armed with machine guns. A Mark II was quickly ordered with a larger three-man crew and a 20mm cannon as the main weapon. The first panzer division was soon formed. Guderian was appointed to command the 2nd Panzer Division, and by late 1938 he had become Commander of Mobile Troops.[6] This period was a time of great optimism and excitement for the German officer corps as massive expansion caused rapid promotion.

There was some resistance to the creation of panzer divisions, but this should not be exaggerated. The panzer force could not have been expanded so fast and could not have assumed a central role in the German army without a great deal of high-level support. The German High Command ensured that panzer forces were developed in a manner that complemented the existing structure of the army, much of which was still tied to marching infantry and horse-drawn artillery. The reformers could also count on the approval of Hitler, who had written in *Mein Kampf*, 'The general motorisation of the world ... in the next war will make its appearance in an overwhelming and decisive form. In this important field Germany has ... shamefully lagged behind.'[7] The main impediments to a more comprehensive mechanisation of the German military between 1933 and 1939 were a lack of raw materials such as oil and iron ore, and the sheer extent of the rearmament programme, which had to expand the existing industrial base and provide for the air force and a steel-consuming navy.

The build-up of the panzer force from scratch was complemented by the formation of a new German Air Force, the *Luftwaffe*. The German military had been at the forefront of aerial warfare from 1914–18, only to see the Treaty of Versailles sweep that away. The *Reichswehr* had contained a small group of air force officers, but the roots of the revived *Luftwaffe* lay more in a strong civilian aviation sector. Versailles treaty restrictions had only applied to civilian aircraft for a short period. By the late 1920s the partly government-owned Lufthansa airline had become the most important civilian air service in Europe. The head of Lufthansa, Erhard Milch, went on to become the State Secretary in the new Nazi Air Ministry. At the outset, the *Luftwaffe* drew heavily on civil aviation for aircrew and industrial plants. Competent army officers were transferred to senior posts in the air force. The *Luftwaffe's* commander, Herman Goering, was able to use his Nazi Party position to gain scarce resources for the rapid expansion of his service.[8]

In the Spanish Civil War from 1936–39 a small military force sent by Hitler to assist General Franco put into practice new army and air force techniques and equipment. The Condor Legion operated both air force and armoured units. The Panzer Mark I, 88mm flak gun, Heinkel bomber and Messerschmitt Bf 109 fighter all made their combat debut in Spain. In August–September 1936 German transport aircraft flew Nationalist troops from Africa to mainland Spain at a vital moment in the conflict. Wolfram von Richthofen, a cousin of the Red Baron and Chief of Staff of the Condor Legion, strongly advocated dive-bombing after it became apparent that high-level bombing was often inaccurate. Abysmal bombing accuracy at night and in poor weather encouraged the Germans to develop a guidance system for blind bombing using radio signals.[9]

General von Thoma later described Spain as 'a European Aldershot' for his tanks. On 12 July 1938 the *News Chronicle* published details of a lecture by General von Reichenau, who claimed that 'two years of real war experience have been of more use to our yet immature *Wehrmacht*, to the offensive power of the people, than a whole ten years of peaceful training could have been'.[10] Large Italian, Soviet and International Brigade contingents added to the multinational flavour of what was predominantly a localised civil war. Ironically, many more Germans and Austrians died fighting against Franco's forces in the International Brigades than in the Condor Legion.[11]

German and Italian bombing of Madrid inspired dire prophecies from resident war correspondents, as did the 26 April 1937 plastering of the town of Guernica by forty-three aircraft. Hundreds of people – mostly civilians – were killed. The *Luftwaffe's* performance in Spain did much to heighten exaggerated foreign estimates of its size and effectiveness. The *Luftwaffe* had become a powerful weapon in international diplomacy. On his return from a meeting with Hitler in September 1938, the British Prime Minister Neville Chamberlain remarked to his Cabinet colleagues that his aircraft bound for London had flown up the Thames. Chamberlain's fertile imagination had foreseen German bombers following the same route. The *Luftwaffe's* twin-engine bombers could certainly hit capitals such as Warsaw, Paris and Prague without much difficulty. In August 1938 the French Chief of the Air Staff returned from Germany to tell the French government that their air force would not last much more than two weeks against the might of the *Luftwaffe*.[12]

The reformed German military could look forward to the early possibility of war as Hitler set about overturning the Treaty of Versailles, and unifying the German peoples of central Europe into a greater Germany. In 1936 the Rhineland was remilitarised; in March 1938 Austria was absorbed; in September 1938 the German-speaking areas of Czechoslovakia were annexed; the rest of Czechoslovakia was dismembered in March 1939. The so-called Rome–Berlin Axis hardened into an alliance, and a new supreme military command – *Oberkommando der Wehrmacht* (OKW) – was formed, under Hitler's leadership, to control all the German armed forces. Hitler was already titular commander of the German armed forces, and he assumed the powers of War Minister as well. In addition to the fighting in Spain, the military manoeuvres caused by the unification of Germany and Austria had taught valuable lessons about the mobilisation of reserve units, and the logistics of mechanised warfare. Transport aircraft had helped carry troops to Vienna.

Hitler's ideas about nationalism and a social-darwinian belief in the strength of the German people were not particularly new. These ideas had powered the Kaiser's Germany a generation before. Hitler, however, had additional plans for large-scale permanent conquest and settlement beyond Germany's eastern borders. *Lebensraum* – or 'living space' – was to be achieved at the expense of Slavic peoples. This philosophy had been set out in the rambling *Mein Kampf*, which had been written (or dictated) by Hitler mainly in 1924 in the prison fortress of Landsberg. As a first decisive step Poland would have to be dealt with, despite the ten year Polish-German non-aggression pact of 1934.

Germany had lost significant eastern border lands to Poland in 1919, in particular the corridor to the Baltic Sea driven across the heartland of eastern Prussia. From late in 1938 the Nazis began to apply pressure to Poland over the status of Danzig, the autonomous city alongside East Prussia established by the Treaty of Versailles. Initial German demands were focused on the return of Danzig, and control of a railway across the corridor dividing the bulk of Germany from East Prussia. After the occupation of Prague in March 1939 Berlin's demands on Poland intensified. Yet Hitler's secret intention was to destroy Poland as a state. He explained to his military commanders on 23 May 1939 that Poland was to be attacked at the first good opportunity. 'Danzig is not the subject of the dispute at all. It is a question of expanding our living space in the East, of securing food supplies, and of settling the Baltic problem.'[13] The political and cultural elite of Poland were to be destroyed and large swaths of territory annexed to Germany. The 'strategic window' when Germany's military lead over its neighbours was greatest seemed to beckon in the summer of 1939. [14]

Shocked by repeated German aggressions, and the recent carve-up of Czechoslovakia in particular, Britain and France guaranteed the security of Poland on 31 March 1939 with a public promise. France and Poland had been military allies since 1921. On 7 April Italy invaded Albania and the Anglo-French guarantee was extended to Greece and Romania. Hitler either disbelieved or did not fear that guarantee. He was keen to test his new war machine and thundered: 'I had experience with those poor worms Daladier [French Prime Minister] and Chamberlain in Munich. They will be too cowardly to attack. They won't go beyond a blockade. Against that we have our autarchy and the Russian raw materials.'[15] The German nightmare of a war on two major land fronts was removed by the signing of a non-aggression pact with Stalin on 23 August 1939, whereby the Soviets would join Germany to partition Poland and received German acknowledgement that the Baltic states were a Soviet sphere. Anglo-French attempts to reach an alliance with the Soviets during 1939 had come to nothing. The Poles would not permit Soviet troops to enter Polish territory, and no meaningful Anglo-French accommodation with Moscow could be arranged without that condition. The Polish Commander-in-Chief, Marshal Edward Rydz-Smigly, had declaimed: 'With the Germans we are risking our freedom. With the Russians we lose our soul.'[16]

A quick German campaign was devised for Poland. OKH – the German army's high command – had begun planning in April 1939. The possibility of Anglo-French intervention made it vital to defeat Poland rapidly. Press correspondents would subsequently popularise this notion with the expression '*blitzkrieg*' (lightning war). In the summer of 1939 the German army was partly mobilised under the guise of routine manoeuvres. Twenty-fifth anniversary commemorations of the German victory over the Russians at Tannenberg in 1914 provided cover to ship extra troops to East Prussia. Annual summer training exercises helped Generals Heinrich von Brauchitsch and Franz Halder, the army's Commander-in-Chief and Chief of Staff, to finalise their schemes.[17]

Two German army groups were to be deployed against Poland under the command of Generals Fedor von Bock and Gerd von Rundstedt; over a million and a half German troops in fifty-four divisions, including six panzer, four 'light' armoured and four motorised infantry divisions. The remaining formations were infantry divisions relying on horse-drawn artillery and supply wagons. As Poland was an agricultural country, motorised units were likely to face serious refuelling, repair and maintenance problems.

Army Group South was to thrust north east from Silesia and Slovakia towards Warsaw, whilst Army Group North advanced across the Polish Corridor to join German forces in East Prussia for a sweep south eastwards. These two giant pincers were to destroy the Polish Army in a campaign of annihilation west of the great rivers of central Poland. A light covering force linked the two army groups and shielded the road to Berlin. According to Captain F.W. von Mellenthin, a staff officer involved in the Polish campaign, 'This conception of a weak centre with two powerful attacking wings was traditional in German strategy, and found its roots in Count von Schlieffen's classic study of Hannibal's victory at Cannae.'[18] Two air fleets totalling over 2000 aircraft were deployed along the Polish frontier, including almost all the *Luftwaffe*'s dive-bombers.[19] A small army group remained in western Germany in case of war with France and Britain, supported by two air fleets relatively strong in fighters.

The Poland that was awaiting the *Wehrmacht*'s onslaught was a relatively new player in the international order. The revival of the Polish state in 1918–19, after an interval of over a century, had been a triumph for Polish nationalism. Poland's western and northern borders had been established by the peace treaties that had ended the First World War. However, to the east a war with the Russians had almost ended in disaster in 1920, only to rapidly reverse course and conclude in victory and large scale territorial conquest. The Polish state's eastern frontiers, established by the Treaty of Riga in March 1921, had annexed large non-Polish minorities. What had started as a desire for self-determination for Poles had degenerated by 1921 into a land grab at the expense of a temporarily weak neighbour. The population of Poland by 1939 was over thirty million, of which only sixty per cent were ethnic Poles.[20] Poland had recommenced its existence with a liberal constitution, but in 1926 Marshal Josef Pilsudski, a popular hero from the war of 1920–21, had backed a coup. A new constitution had strengthened the powers of the executive against parliament. There was broad and enduring support in Poland for Pilsudski's regime.

National survival was vital for the Polish people precisely because they knew it could never be taken for granted. The army played a central role in the Polish state. By the mid 1930s the national government was spending half its budget on the military.[21] The army had thirty active divisions, eleven cavalry brigades, two mechanised brigades and another nine reserve divisions. The Poles had a long military tradition, though mostly in the service of other powers. Senior officers had spent time in either the German, Austro-Hungarian or Russian militaries during the First World War. Leadership at a regimental level was sound, though staff and command training had been neglected. The typical Polish soldier was a tough, well-motivated, sturdy peasant from one of the country's many small farms. A well-developed system of peacetime conscription based on the French model ensured there was a large pool of reservists available to bring the active and reserve divisions up to strength upon mobilisation. In theory Poland had almost two million reservists under the age of fifty. A large force of cavalry armed with sabres, but organised as efficient mounted infantry, had an important role in the army in light of the undoubted success of mounted troops in the campaign of 1920. A lack of roads suitable for motor vehicles in eastern Poland, and the severity of the wet season, were other reasons for persevering with mounted forces.[22]

The Poles were rich in manpower but poor in equipment. Poland was not a 'motorised' society and in 1939 had only a small fraction of the motor vehicles and farm tractors possessed by the peoples of France or Germany. The nation lacked heavy industry to equip the military through local production, nor was the currency sufficiently strong to import large quantities of armaments. The Polish Air Force possessed only 400 largely obsolete aircraft.[23] Many Polish fighters were slow, gull-winged aircraft with a fixed undercarriage. The army's 300 tanks were a mixture of British, French and locally built light tanks. Over 500 two-man tankettes armed with a machine gun served as armoured cars. A Polish infantry division was armed with an effective 37mm anti-tank gun, but the division's forty-eight field guns would be outnumbered by the seventy-four guns of a similar German division. A lack of radio communications equipment hampered the operation of Polish headquarters at all levels.[24]

Marshal Rydz-Smigly, Inspector-General of the Armed Forces since the death of Pilsudski in 1935, faced a difficult challenge in preparing for possible war against Germany. There were few fortifications in western Poland as the Soviet Union had been perceived as the main military threat in the 1920s. The west of the country was flat and an extension of the North German Plain. The Carpathian Mountains in the south, and the Pripyat marshes in the east, would play little role in a war against the Germans. The great rivers running south to north through the centre of Poland were significant military obstacles in flood season but not in summer. Rydz-Smigly decided to deploy his forces along the borders with Germany in a straightforward manner. Seven corps-sized 'armies' lined the frontiers. A force at Gdynia at the northern end of the corridor to the sea, and a general reserve, completed the nine formations that reported directly to the Polish high command in the absence of any intermediate headquarters.[25] If the Germans attacked, the Poles would doubtless be forced to give ground, but possible French retaliation against western Germany, and poor weather late in the year, gave reason to hope for survival.

In a number of respects the Polish strategic plan had been hopelessly undermined by the presence of German forces poised around three sides of western Poland, in an arc from East Prussia in the north to occupied Slovakia in the south. The threat from the south had only come into existence with the final dismemberment of Czechoslovakia early in 1939. The Polish Army was virtually in the jaws of the German pincers from the outset of the campaign. Polish forces in Pomerania, at the entrance to the corridor leading to the Baltic coast, and the western Poznan salient were particularly exposed. The Poles might have concentrated their forces around Warsaw to fight a prolonged battle behind the river system running through the centre of the country. Yet much industry, mines, and a large part of the ethnically Polish population was concentrated in the west of Poland. Cracow was close to the south western frontier. The army had to deploy sufficiently close to the western frontier to permit the mobilisation of reservists in an orderly fashion. There was also the possibility that the Germans might simply occupy lightly defended border regions to undermine Poland, rather as the occupation of the Sudetenland had heralded the destruction of Czechoslovakia.[26]

The invasion of Poland – Case White – had been scheduled for 26 August, but Hitler postponed the operation late on the preceding day after news was received that the British guarantee to Poland had been formally signed. There were problems recalling all German units in time and minor skirmishes took place before news of the cancellation reached all troops. Rumours of the German build-up had been carried into Poland by Polish refugees. High-level German reconnaissance flights across the frontier had become common. Radio silence and the use of telephone landlines by German forces helped to maintain secrecy in respect to the exact timing of the invasion.

The Polish army had partly mobilised during the summer of 1939 for mid-year manoeuvres. Polish general mobilisation was ordered at 1 p.m. on 29 August, but after British and French protests the order was reversed the following morning. The British and French were mistakenly concerned that a premature Polish mobilisation might deepen the crisis. The Poles could not risk offending their allies. Most of the small Polish navy, however, sailed for Britain on 30 August, and the air force was successfully dispersed to its war stations. Perhaps 1,100,000 men were mobilised for the army during the September campaign, but only 700,000 were in position on 1 September.[27]

On the night of 31 August German troops staged a faked attack on a German radio station at Gleiwitz. This was later used in propaganda to justify the war with Poland, as were claims that Germans in Poland were being persecuted.

The invasion began at dawn on 1 September. The German battleship *Schleswig-Holstein*, which had been at Danzig on a courtesy visit, opened fire on nearby Polish fortifications. France and Britain declared war on Germany in support of Poland, though the Anglo-French ultimatums did not expire until 3 September.

On the opening day of war the spearheads of five German armies began to slice through the Polish front. The sheer length of the Polish-German and Polish-Slovakian frontiers meant that defending formations were stretched. Dry September weather promised good flying conditions and the likelihood that rivers would be at their most fordable. Massed tanks and motorised infantry pushed quickly through gaps punched in the Polish front. SS troops followed behind the army to deal with designated enemies of National Socialism.

In the Polish Corridor on the morning of 1 September a thick ground mist had reduced the possibilities of air support. General Guderian oversaw the advance of his XIX Panzer Corps from an armoured command vehicle. Radio-equipped motorised headquarters helped overcome the confusion caused by rapid changes in unit locations. One of Guderian's staff later commented that, 'from the outset it was realised that without a comprehensive communication network, the concept of high mobility and deep penetration by panzer divisions was unthinkable'. As the advance got underway Guderian's vehicle was bracketed by friendly artillery firing into the mist, one of the disadvantages of a senior officer getting close behind the fighting troops.[28]

In the Polish Corridor some panzer units were held up for a number of hours when they ran out of fuel, but by the following day the German Fourth Army had linked up with the Third Army in East Prussia. Two Polish infantry divisions and a cavalry brigade had been broken up in the fighting. The Polish garrison at the northern end of the corridor was isolated. Stories began to circulate in the press of Polish cavalry charging German tanks. Whilst horsemen doubtless manoeuvred in the presence of enemy armoured vehicles, war correspondents who claimed any more than that were either gullible or overly inventive. On the opening two days of the campaign Polish troops in the fortifications at Mlawa, to the immediate south of East Prussia, offered stout resistance to the German invaders. On the night of 2/3 September Polish cavalry managed to penetrate East Prussia, though they were soon obliged to withdraw.

In the south west of the country, Army Group South made good progress on 1 September in clear weather. Cracow fell by 6 September and Lodz came under threat. Armour of the Tenth Army headed directly for Warsaw. After five days of war General Halder at OKH (army high command) wrote in his diary: 'The enemy is practically beaten.'[29] Motorised units could overrun soldiers retreating on foot with alarming rapidity.

The *Luftwaffe* heavily attacked Polish aerodromes, railway stations and rail-track from the outbreak of war. Damage to the railways, often single-track, badly hampered Polish reservists trying to reach their units after the delayed mobilisation. General Wladyslaw Anders recalled that on 4 September:

> I went by car to Mlawa [near the frontier with East Prussia]. I could only get there by a circuitous route, and on the way passed through burning villages. The bodies of many civilians lay in the streets, among them those of children. Once I saw a group of small children being led by their teacher to the shelter of the woods. Suddenly there was the roar of an aeroplane. The pilot circled round, descending to a height of fifty metres. As he dropped his bombs and fired his machine guns, the children scattered like sparrows. The aeroplane disappeared as quickly as it had come, but on the field some crumpled and lifeless bundles of bright clothing remained. The nature of the new war was already clear.[30]

In the heat of summer, refugee columns and cattle blocked roads and threw up clouds of dust.

Heavy air attacks were launched against Warsaw, the outskirts of which were reached by the spearhead of Army Group South on 8 September. Tanks of the 4th Panzer Division entered the south-western suburbs that evening but were beaten back by artillery fire. The defenders hastily threw up barricades and overturned tram cars to block streets. The previous day, the Polish High Command had left Warsaw for Brest-Litovsk, over a hundred miles to the east. Rydz-Smigly's headquarters had been struggling to control so many subordinate formations in a fast-moving campaign. The telegraph and telephone system had broken down.

In the west of Poland the three infantry divisions and two cavalry brigades of the Poznan Army had been bypassed in the opening week of the German offensive. The Poznan Army turned about and began to march eastwards towards Warsaw. They were joined from the north and south by retreating units of other Polish formations. About noon on 10 September this Polish force collided with Rundstedt's Army Group South. The rapid advance to Warsaw had badly stretched German infantry formations trailing in the wake of motorised panzer troops. The German 30th Division was marching north east in columns strung out over twenty miles. An improvised Polish attack fell upon the division and 1500 German prisoners were taken.

Panzer units nearing Warsaw were swung back to support German forces hastily gathering to block the Poznan Army's passage eastwards. A large Polish force was surrounded in the vicinity of Kutno, a town on the River Bzura. After initial attempts to break the German line in a south eastern direction, a further effort was made north eastwards towards the River Vistula on 16 September. This thrust was repelled with heavy losses and the Polish perimeter collapsed the following day. 40,000 prisoners were taken. Some detachments of Poles crossed the Bzura but were broken up east of the river. The Kutno–Bzura battle was proclaimed by the victorious Germans as a 'second Tannenberg'. As this was taking place, the southern arm of Army Group South destroyed Polish forces in the Radom area to capture another 60,000 prisoners.[31]

By 17 September the Germans had thrown a screen around Warsaw. The *Luftwaffe* bombed the Polish capital and the German Third Army approached the suburbs of Praga on the eastern bank of the Vistula. Negotiations to evacuate the civilian population broke down. Guderian's reinforced panzer corps embarked on a wide turning movement far to the rear of the Polish capital. In southern Poland the defending army had retreated eastwards across the San river. A Polish officer wrote that it 'was not like the march of an army; it was more like the march of some biblical people, driven onward by the wrath of Heaven, and dissolving in the wilderness'.[32]

The war in Poland was transformed on 17 September when Soviet forces advanced across Poland's eastern frontier in accordance with the secret clauses of the Ribbentrop-Molotov Pact. The Poles were taken by surprise. The German Foreign Minister had been urging the Soviets to join the campaign from an early stage. The Soviets, however, had delayed their intervention. Major logistical hurdles had to be overcome as fresh formations were hurriedly mobilised in the Russian interior. A local war in the Far East had also been underway against Japan on the border of Manchuria and Outer Mongolia for the past several months. An armistice and cease-fire had only been recently arranged. To justify an invasion of Poland, Moscow simply declared that the Polish state no longer existed. The Soviets claimed they were restoring order and protecting Belorussian and Ukrainian peoples. Britain's treaty with Poland only covered aggression by Germany. Soviet intervention did not result in war with Britain and France.

Two Soviet army groups crashed through negligible resistance in eastern Poland. Between half a million to a million Soviet troops were involved.[33] The Polish High Command's hopes to form a last bridgehead near the Romanian border vanished, as did the possibility of large-scale resistance in the forests and swamps of eastern Poland. The Polish High Command initially ordered its forces to fight the Soviets, but soon rescinded the instruction and advised troops to negotiate with the Red Army. The garrisons of Warsaw and other defended cities were ordered to fight on. Soviet forces cut the route to Romania within days of their invasion, and the door was open to Hungary only for a little longer. Some Polish troops crossed into the Baltic states. In total, the Polish government and up to 100,000 troops escaped to neutral territory, mainly Romania, along with the remaining aircraft of the decimated Polish Air Force.[34]

The River Vistula was the initial German-Soviet partition line. German forces that had advanced as far as the River Bug were ordered to withdraw westwards. Fleeing refugees did not know which way to turn. Some mingling of German and Soviet troops was inevitable but few incidents resulted. General von Bock of Army Group North felt that Soviet troops lacked discipline and were poorly turned out. He was equally unimpressed by the obvious influence political commissars wielded. When the partition line was redrawn further eastwards another round of redeployment was needed. The Soviets received control of 51.6 per cent of Polish territory and 37.3 per cent of the population.[35]

Whilst the Red Army pressed into eastern Poland, the capital was subjected to a steady stream of German air attacks. Leaflets dropped from the air urged surrender. Warsaw's civilian population was 1,300,000 and the pace of the German advance had trapped many inside the city. Perhaps sixty per cent of Warsaw's people lived in one or two room flats, and there were heavy civilian casualties during the siege of such a crowded city. Food supplies ran low and dead horses were stripped of their flesh. The diplomatic colony in Warsaw watched events on the world's behalf until they were evacuated.

Thirteen German divisions and a thousand guns ringed the Polish capital. The defending force was also large, and had been supplemented by local militia and police. On 22 September Hitler observed the shelling of the city from a nearby church tower. He wanted Warsaw captured before the arrival of the Red Army. Preparations were made for an assault and over 400 aircraft took part in a renewed bombing effort. Junkers Ju 52 transports were used to unload incendiaries. Behind heavy artillery fire German troops made cautious gains. On the evening of 26 September the Polish General Juliusz Rommel sent envoys across the lines to meet the Germans. Warsaw capitulated on the afternoon of 27 September. 140,000 Polish prisoners were taken, including thousands of wounded.[36] The nearby garrison of Modlin and a further 24,000 men surrendered in the days ahead. Organised resistance to the dual invasions had ended by early October. Many German troops were soon boarding trains for the return journey to the Reich's western borders.

Along the western frontier of Germany, the French and British did little directly to help Poland during September. Relief and delight in Poland at the Anglo-French declarations of war had been short-lived. Pre-war promises had led the Polish leadership to expect more from their allies.[37] In May 1939, after four days of negotiations, the French Supreme Commander, General Maurice Gamelin, had informed a delegation from Poland's High Command that if Poland was attacked by Germany the French Army would commence limited operations into western Germany three days after mobilisation. A full-scale offensive was promised for fifteen days after mobilisation. In private, however, Gamelin said there was little sense to making pacts with Poland until an agreement could be made with the Soviets that was acceptable to Warsaw. Anglo-Polish military discussions in May and July saw the British promise air action against Germany. In July the Anglo-French-Polish relationship was furthered in a decisive fashion when the British and French gratefully received from Polish codebreakers duplicates of the Polish-built version of the German Enigma machine used to encipher radio messages. For a number of years the Poles had been working hard to build up their capacity for signals espionage.[38]

In contrast to Anglo-French negotiations with Poland, when British and French leaders met there was never any doubt that Anglo-French military commitments to Poland were merely goodwill gestures. A range of British and French political and military figures were aware that no offensive preparations were in place. Anglo-French discussions over the summer of 1939 had decided upon a war strategy that would place an emphasis on economic blockade and the liberation of German-occupied territory after a victorious conclusion to the war had been negotiated. On 28 July the British chiefs of staff had reported that assistance to Poland could only really be made in the air: 'As a general point, we would emphasise that the fate of Poland will depend on the ultimate outcome of the war, and that this in turn will depend on our ability to bring about the eventual defeat of Germany, and not on our ability to relieve pressure on Poland at the outset.'[39] On 27 August Gamelin was alleged to have said, 'I know the Polish Army quite well. Their soldiers are excellent and their officers well up to their job ... The Poles will hold out at least six months and we shall come to their aid through Romania.'[40] Anglo-French diplomatic appeasement of Berlin had thoroughly infected Anglo-French military planning for war against Germany.[41]

On 3 September 1939 German forces in the west had totalled thirty-three divisions. These were backed by a relatively strong air force. The defences of the West Wall were poor in comparison to the Maginot Line and all panzer formations had been sent to Poland. Initially sixty-seven French divisions had been mobilised, but only nine divisions were involved in a hesitant advance beginning on 7 September across the Franco-German frontier towards the outposts of the West Wall and the Saar region. Minor gains were portrayed as triumphs in the Allied press. By 12 September, when Gamelin ordered a halt, French troops had only advanced five miles into Germany. About twenty German villages had been occupied.[42] The lack of intensity to the French attack had very quickly let the Germans know that little was intended. French forces withdrew to the Maginot Line after the collapse of Poland without having made any discernible impact on events in the east.

Poland's leaders had waited in vain for effective intervention by their allies. On 6 September the Polish ambassador to France had requested that air attacks and a land offensive be launched against Germany. On 9 September Gamelin was given a message from Marshal Rydz-Smigly which asked: 'Has the French Air Force yet gone into action against the German Air Force and German territory? I have not yet noticed any lessening of German air activity on the Polish front.' The following day Gamelin replied to the Polish military attaché in Paris, Colonel Fyda:

More than half of our active divisions in the north east are engaged in combat. Ever since we crossed our frontier the Germans have offered us vigorous resistance. None the less we have made progress. But we find ourselves engaged in a war of position against an organised adversary, and I do not yet have at my disposal the necessary artillery ... we can claim with justice to be keeping on our front a large part of the German Air Force. I have therefore exceeded my promise that I would mount an offensive with the main bodies of my forces by the fifteenth day after the first day of Polish mobilisation.[43]

General Stanislaw Burhardt, head of a Polish military mission, arrived in Paris on 10 September to meet with Gamelin.[44]

German commanders were relieved and puzzled that the western Allies had done so little on land during September. When Mellenthin inspected the West Wall's defences after returning from Poland he noted:

Few of the strongpoints were sited to fire in enfilade and most of them could have been shot to pieces by direct fire, without the slightest risk to the attackers. The West Wall had been built in such a hurry that many of the positions were sited on forward slopes. The anti-tank obstacles were of trivial significance, and the more I looked at the defences the less I could understand the completely passive attitude of the French.[45]

Knowledgeable German officers believed that a lot of German territory could have been taken west of the Rhine during September by a determined French offensive. Winston Churchill later suggested that September 1939 would have been the ideal time for Anglo-French forces to move into Belgium to form a more secure western front, if only the Belgian government had been willing to discard its self-delusory neutrality.[46]

On 1 September an American correspondent in Berlin, William Shirer, noted in his diary: 'Curious that not a single Polish bomber got through tonight. But will it be the same with the British and French?' There had been no celebrations in Berlin when war broke out, and considerable public fear of air attack.[47] The German population need not have worried. RAF Bomber Command confined its activities to dropping millions of leaflets over western Germany – so-called 'confetti warfare' – even when it became apparent that Polish cities were being pounded by live munitions. The irony of this was only too apparent and a contemporary joke told the tale of an airman who was chastised for dropping a still tightly tied bundle of leaflets – 'Good God, you might have killed someone!'[48] The French were just as keen to avoid strategic bombing in case the Germans retaliated against an exposed Paris, and, in any case, the French Air Force lacked a strong force of bombers. RAF aircraft attacked German warships in port, though losses were heavy and little damage inflicted. The British government was immensely relieved that London had not come under immediate attack from the *Luftwaffe*.

At sea, however, matters were different for Britain whilst the Polish campaign unfolded. During August submarines had left Germany to cruise Britain's sea lanes. The pocket-battleship *Graf Spee* sailed for the South Atlantic. On the evening of 3 September the submarine *U-30* torpedoed and sank the liner *Athenia*, 250 miles north west of Ireland. 112 people died, including twenty-eight Americans. By the end of September the Royal Navy had destroyed the first two of many U-boats sunk during the war, but forty-one Allied merchant ships amounting to over 150,000 tons had also gone to the ocean's floor. Convoys were swiftly introduced for merchant ships sailing to the United Kingdom, and the large majority of torpedoed ships were not in a convoy at the time of their sinking. The punishment, though, was not all one-way. By the end of September 325 German merchant ships of almost three-quarters of a million tons had been swept from the seas to seek refuge in neutral ports or risk capture by Allied warships. Germany's high seas trade in vital war materials had been stopped.[49]

Some major blows befell the Royal Navy in the early weeks of war. The fleet aircraft carrier *Courageous* was torpedoed on 17 September during an anti-submarine patrol in the Bristol Channel. She was sent to the bottom along with 519 lives. In the early hours of 14/15 October Lieutenant-Commander Guenther Prien's *U-47* penetrated the negligently incomplete defences of the Home Fleet's main anchorage at Scapa Flow in northern Scotland. The old battleship *Royal Oak* was torpedoed and capsized. 833 officers and men died. *U-47* successfully escaped.[50] With the western front inactive, the extent of the war at sea strengthened Britain's position in her alliance with France.

By the end of the short campaign in Poland the defenders' military losses had amounted to 70,000 killed and 133,000 wounded. 700,000 servicemen had been made prisoners of war by the Germans. The Soviets had rounded up another 230,000 prisoners.[51] German officers had been impressed by the courage of the Poles. According to General Erich von Manstein, 'The enemy's losses in blood were undoubtedly very high indeed, for he had fought with great gallantry and had shown a grim determination to hold out in even the most hopeless situations.'[52] The Polish soldier had fought bravely, but the Polish high command had lost control of the battle almost from the outset. The Polish leadership had greatly overestimated their country's military capacity.

German casualties in Poland were 11,000 dead, 30,000 wounded and 3,400 missing.[53] A prominent German fatality had been General Werner von Fritsch, a former commander-in-chief, who had been killed near Warsaw visiting an artillery regiment. The wide gap between German and Polish losses is not hard to explain. The Germans possessed many more tanks and aircraft than the Poles. Hitler had visited Guderian in the course of touring German forces. Guderian had driven him back along the line of advance in northern Poland. They had passed the wreckage and debris of a Polish artillery regiment pulverised on the march. Wrote Guderian: 'At the sight of the smashed artillery regiment, Hitler had asked me, "Our dive bombers did that?" When I replied, "No, our panzers!" he was plainly astonished.'[54] Even an ordinary German infantry division had been able to unleash twice the firepower of a Polish division. The Red Army's casualties in Poland were officially reported as 737 killed and 1,862 wounded.

German losses in armoured fighting vehicles and assault guns had numbered 173, though many more had been damaged.[55] The *Luftwaffe* had lost 285 aircraft and another 279 were badly damaged and written off. Of 435 operational Polish aircraft, ninety-eight were flown by their crews to Romania.[56] The rest had been destroyed. The war, though, was far from over for the Polish armed forces. With the Royal Air Force and Allied armies, Poles would continue to fight Nazi tyranny in several theatres of war in the years ahead.

On 5 October Hitler flew to Warsaw. He told gathered journalists: 'Take a good look around Warsaw. That is how I can deal with any European city.'[57] Photographs of bomb-damaged Warsaw appeared in newspapers in neutral countries to reinforce that point. In addition to unprecedented aerial bombardment of civilian centres, widespread atrocities had taken place behind the front of advancing German forces. Complaints from the army about the conduct of SS troops in Poland had been brushed aside by Hitler. General Halder at OKH recorded in his diary for 10 September that General von Bock had reported: 'SS artillery of the armoured corps herded Jews into a church and massacred them. Court-martial sentenced them to one year's penitentiary.' Senior army commanders made feeble protests, but in practice the army in Poland had willingly cooperated with SS and police auxiliaries at a local level.[58] The German Army had always taken a tough stance against alleged partisans suspected of sniping, whether in France in 1870–71 or Belgium in 1914. Summary executions of Polish prisoners of war also took place during the campaign. In a forest near Ciepielow on 9 September German infantry executed 300 Polish troops after capture. The German commander declared the Poles to be partisans and had them take off their uniform tunics prior to execution.[59]

To an extent that high-ranking German officers would subsequently struggle to acknowledge, the Polish campaign helped to break in the German Army to the world view of National Socialism. Nazi propaganda that the east was inhabited by racial enemies who deserved to be destroyed had often been well absorbed by impressionable young soldiers. This was as important a development for modern warfare as the new fighting methods of *blitzkrieg*.[60]

Poland now faced a partition between the Germans and Soviets. Parts of the German zone – the corridor to the sea in particular – were annexed to the Reich, and the remainder turned into a colony known as the General-Government. Forced labour, 'ethnic cleansing' and executions became commonplace. Polish elite groups, such as the nobility, professions and clergy, were targeted in a deliberate bid permanently to dismember Polish society. The Soviets deported over a million Polish citizens and plundered at will. Polish prisoners, civilian and military, found themselves scattered across the Soviet concentration camp system.[61] Many Polish officer prisoners were murdered by the Soviets, 5,000 at Katyn Wood in April–May 1940 in particular. The bodies of thousands more officer prisoners would never be discovered.

An increasing level of atrocity in Poland was paralleled by events within Germany. A Nazi-directed euthanasia campaign was launched against elderly and physically or mentally handicapped German patients in hospitals and institutions. Hitler backdated a written decree, secretly authorising the programme, to 1 September. The Nazi euthanasia expert Dr Pfannmueller summed up the philosophy behind the euthanasia programme: 'The idea is unbearable to me that the best, the flower of our youth, must lose its life at the front, in order that feeble-minded and asocial elements can have a secure existence in the asylum.'[62] Victims were poisoned and then cremated. There were protests in Germany against these practices, despite the rigours of the Nazi dictatorship, but tens of thousands of people would be killed over the next two years. Among the SS and medical profession, the euthanasia programme created a cadre of men with experience in systematic and bureaucratic killing which would be utilised against other Nazi enemies.

Late in September 1939 it was decided to start the ghettoisation of the Jewish population in German-occupied Poland. The road from random and sporadic atrocity to an organised genocide was well underway. The killing of civilians had become a military operation to be carried out by a part of the German state's military forces, with assistance from other parts of the military when required. By the end of 1939 executions in Poland by the SS and their auxiliaries had probably run into tens of thousands.[63] By the war's end six million Polish citizens would be dead, roughly half Jewish and half ethnically-Polish. This was between a fifth and a quarter of the entire 1939 population, man, woman and child.

The opening phase of war in 1939 had been entirely satisfactory for the German leadership. Poland had been swiftly overrun. Russia had become an ally. In 1914 Russia had been part of an enemy coalition. Hitler's belief in his ability as a strategist had been given a tremendous boost.

The German high command had pushed aside the moral dimension to the army's campaign in Poland, but its operational performance was subjected to a more stringent review. The extent of the victory encouraged panzer commanders to believe more strongly in the destiny of their new technology and methods. It had been generally accepted in the army that tanks were useful in a tactical situation, but the Polish campaign firmly established that panzer forces were an instrument able to deeply penetrate an enemy front.[64] Panzer divisions could pursue a beaten enemy to the point of disintegration, thus turning a battlefield success into a decisive victory of overarching strategic significance. Modern radio communications, motorised supply columns and repair shops had proved as important to success as the specific performance of tanks in close combat. The 'Light' armoured divisions used in Poland were earmarked for conversion and upgrade to panzer divisions. The Panzer Mark IIIs and IVs had performed well and increased production of those types would gradually replace older tanks. 88mm anti-aircraft guns had proved effective weapons when firing directly at ground targets. The *Luftwaffe* learnt how to leapfrog forward to quickly bring captured aerodromes into operation.

The army's review was not confined to the mechanised divisions. The standard of training across the infantry divisions had been patchy. The recently mobilised reserve divisions needed further hard training. Most infantry divisions still literally relied on horse-power to propel their guns and transport. The Polish campaign had revealed problems with the military's supply of horseshoes. Horses requisitioned from German farms had differently sized feet from the standard army horses.[65] This, too, was a problem worthy of serious attention.

In the wake of the fall of Poland there was no possibility of peace between Germany and the Anglo-French coalition. The campaign in Poland had only proved Hitler's regime to be more predatory and less trustworthy than previously believed. From October 1939 two great armies faced each other behind their respective defences along the Franco-German frontier. The 'Phoney War' was in full swing, to provide an absurd contrast to the maelstrom of the Western Front from 1914–1918.

2
The Fall of France

During September 1939 the German Army had rapidly overrun Poland without provoking a retaliatory French attack on the Rhineland. No serious Anglo-French offensive was under consideration in 1939 or even 1940 for that matter. The western allies had agreed to prepare for a long war. The lesson of 1914–15 seemed to be that a unilateral French offensive against Germany would achieve little. The four and a half million French military casualties of the First World War, including over a million and a third dead, made the French reluctant to launch great offensives. They would wait for the British Expeditionary Force to be built up towards maximum strength. Maybe after that something might be attempted.

The French Army sat within the Maginot Line during the winter of 1939–40. The line was a state-of-the-art chain of defensive works built at great cost along the Franco-German border after the French had evacuated the Rhineland in 1930. The Third Republic suffered from many changes of government and too many political parties, but the construction of the Maginot Line had achieved broad support as a prudent defensive measure. The French can hardly be blamed for fortifying a possible and, indeed, likely future battlefield. There were few natural defensible geographic features on the French side of the frontier. The recently regained territory of Alsace-Lorraine was vulnerable and a rich source of iron ore. The French in the 1930s clearly had no territorial aspirations beyond their existing metropolitan borders. The Maginot Line was also a timely post-depression public works programme.[1]

France had a long and distinguished record of using fortifications to defend its borders; from Vauban's fortresses of the reign of Louis XIV to the modern forts of Verdun in 1916. Traditionally the primary aim of frontier fortifications was to gain time for the field army to mobilise, but that goal had given way to the concept of fortifications as an impassable barrier in their own right. The Maginot Line, named after the French War Minister at the time the first phase of the project was approved, has been likened to a land-based fleet of warships. Well-sited and armoured gun turrets were connected by underground railway lines. The garrisons lived and worked in underground barracks and storehouses. The entire length of the line, however, was by no means dominated by sophisticated forts. Existing frontier fortifications were incorporated in the line wherever that was practical. Easily defendable terrain was lightly fortified. The River Rhine was an integral part of the southern end of the line. The main technical criticism of the Maginot Line was that it was a relatively thin chain of fortifications, and lacking the depth of the fortified zones that had become common in France by the later period of the First World War.[2]

The Maginot Line had been built to help make up for the fact that France had only two-thirds the population of Germany. In 1919 the French population had been thirty-nine million as against fifty-nine million Germans. After the annexation of Austria in 1938 the relative populations had worsened, from the French viewpoint, to forty-two million against seventy-six million.[3] The 'hollow years' of 1935–40, caused by the low birth rate during the First World War, hurt France especially, denying the French Army hundreds of thousands of recruits in their fighting prime. In Germany the same problem had been warded off to a substantial extent by a higher birth rate and the acquisition of Austria and the Sudetenland.

The Maginot Line had not been extended northwards along the border between France and Belgium. This was due to a number of factors, including expense, the water-logged nature of parts of the ground and the close proximity of French industry and mines to the frontier. Until 1936 France had a military alliance with Belgium; another reason not to lock Belgium out of the French system of defence. Yet in 1936 the Belgium government had myopically proclaimed their neutrality. The Belgian Army was mobilised in 1939, but to all practical purposes Belgian neutrality equated Nazism with the Anglo-French coalition. That was a poor reward for Anglo-French efforts to liberate Belgium from German occupation in the war of 1914–18.

After the partition of Poland between Germany and the Soviet Union, the question confronting Hitler was what to do next. Hitler turned quickly to the task of defeating France, after which Britain might be compelled to make a separate peace. Then the British overseas empire and the new German empire in Europe could co-exist. On 9 October 1939 Führer Directive No. 6 ordered the German armed forces to prepare plans for an offensive in western Europe, an offensive to win 'as large an area as possible in Holland, Belgium, and northern France as a base for conducting a promising air and sea war against England and as a protective area for the Ruhr'.[4] As in 1914, Belgium was to provide the invasion route into France.

German planning for an attack against France was soon in hand. Hitler wanted to launch an invasion as early as possible. He told his generals: 'For the first time in history we have only to fight on one front. The other is at present open. But nobody can be certain how long it will remain so.'[5] Bad weather and Allied passivity meant there was no urgent reason for a winter attack. Further postponements caused the date for the German offensive in the west to be put back to the spring of 1940. This delay allowed further planning debates to take place within the German military hierarchy. The views of General von Rundstedt of Army Group A and his Chief of Staff, General von Manstein, steadily won over their colleagues on the General Staff. Rundstedt and Manstein had seen the success of mobile forces with their own eyes during the Polish campaign. Rundstedt, in his mid-sixties, had the persona of an unyielding, aristocratic Prussian, but he was adaptable and shrewd. He had spent most of the First World War on the eastern front and was accustomed to the idea of sweeping military manoeuvre.

On 7 February 1940 Rundstedt's Army Group A held a war game at Koblenz attended by OKH's Chief of Staff, General Halder. The outcome of the war game suggested that the plan favoured by Manstein to push panzer and motorised forces through southern Belgium to the River Meuse in northern France was practicable. This thrust would split the Allied front. A week later another war game at a subordinate army headquarters attended by Halder confirmed that impression. In the meantime Manstein had privately explained his plans to an approving Hitler. The Kaiser had become a virtual prisoner of his general staff during the First World War, but Hitler had every intention of being an active player in military planning when he wished.[6]

By late February OKH (army high command) had developed a revised plan known as *Sichelschnitt*, 'the cut of the sickle'. The initial attack, at the northern end of the western front, was to be made against Holland and Belgium by Army Group B. If British and French forces advanced into Belgium in response so much the better; Army Group B might act as a 'matador's cloak' to draw their enemy forward. A small Army Group C opposite the Maginot Line would, it was hoped, be sufficient to keep French divisions fixed in their fortifications. The main attack was to be made by Rundstedt's Army Group A, which was centrally located between Army Groups B and C. Army Group A, with seven panzer divisions, was to drive through the Ardennes Forest in southern Belgium and Luxembourg to north-eastern France and the River Meuse. At a conference on 15 March Hitler asked General Guderian, a panzer corps commander, what might happen afterwards if armour could successfully cross the River Meuse. Guderian replied:

> Unless I receive orders to the contrary, I intend on the next day to continue my advance westward. The supreme leadership must decide whether my objective is to be Amiens or Paris. In my opinion the correct course is to drive past Amiens to the English Channel.[7]

In response, Hitler nodded quietly, but this question was never clearly fixed in advance. That German planning was constantly evolving made it harder for Allied intelligence to decipher their enemy's intentions. The continual postponements of the German offensive across the winter of 1939–40 had undermined specific warnings that were received from time to time.

The French were not afraid of a German attack. Allied confidence was based on the sheer size of the combined British and French Empires and Allied mastery of the oceans. Certainly the loss of Russia to the Nazi camp had been a blow, and the French government's ban of the Communist Party caused discord among its large French following, but French draft evaders in 1939 were no higher than in 1914, perhaps one and a half per cent of recalled reservists. Marc Bloch, the future author of *Strange Defeat*, a condemnation of the French war effort, gave little sign of pessimism in his letters before May 1940.[8]

In the coming battle for France much would depend on the quality of the French Army, its commanders, equipment and methods. Some French divisions were of relatively high quality. These divisions included formations kept up to full strength in peacetime to train the current intake of conscripts, and regular divisions from the garrison of North Africa. There had been a great deal of fighting in Morocco in the 1920s and 1930s, though this did not take place on terrain that was favourable to experiments in mechanised warfare. The French Army was particularly strong in artillery, the dominant arm of 1914–18, but weak in mechanical transport, nine-tenths of which had to be requisitioned from civilian sources.[9] New model 25mm and 47mm anti-tank guns were effective weapons, but there were not enough to adequately equip the whole army. Some anti-tank guns were horse-drawn. Like the bulk of the German infantry, the French infantry was still heavily dependent on their own feet for transport.

Upon mobilisation French military depots had been flooded with reservists. Over half a million men, however, had to be sent back to their jobs in industry, which was both disruptive for combatant formations and a prime demonstration of bureaucratic inefficiency. Reservists were of widely differing quality. After initial military service a Frenchman spent no less than twenty-seven years in the reserve; three in the 'ready' reserve, sixteen in the first-line Series A reserve and eight years in the second-line Series B reserve.[10] Series B men were typically in their forties and this was an indication of the extent to which the French had to stretch their manpower to be competitive in a war against Germany. The British Lieutenant-General Sir Alan Brooke, a harsh judge at the best of times, wrote of a column of Ninth Army Series B men at a 1939 Armistice Day parade:

> Corap [the Ninth Army's commander] requested me to stand alongside him whilst the guard of honour, consisting of cavalry, artillery and infantry marched past. I can still see those troops now. Seldom have I seen anything more slovenly and badly turned out. Men unshaven, horses ungroomed, clothes and saddlery that did not fit, vehicles dirty, and complete lack of pride in themselves or their units. What shook me most, however, was the look in the men's faces, disgruntled and insubordinate looks.[11]

French conscripts had served for three years until the early 1920s, but this had been reduced to only one year by 1930. An unduly short service period did not allow enough time to teach recruits how to use mechanised equipment.[12] Only in 1935 was a two-year period reintroduced to make up for the onset of the 'hollow years'. All too often older Series B men had received little training in the first period of their service and had forgotten what they knew in the years since. New types of equipment were a complete mystery to many reservists.

The Phoney War period did not see much improvement in general troop preparedness, as unusually cold weather in the winter of 1939–40 and work on defences interfered with training. This was especially true for men of the Second and Ninth Armies lining semi-built frontier defences to the north of the Maginot Line. With hindsight, there appears to have been an ominous unwillingness on the part of the French Army's regular cadre to force reservist officers and men through a tough programme of training. The state of virtual truce that held along the active front did little to develop military preparedness either. A British war correspondent asked a French sentry why he did not fire on a German washing himself across a river. He was told, 'if we fire they will fire back'.[13]

Senior officers in the French Army tended to be elderly men who had often already been generals in the First World War. The average age of army commanders was sixty-five, corps commanders sixty, and commanders of divisions were in their late fifties. Partly as a consequence, French military thought had been insufficiently affected by recent military events, particularly the campaign in Poland. So far as the French Army was concerned, Poland was a backward state and not a first-rate power. A similar patronising attitude had been adopted towards the Spanish Civil War, which was dismissed as an old-fashioned conflict between under-equipped infantry, rather than a trial run for new weaponry and methods. The prophetic role played by small numbers of modern aircraft and tanks in Spain was not as obvious to contemporaries as it is today.

The French supreme commander was General Maurice Gamelin, a sixty-eight year-old who had his headquarters, the Grand Quartier General, near Paris at Chateau de Vincennes. Lacking radio communications, the Vincennes headquarters was later described as a 'submarine without a periscope'. Gamelin had passed out top of his class at St-Cyr. He had been a senior staff officer and divisional commander in the First World War. During the 1920s he had headed a military mission to the Brazilian Army and had led the suppression of a major rebellion in Syria, before holding down senior general staff posts from the turn of the 1930s. Gamelin's predecessor at the summit of the French military hierarchy had been General Weygand, who had also been sixty-eight at the time of his retirement.

Gamelin wore a tight tunic and high-laced boots. Andre Maurois wrote of Gamelin: 'His short, stiff moustache, his small eyes and thin-lipped mouth gave him an indecipherable aspect, which no spontaneous gesture served to clarify.'[14] Whilst looking fit for his age, Gamelin was facing the likelihood of retirement at some point during the war. He had few obvious thoughts on mobile warfare or modern equipment and training. He did not visit troops often and frustrated his subordinates with his indecisiveness. His tendency to promote consensus within the military command ensured that the views of his most senior colleagues dominated questions of tactics and organisation. Daladier, one of the Third Republic's many Prime Ministers, is alleged to have said that the supreme commander's words were 'like sand running through one's fingers'.[15] Nonetheless, Gamelin was an intelligent man with cultured interests and a flair for diplomacy. He had absorbed the political atmosphere of the Third Republic well, and kept his headquarters near Paris partly for that reason.

French command arrangements did not make Gamelin's task any easier. As commander of all French land forces, Gamelin was responsible for troops in Syria, North Africa and the Alps facing Italy. To share the burden, and directly face the German threat, General Alphonse-Joseph Georges was appointed commander of the North Eastern Front. Gamelin and Georges, a straightforward soldier, did not see eye to eye. Georges had been badly wounded in a 1934 terrorist attack that had assassinated the King of Yugoslavia and the French Foreign Minister.[16]

In terms of equipment, the French Army had been undermined during the pre-war period by domestic political turmoil that had delayed vitally needed increases in military spending. In 1938 German military spending had been 16.4 per cent of national expenditure, as against 8.5 per cent in France and 8.3 per cent in Britain.[17] A portion of the French military budget had to be invested in a large navy that included seven battleships, with more under construction.

The relatively low level of French military spending hurt the development of armoured vehicles for the army, though a belatedly launched rearmament programme had yielded significant results. By 1940 the French Army had at least as many tanks as the German Army.[18] On paper the French tank force, which comprised 3,063 vehicles by one estimate, compared well to their German counterparts in terms of speed, armour and gun-power.[19] By the spring of 1940 the French Army had three divisions of light and medium tanks (DLMs – *Division Legere Mecanique*).[20] There were another three divisions comprising heavy tanks (DCRs – *Division Cuirassee de Reserve*) and a fourth division was in the process of formation. This would give the French seven specialised armoured divisions. Still, only half of French tanks were allocated to the armoured divisions. Independent tank battalions accounted for the other half of French tanks. These tank battalions were distributed in penny-packets among the infantry divisions.

Nevertheless, though the number of French tanks was impressive by 1940, there were major drawbacks to French tank design that rendered French armoured vehicles dramatically inferior to their marginally less numerous

German counterparts. French tanks had been designed to carry small crews; so small that the fighting power of their vehicles was badly retarded. French light tanks and some medium models only carried a two-man crew. The medium Somua S-35 had a three-man crew, and the heavy Char B1 had a four-man crew.[21] French tanks were also cursed with a one-man turret, meaning that the turret man had to be commander-loader-gunner rolled into one. As a consequence, leadership, rate of gun fire and accuracy were all horribly compromised.

Another design problem with French tanks was that four out of five tanks did not have a radio.[22] Radio was vital to the rapid manoeuvre of a tank formation, and was at least as important to armoured warfare as any other characteristic of tank design. The larger crew in a German tank permitted a specialised radio operator, as well as better handling of the gun and command function. In no sense was the typical French tank of 1940 as effective as a similar weight German tank of the period. The rushed design and creation of French armoured units on the eve of war was the main source of the problems.

The French Army did not stand alone in the defence of their country. As in 1914–18, Britain was committed to the defence of France. Britain, however, did not have army conscription prior to 1939. The mobilisation strength of the British Army consisted of the regulars and reservists available in the United Kingdom and part-time territorials. The raising and training of a large citizen army was likely to take the better part of two years. In the spring of 1940 the British Expeditionary Force in France comprised only 400,000 troops.[23] A number of fresh divisions were being formed in the United Kingdom, but the government had no intention of sending them across the Channel until they had attained a reasonable standard of training and equipment. This was a luxury the French could not afford in respect to their own low-grade divisions.

The most noteworthy thing about the BEF, apart from its limited size, was that it was fully motorised, unlike the German and French Armies. There were few horses left in the British Army and this reflected the great spread of motor transport in British civilian life. In contradiction to this, the development of British armoured forces had lagged well behind the German and the French, though the British had pioneered tank warfare in the First World War.[24] The British had lost their lead in building armoured vehicles in the early 1930s due to cutbacks in military spending and the preferential treatment given to obsolete cavalry regiments. As late as 1935 the Secretary of State for War, Alfred Duff Cooper, had said in the House of Commons that for the cavalry to exchange their horses for motor vehicles 'was like asking a great musical performer to throw away his violin and devote himself in the future to the gramophone'.[25] (Duff Cooper wrote a sympathetic biography of Field-Marshal Earl Haig.) With the survival of the cavalry regiments at stake, decisions had eventually been made to give them light tanks and armoured cars at the expense of creating additional specialised tank units. In the spring of 1940 the BEF had only 300 tanks.

The BEF's commander was Lord Gort, a former Chief of the Imperial General Staff and highly decorated First World War veteran. Gort was well liked by those who knew him. A Frenchman described him as having the personality of 'a jovial battalion commander'. Gort was no intellectual or administrator, nor was he keen on foreigners.[26] In the winter of 1939–40 Gort contributed little to the planning debates of the Allies, his task not made any easier by the multi-layered nature of the French High Command, and his own responsibilities as both an army commander and BEF Commander-in-Chief. Gort could appeal over Gamelin's head to his own government in an emergency.

The BEF was joined in France by a Royal Air Force contingent, but in the air the Allies were at a serious numerical disadvantage relative to the Germans. The French had neglected their air force, whilst the British kept a large part of their powerful RAF in the United Kingdom. In the spring of 1940 the RAF had 456 aircraft based in France, just a fraction of its global first-line strength. The French Air Force had only become an independent organisation in 1933 and had in total 2,330 mostly obsolete aircraft, of which 1,735 were in the European theatre.[27] The French Air Force had been starved of funds, only for that state of affairs rapidly to change on the eve of war. Employment in the French aircraft industry had risen from 35,000 in 1938 to 230,000 in May 1940.[28] New high-performance fighters were on the verge of mass production. In contrast, the *Luftwaffe* had over 4,000 operational aircraft in the western theatre at the start of May 1940, the great bulk of which were modern. Logically, the French neglect of their air force was reflected in a shortage of anti-aircraft guns for the army.[29]

As the Allies were not planning an offensive in 1940, it became a question of waiting for the first German move. Gamelin was counting on the Germans invading Belgium, as they had done in 1914. If that happened, he intended to advance strong forces into Belgium to parry the blow. This would avoid the error of 1914, when French miscalculations had allowed almost all of Belgium and large parts of north-east France to fall into German hands in one swoop. north and central Belgium was the destination for the bulk of Allied forces earmarked for Gamelin's counter-offensive. The forests and hills of southern Belgium were less suitable terrain for a large army.

French planning had been given a jolt when a German aircraft crashed just across the Belgian frontier, near the town of Mechelen-sur-Meuse, on the morning of 10 January 1940. Aboard the aircraft was Major Helmuth Reinberger, the commander of a paratroops school. The pilot had become lost in heavy cloud flying to Cologne and the engine had failed. Despite the ban on carrying secret documents by aircraft, Reinberger had papers in his possession which he was unable to burn prior to capture. The material revealed something of the expected German offensive into Belgium, but German plans seemed also to include an invasion of Holland. This information was discreetly passed to the Allies. Gamelin became convinced that Allied forces should link up with the Dutch in the event of a German invasion. At the northern end of the front the French Seventh Army was detailed to dash all the way to the Dutch border and beyond to Breda. Alas for the French, the Dutch were planning to pull back from their frontier to concentrate on defending the area around Amsterdam, Rotterdam and The Hague.[30]

General Georges was opposed to the Breda thrust, as he felt Holland was too distant, but Gamelin ordered the new plan to be put in place on 20 March 1940. Roughly thirty Allied divisions were ready to advance into Belgium and Holland, whilst forty divisions watched Germany from the Maginot Line and twenty-two divisions were held in reserve.[31] Once the German offensive in the Low Countries had been parried, the French High Command expected that the front would settle down to a new round of static trench-style warfare, and, after an eventual successful Allied offensive, a political settlement would end the war.

Despite his optimistic plans for a counter-offensive into Belgium, in the spring of 1940 another threatening scenario was preying on Gamelin's mind. He believed that the German army group opposite the Maginot Line was almost twice as strong as it actually was. He was concerned that the Germans might try to turn the Maginot Line from the south through Switzerland. Allied estimates of German tank strength were highly alarmist. In April 1940 the Anglo-French liaison committee estimated the Germans to have 5,800 tanks (4,000 Mark Is and IIs and 1,800 Mark IIIs).[32] The *Deuxieme Bureau* (French military intelligence) favoured an even higher estimate. They placed German tank strength at 7,000–7,500. French military intelligence assumed that the Germans attached independent tank battalions to their infantry formations, much as the French Army did. The *Deuxieme Bureau* had a long established habit of exaggerating German strength.[33]

Behind the Allied armies, the political instability of the Third Republic had not been restrained by the advent of war. Paul Reynaud replaced Daladier as French Prime Minister on 21 March 1940, a move ostensibly brought about by disquiet over the failure of the Allies to aid Finland against the Soviets. Daladier was demoted to another senior post within the new government. The Daladier ministry of April 1938 to March 1940 had been relatively long by Third Republic standards, and had successfully driven forward a major rearmament programme. The incoming Reynaud ministry was still settling down when, to the surprise of the Allies, the first German move in 1940 was the invasion of Norway and Denmark early in April. A naval expedition involving almost all German warships, supported by airborne troops, rapidly established a firm grip on Norway's long seaboard. The Royal Navy had been caught unawares in waters they felt they controlled. A small Allied ground expedition to Norway was beset by confusion and had only a limited impact until its eventual evacuation. The German occupation of Norway loosened the Allied sea blockade of the North Sea. Germany's vital supply of iron ore from Sweden was firmly secured.

Unimpressed by Gamelin's dilatory response during the Norwegian campaign, the newly installed Prime Minister Reynaud was keen to replace the Supreme Commander. He told a colleague, 'It would be criminal to leave this nerveless philosopher at the head of the French Army'. Daladier, however, had a long political association with Gamelin and supported the general in Cabinet, threatening to break up the new government by resigning if the Supreme Commander was dismissed. As late as 9 May Reynaud again tried at a Cabinet meeting to secure authorisation to replace Gamelin, and considered resignation himself when he could not secure sufficient support. He was soon to be overtaken by events.[34]

After further postponements, due to poor weather, the great German offensive began on 10 May. Many German commanders were unsure of its prospects. Optimistically, Hitler told his staff prior to the assault: 'You are about to witness the most famous victory in history!' The attack was a surprise. The use of telephone landlines by the German military had eliminated the possibility of Allied intelligence uncovering German plans by intercepting encoded radio signals.[35]

On paper the German Army and the newly expanded alliance of western European states (with the inclusion of Holland and Belgium) fielded armies of similar strength. Of the German Army's 156 divisions, 136 were deployed for the offensive in the west. The remainder were in Scandinavia, Germany and eastern Europe. Allied strength on the western front, excluding a number of French divisions watching Italy, was also 136 divisions: ninety-four French, ten British, twenty-two Belgian and ten Dutch.[36]

During the winter of 1939–40 the *Wehrmacht's* five panzer divisions had been expanded to ten. In May 1940 German tank strength was 2,574.[37] Only 628 of these tanks were medium Mark III and Mark IV vehicles. The rest were light tanks, command tanks and Czech-built tanks. German tank types were mixed within divisions to allow medium tanks to support and protect more vulnerable light tanks. Hitler's pact with Stalin had made possible the massing of the great bulk of the German Army in the western theatre.

The initial German target was the Low Countries. The Belgian Army had a mobilisation strength of 600–700,000. King Leopold III of Belgium, in his late thirties and an old Etonian, directly commanded the Belgian Army, as his father Albert I had done in the First World War.[38] At 4.30 on the morning of 10 May Belgian soldiers garrisoning the fort of Eben Emael, near the junction of the Albert Canal and River Meuse a few miles south of Maastricht, received the shock of their lives when German glider-borne troops landed on the roof of the fort. Gliders towed by transport aircraft were employed, as a parachute drop was likely to disperse the attackers. Eben Emael had not been designed with an assault from the air in mind. The specially trained Koch Storm Detachment used explosive charges to knock out the turrets of the fort. Eben Emael, more powerful than any single Maginot Line fort, surrendered before midday on 11 May, along with a battalion-sized garrison.[39] Airborne troops were also used to seize nearby bridges. German mechanised columns on the ground raced to link up with their airborne comrades. German troops soon began crossing the breach made in the main Belgian defence line. The Belgian authorities had wasted no time inviting Allied forces to enter their country. General Gaston Billotte had been appointed commander of the Allied army group destined to operate in the Low Countries.

The German offensive in the west achieved early success. The Dutch Army was crushed in five days. When the advance guard of the French Seventh Army reached Breda in Holland they met German troops instead of Dutch. Rotterdam was heavily bombed on 14 May, by which time the Queen had already left for Britain in a warship. Nonetheless, the Dutch government, colonial empire, navy and merchant shipping remained with the Allied cause, despite the German conquest of the Netherlands.

The German High Command was pleased with the way events were developing. Hitler later recalled:

> It was wonderful the way everything turned out according to plan. When news came through that the enemy was moving forward along the whole front, I could have wept for joy; they had fallen into the trap ... they had believed ... that we were sticking to the old Schlieffen Plan.[40]

By 12 May the Belgian Army was in full retreat from the Albert Canal towards the left flank of the British Expeditionary Force, which was digging in along the River Dyle in front of Brussels. South of the BEF, the French First and Ninth Armies continued the line to Namur and the southern arm of the Belgian Meuse.

Gamelin had left only weak forces guarding the Ardennes region of Luxembourg and south east Belgium. With fighting underway further north in the Low Countries, this sector became the central pivot of the entire front from the North Sea to Switzerland. Allied commanders, however, believed that the Ardennes forest was too dense for a large mechanised army. But the tanks of seven panzer divisions were moving through the Ardennes, unspotted by Allied aerial reconnaissance. The main German blow was heading towards the junction of the French Ninth and Second Armies.

General Charles Huntziger's Second Army held a sector from the northern end of the Maginot Line at Longwy to the River Meuse near Sedan, the scene of the crushing French defeat at Prussian hands in 1870 that had ended Napoleon III's Second Empire. Huntziger had extensive colonial experience. He was still under sixty years of age and a possible successor to Gamelin. Huntziger's best divisions were on his right flank to guard the immediate northern end of the Maginot Line. Against the Meuse, General Grandsard's X Corps held the left flank of the Second Army's line with, from left to right, the Series B 55th and Series B 71st Divisions and the regular 3rd North African Division. On 12 May the 71st Division was only settling into the centre of the corps line after two nights' forced marching. Grandsard wrote of his Series B troops that:

> cases of ill-will were rare, but the ardour for work, for training and the desire to fight, were even rarer. Nonchalance was general; it was accompanied by the feeling that France could not be beaten, that Germany would be beaten without battle ... the men are flabby and heavy ... In the artillery the men are older, the training is mediocre.[41]

Grandsard's Series B divisions were below establishment in anti-tank guns. The 71st Division was also understrength in men and partly recruited from 'red-tainted' suburbs of Paris.

To the left of X Corps was the right-flank division of the neighbouring Ninth Army. This was also a Series B division. The Ninth Army's commander was General Andre Corap. Corap, sixty-two and heavy in build, had won fame in North Africa in 1926 for his role in the capture of Abd-el-Krim, the leader of tribal forces that had waged a full-scale war against Spain and France. Maurois wrote of Corap that he was 'unmilitary in appearance, and running to fat around the middle. He had trouble getting into a car.'[42] The Ninth Army had pushed its left flank into Belgium to defend the line of the Meuse south of Namur.

Traffic jams in the Ardennes did more to disrupt the advance of the panzer divisions leading Rundstedt's army group than French and Belgian reconnaissance troops on horseback. Guderian, commander of the XIX Panzer Corps, wanted to rush the line of the River Meuse at the first opportunity. Aerial photographs had revealed French frontier defences north of the Maginot Line to be surprisingly weak.[43] Suspicions were starting to deepen within the French High Command as to the direction of the main German thrust.[44]

By 12 May panzer troops had already reached the east bank of the Meuse and the Belgian town of Houx. Major-General Erwin Rommel's 7th Panzer Division captured Houx, after which an undefended weir was discovered that led to an island midstream and a lock gate leading to the other bank. This structure had not been destroyed by the Allies in case it lowered the water level of the Meuse upstream. That night Rommel's divisional motor-cycle battalion crossed the river by the weir to make a small dent in the Ninth Army's line.

There was no time to waste and General Ewald von Kleist, the commander of Army Group A's Panzer Group, ordered Guderian to assault across the Meuse either side of Sedan at 3 p.m. on 13 May. Guderian's panzer corps was the most southern of the three panzer corps approaching the Meuse. On the far side of the river the French could hear the engines of tanks roaring. General Grandsard of X Corps believed that the Germans would have to pause to bring up their heavy artillery and ammunition before crossing the river, but the Germans were planning to use the *Luftwaffe* in that role. This was another unexpected surprise for the Allies in a war proving full of novelties.

In the morning of 13 May German medium bombers attacked the French behind the Meuse without much opposition from Allied fighters. A heavy bombardment by Stuka dive-bombers in the early afternoon sunshine helped directly to soften up the defenders. Sergeant Pruemers of the 1st Panzer Division watched the Stukas.

> Simultaneously, like some bird of prey, they fall upon their victim and then release their load of bombs on the target ... Each time the explosion is overwhelming, the noise deafening. Everything becomes blended together; along with the howling siren of the Stukas in their dives, the bombs whistle and crack and burst ... We stand and watch what is happening as if hypnotised; down below all hell is let loose![45]

The 550-pound bombs were inaccurate but a frightening experience for infantry crouching in their bunkers and trenches. French artillery positions were vulnerable to the unexpected severity of the assault from the air.

German 88mm anti-aircraft guns fired directly at French positions on the far side of the Meuse. These weapons proved to be effective against ground targets. Mid-afternoon, infantry of Guderian's corps began crossing the sixty-yard wide river by rubber boat. Sedan, unlike Houx, was on French territory and there had been twenty years to finish the uncompleted local fortifications. The panzer and motorised infantry making the assault crossing had been well blooded in the Polish campaign, and were as fine a body of 'Special Force' quality troops as could be found in the world of 1940. The German Army magnified its effectiveness by using its very best troops at the lance-point of major operations.

German troops crossing the river were badly shot up in places but sufficient numbers reached the far bank to create a bridgehead. By evening Guderian's corps had a firm foothold across the river, the thrust supported by the elite Grossdeutschland and 1st Rifle Regiments to secure the dominant heights of La Marfee, south west of Sedan. The French 55th Division caved in before the fury of the attack. Panic is alleged to have begun with the artillerymen. The withdrawal of the divisional command post during the night added to the confusion. To the right of the 55th Division, the neighbouring 71st Division also began to give way.

As General Joseph-Aime Doumenc, Gamelin's Chief of Staff, later commented:

> Crediting our enemies with our own procedure, we had imagined that they would
> not attempt the passage of the Meuse until after they had brought up ample artil-
> lery: the five or six days necessary for that would have easily given us time to
> reinforce our own dispositions.[46]

The Germans bridged the Meuse overnight and formed a pocket south of the river, three miles wide and four to six miles deep. Piecemeal counter-attacks by local French reserves had achieved little by the following morning.

On 13 May, whilst Guderian's troops were crossing the Meuse further south, General Rommel personally supervised the reinforcement of his division's bridgehead across the river near Dinant and Houx. Panzers directly fired on French bunkers and machine gun posts across the Meuse as troops paddled on the water in rubber boats. French counter-attacks lacked strength and a bridgehead a couple of miles deep and three miles wide was created. That night it became possible to start ferrying tanks over the river, 120 yards across at this point. In response, the French 1st Armoured Division, newly released from general reserve, began approaching the expanding bridgehead. Zouaves and Algerian Tirailleurs of the 4th North African Division were also sent by General Corap from the Ninth Army's reserve to reinforce an improvised defence line.

The next day, 14 May, Rommel added further to his growing reputation as an energetic front-line commander. The tank in which he was travelling was twice hit by shells. Rommel was wounded in the cheek and the tank had to be abandoned.[47] The panzers carved deeper into the French front. According to the military historian Sir Basil Liddell Hart, the forty-eight year-old Rommel, a Wurttemberger and son of a school teacher, would come to personify the 'dynamism of *Blitzkrieg*'. Both thoughtful and audacious, he was able to base his decisions on what he saw with his own eyes, something that was particularly important as a new form of warfare was unfolding that a senior officer could not have seen earlier in his career.[48] Rommel was not a tank specialist, nor a general staff officer, but he had a brilliant record from the First World War, having won the *Pour le Merite* against the Italians in 1917. He had come to Hitler's attention in 1938 as a colonel who had written a book about his experience as an infantryman. During the Polish campaign Rommel had again been under the Führer's eye as commander of the guard of Hitler's field headquarters. Rommel had subsequently asked for command of a panzer division, as he had been impressed by the tank force's achievements in Poland. Rommel's 7th Panzer Division was understrength in armoured vehicles, with only three of the usual four tank battalions, and half its tanks were Czech tanks. Guderian and Rommel were not the only thrusting panzer leaders, but they would be the most famous of the French campaign.

At Sedan on 14 May the 55th and 71st Divisions continued to fall apart, the first of a steady stream of French divisions to more or less vanish from the order of battle. On the heights beyond the Meuse near Thelonne, Sergeant Schulze of the 10th Panzer Division observed: 'We found their artillery positions left as if they had fled. Some of the guns were still loaded; the enemy had not had time to render the weapons unserviceable.'[49] In the meadows on the banks of the Meuse Guderian saw thousands of French prisoners. He made the vital decision to wheel his panzers westwards, rather than continue to attack southwards from the breach his corps had wrought in the French front.

Allied air forces tried to bomb the German bridges hastily thrown over the Meuse, but the *Luftwaffe* and strong anti-aircraft defences were waiting for the bombers. After noon on 14 May French aircraft attacked and lost heavily. By mid-afternoon it was the turn of the British. Forty of seventy-one RAF bombers were downed; many of them outdated Battles and Blenheims. Total Allied aircraft losses at Sedan were ninety.[50]

When the news of the growing crisis at Sedan reached French commanders they were devastated. In the early morning of 14 May a staff officer recorded the scene at General Georges's North East Front headquarters.

> The atmosphere was that of a family in which there had been a death. Georges ... was terribly pale. 'Our front has been broken at Sedan! There has been a collapse ...' He flung himself into a chair and burst into tears. He was the first man I had seen weep in this campaign. Alas, there were to be others. It made a terrible impression on me.[51]

To the north of Sedan in Belgium, advancing Allied forces had made contact with German troops of Army Group B moving along the traditional invasion route to France. This was where Gamelin had expected the Germans to make their main thrust. The vanguard of the French First Army, two armoured divisions of General Rene Prioux's Cavalry Corps (2d and 3d DLM), met two panzer divisions head-on in the Gembloux Gap. The opposing divisions had a combined strength in excess of a thousand tanks.[52] This was good tank country and combat began on 12 May. On 13–14 May fierce tank-versus-tank fighting took place whilst the infantry divisions of the French First Army came into position behind their screen of armour. The Cavalry Corps, some of France's best troops, performed steadfastly at Gembloux. French tanks were a match for German tanks in some respects, though cooperation between French tanks was hampered by a lack of radios. At times commanders had to run from one tank to another and hammer on the hatches to give an order.[53] On 15 May a concentrated German attack was held with difficulty at Gembloux by French infantry and guns, but that evening the order came to begin a withdrawal towards the Franco-Belgian frontier. The fighting in central Belgium had held the attention of valuable Allied forces at a critical time.

On a tactical level the fighting at Gembloux had revealed a crucial aspect of tank combat, namely that the army that won the day was able to recover its damaged armoured vehicles. A victorious armoured division could self-regenerate with repaired tanks. Only a quarter of vehicles lost to either combat or mechanical breakdown were beyond repair. On the other hand, the army that quit the field was able to salvage very little. When the French withdrew from Gembloux, damaged or broken-down tanks had to be abandoned. The French 3d DLM lost half to two-thirds of 150 Hotchkiss light tanks and thirty of eighty-seven Somua medium tanks. German effective losses were a good deal fewer. Early on 16 May the 3rd and 4th Panzer Divisions listed just forty-nine tanks destroyed. The same report listed 20–25 per cent of tanks in the 3rd Panzer Division and 45–50 per cent of tanks in the 4th Panzer Division 'unfit for action'.[54] But most of those tanks were reparable in mobile field workshops and fought again in the campaign.

Once the French line behind the Ardennes had been broken, German tanks poured through the gap and raced westwards. In the early hours of 15 May General Corap asked for permission to retire his Ninth Army from the Belgian Meuse to the French frontier. On that day Rommel's tanks came upon the French 1st Armoured Division's heavy Char B1 tanks whilst refuelling and dealt them a heavy blow in piecemeal fighting. By the end of 15 May Rommel's division had advanced another seventeen miles. The Ninth Army disintegrated as it tried to retreat in the face of a fast-moving adversary. General Reinhardt's XLI Panzer Corps, the central of the three panzer corps emerging from the Ardennes, pushed forward rapidly beyond the Meuse to join the fray. A member of the 6th Panzer Division recalled:

> A perfect road stretched before us with no enemy fliers over us. The air was completely dominated by our own fliers. A wonderful feeling of uncondi-
> tional superiority. We rushed on at 50 mph to Montcornet on the Serre. In
> front of the town there was a short collision with a French company, who gave
> themselves up almost without fighting.[55]

Gamelin's headquarters at Vincennes continued to misread German intentions. French reinforcements were deployed to cover the northern flank of the Maginot Line.

In London the British government and public anxiously followed events on the Continent. Chamberlain had been forced to resign and the new Prime Minister, Winston Churchill, lost no time unleashing his rhetoric to stiffen national morale. In the House of Commons on 13 May Churchill had stated:

> You ask, what is our policy? I will say. It is to wage war, by sea, land and air, with all
> our might and with all the strength that God can give us; to wage war against a mon-
> strous tyranny, never surpassed in the dark, lamentable catalogue of human crime.

The war aim of Churchill's government was 'victory at all costs, victory in spite of all terror, victory however long and hard the road may be; for without victory there is no survival'.[56] RAF bombers would soon commence night bombing of industrial targets in western Germany. Across the Channel, though, the French leadership was not feeling so resolute.

On the morning of 15 May French Prime Minister Reynaud called Churchill by telephone:

> I was woken up with the news that M. Reynaud was on the telephone at my bedside. He said in English, and evidently under stress. 'We have been defeated.' As I did not immediately respond he said again: 'We are beaten; we have lost the battle.' I said: 'Surely it can't have happened so soon?' But he replied: 'The front is broken near Sedan; they are pouring through in great numbers with tanks and armoured cars.'

Churchill flew to Paris the following afternoon.

On 16 May Gamelin met Reynaud, Churchill, Daladier and other high officials at the Quai d'Orsay, the French foreign ministry. Outside the building official documents were already being thrown onto bonfires. According to Churchill, 'Utter dejection was written on every face'. Gamelin explained that a hole fifty to sixty miles wide had been torn in the front around Sedan. Armour and motorised German formations were pouring through the gap towards either the Atlantic coast or Paris. Churchill asked Gamelin, 'Where is the strategic reserve?' Gamelin turned to him with a shrug and said, 'There is none.'[57] The war had started badly in 1914, but the pace of events in that year had not been so rapid.

Generals Gamelin and Georges worried that the Germans would immediately direct their forces on Paris, but German tanks and motorised infantry headed westwards from Sedan. The terrain of northern France and the spring weather was ideal for mechanised formations. In glorious sunshine the columns strained their supply lines to the limit. Tanks refuelled at public petrol stations and soldiers milked untended cows. Guderian travelled with the advance guard in his command vehicle. Long columns of refugees clogged the roads. Towns emptied and millions would eventually be on the move, their belongings staked on all manner of carts and vehicles. Rumours of a fifth column and fear of air attack added to the atmosphere of panic.

The pace of the advance began to cause Rundstedt and other senior German commanders concern given the sheer length of the flank they were offering to a French riposte from the south. General Halder at OKH wrote in his diary for 17 May:

> An unpleasant day. The Führer is terribly nervous. Frightened by his own success, he is afraid to take any chance and so would rather pull the reins on us. Puts forward the excuse that it is all because of his concern for the left flank!

Rundstedt later commented:

> I knew Gamelin before the war, and, trying to read his mind, had anticipated that
> he would make a flank move from the Verdun direction with his reserves. We esti-
> mated that he had thirty to forty divisions which could be used for the purpose.
> But nothing of the sort developed.[58]

French attempts to organise forces to contain the breakthrough were slow and
weak. Generals using field telephones and dispatch riders to communicate with
their front-line troops struggled to respond, especially as headquarters were
constantly changing location. General de Gaulle, in command of the newly
formed 4th Armoured Division, launched a series of local attacks against the
southern flank of the 'Panzer corridor', but these were only pin-pricks.

German infantry divisions marched forward along roads carrying French
soldiers marching in the other direction as prisoners. General Giraud, the
dismissed Corap's replacement in command of the Ninth Army, was captured
in the confusion. The French pilot Antoine de Saint-Exupery recorded his
impressions of the scene from the air:

> A French army, even though it seems to be virtually intact, has ceased to be an
> army. It has been transformed into clotted segments. The armoured divisions
> play the part of a chemical agent precipitating a colloidal solution. Where once
> an organism existed they leave a mere sum of organs whose unity has been
> destroyed.[59]

German tanks crossed the Picardy plain and the Canal du Nord. Battlefields
of the First World War were quickly traversed. The German thrust seemed
undiminished in strength. On the evening of 20 May troops of the 2nd
Panzer Division reached the Atlantic coast. Ominously for the forty-five
Allied divisions now cut off, late the next day Guderian received orders to
turn northwards.

On 18 May Prime Minister Reynaud asked Marshal Petain, formerly
ambassador at Madrid, to be his deputy. General Maxime Weygand was recalled
from Syria to replace Gamelin late on 19 May. Reynaud had decided to turn
to the heroes of the past rather than promote a current army or army group
commander. Weygand was a small and energetic man, but it would take time
for him to assess the situation after taking command in the early morning of
20 May.[60] He had been Marshal Foch's Chief of Staff during the First World
War and French Army commander from 1931–35. He had been recalled from
retirement in 1939 for a posting to Syria.

At the age of seventy-three Weygand was to replace the sixty-eight year-
old Gamelin. The latter's response to the growing crisis had appalled his
colleagues. Gamelin had been responsible for the ill-fated decision to push

strong forces into Belgium, and he had then abdicated command to Georges to salvage the situation. In ten days the French Army had lost no less than fifteen divisions routed and dispersed. Only on 19 May had Gamelin for the first time intervened to order Georges to launch converging attacks across the corridor leading to the Atlantic.

In Britain, the War Cabinet had met on 19 May and decided that the Chief of the Imperial General Staff, Field-Marshal Sir Edmund Ironside, should go to France personally to instruct Lord Gort to link back up with the main French army to the south. On 20 May the War Cabinet ordered Admiral Bertram Ramsay at Dover to begin preparations to evacuate the BEF if the need arose. Ironside, a man of 6 feet 4 inches, was in France by 20 May and he 'found Billotte [the northern army group's commander] and Blanchard [the French First Army's commander] at Lens, all in a state of complete depression. No plan, no thought of a plan. Ready to be slaughtered. Defeated at the head without casualties. Tres fatigues and nothing doing. I lost my temper and shook Billotte by the button of his tunic. The man is completely beaten.'[61] Ironside had no fresh forces of his own to contribute, however; just his own imposing personality.

On 21 May a British counter-attack was made, to the west of Arras, against the northern flank of the German breakthrough. Infantry supported seventy-four slow but heavily armoured tanks of the 1st Army Tank Brigade. Rommel's panzer division took the blow, during the course of which an ADC was killed at the general's side. The attack had a local impact and anxiety was caused among German commanders who had been waiting for a coordinated Allied counter-offensive. Also that day, General Weygand visited the northern army group and met King Leopold and Billotte at Ypres. The men could agree on little. To make matters worse, Billotte was mortally injured in a traffic accident returning to his headquarters. The situation further drifted until General Blanchard was confirmed as his replacement. On 25 May Major-General Sir Edward Spears, Churchill's liaison officer with the French government, heard Weygand tell Prime Minister Reynaud that the French Army was twenty years out of date. 'This war is sheer madness, we have gone to war with a 1918 army against a German Army of 1939.'[62]

On 22 May Guderian's panzer corps began driving northwards along the coast of north-west France towards the ports of Boulogne, Calais and Dunkirk. The Allied army group in the north was in danger of encirclement. British troops at Boulogne were evacuated on the night of 23/24 May, though French troops held out in the citadel until the morning of the 25th. By 24 May both Guderian's and Reinhardt's panzer corps had established a number of bridgeheads across the Aa Canal, on the south western approaches to Dunkirk.

Salvation, though, was at hand for Allied troops. Hitler and Rundstedt conferred on the morning of 24 May. The discussion focused on the vulnerability of the long corridor to the sea, with its extended flanks to the north and south.

Both men were separately concerned by this matter. The marching infantry was being left far behind. Rundstedt did not disagree with Hitler's desire to halt the panzers' northward drive.[63] The halt would give the infantry a chance to consolidate the flanks of the corridor, and give the tanks a chance to refit for a renewed offensive southward into central France. Goering had boasted that the *Luftwaffe* would disrupt and wreck any evacuation from a Channel port. Given the *Luftwaffe's* success at blasting Warsaw and Rotterdam, there was the distinct possibility that a harbour such as Dunkirk could be knocked out. Flanders was not the best terrain for tanks either. Bock's infantry of Army Group B were to deal with the northern Allied pocket. Generals Keitel and Jodl, the chiefs of Hitler's OKW (Supreme High Command), agreed with Hitler's decision, as was invariably the case.

At OKH (Army High Command) Generals von Brauchitsch and Halder were furious at the order to halt. Halder grimly noted that the panzers had been halted 'upon direct orders of the Führer! Finishing off the encircled enemy army is to be left to air force!!' Halder was not persuaded that Flanders was unsuited to tank warfare, and the *Luftwaffe* might well be frustrated by bad weather. Halder remarked that:

> these orders from the top just make no sense. In one area they call for a head-on attack against a front retiring in orderly fashion and still possessing its striking power, and elsewhere they freeze the troops to the spot when the enemy rear could be cut into anytime you wanted to attack.[64]

The order to halt panzer formations driving north was only rescinded on 26 May. In the time granted by the halt, many Allied troops were able to withdraw from the pocket extending south of Lille to a more defensible bridgehead around Dunkirk, a locality full of canals and dikes.

In Paris General Spears met Reynaud, Weygand and other senior French leaders to discuss the crisis.

> I suddenly realised with a clarity that had never before been vouchsafed me in all the long years I had worked with the French Army that to them the sea was much the same thing as an abyss of boiling pitch and brimstone, an insurmountable obstacle no army could venture over ... To fall back to Dunkirk represented retiring into a fortress, which might be supplied by sea, but from which there was no retreat.[65]

On 26 May the War Office in London approved Gort's decision to retire on Dunkirk. Later that day fighting ended at Calais, where a small Allied garrison had held up a superior German force for a critical period. On the afternoon of 27 May Gort received an order to evacuate as much of his force as possible. For the past week shipping had been gathering at Dover under the command of

Admiral Ramsay. The ports of south-east England had been stripped of vessels able to make a Channel crossing.

Initially London had expected to lose most of the BEF in the disaster looming on the Continent. German commanders did not believe a large evacuation to be possible either, and were slow to realise it was underway. That so many Allied troops were eventually saved was greatly aided by the fine fighting performance of the French First Army. On the evening of 28 May the French about Lille, and the Anglo-French defenders of the funnel between Lille and Dunkirk, held the attention of a series of panzer divisions.[66] Almost half the French First Army was cut off around Lille, but they fought on for several more days. General Prioux and the bulk of two corps were taken on 29 May. The garrison of Lille under General Molinie, pushed by the Germans into the suburbs, capitulated on the evening of 31 May. In his memoirs Churchill judiciously acknowledged that, 'These Frenchmen, under the gallant leadership of General Molinie, had for four critical days contained no less than seven German divisions which otherwise could have joined in the assaults on the Dunkirk perimeter'.[67] The fighting had been marred by SS executions of prisoners. On 27 May ninety-seven British prisoners had been executed but two men of the Royal Norfolk Regiment had survived to tell the tale.

The Dunkirk perimeter's main line of defence was the Bergues-Furnes Canal, the approaches to which lay across low, open countryside. Inundation along the Yser Canal helped to anchor the eastern flank of the perimeter. Burning oil tanks cast a pall of smoke over the town of Dunkirk. The confused German command structure around Dunkirk made it difficult to launch coordinated attacks, but the northern pocket soon ceased to be the most immediate German priority.[68] On the night of 28 May Guderian's corps had been ordered out of the line, followed by Reinhardt's corps the next day. The panzers had been turned south for the next round of the battle with the main body of the French Army.

The surrender of the Belgian Army in the early hours of 28 May had certainly not helped the Anglo-French cause at Dunkirk. The Belgian front in the north-east corner of the Allied pocket had been crumbling over the previous two to three days, though at no faster a rate than at other places in the Allied pocket. King Leopold's surrender as Commander-in-Chief did not involve his government, which stayed in the war. The combination of French defeatism, the impending British flight from the Continent and the collapse of the Belgian military's supply network in the last unconquered corner of Belgian territory had been all too much for the King. The Belgians had been without air cover for a number of days and their contracting sector was full of refugees. Reynaud lost no time in roundly condemning King Leopold on the radio. 'The King of the Belgians has betrayed us. Three weeks ago he begged us to fly to his help; today, without a word of warning, he has capitulated.'[69]

Strong RAF air cover over Dunkirk made the *Luftwaffe's* task more difficult, as did intermittent poor weather, especially on 28 and 30 May. The commander of *Luftflotte 2*, General Kesselring, pointed out to Goering that his squadrons were understrength, and starting to operate away from their permanent bases in Germany. Allied troops on the ground saw little of the aerial battle above the clouds or beyond the perimeter, but they did see the *Luftwaffe's* dive-bombers hurtling downwards. When shipping was sunk at night, quickly or alone, losses in troops and sailors were heavy. For instance, the destroyer HMS *Wakeful* was broken in two by a submarine's torpedo in the middle of the night with 650 troops aboard. There were few survivors. The heaviest naval losses were on 29 May and 1 June, when the weather was best from the *Luftwaffe's* viewpoint. 1 June dawned with mist and low cloud, but this was followed by sunshine. Ju 87 Stuka dive-bombers managed to attack shipping between RAF patrols. A number of ships were sunk but almost as many troops were evacuated as on the previous day. Nonetheless, Admiral Ramsay decided to halt the evacuation by daylight and limit it to the cover of night from that time onwards.[70]

The troops were embarked from Dunkirk harbour and beaches east of the town in a reasonably ordered manner. Beach sand fortuitously muffled the explosions of bombs. The French were slow to be involved in the evacuation. General Blanchard had little confidence in the operation and was reluctant to act without direct orders. Only on the afternoon of 29 May did Weygand order the evacuation of the First Army, though he had been informed three days before that the British government had ordered the BEF's departure.[71] From that time forward Gort agreed that the evacuation should be evenly split between the remaining British and French troops.

Marc Bloch, the French historian and a war-time staff officer, was among those evacuated from Dunkirk.

> I have a very vivid memory of the ruined town with its shells of buildings half-visible through drifting smoke, and its clutter, not of bodies, but of human debris, in the streets. I can still hear the incredible din which, like the orchestral finale of an opera, provided an accompaniment to the last few minutes which we spent on the coast of Flanders.[72]

40,000 French troops were captured when Dunkirk surrendered on 4 June.

338,226 Allied troops were evacuated in Operation Dynamo from 27 May to 4 June, over forty per cent of whom were French. (The French troops were mostly relanded in south-western France when shipping became available.)[73] Over 800 vessels had been involved in the evacuation, including all available civilian passenger ferries. Seventy-two ships are known to have been lost to hostile action, including six British and three French destroyers. Another nineteen British destroyers had been damaged.

Dunkirk may have been a triumph of sorts for Britain, but Churchill told the House of Commons on 4 June: 'We must be very careful not to assign to this deliverance the attributes of a victory. Wars are not won by evacuations.'[74] The evacuation had only been possible because almost all equipment had been abandoned. On 2 June General von Bock wrote in his diary after a tour of the Dunkirk front.

> The scene of the roads used by the English retreat was indescribable. Huge quantities of motor vehicles, guns, combat vehicles, and army equipment were crammed into a very small area and driven together. The English had tried to burn everything, but in their haste they succeeded only here and there. There lies the material of an army whose completeness of equipment we poor wretches can only gaze at with envy.[75]

The French leadership felt that the British evacuation ensured the collapse of the Dunkirk pocket sooner than might otherwise have been the case. That was true, but the panzer divisions had already been turned south for the next and final phase of the campaign. It is unlikely the BEF's evacuation delayed the moment that blow was to fall by as much as a day.

General Weygand – 'a doctor called in at the last moment to heal a man dying of an incurable disease' – prepared to fight the Germans on a line running across central France behind the Somme and Aisne rivers. The French Army had lost thirty divisions in the north, along with the Belgian and Dutch Armies and the great bulk of British troops. By one count Weygand still had forty-nine divisions along the Somme and Aisne, seventeen divisions in the Maginot Line and other forces facing the Italian border.[76] The French government left Paris for the south of the country.

At the western end of the Somme–Aisne line Bock's Army Group B began to attack on 5 June. At first the panzer divisions were held by French troops south of German bridgeheads over the Somme at Amiens and Peronne, but further west German troops broke the front of the French Tenth Army and drove southwards. By 12 June those Allied divisions between the breakthrough and the coast had been cut off and forced to surrender, including the bulk of the 51st Highland Division at St-Valery-en-Caux. Rommel's division was again at the forefront of operations. The pursuit continued deep into south-west France.

Rundstedt's Army Group A attacked across the River Aisne on 9 June. Guderian's panzer group broke through the French front after German infantry had established a bridgehead across the river. Paris was declared an open city on the night of 11 June and occupied by German forces three days later as refugees poured southwards. Verdun fell quickly to the triumphant Germans, who continued their pursuit to the Swiss border to pin 400,000 French troops against the Maginot Line from the rear. British forces in south-west France were rescued in another major evacuation. South of the Somme the Royal Navy embarked 191,870 troops, including many Poles. Tragically, at Nantes on 17 June the liner *Lancastria* was sunk amid a giant pool of burning oil. Nearly 3,000 of 5,800 aboard died.[77]

On 10 June Italy had belatedly joined the conflict. Hitler commented: 'First they were too cowardly to take part. Now they are in a hurry so that they can share the spoils.'[78] Churchill and the United States President, Franklin Delano Roosevelt, were equally contemptuous in their recorded remarks. A small French army blocked the progress of a much larger Italian force.

As the news from the battlefield worsened, Marshal Petain, France's eighty-four year-old First World War leader, formed a new government with Weygand as Minister of Defence. Reynaud had resigned on 16 June. The support of his colleagues had ebbed away. Petain's government made a number of key political decisions. The government would not leave metropolitan France for the safety of northern Africa, and Churchill's offer of political union between France and Britain was rejected. General de Gaulle, who had been appointed Under Secretary of State for National Defence, was one of the few members of the government to advocate fighting on. He left for London to lead the Free French movement.

Both Petain and Weygand wanted the war ended by a political agreement, rather than have the army endure the dishonour of surrender in the field in isolation from the government. They were determined that the army's defeat be portrayed as a state failure. The dismissed Gamelin also embraced this line of thinking. According to Gamelin, defeat was the consequence

> of all French policy, domestic and foreign, since 1919, the consequences of which unfolded inexorably ... I am personally convinced that our defeat is not a simple military one ... but rather the result of many causes. The whole nation has paid for so many accumulated mistakes.[79]

Petain had never been a great admirer of the Third Republic and had little liking for the British either. His pessimism was only enhanced by a not-so-secret admiration for fascism. On 17 June the French government approached the Germans for an armistice.[80]

Hitler and other Nazi leaders met the French delegation at Compiegne on 21 June. French peace emissaries led by General Huntziger were taken by the Germans to sign the armistice in the railway carriage in which the German delegates had signed the November 1918 armistice. The surrounding site had been turned into a museum and an inscription on an adjacent granite memorial read: 'Here on the eleventh of November 1918 succumbed the criminal pride of the German Empire ... vanquished by the free peoples which it tried to enslave.' Terms were signed on the evening of 22 June, and were to come into force early on 25 June after a Franco-Italian armistice had been arranged.

The armistice terms involved occupation and reparations. Petain's government remained in control of southern France, but the Germans occupied northern France, Paris and the west coast. The French Army was reduced to 100,000 men and French military prisoners were to remain in German hands until a formal peace was concluded. The Germans had to concede France its fleet and empire, as those things remained out of reach. (Italy received little from France.) These were harsher terms than 1918, but the 1940 settlement reflected the military reality that France had been decisively defeated. In Paris, German troops marched down the Champs-Elysees in a victory parade. German soldiers with cameras played the part of tourists in the virtually undamaged great city.

The fall of France in 1940 has been described as the greatest surprise in modern history. Warfare would never be the same again. The campaign was an abrupt disjunctive in military affairs. France had been one of the greatest powers for over three hundred years. The defeat in the war of 1870–71 had been a setback, but the building of a new colonial empire and victory in 1918 was felt to have expunged the stain.[81] When France formally surrendered, German forces had achieved in a campaign of six weeks the goal which had eluded them for over four years in the First World War. In 1940 the Germans had routed the armies of four western European states though they had no significant numerical superiority.

The costs of the brief campaign had not been cheap. French losses had been 90,000 killed, 200,000 wounded and 1,900,000 prisoners. The Germans had lost 27,074 killed, 18,384 missing (presumed dead) and 110,034 wounded. The British Expeditionary Force had lost 68,111 men killed, wounded or taken prisoner.[82] 900,000 men of the Belgian and Dutch forces had been killed or captured. Among the German dead was Prince Wilhelm of Hohenzollern, the grandson of the Kaiser.[83]

Allied equipment losses had been catastrophic. Few British guns or vehicles sent to France returned to the United Kingdom. 7,000 French 75mm. field guns had been captured. Some of these guns would be gratefully turned against Allied troops in other campaigns.[84] Captured French equipment would be given to Germany's eastern European allies. German tank losses for the campaign had been 753: 127 for 10–20 May, 485 for 21–31 May, 85 for 1–10 June and 56 for 11–30 June. Many other tanks had been damaged.[85] These figures reveal that far and away the toughest part of the campaign had been the fighting against the well-armed French First Army and BEF in the shrinking northern pocket. The figures might also be used as evidence to support an unflattering assessment of the French Army in other segments of the campaign. By one estimate the German military had only needed to consume thirty per cent more ammunition to overrun France and the Low Countries than had been required in the Polish campaign.[86] The *Luftwaffe* had lost 1,284 aircraft in France. In May and June 1940 the RAF had lost 959 aircraft.[87] The French Air Force, like the French armoured force, had been substantially destroyed.

In a general sense the defeat for France in 1940 might be explained by the extent to which it lacked the support of the allies it had possessed from 1914–18. Throughout the First World War the Russians had engaged a large German army. By late 1918, only forty per cent of Allied troops in France and Belgium had been French. The bulk of the rest had been British and American. As well as lacking effective allies in 1940, France had suffered from a serious manpower shortage before the first shot had been fired. At the outset of war France had relied on brittle Series B divisions manned by middle-aged personnel. This was a direct consequence of France's smaller population relative to Germany.

The conduct of General Gamelin as Supreme Commander has long puzzled military historians. North-East Front CIC General Georges contributed little to improve matters. In the teeth of a well-prepared German offensive, Gamelin rashly committed the Seventh Army, which might logically have augmented a strong central reserve, to a dash for the Belgian-Dutch frontier on the extreme left of a long front. That reckless commitment was made before the main direction of the German offensive was clear. Gamelin's initial deployment was so riddled with mistakes as to have ensured a bad defeat in any era of warfare.[88] The existence of the Maginot Line seems to have encouraged Gamelin to gamble in the Low Countries. The significance of the centrally located Ardennes slipped from the mind of the French High Command, as it had from the minds of the builders of the Maginot Line.

To compound problems for the French, their German counterparts did almost everything right. The extraordinary concentration of German tank strength on a narrow front may have won the Germans victory even if they had advanced by the more obvious route through central Belgium. How would the Allies have coped if the bulk of the panzer divisions had been deployed between Antwerp and Namur, instead of the Ardennes? No matter how French mechanised forces had been arranged, it is hard to see how they could have fielded enough fighting power to match a massed phalanx of panzer divisions anywhere in the Low Countries.

An appalling display of generalship and military incompetence directly encouraged a spineless performance by the French political leadership to deepen the consequences of defeat. A better military performance might not have saved metropolitan France for long, but it might have caused a more spirited political resistance. The French government might have continued the war from their North African colonies in different circumstances. A surprisingly large force, far greater than embarked at Dunkirk, could have been evacuated by Anglo-French shipping from western and southern France if the political will to fight on had existed. The Dutch fought on against Nazi Germany despite the loss of the Netherlands.

The fall of France was so sudden and dramatic that it had an impact on all major powers. For the British the fall of France shifted the focus to their own survival. The Americans were pushed into an increasingly difficult position by every German triumph. The United States was already committed to the Allied war effort by the huge munitions contracts placed by the British and French governments with American industry. That had only been possible as such contracts were in accordance with the United States government's foreign policy. If Allied warships fell into German hands this might directly threaten the United States, which already had a combatant Canada lying on its northern border and the British Caribbean to the south east. President Roosevelt and Congress agreed to a massive building programme for the United States Navy – the Two Ocean Navy Bill. For the Soviet Union, Germany's success put paid to hopes that Germany, France and Britain might exhaust themselves in a long war of attrition. Stalin, nonetheless, took advantage of the situation to expand the Soviet sphere by seizing the Baltic states and annexing the Bessarabian region of Romania.

In Germany the fall of France was greeted as a triumph to avenge the defeat of 1918. The exiled Kaiser in Holland sent Hitler his congratulations. Twelve new field-marshals were created, though Halder was left off the list. The Kaiser had made only five field-marshals in the First World War. (Even Ludendorff had missed out.) The National Socialist hold over the German people reached a new peak. Hitler acquired enormous authority within the armed forces for the success in France; and not without good reason. Hitler was now a true warlord and supreme commander.

Neutral countries and conquered territory were drawn into the orbit of the German war economy. The Nazis were determined to prove that the benefits of rapid conquest could outweigh the costs. An autarchic economic system had to acquire new territory to expand.[89] During the 1930s a lack of oil, iron ore and foreign exchange had constrained German potential. There was no oil in western Europe. Yet the conquest of France and the Low Countries transformed the situation for Germany in respect to iron ore and foreign exchange. In 1938 Germany had less than one per cent of the world's gold and financial reserves.[90] It was vital for Berlin to be able to use the power of a conqueror to bypass that problem by introducing false financial mechanisms to obtain goods and services from outside the Reich. In 1940 Germany was already benefiting greatly from the raw materials of Romania and Sweden, and the industry of Czechoslovakia and Switzerland. Access to the resources and industry of France and the Low Countries introduced the possibility that Germany might now have the economic base needed to be a genuine world power. Nazism might be secured for generations to come. For instance, whereas in 1939 German industry produced 22.5 million tons of raw steel, in 1941 the figure would be 32 million tons.[91] New output was channelled into military production to have a much greater impact than those overall figures imply. The iron ore of Alsace-Lorraine, over 13 million tons in 1928, played an important role in that process.[92]

The part that France would now play in the Axis war economy cannot be underestimated. In 1938 only 3.7 per cent of German imports had been from France. By 1942 that figure would rise to 16.6 per cent. By late 1942 the number of French workers in Germany would rise to an industrial army of 1,341,000. Among foreign workers and prisoners, these Frenchmen would play a disproportionate role in the expansion of German military industries as they were from a developed industrial economy. By 1943, by one possibly exaggerated estimate, Germany would be using forty per cent of French resources in the Axis war effort. The fall of France did more than take a major military force and war economy out of the Allied camp; it added a major war economy to the Axis cause.[93]

Germany's success also provided opportunities for her Axis partners. In October 1940 an emboldened Mussolini invaded Greece from Albania. In the Far East, in September 1940 Japan forced a military presence upon the Vichy-loyalist officials of French Indochina in the north of the colony. These Axis countries would take war to Africa, the Middle East and the Asia-Pacific regions as a direct consequence of Germany's spectacular success in France.

Still, to a degree yet to be appreciated, the 'Franco-German duel' which had just been decided in Germany's favour was not quite as final as in previous generations.[94] The war did not conclude with a decision in the battle between France and Germany, as had been the case in 1871 and 1918. Other players had to be taken into account. Britain was unwilling to accept the outcome of 1940, and fought on in a bid to re-win the result of 1918. At a diplomatic and ideological level, neither the United States nor the Soviet Union accepted the result of 1940.

The fall of France did not end the Second World War but it ensured that the war would be a dramatically different war from the previous conflict of 1914–18. The genie had been let out of the bottle. The Second World War was now destined to continue its course on a much broader geographic canvas, causing great destruction and loss of life. So much of that could not have happened without the fall of France.

3
The Battle of Britain

The Battle of Britain arose from the strategic problem Germany confronted after France had been defeated. The fall of France had made Germany master of continental Europe. Those countries still neutral were powerless to interfere. Yet Hitler faced the immediate dilemma of what to do about Britain, the defeated France's principal ally. Immediately after the Dunkirk evacuation the under-equipped and semi-trained British Army was vulnerable, but the stormy waters of the English Channel lay between Britain and the German military, as did the Royal Navy and Royal Air Force.

Hitler was ready to make some sort of peace with Britain, and, just as the French had retained their empire, the British would have been allowed to keep theirs. Given the policy of appeasement pursued by the British government for much of the 1930s, it was not entirely unrealistic for Hitler to believe that a settlement was possible. After the armistice with France had been agreed, Hitler had told General Jodl at OKW (Supreme High Command): 'The British have lost the war, but they don't know it; one must give them time, and they will come round.'[1] A vague peace offer made by Hitler during a 19 July speech before an assembly in the *Reichstag* was, however, rebuffed by the British government. By late July it was clear that the war would continue. From the British government's viewpoint there were no acceptable terms available, nor any reason to believe that the regime in Berlin could be trusted. Discussions within the British government as to whether the war should be continued had been quickly resolved in the affirmative. Only a small proportion of Britain's armed forces had been involved in the fall of France. The defeat of France had in no sense encompassed the defeat of the British armed forces.

On 2 July 1940 Hitler had ordered detailed plans for an invasion of Britain. Hitherto OKW had made no contingency plans for Britain, as the problem of conquering France had appeared so immense. The planned invasion was code-named Operation Sea Lion. Führer Directive No. 16 stated:

Since England, despite the hopelessness of her military situation, still shows no signs of a desire to come to terms, I have decided to prepare and, if necessary, to carry out a landing operation against her. The aim of this operation is to elimi-nate the English homeland as a base from which the war against Germany can be continued and, should it prove necessary, to occupy the country completely.[2]

The British Channel Islands, close to the French coast, had already been swiftly occupied.

The German Navy was not enthusiastic about Operation Sea Lion. Germany had lost its fleet after the First World War. The Anglo-German Naval Treaty of 1935 had allowed for a German surface fleet thirty-five per cent of the Royal Navy's, but the building of a new fleet had not been a priority when Germany rearmed as a land power in the mid to late 1930s. Only in 1939 did Hitler embrace an ambitious plan for naval building intended to stretch well into the 1940s. At the outbreak of war the Commander-in-Chief, Admiral Erich Raeder, had said:

> As far as the navy is concerned, it is of course by no means ready for the big war against Britain ...The surface ships are so few and so weak compared with the British fleet that, even if fully committed, they would only be able to show that they know how to die with honour.[3]

In September 1939 the *Kriegsmarine* had just one-eighth of the Royal Navy's surface fleet. Fifteen British battleships and battlecruisers, seven aircraft carriers, fifteen heavy cruisers, forty-nine light cruisers, 192 destroyers and sixty-two submarines had faced a German fleet of two battlecruisers, three pocket battleships, one heavy cruiser, six light cruisers, twenty-one destroyers, twelve torpedo-boats and fifty-seven U-boats.[4]

To make matters worse for Admiral Raeder, many of his small fleet of warships had been lost or damaged in the Norwegian campaign, in addition to earlier war losses. (The pocket battleship *Graf Spee* was famously scuttled in South American waters on the evening of 17 December 1939.) Two-thirds of the German surface fleet had been sunk or damaged in the invasion of Norway. British naval losses had been similar in numbers of ships, but the British were far more able to absorb the cost. Excluding several large warships out of action for repair work, the German Navy had only one heavy cruiser, two light cruisers, four destroyers and nineteen torpedo boats available in the summer of 1940. At the very least Raeder wanted Hitler to postpone an invasion until the spring of 1941, when repaired ships might be again available. Raeder's preference was to bring Britain down by blockade. His pessimism was shared within the navy. An officer based at occupied Dunkirk, Lieutenant-Commander Heinrich Bartels, was asked by Raeder during an inspection tour what he thought of the invasion's prospects. Bartels remarked: 'Herr Grossadmiral, the thing will be a flop from the start.'[5] Nonetheless, in preparation for Operation Sea Lion, Europe's waterways were stripped of thousands of barges, tugs and merchant craft.

The German Army was far more optimistic that they could fulfil their role in Sea Lion. After their victory in France, the confidence of German generals could not have been higher. At first the English Channel had seemed no more than a wide river. On 12 July General Jodl spoke of 'a huge river crossing on a broad front, in which the *Luftwaffe* would be allotted the role of artillery'.[6] General Halder at OKH (Army High Command) was thinking along similar lines. Halder was planning to land on a long, discontinuous front on the coast of south-east England from ports in an arc between Cherbourg and Rotterdam. A broad front invasion would divide and dissipate British reserves. The first assault wave of thirteen divisions was to comprise 250,000 men, 650 tanks, 60,000 horses and 30–40,000 motor vehicles.[7] Another seventeen infantry, six panzer and three motorised divisions were to follow as reinforcements. The many horses among the force gave the planned invasion something in common with the army of William the Conqueror, in addition to their shared objective of carrying England.

If the German Army could have landed on the coast of Britain in strength in 1940 they would very likely have won a swift victory. The Germans respected the individual British soldier but did not rate British Army commanders highly. Rundstedt believed: 'Once we can gain a foothold on the enemy coast with strong forces and are advancing inland our superiority in this form of operation will show itself clearly.'[8] By the end of July, however, OKH was already distracted by the possibility of an attack on Russia, and the difficulties facing the German Navy were becoming increasingly apparent. The Naval Operations Staff informed Halder that ten days would be needed to ship the first wave of assault troops across the Channel. If the landings were to take place, Raeder wanted the troops to disembark on a narrow front to facilitate the protection of convoys at sea by minefields, submarines, aircraft and warships. A furious Halder noted: 'If that is true, all previous statements of the navy were so much rubbish and we can throw away the whole plan of an invasion.' Two days later Halder noted that many of the river barges in which it was planned to embark troops were not seaworthy and hardly suitable for landing troops on open beaches.[9] Lack of suitable craft was also likely to limit the number of tanks that could support the initial invasion. On 30 July Halder acknowledged: 'The navy in all probability will not provide us this autumn with the means for a successful invasion of Britain.'[10]

The British government knew little of the doubts of German military planners. Across the summer of 1940 the British people braced themselves for the shock of invasion. This kind of crisis, which had not arisen during the First World War, recalled to mind the days of the Spanish Armada of 1588 and Napoleon at the peak of his power. The country was gripped by fifth column mania. People looked skywards wondering when Nazi paratroopers would descend. Orders were given that church bells should not be rung, except as a signal for invasion.

Britain did not have peacetime army conscription until early 1939. The British Army in 1940 was still in the process of absorbing hundreds of thousands of national servicemen. The troops returning from Dunkirk formed only a small part of the whole force. By June 1940 the army was 1.65 million strong, and would grow to over 2 million men. In May local volunteers began forming the organisation that would become the Home Guard. Army units were short of equipment and coastal defences were rudimentary. It would take months of production to replace the stocks of equipment left behind in France by the BEF.[11] The British Army was far weaker in terms of equipment and training than the French Army, which the Germans had recently beaten so rapidly.

On 4 June in the House of Commons Prime Minister Churchill made clear the view of his government regarding the German threat:

> We shall fight on the beaches, we shall fight on the landing grounds, we shall fight in the fields and in the streets, we shall fight in the hills; we shall never surrender, and even if, which I do not for a moment believe, this island or a large part of it were subjugated and starving, then our Empire beyond the seas, armed and guarded by the British Fleet, would carry on the struggle, until, in God's good time, the New World, with all its power and might, steps forth to the rescue and the liberation of the Old.

On 18 June, the anniversary of the battle of Waterloo, Churchill made another famous speech in Parliament, which was later broadcast on the radio. Churchill declaimed:

> What General Weygand called the 'Battle of France' is over. I expect that the bat- tle of Britain is about to begin. Upon this battle depends the survival of Christian civilization. Upon it depends our own British life and the long continuity of our institutions and our Empire. The whole fury and might of the enemy must very soon be turned on us. Hitler knows that he will have to break us in this island or lose the war. If we can stand up to him all Europe may be free, and the life of the world may move forward into broad, sunlit uplands; but if we fail then the whole world, including the United States, and all that we have known and cared for, will sink into the abyss of a new dark age made more sinister, and perhaps more pro- longed, by the lights of a perverted science. Let us therefore brace ourselves to our duty and so bear ourselves that if the British Commonwealth and Empire lasts for a thousand years men will still say, 'This was their finest hour'.

Aside from Churchill's oratory and resolute leadership, Britain's traditional strength was its navy. Four flotillas of destroyers were available at ports in southern Britain, with the heavy units of the Home Fleet based in the north of the country. From Scotland the Home Fleet could sweep down to destroy the transports of a weakly escorted invasion force. The supply and reinforcement route for Sea Lion could be steadily attacked for as long as an invasion campaign lasted. If the ships of the Mediterranean Fleet were brought back to Britain, the Royal Navy's margin of superiority over the German Navy would become even more extreme.

In preparation for the worst, the British government battened down the hatches of state. Britain's gold and foreign exchange reserves were sent to Canada, and the troublesome Duke of Windsor despatched to govern a distant minor colony. On 30 June Churchill received the assent of his Cabinet to use poison gas against an invasion force.[12] As the shock of France's collapse wore off the popular mood in Britain became less bleak. Notwithstanding the backsliding of the interwar period, the British people had a proud military and imperial tradition and responded well to strong political direction.

The British government's international problems did not just involve the Germans. In the Mediterranean and Africa, Italy posed a threat to Malta, Egypt and other colonies. There was anxiety in London as to Spain's intentions towards Gibraltar, and about Japan's ambitions in the Far East. The Irish Free State, though still a dominion of the British Empire, had no intention of allowing British forces access to naval and air bases in the south of the country. One of the most pressing problems was the attitude of the new French government. France had broken off her alliance with Britain to make a deal with Germany. There was no reason to trust anyone who had made deals with the Nazis. Churchill's government were alarmed that the French fleet might fall into German control, though the leadership of the French Navy had determined to scuttle their ships rather than let that happen. In theory, if the French fleet was combined with the Italian fleet and Germany's remaining surface warships, there was the possibility that the Royal Navy might be beaten. Indeed, Mussolini had pressed Hitler to seize the French Navy. There was no telling exactly what attitude Petain's government at Vichy would take in the future, and German airborne forces had descended on Norway and Holland without warning. The same fate might befall French North Africa, with or without the cooperation of the Vichy regime.[13] As Churchill later stated: 'In a matter so vital to the safety of the whole British Empire we could not afford to rely on the word of Admiral Darlan' [the French Commander-in-Chief]. The British government determined to secure the disarmament of the French fleet, preferably by agreement, but by force if necessary.

Early in July 1940 French warships were based at Toulon in the south of France, and at a number of ports in French North Africa, the West Indies, southern England and Egypt. At Alexandria French warships were neutralised by agreement, and shipping at Plymouth and Portsmouth was seized. The main concentration of French capital ships was at Mers-el-Kebir near Oran, Algeria. A Royal Navy squadron, Force H, commanded by Vice-Admiral Sir James Somerville, sailed from Gibraltar to secure the submission of this force. Somerville had orders to attack if all else failed. An ultimatum was presented to the local French commander on 3 July, but poorly conducted negotiations during the day for an agreed form of demobilisation failed with faults on both sides.

Finally, Somerville, under heavy pressure from London, reluctantly made good his threats to attack. British and French forces were about to fire on each other for the first time since Waterloo. Just before 6 p.m. a bombardment was begun by the battlecruiser *Hood* and battleships *Valiant* and *Resolution*. This soon yielded savage results. French ships in the cramped port were unable to return fire effectively. The old battleship *Bretagne* blew up and capsized. A pall of smoke spread over the harbour. The battleship *Provence* was set afire and ran aground; the battlecruiser *Dunkerque* was damaged. 1,297 French sailors were killed. The battlecruiser *Strasbourg* escaped to Toulon, as did other warships based at North African ports. At Dakar, the new battleship *Richelieu* was attacked and damaged on 8 July by Royal Navy torpedo-bombers. According to Churchill: 'It was made plain that the British War Cabinet feared nothing and would stop at nothing.'[14]

In the summer of 1940 the powerful German Army in northern France was prevented from overrunning Britain by the English Channel and the strength of the Royal Navy. But as recent events in Poland, France and Holland had shown, air power had arrived as a major force in military operations. Could the German air force, the *Luftwaffe*, win dominance over southern England sufficient to make an invasion possible in spite of other obstacles? On 31 July Hitler met with senior commanders at the Berghof in the Bavarian Alps. Raeder felt that mid-September was the earliest possible invasion date. Hitler told his apprehensive naval commander: 'If the effect of the air attacks is such that the enemy air force, harbours, and naval forces are heavily damaged, Operation Sea Lion will be carried out in 1940.'[15] (The conference soon turned to a discussion mostly dealing with the Russians.) On 1 August Führer Directive No. 17 instructed the *Luftwaffe* to 'overpower the English air force with all the forces at its command in the shortest possible time. The attacks are to be directed primarily against flying units, their ground installations, and their supply organisations, but also against the aircraft industry.'

Reichsmarschall Goering, head of the *Luftwaffe*, did not hesitate to assure Hitler that the RAF would be badly beaten. Goering had told his commanders at a meeting on 11 July:

> When the time comes, the enemy aircraft industry and air force must be destroyed at the earliest possible moment by the first blows of the attack. The defence of Southern England will last four days and the Royal Air Force four weeks. We can guarantee invasion for the Führer within a month.[16]

To pave the way for a successful invasion, at the very least the *Luftwaffe* needed to drive the RAF out of south-east Britain. In a new white uniform, Goering told his commanders at The Hague on 1 August:

> The Führer has ordered me to crush Britain with my *Luftwaffe*. By means of hard blows I plan to bring this enemy, who has already suffered a moral defeat,

down on his knees in the nearest future, so that an occupation of the island by our troops can proceed without risk.[17]

Soon Goering was boasting that air attacks in isolation might bring Britain to its knees.[18]

The extraordinary personality of Goering, the freshly promoted six-star *Reichsmarschall* of all the armed forces, cast a large shadow across the *Luftwaffe's* conduct of the coming campaign. Born in Bavaria in 1893, the son of a senior government official, Goering had been an acclaimed fighter pilot during the First World War, leading *Jagdgeschwader* 1 after the death of Manfred von Richthofen, the Red Baron. Joining the Nazi Party in 1922, Goering had been wounded the following year in the putsch in Munich and had become addicted to morphine during a difficult period of recovery. He became a crucial political figure in the Nazi government after 1933, becoming Air Minister in that year and *Luftwaffe* Commander-in-Chief in 1935.[19] Ruthless, energetic, charming, corrupt and ambitious, as an air force commander Goering lacked knowledge of contemporary technology and of the duties of a senior commander.[20] His lack of interest in long-term planning was only matched by his lack of interest in day-to-day operations. Morphine may have falsely boosted his confidence. His time was also in short supply, given his hobby of collecting plundered art and responsibilities for the direction of the German war economy. His fancy uniforms and pot-belly were symptoms of his notorious love of high living.

For the *Luftwaffe*, the campaigns against France and Britain overlapped. Of the *Luftwaffe's* aircraft available at the start of May, 1,428 had already been destroyed by the end of June.[21] Three *Luftflottes* (air fleets) were to be involved in the attacks on Britain. *Luftflotte* 2 was led by Field-Marshal Albert Kesselring, a former artilleryman who had only transferred to the Air Ministry in 1933 after a long army career. *Luftflotte* 3's commander was Field-Marshal Hugo Sperrle, a large, tough-looking, former airman. He had commanded the Condor Legion in Spain. *Luftflotte* 5 was based in Scandinavia, though that was too distant for single-engine fighters to reach Britain and return safely. German aircrew were well trained and experienced, and possessed the high morale typical of the German armed forces. Aircrew numbers had been augmented by prisoners released after the fall of France.

The mainstay of the German single-engine fighter force was the Messerschmitt Bf 109. The Bf 109 was powered by a Daimler-Benz engine and armed with two machine guns and two 20mm cannons. A fast aircraft able to level fly at 350 mph, it was especially nimble at high altitudes due to a supercharged engine. The main problem with the Bf 109 was a low level of production. 1,870 German single-engine fighters would be produced in 1940. This was less than half the total the British would manage to build.[22] The Bf 109 was supported by the Messerschmitt Bf 110 twin-engine 'heavy-fighter'. The Bf 110 was fast, well armed and capable of flying long distances. It lacked, however, manoeuvrability in close combat and the acceleration needed to escape a pursuer.

Apart from the Stuka dive-bomber (Junkers Ju 87), the *Luftwaffe*'s twin-engine bomber force relied on the Dornier Do 17 'Flying Pencil', Heinkel He III and the new Junkers Ju 88A. The Dornier only carried a bomb load of 2,200 lbs, but the other types could carry double that load. The *Luftwaffe* lacked effective armour-piercing anti-shipping bombs and torpedoes at this stage of the war. Radio communications between airborne *Luftwaffe* formations and ground bases was less comprehensive than the RAF's still incomplete network.

The *Luftwaffe*'s intelligence organisation was a lean outfit headed by Major Beppo Schmid. On 16 July Schmid presented an intelligence paper that seriously under-rated the RAF. Schmid claimed the Bf 109 was appreciably superior to British fighters. The report showed no awareness that the RAF was heavily dependent on a radar network. The Germans had been generally unimpressed by British radar equipment captured in France. British fighter production was estimated to be only 180–300 a month.[23]

In opposition to Goering's *Luftwaffe*, the RAF's Fighter Command was chiefly responsible for the air defence of Britain. This was not the first time Britain had come under air attack. During the First World War Zeppelin airships and Gotha bombers had raided Britain. In the 1930s the obvious vulnerability of London to air attack, exaggerated estimates of *Luftwaffe* expansion, and the publicity given to the bombing of civilian centres in Abyssinia, Spain and China had all been spurs to air defence. Late in 1937 the Chamberlain government had decided, partly for financial reasons, to boost fighter production at the expense of bombers. In 1938 the RAF had received thirty-six per cent of an increased military budget. 1938 had also been the year when large numbers of new Spitfire and Hurricane fighters began reaching operational squadrons. The era of biplane fighters had finally ended. Spitfires and Hurricanes mounted batteries of machine guns in their wings to create a weapon that could blow hostile bombers out of the sky.[24]

In 1936 the RAF had been reorganised into four commands based on aircraft type – Fighter, Coastal, Bomber and Training Command. Fighter Command's first leader, Air Chief Marshal Sir Hugh Dowding, a dull but intellectually flexible man, backed the drive to produce high-speed fighters and a chain of radar stations.[25] Dowding, born in 1882, had begun his military career in the artillery, before transferring to the Royal Flying Corps to achieve senior rank by 1918. A prosperous postwar career had followed, and by 1930 Dowding had become the member of the Air Council responsible for supply and research. Dowding was an aloof non-drinker. He had lost his wife after a brief marriage and had a son who was a pilot. As head of Fighter Command, Dowding's appointment had only been extended to March 1940 as his intended successor had a serious accident. His term had then been extended to 14 July at the last minute and then extended again to 31 October.

The building of a network of RDF – radio direction finding – stations along the coast of Britain facing continental Europe had been a project requiring the cooperation of scientists, and military and civilian leaders. The general idea of using radio equipment to track the movements of an enemy force had not been original. During the First World War a network of Admiralty stations had listened to the radio traffic of the German fleet to help determine its location and intentions.

The newly invented radar equipment of the late 1930s was especially suited to coastal locations as the flat sea had few obstructions. The radar chain had been rapidly expanded during 1938–39 as a sense of approaching war had rightly intensified. Radar transmitters sent a radio pulse into the air which was reflected back to the transmitter if it struck a solid object. The object was then displayed as a blip on a cathode ray tube. The time it took for the signal to return to the station was measured to give an approximate distance. Fog, darkness or cloud did not block the signals. The radar stations were effective out to an average range of eighty miles, but aircraft below a thousand feet could not be detected. A second chain of stations was built after the war started to track low-flying aircraft and shipping out at sea.

The information received at the radar stations was relayed by telephone to Fighter Command headquarters at Bentley Prior near London, where it was 'filtered', following which aircraft were plotted on a large map table. Radar information was used to send defending fighters to intercept incoming aircraft. Centralised two-way radio systems controlled and coordinated fighters in the air. Radar and radio combined to cope with the increased 'velocity of combat' caused by new high-speed fighters.[26] The radar chain reduced the need to fly standing patrols for reconnaissance purposes. Radar, however, was not without its problems. The height, size and nationality of formations of aircraft located could all be misread. Needless to say, the counters on the plotting table might fall uncomfortably behind events without warning.

If modern technology failed, the Observer Corps was in place as a support. 30,000 watchers at a thousand posts were available to scan the skies for aircraft. On a cloudy or rainy day the observers had to interpret the sounds of engines. Information was telephoned to local headquarters and passed up the command chain to be collated alongside other sources of intelligence. In support of Fighter Command were almost 2000 light and heavy anti-aircraft guns. Barrage balloons were deployed to protect key targets from low-flying aircraft.

Fighter Command was divided into four groups. Each group was then divided into sector stations controlling two or more squadrons. The most important group was No. 11 Group in south-east England. No. 11 Group was commanded by a tough, reserved New Zealander, Air Vice-Marshal Keith Park, whose headquarters were at Uxbridge. Park, a tall man and son of a Scot, had been a gunner at Gallipoli. He had transferred to the Royal Flying Corps after recovering from wounds received during the Somme battles of 1916. A successful fighter pilot in his own right, Park had commanded a squadron in 1918 and had attended the Red Baron's funeral. In 1938 he had become Fighter Command's senior Air Staff Officer. He was appointed to No. 11 Group by Dowding in April 1940, and enjoyed excellent relations with the head of Fighter Command. On average, the forty-eight year-old Park flew a Hurricane fighter twice a week to gain experience of modern aircraft. During 1940 Park was responsible for making many complicated tactical decisions on a daily basis.

Three other fighter groups supported No. 11 Group. Air Vice-Marshal Trafford Leigh-Mallory, a specialist in army cooperation work, had command of the midlands-based No. 12 Group. No. 10 Group covered south-west England. No. 13 Group was based in northern Britain.[27]

During 1940 Britain would produce 4,283 single-engine fighters. In February 1940 only 141 fighters had been built, but by July the figure had risen to almost 500 a month. The appointment of Lord Beaverbrook as Minister of Aircraft Production had given fresh impetus to the task, though Beaverbrook would get the credit for a lot of work already underway. On 19 June Fighter Command had 768 fighters with operational squadrons, of which 520 were fit for operations. By 9 August those figures would rise to 1,032 and 715.[28] Hurricanes and Spitfires comprised the great bulk of fighter aircraft, the Hurricane being more numerous. Both aircraft were powered by the Rolls Royce aero-engine and mounted eight Browning machine guns, four in each wing. The Vickers Supermarine Spitfire was a graceful and charismatic aircraft that had successfully incorporated the aerodynamics of high-speed seaplanes. The Hawker Hurricane lacked beauty but was a sturdy machine.

British pilots in 1940 were a mixture of regulars, reservists and auxiliary air force personnel. Large numbers of Poles, Czechs, Canadians, New Zealanders and other nationalities complemented the British-born majority of RAF fighter pilots. During the summer and autumn of 1940 Fighter Command's strength hovered between fifty and sixty squadrons. Over twenty of these were in No. 11 Group. Neighbouring squadrons in No. 10 and No. 12 Group were available to assist No. 11 Group. More distant stations and No. 13 Group in northern Britain formed a reserve which could be drawn upon when needed. Pilots from Coastal and Bomber Command and the Fleet Air Arm were transferred to Fighter Command to bolster numbers.

The 'Battle of Britain' was revolutionary as it was primarily fought between two combatants in the air. In previous campaigns aircraft had played supporting roles to soldiers on land and shipping on the surface of the sea. The summer of 1940 was frequently good for flying, though indifferent periods gave regular rest to combatants. On 20 July, in France and the Low Countries, the *Luftwaffe*'s 2nd and 3rd Air Fleets comprised 2,600 aircraft, a figure which included 1,131 bombers, 316 dive-bombers and 809 single-engine fighters.[29] *Luftflotte* 5 in Scandinavia had another several hundred aircraft.

From the first half of July to early August a fight for air space over the English Channel developed as the German leadership planned for Sea Lion. English south coast towns such as Plymouth and Dover were raided, as were regular convoys bound for the Thames estuary. Some merchant ships were sunk, though the failure of the *Luftwaffe* quickly to halt the convoys suggests their capacity to sink the Royal Navy's much faster warships was limited. By the end of July the Channel convoys had been discontinued, only to be resumed on 8 August. That day General Wolfram von Richthofen's Stukas hammered shipping with great success. [30]

In the battles over the Channel the British were given the opportunity to refine their fighting tactics and the operation of the radar system. In Spain and France German fighter pilots had adopted loose formations based on pairs of aircraft. Pilots could thus spend more time watching the sky around them, rather than concentrating on maintaining station in a larger formation. RAF pilots learnt to imitate that practice, and dispensed with pre-war tactics based on sections of three and close squadron formations. Obsolete aircraft were severely dealt with by high performance fighters. On 19 July an RAF squadron of two-seater Boulton Paul Defiants was decimated.

German reconnaissance in British air space was hurt by the radar interception of aircraft sent on scouting missions. On 11 July Squadron Leader Douglas Bader, the commander of No. 242 Squadron, downed a lone Dornier on a weather reconnaissance flight. On the same day another famous pilot, Squadron Leader Peter Townsend, the commander of No. 85 Squadron, also encountered a lone Dornier. Townsend shot up the bomber, but the German aircraft returned to France after stopping his Hurricane's engine with return fire. Townsend had to be rescued from the sea by a trawler. [31]

Early in August Goering ordered that the tempo of operations be stepped up in pursuance of the objectives of Führer Directive No. 17. A month-long campaign of attrition in the skies over south-east England was soon underway. The Germans were not oblivious to the significance of British radar stations. From France observers could see the masts of the Dover station. On 12 August Bf 110s bombed the Dover station and other stations with good effect. The 350-foot radio masts were hard to damage, but station buildings were more vulnerable. At a command conference in Germany Goering commented on 15 August: 'It is doubtful whether there is any point in continuing the attacks on radar sites, in view of the fact that not one of those attacked has so far been put out of action.' The Germans assumed that radar station control rooms were deep underground and protected from bombing. This was not the case and *Luftwaffe* priorities might have been different if that neglect had been known. [32]

The main *Luftwaffe* effort of the campaign, Operation Eagle, began on 13 August, a day marred by poor morning weather. On 15 August the *Luftwaffe* dispatched 520 bombers and 1,270 fighters and fighter-bombers across the Channel. Goering instructed that 'operations are to be directed exclusively against the enemy air forces ... Our night attacks are essentially dislocation raids made so that enemy defences and population shall be allowed no respite.'[33] German bombers and Bf 110s attacked targets in northern Britain from Scandinavia. Total RAF claims for 15 August were 182 German aircraft destroyed and another fifty-three probably destroyed. This was an exaggeration and postwar British estimates of German losses for that day would be revised down to seventy-five.[34]

As German bombers pushed further inland the relatively short range of the Bf 109 fighter became a problem. Pilots who misjudged their fuel supply had to ditch in the Channel or crash land in France. Adolf Galland, one of the *Luftwaffe's* foremost aces, later remarked: 'The German fighters found themselves in a similar predicament to a dog on a chain which wants to attack the foe, but cannot harm him because of his limited orbit.'[35] The Bf 109 was marginally superior to the Hurricane in performance but no better than a match for the Spitfire.[36]

The balance of losses during the early period of the campaign had favoured Fighter Command. Nonetheless, many *Luftwaffe* leaders felt that the fight was progressing well. At a conference on 19 August the *Luftwaffe* Air Staff estimated that from 1 July to 16 August 770 of 900 RAF fighters had been destroyed. 300 of those aircraft were assumed to have been replaced, leaving just 430 remaining. General Halder at OKH noted in his diary that from 8 to 26 August the *Luftwaffe* had lost 169 of 1,464 fighters and 184 of 1,800 bombers, a little over ten per cent of the combined totals. Of 1,515 first- and second-line RAF fighters, 791 were claimed as destroyed, a loss rate of fifty per cent.[37]

Exaggerated claims were also made for the number of RAF airfields put out of action. Airfields were hard seriously to damage, as many had no paved runways. Pre-jet era aircraft were well able to fly from grass fields, especially during the summer. In selecting targets, the *Luftwaffe* displayed a poor understanding of the vulnerability of the British aircraft industry. The Spitfire and Hurricane used a Rolls-Royce aero-engine. There were only two factories building those aero-engines, one of which was in Derby. At Southampton, on the exposed south coast, was an important airframe factory for the Spitfire that ought to have received closer attention from *Luftwaffe* bombers.[38]

On 20 August Hitler observed realistically to his staff: 'The collapse of England in the year 1940 is under present circumstances no longer to be reckoned on.'[39] The campaign against Britain was not, however, to be relaxed and a renewed *Luftwaffe* offensive against Fighter Command airfields began late in the month. German fighters were concentrated in the Pas de Calais to strengthen the escort given to bomber formations. This concentration of force began to achieve results. No. 11 Group airfields were pounded by bombers. From 24 August into early September the RAF suffered serious losses. In thirteen days 466 RAF fighters were destroyed or damaged and 231 pilots killed or wounded.[40] For a time losses ran well ahead of replacements.

The duration of flight training courses was slashed to maintain a supply of fresh pilots.[41]

As the campaign wore on patterns of aerial combat began to become apparent, besides the vapour trails created visually at high altitudes. RAF and *Luftwaffe* fighter pilots sometimes had to fly several sorties a day. Some squadrons had alarmingly high losses, depending on the quality of that unit's leadership and luck. Over half of pilots in downed fighters survived, often uninjured but sometimes with terrible burns. A substantial minority of aircraft were lost in accidents rather than combat. Lack of sleep, fatigue and the loss of friends and comrades ground down the nerves of aircrew. Cloud and rain, though, cut back flying on some days to provide a break from combat.

New 'aces' began to achieve the kind of fame First World War flyers had attained. By the end of 1940 Major Werner Molders had been credited with fifty-five victories. Captain Helmut Wick also managed to reach the fifty mark, before parachuting to his death in the Channel. Major Adolf Galland was another of the *Luftwaffe*'s highest scoring pilots. Squadron Leader Douglas Bader achieved legendary status thanks to his tin legs and forceful leadership. Among the highest scoring RAF pilots was a Czech serving in a Polish squadron, Sergeant Josef Frantisek. The only Fighter Command pilot awarded a Victoria Cross during the campaign was Flight Lieutenant James Nicholson. He was shot down by Bf 109s as he continued to attack another German aircraft. Nicholson baled out badly burnt only to be wounded again, as he descended by parachute, by shot gun pellets fired by British troops on the ground. The South African Flight Lieutenant 'Sailor' Malan probably damaged Molders's Bf 109 in one particular combat. The finest and more senior pilots tended to monopolise the best aircraft and gained the services and protection of the most experienced wing-men and ground staff.

As in the 1914–18 war, pilots needed superb eyesight, experience and youth. The advantages of height, calculated judgement, blinding sunlight in the eyes of an opponent and willingness to close to point-blank range before opening fire were vital. Three and a half per cent of RAF pilots made thirty per cent of the claims.[42] Expert pilots took a terrible toll of the less capable or inexperienced. Part of the so-called 'romance' of aerial combat was the extent to which good pilots were able to live to fight another day. In comparison to 1918, by 1940 the speed of aerial combat had greatly increased. There were fewer duels and more ambushes as closing speeds reached unprecedented levels.

Air Vice-Marshal Park, who was mainly responsible for the detailed fighting of the air battle, displayed a sound understanding of its evolving tactics. Park determined to send a stream of squadron-sized formations against incoming raiders to break up *Luftwaffe* formations at an early opportunity. There was seldom time to assemble more than a pair of fighter squadrons within No. 11 Group's area. Park's headquarters received good cooperation from No. 10 Group squadrons, which helped to protect exposed No. 11 Group aerodromes.

The same level of cooperation was not received from Leigh Mallory's No. 12 Group. This group got into the habit of assembling a 'big wing' of three or more squadrons, often led by the pugnacious and impatient Bader. The Air Ministry and politicians were lobbied by No. 12 Group in support of their methods. The 'big wings', however, wasted time forming up, often failed to make contact and posted ridiculously high claim scores as so many aircraft were milling about in the sky. Leigh Mallory's attitude towards Dowding verged on insubordination, and Park's requests of No. 12 Group were often ignored. Park became concerned that, whereas No. 13 Group in northern Britain was sending its best squadrons to reinforce No. 11 Group, when No. 12 Group was required to rotate squadrons southwards inexperienced units were sent to incur unnecessarily heavy losses.[43] It was remiss of Dowding not to intervene and firmly coordinate the activities of his bickering group commanders.

The extent of pilot claims began to cause problems for ground-based intelligence staffs and commanders. Speed and altitude made it hard for pilots to know the exact fate of a damaged victim. In a crowded sky several pilots might claim to have fired the fatal burst at a downed enemy. The *Luftwaffe* was completely dependent on pilot claims for information as the fighting was over British territory. For instance, on 15 August *Luftwaffe* pilots claimed ninety-nine RAF aircraft shot down, whereas the actual figure was less than half that total. The demands of London-based political and military leaders, and the need to provide propaganda, did not make the task of RAF air intelligence an easy one. The Air Ministry in particular seems to have had problems drawing a distinction between intelligence and propaganda. Tallies of claims tended to acquire a quasi-official status as they were released to the press and the BBC radio service for speedy publication. During the second week of August only fifty-one *Luftwaffe* wrecks were found against armed forces claims of 279, which could hardly be reconciled even after adding those German aircraft that might have crashed in the Channel and France. An investigation by Fighter Command headquarters later found that from 8 August to 11 September 1,631 enemy aircraft had been claimed destroyed, along with 584 'probables', but only 316 wrecks on the ground could be counted.[44] At one point Dowding felt compelled to protest to the Secretary of State for Air that inflated published claim tallies were misleading the public.

On the night of 24/25 August *Luftwaffe* aircraft bombed London. The British responded by raiding Berlin the following night. RAF attacks on Berlin were petty but made an impact. They provided a propaganda argument to justify a shift in German air strategy.[45] Hitler told the *Reichstag* on 4 September, 'Mr Churchill is demonstrating his new brainchild, the night air raid ... When they declare that they will increase their attacks on our cities, then we will raise their cities to the ground. We will stop the handiwork of these night air pirates.' Churchill had once referred to London as 'a tremendous fat cow tied up to attract the beasts of prey'. The London docks were an obvious and legitimate military target.

On 7 September Goering's personal train came to the Pas de Calais. On cliffs near Kesselring's *Luftflotte 2* advance headquarters, Goering and other senior officers were photographed watching heavy formations flying over the Channel on the first massive raid against London. The British capital was at the limit of a Bf 109's range, especially when wasting fuel flying zigzags to escort slower bombers. The high-flying force reached its target late in the afternoon, largely unopposed, as Fighter Command's controllers had expected it to attack aerodromes north of the Thames. Air Vice-Marshal Park had been at a conference at Fighter Command headquarters as the raid came over.[46] An invasion alert on the ground added to the occasion. London's dock area was set on fire and burned through the night as more bombers arrived to deliver their loads. Park inspected the scene that evening from the cockpit of his personal Hurricane.

The raids on London took the pressure off Fighter Command's airfields, though not the pilots. Park later asserted: 'Had the enemy continued his heavy attacks against Biggin Hill [an important air base] and the adjacent sectors and knocked out their operations rooms or telephone communications, the fighter defences of London would have been in a perilous state during the last critical phase when heavy attacks were directed against the capital.'[47] Further raids on London on 9 September were more effectively intercepted by RAF fighters.

A particularly heavy raid was made on 15 September, later to be known as 'Battle of Britain Day'. Radio activity and radar information had indicated that large bomber formations were assembling over France and the Channel. The bomber formations were mostly broken up heading to London. British pilots claimed to have destroyed 185 German aircraft. The real German loss figure was in the region of sixty, but even that rate of casualty was unsustainable for the *Luftwaffe's* bomber force. During the fighting Churchill visited Park's operations room fifty feet below ground. It had to be explained to the Prime Minister that his cigar smoke was too much for the air-conditioning system to cope with.[48] From 7 to 15 September Fighter Command lost 120 aircraft in exchange for 298 German aircraft of all types.[49] After a pause in the air battle, on 27 and 30 September large numbers of aircraft again took to the skies for fierce engagements.

Fighter pilot losses for the past two months had been heavy for both sides. In August the RAF had lost 237 Hurricane and Spitfire pilots – twenty-six per cent of the total – and 264 in September – twenty-eight per cent of the total. 168 Bf 109 pilots had been lost in August and 229 in September, fifteen and twenty-three per cent of the respective monthly totals.[50] The way in which Dowding had husbanded his resources to fight a long campaign of attrition had probably given the *Luftwaffe* the impression that Fighter Command was low in numbers.[51] Dowding certainly had an exaggerated sense of the *Luftwaffe's* strength. RAF air intelligence had estimated German aircraft production for 1940 as twice the actual figure. German first-line aircraft strength during August had been estimated as 5,800, but in September the true figure was only 3,051.[52]

As the air battle had unfolded, British officials had looked carefully for signs of impending invasion. Were German preparations just a bluff? By late August the *Wehrmacht* had finally agreed upon an invasion plan for a landing along a narrow part of the coast of Kent and Sussex from Folkestone to Brighton. Once a bridgehead had been secured, mechanised forces were to advance inland to outflank London from the west. A grand total of 4,000 barges, motor-boats, tugs and transports had been requisitioned from Europe's waterways.[53] By early September Britain's Home Forces could call on twenty-seven infantry divisions, of which only twelve were reasonably well equipped. Two armoured divisions and four tank brigades had been formed to combat the might of the panzer arm.

The British government's Code and Cipher School at Bletchley Park had begun to regularly break the *Luftwaffe's* radio transmitted Enigma machine-cipher during the Norwegian and French campaigns, but after the fall of France the *Luftwaffe* had reverted mostly to landline communications. Detailed information about current strengths and losses was relayed by a secure telephone system. It would be some months before the codebreakers were able to usefully decode the German Navy's Enigma machine-cipher.[54] The British never received any sign of a date or place of invasion. Aerial reconnaissance of Channel ports during July had not indicated the assembly of invasion shipping. At the end of August aerial reconnaissance had found only eighteen barges at Ostend, but within a fortnight that figure had shot up to 270. It finally became apparent that an invasion fleet was being gathered. The bodies of forty German soldiers had been recently washed up on the south coast of England, the victims of accidents during embarkation exercises. Bomber Command was directed to attack the concentrations of barges and sank or damaged at least a tenth of the targets on offer.[55]

At night the Royal Navy sent valuable warships into the Channel to bombard and harass invasion shipping. On the night of 8 September ships of the 2nd Cruiser Squadron bombarded Boulogne harbour in thick weather. Two nights later destroyers menaced Calais and Ostend. Light forces conducted regular night sweeps in September and October. Early on the morning of 11 October the old battleship *Revenge*, accompanied by a strong escort, shelled Cherbourg.[56] The impractical nature of Operation Sea Lion is made evident by these night activities of the Royal Navy.

In five ports from Flushing to Boulogne about a thousand barges were discovered by aerial reconnaissance on 18 September. Yet that figure had fallen to 691 by late September and 448 in October. Evidently the German invasion fleet was being broken up as rapidly as it had assembled. Indeed, on 17 September Hitler had ordered a postponement of Sea Lion and the partial dispersal of the fleet. He had once remarked to his naval adjutant, Lieutenant

Karl von Puettkammer, 'We have conquered France at the cost of 30,000 men. During one night of crossing the Channel we could lose many times that – and success is not certain.' On 12 October Hitler postponed the operation to the coming spring. Only the threat was to be maintained across the winter.[57]

The postponement of Sea Lion allowed *Luftwaffe* commanders to wind down the campaign against Britain by daylight. A frustrated Major Galland had told Goering that, 'British plane wastage was far lower and production far higher than the German intelligence staff estimated and now events were exposing the error so plainly that it had to be acknowledged.'[58] Earlier in the campaign a pilot had tried to explain to Goering that the Spitfire was an excellent aircraft. He had been told in reply: 'If that is so, I will have to send my Air Inspector General before the firing squad.' During October *Luftwaffe* medium bombers were withdrawn from day operations. As the weather deteriorated, high-flying Bf 109s ranged across south-east England in a fighter-bomber role. At the end of October the British government came to the conclusion that invasion was now 'relatively remote'. By November the air battle by day had petered out.[59]

For the British people victory in the daylight air battle greatly reduced fears of invasion. And there had been much of which to be afraid. The Nazis had already appointed a secret police chief for occupied Britain, and a list of persons to be arrested had been drawn up. It had been intended to deport and intern large numbers of males of military age.[60] The worst of the invasion threat may have passed, but in October the night-time bombing of London and other cities and towns was only just beginning. Stanley Baldwin had once famously made the point in parliament: 'I think it well ... for the man in the street to realise there is no power on earth that can protect him from bombing, whatever people may tell him. The bomber will always get through.' From October 1940 to May 1941 the *Luftwaffe*'s 'Blitz' on Britain caused great destruction to civilian life and property. By night German bombers could fly more slowly at lower heights, and thus carry heavier bomb loads than by day. Britain's air defence failed to function effectively during the hours of darkness. RAF night-fighters were often obsolete and lacked efficient airborne radar sets. Anti-aircraft fire was less of a concern to *Luftwaffe* bomber crews than accidents caused by variable winter weather.

Luftwaffe aircrew used direction finding beacons for night flying navigation. The RAF's Bomber Command was only starting to come to terms with night flying navigation, but the *Luftwaffe* had given this matter a great deal of thought during the three-year Spanish Civil War. The so-called *Knickebein* ('crooked leg') system for blind bombing worked by bombers flying along a radio beam directed at the target. When the target was reached the bomber crossed an intersecting radio beam. The sound in the radio operator's ear-phones changed to indicate this had happened. The bombs could then be dropped accurately to within a square mile. By studying captured German equipment and interviewing prisoners, information was gradually assembled about the *Knickebein* system. British scientists had occasional success jamming German navigation signals.

Luftwaffe bombing was principally directed against London, but on the night of 14/15 November 450 aircraft struck Coventry. Fighter Command night-fighters failed to make a single claim that night. Incendiaries effectively marked the target and the town centre was burnt out. Birmingham, Liverpool, Glasgow, Plymouth, Belfast, Southampton and Bristol all received severe attention in the months ahead. The worst of the winter's weather proved to be the best ally of Britain insofar as it curtailed the *Luftwaffe's* operations. On the night of 16 April 685 German aircraft attacked London.[61] The last heavy London raid was on 10/11 May.

Pre-war estimates of the number of civilian casualties that might be caused per ton of bombs dropped from the air proved far too high, yet the cost was still very heavy. From July to December 1940 23,000 British civilians were killed by hostile bombing and over 32,000 seriously injured. A similar figure was the toll for the early months of 1941. For the whole war 60,595 civilians in Britain would be killed by enemy action.[62] The great bulk of these occurred during the Blitz of 1940–41.

The bombing was tragic for individuals directly affected, but in an overall sense civilian morale held up surprisingly well. The enemy's occupation of the night skies was only temporary and occasional. At the conclusion of every single raid the people on the ground remained in possession of their territory whilst the bombers beat a hasty retreat to their bases. The psychological significance of this had been under-appreciated by pre-war experts. An effort by individual civilians to maintain their normal routine was the best defence against demoralisation, as is so often the case when a person is faced by a crisis in their life.[63] The Blitz was important to the idea that Britain was fighting a 'people's war'. Bombing destroyed and damaged many buildings but lacked accuracy and a systematic focus on specific industrial targets. No more than a small dent was made in the British war economy. The Blitz ended when the *Luftwaffe's* bombers were moved to eastern Europe for the campaign against the Soviet Union. One of the most important consequences of the Blitz was that it helped shore up the moral and political case for the retaliatory bombing of Germany.

The overall 'Battle of Britain' – Sea Lion, the daylight air campaign and night Blitz – was Germany's first major setback in the war. The *Luftwaffe's* aura of invincibility was punctured, whereas the RAF was cast in the role of national saviour. With hindsight the *Luftwaffe* entered the air war against Britain without any appreciable advantages. Operational surprise was hard to achieve given Fighter Command's radar network. The Germans had a large fleet of medium bombers, but the two sides had a similar number of fighters. From 1 July to

1 October the *Luftwaffe's* single-engine fighter strength fell from 893 to 700; whereas from 6 July to 28 September RAF fighter strength rose from 871 to 1,048. Pilot availability for the two air forces showed the same trend.[64]

Goering's flawed campaign had been too improvised. The *Luftwaffe's* commanders never concentrated their attacks on a specific target for long. The list of alternating priorities lurched between airfields, industry, London and airborne RAF fighters. The knowledge within the German High Command that Sea Lion probably would not go ahead had contributed to the *Luftwaffe's* shambolic approach to the campaign. The RAF, however, did not know the precise state of Germany's invasion plans. It could focus on the straightforward task of shooting down as many German aircraft as possible.

Overall 'scores' for aircraft destroyed during the British-designated 'Battle of Britain' period have proved controversial. The post-war British tallies from 10 July to 31 October were 1,733 *Luftwaffe* and 915 RAF aircraft destroyed.[65] But these figures only include RAF Fighter Command losses, whereas Bomber Command and Coastal Command losses should also be counted in the tallies. During the campaign, by one set of figures, Bomber Command and Coastal Command lost 376 and 148 aircraft respectively. More Bomber Command than Fighter Command aircrew were killed during the battle period.[66] It is hard to see why RAF bomber and reconnaissance aircraft losses should be deleted from evaluations of the United Kingdom's air battle for survival. All German aircraft types – fighters and bombers – are included when British historians tally up *Luftwaffe* losses. German crash landings and air accidents in France and the Low Countries have also found their way into the totals. Similar RAF mishaps appear to have been treated by British historians differently.

Dowding was replaced on 25 November 1940, and Park lost his post soon afterwards on 18 December. Park wrote in 1968: 'To my dying day I shall feel bitter at the base intrigue which was used to remove Dowding and myself as soon as we had won the battle.'[67] The growing weight of German night bombing and Fighter Command's inability to combat the Blitz had damaged the standing of both men. When the Air Ministry's account of the 1940 campaign was published in March 1941 Dowding was not mentioned, though Goering's role was emphasised. Given the patience British political and military authorities have often shown failing commanders, it is puzzling that Dowding and Park were abruptly discarded. In hindsight both Fighter Command and No. 11 Group headquarters had been awkwardly close to the Air Ministry and government in London. The incumbents were thus subjected to a level of scrutiny not cast on commanders in more distant theatres of war. In the case of Park, the Battle of Britain was the only the first instalment in a distinguished command career that included postings to Egypt, Malta and South-East Asia.

Victory in the Battle of Britain secured the United Kingdom from invasion. The Germans in 1940 were masters of land warfare, but Britain's survival depended on sea power and the Royal Air Force. The Battle of Britain became mid twentieth-century Britain's equivalent of a Trafalgar or Waterloo.[68] British success in staving off the threat of invasion boosted United States support for Britain, and provided the eventual land bridge for direct American intervention in north-west Europe. Even if Britain had been successfully invaded, it might not have been knocked out of the war. The British government and navy might have sailed to Canada. The British Empire straddled the globe and had considerable military and economic potential without the United Kingdom.

The ongoing war against the British Isles proved a major drain on German resources. This was the most important consequence of Britain's survival. With Britain safe from invasion, there was still one great power located in Europe opposed to Nazi Germany. So long as Britain was in the war, there was a focal point, both in psychological and practical terms, upon which anti-Nazi forces could concentrate. Historically, Britain's secure strategic position had usually allowed it to determine who would be the victor in a major war on the European Continent. Britain's failure to make peace doomed the Germans to repeating the 1914–18 error of fighting a war on more than one major front when the Soviet Union was invaded in June 1941. When Napoleon had been unable to invade Britain, he too had turned eastwards to Russia.

4
The Battle of the Atlantic

Whilst the *Luftwaffe* launched air attacks on Britain, and Operation Sea Lion was planned and postponed, the German Navy had been pursuing a campaign to reduce Britain by submarine blockade. On the surface of the ocean the Germans were no match for the Royal Navy, but beneath the waves it was a different story. Britain, as a heavily populated island kingdom, imported over half its food, almost all oil products and many other raw materials. If the Germans could devastate Britain's merchant fleet, the British war effort might be paralysed and the general population subjected to severe food shortages.

Whereas the sheer scale of the assault on Britain by Goering's *Luftwaffe* was a new phenomenon, a major submarine campaign had been waged by Germany against British trade during the First World War. German submarines had sunk 12.8 million gross tons of Allied and neutral shipping from 1914–18.[1] Despite the extent of those losses, the U-boat menace had been overcome successfully. The belief that Britain had been brought to the brink of starvation in 1917 was a myth, though there had briefly been an unseemly degree of panic in naval and government circles. On a grand strategic level, the U-boats' 'piratical' actions in the Atlantic had been a prime reason for the United States entry to the war in April 1917, which in turn had been vital to bringing about an armistice to end hostilities in western Europe in November 1918.

During the interwar period, the Royal Navy had devoted its philosophical energies to re-fighting the battleship engagements of Jutland. Anti-submarine warfare had been swiftly forgotten. An interest in the seemingly dull work of safely convoying merchant shipping was liable to damage an officer's career. The Naval Staff's historical section had lacked sufficient personnel even to finish its study of the convoy battles of 1917–18 by the eve of the Second World War. Until the late 1930s the Admiralty had placed limitations upon submarine participation in night exercises for reasons of safety. In 1939 the Royal Navy had high hopes that new and insufficiently tested sonar technology – underwater radar – would counter the submarine menace.[2]

Meantime, in Germany the Treaty of Versailles had banned submarines, but during the 1920s commercial joint ventures with firms in Holland, Spain, Sweden, Finland and Turkey had allowed German technical experimentation to continue.[3] The 1935 Anglo-German Naval Treaty had conceded the Germans forty-five per cent of the Royal Navy's submarine tonnage. The

Nazi government had kept that commitment as continued good relations with Britain was of great importance during the rearmament period. Unrestricted submarine building by Germany might have changed the nature of international relations in the late 1930s as such a programme could only be construed as a threat to Britain. Not until early 1939 did Hitler change naval policy given Britain's persistent interference in the affairs of central and eastern Europe. A new construction programme – Z Plan – envisaged the building of a large fleet of U-boats, but that programme was still getting underway when war began.[4] In September 1939 Germany had fifty-seven U-boats, many of which were small, short-range boats. (Coincidentally, Britain also had fifty-seven submarines at that time and France had seventy-eight submarines).

Commander-in-Chief Admiral Raeder accepted the need for a fresh submarine war against Britain, despite the failure of the 1917–18 campaign. The Berlin government was willing to risk possible negative effects on neutral and United States opinion. Already sixty-three years old in 1939, the aloof Raeder was relatively apolitical, having been appointed naval commander prior to the Nazi assumption of power. Critically, in the rough and tumble of Nazi politics, Raeder had lost the battle with Goering for control of aircraft. The German navy had no air arm of its own and would rely on the *Luftwaffe* for air support.

Several years before the war Raeder had appointed Karl Doenitz commander of U-boats. Doenitz had been born in 1891 near Berlin and was the son of an engineer. He had spent the first half of the First World War as a signals officer on a light cruiser in the Mediterranean and Black Sea, before transferring to submarines at the end of 1916. In 1917 Doenitz had been an officer of *U-39*. This submarine had been commanded by the 'ace' Walter Forstmann. *U-39* sank eight ships on Doenitz's first patrol with her in the Mediterranean. Fourteen ships had been sunk on the submarine's next patrol. One victim had been carrying 1,000 Italian soldiers and virtually all drowned. Doenitz had later commanded U-boats with modest success until disaster struck on 4 October 1918 when his *UB-68* went out of control after attacking a convoy. The damaged boat had come to the surface close to Allied warships and had to be scuttled. Doenitz and most of his crew had been rescued.[5]

During the 1920s and 1930s Doenitz became a great believer in the tale that submarine warfare had taken Britain to the brink of defeat in 1917. If a great fleet of new U-boats could sink a million tons of shipping a month, disaster might loom for Britain in the next war. Doenitz's personal experience as a U-boat officer during the First World War probably over-influenced his thinking about the potential of submarine warfare. 'The enemy merchant navies', wrote Doenitz, 'are a collective factor. It is therefore immaterial where any one ship is sunk, for it must ultimately be replaced by new construction. What counts in the long run is the preponderance of sinkings over new construction.'[6] The single-minded Doenitz was not inclined to believe rumours in the late 1930s that the British had solved the problems of producing an effective sonar. 'I did not consider that the effective working of ASDIC [Allied Submarine Detection Investigation Committee] had been proved, and in any case I had no intention of allowing myself to be intimidated by British disclosures.'[7]

Doenitz had placed his faith in ocean-going U-boats, 750- or 1,000-ton vessels. The medium Type VII C had a maximum speed of seventeen knots on the surface. It could make seven and a half knots submerged and carried at least a dozen torpedoes for firing from bow tubes. An oil-fuelled engine powered a U-boat on the surface, but once submerged propulsion by electric batteries was needed to avoid eating into the crew's oxygen supply. The batteries were recharged as the submarine ran on the surface. A U-boat dived as deeply as its hull could safely withstand – perhaps to a maximum of 600 feet – by filling ballast tanks. The submarine rose again by blowing the water out of the tanks.

Doenitz believed that advances in radio technology would make it possible for a land-based headquarters to organize attacks by a number of U-boats against a single convoy of merchant ships. A chain of patrolling U-boats could watch a wide expanse of ocean. If a convoy was sighted the news would be relayed to U-boat headquarters, which in turn would use that information, and anything else uncovered by German intelligence, to direct U-boats into the path of that convoy for a night attack. Doenitz had told a fellow admiral in 1939: 'It is clear that the attack on British sea communications alone can have a "war decisive" effect in a naval war against Britain.'[8] The Germans were aware that the British might be able to detect and track the transmission of U-boat radio signals, but so long as the code was secure that could be tolerated.

Upon the outbreak of war, unrestricted submarine warfare, which is the sinking of Allied merchant shipping on sight, had become the norm. To maintain a flow of imports, Britain, the original home of the industrial revolution, had the largest merchant fleet in the world. Almost one-third of the world's merchant tonnage was British, about 3000 ships. This was more than twice the tonnage of the next largest national merchant navy (which belonged to the United States). Over 190,000 volunteer seamen manned the merchant fleet, of whom roughly seventy per cent were British nationals, five per cent foreigners and twenty-five per cent 'lascars' originating mainly from India and China.[9] British trade was organised by a Ministry of Shipping and backed by a government insurance scheme. Civilian merchant seamen would be subject to conscription to the Royal Navy if they stopped sailing, and were lured on by payment of high wages and war bonuses.

Convoys had been quickly introduced on the most important routes to the United Kingdom. Convoys had unequivocally proved their value in the First World War. In practise it was easier for a defender to protect merchant shipping if it was grouped together, and harder for an attacker to locate prey if ships did not sail independently along a known trade route. A submarine might surprise a convoy with its initial attack, but the naval escort could then counter-attack to force the submarine to submerge whilst the convoy sailed on. Escort warships carried depth charges – canisters of explosive – to lob into the water above the suspected location of a submarine. Delays caused in assembling, sailing and unloading convoys in crowded ports cut the cargo-carrying capacity of Britain's merchant fleet by up to one-third.[10] It might take days or weeks for a convoy to be gathered. This had been a heavy one-off cost British trade had to absorb at the outset of war. Government enforced rationing of civilian goods had been designed to cope with a reduction in trade that was inevitable.

In the winter of 1939–40 the Germans had been able to do British shipping only limited damage as the English Channel had been blocked by mines and other anti-submarine measures. U-boats had to waste valuable time and fuel sailing around the north of Scotland. Faulty torpedo detonators had also caused problems during this period and had saved more than one large British warship. After the Norwegian campaign a German study had found torpedo failure rates to be as high as thirty per cent. German torpedoes had also proved disappointing in their destructive power, especially against large merchant ships. An analysis of torpedo hits conducted later in the war would conclude that only forty per cent of torpedoed ships had been sunk by a single torpedo. The rest had needed either more than one torpedo to sink or had been merely damaged. Doenitz would acknowledge that during the early period of the war, 'the effectiveness of our torpedoes was no greater than it had been in the First World War'.[11] For the first nine months of the Second World War British merchant shipping losses had been covered by new construction and captured German shipping.

In 1940 submarines quickly became the overwhelming focus of the German naval war effort. The pressures of war had caused Hitler to abandon the ambitious Z Plan ship-building programme. Only warships already partly built were to be completed, along with a limited number of small coastal warships. U-boat construction, however, was to continue faster than ever. Hitler had accepted Raeder's argument that the moment was opportune for a strong commitment to submarines. A plan had been drawn up to build twenty-nine U-boats a month. In March 1940 this figure had been reduced to the still substantial figure of twenty-five.[12]

After the fall of France the Germans were able to base submarines on the Atlantic coast of western Europe. This further encouraged the German High Command to continue with a major and sustained commitment to submarine warfare. The U-boat campaign was elevated into the front rank of the Nazi war effort. From French bases U-boats were able to range far out into the Atlantic to get astride shipping routes to Britain from South America, the Indian Ocean and North America. Doenitz's headquarters was relocated to a chateau in Brittany. U-boat pens with twenty-six foot thick concrete roofs were constructed at ports such as Brest, Lorient, St Nazaire and Bordeaux. The RAF did little to bomb these pens whilst they were under construction, and they were well-neigh invulnerable once completed. According to Lothar-Guenther Buchheim, a wartime artist and future author of *Das Boot*:

> The string of bases at the Navy's disposal now stretched from the Arctic Sea to the Bay of Biscay. The age-old handicap of having to operate exclusively out of the 'liquid triangle' of the North Sea was thus removed. The enemy could no longer lie in ambush as German ships departed or bar their way home.[13]

For decades the Royal Navy had sat astride the route from Germany to the great oceans of the world. German naval officers were excited and intoxicated to break free of that situation. The British government had made matters worse by foolishly surrendering rights to military bases in southern Ireland in 1938.[14]

In August 1940 Hitler declared Britain to be under total blockade. All shipping, enemy or neutral, was to be attacked on sight. A four month period followed in the autumn of 1940 that German submariners would call the 'happy time'. From June to September submarines sank 274 ships for the loss of just two U-boats.[15] This toll of shipping greatly bolstered Doenitz's faith in the submarine as a war-winning weapon. He was impatient that at such a vital time so much of Germany's planned U-boat armada was still under-going construction. The time needed to build a submarine and then train a crew might take from one to two years. Submarine construction was a specialized form of industry, and German shipyards were on the verge of achieving a greatly expanded rate of output. In the first half of 1940, on average only two U-boats a month had been launched. This figure jumped to six a month in the second half of 1940. In the first half of 1941 thirteen U-boats a month would be launched, and, ominously, that figure would rise again to twenty a month in the second half of 1941.[16]

The autumn of 1940 began to feature so-called wolf pack attacks on convoys by a group of U-boats. For instance, on the night of 21/22 September five U-boats attacked a convoy of fifteen ships. No less than eleven ships were sunk in the ensuing battle. A few weeks later the same fate befell convoy SC 7, which comprised thirty-four merchant ships and five escorts. From the night of 16/17 October U-boat attacks and poor weather dispersed the convoy as it neared western Scotland. In total seventeen ships were sunk and another two were damaged. A wolf pack had the potential to devastate a convoy to the point of achieving a strategic outcome. Aces in command of particular submarines began to establish formidable reputations. Veteran U-boat commanders sometimes had the nerve to sail down a file of shipping within a convoy to sink several ships in succession. By the war's end two per cent of commanders would account for thirty per cent of sinkings.[17]

The Royal Navy was badly stretched in the autumn of 1940. The number of warships available for escort duty had been reduced by the losses of the

Norwegian campaign and Dunkirk evacuation. The convoy system was far from comprehensive at this time and the U-boats took full advantage of that. From mid-July to mid-December 1940 the number of ships sunk sailing independently was twice as many as was sunk sailing in convoy.[18] Up to August 1940 *B-Dienst* – the German Naval Radio Monitoring Service – was able to read up to half of the Royal Navy's less important signals traffic. A relatively straightforward Administrative Code had been broken pre-war. The knowledge gained from that had permitted the penetration of other ciphers, though the code used by the most senior Royal Navy commanders had remained secure. Royal Navy ciphers were changed periodically but German intelligence continued to profitably monitor British merchant navy radio traffic. Information about when a convoy left port, and its course, was valuable to U-boat headquarters.

In the First World War aircraft had played an important reconnaissance role in the Allied campaign against submarines. Yet the Royal Naval Air Service had been lost to the RAF and the campaign in the Atlantic had started poorly for the RAF's Coastal Command, which was responsible for land-based maritime operations. At the start of the war Coastal Command's principal aircraft had been the relatively short range Avro Anson. The twin-engine Anson was armed only with 100-pound bombs, though the experience of the First World War had long ago revealed that a 500-pound bomb was needed to sink a submarine. That impression had been confirmed when a British submarine was accidentally hit by an RAF 100-pounder to suffer only slight damage.[19] In 1940 Coastal Command aircraft lacked effective navigation equipment, modern bomb sights, a low-reading altimeter, night illuminants and effective depth charges. The ASV Mark I radar (Air to Surface Vessel) was so unreliable that waves could disrupt the signal.

The main problem for Coastal Command was the unwillingness of the Air Ministry to give it a share of the new four-engine bombers coming into service. Four-engine aircraft were essential for long flights over a great ocean like the Atlantic. In June 1940 only five to ten per cent of Coastal Command aircraft had an outward range of over 500 miles. When the Admiralty called for the expansion of Coastal Command, the Air Minister, Sir Archibald Sinclair, replied on 5 November 1940 that 'any undue expansion of the naval cooperation force would inevitably hamper the building up of Bomber Command's strength and would sacrifice the possibility of its being employed effectively on offensive operations'.[20]

As the war at sea grew in scale, the suffering was shared by all combatants. Slow-moving merchant ships and crews were passive victims, plying their peacetime trade in very different circumstances. Tell-tale smoke streaming from ships' stacks gave away a convoy's location at an alarming distance. For a merchant seaman, night-time explosions, sheets of flame and a hurried escape from a burning ship might be followed by days adrift in leaky lifeboats and rafts, with little food and water and other sailors slowly losing their minds. Damaged ships and boat-loads of survivors might vanish from a convoy during the night. The ruthlessness involved in sinking unarmed merchant ships was highlighted when they were sunk alone without a swift escort at hand to rescue the crew. On average over forty per cent of a merchant crew died when a ship was sunk.[21] Winter storms, fog or high seas reduced the submarine threat, though a convoy might be scattered by the elements. Extraordinary as it may sound, until mid-war a British merchant seaman's pay was stopped from the moment his ship was sunk.

Escort commanders, usually sailing in old destroyers, corvettes and sloops faced great challenges in 1940–41. A few escorts might have to cover a convoy of forty to fifty ships, drawn up in columns 1,000 yards apart. A ship-borne sonar mounted in a retractable dome under an escort warship could locate submarines by bouncing a radio signal off a submerged object, but it could not give an accurate depth reading and failed at very short ranges. At the start of the war the Royal Navy was over-confident in its ASDIC (sonar) sets, which proved to be of little use against U-boats operating on the surface at night. In the dark, the low silhouette of a U-boat had to be spotted by eyesight. Escorts were manned by a cadre of regulars and reservists, but mostly by war service personnel still learning their trade.

Below the waves, bearded and unwashed U-boat crews worked in cramped quarters, breathing fouled air and able to hear the churning propellers of hunting warships above. In reality, U-boats spent most of their time cruising on the surface as a submersible torpedo-boat. An average U-boat patrol lasted about two months. A submarine was claustrophobic at the best of times and offered a poor chance of survival if its hull was cracked open by a depth charge explosion. Less than one-third of a crew could hope to survive if the boat was sunk. Shared danger and enforced intimacy bred a strong camaraderie among crews. Successful commanders were highly decorated and lauded in the German press.

During 1940 almost four million tons of Allied and neutral merchant shipping had been lost, of which a little less than 2.2 million tons had been sunk by submarines.[22] The Germans had no intention of letting up the pressure in 1941. Führer Directive No. 23 of 6 February 1941 stated:

> Contrary to our former view the heaviest effort of our war operations against the English war economy has lain in the high losses in merchant shipping inflicted by sea and air warfare ... A further considerable increase is to be expected in the course of this year by the wider employment of submarines, and this can bring about the collapse of English resistance in the foreseeable future.

German warships added to British worries at sea by making regular forays into the Atlantic during the early period of the war. Late in January 1941 the battlecruisers *Scharnhorst* and *Gneisenau* set sail to destroy any shipping they happened upon. The sinking of the battleship *Bismarck* in May, however, was an undeniable British victory over the surface raider threat.

The British war effort in the Atlantic was coordinated by the Admiralty in London and naval headquarters at Plymouth and Liverpool. At the summit of government, a War Cabinet 'Battle of Atlantic Committee' began to meet under Churchill's chairmanship in March 1941. Britain was not entirely alone either. In 1940 the United States had built almost a million tons of merchant shipping, and preparations had been made for a huge expansion of ship building in response to the mounting U-boat crisis. In September 1940 the Roosevelt administration had agreed to transfer fifty old destroyers to the Royal Navy in exchange for basing rights on British territory in north and central America. The Royal Canadian Navy was in the process of a massive expansion that would eventually see it undertake a large part of the North Atlantic's convoy escort work.

In the spring of 1941 the campaign in the Atlantic intensified as winter storms abated. In March five U-boats were sunk in fifteen days, including the boats of three famous aces. Otto Kretschmer sank forty-five ships until he was made POW after *U-99* was destroyed. *U-47*, which had sunk *Royal Oak* in Scapa Flow in 1939, was depth-charged by the destroyer *Wolverine*. An orange glow deep in the water indicated the complete destruction of the submarine and its crew. *U-47*'s commander, Guenther Prien, had been third on the list of tonnage aces. These successes for the Royal Navy proved to be only a temporary respite and losses soon began to approach those of the previous autumn. Doenitz had widened the zone of U-boat operations and before long there were heavy losses off Freetown in West Africa. Doenitz's son-in-law, Lieutenant Hessler of *U-107*, sank fourteen ships on a single extended voyage off West Africa. Doenitz began to assemble wolf packs in the North Atlantic far out at sea in a bid to destroy convoys over a battle of several day's duration.[23]

The cause of convoy protection was also hurt by the belated appearance of the *Luftwaffe*. In late 1940 thirty Focke-Wulf FW200 Condor aircraft had been based near Bordeaux. The Condor was a modified airliner and benefited greatly from the typical convoy's lack of anti-aircraft weaponry and air support. The Condor's outward range of 1,000 miles was far enough to make a 2,000 mile one-way flight across the Atlantic from France to Norway. Any one of its four 550-pound bombs could cripple or sink a merchant ship. Convoys sailing between Britain and Gibraltar were especially vulnerable to location and attack by German aircraft. In January and February of 1941 U-boats sank sixty ships and Condors accounted for another forty-seven.[24] Much more might have been achieved had Goering and Hitler taken a greater interest in the air war against Allied merchant shipping.

U-boat operations in the Atlantic were coordinated by a stream of radio messages between submarines and U-boat headquarters in France. British signals experts and code breakers monitored U-boat radio communications.

This was not a new technique for the British in a naval war against Germany. During the First World War a secret department in the Admiralty known as Room 40 had successfully brought together civilian professionals and military officers to detect German radio transmissions and break German naval codes. In the war beginning in 1939 a new challenge faced British signals experts in the form of the Enigma machine, an electro-mechanical enciphering apparatus with interchangeable rotors. The Enigma machine was battery-powered and highly portable. A signaller encoded a message by typing it on an ordinary keyboard. The Enigma machine's rotors and connectors scrambled and encoded the message depending on the settings of the machine. A receiving signaller could decode the message by putting it through his Enigma machine using the same settings. The rotor settings might be changed every twenty-four hours, and the Germans believed that would thwart codebreakers.[25] The British effort against Enigma signals was known as 'Ultra', which referred to the highest level of security classification.

Enigma-generated signals could be decoded by capturing a schedule of machine settings or by breaking into the code by means of slack operating procedures, such as the repeating of parts of standard messages at the same time each day. Young German naval signallers, tossed by the high seas whilst crouched over their Enigma machines, tended to be more careless than their land-based colleagues. Another Achilles heel to the Enigma machine was the fact that it was an adapted version of a machine available on the commercial market in the 1920s. During the 1930s Polish mathematicians had worked to break into German codes and in 1939 the British had received a Polish-built copy of an Enigma machine.

During the first half of 1941 the effort to break the naval Enigma had been pushed forward rapidly when several German vessels were captured, in particular *U*-110 on 9 May 1941. In June all eight German supply ships operating in the Atlantic in support of the U-boats were sunk as a result of Ultra information and good fortune. In consequence, German naval intelligence was forced to review the security of naval signals, only to conclude that nothing was amiss.[26] There were other occasions when Doenitz's or Raeder's staff were suspicious of the security of their signals, but flawed internal investigations continued to give the all clear.

The availability of a regular flow of timely Ultra information allowed the Admiralty to re-route convoys away from located U-boat patrol lines. This was a strong benefit as the number of U-boats available to Doenitz was steadily rising. The U-boat fleet had only increased to sixty-four by the autumn of 1940, but U-boat numbers had risen to 113 by April 1941 and to 198 by October of that year. The enormous U-boat construction programme was paying dividends, though many were still undergoing trials and crew training. Part of the explanation for rising U-boat numbers was that so few had been sunk. The Allies had only managed to sink nine German submarines in 1939 and twenty-four in 1940. For the first nine months of 1941 the Allies maintained that mediocre record.

Unexpectedly, from the German viewpoint, even though the number of U-boats at sea rose during 1941, merchant ship sinkings by U-boats fell dramatically in the second half of the year. From July 1940 to June 1941 average monthly losses to U-boats in the Atlantic had been 263,000 tons. Yet this figure fell to a monthly average of 103,000 tons from July to December 1941. The emptiness of the oceans was uncanny and U-boats were simply not sighting North Atlantic convoys that were obviously sailing on a regular basis. Doenitz was suspicious and observed wryly on 19 November 1941: 'Chance does not always come down on one side.'[27] Ultra information, and the re-routing of convoys away from Ultra-located wolf packs, has been given most of the credit for the drop in merchant ship sinkings in the second half of 1941. By one estimate Ultra saved one and a half to two million tons of shipping, over 300 ships.[28] There were, however, other relevant factors. Firstly, the number of escorting warships rose during 1941 thanks to new construction, the release of destroyers from anti-invasion duties and United States' involvement. Secondly, from 18 June 1941 the speed limit for merchant ships sailing independently was raised from thirteen to fifteen knots. This relatively small rise was towards the threshold of a U-boat's maximum speed on the surface. 120 independents had been lost from April to June (sixty-six per cent of losses to submarines in the Atlantic), but only twenty-five independents were lost from July to September (24.3 per cent).[29] Thirdly, from September 1941 U-boats began to be transferred to the Mediterranean Sea and Norwegian waters. Towards the end of the year the seas around Gibraltar would become the focus of submarine activity. Ultra's golden run in the Atlantic would be brought to a close at the start of February 1942 when a fourth rotor was brought into use on naval Enigma machines. Codebreakers were blinded as this caused a dramatic increase in enciphering possibilities.

The United States Navy had been patrolling the western Atlantic since the spring of 1941. USN forces had been based at Newfoundland from May and Iceland from July. Washington was of the view that if they were going to ship supplies to Britain that material needed to safely reach its intended destination. President Roosevelt said of the U-boats: 'When you see a rattlesnake poised, you don't wait until it has struck before you crush it.' On 20 June 1941 *U-203* happened upon American warships in the German designated zone of Atlantic operations. The submarine tried to torpedo the battleship *Texas* but failed to gain a good firing position. When the German Naval Staff reported this to Hitler he banned attacks on American warships. British radio intercepts and decoding efforts revealed the extent to which the Germans wanted to avoid incidents in the Atlantic involving the Americans. This may well have encouraged Roosevelt to increase the United States Navy's involvement in the Atlantic. In September the USN began escorting British convoys in the western Atlantic as far as Iceland. Certainly the re-routing of convoys based on Ultra information helped to hold down the number of American-German clashes at sea, though it could not prevent them entirely.[30] In October two American destroyers were torpedoed, one of which sank. Raeder and Doenitz were greatly concerned by Washington's creeping involvement in the Atlantic campaign, but there is no evidence that Roosevelt was planning a declaration of war against Germany.

1941 was another poor year for the RAF's Coastal Command. In 1940–41 less than twenty per cent of U-boats destroyed were sunk by air attack.[31] By 1941 four-engine Halifax bombers were coming into operational service, but Coastal Command saw little of these aircraft, which went to Bomber Command. The leaders of the RAF held out against giving Coastal Command more than a minimum of resources. The First Sea Lord, Admiral Sir Dudley Pound, was not an effective lobbyist, and Churchill was committed to the strategic bombing of occupied Europe. Air Vice-Marshal Sir Arthur Harris, when he was Deputy Chief of the Air Staff, had opposed the diversion of heavy bombers to Coastal Command, commenting that 'twenty U-boats and a few Focke-Wulf in the Atlantic would have provided the effective anti-aircraft defence of all Germany'.[32] Pressure was applied to Bomber Command to attack shipyards building U-boats and the concrete pens in French ports that based the submarines. Yet from 1940–42 only three to four per cent of bombs dropped on Axis Europe were targeted on submarine pens and shipyards. The limited *Luftwaffe* involvement in the Atlantic made it easier for RAF commanders to argue that their efforts were better needed elsewhere. The number of aircraft lost by Bomber Command over the Continent in a typical fortnight would have made a significant difference to convoy protection in the Atlantic. Only in September 1941 did No. 120 Squadron commence operations flying B-24 Liberators out of Iceland and Northern Ireland. The Mark III four-engine Liberator fitted extra fuel tanks to extend its range to 2,400 miles. Otherwise a Liberator could still manage an impressive 1,800 mile-round journey.[33]

In the later half of 1941, Doenitz was forced to accept the diversion of part of his fleet away from the North Atlantic. In September Hitler ordered that six U-boats immediately head for the Mediterranean through the eight mile-wide Gibraltar strait to support the faltering Italian war effort. Hitler was concerned at the level of loss being inflicted on Italian convoys to North Africa and the extent of the Royal Navy's supremacy in the Mediterranean. In November Hitler dispatched an air fleet headquarters to the Mediterranean (from Russia) to build up the *Luftwaffe*'s effort to contest the skies between Sicily and North Africa. More U-boats were sent to the Mediterranean in November and December, and Doenitz was obliged to deploy another half a dozen U-boats to the seas to the west of Gibraltar. Twenty-three U-boats had reached the Mediterranean by December. Others had been sunk or turned back making the attempt.[34]

Doenitz was opposed to sending his U-boats to the Mediterranean. He knew that the great bulk of British reinforcements to the Middle East were sailing around South Africa and not through the Mediterranean. RAF squadrons and RN submarines at Malta were the main problem for Italian convoys in the central Mediterranean, and that was not something U-boats could directly combat. Doenitz was also convinced that given the currents and defences of the Gibraltar strait, U-boats sent to the Mediterranean would never return. The current flowing into the Mediterranean helped to carry a submarine, submerged or on the surface, through the strait, but the nights were too short to allow a submarine to travel in the other direction against the current.

In the short term, however, the pay-off for Hitler's plan was considerable. On 13 November a U-boat sank the aircraft carrier *Ark Royal* as she returned to Gibraltar from a Malta reinforcement operation. Only one crewman was killed but fires got out of control to doom the fleet carrier. On 25 November, in the eastern Mediterranean, the battleship *Barham* was torpedoed and rolled over to explode with heavy loss of life. 862 officers and men were killed. *U-331* dived to a record depth of 820 feet to make a successful escape from *Barham's* escorting destroyers.[35] More British warships were lost in the Mediterranean during December. The cruiser *Neptune* struck mines north of Tripoli and capsized. There was only one survivor from a crew of 764. On the night of 18/19 December Italian frogmen successfully mined the battleships *Queen Elizabeth* and *Valiant* in Alexandria harbour. The Royal Navy had effectively lost control of the Mediterranean at a vital time.

At the Admiralty, the shifting of the focus of the U-boat war to Gibraltar and the Mediterranean had become painfully apparent. The rising number of U-boats operating in waters near Gibraltar had made the safe passage of convoys to and from that location more difficult to arrange. For example, HG 75 had been a homeward-bound convoy from Gibraltar. It had an escort of thirteen warships for seventeen merchantmen and sailed from Gibraltar on the evening of 22 October. The convoy had been attacked by five U-boats until the night of 27/28 October. A destroyer and four merchant ships had been sunk. At his headquarters in France, Doenitz had estimated the convoy's losses to be twice as high as the true toll.[36]

By 1941 certain U-boat commanders had proved themselves to be experts, and, similarly, on the Allied side there were escort groups more effective than others due to better leadership, training and experience. On 14 December 1941 convoy HG 76 set out from Gibraltar for Liverpool protected by such an escort group. Signals intercepts and recent convoy experience on the Gibraltar run had warned that strong U-boat opposition was to be expected. Thirty-two merchant ships were escorted by Commander Frederic John Walker's 36th Escort Group, which comprised two sloops and six corvettes. Another eight destroyers, sloops and corvettes had been added to the group for the opening phase of HG 76's passage. The convoy's merchant ships formed five columns, surrounded by the escorting warships deployed to form an inner and an outer screen. The experience of convoy HG 76 proved to be among the most important of all the many engagements fought between a convoy and a wolf pack. The U-boat war was a long campaign of attrition, but a close examination of HG 76 reveals much about that long campaign's likely outcome.

Walker's escort group had been joined by the *Audacity*, the Royal Navy's first escort aircraft carrier. Late in 1941 the Royal Navy had a dozen escort carriers on order from British and American shipyards. *Audacity* – with a crew of over 200 and a top speed of fifteen knots – had been recently converted from the captured German merchant ship *Hanover*. The superstructure had been razed and replaced with a wooden flight deck. Six aircraft were parked on the deck and arrester wires were employed to catch an aircraft as it landed. *Audacity* carried Martlets, the British version of the American Grumman Wildcat, a fighter capable of a maximum speed of over 300 mph. *Audacity*'s maiden voyage had been a recent outward bound convoy to Gibraltar and the Martlets had marked the occasion by shooting down a Condor bomber.

HG 76's Commander Walker – the son of a naval officer – was a tall, argumentative, formidable-looking man, with dark, bushy eyebrows and a strong jaw often used to clench a pipe. Walker had taken an interest in anti-submarine warfare on a destroyer in the First World War. He had made that his specialisation during the 1920s and his career had suffered accordingly. After a spell as second-in-command of a battleship in the mid-1930s, Walker had become commander of the Anti-Submarine Warfare School in the spring of 1937. In that post he had been passed over for promotion to the rank of captain, which shows how lowly the Admiralty had regarded convoy escort work at that time.[37] From 1939 to early 1941 Walker had been anti-submarine officer at the naval headquarters at Dover. He had then taken command of a sea-going escort group. During a brief training period Walker had laid out some clear instructions for his commanders. Sighted U-boats were to be counter-attacked with depth-charges at the first opportunity. Walker's 1,190-ton sloop *Stork* had been launched in 1936, carried a crew of 125 and was able to make eighteen knots. That was a good deal slower than a fleet destroyer but more than enough to shepherd a convoy typically sailing at less than ten knots. The corvettes of the escort group had been launched in 1940 or 1941. The 36th Escort Group had taken a convoy from Liverpool to Gibraltar at the end of November. Heavy storms had discouraged U-boat attack and the voyage had been uneventful.

Convoy HG 76 headed north west from Gibraltar into the Atlantic on the afternoon of 14 December. Aircraft flying from Gibraltar – Swordfish, Hudsons and Catalinas – were able to provide air cover at the outset. The convoy was sighted by a U-boat preparing to make a run through the Gibraltar strait. German spies in Spain and French Morocco wasted no time in filing their own reports. Doenitz soon knew that the convoy comprised over thirty merchant ships, though agents' estimates of the escort only claimed the presence of the aircraft tender *Unicorn* (and not *Audacity*). HG 76 would receive a hot reception as it headed homeward. Doenitz had a group of U-boats deployed across the route from Gibraltar to Britain.[38]

Poor visibility on 15 December made for a quiet first full day at sea for HG 76. On the afternoon of 16 December *U-131*, commanded by Fregatten Kapitan Arend Baumann, spotted the convoy and dived for safety only to re-surface amid the ships and have to dive again. At U-boat headquarters, Doenitz and his staff ordered reinforcing submarines to join Baumann.

At dawn on 17 December the convoy was beyond the range of Gibraltar-based aircraft. That morning a Martlet from *Audacity* found *U-131* shadowing the convoy. Taking advantage of the escort's strength, Walker and *Stork* led four other warships to hunt the submarine. A U-boat's slow speed under water made it vulnerable to counter-attack if located. Sonar contact was made and *U-131* was damaged by depth-charges and forced to the surface after two hours as attempts at repairs had failed. *U-131* tried to escape on the surface only for the warships to follow in pursuit firing their main guns. The battle had become a surface engagement. A Martlet arrived to strafe the submarine but the steady-nerved deck crew shot it down and killed the pilot. When the gunfire of the warships grew too severe, Baumann and his crew abandoned their submarine in a timely fashion. All forty-eight German crew were rescued. The successful hunt had taken eight hours from the time Walker's small flotilla had left the convoy till their return.[39]

At dawn on the morning of 18 December Commander Wolfgang Heyda's *U-434* was sighted shadowing the convoy from astern and attacked by the destroyer *Stanley*. Other warships quickly joined the hunt. Several dozen depth-charges were dropped to cause critical damage to the submarine. Aboard *U-434*, lighting was lost, there was steady flooding and a torpedo exploded in the stern tubes. Commander Heyda ordered the ballast tanks to be blown and the submarine came to the surface with a bounce. The destroyer *Blankney* lowered a whaler to send a boarding party, but scuttling charges had been set on the submarine and *U-434*'s crew hurriedly abandoned ship. Heyda and forty-one crewmen were rescued; only four men were lost. The crews of *U-131* and *U-434* had been fortunate. Survival rates on lost submarines were typically much lower. Both U-boats had been on their maiden cruise.[40]

Two *Luftwaffe* four-engine Condors were driven off by the *Audacity*'s fighters on 18 December to again prove the value of aircraft to a convoy's defence. Still, the convoy's good fortune could not last indefinitely in the face of determined attack. Six escort warships departed for other duties as HG 76 moved further away from Gibraltar.

In the early hours of 19 December, a fine night beneath a pale moon, *U-574*, commanded by Lieutenant Dietrich Gengelbach, attacked the convoy. *U-574* had been in contact with the convoy since late on the 16th. *Stanley* was a former American four-stack destroyer on station two miles astern of the convoy. *Stanley*'s lookouts spotted a submarine on the surface in the moonlight. The destroyer was turned to mount an attack. Six miles away aboard *Stork*, Walker received a signal from *Stanley*, 'Torpedoes passing from astern.' Just after that, the destroyer's magazine exploded. Walker later wrote: 'At the moment when everything seemed to be sorting itself out ... I had my glasses on her, she went up, literally, in a sheet of flame hundreds of feet high. She thought the torpedoes were passing her.'[41] *Stork* and other escorts headed towards the rapidly sinking destroyer, firing star-shells to light up the area.

The crew of U-574 did not have long to celebrate their victory. The higher speeds of the surface escorts brought them quickly into range for a sonar contact. *Stork* dropped a heavy pattern of depth-charges. The damaged U-574 was forced to the surface 200 yards away. Walker's battle report told the story of what happened next.

> As I went in to ram he ran away from me and turned to port. I followed and I was surprised to find later that I had turned three complete circles, the U-boat turning continually to port just inside *Stork*'s turning-circle at only two or three knots slower than me. I kept her illuminated with snowflakes and fired at him with the four-inch guns until they could not be sufficiently depressed. After this the guns' crews were reduced to fist shaking and roaring curses at an enemy who several times seemed to be a matter of feet away rather than yards.[42]

Stork's first lieutenant mounted a machine gun on the bridge screen to shoot up the submarine's conning tower. Finally *Stork* caught up with U-574 and completed a successful ramming. The submarine scraped along the bottom of the sloop and was destroyed by depth charges as it fell astern. *Stork*'s bow was crushed by the collision and the sonar dome underneath the warship was smashed. *Stork* and other ships rescued a number of survivors. Sixteen Germans and twenty-eight British sailors were saved from U-574 and *Stanley*.

The night's events were not yet over. Amid the commotion, the convoy's first merchant ship was torpedoed by U-108. The crew of thirty-nine took to their lifeboats and the crippled freighter had to be finished off by the gunfire of an escort. At dawn Walker received a signal from the Admiralty that six U-boats were believed to be nearby. That day, 19 December, Martlets drove off menacing Condors, shooting down two and damaging a third. In the early evening a U-boat was spotted by an airman fifteen miles away. The submarine was pursued by warships from the escort without contact being made.[43]

On 20 December U-boats sighted ahead of the convoy were forced to dive by the *Audacity*'s Martlets. The following morning U-boats astern of the convoy were again forced to dive. *Luftwaffe* reconnaissance aircraft had spotted another convoy heading south to Gibraltar but Doenitz had decided to continue the battle against HG 76. He despatched three more U-boats – U-71, U-567 and

U-751 – to reinforce the wolf pack. Doenitz helpfully signalled his commanders: 'Given equal firing opportunity, sink the aircraft carrier first. You'll find it easier then.'[44] Easier said than done perhaps, yet this is a good example of the way in which Doenitz closely monitored battles underway at sea. Seldom in the Second World War did such a senior commander give regular instructions to relatively junior officers in close contact with an enemy.

On the night of 21/22 December U-boats closed in again on HG 76, which was off the Portuguese coast. *U*-567, commanded by Kapitanleutnant Engelbert Endrass, sank a second merchant ship. The freighter was carrying iron ore and plunged rapidly down into the ocean's depths, leaving behind only four survivors. At about the same time, Kapitanleutnant Gerhard Bigalk's *U*-751 managed to execute Doenitz's recent advice. At 11 p.m. *Audacity*, ten miles away from the convoy, reported that she had been torpedoed. Walker's report stated:

> For the last three nights, *Audacity* with one corvette had zig-zagged independently well clear of the convoy. Before dark to-night she had asked for a corvette and proposed to operate on the starboard side of the convoy. I had regretfully refused the corvette since I had only four escorts immediately around the convoy. I also suggested she should take station to port of the convoy since I anticipated any attack from the starboard side. *Audacity* replied that the convoy's alterations of course to port would inconvenience her and eventually she went off to starboard alone. I should have finally ordered her either on to the port side or into the middle of the convoy and I feel myself accordingly responsible for her loss.[45]

Audacity's Commander D.W. Mackendrick was marginally senior to Walker. Despite his post as convoy escort commander, Walker had been reluctant to indulge in a public dispute by signal. Three torpedoes cut the carrier in half and the pieces sank separately in ten minutes. *Audacity* had no hull armour. Aircraft on the flight deck broke from their tethers as the ship listed to crash into the sea and men trying to get clear of the ship. Most of the crew survived but many lives were lost, including Mackendrick's. Bigalk of *U*-751 hopefully speculated by signal that he had sunk a *Formidable*-class fleet carrier, though German naval intelligence was more inclined to think that an aircraft tender had been his victim.[46]

As rescue work for *Audacity*'s crew continued, a submarine was sighted and attacked by the sloops *Deptford* and *Stork*. This was Kapitanleutnant Endrass's *U*-567, which dived and was depth-charged by *Deptford* several times. The sonar contact vanished from the screen of the sloop's equipment. No wreckage or survivors were found and the Admiralty was undecided if a submarine had been sunk. It took postwar study to confirm the kill. Endrass was an authentic U-boat ace, having sunk twenty-five ships. He had been first lieutenant of *U*-47 when that boat had successfully penetrated Scapa Flow to sink the *Royal Oak*. Like Prien and *U*-47, Endrass's submarine was lost with all hands. Possibly the toughest U-boat commanders were overly reluctant to re-surface once they had suffered damage. *Deptford* completed an eventful night by ramming *Stork* in the gloom, believing her to be a U-boat.[47]

At 10.54 a.m. on 22 December the convoy was finally met by a four-engine Liberator of No. 120 Squadron, 750 miles from its Ulster base. It helped to drive off a German aircraft and a U-boat. In the afternoon another Liberator appeared on station to force more submarines to submerge. A four-engine aircraft could circle over a convoy for several hours. The convoy sailed on to Britain. The last noteworthy incident for HG 76 was when the crew of one particular merchant ship abandoned their vessel at night as they thought they had rammed a U-boat. The confusion had been caused by heavy seas and the embarrassed crew were returned to their ship by escorting vessels.[48]

An epic convoy battle had come to an end. In a week-long encounter a large wolf pack had pursued HG 76. Many attacks had been mounted. Four U-boats had been sunk in return for the sinking of two warships and two merchant ships. A loss ratio of one U-boat for each Allied surface vessel sunk constituted a terrible defeat for Doenitz. During 1941 as a whole, each U-boat destroyed had been traded for the sinking of a dozen merchant ships, as well as additional Allied warships.[49]

A gloom fell upon U-boat headquarters which had, after all, played an important and direct role in coordinating the battle against HG 76. Doenitz recorded in his memoirs: 'After this failure and in view of the unsatisfactory results of the preceding two months my staff was inclined to voice the opinion that we were no longer in a position successfully to combat the convoy system.'[50] The resilient Doenitz consoled the doubters by pointing out that the escort defence of HG 76 had been freakishly strong. The seas had been calm, air cover had been continuous and the escort had been commanded by a man of above-average skill. In addition, Doenitz consistently inflated estimates of sinkings to support his generally buoyant analysis of the U-boat campaign. Allied and neutral merchant shipping losses for 1941 would tally up to 4.3 million tons, however, this was only ten per cent higher than 1940 despite a greatly expanded submarine fleet. [51] New merchant shipping and shipping purchased, leased or seized from other nations had added almost six million tons to the British merchant fleet from 1939–41.[52]

The outcome of HG 76's voyage was far more encouraging from the viewpoint of the Admiralty in London. Walker had shown that the tactical solution to defeating the U-boat menace was unquestionably available, so long as the British government was willing to invest in the necessary convoy escorts and long-range aircraft for Coastal Command. There was nothing fundamentally different about a U-boat in 1941 compared to 1918. A long inter-service fight still lay ahead to win enough four-engine aircraft for convoy protection.

Commander Walker, soon to be belatedly promoted captain, went on to be the most successful of U-boat hunters and would be among the most decorated

men in the British armed forces. Ironically, a son of Walker would be killed in
a Royal Navy submarine in the Mediterranean in 1943. Walker did not survive
the war either. He died of a cerebral thrombosis in July 1944 at the age of forty-
seven, possibly brought about by the strain of a long war.

Salvation, though, was at hand for Britain in a grand strategic sense with the
entry of the United States to the war in December 1941. From January 1942
the hub of the U-boat offensive would shift away from the Mediterranean and
Gibraltar route. The entry of the United States to the war altered priorities.
Initially the sinking of Allied merchant ships would increase in 1942 as a
broader range of targets could be legitimately attacked. Yet the most important
American contribution to the war against U-boats would be merchant ship
construction. In August 1941 the first Liberty-type cargo ship had been
launched, a ship mass-produced by welding together prefabricated components.
Once United States shipyards began building merchant ships on a massive scale,
the rate of new launchings outran sinkings by a huge margin. As in the First
World War, U-boats could not catch fast troop transports carrying American
troops across the Atlantic to Europe. Great liners such as *Queen Elizabeth* and
Queen Mary could cross the Atlantic at an average speed of twenty-six knots,
and did not even require an escort for much of the voyage.[53]

One of the least acknowledged, yet no less decisive, aspects to the Atlantic
battle was the extent to which Britain had been able to keep functioning as
a mobilised military society on a far lower level of imports than had been
predicted at the outbreak of war. In 1938, 91,880,000 net tonnage of shipping
had docked at Britain. This figure had dropped to 41,660,000 in 1940 and had
dropped again to 25,496,000 in 1941.[54] But the slashing of imports to Britain
did not critically damage the nation's war effort.

On the other hand, the U-boat campaign had a significant and under-
appreciated impact on the German war effort. With limited resources at their
disposal, the Germans had to make definite choices regarding the weapon
systems in which they invested. Given his relatively strong position in the
gloomy world of National Socialist politics, Doenitz had been well placed to
get a very good deal for his command. He had pushed hard and successfully to
gain increased quotas of steel and other resources needed to build the U-boat
fleet. At the close of 1941 the U-boat fleet was stronger than ever, despite its
failure to achieve results at a strategic level.

U-boats were constructed in coastal cities such as Hamburg, Kiel, Bremen
and Danzig, but prefabricated steel sections and diesel and electrical motors
were built in factories in cities such as Berlin. The tentacles and impact of
the U-boat industry stretched well beyond the northern German ports. The
Germans might have built thirty medium tanks for each U-boat constructed.[55]
During 1941 199 U-boats had been commissioned and that figure would rise
to 238 in 1942. But during 1941 tank production had been only 3,245 and that

figure would only rise to 4,137 in 1942. Aircraft and ammunition were the largest items in German arms production, yet naval vessels were a surprisingly high and consistent priority. Naval vessels were a higher priority in terms of cost than panzer equipment in all years from 1940 to 1943; by a margin greater than double in 1940 and no less than triple in 1941.[56] The great investment in U-boats was all the stranger given Hitler's ongoing ambivalence towards Britain. On 27 October 1941 Vice-Admiral Fricke, the Chief of the Naval Staff, had met with Hitler and in the course of discussions had given the view that 'the complete overthrow of Britain was necessary to secure the European new order'. In reply Hitler had said that he was 'even now ready at any time ... to conclude peace with Britain, as the European space which Germany has secured for itself through the conduct of the war so far is sufficient for the future of the German people'.[57]

After the invasion of Russia in June 1941, tanks and armoured vehicles would be vital to winning a land war in eastern Europe, not Doenitz's U-boats, which could neither storm Moscow nor scale the Urals. The *blitzkrieg* – which had made European land warfare in 1940 so different from 1914–18 – had been all about a new generation of armoured fighting vehicles, not submarines. Hitler had allowed the Third Reich to make a massive commitment to submarine warfare without understanding just what a big impact that might have on his plans for further conquests. Ultimately, the Germans were too central European in outlook to understand the vast costs of a genuine commitment to sea power. As in the First World War, from 1939–45 Berlin devoted too much to supporting unrealisable naval ambitions, whilst the true contest for victory or defeat was predictably decided on land.[58]

5
Operation Barbarossa:
The Invasion of Russia

With France conquered, and Britain seemingly contained by aerial bombardment and submarine blockade, Hitler turned his attention to the further expansion of Germany's territory in eastern Europe. Soon after the French campaign Albert Speer had overheard Hitler say to General Keitel: 'Now we have shown what we are capable of, believe me, Keitel, a campaign against Russia would be like a child's game in a sandbox by comparison.'[1] The dismemberment of Poland had already begun to turn Hitler's desire for eastern conquest into reality.

During July 1940 OKH (Army High Command), at Hitler's orders, had begun preparing a preliminary study for a campaign in western Russia. At a 31 July conference Hitler revealed his intentions to his commanders. General Halder recorded a summation of the Führer's ambitions: 'The sooner Russia is crushed the better. Attack achieves its purpose only if Russian state can be shattered to its roots with one blow. Holding part of the country alone will not do. Standing still for the following winter would be perilous.'[2] For Hitler a one-front war had always meant one major land front. Hence the sea war against Britain could be disregarded when making calculations for Russia.

The Soviet Union's occupation of the Baltic states and eastern Poland, and the annexation of Romania's Danubian provinces in June 1940, had revealed Stalin's determination to exploit conditions of general war in Europe. But Hitler's planning for a Russian invasion should not be regarded as a pre-emptive strike in response to Soviet posturing. The invasion was to be a high stakes gamble to aggressively create a greatly expanded German empire. In *Mein Kampf* in the early 1920s Hitler had stated his views only too clearly.

What importance on earth has a State in which the proportion between the size of the population and the territorial area is so miserable as in the present German Reich? At an epoch in which the world is being gradually portioned out among States many of whom almost embrace whole continents one cannot speak of a World Power in the case of a State whose political motherland is confined to a territorial area of barely five-hundred-thousand square kilometres.[3]

Hitler did not believe that world power could be achieved by repeating the policies pursued by the Kaiser's Germany prior to 1914. The needed raw materials and agricultural lands lay in the east.

Hitler believed that Bolshevism and the Jews had destroyed the 'Germanic nucleus' that had underpinned Russia's traditional governing class. Russia was now 'ripe for dissolution'.[4] Hitler had prophesied in *Mein Kampf* that a victory over France in another war would be 'nothing more than a means which will make it possible for our people finally to expand in another quarter'. After he had achieved power, Hitler indiscreetly told a rally at Nuremberg in 1936: 'If we had at our disposal the incalculable wealth and stores and raw materials of the Ural Mountains and the unending fertile plains of the Ukraine to be exploited under National Socialist leadership ... our German people would swim in plenty.'[5] If the Germans could destroy the Soviet state, and conquer its valuable western territories, the Nazi empire would straddle the Eurasian land mass. Britain might be compelled to make peace as no other potential European allies would be available. If Berlin could control the industrial resources of western Europe and the raw materials and agricultural lands of eastern Europe, a Nazi super-state could be established. Germany could then turn to the task of building a great blue water fleet, which, with the aid of the Japanese navy, might be sufficient to face down the United States and force it to accept the dominant global position of the Axis.[6] A thousand-year Third Reich beckoned. A demographic revolution would transplant German settlers to the east at the expense of Slavs and Jews. The humiliations of 1918–19 for Germany might be prevented from ever occurring again.

Meantime, whilst the Battle of Britain had unfolded, in continental Europe there had been a lull until Mussolini had chosen to attack Greece from occupied Albania on 28 October 1940. This reckless act gave the British the opportunity to dispatch RAF units to Greece. Mussolini had not told the Germans of his plans. A political crisis in Romania in September caused further upheaval in south-east Europe. A contingent of German troops entered Romania to secure its oilfields and support the new government of General Antonescu.

Despite the fact that secret planning for an invasion of Russia was well underway, on 12 November 1940 Soviet Foreign Minister Molotov visited Berlin for two days of discussions. Hitler questioned his visitors to uncover Soviet intentions. Molotov indicated that Stalin wanted to annex Finland and make Bulgaria and the Dardanelles a Soviet sphere of influence. These schemes clashed with Nazi plans for eastern Europe and the Germans advised that the Soviets should expand towards the Indian Ocean and Persian Gulf instead. The meeting yielded few concrete results. Hitler proceeded to ignore the suggested question of Soviet membership of the Axis, though a new economic agreement advantageous to Berlin would eventually be signed on 10 January 1941.[7]

In preparation for a Russian campaign it was intended to increase the strength of the German army to 180 divisions. Western Europe could thus be garrisoned, whilst a large field army was readied for operations in eastern Europe. The number of panzer divisions would rise from ten to twenty. This would be achieved primarily by halving the number of tanks in each division. Führer Directive No. 21, issued on 18 December 1940, outlined the plan for Operation Barbarossa. 'The German *Wehrmacht* must be prepared to crush Soviet Russia in a quick campaign even before the conclusion of the war against England.' The name chosen for the operation had a medieval ring. In 1189 Frederick I Barbarossa (Red Beard), Emperor of Germany, had led the Third Crusade against the Muslim armies of Saladin that had taken Jerusalem.

Preparations for Operation Barbarossa were to be completed by 15 May 1941. The Red Army was to be destroyed in western Russia, following which:

> By means of a rapid pursuit a line is then to be reached from beyond which the Russian air force will no longer be capable of attacking the German home territories. The final objective of the operation is to be the attainment of a line sealing off Asiatic Russia ... From such a line the one remaining Russian industrial area in the Urals can be eliminated by the air force, should the need arise.

Hitler hoped that if the *Wehrmacht* could advance to a line running from Archangel on the Arctic Circle to Astrakhan on the Caspian Sea the Soviet Union might be collapsed. The Red Army was to be destroyed before its immense manpower reserves could be fully mobilised. Barbarossa would cause a repeat of the chaos that had engulfed Russia in 1918 when German forces had pressed eastwards in the wake of the signing of the Treaty of Brest-Litovsk with the new Bolshevik government. Kiev, Kharkov, the Donetz basin and Crimea had been occupied. By September 1918 German forces had even reached the oilfields of Baku. The mobilisation of twelve million soldiers had not saved Russia from defeat in the First World War. It is important to bear in mind that Hitler was proposing to repeat in 1941 what Germany had achieved in Russia only twenty-three years before. Why could such feats not be repeated? In the collective memory of the German leadership the relatively recent events of 1918 loomed a good deal larger than historical examples from a distant 1812, when Napoleon had unsuccessfully invaded Russia.

Hitler worked hard to persuade his generals that a Russian campaign would be a great success. On 5 December 1940 he told Field Marshal von Brauchitsch and General Halder that the Russian army 'would suffer an even greater collapse than that of France'. On 9 January 1941 Hitler described Soviet forces as 'a clay colossus without a head'.[8] On 1 February Field Marshal von Bock recorded:

> The Führer ... regards Russia's collapse as a foregone conclusion ... I remarked that we can defeat the Russians if they stand and fight, but it may be difficult to convince them to talk in terms of peace. The Führer replied that we are militarily and economically in excellent condition and if the Russians continue to resist ... we

will simply advance all the way to Siberia ... 'Nevertheless', I told him, 'we should be prepared for reverses.' Hitler replied pointedly, 'I am convinced that they will think a hurricane has hit them.'[9]

In Berlin on 30 March Hitler instructed a large gathering of senior officers: 'We have the chance to smash Russia while our back is free. That chance will not return so soon. I would be betraying the future of the German people if I did not seize it now!'[10] Hitler's belief in the racial supremacy of the German people was a factor in his military calculations. After destroying the Soviet Union Hitler daydreamed of further conquests in the Mediterranean and Middle East, and successful advances across central Asia.

Purely operational factors were to be the servant of the overriding ideological goals of Operation Barbarossa. Hitler had determined that a five-month campaign could subdue Russia politically; hence preparations for Barbarossa did not need to be dramatically different from those made to invade western Europe in May 1940. Nazi Germany had yet to fully mobilise its war economy and there would be significant equipment and munitions shortages if Russia was not knocked out in a one-stage campaign. But logistics had long been the Achilles heel of the German Army. Shortcomings in transport and supply had played important roles in the failure of German offensives in western Europe in 1914 and 1918. The 'German way of war', developed since the mid-nineteenth century, had been to use the Reich's excellent railway system to mobilise forces for invasions of next-door neighbours. In some respects the German Army's experience of warfare was short-lived and simplistic, when compared to the global experience acquired by an institution such as Britain's Royal Navy over a much longer period.

In the autumn of 1940 German troops and headquarters had begun moving eastwards. The preparations in France for Operation Sea Lion had provided cover at the outset. Three Axis army groups were to thrust at Leningrad, Moscow and Kiev respectively. Panzer divisions were to bypass and encircle the bulk of the Soviet army in the frontier region. The infantry would then reduce the pockets. According to Halder:

> By any attack against the Russian army, one must avoid the danger of simply push-ing the Russians back. We must use attack methods which cut up the Russian army and allows its destruction in pockets. A starting position must be created which allows the use of major envelopment operations. When the Russians are hard hit by these desperate blows, a moment will come when, as in Poland, the travel and communications networks will collapse and create total disorganisation.[11]

Halder wished to capture Moscow at an early stage. As well as being a centre of political power, Moscow was the hub of the Russian transport system and an industrial centre. There was no agreement between OKH (army high command)

and OKW (Supreme High Command) regarding the relative importance of Moscow or other objectives in Russia's interior. Both headquarters, however, shared the hope that the campaign would be a mopping up exercise after the initial round of frontier battles. The second half of 1940 was a time of great optimism at the highest levels of the German government and military. It was not an atmosphere conducive to realistic planning, and certainly contingency planning for setbacks was a very low priority.[12]

In tandem with the military invasion, Nazi Germany had other ruthless plans for the occupation and administration of conquered eastern territory. The Communist Party cadre and Jews were to be liquidated by *Einsatzgruppen* – 'Special Employment Units' – and the rest of the Slavic population enslaved in a terror state run by the SS. Hitler lectured his generals about the need for a merciless approach.

> We have to free ourselves from ideas of soldierly camaraderie. A communist is not and can never be considered a fellow-soldier. This war will be a battle of annihilation ... It will be very different from the war in the West. In the East harshness will guarantee us a mild future. Military leaders must overcome their reservations.[13]

This policy was an extension of what had been taking place in Poland since late 1939. German officials already working in occupied parts of eastern Europe were well familiar with those policies. Sheer brutality might even hasten the collapse of Soviet society. Terror policies were in fact the cornerstone to the German political strategy for Barbarossa.

In the spring of 1941 Barbarossa planning was interrupted as Italy's ongoing war with Greece was going badly. The Balkan's chief value to Germany was the Ploesti oilfields in Romania, Germany's main source of natural oil. The RAF in Greece might start to bomb the oilfields. In North Africa the Italian invasion of British-occupied Egypt had also been a failure. Hitler felt compelled to come to his ally's aid. The vanguard of the Afrika Korps, commanded by General Rommel, arrived at Tripoli on 12 February. The mercurial Rommel would not be available for Barbarossa.

To make Mediterranean affairs even more complicated for Berlin, London decided to send an army to Greece. This made up Hitler's mind to seize the Balkan region to secure the southern flank to Operation Barbarossa. German troops were already stationed in Romania and on 1 March Bulgaria joined the Tripartite Pact. On 6 April a German army group invaded Yugoslavia from Romania and Bulgaria. Yugoslavia and Greece were quickly overrun. The bulk of the British expedition was withdrawn by sea. German forces captured over half a million prisoners in the brief campaign at negligible cost. On the whole, the Soviets chose to see German actions in the Balkans as designed to expel British influence.

On 20 May an assault on Crete spearheaded by paratroopers led to further bitter fighting and another British defeat and evacuation by sea. Crete was one of the Royal Navy's bloodiest engagements of the war. The Afrika Korps advanced to the Egyptian frontier and laid siege to Tobruk in eastern Libya. There was, though, one positive operational outcome for the Allies in this dark period. Heavy losses among the German parachute force at Crete caused Hitler to shy away from further airborne operations. This quite possibly saved Malta from attack.[14] The grounding of German paratroopers was also a loss for Barbarossa. The Russian invasion was bound to offer splendid opportunities for airborne drops in support of the panzer spearheads.

The final date for launching Barbarossa proved to be 22 June, rather than a month earlier as implied in the original Barbarossa directive. The Balkans campaign was one of several factors that delayed the launching of Barbarossa, though it was not the most important by any means. The sheer scale of preparations, delays in equipping an expanded German Army and widespread spring flooding in Poland were the main factors determining the final invasion date. The principal impact of the Balkans campaign on Barbarossa was the extent to which it distracted overworked senior commanders and staffs from detailed planning for the Russian campaign. This is amply borne out by the amount of attention Halder's war diary gives to events in the Mediterranean and Balkans during the spring of 1941. All of that effort could have gone into more detailed study and discussion of the operational and logistical requirements of Barbarossa, one of the great military gambles in modern history.

German expectations for Barbarossa in the spring of 1941 were high. Hitler told Field Marshal von Rundstedt, designated commander of Army Group South: 'You have only to kick in the door and the whole rotten structure will come crashing down.' Most German leaders were confident of a quick victory, as were many western and neutral observers. British and American military leaders gave the Soviets little chance of survival. In the First World War the Germans had failed in France but had knocked Russia out of the war. In 1940 France had been defeated, and Russia did not appear to pose an insurmountable problem. The Soviet system was believed to be fragile.

In reality the German High Command had an incomplete understanding of the Soviet military. Aerial photography and radio listening had gleaned only finite information given the geographic depth of the Soviet Union. Espionage was exceedingly difficult in the Soviet police state. The German military attaché in Moscow, General Koestring, claimed: 'It would be easier for an Arab in flowing burnous to walk unnoticed through Berlin, than for a foreign agent to pass through Russia.'[15] Captured Polish and French intelligence material had not revealed anything new. High-level Soviet codes were secure.

Economic intelligence of the Soviet Union was also poor. German economists were aware of the obvious Soviet centres of industry in Leningrad, Moscow, Ukraine and the Donetz Basin. But far less was known about industry further east in the Urals, along the Trans-Siberian railway and in the central Asian republics. During the 1930s Moscow had claimed to have expanded the Soviet Union's heavy industries, but little was known about the detail of those claims. Given the limited nature of Soviet international trade, the statistics commonly used for assessing the strength of a foreign economy hardly existed. It also suited the Germans to believe that the Russian economy had not changed dramatically since 1917. If the Soviets were still heavily reliant on their western regions economically, the Red Army would have to fight to defend those western regions. If that were true, the Red Army and Soviet economy might both be conveniently destroyed in a single great campaign.

Führer Directive No. 32 of 11 June 1941 predicted that about sixty divisions and an air fleet would be sufficient to maintain Axis supremacy in Russia after victory had been won. Expeditions by motorised columns would be needed from time to time to crush the embers of opposition.[16] It would then be possible to initiate operations from Bulgaria across Turkey – with Turkish permission or without – aimed at the British position in Egypt. 'If the collapse of the Soviet Union has created the necessary conditions', stated Directive No. 32, 'preparations will be made for the despatch of a motorised expeditionary force from Trans-caucus against Iraq.'[17] After the Soviets had been crushed, Berlin would also place Spain under redoubled diplomatic pressure to permit an attack on Gibraltar and the establishment of bases across the strait in western Africa.

The Soviet Union's Red Army of 1941 was a different beast from that envisaged by German military planners. From its beginnings the Red Army, with its origins in a tumultuous civil war, had been a political as well as a military organisation. The 1917–21 civil wars had sternly tested the Bolshevik Party's ability to defend itself from internal and external opponents. In the new Soviet Union state-directed paranoia and militarism was justified by the never-ending need for vigilance. The Georgian Joseph Stalin, from his power base as General Secretary of the Party, had come to dominate the Soviet leadership after the death of Lenin. Stalin, an enigmatic, egotistical, dull and heartless man, had spent his youth adrift in a world of police spies. He had developed a ruthless, untrusting nature.[18]

At the end of the 1920s, with the advent of the first 'five-year plan', Stalin had initiated a huge effort to expand the Soviet Union's industrial base and stock of military equipment. Steel output of 4.3 million tons in 1928 had risen to 18.1 million tons by 1938. In 1928 the Red Army had ninety-two tanks, but in 1938 the Red Army had over 7,000 tanks, the largest figure of any nation. The first Soviet armoured divisions pre-dated the first panzer division. The Red Air Force had also been greatly expanded across the 1930s. The proportion of national product spent on the military by the Russian state had been 5.2 per cent in 1913, but by 1932 that figure had risen to nine per cent and in 1940 was nineteen per cent.[19] The Soviet state was virtually on a war-footing before the German invasion could begin. This is hardly surprising. After all, one of the guiding principles of Marxist-Leninist thought was that the capitalist and communist systems were incompatible. Collision one day was inevitable.

Nonetheless, the military benefits of industrial expansion had been greatly compromised by the inhumanities of the Soviet regime. The policies whereby agricultural communities had been forcibly 'collectivised' in the early 1930s had directly brought about famine. Seven million people are believed to have died. Most deaths occurred in the Ukraine, where security police prevented the delivery of food to politically troublesome areas.[20] Stalin had also become increasingly determined to hunt down and destroy any potential internal enemies. It had been bizarre but logical to search for potential enemies in the ranks of the administration and armed forces. In 1937 alone Stalin's purge may have killed a million people, with many more beginning to pass through or die in the Siberian concentration camps. The purges of the 1930s recreated the dynamic, violent, revolutionary atmosphere of the civil war. This in itself seems to have had a narcotic-like attraction for dedicated revolutionaries.

The military leadership had not been spared by the purge. Stalin greatly feared a military coup. By the autumn of 1938 three of five marshals were dead, as were thirteen of fifteen army commanders, and several hundred corps, divisional and brigade commanders. Up to 35,000 military officers were purged, about half the total officer corps. Those not executed were exiled to the labour camps. Remaining senior army commanders had passed Stalin's test of political loyalty, though nobody could tell for sure how or why. Possibly key survivors had been associated with Stalin's faction in past intra-party disputes. The German General Staff believed that the purges, about which information was available through military channels, had done appalling damage to Soviet military potential. That, however, was only partly true. Most of the purged officers in the camps would eventually be reinstated as war loomed. Younger officers were rapidly promoted to replace their vanished and sometimes incompetent seniors.[21]

The performance of the Red Army in its next major campaign, however, had not been encouraging. In the Winter War beginning late in 1939 the Soviets used over a million men against a Finnish force never more than 200,000 strong. The Red Army was badly outmanoeuvred and indulged in clumsy massed frontal attacks that incurred heavy losses, amounting to 200,000 killed and wounded by the war's end in March 1940.[22] By contrast, in the Far East during the summer of 1939 General G.K. Zhukov had made effective use of massed armoured vehicles to defeat a Japanese force in a brief border conflict.

There had been some reorganisation of the Red Army after the Finnish debacle. The pact with Germany gave the Soviets breathing space in which to accelerate their military build up. The army was greatly expanded during 1940–41. Traditional military discipline was restored and the powers of political officers curtailed. In 1937 the Red Army had one and a half million men under arms. By May 1941 that figure had reached five million. As the saying goes, quantity has a quality all of its own. Fatalistic, patriotic, sentimental, tough, semi-literate and volatile, the Red Army's peasants and workers were fine potential soldiers. The army was also a true 'imperial' army. In 1940 Russians comprised only fifty-eight per cent of the Soviet population. Ukrainians, Belorussians and numerous Asian peoples provided a large minority of the Red Army's rank and file.

In theory, the Soviet tank park in 1940 was larger than the tank forces of the rest of the world combined. Various estimates of numbers hover about the 20,000 mark, though most of these vehicles were obsolescent light tanks. On the eve of Barbarossa fewer than 2,000 Soviet tanks were new-model medium T-34s (30.9 tons) or heavy KVs (47.5 tons). Soviet industry, though, was gearing up to specialise in building those types, which were planned to dominate future production.[23] General D.G. Pavlov, the chief Soviet adviser to the Spanish republic, had returned from Spain to inform Stalin that Soviet mechanised corps should be broken up into smaller tank units. Acting on Pavlov's advice, the Red Army had distributed many of its tanks among the infantry, but after the fall of France an effort was made to rebuild larger armoured formations.[24]

In June 1941 the Soviets were defending western frontiers newly acquired since 1939. Frontier defensive works were far from complete. Stalin had received many warnings of gathering German forces from his agents and foreign governments, but he regarded those reports as 'provocative misinformation'. Hitler's deputy, Rudolf Hess, had dropped by parachute into Scotland on 10 May 1941 to further tarnish the credibility of British information given to Moscow. The deputy Führer had told his interrogators that he wanted to bring about peace between Germany and Britain. He does not seem to have disclosed anything about the imminent Operation Barbarossa. Both London and Berlin concluded that Hess was deranged.

Yet Stalin continued to appease Hitler. Shipments of Soviet oil, grain and minerals, under the terms of the 1939 Molotov-Ribbentrop Pact and subsequent agreements, continued right up to June 1941. Stalin, as the world's most prominent practising Marxist, may even have thought that giving Germany the raw materials the Nazis wanted would tame the acquisitive desires of a capitalist state.[25] He certainly lacked honest advisers given the potential fate of dissenters. On 13 April Stalin had signed a neutrality pact with Japan. He had personally seen Foreign Minister Matsuoka depart at Kazan railway station in Moscow for the return journey eastwards. This was another piece of diplomatic reinsurance.

Stalin may have doubted whether the Germans were sufficiently ready to attack Russia in 1941. He also may have hoped that the Balkans campaign had sated Hitler's appetite for conquest for that year. It has been suggested that Stalin did not want to repeat the Russian mistake of 1914, when the Tsar had fuelled an international crisis by ordering a general mobilisation. In the spring of 1941 German reconnaissance aircraft had been increasingly active over western Russia, but Soviet aircraft and anti-aircraft guns were forbidden to interfere with those activities. There has never been any indication that the Soviets were preparing a pre-emptive attack, nor did the Germans ever believe that to be the case. The likely explanation for Soviet passivity is the simplest: Stalin felt the Soviet Union was unready for all-out war with Germany in 1941. His actions to delay the outbreak of war stemmed from that premise.

The force Hitler assembled to invade Russia numbered almost four million men, including over three million German troops supported by 3,350 tanks. The 151 German divisions included nineteen panzer and fifteen motorised divisions.[26] Almost half the tanks were light vehicles or Czech-built tanks, but the proportion of medium tanks in the panzer force had risen since the previous year. German tank production in 1941 would more than double that of 1940. 600,000 motor vehicles were supplemented by 600,000 horses to haul the transport of unmotorised formations. Captured French motor vehicles and anti-tank guns were pressed into service. The presence of so many horses showed that the supply methods of the nineteenth century were still being partly employed to push forward an advanced mid-twentieth century war machine. Romanian troops, and later Finnish, Hungarian, Slovak, Italian and Spanish volunteer forces would also take part in Barbarossa. The Axis satellites were to contribute the equivalent of forty divisions.[27] *Einsatzgruppen* were assembled to sweep the countryside behind the advancing army for enemies of National Socialism.

This German force was not much larger than that used in May 1940 to invade western Europe, though the space to be conquered was much greater. The demands of the Mediterranean and western theatres had absorbed the increases in the *Wehrmacht* instigated over the previous twelve months. Fifty-five German divisions remained in the non-eastern theatres (thirty-eight in France and the Low Countries, eight in Scandinavia, seven in the Balkans and two in North Africa). A major weakness of the *Wehrmacht* in mid-1941 was a lack of replacements, both in men and equipment. The losses in the war thus far had not been high enough to encourage the building of a strong replacement system.

Two-thirds of the *Luftwaffe*'s first-line strength was to support Barbarossa, 2,770 of 4,300 aircraft. Over 1,000 aircraft remained in the Mediterranean theatre and western Europe. The *Luftwaffe* was still a tactical army-support air force without heavy bombers. Goering's air force had stagnated over the previous twelve months due to heavy losses in the sustained campaign against Britain. German aircraft production of 10,247 in 1940 would only rise to 12,401 in 1941; not because more was not possible, but because the need for more aircraft was wantonly underestimated.[28]

The operational plan for Barbarossa aimed to punch gaps in the Russian front. Panzer divisions were to thrust into the Russian interior to encircle large pockets of Soviet troops. Of the four panzer groups available, Army

Group Centre had two and the other army groups one each. A panzer group comprised from two to four corps of panzer and motorised divisions to create a fearsome strike force. Apart from the Pripet Marshes, western Russia had few major geographic obstacles. The lack of good roads, dense forests, and the rains of autumn and snows and cold of winter were the principal environmental threats. Dangerously, the three army groups of Leeb, Bock and Rundstedt were to advance on diverging axes. From north to south, the eastern front was 1,300 miles long at the outset, but would grow to 2,000 or even 2,500 miles as the advance progressed. Barbarossa could not hope to replicate the main feature of the May 1940 offensive, which had been the concentration of panzer forces for a single dramatic thrust. On the other hand, the roads and railways leading into Russia may not have been sufficient to supply a greater concentration of force.[29]

Reports to Moscow on the eve of the invasion were alarming. The Germans had cut the telephone lines at the border and a German deserter had warned of imminent attack. Nonetheless, tactical surprise was achieved. Border guards were soon overwhelmed on the morning of 22 June. Identified defensive works received a deluge of German shells and bombs. The frontier city of Brest-Litovsk was isolated on the first day. Soviet forces were concentrated close to the frontier in exposed positions. Soviet airfields in western Russia were hammered by the *Luftwaffe*. An estimated 1,200 Soviet aircraft were destroyed on 22 June, many caught lined up on their bases.

Italy and Romania also declared war on the Soviet Union. Finland, Hungary and Albania did the same in the days ahead. In Britain, Churchill promised in a radio broadcast to give the Soviets any possible aid. Out of necessity, Churchill's government chose to ignore the support Stalin had given Hitler over the previous two years.

Field Marshal von Bock's Army Group Centre controlled Panzer Groups 2 and 3, commanded by Generals Guderian and Hoth. Bock was a tall, slender, clever and overbearing Prussian. He had been a senior staff officer at an army group headquarters during the First World War. General Blumentritt, the Fourth Army's Chief of Staff, wrote of Bock: 'He was vivacious, often sarcastic, and expressed his thoughts clearly and well. He did not look his age and might have passed for a man of forty. However, his health was not perfect, for he suffered from frequent stomach pains.'[30] Bock's tanks quickly opened gaps in the Soviet front and motorised troops rushed eastwards up to fifty miles a day. Panzer commanders led their battle groups towards their objectives without unduly worrying about the progress of flanking units. Opposing Soviet tanks were often poorly maintained. For example, fifty per cent of the 22nd Mechanised Corps' tank losses were the result of breakdown.[31] Some Soviet formations only had maps of German territory. The NKVD – Stalin's secret police – killed their prisoners, civil and military, as they retreated, whilst advancing Nazi security units began their slaughter of Jews and Communist officials.

By the end of June the panzer pincers of Army Group Centre had closed around Minsk, 200 miles behind the original front line, trapping all four armies of the Soviet Western Front army group. The tanks and infantry of the panzer and motorised divisions blocked escape routes eastwards. German infantry divisions behind the spearheads marched forward, up to twenty miles a day along rough roads in the heat, to seal off and crush the surrounded pockets in fighting that was often fierce and protracted. Soviet formations disintegrated when fuel, food and ammunition began to run out. In eighteen days Army Group Centre advanced 360 miles to overrun Belorussia and inflict on the Red Army 400,000 casualties. 4,800 Soviet tanks were destroyed or captured.[32] General Pavlov, the commander of the Western Front army group, and a number of other senior officers, were later executed as punishment for the defeat and their alleged 'criminal behaviour in the face of the enemy'.

Nonetheless, German encirclement operations were only partly successful as the panzer and infantry formations were advancing at such different speeds. Sizeable Soviet forces escaped through loose cordons around pockets. Reading reports on the campaign from a distance, Halder noted that Russian troops were fighting strongly, though often inexpertly. German commentators had not been so complimentary about French troops in 1940. The method of Russian counter-attack was described by Halder. 'Three-minute artillery barrage, then pause, then infantry attacking as much as twelve ranks deep, without heavy weapon support; the men start hurrahing from far off. Incredibly high Russian losses.'[33]

Stalin was at first stunned by the turn of events, though he recovered to make his first war broadcast to the Soviet people on 3 July. He appealed to patriotism rather than Marxism and narrow party loyalty. In the weeks ahead Stalin appointed himself head of the Soviet High Command. The terror apparatus of the NKVD and party helped to mobilise the nation when enthusiasm was lacking.

Political commissars with the troops lashed their charges with warnings of the fate that would befall them as German prisoners. The threats were not misplaced. Of 5.7 million Soviet prisoners taken in the war, the bulk in the opening Barbarossa campaign, at least two-thirds would die in captivity. Stalin's son Yakov was among those taken prisoner early in July 1941. Absurdly, Yakov's wife was arrested and sent to a labour camp for two years as punishment for her husband's capture. (Yakov was shot dead by a camp guard in 1943). The *Wehrmacht* had not made adequate preparations for the many prisoners they had expected to capture. Many simply died in holding camps. As prisoners grew weaker from malnourishment and disease they became unfit for work. This diminished the incentive for occupation administrators to intervene and make use of the captives. Goering even made jokes about cannibalism in prisoner of war camps. Things would only have gone too far in Goering's

view if the prisoners started to eat their guards. Not all Soviet troops from
shattered formations were rounded up. That was too big a task for a German
Army continuing to push eastwards with all its energy. Perhaps a quarter to half
a million Soviet troops remained free behind German lines in the autumn of
1941 to provide a nucleus for a growing partisan movement.[34]

On 3 July Halder diarised:

> On the whole, then, it may be said even now that the objective to shatter the bulk of
> the Russian army this side of the Dvina and Dnieper has been accomplished ... It is
> thus probably no overstatement to say that the Russian Campaign has been won in
> the space of two weeks. Of course, this does not yet mean that it is closed. The sheer
> geographical vastness of the country and the stubbornness of the resistance, which is
> carried on with all means, will claim our efforts for many more weeks to come.[35]

Halder optimistically believed that newly raised Soviet formations were likely
to be ineffective for lack of officers, specialists and artillery. Propaganda Minister
Goebbels announced that, 'The eastern continent lies like a limp virgin in the
mighty arms of the German Mars.' Looking ahead, Hitler decided to level
both Moscow and Leningrad after they were captured 'so as to relieve us of
the necessity of having to feed the populations through the winter'.[36] In the
expectation of victory, on 14 July Hitler ordered a shift in armaments production
away from the army and towards the navy and air force. This decision would
have to be overturned later in the year, but not before a sizeable dent had been
made in the production of army weaponry.

By 9 July Soviet forces west of Minsk had been cleaned up and Kluge's
Fourth Panzer Army, which included Army Group Centre's panzer forces,
pressed onwards towards Smolensk, two-thirds of the way to Moscow and
the last major city before the capital. German tank formations lunged beyond
bypassed Soviet troops, and marching German infantry toiled forward in the
hot sun, labouring under heavy equipment. They had to fight at short notice
when enemy troops were encountered. In the Smolensk encirclement battles
lasting into early August, Army Group Centre took another 300,000 prisoners
and destroyed or captured over 3,000 tanks.

Whilst Army Group Centre advanced towards Moscow, Army Group North
made steady progress through the Baltic States. The forests and swamps of
northern Russia was not good ground for mechanised units. There were no
great encirclement victories in the broken terrain of the region but three Soviet
armies were forced to retreat in disorder. Field Marshal von Leeb's troops had
their sights firmly set on Leningrad. Tens of thousands of Soviets civilians were
rounded up to build field works on the approaches to the threatened city. Naval
guns from the Baltic Fleet were incorporated in the defences. On 26 September
the Germans reached Lake Ladoga behind Leningrad. A 900-day siege of the
city would soon get underway.

To the south of the Pripet Marshes, Rundstedt's Army Group South had not maintained nearly the same rate of advance as their counterparts to the north. One-third of the army group's tank strength had only returned from the Balkans campaign after Barbarossa had commenced. Mechanised formations had high rates of vehicle break-down because of their Balkans service. The forces of the Soviet Southwestern Front army group were relatively strong, but they gave ground before German attacks and suffered heavy losses.[37]

Overall, the first three weeks of Barbarossa had proved a success, but things had not gone all the Germans' way. Heavy local fighting up and down the front had drained German strength, and the spearheads had become increasingly dispersed in the vast regions of the Russian interior. German losses to 13 August tallied up to almost 390,000 killed, wounded and missing. Armoured divisions had been reduced to sixty per cent of their starting strength.[38] It was a testament to the skill of the panzer leadership that they kept pushing forward so swiftly as their strength ebbed. German production of tanks and assault guns was running at only 250 a month, a dangerously low level of output given the rates of loss already apparent on the eastern front. The different railway gauge in Russia delayed full utilisation of rail transport in the occupied regions.

The vital question was whether or not the Soviet Union would be able to fully mobilise its vast manpower reserves before the Germans could overrun the main population centres. By the end of June 5.3 million reservists had been recalled to create new formations. Thirteen new armies had been formed in July and another fourteen in August. An additional three and a half million recruits would be absorbed from July to the start of December. At the beginning of 1940 the Red Army had 117 divisions. That figure had been hastily expanded to 232 divisions by June 1941. Yet by the end of 1941 a staggering 592 divisional-sized formations would be formed, far in excess of German estimates of Soviet capacity.[39]

On the industrial front, from July to November 1941 over 1,500 Soviet armaments factories would be dismantled and hastily relocated eastwards to the Volga region, Siberia and central Asia. The moving of a factory might take the loads of thousands of railway wagons and months to complete. In the meantime arms production fell by between thirty and eighty per cent for many types of equipment. Unbeknownst to German intelligence, up to a third of Soviet industry had been based in the eastern regions before the outbreak of war. The necessary infrastructure already existed in the east to receive the relocated factories.

General Halder and his OKH staff were keen for Army Group Centre to push onwards towards Moscow so as to defeat Soviet reserves on that front. Hitler had other ideas. He doubted the profitability of a further immediate round of attacks on the highway to the Kremlin. On 19 July Führer Directive

No. 33 ordered Army Group Centre's mechanised formations to aid their neighbouring army groups. Directive No. 34, however, postponed the decision. Hitler visited the headquarters of Army Group Centre on 4 August for discussions that still did not firmly clear up the issue. Meanwhile Halder's optimism of the early weeks of Barbarossa rapidly melted away. He wrote in his diary on 11 August:

> The whole situation makes it increasingly plain that we have underestimated the Russian colossus ... At the outset of the war, we reckoned with about 200 enemy divisions. Now we have already counted 360. These divisions indeed are not armed and equipped according to our standards, and their tactical leadership is often poor. But there they are, and if we smash a dozen of them, the Russians simply put up another dozen. The time factor favours them, as they are near their own resources, while we are moving farther and farther away from ours.[40]

On 23 August a frustrated Halder visited Bock's headquarters. Halder, Bock and Guderian wanted a renewed advance on the central front. It was agreed that Guderian should immediately fly with Halder to visit Hitler's OKW headquarters at Rastenburg for some discrete lobbying. Upon arrival at OKW, Guderian dropped plenty of hints about his views and Hitler proved willing to debate the subject. He listened to Guderian and responded by saying that his commanders 'know nothing about the economic aspects of war'. In Hitler's assessment, Germany needed the economic resources of the Ukraine, and from the Crimea the Red Air Force might attack Romania's oil fields. Hitler probably felt that enough time still remained before winter to capture both the Ukraine region and Moscow. Halder offered to resign as an expression of his disagreement with Hitler's plan to divert forces from the central front to the Ukraine. Halder wrote that 'history will level at us the gravest accusation that can be made of a high command, namely that for fear of undue risk we did not exploit the attacking impetus of our troops'.[41] The resignation was rejected. In Hitler's view, the army's chief of the general staff could no more be permitted to resign and walk away from his post than the humblest front-line infantryman.

The pause on the front of Army Group Centre from late July to early September has often been portrayed as purely the result of Hitler's intervention, but Bock's army group had begun to confront crippling supply problems due to its rapid advance. The pooling of scarce transport had helped to keep German formations moving forward, but this ad hoc system was on the verge of breaking down. Heavy but poorly coordinated Soviet counter-attacks had also kept the central front aflame.[42]

The offensive in the Ukraine authorised by Hitler went ahead. Late in August Army Group Centre's Panzer Group 2 headed south to cut into the long exposed flank of Soviet forces holding up Army Group South. The flat steppe of the Ukraine favoured rapid mechanised thrusts and Stalin had insisted that Kiev be strongly defended. By 15 September Guderian's tanks had linked up with panzer divisions of Army Group South to surround a vast Soviet force at Kiev. Resistance in the pocket was overwhelmed in the next ten days. 665,000 Soviet prisoners were taken in one of the most immense victories in battlefield history. The Kiev 'cauldron' opened the way for further advances to the Donetz basin and more large hauls of prisoners. Odessa, on the Black Sea coast, was captured by Romanian troops. Sevastopol in the Crimea was besieged. New Jewish populations fell into German hands in the Ukraine. In a ravine at Babi Yar near Kiev over 33,000 Jews were killed in two days, one of the largest massacres of Jews outside of the concentration and death camp system. German commanders at all levels turned a blind eye to the activities of killing squads.

At the northern end of the front German operations continued to clear the approaches to Leningrad. The city was blockaded, though the blockade was incomplete as the rear of Leningrad was covered by Lake Ladoga. The Finnish army to the north west of the city did not move beyond Finland's 1939 frontiers.

General Zhukov, still only forty-three years of age, was placed in charge of Leningrad's defences during the vital September period. The son of a shoemaker, Zhukov had been conscripted into the Tsarist army in the First World War, and had been a cavalryman in the Red Army during the civil war. He became a committed Communist and managed to both study military science in Germany in the early 1930s and escape the purges in Russia of the late 1930s. Zhukov had fought a successful campaign in the Far East against the Japanese in 1939. He was an educated man though he presented a harsh and domineering face to the world. General Rokossovsky later remarked:

> Zhukov was always a man of strong will and decisiveness, brilliant and gifted, demanding, firm and purposeful. All of these qualities, unquestionably, are neces-sary in a great military commander and they were inherent in Zhukov. It is true that sometimes his toughness exceeded what was permissible.[43]

Zhukov was a sensible rather than a brilliant strategic thinker. He was willing to stand up to Stalin, and could bear the burden of great responsibility.

German attacks bogged down before Leningrad and the local terrain was not favourable to tank warfare. Rains and flooding liquefied dirt roads. A German directive of 22 September stated:

> The Führer has decided to erase the city of Petersburg (the cradle of Bolshevism) from the face of the earth. I have no interest in the further existence of this large city after the defeat of Soviet Russia ... We propose to blockade the city tightly and erase it from the earth by means of artillery fire and continuous bombardment from the air.[44]

During October the blockade was tightened and by the start of November a population of over three million had food supplies for only seven days.

The factories of Leningrad, one of the Soviet Union's most important pre-war industrial centres, carried on until they ran out of materials and power. Dmitri Shostakovich wrote his Leningrad Symphony to encourage the citizenry. Once Lake Ladoga froze it became possible to haul supplies over the ice and into the city by truck. It took a long time, though, to develop the route and the level of relief was not enough. Famine caused slow starvation and death from disease and exposure. Over a million Leningrad citizens would die before the blockade ended, many during the fearsome winter of 1941–42. More civilians might have been evacuated prior to Leningrad's investment, but that would have left the authorities open to potentially fatal accusations of defeatism.

With most of the Ukraine in German hands, and a large part of Army Group North settling in front of Leningrad, the major threats to the northern and southern flanks of Army Group Centre had been removed. Hitler now gave his generals permission to advance to Moscow. Panzer Group 4 was transferred from Army Group North to strengthen Army Group Centre. Bock told a conference on 29 September that Moscow had to be taken by mid-November and the start of winter. The goal was less than 100 miles away, but the weather was already starting to get disconcertingly cold for German soldiers unused to how quickly winter arrived in Russia.[45]

Three Soviet army groups were covering the central front, but Bock's Army Group Centre had fourteen panzer divisions and over 1,000 tanks. Stocks of equipment and supplies had been rebuilt during the period of the Kiev diversion. Panzer Group 2 only had fifty per cent of its authorised tank strength, but the other panzer groups were in better shape. The main blow of the new offensive kicked off on 2 October. Within a week another spectacular encirclement victory had been won between Smolensk and Vyazma. Panzers entered Orel with the street cars still running. Zhukov was hastily recalled from Leningrad to take command at Moscow. On 5 October the German Army's Quartermaster-General Wagner wrote: 'Our impression is that the final great collapse is immediately ahead, and that tonight the Kremlin is packing its bags.'[46] Later in the month, further encirclements by Army Group Centre crippled the Soviets' Briansk Front army group. At Vyazma and Briansk the Red Army lost another million men, of whom 688,000 were made prisoners of war.

By the end of October half of the Soviet Union's industrial capacity had been overrun. But there was no question of an eleventh hour political settlement with Berlin as Stalin had already risked that option from 1939 to June 1941 with a conspicuous lack of success. The Soviet leadership issued orders to start the evacuation of ministerial officials from Moscow. Lenin's body was removed from his mausoleum in Red Square and shipped eastwards as well. A state of siege was declared in the capital. A brief panic among the citizenry may have been caused by Molotov's warning to the British and American embassies that they should ready their staff for evacuation. Stalin had decided to stay in the city himself and that was an important symbolic gesture. The population was combed to form fresh militia and labour units, whilst NKVD troops brutally restored public order with summary executions. On 7 November Stalin held a parade through Red Square to commemorate the October Revolution. He called for redoubled efforts from his embattled people. The deeds of patriotic Russian generals who had resisted Napoleon's invasion were invoked.

The *rasputitza*, the period when rain turned roads to mud, impeded operations from mid-October to mid-November for men, animals and wheeled vehicles alike. During this time the first heavy snow falls of the season appeared but accompanying frosts re-hardened the muddy ground for German tanks. Bock's casualties were mounting and only a trickle of replacement troops and new equipment had arrived to make up losses. The *Luftwaffe* was steadily wasting away and there could be no aerial blitz on Moscow. Only a little over half of remaining aircraft were serviceable enough to fly. Airfields and maintenance facilities deep inside Russia were poor.[47]

The *Wehrmacht*'s final push towards Moscow began mid-November and was planned to encircle the city from north and south. Not all German generals wanted to continue the offensive but Halder, Bock and Hitler were willing to press onward. To Halder the capture of Moscow was a vital strategic objective. To Hitler, the capture of the capital was the last chance of the season to inflict a shattering psychological blow to the Soviet system. On 13 November Army Group Centre's Chief of Staff concluded: 'The danger we might not succeed must be taken into account, but it would be even worse to be left lying in the snow and the cold on open ground only thirty miles from the tempting objective.'[48] To thwart the Germans, the Soviet High Command had been able to form another nine reserve armies by drawing on troops assembling in the Volga, Caucasus, Siberia, central Asia and Urals. These troops were hastened forward to shore up the defences of the capital. The Russian state was still functioning effectively to maintain a flow of troops and weaponry to the firing line. The Red Army continued to counter-attack at regular intervals. A Mongolian cavalry division made a wasteful mounted charge on 16 November. Horses and riders were mown down crossing snow-covered fields.

Late in November the Germans pressed forward again. To the immediate north of Moscow, Panzer Groups 3 and 4 crossed the Moscow-Volga Canal to reach twelve miles from the city centre. Legend has it that German officers saw the golden domes of the Kremlin through their field glasses. From the forests around Moscow German troops could see Soviet anti-aircraft shells bursting over the city at night. The thrust made by the weaker forces of Guderian's southern pincer struggled to make as much progress as the northern pincer. Guderian's panzer group was stopped at Tula still some distance from the capital.

General Winter had now arrived in full fury. Temperatures of minus twenty degrees Celsius and high snowdrifts hampered the exhausted Germans at every step. Lack of winter clothing and appropriate boots was a symptom of the extent to which the German Army was short of virtually all categories of equipment. On 4 December there were blizzards and a cold blast of minus thirty-five degrees Celsius. The *Luftwaffe* was grounded by the weather. General Blumentritt recorded that 'the ghosts of the Grand Army and the memory of Napoleon's fate began to haunt our dreams ... Comparisons with 1812 multiplied'.[49] Army Group Centre was worn out, and scant reinforcement was at hand. For example, the 6th Panzer Division had fewer than 1,000 infantrymen fit to fight.

On 1 December Bock advised Halder that it was time to halt the offensive. His army group was too weak to take Moscow and on the point of exhaustion. 'The fighting of the past fourteen days [wrote Bock] has shown that the notion that the enemy in front of the army group had "collapsed" was a fantasy.'[50] The previous day Bock had told Field Marshal von Brauchitsch, the army's Commander-in-Chief, that 'there exists the danger of a brutish, chest-to-chest struggle, such as occurred at Verdun twenty-five years ago. I have no desire to be a participant in that kind of struggle.' Halder observed that the eastern army was short of 340,000 men, which was equal to fifty per cent of the total infantry strength.

As the German advance lost momentum, Zhukov asked the Soviet High Command to authorise a counter-offensive. 'The enemy is exhausted. But if we do not now liquidate the dangerous enemy penetration, the Germans will be able to reinforce their force in the Moscow region with large reserves at the expense of their northern and southern groups of forces.'[51] On the morning of 30 November, Stalin, the Supreme Commander, ordered Zhukov to move onto the offensive. All new units were to be thrown into the attack. During the preceding weeks the Soviets had withdrawn the best of their troops stationed in Siberia and brought them to the Moscow front. The credit for this is sometimes attributed to information supplied by the spy Richard Sorge. Sorge, a confidant of the German ambassador in Tokyo, is said to have informed his controllers that Japan was determined on war in South-East Asia instead of attacking the Soviet Union. The obvious desperation of the situation before Moscow, however, provides a more persuasive explanation than a lurid spy story. Trained Soviet manpower withdrawn from Siberia was replaced by recruits to keep troop strength facing the Japanese in the Far East reasonably steady. Strong Soviet forces also remained in the Caucasus to guard against the unlikely contingency of Turkish intervention. Notwithstanding that, by early December the Red Army had over a million men in the Moscow region. As Moscow was the hub of the Russian road and rail network, this was an ideal place for Soviet forces to gather.

On 5 December a major Soviet counter-offensive was opened against the two stalled German pincers reaching out to seize Moscow. The timing was superb. Army Group Centre was spent and frozen in position. Surprised German commanders had believed that the Soviets were without large reserves. German forces, especially in the bulges threatening Moscow, were compelled to retreat. Men from broken units trudged back through the snow, leaving behind heavy equipment and vehicles that had broken down. Lubricant fluid in guns froze and frost bite casualties from unsuitable boots mounted. German infantry were placed in jeopardy as the shell of the standard German anti-tank gun struggled to penetrate the armour of Soviet T-34 and KV tanks. The attacking Soviet units were fresher and better equipped. The danger of a German collapse was in prospect.

On 8 December Bock wrote: 'We underestimated the strength of the enemy, his ability to recuperate after suffering losses that would have toppled almost any other nation, and his great reserves in manpower and material.' Bock still regretted the diversion of his armoured forces to the Ukraine back in September. 'We could have finished the enemy last summer. We could have destroyed him completely. Last August, the road to Moscow was open, we could have entered the Bolshevik capital in triumph and in summery weather ... Now all of us are paying for that mistake.'[52] A swath of German generals were sacked or granted sick relief during this critical period, including Bock, Guderian, Brauchitsch and Rundstedt. With Brauchitsch's resignation, Hitler assumed the role of army Commander-in-Chief.

At his distant headquarters, Hitler refused to authorise a general retirement in the face of the Soviet counter-offensive. He was keenly aware that Napoleon's army had disintegrated during its retreat from Moscow in the winter of 1812. The over-stretched Germans lost ground but were able to slow the Soviet advance by fighting delaying actions in the towns and villages dotted along their principal lines of communication. Housing and farm buildings were important to troops as shelter from the elements. The pace of combat was disrupted by the cold and snow. Combat at night became less frequent. Vehicles stalled, weapons might not fire. As a rule bad weather favours a defender, and in this phase of the campaign that was to the Germans' advantage. Deep snow made it difficult for the Soviets to envelop German rearguards. Both the Red Air Force and the *Luftwaffe* were grounded by the climate. Army Group Centre was pushed back in places almost as far as Smolensk, its front held by a maze of improvised units formed from the survivors of larger formations.

A big hole had been torn in the German front between Army Groups North and Centre. At Demyansk a pocket of 95,000 men had been trapped behind Soviet lines. Field Marshal von Leeb asked permission to withdraw from Demyansk. Hitler refused the request and Leeb's resignation was accepted. The *Luftwaffe* resupplied the encircled pocket, loosing many Ju 52 Junkers transports in the process.

Zhukov had wanted to focus the counter-offensive upon Army Group Centre, but Stalin ordered wasteful attacks along large parts of the front from Leningrad to the Crimea. He wrongly felt that a great opportunity had presented itself for a war-winning victory. In territory retaken by the Soviets, civilians told a brutal tale of life under Nazi occupation. The eastern front only stabilised during February after the Red Army had exhausted its strength. The combatants drew breath and counted the cost.

In six months the Germans had advanced 720 miles on a 1600-mile front and had killed or captured at least five million Soviet troops. Forty per cent of the Soviet population had been overrun. The Red Army had lost more than 20,000 tanks.[53] By February 1942 it is likely that 2.8 million Soviet prisoners of war had already died from starvation, disease, atrocity and exposure. High death rates among Soviet prisoners held in Greater Germany reveal that the neglect of prisoners was often deliberate, and not necessarily the result of an 'emergency situation' deep inside occupied Russia.[54] Coincidentally, in Berlin, on 20 January 1942 the infamous Wannsee conference was held to coordinate government agencies for the implementation of the 'Final Solution' to the Jewish question.

Yet there can be no doubt that Barbarossa had failed. The Soviet state was still in existence; a vast Red Army remained in the field; Soviet resistance had not cracked. By the end of 1941 German casualties had amounted to over 830,000.[55] *Wehrmacht* equipment losses had crippled mechanised formations. By January 1942 losses of armoured vehicles had risen above 3,000 but replacements received had been less than a quarter of that figure. Losses of all categories of motor vehicles had been heavy and most were not replaced. The Nazi regime had not prepared for a long attritional war. The creators of *blitzkrieg* lay stranded in the snow deep inside Russia, more closely resembling a German army of 1917 than 1941.

Why did the German invasion fail? It has been argued that an advance deep into Russia was simply beyond the logistical capacity of the German military. Less than a fifth of German divisions were fully motorised. Parts of Hitler's army were almost as dependent on their feet and animals as Napoleon's army of 1812. The Soviet rail system was too limited to make up for what the German Army lacked in motorised equipment. The German Army was unaccustomed to the logistical demands of fighting wars a long way from central Europe.[56] The campaigns in Poland and France had not exposed the *Wehrmacht*'s lack of motorised transport.

Would the capture of Moscow have made a difference? In 1812 the French had captured the city only for the Russians to withdraw their army further eastwards out of harm's way. All the indications suggest that the fall of Moscow in 1941 would not have been a decisive blow against the Soviet regime. The soul of Stalin's state was not encompassed by a single city. As in 1812, the Red Army would simply have retired further eastwards. Possession of Moscow would not have directly helped the Germans to capture the vital Soviet oilfields of Central Asia.

Did the Germans miss an opportunity by not involving Japan in the Barbarossa invasion? Japan had not been informed about Barbarossa in advance. Japanese Prime Minister Prince Konoye had been mortified by the news. Once Barbarossa was underway, Foreign Minister Ribbentrop had urged Tokyo to attack Russia. On 10 July he had told the German ambassador to Japan: 'The natural objective still remains that we and the Japanese join hands on the Trans-Siberian railway before winter starts.'[57] But the Japanese were only mildly pressured to join the campaign. Hitler and his closest advisers had always seen Japan's primary role in the Axis as a counter-weight to the United States, and not as a participant in what was primarily an eastern European problem. If Japan had attacked, it is debatable whether a poorly equipped sixteen-division force in Manchuria could have advanced far across the expanses of Siberia in the face of a large Soviet army.

The failure of the Barbarossa campaign revealed that Germany was still a European power and not a potential world power, something to which the German leadership had aspired since the late nineteenth century.[58] The Soviet Union did not collapse politically as it was governed by a dictator as ruthless and uncompromising as Hitler. Stalin and his fellow Bolsheviks had already spent years building a militarised society to wage war upon their own people. Stalin certainly did not underestimate the Germans. This was partly a consequence of the Germans' well-deserved military reputation, but Stalin was also inclined to solipsism. In other words, Stalin was strongly inclined to believe that his enemies were every bit as effectively brutal and calculating as himself.[59] Hitler did not necessarily see other people that way. According to Albert Speer:

Hitler actually knew nothing about his enemies and even refused to use the information that was available to him. Instead, he trusted to his inspirations, no matter how inherently contradictory they might be, and these inspirations were governed by extreme contempt for and underestimation of the others.[60]

Hitler's ideologically driven contempt for Soviet society had undermined the level of strategic and logistical preparation for Barbarossa.

Whether a better prepared *Wehrmacht* could have knocked out the Soviet Union in the circumstances of 1941 is doubtful, but they certainly could have damaged the Soviet state to a greater extent. That would have significantly altered the shape of future campaigns on the eastern front to the Germans' advantage. The sufferings of the many millions of people engulfed by Hitler's war would have been further deepened.

6
Pearl Harbor

The failure of Operation Barbarossa takes the chronological narrative of the Second World War to the end of 1941. The next step that needs to be taken is a consideration of the entry of Japan and the United States to the conflict. But a full scale war in eastern Asia, involving Japan and China, had broken out in 1937. The international struggle for the Asian mainland began over two years before the German invasion of Poland and the start of another major war in Europe.

In the early 1930s the Japanese had seized the whole of Chinese Manchuria. Further Japanese encroachments in northern China eventually led to war with the Nationalist regime of Generalissimo Chiang Kai-shek in July 1937. A protracted campaign to capture the international city of Shanghai at the mouth of the Yangtze river was followed by a Japanese advance inland to capture the Nationalist capital of Nanking. The so-called 'Rape of Nanking' of December 1937 ruined Japan's international reputation and did not create the conditions for the resumption of peace. The Japanese sought to sponsor a new Chinese government that would accept their domineering influence over large parts of China.

In the absence of international intervention, the Chinese Nationalists had no strategic alternative other than to trade space for time, and trust that China's vast terrain and populace would soak up and over-stretch the occupying forces of Japan. Japanese troops proved unable to penetrate the deep interior of China and a stalemate set in during 1938. Untold death and suffering was inflicted upon a Chinese population dependent upon a fragile agricultural economy. At Chungking, 900 miles up the Yangtze from Wuhan, Chiang's government was virtually invulnerable except to bombing raids. The conflict had acquired a scale and complexity beyond the previous experience of the Imperial Japanese Army, the commanders of which had no tenable plan for victory.

By 1940, after three years of war in China, the Japanese leadership had clarified their long-term goal for the Asia-Pacific region, which was the creation of a Japanese-dominated 'Greater East Asia Co-prosperity Sphere'. This sphere was to embrace Manchuria, Korea, China and South-East Asia. Obviously, this programme ran counter to the interests of the western powers. Britain and Holland were not going to give up their colonies without a fight. Likewise the United States was opposed to Japan's policy in China, and Washington was responsible for the defence of the Philippines. Yet the position of the United

States in Asia was contradictory. From 1937 to 1941 America exported vast quantities of iron and oil to Japan, most of which was known to be earmarked for military consumption. United States trade and investment with Japan was five to six times greater than with China. President Roosevelt had declined to invoke the Neutrality Acts to halt this trade as it would antagonise Japan, was bad for business at a time of depression and might also legally halt any aid to the Chinese Nationalists.[1]

Japan's path down the road to an expanded war had been greatly accelerated by the example and support of Germany. The fall of France had demonstrated that Germany was the strongest power in Europe. Germany needed like-minded allies, and in September 1940 the Japanese had signed the Tripartite Pact. As a member of the Axis, Japan had the prospect of German assistance in the event of war with the United States. Tokyo was counting on Nazi Germany maintaining its triumphal progress.

The April 1941 non-aggression pact between Japan and the Soviet Union had been intended to diminish the threat of war in north-east Asia. Relations between Tokyo and Moscow had been poor for a number of years. The pact, however, was soon undermined by the actions of Berlin. The unforeshadowed German invasion of the Soviet Union in June 1941 caused considerable disquiet in Tokyo. Despite misgivings, the Konoye cabinet proved willing to consider war against the Russians if a favourable opportunity presented itself. Japanese forces were rapidly redeployed and the Kwangtung Army in Manchuria was more than doubled to reach a strength of over 700,000 by mid-September.[2] The failure of the Germans to cripple the Red Army rapidly, and the early onset of winter in Siberia, caused Japan's leadership to abandon plans for intervention and give their full attention to relations with China and the United States.

International tensions in the Asia-Pacific region leapt alarmingly late in 1941 after a Japanese occupation of southern Indo-China caused the United States finally to impose a de facto trade embargo. Japanese incursions in northern Indo-China the previous year had been explained away as part of the blockade of Nationalist China, but Japanese bases in southern Indo-China seemed to be directed at the rest of South-East Asia. The British and Dutch also ended trade with Japan in support of America. American oil and scrap iron had been vital to the Japanese war effort. During the 1930s half of Japan's oil had been imported from America, and by 1940–41 this had risen to eighty per cent as Japan had sought to build its oil reserve. A Japanese admiral said of the embargo: 'There is [now] no choice but to fight and break the iron chains strangling Japan.' By mid-1941 Japan's oil reserve was only enough for two years at normal rates of consumption. In the autumn of 1941 Japan and the United States conducted diplomatic negotiations in a bid to resolve the dispute, but Washington would only resume full trade relations with Japan if Tokyo dramatically reversed its policy towards China and Indo-China.

Whereas the war in China and military preparations in Manchuria was clearly an army responsibility, the Imperial Japanese Navy was destined to play the foremost role in any conflict with the United States. The commander of Japan's fleet in 1941 was Admiral Isoroku Yamamoto. Born in 1884 and the son of a village schoolmaster, Yamamoto had been present as an ensign at the 1905 battle of Tsushima Straits, the new Imperial Navy's decisive victory over Tsarist Russia. He had lost two fingers in the action and had suffered numerous wounds on the lower half of his body. Standing five feet three inches tall, the broad-shouldered Yamamoto had considerable drive and willpower, tempered by intelligence and sensitivity. He was fond of a variety of gambling games, especially poker and bridge.

Japan's limited involvement in the First World War had not left a personal imprint on Yamamoto. To widen his knowledge of the world, the navy had sent him to study the English language in the United States. Yamamoto had been naval attaché at Japan's Washington embassy from 1926–28 and a delegate at the 1930 London Naval Conference.[3]

Yamamoto's interest in air power had been fostered when he was executive officer at an important naval air station. He had later commanded an aircraft carrier and a carrier division for brief periods, though he never qualified as an aviator. Yamamoto became a keen advocate of aircraft carrier warfare. The vast Pacific Ocean had few air bases. Fleets would self-evidently need to supply their own air cover. As Japan did not have an independent air force, both the Japanese army and navy had developed their own air services.

In August 1939 Yamamoto had become Commander-in-Chief of the Combined Fleet. As Vice-Minister of the Navy in the late 1930s, he had already established a presence in government circles. During this period the navy had received four new fleet aircraft carriers and several new light fleet carriers as the restrictions of the Washington Naval Treaty were thrown off. Japanese naval aviation had been heavily involved in the China war. From 1937–41 over 550 naval aircraft were destroyed in China. Japanese aircraft carriers conducted many operations exclusively against Chinese land targets. Some Second World War aces achieved their first victory in Chinese skies.[4] Off the coast of China, the Imperial Japanese Navy had learnt much about the benefits of concentrating carriers, in contravention of the received wisdom that carriers should sail in separate squadrons to reduce their collective vulnerability.[5] IJN carriers had become accustomed to operating apart from battleships in pursuit of aims that went far beyond providing air cover for big-gunned warships.

The carrier-based First Air Fleet comprised 500 pilots, each with an average of 800 flying hours. The navy's land-based Eleventh Air Fleet was available to support other maritime operations. Japanese naval aviation, however, was not without faults. Japanese fighters lacked effective airborne radio and ninety per cent of aircrew were enlisted men rather than officers, which unduly reduced the influence of aircrew in the naval chain of command.

Yamamoto knew that the odds of Japan fighting a successful war against the United States were not slim, nor did he approve of Japan's Axis membership. Nonetheless, Yamamoto regarded the United States' naval building programme inaugurated in the summer of 1940 as a definite threat. He told Prime Minister Konoye shortly after Japan had joined the Axis: 'If I am told to fight regardless of consequence, I shall run wild considerably for the first six months or a year, but I have utterly no confidence for the second and third years.'[6] The traditional Japanese naval plan for a war against the United States was to fight a defensive campaign in the western Pacific as the American fleet advanced towards the Philippines. Yet in April 1940 the United States Pacific Fleet had left California for scheduled manoeuvres in the central Pacific, at the end of which the fleet had remained at the hitherto advance base of Pearl Harbor. In the central Pacific, Pearl Harbor was a far more exposed location than the ports of California. The relocation of the United States Pacific Fleet to Hawaii opened up the possibility of a Japanese pre-emptive strike by carrier aircraft. If the United States Navy was temporarily crippled, Japanese forces might overrun South-East Asia and its oil and other raw materials with impunity. And Japan was no stranger to surprise attacks. In 1904 a surprise attack on Port Arthur had begun the war with Russia without a preceding declaration.

Yamamoto had first discussed a possible attack on Pearl Harbor with his Chief of Staff as early as March and April of 1940. Hawaii was 3,900 miles from Japan. A strike across such a distance would require a great deal of preparation. Meanwhile, the success of British carrier aircraft against the Italian fleet at Taranto had been an encouraging development. On the night of 11 November 1940 RAF torpedo-bombers had been launched by the Mediterranean Fleet against the southern Italian port of Taranto. The twenty-one torpedo-bombers had dropped parachute flares to illuminate an assault that had damaged or sunk three of Italy's six battleships. Torpedoes dropped from aircraft had functioned effectively, and had not become stuck in the mud at the bottom of the harbour. The Italians at Taranto had been without an effective radar system. Torpedo nets in the harbour had also been incomplete. This was the first aircraft carrier strike against an enemy fleet sheltering behind the defences of a major home port. The successful raid on Taranto helped to give the British naval superiority in the Mediterranean for months to come; though with hindsight the raid's impact on Japanese thinking may have been its most important outcome. Yamamoto is known to have called for reports on the Taranto raid from the naval attaches in Rome and London.[7]

At the start of 1941 Yamamoto and his staff began drawing up detailed contingency plans for a strike at Pearl Harbor. This planning was a tightly guarded secret even within the naval establishment. In January Yamamoto wrote to the Navy Minister to propose an attack on Pearl in the event of war with America and Britain. 'We should do our best ... to decide the fate of the war on the very first day.'[8]

The Japanese naval intelligence effort at Hawaii was stepped up in preparation for a possible attack. The city of Honolulu on Oahu Island had a multi-racial population with a large Japanese minority. A Japanese agent could thus operate with considerable freedom. Takeo Yoshikawa, after intensive training by naval intelligence, was appointed to the Foreign Office and arrived at Honolulu in March 1941 under the cover of a routine diplomatic post. Yoshikawa sent regular reports back to Japan on the composition and movements of the United States Pacific Fleet, the ships of which were clearly visible to any civilian gazing down from the high ground overlooking Pearl Harbor.

In the closing months of the year, Japan's leadership made the final decisions needed for war with the western powers and the invasion of South-East Asia. The main Japanese objectives in South-East Asia were the oil and raw materials of Dutch and British colonial territory. The American-occupied Philippines lay astride the routes to South-East Asia and it made no sense not to involve the United States in the initial round of aggression.

The Naval General Staff had ongoing doubts about the impending raid on Pearl and Yamamoto had to keep working hard to justify the attack. He claimed, 'The presence of the US fleet in Hawaii is a dagger pointed at our throats. Should war be declared, the length and breadth of our southern operations would immediately be exposed to a serious threat on its flank.'[9] Yamamoto had to threaten resignation to secure the Naval Staff's final agreement. In October the government in Tokyo gave final approval to the plan. The politically powerful Army General Staff had raised few objections as they were not required to provide troops for the operation. A troop landing at Hawaii had not been seriously considered as South-East Asia was the main objective. The size of the American garrison on the Hawaiian Islands was another deterrent. As Britain had few large warships in South-East Asia, Japan's fleet carriers would not be needed in that region. Land-based aircraft, many flying from newly developed aerodromes in Indo-China, would be sufficient to cover invasion transports destined for Malaya, Thailand and the Philippines.

The Japanese undertook detailed planning for the attack on Pearl Harbor. War games conducted in Tokyo yielded promising results, though there were bound to be significant losses if the fleet was discovered on the approach leg. Commander Minoru Genda, a senior staff officer of the First Air Fleet, played a key role in planning for the operation. Lieutenant-Commander Mitsuo Fuchida was transferred to the fleet carrier *Akagi* from a staff posting to be informed that he would be leading the assault. The carrier air groups trained for an attack on an enemy fleet in port.

Nearing winter monsoons, and Japan's falling fuel stocks, heralded the final approach of war in the Pacific. Diplomatic negotiations in Washington had become irrevocably deadlocked. Sunday 7 December was the date chosen for the attack on Pearl Harbor, as agents had reported that the main body of the fleet would be in port on a Sunday. The United States Pacific Fleet had a firmly established routine.

Pearl Harbor was at Oahu, the third largest of the eight major Hawaiian islands. The Hawaiian archipelago is a series of volcanic mountain-tops arranged in a crescent stretching for hundreds of miles. The blue sea, white surf and island greenery create a setting of great beauty. In May 1940, shortly after the fleet had first moved from California to Hawaii, the commander of the fleet, Admiral J.O. Richardson, had been told by Admiral H.R. Stark, Chief of Naval Operations in Washington: 'You are there because of the deterrent effect which is thought your presence may have on the Japs going into the East Indies.'[10] Richardson had been replaced at the end of his first year in command, as he wanted to retain the Californian ports as the fleet's principal base. President Roosevelt had supported the fleet's relocation to Hawaii and had been angered at Richardson's attitude.

Admiral Husband E. Kimmel became the new Commander-in-Chief United States Fleet on 1 February 1941. On the same date Admiral Ernest J. King was made Commander-in-Chief Atlantic Fleet. Prior to appointment to the highest seagoing post in the navy, Kimmel had been a rear-admiral of cruisers. Kimmel, an energetic and devoted officer, directed his attention to preparing the fleet to fight a mid-ocean battle in accordance with the offensive strategy that had come to dominate American naval thinking in the interwar period. Kimmel would later say that he believed a submarine attack in the Hawaiian area by a hostile power was the most likely local danger. An attack by aircraft was a possibility, but 'I felt also that the danger of torpedo plane attack in Pearl Harbor was nil because I believed that torpedoes would not run in the shallow water in that harbour'.[11] Pearl Harbor was particularly shallow, less than half as deep as Taranto harbour. Pearl was also a cramped harbour with a narrow entrance and that discouraged the use of anti-torpedo nets. Kimmel moved his headquarters from the fleet's flagship *Pennsylvania* to the more spacious submarine headquarters ashore.

On 5 February 1941 Major-General Walter C. Short arrived at Honolulu to take command of army forces at Hawaii. Army ground forces at Oahu were 58,000 strong and included the 24th and 25th Divisions. The protection of the fleet's base at Oahu was the Hawaiian army garrison's foremost duty. Kimmel and Short were undoubtedly on good terms. In May 1941 the army's Chief of the General Staff, General George C. Marshall, assured Roosevelt that Oahu was the 'strongest fortress in the world'. Oahu was the greatest concentration of American military strength in 1941.

Through 1940–41 the United States had acquired new defence responsibilities as the military situation worsened for Britain in its war against Germany. The United States Navy became engaged in the U-boat war in the Atlantic. In the middle of 1941 three battleships and a large aircraft carrier were transferred from the Pacific Fleet to the Atlantic Fleet. Battleships were not needed for anti-submarine warfare, but there was the possibility of an encounter with a German surface raider.[12] Kimmel divided his reduced fleet into three task forces: a fast carrier force, an amphibious force and a battleship force. The carrier force – Task Force 2 – was commanded by Vice-Admiral W.F. Halsey. The battleships and aircraft carriers were put in separate task forces, as the old battleships were too slow to keep pace with the carriers.

During 1941 efforts were made to build up American forces in the Philippines, which had hitherto been held at a token level in accordance with provisions of the expired Washington Naval Treaty. The archipelago seemed indefensible, but on 26 July Roosevelt ordered that the Philippines armed forces be incorporated into the United States military. General Douglas MacArthur took command at a unified Far East headquarters. Plans were made to base 300 B-17 four-engine bombers in the Philippines. Only thirty-five B-17s had arrived by December 1941, but their long range was a direct threat to a number of Japanese interests, including the life of the Emperor.[13] The build-up in the Philippines diminished Hawaii's status as America's most important Pacific outpost. The Philippines assumed elements of that role.

Though the two countries were not at war, American code breakers had been deciphering the code used by the Japanese diplomatic service. These deciphered messages were only seen by the most senior officials in Washington. From August 1940 the Japanese diplomatic J-19 cipher had been regularly broken, meaning that the traffic from Tokyo to the Japanese ambassador in Washington could be monitored. The deciphering project was code-named 'Magic'. Details of J-19 were changed daily to make deciphering a laborious task, and the code was used globally by many Japanese officials to create a large volume of material. The Imperial Japanese Navy's operational JN-25 code remained secure, but work was underway in a bid to break into that code.

On 24 September 1941 the Japanese Foreign Ministry requested of the Honolulu consulate that extra reports be forwarded about warships at Pearl. This message was recorded by American intelligence and sent to Washington to be deciphered, as Hawaii lacked that capability. Kimmel's intelligence officer, Lieutenant-Commander E.T. Layton, later commented: 'The Pacific Fleet, the principal instrument of our military power in the Pacific, was not equipped to monitor the enemy beyond its harbour wall.'[14] In Washington low priority Magic material might take a fortnight for decryption. Material from Honolulu was often mixed in with intercepts from Japanese diplomats in Panama, California and elsewhere. Only limited deciphered Magic material from the Honolulu consulate – some of which obviously focused on the activities of the fleet – was sent back to Hawaii. Within the army, Chief of Staff General Marshall kept a very tight control over Magic material leaving Washington.[15]

Thanks to the Magic code-breaking effort, the American leadership in Washington knew that the Japanese had set a deadline at the end of November for diplomatic negotiations to succeed. As negotiations between Japan and the United States neared final collapse, on 27 November 1941 Admiral Stark sent a message to the naval commanders in the Philippines and Hawaii.

This dispatch is to be considered a war warning. Negotiations with Japan looking toward stabilisation of conditions in the Pacific have ceased. An aggressive move by Japan is expected within the next few days. The number and equipment of Japanese troops and the organisation of naval task forces indicates an amphibious expedition against either the Philippines, Thailand or Kra Peninsula or possibly Borneo. Execute appropriate defensive deployment.[16]

Admiral Kimmel ordered that anti-submarine measures be stepped up and suspicious submarines were to be depth-charged. Kimmel subsequently said that, even after receiving the 27 November dispatch, he continued to believe 'there was a very good chance that a mass submarine attack would occur in the Hawaiian area. I thought an air attack was still a remote possibility.'[17]

It seems likely that Admiral Stark and other senior naval officers in Washington believed that a flow of background Magic information was being sent to commanders at Hawaii. That was simply not the case.[18] The warning to Kimmel stated that negotiations had 'ceased', but he was not provided with the Magic intercepts that would have clearly shown how tense Japanese-American relations had become. The 'war warning' from Stark did not indicate Hawaii to be a specific target, and, if anything, diverted attention away from Hawaii to places in South-East Asia, thousands of miles distant.

The divided chain of command at Hawaii did not help matters. Where responsibilities began and ended or overlapped was not always clear. Kimmel was responsible for the fleet at sea, but the army was responsible for the safety of naval shipping in harbour in conjunction with Rear-Admiral C.C. Bloch, who commanded the shore-based Fourteenth Naval District headquarters. Bloch was a sixty-three year-old former commander of the United States Fleet enjoying a final posting prior to retirement. By early December the army's General Short had instituted an Alert No. 1, which was an alert against ground sabotage and espionage by Japanese elements of the local population. An Alert No. 3 was a warning against all-out attack, but that was not activated. To the extent that the army and navy at Oahu had difficulties effectively coordinating their activities, this merely reflected the service divisions evident in Washington. Stark and Marshall had not worked together to send a single set of instructions to Kimmel and Short.

Responsibility for aerial reconnaissance at Hawaii was particularly convoluted. In 1941 the United States did not have an independent air force. Aircraft at Oahu were controlled either by the navy or the army's 'Hawaiian Air Force'. By mutual agreement, the navy was responsible for long-range reconnaissance using a restricted number of Catalina flying-boats that might patrol 7–800 miles from Oahu. At this stage of the war aircrew relied on binoculars to search for shipping in sometimes stormy conditions. Obviously by night little could be seen. As Hawaii was an island group in the centre of a large ocean, there was a need to mount reconnaissance patrols in a 360 degree arc, which further stretched resources. Training and maintenance also took a toll on reconnaissance units. Kimmel did not deploy a picket line of submarines and small warships around Hawaii to supplement what proved to be a highly ineffective programme of aerial reconnaissance. On the morning of 7 December only three Catalinas were due to fly a dawn patrol to the south of Oahu. Four other Catalinas were scheduled to take part in submarine exercises to the east of Oahu.[19]

Blithely unaware of Japanese plans, American commanders at Hawaii were confident of their invulnerability. On 6 December Kimmel told a journalist in a private interview that Japan would not risk war in the Pacific so long as the Soviet Union remained undefeated to their rear. Vice-Admiral W.S. Pye, the next most senior naval officer to Kimmel, commented to another officer: 'The Japanese will not go to war with the United States. We are too big, too powerful and too strong.'[20] That same day it was reported to Kimmel that the Japanese were burning papers outside their consulate in Honolulu, though there had been other reports of such a happening during the past year.

On 6 December Kimmel and Pye were informed that Japanese forces had been sighted moving in the Gulf of Siam. British commanders at Singapore believed that a Japanese troop convoy was in the South China Sea, probably destined for Thailand or possibly Malaya. Aerial reconnaissance had spotted the transports and their naval escort. The information had been passed from London to Washington. Ominously, at least in hindsight, the navy's Combat Intelligence Unit had no idea of the location of Japan's six fleet carriers, as their radio call signs could no longer be detected.[21]

Japanese officials at the Honolulu consulate had been busy during the early days of December. On 2 December a message had been sent from Tokyo in J-19 code. 'Wire me in each case whether or not there are any observation balloons above Pearl Harbor or if there are any indications that they will be sent up. Also advise whether or not the warships are provided with anti-torpedo nets.'[22] This message was recorded by the army at Hawaii and sent undecoded by surface mail to Washington, which took many days. On 6 December the Japanese consulate at Honolulu had replied that there was no sign of any balloon equipment and had added: 'I imagine that in all probability there is considerable opportunity left to take advantage for a surprise attack against these places.' The message had gone on to say: 'In my opinion the battleships do not have torpedo nets.' Another message sent that day had noted, 'It appears that no air reconnaissance is being conducted by the fleet air arm'. The operational nature of the messages of 6 December is not hard to discern. The messages were intercepted by an army signals station in San Francisco and forwarded to the War Department, where they were not decoded until 8 December.[23]

Agent Yoshikawa spent the afternoon of 6 December in a taxi having a last look at the fleet at its moorings. He then went to the commercial telegraph office and, shortly after 6 p.m., sent a message to his superiors that nine battleships were in harbour, though the heavy cruisers and aircraft carriers were absent.[24] The fleet carrier *Enterprise* had left Pearl on 28 November to ferry fighter reinforcements to Wake Island. On 5 December *Lexington* had sailed to ferry aircraft to the island outpost of Midway. These task forces were by default providing Oahu with reconnaissance cover to the west and north west. The missions of *Enterprise* and *Lexington* show that Kimmel was willing to use his aircraft carriers in independent roles. A third fleet carrier, *Saratoga*, was on the west coast for repairs.

A task force of six large Japanese aircraft carriers, two battleships, escorting warships and support ships had put to sea on 26 November from Tankan Bay in the isolated Kurile Islands to sail several thousand miles across the empty, stormy, foggy north Pacific towards Hawaii. The fleet at sea was led by Vice-Admiral Chuichi Nagumo, the commander of the carrier strike force. Nagumo was an expert in torpedo warfare and had come to command carriers primarily by virtue of seniority. He had his doubts about the operation and had been in his post for only eight months.[25] On 23 November Nagumo had discussed contingencies with his commanders in the event of the task force's discovery. If the carriers were found by the Americans on the day of the raid the operation would continue. If discovery occurred a day earlier a decision would be made according to circumstance. If the task force was discovered two days before X-Day or earlier, the operation would be abandoned. According to Lieutenant-Commander Fuchida, who was to lead the raid, if the main units of the American Pacific Fleet were not at Pearl, 'we would have scouted an area of about 300 miles around Oahu and were prepared to attack. If the American fleet could not be located, we were to withdraw.'[26]

Strict radio silence was maintained at sea. On some ships this was taken to the point of dismantling the Morse code sending key to reduce the possibility of accidental signalling. False naval radio traffic was broadcast in Japanese home waters to mislead electronic eavesdroppers. A destroyer screen fanned out ahead of the task force. Tankers and supply ships were detached along the route after re-supplying was completed. The officers and sailors of the task force were finally told of their destination and the magnitude of their mission. Commanders and flying officers had been briefed a month earlier. In Japan, the Emperor was kept informed of the task force's progress.

The fleet carriers *Akagi* (*Red Castle*) – Nagumo's flagship – and *Kaga* (*Increased Joy*) had been converted from the hulls of a battlecruiser and battleship respectively in the 1920s. *Hiryu* (*Flying Dragon*) and *Soryu* (*Green Dragon*) had been completed in 1938. *Shokaku* (*Soaring Crane*) and *Zuikaku* (*Happy Crane*) were the largest and newest fleet carriers. The carriers' air groups boasted a total of 423 aircraft. This was the finest naval air force in the world. The strike force was to comprise 'Zero' or 'Zeke' fighters (Mitsubishi Type 00), 'Val' dive-bombers (Aichi Type 99) and 'Kate' high-level or torpedo-bombers (Nakajima

Type 97). Japanese aircraft had been given quasi-official nicknames by the American military. The Zero fighter had acquired its nickname as the year of its introduction, 1940, was the Japanese year 2600. '00' was marked on the fuselage. The Zero was the first carrier-borne fighter at least to match the performance of a land-based fighter.[27]

Aircrew anxiously studied maps and models of Pearl. If torpedo nets were protecting shipping, Japanese commanders intended that the dive-bombers in the task force inflict the bulk of the damage. As American battleships were reported to be moored in pairs, the inboard ship would require dive-bombing in any case. All torpedo-bombers would fly in the first wave of the attack. Wooden extensions had been fitted to aerial torpedoes to stop them running too deep in the shallows of the harbour. The high-level bombers would need to drop their bombs from at least a height of 10,000 feet to penetrate deck armour. The bombs to be dropped were modified armour-piercing naval shells. An aluminium shock-absorbing plug had been positioned to detonate the charge after the deck armour of a ship had been penetrated, rather than on first impact.[28]

Admiral Yamamoto had remained at his headquarters in Japan aboard the battleship *Nagato*. Once the political leadership had decided on war and received the Emperor's approval, on 2 December Yamamoto signalled 'climb Mount Nagata' to the task force to indicate the operation was to proceed. A large force of Japanese submarines, five of them carrying midget submarines, was already in position around Hawaii. Air officers such as Genda and Fuchida were appalled by the prospect that the submarines might expose the impending attack before the carrier force had arrived. Yamamoto, though, had decided to involve submarines in the plan as an air attack might not be enough to complete the American fleet's destruction.

On 3 December the fleet was 900 miles north of Midway Island, after a voyage across an empty and stormy ocean. By early on 6 December the task force was 575 miles north of Oahu and sailing south at twenty-four knots. For encouragement, *Akagi* flew a signal very similar to the signal Admiral Togo had hoisted before the 1905 Tsushima Straits battle. 'The rise and fall of the Empire depends upon this battle. Every man is expected to do his utmost.' Yamamoto had told task force officers in an address before sailing: 'You must take into careful consideration the possibility that the attack may not be a surprise after all. You may have to fight your way in to the target.' But radio transmissions at Hawaii suggested to the approaching Japanese that a peacetime routine still prevailed. At 1.50 a.m. on 7 December the task force received a message from Imperial General Headquarters with information of the American fleet at Oahu. The American aircraft carriers had left Pearl Harbor, though the battleships and two heavy cruisers were in port. In addition, the message reported that there were no indications of oceanic patrol flights around Hawaii.

Early on Sunday 7 December, on the pitching decks of Nagumo's carriers, 183 aircraft were readied for launch. These were the first wave of the attack destined for Pearl Harbor, now about 250 miles to the south. The skies were dark and overcast. The timing of the launch was intended to coincide with a lightning sky and avoid the confusion of a night operation. On *Akagi* aircrew had gathered beforehand to hear speeches and drink traditional toasts in sake. Airmen had tied cloth headbands around their leather helmets bearing the characters 'Certain Victory'. Intelligence reports had recently confirmed the absence of torpedo-nets. Two reconnaissance floatplanes had been flown off heavy cruisers at 5.30 a.m. to scout ahead. This posed a risk to the operation's security, but Japanese commanders wanted visually to confirm the situation at Oahu.

The first wave comprised forty-three fighters, forty-nine high-level bombers, fifty-one dive-bombers and forty torpedo-bombers. Seamen crowded the decks to watch the launch and shout banzais in appreciation. The main launching began about 6 a.m. and fifteen minutes later the force, led by Fuchida in a high-level bomber, set course for the blue-green hills of Oahu. The aircraft flew in layers from 9,000 to 14,000 feet. Aircrew were able to tune their radio receivers to pick up a Hawaiian station playing a Japanese song. The sun rose brilliantly. It bore a resemblance to the Japanese naval ensign if an observer wished to look for that omen.[29]

The Japanese task force had no need to fear detection by American reconnaissance aircraft. That morning only a few Catalina flying-boats were conducting routine patrols near Hawaii, and none were patrolling to the north of Oahu. There were no American fighters on standby for immediate take-off. The Japanese ambassador in Washington had been instructed by Tokyo to sever negotiations that day at 1 p.m. Washington time (7.30 a.m. Hawaiian time). This information had been intercepted and quickly decoded, as the ambassador's traffic was of the highest priority for decryption. This last-minute intelligence coup did not generate any fresh, timely information for the commanders at Hawaii. A delayed message about the final collapse of negotiations sent by General Marshall only reached the Pearl Harbor commanders during the afternoon of 7 December. It would have been possible for Stark and Marshall to telephone Hawaii, though Marshall was to say that he did not believe the lines to be secure. He also later acknowledged that he would have called the Philippines first if he had felt the need for urgent discussions with commanders in the Pacific.[30]

A radar system comprising five mobile stations had been established at Oahu in August 1941, but the posts only operated from 4 a.m. to 7 a.m. This was a full year after a comprehensive radar system had played such an important role in the Battle of Britain. Just after 7 a.m. radar operators at Opana station, which had yet to close down as scheduled, saw pulses on the screen that signified a large formation of aircraft 130–140 miles to the north. Privates Lockard and

Elliott alerted a duty officer at 7.25 a.m. but were told by Lieutenant Kermit Tyler that the planes were probably American B-17s arriving from California. All of the personnel involved in these exchanges were inexperienced. The operators did not say how unusually large the incoming flight appeared, nor does the duty officer appear to have asked about such details.[31] The unidentified blips grew steadily closer as the next hour wore on. Even a very short period of warning time might have allowed warships fully to man their anti-aircraft weapons and shut watertight doors and hatches below deck.

The radar interception of a strong force of approaching aircraft was not the first indication that something unusual was afoot. Earlier that morning a hostile submarine had been attacked by a destroyer with depth charges as it tried to sneak through the entrance to Pearl Harbor. At 3.58 a.m. the destroyer *Ward* had been informed by a nearby minesweeper that an object that might be a submarine had been sighted. No report had been forwarded to the naval district headquarters and a sonar search of the area located nothing. Shortly after 6 a.m. three Catalinas had taken off for a routine patrol to the south of Oahu. By 6.30 a.m. a probably hostile submarine had been sighted shadowing the repair ship *Antares*. The nearby destroyer *Ward* had made the sighting as well and promptly attacked with depth charges and gun fire. The Catalina also dropped depth charges and an oil patch was spotted on the surface. The Catalina's pilot, Ensign William P. Tanner, reported what had happened to the Ford Island air base's command centre. At least one submarine did enter the harbour and was later sunk. Prior to this attack the Americans knew nothing about Japan's 'midget' submarines. With hindsight it seems absurd that the Japanese had risked compromising the secrecy of the overall plan to accommodate secondary suicide missions by midget submarines.

In the operations office of the Fourteenth Naval District a message of a destroyer's attack on a submarine was received at 6.53 a.m. 'We have attacked, fired upon, and dropped depth charges upon submarines operating in defensive sea area.'[32] The information of this extraordinary encounter was passed up the chain of command, but calamitous delays were caused by requests for confirmation and an overall lack of urgency. Ensign Tanner's message to Ford Island was passed upwards as well and culminated in a staff officer calling Kimmel at 7.30 a.m. with news of an attack on a submarine. Admiral Kimmel and General Short had been due to play golf that morning.

By this time the opportunity for the Americans to take advantage of signs of impending attack had passed. The Japanese airborne strike force was on its final run to Oahu. At 7.49 a.m. Fuchida gave the attack signal. The message 'Tora, Tora, Tora' was sent back to Nagumo's task force at 7.53 a.m. to tell them that surprise had been achieved. The signal was picked up on Yamamoto's flagship on the far side of the Pacific. Agents had given reasonably precise information of the likely location of shipping within the harbour. Pilots had been preparing for weeks with that in mind. Declared Fuchida: 'Below me lay the whole United States Pacific Fleet in a formation I would not have dared to dream of in my most optimistic dreams.'[33] Seventy naval combat ships and twenty-four naval auxiliary ships were in port that Sunday morning, including eight battleships and two heavy cruisers. Commander Itaya, the leader of one formation, recalled:

> Pearl Harbor was still asleep in the morning mist. It was calm and serene inside the harbour, not even a trace of smoke from the ships … fine objectives of attack in all directions. In line with these, inside the harbour, were important ships of the Pacific Fleet, strung out and anchored two ships side by side in an orderly manner.[34]

One battleship was in dry-dock but the other seven were moored on the south east side of Ford Island, either in pairs or singularly, 'just like toys on a child's floor', said another Japanese pilot. As was usual, the Sunday morning routine saw American naval officers at breakfast in their wardrooms. Seamen were at rest or undertaking cleaning duties.

The torpedo-bombers were to lead the attack, but due to a misunderstanding of a signal flare fired by Fuchida the dive-bombers went for their targets at about the same time. Some Japanese aircraft headed for the naval airfield at Ford Island, in the middle of the harbour. The first bombs of the Pacific War fell on the airfield. At 7.58 a.m. Ford Island's command centre broadcast the soon-to-be famous message: 'Air Raid, Pearl Harbor. This is no Drill.' Church bells were starting to ring in distant Honolulu. When the Ford Island warning message reached Washington, it was handed to Navy Secretary Knox. He blurted out, 'My God! This can't be true, this must mean the Philippines!'

That Sunday morning over half of officers and ninety per cent of enlisted men were aboard the vessels moored on Battleship Row. A limited number of anti-aircraft guns were continuously manned with a restricted supply of ammunition. The first wave of sixteen low flying torpedo-bombers, the rising sun painted under their wings, swooped in from the north west towards Ford Island. Battleship Row lay on the south-east side of the island, but moored on the north-west side was the decommissioned battleship *Utah* and light cruiser *Raleigh*. Half a dozen torpedoes were dropped at these tempting targets. Just before 8 a.m. a torpedo hit was scored on *Raleigh*. Two hits were made on *Utah*, which was still in service as a target and training ship. *Utah* capsized in ten minutes and fifty-eight of her crew died. Later in the raid an armour-piercing bomb landed on *Raleigh*, only to go right through the ship and explode on the harbour bottom beneath.[35]

The torpedo-bombers flew over Ford Island to attack next warships moored against the south side of Pearl Harbor. The light cruiser *Helena* – moored inboard of the minelayer *Oglala* – was hit by a torpedo that had passed underneath the minelayer. The blast blew in the thin plating of *Oglala*, which flooded and later capsized. Just as *Utah* had not been a designated target, *Helena* may also have been attacked by mistake, as she was in a berth previously occupied by the fleet flagship *Pennsylvania*. Five of the torpedo-bombers arriving from the north west did not drop their torpedoes. They swung around to join another twenty-four torpedo-bombers approaching to attack Battleship Row directly.[36] By now ships' sirens were sounding general quarters and once somnolent companies were abuzz with activity.

The main wave of torpedo-bombers ran towards Battleship Row at high speed. Huge water spouts rose into the air when torpedoes hit their target. Japanese torpedoes were the most effective in the world. The bulk of the torpedoes were aimed at *Oklahoma* and *West Virginia*. Low-flying aircraft with gleaming rising sun insignia skimmed clear of the battleships after dropping their ordnance. American anti-aircraft guns and machine guns came into action amid the sounds of bursting bombs. Fuchida was impressed by the speed at which the smoke puffs of anti-aircraft shell-fire appeared in the sky.

Dive-bombers and high-level bombers joined the fray. A forward magazine of *Arizona* was penetrated by an 800-kilogram bomb dropped by a high-level bomber.[37] The resulting explosions – which were caught on film – threw an orange-black column of flame and smoke 1,000 feet into the air, 'like a million Fourth of Julys'. Japanese aircraft were bounced by the shock waves. The front end of *Arizona* was demolished. Debris from the explosion, human and material, rained down. Living men were blown clear of the ship. Four out of five men aboard were killed by blast, burns and drowning. The wrecked *Arizona* quickly sank to entomb much of her crew. The ship's captain was killed along with Rear-Admiral Isaac C. Kidd, the commander of Battleship Division 1.

Oklahoma soon capsized after flooding caused by three almost simultaneous torpedo strikes. The ship stopped rolling when her masts hit the bottom of the harbour. Survivors clambered up the hull of the stricken ship as she rolled but over 400 of *Oklahoma*'s crew died.[38] Astern of *Oklahoma*, *West Virginia* was also struck by a number of torpedoes. It took deliberate counter-flooding by quick-thinking junior officers to avoid the fate of *Oklahoma*. Two hits on *West Virginia* by dive-bombers added to the chaos. The ship sank into the mud of the harbour floor on an even keel with her upper deck above water. She was engulfed by fire as her paintwork burned. 105 men died on *West Virginia* and her rapid demise had been hastened by the number of hatches and passageways left open inside a ship taken by surprise. A fragment from a bomb hit on *Tennessee* moored alongside killed *West Virginia*'s Captain Mervyn S. Bennion.

California was the flagship of Vice-Admiral Pye. A bomb hit caused an anti-aircraft ammunition magazine to explode with devastating effect. Many watertight inner hatches were open due to an ongoing inspection process. Light and power was lost when salt water got into the fuel system. Leaking oil from damaged tanks flowed into the surrounding water and caught fire to engulf the stern of the ship. Bomb and torpedo hits left *California* settling on the bottom of the shallow harbour with ninety-eight dead.

Moored inboard of sister ships and thereby protected from torpedoes, *Tennessee* and *Maryland* received bomb hits, though the latter in particular suffered only minor damage. *Nevada*, which had been moored astern of *Arizona*, prepared hurriedly to get underway as she had two hot boilers at the time of the attack. *Nevada* received two or three dive-bomber hits and a torpedo strike that tore a gash in the ship's side forty-five feet long. *Vestal*, a repair ship, was moored outboard of *Arizona* and received two bomb hits. She got underway but had to be beached heavily flooded. After dropping their bombs and torpedoes, Japanese aircraft swooped back across the harbour to strafe targets of opportunity.

The attack lasted less than an hour before Japanese aircraft began the return flight to their carriers. Only nine aircraft had been downed by American fire or accident. Surprisingly, during the later part of the assault a dozen four-engine B-17 bombers had arrived from the United States mainland to land on Hickam Field, despite the prevailing chaos. Oil gushing from the damaged warships would burn for many hours. A stunned Kimmel had watched the sudden attack on Battleship Row. 'I knew right away that something terrible was going on, that this was not a casual raid by just a few stray planes. The sky was full of the enemy.'[39] General Short subsequently remarked: 'I heard the first bombs, and my first idea was that the Navy was having some battle practice.'

There was a lull in the battle from about 8.35 a.m. to 8.55 a.m., when a second wave of 170 Japanese aircraft arrived to add to the tumult. The second attack force comprised eighty Val dive-bombers, forty Zeros and fifty high-level Kate bombers. Fuchida had remained on the scene, determined to direct the entire operation. As the second wave arrived, a great pyre of smoke was rising from Battleship Row. The growing pall of smoke obscured targets. The anti-aircraft fire of the thoroughly alerted defenders became intense.

Second-wave Japanese aircraft quickly focused on the slow-moving *Nevada* as she made for the harbour entrance. A number of bombs missed but the ones that hit wrecked the fore part of the ship with heavy loss of life. She received orders to beach from the navy yard signal tower to avoid blocking the narrow channel entrance. *Nevada* ran aground on Hospital Point. Her short cruise with her ensign flying was an inspiring moment for onlookers on an otherwise grim day. Some smaller warships managed to successfully run out of harbour during the second attack.[40]

The flagship *Pennsylvania* was bombed in dry-dock on the south side of the harbour. Two destroyers in the same dry-dock were wrecked. In a floating dry-dock a magazine in the destroyer *Shaw* exploded with spectacular effect. The light cruiser *Honolulu* and seaplane tender *Curtiss* were also damaged. A naval officer arriving at Pearl Harbor during the second attack, Lieutenant-Commander H.F. Pullen, recorded the scene:

The water was afire; *Arizona* was ablaze; the smoke rose high and black over the Navy yard; then there was that umbrella of black bursts overhead, and straight ahead the pyre of burning ships, with huge, terrific black clouds of burning oil. Interspersed with the explosion of the bombs and guns was the speed of the flames moving across the water and directing long fingers of flame at me.[41]

The second attack featured more misses than hits on warships. The raid was over by 10 a.m.

The fleet was not the only principal target of the Japanese attack. Military air bases at Pearl Harbor and elsewhere on Oahu had also been devastated by the raiders. Major-General F.L. Martin's Hawaiian Air Force had been crippled. Wheeler Field in the centre of Oahu had been a principal target for dive-bombers. Hickam Field to the immediate south of the Naval Station had also taken a pounding. Aircraft had been caught on the ground parked wing-tip to wing-tip for fear of sabotage. Only a handful of American fighters had managed to get into the air to dogfight with the Japanese.

The estimates of the number of destroyed and damaged American aircraft vary. By one estimate, of 169 naval aircraft at Oahu eighty-seven were destroyed by the raiders. Of the 231 army aircraft, sixty-four were destroyed and as many damaged.[42] During the raids eighteen American Dauntless dive-bombers had arrived to land at Ford Island from the fleet carrier *Enterprise*, which was returning from her westward journey to Wake Island. *Enterprise* was about the same distance to the west of Pearl as Nagumo's carriers were to the north. Zeros had shot down four of the Dauntlesses, friendly fire had accounted for another and a sixth had crash-landed.

In the entire attack, twenty-nine Japanese aircraft and fifty-five aircrew were lost. Another seventy-four aircraft were damaged and some of these were thrown overboard. One large and five midget submarines were also destroyed in the operation. A Japanese crewman was taken prisoner from a beached midget submarine after being rendered unconscious by fumes. He was nicknamed 'Prisoner Number One' by his captors and promptly requested to be killed.[43]

All eight United States battleships at Pearl were sunk or damaged in the raid. 2,403 Americans were killed and 1,178 wounded. Over 1,100 men died on *Arizona*. A number of cruisers, destroyers and other ships had also been sunk or damaged. The last sailors to die trapped in the hull of *Oklahoma* may have survived a fortnight until about 23 December. Eighty per cent of fatalities were naval personnel. The United States Navy suffered three times as many killed in action at Pearl Harbor as had been killed in action during the Spanish-American War and First World War combined.[44] After the raid, the towers of *Arizona* could still be seen above the surface of the water. The waves lapped the sunken *West Virginia*'s main deck.

Fuchida's aircraft had spent over two hours above Oahu and was the last to depart the scene. He did not encounter any American aircraft throughout this period and returned to *Akagi* around noon. He was later to claim that he recommended a third attack, but there is no independent confirmation of that.[45] At 1.30 p.m. Nagumo's carriers began to retire northwards. A relieved Nagumo elected to withdraw his fleet to safety rather than stay near Hawaii to hunt down the absent American carriers or launch further strikes against Pearl's shore installations. In Japan Yamamoto declined to intervene to order Nagumo to change his decision. The admiral told a member of his staff: 'Nagumo is thousands of miles away. He may have information we do not have. He must fight his own battle. I have complete faith in him.'[46] There had been little in the way of contingency planning by Yamamoto's Combined Fleet headquarters for the eventuality of the strike proving to be a great success.

Many American commanders at Oahu, including Kimmel and his Chief of Staff, had expected further Japanese air attacks. There was the possibility that an amphibious landing might be part of the Japanese plan. Kimmel signalled Admiral Halsey in *Enterprise* that enemy aircraft carriers were possibly to the south of Oahu. Halsey was instructed to investigate in that direction. *Lexington*, en route to Midway, was ordered to return and join Halsey.[47] Kimmel was still unsure from which direction the raiders had come even after the raid had been completed.

The disaster had been a terrible blow for Admiral Kimmel. Numerous observers had noted his obvious distress as he had watched events unfold from his office in the submarine base. During the raid the fifty-eight year-old Kentuckian had been hit in the chest by a spent bullet that had come through the window glass. Kimmel had commented to a nearby staff officer: 'It would have been merciful had it killed me.'[48] False alarms further stretched American nerves for the rest of 7 December. After dark senior officers on *Enterprise* unwisely flew off another six aircraft to land at Ford Island. Three Wildcats were shot down by panicky anti-aircraft gunners and another crashed in the night.[49]

To make matters worse for America, when daylight reached the Philippines on the other side of the international date line (8 December), the United States Army Air Force lost half its strength on the ground on the opening day of combat. Advance warning that an assault was coming did not make much of a difference. Before long the small United States Asiatic Fleet had to seek refuge away from the Philippines.

There were numerous courts of inquiry and official investigations into what had gone wrong for the Americans at Pearl Harbor. President Roosevelt and his advisers were shocked that commanders at Oahu could have been so complacent. The threat of war with Japan at the start of December 1941 had been obvious. Kimmel's battleships had been neatly moored in port on a Sunday morning as if the world was in the middle of a period of extended peace. Senior officers at Hawaii seemed convinced of their invulnerability, despite the great wars currently underway in Europe and Asia.

The Roberts Commission began hearings in Hawaii late in December. A process was underway by which Kimmel and Short would endure public disgrace, whilst significant failings in Washington were glossed over in the interests of the ongoing prosecution of the war. At the hearings Short conceded that he did not realise that the navy had so badly neglected long-range aerial reconnaissance around Oahu. Short agreed that he might have adopted a higher category of alert prior to 7 December. In turn, Kimmel conceded he knew little about the patchy nature of Hawaii's radar system. He admitted that he had been completely wrong about Pearl Harbor being too shallow for aerial torpedoes. Investigators found that torpedo nets had not been deployed for reason of inconvenience. The complete failure of reconnaissance to the north of Oahu suggests a failure of conception rather than execution. There had undoubtedly been local operational failings at Pearl Harbor. Kimmel and Short would primarily be sacked for those failings.

Nevertheless, Washington officials had contributed little to the safety of the fleet at Oahu, as they had shared so many of the assumptions of Kimmel and Short. Hawaii and Washington-based commanders had all assumed that, in the event of war, the Japanese would use their fleet aircraft carriers to cover an invasion of South-East Asia. Hawaii had seemed too distant from the East Indies to need simultaneous neutralisation. The Americans did not appreciate that the Japanese had the operational skill to undertake such divergent tasks at the same time.

Despite considerable goodwill, Hawaii and Washington had failed to coordinate their activities. Not until 1944 did Kimmel see the Magic decrypts relevant to Hawaii that a competent national intelligence organisation should have sent him in 1941.[50] Washington was to blame for moving too slowly to provide their most important military base with comprehensive radar coverage. Some sort of joint service air command to defend Hawaii against air attack seems obvious in hindsight. In 1941 officialdom was aware that the army and navy struggled at times to cooperate, but it was felt that the world still moved sufficiently slowly to accommodate the idiosyncrasies of separate armed services. The speed of operations exhibited at Pearl Harbor made it clear that the United States government and military needed quickly to move into the era of combined services warfare.

The raid on Pearl Harbor was a tactical victory for the Japanese, but strategically the benefits of the attack were of lesser significance. A Japanese amphibious landing on Oahu had never been a realistic proposition. The American garrison was too large for a successful invasion. The vast fuel dumps at Pearl remained intact after the raid. Lieutenant-Commander Layton, Fleet Intelligence Officer, said of the two oil tank clusters to the east and west of the naval station: 'They were all right above ground and in plain sight. Such an attack would have required no special strategy by the Japanese.'[51] More importantly, American aircraft carriers away at sea escaped damage. The raid had proved that carriers mattered more in oceanic naval battles than battleships. The main reasonable criticism of the Japanese conduct of the raid is that they might have allowed a longer cruising period off Oahu to reap fully the rewards of initial victory. Of the battleships damaged in Pearl Harbor on 7 December, only *Arizona* could not be refloated, and *Oklahoma* was the only other battleship unable to rejoin the fleet as a fighting ship. *Maryland* would be repaired by February 1942.

On 17 December Admiral Chester Nimitz replaced the disgraced Kimmel at Oahu. Nimitz later commented:

> It was God's mercy that our fleet was in Pearl Harbor on December 7, 1941. Had Kimmel had advance notice that the Japanese were coming, he most probably would have tried to intercept them. With the difference in speed between Kimmel's battleships and the faster Japanese carriers, the former could not have come within rifle range of the enemy's flattops. As a result, we would have lost many ships in deep water and also thousands more in lives.[52]

The loss of the battleships at Pearl pushed American commanders towards building up a submarine campaign against Japan, since many submarines were available and they did not require a large supply of oil.[53] The sudden loss of so many battleships would by necessity see a dramatic change in American naval doctrine to enshrine the aircraft carrier as the new heart of the fleet. And reinforcements were at hand. The aircraft carrier *Saratoga* soon returned to Hawaii from the west coast. The aircraft carrier *Yorktown* and three battleships were ordered from the Atlantic Fleet to enter the Pacific.

Above all else, the Pearl Harbor raid pushed America into a war against Japan. That Japan attacked both Hawaii and the Philippines made war doubly certain. A surprise attack only on the Philippines would have been more than sufficient. On 8 December President Roosevelt asked Congress to ratify the state of war with Japan that had existed since the previous day's attack on Pearl Harbor. There was no possibility of a compromise settlement in the wake of the attack. Washington could never trust Tokyo again until the Japanese had been beaten to their knees. This attitude was summed up by Admiral Halsey when *Enterprise* returned to Pearl on the afternoon of 8 December. Halsey surveyed the wreckage and exclaimed, 'Before we're through with 'em, the Japanese language will be spoken only in hell!'[54]

Germany quixotically declared war on America in support of Japan. If Germany had not declared war against the United States there is no way of knowing if Roosevelt would have asked Congress to declare war against Germany. By December 1941 it looked as though Britain and the Soviets might be able to survive against Germany without direct American intervention. It might have been tempting for Washington to throw America's main weight against Japan before dealing with Germany.[55]

The turn of events had certainly brought global war about unexpectedly. Hitler had to ask where Pearl Harbor was located when he was told of the Japanese raid.[56] Despite that, Germany's decision for war with America was taken quickly, as Berlin had been worried that the United States and Japan might come to an agreement. The Soviet-Japanese non-aggression pact had been an unpleasant surprise and Nazi leaders did not want the Japanese making peace with anyone else. Assurances had been given to Tokyo that Germany was willing to support Japan in a war against the United States. Hitler had long foreseen an eventual war with America. Germany would need the Japanese navy to be actively involved in that conflict.

Hitler had always under-rated American potential. He had told Goebbels on 8 May 1941 that with all the raw materials of Europe for Germany to draw on, United States production was not to be feared. Hitler had once said of the United States: 'What is America but millionaires, beauty queens, stupid records and Hollywood?'[57] Speer summed up Hitler's views of the United States as follows:

> The Americans had not played a very prominent part in the war of 1914–18, he [Hitler] thought, and more over had not made any great sacrifices of blood. They would certainly not withstand a great trial by fire, for their fighting qualities were low. In general, no such thing as an American people existed as a unit; they were nothing but a mass of immigrants from many nations and races.[58]

Hitler was unaware that America had played a decisive role in securing an armistice in western Europe in 1918.

Tokyo and Berlin hoped that America would be divided and demoralised by a sudden attack. That could not have been further from the truth. On 7 December 1941 the United States was summoned forth to become the greatest power on earth, a role it had previously shied away from. This was a great turnabout from the period of the Great Depression of the 1930s. The crash and turbulence of the United States economy from 1929 all the way down to 1939 had encouraged the contempt and opportunism of potential enemies. Hitler still clung to the traditional view that the fate of the world could only be decided by a contest for the leadership of Europe. Paradoxically, Hitler and his followers were fighting to establish Germany as a global power in a world of which they knew relatively little compared to their opponents in London and Washington.

Whilst Nagumo's fleet retired from Hawaiian waters, on the Asian mainland Japanese forces were poised for an immediate assault on the British colony of Hong Kong. On China's south coast, already surrounded by Japanese troops, Hong Kong had never been expected to hold out long. Further north Shanghai had been declared an open city. The British and United States garrisons had already been withdrawn. The Shanghai Volunteer Corps was not mobilised.

The outlook for Allied forces in South-East Asia was grim. Fifty days had been allotted by the Japanese High Command for the conquest of the Philippines; a hundred days for Singapore; 150 days for the Dutch East Indies. In many respects that timetable would be met. The Royal Navy would be swept from the region. The Japanese invasion of South-East Asia proved to be a colossal success. Battered United States naval forces at Hawaii would be unable to retard Tokyo's progress southwards.

7
The Battle of Midway

Once the Japanese had captured all their objectives in South-East Asia and the western Pacific, the question posed itself, what should be done next? Japan's leadership was in general agreement that it was necessary to continue offensive action to maintain momentum and initiative. It was too early to expect a favourable settlement with the United States. The low cost of the first round of victories had been a great encouragement, but the army had only limited troops available for further operations. The bulk of the army was deployed in China and Manchuria and there was no prospect of that changing in the near future.

The Imperial Japanese Navy was more prepared for further fighting against the western powers, Japan's principal naval enemies. Port Darwin had been raided by carrier aircraft on 19 February 1942 to neutralise Allied forces in northern Australia. Japanese forces were landed on the north coast of New Guinea in March. Port Moresby, on the south coast of Papua New Guinea, was a port from which the Japanese might menace Australia and other islands in the south-west Pacific. After some weeks' debate among army and navy planners, on 15 March Imperial General Headquarters in Tokyo decided to capture Port Moresby and the Solomon Islands, after which the Naval Staff wanted to take Fiji, Samoa and New Caledonia to isolate Australia from the United States.[1]

Early in April Admiral Nagumo's carrier task force struck Ceylon to drive the Royal Navy's Eastern Fleet away to the coast of Africa. This was the first time for over a century and a half that the British had suffered a defeat in the Indian Ocean. The Japanese presence in the Indian Ocean, however, was only transitory. The army did not want to land troops on Ceylon or the coast of south-east India. In the spring of 1942 the Japanese leadership firmly decided that linking up with the Germans, whether in the Indian Ocean or Siberia, was not a realistic policy.

In contrast to the wishes of the Naval Staff, Admiral Yamamoto and the Combined Fleet's staff wanted a fresh offensive in the central Pacific to destroy the United States Pacific Fleet. Early in April Yamamoto forced a showdown with his rival commanders in Tokyo. In theory the Naval Staff were in charge of strategy, but after the Pearl Harbor success Yamamoto had become dominant in Japan's councils of war. He was at the peak of his power and prestige.

Eventually the Naval Staff gave way so long as they could continue to develop their preferred set of operations in the south-west Pacific in tandem with Yamamoto's scheme. The compromise between the Naval Staff and Yamamoto caused Japanese naval forces to be divided at a vital time in the conflict.

The Naval Staff's capitulation to Yamamoto had been influenced by a recent American air raid on Tokyo. A United States carrier task force had sailed deeply across the northern Pacific towards Japan until sighted by a picket boat. On 18 April twin-engine bombers commanded by Lieutenant-Colonel James Doolittle had been daringly launched from the aircraft carrier *Hornet*. What had especially caught the Japanese by surprise was the fact that the bombers were launched at 700 miles range, after which the carrier task force turned away. The aircraft were on a one-way journey. The sixteen bombers hit Tokyo and then flew on to China. Only limited damage was caused by the raiders but they had threatened the life of the Emperor. A blow had been struck against the honour of the Japanese military. According to a Combined Fleet staff officer, the raid 'passed like a shiver over Japan'. The operation had been a propaganda exercise from the Allied view point, but it had exposed a gap in the Japanese defensive perimeter. Offensive action in the central Pacific by the Combined Fleet would help to seal that gap. The Naval Staff suggested to Yamamoto that if the Aleutians were captured in the far northern Pacific near Alaska that would help further to shield the home islands of Japan.[2]

As Yamamoto and the Combined Fleet developed plans for a major operation in the central Pacific, the Naval Staff's plan to seize Port Moresby by sea invasion was set in motion. An amphibious force left Rabaul on 4 May. A smaller force was detached to occupy Tulagi in the southern Solomons opposite Guadalcanal Island. The troop convoy bound for Port Moresby had a destroyer screen and a covering force that included the light carrier *Soho* and four heavy cruisers. *Soho* had been converted from a submarine tender and carried twenty-one aircraft. A strike force based around the fleet carriers *Zuikaku* and *Shokaku* was to sail around the Solomons into the Coral Sea to seek out and engage any Allied warships in the region. *Zuikaku* and *Shokaku* had been detached from the force returning from the Indian Ocean. Australian troops were holding Port Moresby and a New Zealand garrison was at Fiji. Under an agreement between the United States and Britain, the waters off the coast of eastern Australia were an American responsibility. The Americans had steadily reinforced the south-west Pacific in the early weeks and months of 1942, partly to begin building a line of communication to the beleaguered Philippines garrison. General Douglas MacArthur, evacuated from the Philippines to Australia, had taken command of Allied forces in the South-West Pacific.

At Hawaii, Admiral Chester Nimitz was both commander of the Pacific Fleet and overall theatre commander for the central Pacific. Aged fifty-seven, Nimitz was an even-tempered man, with white hair and light blue eyes. He had a reputation for sound judgement and a willingness to take the fight to the enemy. The softy-spoken admiral had been instructed to both protect Hawaii and maintain the route through the south-west Pacific to Australia.

The fleet carrier *Saratoga* had been torpedoed by a Japanese submarine on 11 January, but *Hornet* and *Yorktown* had entered the Pacific from the Atlantic to join *Enterprise* and *Lexington* and the rest of the Pacific Fleet. The United States Navy's fleet carriers were the equal to those of Japan, ship for ship. During the interwar period, the possession of the Philippines and Hawaii had encouraged the Americans to take an 'oceanic' view of carrier warfare.[3] Japan and the United States had constructed large carriers to embark as many aircraft as possible, in contrast to British carriers that had armoured flight decks but only space for limited numbers of aircraft.

The tough assignment confronting Nimitz was made a good deal easier when intelligence intercepts successfully uncovered the main features of the up-coming round of Japanese operations. In the lead up to the Pearl Harbor raid the Imperial Japanese Navy's operational code JN-25 had not been sufficiently penetrated, but the codebreakers of Commander Joseph Rochefort had cracked large parts of the code by the spring of 1942. This information was combined with radio traffic analysis to build up a reasonably complete intelligence picture. Radio traffic analysis involved plotting the location and volume of enemy radio signals. A sense of enemy dispositions was gained through the detection and plotting of the call signs of particular ships.

Armed with the knowledge that the Japanese had planned for offensive operations in the south-west Pacific, Nimitz ordered Rear-Admiral F.J. Fletcher to operate in the Coral Sea with *Yorktown* and *Lexington*. When Halsey's *Hornet* and *Enterprise* returned to Pearl Harbor from the Doolittle raid on Tokyo they were also ordered to start the long voyage to the south-west Pacific after a short refit.

The Japanese plan to occupy Tulagi, near Guadalcanal, was successfully undertaken by 3 May to alert Admiral Fletcher that his enemy was on the move. Early on 6 May – the day Corregidor fell, the last American bastion in the Philippines – Allied aircraft discovered a Japanese troop convoy off eastern New Guinea, possibly headed for Port Moresby. The next morning the light carrier *Soho*, which was part of the convoy's covering force, was attacked and sunk by Fletcher's aircraft. A triumphant American famously signalled, 'scratch one flattop'.[4] In turn, the Japanese spotted the carriers of Fletcher's task force. A strike was launched but poor visibility and American fighters thwarted the attackers. Several Japanese aircraft were shot down trying mistakenly to land on American carriers as poor weather closed in.

On the morning of 8 May, however, each fleet attacked the other's carriers. *Shokaku* was badly damaged by three bomb hits, though a nearby *Zuikaku* was protected by a rain squall. Seventy Japanese aircraft jumped the American carriers. *Lexington* was badly damaged and would later be engulfed by fire after the explosion of gasoline vapours. She had to be abandoned and was torpedoed by a USN destroyer as rescued crew looked on. With *Lexington* sunk, Fletcher prudently withdrew, as did the battered Japanese fleet. Japanese plans to take Port Moresby from the sea were shelved. Aircrew losses in the Coral Sea had been heavy for both sides. The damaged *Shokaku* lost thirty per cent of her air group; the undamaged *Zuikaku* lost forty per cent.

The Coral Sea engagement had been a stalemate in a tactical sense, but it was a strategic victory for Allied forces and more or less ended the likelihood of Australia facing large hostile landings. Neither fleet's ships had sighted the other and for that reason the battle was a revolutionary turning point in the history of naval warfare. The brigade-strength Australian garrison at Port Moresby would have been hard pressed to repel the Japanese amphibious force if it had landed. Nimitz and the United States Navy had staked a great deal in the south-west Pacific to win an important victory for the Allied cause.[5]

Admiral Yamamoto's central Pacific operation went ahead within a few weeks of the Coral Sea engagement. The plan was to attack Midway Island, 1,100 miles north-west of Hawaii. This was intended to draw the United States Pacific Fleet into a major battle. A Japanese attempt to capture Midway would be a direct threat to Hawaii. That was something the usually aggressive Nimitz could be relied upon to contest.

A full moon was best for an assault landing at Midway. Any delay would mean postponement for a month until the following full moon. Yamamoto was not prepared to tolerate that. The rush to launch the operation to catch the early June moon meant that none of the surviving Japanese carriers from the Coral Sea battle could take part in the attack on Midway. *Shokaku* needed repairs and *Zuikaku*'s air group had been crippled by heavy losses. Past success, however, caused Yamamoto to fall prey to hubris and he was not unduly concerned at the likely absence of two fleet carriers. Staff officers suggested concentrating spare aircrew and aircraft on *Zuikaku* but Yamamoto was content to keep her in reserve at Japan. Comfortingly, reports had been received that two American carriers had been sunk or badly damaged in the Coral Sea.

Yamamoto, who had commanded the Pearl Harbor raid from Japan, had made the battleship *Yamato* the Combined Fleet's floating headquarters. The Midway operation was to involve eight aircraft carriers, four large and four small, which were to be joined by no less than eleven battleships, including *Yamato*. Yamamoto was alleged to have once said that battleships were no more useful a weapon than a samurai sword.[6] But the new super-battleship *Yamato* could hardly be ignored. *Yamato* displaced 70,000 tons and was armed with 18.1 inch guns, the largest of naval artillery. She had been designed to displace a greater tonnage than any warship the Americans could pass through the Panama Canal. The advent of a new class of super-battleship confused Japanese naval thinking at a time when aircraft carriers had become crucial to Pacific Ocean warfare, a fact the Japanese had themselves demonstrated.

The detail of Yamamoto's plan for the Midway operation was complicated. The Combined Fleet was divided into several battle groups and spread across thousands of miles of ocean. The plan called for Admiral Nagumo's four fleet carriers to strike at Midway from the north west. The following day a landing force was to close on the island from the south west. The invasion transports carried 5,000 troops. Yamamoto's main force of battleships was to sail 300 miles behind Nagumo's carrier force. This was too distant for the battleships to take part in a pre-invasion bombardment of Midway.[7] Two of the small aircraft carriers were to assist a force destined for the Aleutians at the far top of the Pacific Ocean. This force was to raid the American base at Dutch Harbor and occupy the western Aleutian Islands of Attu and Kiska.

The Japanese plan was to first neutralise Midway, and then destroy the American fleet presumed to be coming to Midway's relief. This plan pushed Nimitz's carriers back to the status of a secondary objective. In reality the American carriers were the most dangerous enemy the Japanese had ever faced. Japanese intelligence estimated that two or three American carriers might be close to Hawaii. Hard-headed analysts accepted that one of the American carriers claimed sunk in the Coral Sea by Japanese aviators may have been only lightly damaged.[8]

In order to save time, the Combined Fleet unwisely sent the order for the Midway operation by radio to many units already at sea. A new Japanese naval code was on the verge of introduction, but this had been delayed due to difficulties in distributing codebooks caused by Japan's rapidly expanding empire. At Hawaii and Australia codebreakers soon uncovered Japanese plans, as had been the case in the lead up to the Coral Sea battle. Lieutenant-Commander E.T. Layton of Pacific Fleet intelligence was able to tell Nimitz that a major Japanese offensive was imminent. By late May the date, place, timing and rough Japanese order of battle for the Midway operation had been plotted. The Aleutians' thrust had also been detected but was rightly interpreted as an operation of secondary importance.[9]

Senior American officers were at first distrustful of information that claimed that the bulk of the Japanese navy was to be used merely to capture Midway atoll and part of the icy Aleutians. To gain additional confirmation that Midway was the main Japanese objective, towards the middle of May the Midway garrison was asked, with Nimitz's permission, to send an uncoded signal to Oahu falsely announcing that their water distillation plant had broken down. American codebreakers believed that the Japanese referred to Midway as 'AF' in their signals, and 'AF' was known to be the objective of the up-coming operation. Within two days Japanese messages were picked up advising that 'AF' was short of water. There could be little further doubt. Outstanding intelligence work allowed Nimitz to concentrate his scarce resources at the most critical location. All American fleet carriers were recalled to Hawaii from the south-west Pacific.

On 18 May Nimitz held a planning conference. It was decided to reinforce the Midway garrison and send only a token naval force towards the Aleutians.[10] To deploy against the might of the Imperial Japanese Navy, the Americans at Pearl Harbor had three fleet carriers and a number of smaller warships. The three available fleet carriers were *Hornet*, *Yorktown* and *Enterprise*. As for the USN's other fleet carriers; *Lexington* had been sunk in the Coral Sea, *Saratoga* was under repair, and *Wasp* had recently undertaken a convoy operation in the western Mediterranean to beleaguered Malta. Whereas Yamamoto was intending to deploy his battleships at the centre of his seagoing fleet, Nimitz prepared for the coming campaign by sending his battleships to California. Nimitz was content to send them far from Hawaii given the battleships' voracious consumption of oil and poor speed. In 1942 the United States produced two-thirds of the world's refined oil, but that oil still had to be hauled to Hawaii where it was in short supply. As in the Coral Sea battle, the United States Navy was to fight at Midway without a single battleship, the traditional heart of the fleet.[11]

Yorktown had been damaged in the Coral Sea and she arrived back at Pearl Harbor on 27 May bearing the scars of the battle. Repair work proceeded swiftly and *Yorktown's* damage proved less than initially feared. Naval aviators from *Saratoga's* air group were used to reinforce *Yorktown's* air group, which had been depleted in the Coral Sea fighting. American aircrew were an elite group of men, though in comparison with the Japanese some lacked battle experience.

Midway atoll comprised two small islands, one of which held an airfield. The islands added up to less than two square miles of land.[12] A reef lapped by waves surrounded the atoll to form a large lagoon. The atoll's air units operated about as many aircraft as a fleet carrier, though some were twin- or four-engine bombers. By June 3,000 troops had been sent to Midway, which had become crowded. The garrison, many of whom were Marine Corps personnel, threw up barbed wire entanglements, dug posts and erected anti-aircraft batteries.

Nimitz knew that the main Japanese carrier force could be expected to approach Midway from 3 June onwards. He sent his carriers to empty ocean to the north east of Midway, far from the prying eyes of Japanese aerial and submarine reconnaissance. Task Force 16, comprising *Hornet* and *Enterprise*, had sailed on 28 May accompanied by a force of cruisers and destroyers. In the absence of a hospitalised Admiral Halsey, who was suffering from a massive case of dermatitis, Nimitz had appointed Rear-Admiral Raymond A. Spruance to command Task Force 16. Halsey had recommended Spruance as his replacement. Spruance struck many as a cold and remote man, and he was not interested in personal publicity. He was not an aviation specialist but he had been on previous carrier task force operations as a cruiser division commander. He was thus as familiar with carrier operations as any other commander. Admiral Fletcher in *Yorktown*, the main component of Task Force 17, was in overall command of the two task forces.

The three American carriers embarked a total of 233 fighters, torpedo-bombers and dive-bombers. The Grumman Wildcat fighter was not quite a match for the Zero but was a well-armed machine. The Douglas Dauntless dive-bomber/scout plane was also an effective aircraft. On the other hand, the Douglas Devastater torpedo-bomber was too slow for combat in 1942. It was over 100 mph slower than a Zero and its prospects of surviving serious combat were bleak.

Nimitz instructed Fletcher and Spruance: 'In carrying out the task assigned ... you will be governed by the principle of calculated risk, which you shall interpret to mean the avoidance of exposure of your forces to attack by superior enemy forces without good prospect of inflicting, as a result of such exposure, greater damage on the enemy.'[13] American intelligence estimated that the Japanese would bring four to five carriers and two to four battleships against Midway. On 31 May Task Force 16 was in position 325 miles north east of the atoll. Fletcher's Task Force 17 joined its sister task force on 2 June. The task forces cruised about ten miles apart and had not been sighted by Japanese submarines. *Yorktown* was responsible for reconnaissance and local fighter defence (CAP – combat air patrol) for both task forces, leaving the air groups of *Hornet* and *Enterprise* ready for a concentrated strike once the Japanese carriers had been located.[14] Eleven American submarines were also lurking west of Midway. Japanese carriers did not have radar, whereas the base at Midway and American carriers had the advantage of that equipment.

The task forces of the Japanese Combined Fleet had left port late in May. The main body included Yamamoto's flagship and the small aircraft carrier *Hosho*, which had been taken off training duties. The First Carrier Striking Force comprised the fleet carriers *Akagi*, *Kaga*, *Hiryu* and *Soryu*, each carrying a mix of fighters, dive-bombers and torpedo-bombers – 272 aircraft in all. The Midway Occupation Force was directly supported by the small carrier *Zuiho*, though she only carried trainer aircraft. The carriers with the Aleutian force – *Ryujo* and *Junyo* – carried another fifty-one aircraft.[15] *Junyo* was well short of her full complement of aircraft. Many of the larger warships carried two or three reconnaissance seaplanes. Across the fleet these added up to over 100 aircraft.

The fleet observed radio silence during the seven day voyage across the Pacific. Heavy fog helped to shield the ships, and was so thick search lights had to be exposed to prevent collision. Commander Fuchida, who had led the Pearl Harbor raid, had been struck down by appendicitis. He had been operated upon, but remained unfit to take part in flying operations. Commander Genda of the First Air Fleet's staff had been laid low by pneumonia to further deplete the Japanese air warfare brains trust at the outset of a vital operation. Nagumo was not a pilot and only one of his four carrier captains was an aviator.[16]

During the voyage the Japanese had detected heavy radio traffic at Pearl Harbor, though they were unable to obtain more precise information as to American intentions. A plan for a reconnaissance flight over Pearl by long-range flying boats had fallen apart when submarines had been unable to make a necessary refuelling rendezvous as American ships were in the vicinity. Japanese agents at Oahu had long since been neutralised, and the submarine cordon put in place between Hawaii and Midway arrived in position too late to sight the departure of the American carrier task forces. Still, poor Japanese sources of intelligence were amply counter-balanced by abundant self-confidence and hubris.

From Midway Catalina flying-boats flew regular reconnaissance missions far to the west in a bid to find the Japanese forces expected to close on the atoll. This was very different from the weak American reconnaissance effort on the eve of the Pearl Harbor raid. At 9 a.m. on 3 June the transports of the Midway Occupation Force were spotted by the crew of Ensign Jack Reid's Catalina, 700 miles west-south-west of Midway. The ships were attacked by Midway-based B-17 heavy bombers later in the day, though little damage was inflicted. American commanders correctly assumed that the Japanese force that had been located was only the landing force and not Nagumo's carriers, which were always most likely to be in the empty ocean to the north west of Midway. Nagumo's Carrier Striking Force was shielded by a weather front, and continued to sail towards Midway during the night of 3/4 June believing that the Americans did not know they were coming.[17]

In the Aleutians the Japanese raided the air base at Dutch Harbor on 3 June. Attu and Kiska, the islands intended for occupation, were uninhabited. The raid was not particularly effective. A Zero that crashed on land in an intact state was recovered and would be closely studied by American design engineers. The battleships of the Aleutians Guard Force had parted company with Yamamoto's Main Force on 3 June and would be sailing pointlessly between the Aleutians and Midway during the upcoming battle.[18]

On the morning of 4 June Nagumo's carriers were within range of Midway. Sunrise was at 4 a.m. The new day promised excellent flying weather with some light cloud. The Carrier Striking Force had fewer aircraft than had been ready at dawn the previous 7 December due to the absence of *Shokaku* and *Zuikaku*.[19] Half of the available strike force began launching at 4.30 a.m. to attack Midway, 240 miles distant, whilst the other half stood in readiness to attack enemy shipping. Lieutenant Joichi Tomonaga from *Hiryu* led the attack in the absence of Fuchida. Thirty-six Val dive-bombers, thirty-six Kate high-level bombers and thirty-six Zero fighters set out, red and green navigation lights flashing, on the flight to Midway. A strong fighter escort flew with the bombers at the expense of the carriers' defensive air cover. The First Air Fleet was experienced at attacking shore targets, having raided Pearl Harbor, Port Darwin, Ceylon and other places.

Meanwhile, seven Japanese scout planes were launched to search the area for American warships. Nagumo and his staff assumed there were no American carriers nearby; otherwise a greater reconnaissance effort might have been made.[20] Only a one-phase reconnaissance pattern was launched, meaning there was no plan to send out a second wave of aircraft to re-search ocean covered by the first pattern.

After the Japanese force was airborne and heading for Midway, an American search plane from Midway located the Japanese carriers. The American search plane's crew was also able to report that a Japanese air strike was heading on a bearing towards Midway. On *Enterprise* the report of enemy aircraft heading for Midway was overheard, and from the bearings given the location of the Japanese carriers was approximated. Fletcher signalled by flash to Spruance: 'Proceed south-westerly and attack enemy carriers as soon as definitely located. I will follow as soon as planes recovered.'[21] Fletcher held back the air group of *Yorktown* in case further Japanese carriers were sighted emerging from the weather front. *Yorktown* also had to recover the search aircraft sent out pre-dawn and relieve the Combat Air Patrol over the task forces.

The commander of the Midway air group launched a strike on the located Japanese carriers. These aircraft got clear of Midway before the Japanese air strike reached the atoll at 6.30 a.m., their presence already detected by radar. Japanese naval aviators had little difficulty knocking down the obsolete defending Marine Corps fighters flown by inexperienced pilots. Buildings were damaged by Japanese bombs, but the intruders did not do the airfield much harm. Anti-aircraft fire took its toll and half a dozen Japanese aircraft were downed.

Over Midway the aircraft of Lieutenant Tomonaga, the strike force commander, was hit by ground fire. Bullets holed a fuel tank and put the radio transmitter out of action. Tomonaga wrote on a small blackboard, 'There is need for a second attack wave', and held it up alongside another aircraft, the radio operator of which sent the message onwards. This message put Nagumo in a difficult position as the invasion force could hardly approach the atoll in the face of an unsuppressed air defence. The second half of Nagumo's strike force was sitting on his carriers awaiting orders, armed with anti-shipping bombs and torpedoes. But another strike at Midway would necessitate the re-arming of those aircraft with the high explosive bombs needed to damage a land target. That would take time. As his scout planes had not reported any sightings, at 7.15 a.m. Nagumo, with Genda's agreement, ordered the waiting aircraft to be re-armed for another strike at Midway.[22]

To further complicate matters, the first American bombers from Midway soon arrived without fighter escort to attack the Japanese carriers. Four medium B-26 Marauder bombers and six Avenger torpedo-bombers scored no hits and lost half a dozen of their number. An Avenger crashed on *Akagi* without causing significant damage. The ability of the Midway base to launch these attacks may have confirmed Nagumo's impression that Midway needed a second strike. Preparations for that continued.

As Japanese aircraft were being hurriedly rearmed on the decks of the carriers, at 7.28 a.m. a scout plane launched from the cruiser *Tone* signalled that ten ships, 'apparently enemy' had been sighted 240 miles to the north east of Midway. The scout plane had been late launching due to a faulty catapult. The message took some more valuable minutes to reach Nagumo from the flagship's radio room. This was the first news Nagumo had received that American warships were within range. He ordered a halt to the re-arming of aircraft for a second strike on Midway at 7.45 a.m. and instructed the scout plane's crew: 'Ascertain ship types and maintain contact.'[23]

More American Midway-based aircraft arrived to attack the Japanese fleet carriers. Staggered launch times and different aircraft speeds had caused squadrons to arrive in waves at different times. At 8.10 a.m. fifteen B-17s bombed the carriers from 20,000 feet without scoring any hits, though several were claimed by aircrew and the warships had to undertake wild evasive action. Before long sixteen Marine Corps Douglas Dauntless dive-bombers commanded by Major Lofton Henderson launched a shallow glide-bombing attack. The squadron was too inexperienced to attack by means of a steep dive. Half the aircraft were picked off by defending fighters and anti-aircraft fire. They did not hit their targets. Attacks by eleven old Vindicator dive-bombers failed to score any hits either. Japanese watchers were unimpressed by the performance of the American aviators. The series of attacks by Midway-based aircraft concluded without causing Nagumo's carriers worthwhile damage.

Whilst this series of attacks was underway, the Japanese scout plane had reported back to Nagumo's flagship at 8.09 a.m.: 'Enemy ships are five cruisers and five destroyers.' But ten minutes later came the ominous message: 'Enemy force accompanied by what appears to be an aircraft carrier bringing up the rear.'[24] Rear-Admiral Tamon Yamaguchi, commanding Carrier Division Two in *Hiryu*, advised Nagumo by lamp signal to launch an immediate attack with whatever aircraft were armed with anti-shipping ordnance and ready to fly. The cautious Nagumo, however, decided against launching an attack without a fighter escort. Rear-Admiral Ryunosuke Kusaka, the First Air Fleet's Chief of Staff, later commented: 'I was not entirely against his [Yamaguchi's] view of launching the attack force without re-equipping, but I couldn't agree with him on the point of letting them go without fighter cover, because I witnessed how enemy planes without fighter cover were almost annihilated by our fighters mercilessly.'[25] It was now necessary to clear the decks of the carriers so that the Midway strike force could land before running out of fuel. Some of the Zeros patrolling over the carriers also needed to land to refuel. Nagumo decided to recover the Midway strike force and reorganise his air groups to launch a balanced strike at the sighted American carrier. At 8.37 a.m. the signal was given to begin landing the Midway strike force. The carriers' hanger decks became littered with munitions and fuel as preparations went ahead for the next round of operations. The last aircraft landed on *Akagi* at 9.18 a.m. Nagumo's staff made plans to start launching a new strike at 10.30 a.m.

At this time Admiral Spruance's Task Force 16 was steaming in ocean to the north east of Nagumo. The American carriers had only one target to focus upon, namely the Japanese carriers. Each American carrier had an air group of seventy to eighty aircraft. Spruance, in consultation with his Chief of Staff, decided to begin the launch of his aircraft at 7 a.m., when his task force would be 150 miles from the reported location of the Japanese. Task Force 16 would need to turn away from the Japanese and sail into the wind to launch aircraft. It would take up to an hour to launch all aircraft, meaning that the carriers would be about 175 miles from the Japanese by the time the launch had been completed.[26] This was an extreme range for some American aircraft, but Spruance wanted to hit the Japanese carriers while they were still recovering the force known to have been sent to attack Midway.

Spruance's powerful strike force of sixty-seven dive-bombers, twenty-nine torpedo-bombers and twenty fighters began launching from *Enterprise* and *Hornet* just after 7 a.m. as planned. Aircraft heavily laden with fuel and weaponry staggered off moving flight decks.[27] Some fighters were retained as a combat air patrol. An impatient Spruance ordered the first batch of aircraft to head off for their target before the total force had completed its launch.

Admiral Fletcher delayed launching *Yorktown*'s air strike in case further reports were received of other Japanese carriers, but around 9 a.m. he finally dispatched his torpedo-bombers and half of his dive-bombers with a small fighter escort. The squadrons of Task Forces 16 and 17 were launched at different times, from different carriers, and soon became widely separated. As Nagumo had started to sail back north east – rather than the predicted south east – this further confused the navigation of American aviators. Nagumo had changed course by ninety degrees as scout planes had warned of approaching American aircraft.

When the first of the aircraft from *Hornet* and *Enterprise* reached the estimated position of the Japanese carriers they found the ocean empty. *Enterprise*'s fighters returned to their carrier when they ran short of fuel. *Hornet*'s dive-bombers and fighters elected to turn south towards Midway to search in that direction. Some of *Hornet*'s dive-bombers landed at Midway and others returned to their carrier, but all of *Hornet*'s Wildcat fighters had to ditch in the ocean when their fuel ran out.

Hornet's torpedo-bombers, unlike other *Hornet* squadrons, had turned north from the empty rendezvous point as smoke was seen on the horizon. The previous evening the squadron's Commander John C. Waldron had advised his aircrew not to pass up the opportunity to write to their families. *Hornet*'s Torpedo Squadron 8 found their target and attacked, but all Devastators were shot down by Zeroes and anti-aircraft fire. The squadron was wiped out but for one survivor, Ensign George Gay. All the rest of the thirty aircrew died. An injured Gay climbed out of the wreckage of his aircraft and clung onto floating debris amid the Japanese fleet. *Enterprise's* and *Yorktown's* torpedo-bombers were dealt with in an equally savage manner. Twenty of twenty-six aircraft were shot-down. Some torpedoes were dropped but no hits were scored. It had been a remarkable disaster.

At 10 a.m. Nagumo was confident the day was progressing well. The aerial combat had enthralled spectators on the carriers and the ocean surface was littered with the wreckage of American aircraft. At 10.20 a.m. Nagumo gave the order to launch the planned strike against the American carrier force. On the deck of *Akagi* pilots were warming their engines. The great ship turned into the wind; the first Zero flew off; then everything was changed.

What caught out Nagumo's carriers was the late arrival of *Enterprise's* dive-bomber group, which had been guided to the target at the eleventh hour by luck, guesswork and brilliant visibility once the clouds had cleared. Lieutenant-Commander Wade McClusky's force of Douglas Dauntless dive-bombers had failed to sight the Japanese fleet at the original projected point of interception. McClusky had decided to fly on for thirty-five miles and then turned his force to fly in a north westerly direction. Sweeping on, searching the empty ocean, McClusky's dive-bombers had chanced upon the Japanese destroyer *Arashi* at 9.55 a.m. *Arashi* had been detached from Nagumo's main fleet to hunt an American submarine. *Arashi*, having failed to destroy the submarine, was sighted speeding in a northerly direction to catch up with the carriers. Seeing the white trail of the destroyer through a break in the clouds, McClusky correctly guessed she was hurrying to rejoin a larger force and plotted a similar course.

Coincidentally, *Yorktown's* dive-bombers and fighters were also closing on Nagumo's fleet at this time. Lieutenant-Commander Maxwell F. Leslie's dive-bombers had taken off well after McClusky's force, but Leslie's navigation to locate the Japanese carriers had been guided by better information. Leslie's own aircraft had lost its bomb soon after take-off due to an equipment malfunction, as had three other aircraft.

It was 10.25 a.m. when the American dive-bombers attacked Nagumo's carriers. The recently concluded series of doomed torpedo-bomber attacks had drawn down and scattered the thin umbrella of defending Zeros. Diving at a seventy degree angle, McClusky's dive-bombers were able to release their armour-piercing 500 or 1,0000-pound bombs over the decks of the carriers before the Zeros could catch them. Commander James Thatch, a *Yorktown* fighter pilot, was battling for his life amid a 'beehive' of Zeros when he caught a glimpse of the cascading dive-bombers. 'I saw this glint in the sun and it just looked like a beautiful silver waterfall; these dive-bombers coming down.'[28] Three aircraft let their bombs go above the flagship *Akagi* at 2,500 feet. On the deck of *Akagi* Fuchida fell to his knees when he heard a lookout suddenly give warning of dive-bombers. The Japanese carriers had no radar and mediocre anti-aircraft armament. The first bomb missed but the other two struck the flight deck to penetrate to the hanger deck and ignite a store of torpedoes. The hanger deck was littered with munitions and secondary explosions soon had flames sheeting skywards. Heated machine guns sprayed bullets in all directions. Aircraft and men were blown off the flight deck and into the sea. Fuchida recorded:

> Looking about, I was horrified at the destruction that had been wrought in a matter of seconds. There was a huge hole in the flight deck just behind the amid-ships elevator. The elevator itself, twisted like molten glass, was drooping into the hanger. Deck plates reeled upward in grotesque configurations. Planes stood tail up, belching livid flame and jet-black smoke. Reluctant tears streamed down my checks as I watched the fires spread.[29]

The smoke and heat of the fires overwhelmed the valiant attempts of fire-fighting parties to bring them under control. As fire threatened the bridge, Nagumo was persuaded to leave the flagship. He and his Chief of Staff climbed through a window on the bridge and transferred to a waiting light cruiser. The official portrait of the Emperor was moved to a destroyer. *Akagi* had a single fire-extinguishing system. When the main pump was damaged the water supply failed.[30]

Bomb hits doomed *Kaga* about the same time. The island superstructure rising above the flight deck was wrecked by explosions. A small fuel truck blew-up near the bridge, throwing a sheet of flame into the structure. Most men on the bridge were killed or wounded, including the captain. Secondary detonations among munitions on the flight and hanger decks did enormous additional damage. Fire-fighting pumps and hoses were broken by bomb blasts.

Dive-bombers from *Yorktown* chimed in to deliver a lethal dose of bombs to the carrier *Soryu*, the third carrier to be attacked. The seventeen Dauntlesses probably scored only three hits, but that was enough. The first hit blew an elevator against the bridge. So bad was the damage on *Soryu* that within twenty minutes the ship was ablaze. The pilots of the Zeros caught so badly out of position by the dive-bombers' attack pursued the retreating American aircraft, many of which were shot down endeavouring to return to their carriers.[31]

Hiryu, the last remaining Japanese fleet carrier, escaped attack and became separated from her burning sisters in the course of evasive manoeuvres. About 11 a.m. *Hiryu* launched the first of a two wave counter-attack against the American carriers. Lieutenant Tomonaga led both attacks. He may have left for the second strike without enough fuel for the return journey due to a damaged wing tank. *Yorktown* was found by the Japanese in the early afternoon. The attacks were pressed home with determination. One Japanese pilot was seen shaking his fist as he pulled up over *Yorktown*. The American carrier was badly damaged by three bombs in the first attack and two torpedoes in the second attack. Japanese aircraft losses were also very heavy. Some Japanese wrongly believed that the two attacks on *Yorktown* had disabled two different American carriers.[32] *Yorktown* was crippled but did not sink. Two days later the Japanese submarine *I-168* would torpedo her again, and the carrier would sink early the following morning. A destroyer alongside the carrier at the time *I-168* struck had her back broken by the same salvo of torpedoes.

Hiryu became the main focus for the next round of American air attacks. Mid-afternoon on 4 June a scout found *Hiryu* only 110 miles to the west. After the American strike force had found her about 5 p.m., the carrier was quickly crippled.

Aboard *Yamato*, far to the rear, a signal officer handed Admiral Yamamoto a radio message that three of Nagumo's fleet carriers had been heavily damaged by bombing and were ablaze. The admiral groaned as he read the message. He and his staff were shocked by the news. Yamamoto ordered his battleships towards Nagumo's stricken carrier striking force. News that an American carrier had been badly, perhaps fatally damaged, was encouraging, but late in the afternoon came a report that *Hiryu* had also been crippled. A staff officer asked Yamamoto, 'But how can we apologise to His Majesty for this defeat?' The admiral replied: 'Leave that to me. I am the only one who must apologise to His Majesty.'[33]

The blazing and crippled Japanese carriers were slow to sink. Attendant destroyers, on a warm summer's day, rescued the crews, some of whom had suffered terrible burns in the raging fires. *Soryu's* Captain Ryusaku Yanigimoto refused to leave his ship despite efforts to persuade him. He was last seen singing the national anthem amid enveloping smoke. *Soryu* finally went under at 7.15 p.m.; *Kaga* sank at 7.25 p.m.; *Akagi* was scuttled before the next dawn. Combined Fleet staff had worried that the crippled *Akagi* might 'become a museum piece in the Potomac River' if she was not sunk. At 8.20 a.m. on 5 June *Hiryu* was also torpedoed by Japanese destroyers to send her to a watery grave. On *Hiryu* Captain Tomeo Kaku and Admiral Tamon Yamaguchi had waited for their end on the bridge. An officer ordered to abandon ship overheard Yamaguchi say as the ship listed: 'Let us enjoy the beauty of the moon. How bright it shines.'[34] Another account says the two men joked of using the ship's payroll to buy a better billet in hell. The suicide of an admiral as gifted as Yamaguchi was a definite benefit to the Allied cause.

Yamamoto still had a powerful fleet under his command, but he was reluctant to continue the campaign after losing four fleet carriers. The force sailing to the Aleutians was too far away to quickly rejoin the main force. Yamamoto broke off the battle during the night as he knew his fleet would probably be attacked by American carrier aircraft the next morning. Unwilling to risk facing the gunpower of Japanese battleships in a night action, Spruance had also retired away from his opponent during the early part of the night. Some of Spruance's aviators felt their task force should have aggressively steamed west during the night for a dawn air strike at whatever targets were on offer.[35]

During the night the Japanese heavy cruiser *Mikuma* was damaged in a collision. She was sunk the next day with heavy loss of life by American aircraft. Aerial photography vividly captured the listing and burning ship, images of which featured in Allied newspapers reporting the Midway triumph. At sunset on 6 June the American task forces turned back for Pearl Harbor. As in the Coral Sea fighting, the surface ships of the two fleets at Midway had never been within visual distance of each other.

On 7 June the islands of Attu and Kiska in the western Aleutians were occupied by a Japanese landing force. The weather was so poor in the region that it was several days before American reconnaissance could confirm that the ungarrisoned islands had been lost. Three of the last combatants to die as a result of the Midway operation proved to be captured American airmen. As the Combined Fleet retired, one of the Americans was beheaded and the other two were tied to heavy objects and thrown overboard.[36]

The balance of losses in the fighting had strongly favoured the United States. 3,000 Japanese servicemen had died; four fleet carriers and a heavy cruiser had been sunk; four veteran air groups had been devastated. By comparison, American fatalities were only a tenth of the Japanese toll. *Yorktown*, a destroyer and 147 aircraft had been destroyed in the battle.[37]

After the Pearl Harbor raid Yamamoto and the Japanese leadership had wasted almost six months before launching another central Pacific offensive. Nimitz thought they had waited far too long.

> All the time the main enemy of Yamamoto's Combined Fleet was the U.S. Navy at Pearl Harbor which the Japanese left alone after their quick hit-and-run raid. The fact that the Japanese did not return to Pearl Harbor and complete the job was the greatest help for us, for they left their principal enemy with the time to catch his breath, restore his morale and rebuild his forces.[38]

Thanks to the triumph of Allied code-breaking, Nimitz had possessed the information he needed to risk his main carrier force in an engagement to defend Midway. Good intelligence allowed him to concentrate limited forces at the most important place. Nimitz believed: 'Had we lacked early information of the Japanese movements, and had we been caught with carrier forces dispersed … the Battle of Midway would have ended differently.' Admiral Fletcher commented in a similar vein: 'After a battle … people talk a lot about how the decisions were methodically reached, but actually there's always a hell of a lot of groping around.'[39] Thanks to America's vast ship-building programme, Nimitz was well aware that he was only gambling with the first of many American fleets. That must have been a comforting thought when it became necessary to take important command decisions. Nonetheless, American commanders took their chances aggressively, in combination with a number of other favourable factors, to doom the Combined Fleet to defeat at Midway.

Yamamoto has been greatly criticised for unnecessarily spreading his fleet across the Pacific in several forces. So confused was the Combined Fleet's deployment that numerical superiority was turned into near parity of forces at the decisive point. Yamamoto had further confused matters by giving Nagumo's carrier force two difficult and contradictory tasks. Nagumo had been ordered to both suppress Midway and sink the American carriers. Yamamoto and his Combined Fleet staff conveniently assumed that the surprised American carriers would only put in an appearance after Midway had been devastated. If all eight Japanese carriers had been concentrated together the battle might have been a different story. The four smaller carriers, however, only shipped as many aircraft as a single fleet carrier, and their potential impact should not be exaggerated. The smaller carriers might best have been used to strike Midway, leaving the four fleet carriers exclusively to hunt for the American carriers instead of wasting their strength against the atoll.

Yamamoto might also have integrated his battleships and the carrier striking force into a single fleet. *Yamato* and other warships could have helped thicken the anti-aircraft screen of the carriers. The reconnaissance floatplanes carried by the battleships and heavy cruisers might have supported the carriers' air groups. Instead Yamamoto's heavy units had pointlessly stayed far to the rear of Nagumo's carriers.

Admiral Ugaki, Yamamoto's Chief of Staff, later observed:

> In all sea battles since the outbreak of war – namely, the Pearl Harbor attack, the attack upon Port Darwin or the attack upon Ceylon – we achieved brilliant success under circumstances where no powerful enemy air force was in the operational area. It was just like striking a sitting enemy.[40]

Ugaki also wrote with perception: 'There are questions as to whether the enemy knew our plan, apart from its extent.' Japanese preparations for the Midway operation had certainly been sloppy and arrogant. With hindsight, war games carried out by the Combined Fleet had been hopelessly rigged to suit the convenience of the planners. In all likelihood the attempted landing at Midway would have been a disaster. The defending American garrison was too strong for the relatively weak Japanese invasion force.

After the event, many Japanese officers regretted that Midway had been attacked before at least one of the two fleet carriers involved in the Coral Sea battle became available. Six months of victories had led to over-confidence, the so-called 'victory disease'. A long chain of victories against surprised or weak opponents had meant that the Imperial Japanese Navy had not learnt how to properly plan and carry out operations in the face of what proved to be a first-class opponent. Yamamoto seems to have acquired an aura of invincibility that placed his conduct beyond criticism. In reality, Yamamoto had few ideas about the complicated tactics of carrier warfare. This was probably why he had been content to leave so much in Nagumo's hands.

The Japanese authorities tried to portray the battle as a victory. The returning fleet's crews were confined to base or dispersed overseas to keep news of the defeat away from the civilian population. According to Vice-Admiral Nobutake Kondo, commander of the Midway invasion fleet, 'Our forces suffered a defeat so decisive and so grave that details of it were kept a guarded secret of a limited circle even within the Japanese navy. Even after the war, few among high-ranking officers were familiar with the details of the Midway operation.'[41] Nagumo, despite losing all four of his fleet carriers, was allowed to retain his position. On 10 June Imperial headquarters announced that in a recent fleet engagement two American and one Japanese aircraft carriers had been sunk. Propaganda aside, there was no chance of Japan replacing the carriers lost at Midway until 1944. An under-developed pilot training system also meant that the aircrew lost at Midway would take time to replace. Pilot loss rates in the China war since 1937 had not encouraged the Japanese to build up the training establishments needed for an aerial war against a western opponent.

After Midway the Japanese sat back on the defensive. Post-war Japan's former Navy Minister, Admiral Yonai, was asked to nominate the turning point in the Pacific war. Yonai replied: 'Once the war had started, I would pick either Midway or our retreat from Guadalcanal as the turning point, after which I was certain there was no chance for success – I pick Midway principally from the naval standpoint because of the heavy fleet losses suffered there.' At the start of June 1942 the Japanese navy had been at the peak of its fortunes. With the loss of four fleet carriers, however, the weapons system that had raided Pearl Harbor had been dismantled. Admiral King, Chief of Naval Operations in Washington, said of the Midway battle that it had 'restored the balance of naval power in the Pacific'.[42] Midway cost the Japanese the strategic initiative at sea.

In hindsight, the United States Navy cast off any claim to the status of an underdog after the victory at Midway. Yet every top dog has to win its way upwards at some point. Midway was the place at which American naval power moved into the ascendancy. The Coral Sea and Midway battles also made it clear that Britain's Royal Navy was passing back to the status of a second rank naval power. British Commonwealth warships had only a minor presence in the Coral Sea and no presence at Midway, even though Japan was the Axis power with the strongest surface fleet and a great deal of British colonial territory remained at risk in the Far East.

Once the situation in the Pacific came under control, Washington was able to pursue the 'Germany-first' strategy agreed with Churchill. The Japanese would never venture strong forces into the central Pacific or Indian Oceans again. The American fleet carrier *Saratoga* arrived at Pearl Harbor shortly after the Midway battle. She had recently completed repairs in California. The fleet carrier *Wasp* soon entered the Pacific through the Panama Canal from the Atlantic Fleet. Nimitz already had replacements for the two carriers lost in the Coral Sea and at Midway.

On 7 August 1942 the Americans took an early advantage of their victory at Midway by returning to the Coral Sea region and landing marines at Guadalcanal and Tulagi, at the southern end of the Solomon Islands. The convoy enjoyed an escort that featured the carriers *Saratoga*, *Wasp* and *Enterprise*. This set in motion a unique campaign of operations on land, at sea and in the air. To their surprise, the Japanese found themselves drawn into a defensive battle of attrition, the losses of which the Americans were more able to absorb. The course of the war in the Pacific was changing.

As for Admiral Yamamoto, the badly defeated commander at Midway, a further costly defeat at Guadalcanal caused him more anguish. He wrote of the campaign: 'Guadalcanal was a very fierce battle. I do not know what to do next. Nor am I happy about facing my officers and men who have fought so hard without fear of death.'[43] Yamamoto met his own end in an American attack on his aircraft at Bougainville on 18 April 1943. United States codebreakers had discovered his whereabouts and, as at Midway, signals intelligence played a major role in Yamamoto's downfall.

8
El Alamein

By the summer of 1942, the continents of Europe and Asia, and the great oceans of the Pacific and the Atlantic, had been engulfed by war. The conflict had entered the Indian Ocean and was touching the fringes of the continents of North America, South America and Australia. The globe's remaining inhabited continent, Africa, had also been drawn into the war. This was hardly surprising as it was only separated from Europe by the Mediterranean, the largest of the world's inland seas. The terrain of northern Africa was mostly sand and rock. In the 1940s the region was sparsely populated outside the Nile delta. Yet northern Africa was one of the paths to the Middle East, a vital strategic junction of three continents.

The Suez Canal had been opened from the eastern Mediterranean to the Red Sea and Indian Ocean as far back as 1869. Britain had invaded and occupied Egypt in 1882 partly to secure the canal from rivals. Since that time Britain had gained possession of a series of colonies and protectorates in the region. The Middle East theatre had seen important campaigns during the First World War between British and Ottoman forces. Egypt had ceased to be a British protectorate in 1922, but Britain had retained the right to base troops in the country and the Suez Canal continued to be a vital artery between Europe and the Far East and India. The early development of western oil interests in the Persian Gulf had created an additional strategic motive for the British presence in the Middle East.

The Second World War came to the Middle East in June 1940 when the French armistice with Germany and Italy's entry to the conflict threw Britain's position in the Mediterranean suddenly into jeopardy. Mussolini wanted to use his colonial bases in Africa to turn the Mediterranean into an Italian lake at Britain's expense. Churchill's government was determined to maintain Britain's position in the Middle East, and had no intention of retreating in the face of the Italian threat. Northern Africa and the Middle East may not have been vital interests for Germany, but for Britain and Italy the opposite was the case.[1]

After the defeat in France, the Middle East had remained a viable theatre for British ground forces. Lying at the geographic centre of the British Empire, Egypt and Palestine began to receive reinforcements from India, Australia, South Africa and New Zealand. Regular convoys from the United Kingdom added troops to the already large British garrison in the region. From June 1940

Britain's Middle East Command was opposed by large Italian colonial armies stationed in Libya and Abyssinia.

The size of the armies involved in the campaigns in North Africa was not large compared to the campaigns in Europe. This made the conflict more personalised and gladiatorial, like the battles of an earlier era. Away from the Nile delta and land of the Pharaohs, the deserts of North Africa were a sea-like wasteland, with few towns or geographic features of significance. The flatness of the desert gave tactical significance to mere folds and undulations in the ground. Dust and shimmering haze might temporarily disrupt otherwise good lines of visibility across a bleak and gritty landscape.

The desert had few natural resources apart from 'camel dung'. Every ton of material had to be shipped to the region and hauled by road in the absence of railways. Even the distribution of water posed a constant problem, as water springs and palm tree-lined oases were far and few between. War in the desert had the illusion of simplicity but the broader Mediterranean theatre featured the intertwining of land, sea and air fighting to create the most modern of conflicts.[2]

Not long after Mussolini's entry to the war, a series of Italian defeats on land caused a crisis for the Axis in North Africa. From December 1940 to February 1941 outnumbered British imperial forces advanced 500 miles across the wastes of western Egypt and eastern Libya in a campaign that resulted in the capture of 130,000 Italian prisoners. Jokes about Italian tanks having five reverse gears began to gain currency. Meanwhile, in east Africa British forces from the Sudan and Kenya had developed another successful offensive in Italian Abyssinia. There was heavy fighting at Keren in February and March 1941 and the capital of Abyssinia, Addis Ababa, fell on 6 April.

An alarmed and angry Hitler knew that he had to prop up Mussolini in North Africa. Late the previous year General Ritter von Thoma had visited Libya and had reported that only motorised German forces would be useful in the barren wastelands of North Africa. Hitler reluctantly decided to dispatch General Erwin Rommel and a panzer corps to Tripoli. Rommel arrived in Africa on 12 February and his command became known as the Afrika Korps. The Afrika Korps would need ten times as many motorised vehicles as a standard German corps in Russia.[3]

The charismatic and self-confident Rommel went on to achieve enduring fame in North Africa. In his high-peaked hat with sand goggles, field glasses slung around his neck, Rommel conformed to a heroic-style of personal leadership that was thought to have vanished in the maelstrom of the First World War. In France in 1940 Rommel had already revealed his flair as a tactician, often in the face of grave logistical difficulty. An Afrika Korps staff officer, Major von Mellenthin, described Rommel as a stiff, blunt and difficult man to work with. 'He spared those around him as little as he spared himself. An iron constitution and nerves of steel were needed.'[4] Rommel's intention to use panzer forces to penetrate deep into an enemy's rear had the potential to create strategic opportunities where they could not otherwise have existed.

Rommel's Afrika Korps and accompanying Italian troops launched an offensive in Libya in late March 1941. Rommel's forces quickly achieved success. Tobruk was besieged and British troops were pushed back to the frontier of Egypt. A British expeditionary force was also driven out of Greece and Crete during April and May. Surprisingly, the British position in the Middle East steadily recovered across the following months as Hitler's invasion of the Soviet Union ensured that few reinforcements were available for Rommel. There was never any possibility of the Mediterranean supplanting eastern Europe as the most important theatre in German strategy. According to Thoma, a 'great pincer movement against the Middle East ... was never a serious plan. It was vaguely discussed in Hitler's entourage, but our General Staff never agreed with it, or regarded it as practicable.'[5]

Across the middle months of 1941, the 9th Australian Division and other British units continued to hold out at Tobruk. British forces also fought brief campaigns to secure Iraq, Syria, Lebanon and Iran for the Allied cause. Middle East Command was now able to focus its energies against Rommel in the deserts of Libya. And British reinforcements had continued to flow into the Nile delta. From June 1941 to June 1942 Middle East Command expanded from 550,000 to 820,000 men.[6] On 18 November 1941 Operation Crusader was launched by the newly named Eighth Army to relieve Tobruk. The port was recaptured and an advance made as far west into Libya as El Agheila. Yet the Eighth Army was bundled back to Gazala in January 1942, not far to the west of Tobruk. In the Far East, the Japanese entry to the war saw a number of veteran divisions sail from the Nile delta for India and the Far East.

In the House of Commons, on 27 January 1942, Churchill unwisely said of Rommel: 'We have a very daring and skilful opponent against us, and, may I say across the havoc of war, a great general.' The Afrika Korps's commander had certainly caught the imagination of his enemies. Rommel launched a new offensive on 27 May 1942. Making good use of the open desert stretching to the south, Afrika Korps routed the British by driving into the rear of the main Eighth Army defensive line at Gazala. Uncoordinated and piecemeal British counter-attacks caused the Afrika Korps few serious problems. The Eighth Army's tanks, infantry and artillery failed to cooperate effectively, whereas the Germans managed to combine their arms into an ensemble. Rommel's aggressive and personal command methods proved a triumph.

By 21 June Tobruk had fallen, its garrison ignominiously surrendered. Another 33,000 prisoners were taken, including the 2nd South African Division, the loss of which was a terrible blow to that dominion. Rommel's forces also captured at Tobruk 1,400 tons of fuel, 5,000 tons of stores and 2,000 vehicles.[7]

Axis planning earlier in the year had included speculative preparations for an assault on Malta once British forces had been cleared from Libya. Italian military leaders and Field-Marshal Kesselring, whose *Luftwaffe* forces faced Malta, were keen to go forward with the aerial and sea assault. Hitler and other German officials were less keen on the project and plans had never been finalised. There were doubts as to whether the Italian Navy would be up to the challenge. At Rommel's urging Hitler quickly authorised a pursuit of routed British forces deep into Egypt. Rommel was promoted to field-marshal. At that time a major German offensive in Russia was getting underway, and it was logical for Hitler and his OKW headquarters to support similar offensive operations in North Africa. Malta would not be attacked and instead was to be contained by a renewed aerial offensive mounted from bases in Sicily. Captured supplies, the opening of the port of Tobruk, and the air route from Crete would be utilised to meet the logistical demands of an invasion of Egypt.

Churchill was in Washington staying at the White House at the time of Tobruk's fall. Roosevelt generously offered immediately to send 300 new-model Sherman tanks to the Middle East. Churchill wrote of the loss of Tobruk: 'This was one of the heaviest blows I can recall during the war.'[8] The defeat was unexpected and the reputation of British arms had been badly tarnished. The Prime Minister's bitter memory of the rapid fall of Singapore the previous February was still fresh. General Sir Claude Auchinleck, Commander-in-Chief Middle East, dismissed the Eighth Army's commander. Auchinleck vacated his headquarters in Cairo to take personal charge of the Eighth Army as it streamed back across Egypt towards the Nile delta.

The sudden loss of Libya and western Egypt exposed British convoys sailing to Malta to great risks. In mid-June, of seventeen transports sailing in two convoys only two reached Malta. The rest were sunk or turned back. In August the aircraft carrier *Eagle* would be sunk escorting another Malta convoy sailing from Gibraltar. Nonetheless, British submarines and aircraft operating from Malta continued to punish Italian convoys sailing to North Africa. They sank thirty-seven Axis ships sailing for North Africa from June to September, with losses varying from a low of six per cent of all cargo in July to a high of twenty-five per cent of general cargo and forty-one per cent of fuel in August. The official Italian naval history would later conclude that over sixteen per cent of all war-time shipping carrying supplies to North Africa was sunk.[9] The battle in the sea lanes around Malta had a constant impact on the logistics and strategy of the North African campaign.

El Alamein was fifty miles west of Alexandria and the fringe of the Nile delta. It was the last defensible position of any significance west of those places, and the logical place for the Eighth Army to make a determined stand. There were few organised posts at El Alamein in June 1942 and certainly no 'line' existed, though that was confidently broadcast to the world by Allied radio and press agencies. The Royal Navy was forced to evacuate Alexandria on 2 July. In Cairo British diplomats and headquarters staff made bonfires of official documents, to create a local 'Ash Wednesday'. Egyptian nationalists became quietly enthused and rumour said that Shepheard's Hotel was preparing a suite for the arrival of Rommel. The cities of the Nile delta were prizes worth taking. Afrika Korps radio broadcast on 1 July that the ladies of Cairo and Alexandria were to 'make ready to receive them to-night'.[10] If the Eighth Army failed to hold its ground at El Alamein it might next be necessary to retreat beyond the Suez Canal to Palestine and southwards along the Nile valley to the Sudanese frontier.

The El Alamein position took its name from a wayside railway station, south of which was a thirty-eight mile gap between the coast and the Qattara Depression. The coastal gap formed a funnel for an invader crossing Egypt. A steep rocky escarpment at the southern end of the gap fell 700 feet to the Qattara Depression, a vast salt marsh stretching southwards to the great Sand Sea. Motor vehicles became bogged in a salt marsh, which effectively made the Qattara Depression impossible for mechanised formations. Much of the thirty-eight mile gap was very flat, barren, stony and broken by ragged thorn bushes. Occasional low ridges and small hillocks of hard limestone provided good going for vehicles. Ruweisat, Miteiriya and Alam el Halfa ridges were low features, but were high enough to matter in a landscape in which men typically hugged the earth. There was a single coastal road lined by a few houses and fig orchards.

Rommel had every reason to chance his arm to keep the beaten Eighth Army on the run as it wearily retreated along the coastal road. He wasted no time preparing to attack El Alamein, though the Afrika Korps was at the end of a long and precarious supply line. Mellenthin observed: 'It is quite possible that if Rommel had got his divisions across the British rear, they would have been stampeded once more into a headlong flight.'[11] From 1–3 July Rommel probed and attacked the El Alamein position with his advanced guard. Weak German columns were halted by fighting with 'boxes' of South Africans, Anglo-Indians and New Zealanders, who were supported by an assortment of British armoured units. On 2 July Rommel's panzer divisions had only twenty-six tanks fit to fight and, unsurprisingly, the following day he called off his half-hearted offensive.[12] General Auchinleck was aware of the weakness of Rommel's forces due to Ultra signals intelligence and his army's wireless intercepts. He quickly moved to counter-attack using fresh formations brought up from Palestine.

For the rest of the month of July the Eighth Army launched a series of attacks. Signals intelligence helped to identify the location of Italian formations and these were targeted by preference. The Eighth Army's infantry fought effectively but the Royal Armoured Corps was still regularly outwitted by the Afrika Korps, as had been the case at Gazala. The New Zealander's Brigadier Howard Kippenberger commented:

> At this time there was throughout Eighth Army, not only in the New Zealand Division, a most intense distrust, almost hatred, of our armour. Everywhere one

heard tales of the other arms being let down; it was regarded as axiomatic that the tanks would not be where they were wanted in time.[13]

On the last day of July Auchinleck called off his offensive, his army exhausted. He reported to London on 31 July that since the start of the month the Eighth Army had lost 13,250 killed, wounded and missing.

Despite the development of a stalemate at El Alamein during July, the summer of 1942 had been a time of triumph for the Afrika Korps. From 26 May to the end of July, 60,000 prisoners had been taken and total Eighth Army losses had amounted to 80–90,000. Axis casualties for the same period had been a modest 2,300 Germans killed, 7,500 wounded and 2,700 prisoners. Italian losses were 1,000 killed, 10,000 wounded and 5,000 prisoners.[14]

Big changes were afoot for Middle East Command. On 25 July the vital decision was taken by British and American leaders to invade French North Africa at the Atlantic end of the Mediterranean. This promised a dramatic change to the course of events in northern Africa. Early in August Churchill and the Chief of the Imperial General Staff, General Sir Alan Brooke, flew to Cairo. (Churchill would later fly on to visit Stalin in Moscow). Churchill had decided to replace Auchinleck with Lieutenant-General Sir Harold Alexander. Churchill wrote that dismissing Auchinleck was like 'shooting a noble stag', but his experience of the First World War had taught him that mediocre generals seldom improved their performance and should not be persevered with. Auchinleck had held Rommel at El Alamein in the July battles, but the disasters of May–June had been a humiliation for British arms and he could not escape his share of responsibility. Churchill was a great admirer of the aristocratic Alexander, who had displayed common sense and ambassadorial calm in the most trying of circumstances at Dunkirk in 1940 and during the retreat from Burma earlier in 1942. The Eighth Army's new commander was to have been General Gott, but he met an untimely death when his aircraft was attacked and crashed. The appointment was given instead to Lieutenant-General Sir Bernard Montgomery. Shortly after Montgomery's arrival the New Zealanders' General Freyberg told his new boss: 'I feel terribly sorry for you. This is the grave of lieutenant-generals. None of them stays here more than a few months.'[15] The British needed success in the autumn of 1942 after almost three years in which they had lost most of their battles in most theatres of war. The fiasco of the 19 August Dieppe raid was more bad news for British leaders and commanders privy to full knowledge of what had gone wrong.

The advent of Montgomery, who assumed command on 13 August, introduced a new element into the desert war. 'Monty', the son of a Church of England bishop and a domineering mother, had been born in 1887. He was a dedicated, wilful and single-minded professional soldier, with a strong belief in organised, planned battle. He was a thin man and a little below middle height.

He had a rasping voice and sharp features that the ill-disposed would call 'rat-like'. Montgomery had been seriously wounded early in the First World War and had spent the rest of that conflict as a staff officer. During the interwar period he had twice been an instructor at Staff Colleges. He was a natural teacher.

Montgomery was familiar with the Middle East. As a battalion commander at Alexandria in the early 1930s, he had taken part in night exercises in the desert. In the late 1930s Montgomery had commanded a division in Palestine during the Arab revolt. He again proved himself as a successful divisional commander in the Dunkirk campaign, and was quickly promoted within Home Forces to head South-Eastern Command. Montgomery seldom missed opportunities to add to his reputation within army circles for eccentricity and controversy.

The new general quickly imposed his personality on the Eighth Army. He sought to raise morale among his soldiers. This was overdue and there was no denying the moral supremacy Afrika Korps had established. An Eighth Army Chief of Staff wrote of British forces: 'Their morale had not been broken. There was, however, what can be described as a state of bewilderment ... There appeared to be a sort of craving for guidance and inspiration.'[16] In a round of addresses given to his troops, Montgomery asserted that they would 'hit Rommel and his army for six right out of Africa'. The message was simple and the willingness of a commander to meet and talk to his troops had an invigorating and refreshing effect on men unused to such conduct. Montgomery believed that effective public relations were a legitimate part of leadership. A senior German officer commented that, 'The war in the desert ceased to be a game when Montgomery took over.' Montgomery was also an infantryman in the best sense of the word. In his Eighth Army the infantry would be the premier arm. Other arms would be compelled to support the infantry, not the other way around. A new tactical headquarters of caravans and vehicles was set up near the coast and the headquarters of the Desert Air Force. Montgomery had been on the receiving end of the *Luftwaffe* at Dunkirk and he was undoubtedly an 'air-minded' general. New staff officers and subordinate commanders were appointed as the new broom continued his sweep.

In time Montgomery's behaviour would reveal an egotism and boastfulness that would compromise his relations with other senior commanders. An early indication of this was exaggerated claims by Montgomery that Auchinleck had been seriously contemplating a withdrawal into the Nile delta. Contingency plans had been made, and panicky burning of documents had taken place at rear headquarters, but Auchinleck had fought a hard though costly battle to hold the Alamein gap.[17] Montgomery was fortunate to inherit a stable front, a short supply line and an Eighth Army that was larger and better equipped than ever before. Over 800 new tanks would be unloaded in the delta in August and September, over half from the United States, to make up for the terrible losses of the summer in Libya.[18] General

Alexander, Middle East CIC in Cairo, left Montgomery to his own devices, which entirely suited the Eighth Army's commander.

Meantime Rommel was struggling to build up his supplies now that he was 1,200 miles from his main base at Tripoli. Nonetheless, he decided to resume the offensive. The next full moon for night operations would be in late August. Speed was vital as a reinforced Eighth Army might be too strong to attack by the following full moon period. Rommel recalled: 'We had to expect that a large convoy of well over 100,000 tons, laden with a cargo of the very latest weapons and war material for the Eighth Army, would arrive in Suez at the beginning of September.'[19] The chances of Afrika Korps personnel playing tourist at the Pyramids were lengthening.

Repairs had raised Afrika Korps tank strength above 200. Italian mechanised divisions possessed another 240 medium tanks. During the recent summer offensive, many panzers broken down, battle damaged, or run out of fuel had been recovered by workshop units. Only a minority of tanks put out of action had been knocked out beyond repair. Successful *blitzkrieg*-style warfare, whether in France, Russia or North Africa, always depended on the German Army's ability to repair damaged vehicles. Though as Mellenthin succinctly put it, 'An armoured division without petrol is little better than a heap of scrap iron.'[20] Fuel for Rommel's tanks was in short supply and oil had to be borrowed from *Luftwaffe* reserves.

On the night of 30/31 August Axis forces began a new offensive on the southern part of the El Alamein front. Montgomery had expected this. Aerial reconnaissance, common sense, and wireless intercepts had all pointed to the likelihood. Ultra signals intelligence had added to the warning signs, though without making a decisive difference. Montgomery had withdrawn his left-flank XIII Corps to face southwards from the Alam el Halfa ridge. Panzer and Italian mechanised divisions slowly advanced across the mostly vacated southern part of the El Alamein front. Thick minefields and air bombardment by flare-light on the opening night caused many delays. Rommel considered calling off the attack the following day, but subordinate commanders persuaded him to continue.

Rommel's plan was to make a deep encircling movement behind the Eighth Army, but when the Afrika Korps wheeled northwards they came up against British infantry and tanks on rising ground at Alam el Halfa. Axis mechanised forces were unable to penetrate the Eighth Army's front, and on the morning of 2 September Rommel ordered his forces to begin a gradual withdrawal back to their starting positions. Constant RAF attack, though doing little damage to armoured vehicles, steadily attrited soft transport and troops. A poorly executed British counter-attack on the night of 3/4 September was stopped in its tracks and by 7 September the battle was over.

British losses at the battle of Alam el Halfa were 1,750 officers and men; the Germans and Italians lost 3,000 casualties.[21] Thirty-eight German tanks had been destroyed. British tank losses were higher but could be replaced. Most damaged panzers were recovered during the retreat and towed away for repair. The battle had been the Eighth Army's most polished performance to date, and was a grand improvement compared to the defeats of the previous several months. Montgomery has been criticised for not launching a general counter-attack on either 1 or 2 September, when the Afrika Korps was at its most vulnerable. That kind of criticism, however, is unreasonably perfectionist. Montgomery had good reason to doubt whether his army could fight a successful mobile engagement.

After the Alam el Halfa battle, Montgomery resumed preparations for the Eighth Army's planned offensive. Alexander and Montgomery held out against Churchill's desire for an attack in the late September full-moon period and 23 October was chosen as the start date.[22] The Torch amphibious landings in Morocco and Algeria were due in November. There was the possibility that a timely victory in Egypt might help to deter the Vichy authorities in French North Africa from opposing the Torch landings.

Montgomery drew up his plans for the attack. In the northern sector of the El Alamein front, XXX Corps was to punch a hole in the Axis defences for the armoured divisions of X Corps to pass through, whilst to the south XIII Corps conducted diversions on a narrow front. X Corps had been formed as an armour-heavy 'corps de chasse' in imitation of the Afrika Korps. XXX Corps, under the command of Lieutenant-General Sir Oliver Leese, a guards officer newly arrived in the Middle East, had five infantry divisions and two armoured brigades; X Corps comprised two armoured divisions; XIII Corps comprised one armoured and two infantry divisions. In an address typical of many given, the Eighth Army's commander spoke of the coming 'dog-fight' after the break-in assault. 'Our men must be sent into the fight with the light of battle in their eyes and imbued with the burning desire to kill Germans.'[23] The frankly combative Montgomery did not mince his words.

The Eighth Army had over 1,000 tanks with front-line units. One-quarter of the tanks were new Shermans from the United States. In addition, Middle East Command had plentiful reserves of tanks, whereas the Germans had virtually none. The 2,500 tanks shipped to the Middle East in the first nine months of 1942 was not far short of total German tank production for the period, the bulk of which was destined for Russia.[24] Montgomery intended to maintain a tight control over his armoured formations, about half of which were cavalry units and the other half battalions of the Royal Tank Regiment. The 75mm gun of the Sherman and Grant tank could engage enemy anti-tank guns at long range, meaning there was less need for wild, cavalry-style rushes to close the range before opening fire.[25] The tanks were backed by over 900 guns and 1,400 anti-tank guns, including many new six-pounder anti-tank guns. The artillery was overwhelmingly composed of standard twenty-five-pounder field guns. Only one in twenty guns was a heavier 4.5- or 5.5-inch calibre.

The Desert Air Force, which now included United States units, was well placed to guarantee dominance of the air. The Desert Air Force comprised 420 fighters and 150 light bombers, and comfortably outnumbered the 350 serviceable Axis aircraft available in Egypt. Middle East Air Command controlled another seventy Wellington medium bombers. Half of RAF fighters were older model Hurricanes and the Desert Air Force had a strong South African element. Mid-October saw the start of a major *Luftwaffe* offensive against Malta. *Luftwaffe* forces employed in that offensive were greater than those supporting the Afrika Korps.[26]

It was difficult to hide preparations for an attack in the open desert, but dummy camps were constructed to give the impression that an assault was brewing at the southern end of the front, the usual sector for an offensive in North Africa. False radio traffic and vehicle movement, and poorly camouflaged dummy gun and tank positions added to the deception. Strict rules were enforced concerning wireless traffic, which by its volume could reveal where units were gathering. Troops were rotated out of the front line to undertake training for the upcoming attack. In the desert it was possible to rehearse attacks over ground very similar to intended objectives. This was especially valuable for newly arrived formations like the 51st Highland Division. Navigation by night across a landscape with few landmarks needed a great deal of practice.

Engineers and other teams prepared for the extensive mine clearance work that lay ahead. In the autumn of 1942 it was still reasonably safe for a man to walk through an anti-tank minefield as his weight would not be sufficient to activate a mine. Yet an anti-tank mine might be attached to a booby trap to discourage lifting. About 500 electronic mine detectors were available. This was not sufficient and some of the work of finding anti-tank mines would have to be carried out by lines of men prodding the ground with a bayonet step by step. The fiendish anti-personnel S-mine was beginning to make an appearance in the desert. The S-mine was a small mortar that launched a bomb several feet into the air before exploding.

The German-Italian army at El Alamein comprised four German and eight Italian divisions. Of those divisions, two German and two Italian divisions were armoured formations. The German 164th Division and Ramcke's parachute group had recently arrived via Crete to boost the German infantry component of the army. Rommel had 278 Italian medium tanks and 218 Panzer Mark IIIs and IVs. Eight-six 88mm anti-tank guns were supported by several hundred lighter calibre anti-tank guns.[27]

Middle East Command as a whole enjoyed a considerable numerical superiority over Axis forces in Egypt, but the relative numbers of infantry battalions in the front-line was not so unbalanced. Rommel had everything in the shop window, including all available Italian formations. Italian forces were handicapped by outdated equipment, second-rate tanks, a lack of transport and poor relations between officers and good-natured peasant soldiers. On the other hand, German commanders felt that divisions from northern Italy were more technically literate than their southern comrades. Mechanised Italian divisions received better quality recruits and had learned a lot by working directly with panzer units.[28] The newly arrived Folgore division had been trained for airborne operations and was a cut above the usual Italian standard.

General Warlimont, Field-Marshal Keitel's deputy at OKW, had recently visited Africa for discussions with Rommel. According to Mellenthin, Warlimont 'stressed the importance of our remaining at Alamein, in view of Kleist's impending invasion of Persia from the Caucasus'.[29] Though a powerful British offensive was looming, there was no chance of Hitler authorising a voluntary retreat from Egypt to Libya.

The supply problems of Rommel's army grew more severe the longer it remained in Egypt. The situation had worsened during September as twenty per cent of military cargo had been lost at sea between Italy and Africa. This figure would rise to forty-four per cent in October, well above the average loss rate. Oil stocks, in particular, were running low.[30] Rommel had 'stretched the elastic' of his supply line taunt, and he was continually anxious about the margin of logistical support behind Afrika Korps. Rommel's logistical problems, however, should not be exaggerated. Axis forces could never have established themselves at El Alamein if essential questions of supply and transport had not been adequately solved.

Late in September Rommel left his army to seek medical treatment in Germany. The Field-Marshal had been suffering from a stomach complaint and low blood pressure, not least because of the stressful manner in which he conducted operations. He was replaced by General Georg Stumme, a recent arrival to Africa. Stumme oversaw final preparations to parry the expected British offensive. Rommel hoped that the Eighth Army would not attack until the November full-moon period. Prior to departure he is alleged to have said, 'If I were Montgomery we wouldn't still be here!' In Berlin Hitler presented Rommel with his Field-Marshal's baton. Rommel commented to his wife, 'I would rather he had given me one more division.'[31] Hints were thrown out to Rommel, as he set off for the Austrian Alps to recuperate, that his next command appointment might be in Russia.

Once forced firmly onto the defensive, Axis troops put enormous work into deepening existing minefields – 'devil's gardens' – and laying new fields. The chief German engineer estimated that 445,000 mines were laid. Only three per cent of these were anti-personnel mines as in the desert it was more important to stop the progress of vehicles than men.[32] There were two main belts of mines, connected by intersecting fields laid to prevent motorised formations from fanning out if they penetrated the first main belt. In total the belts varied from two and a half to four and a half miles in depth. A line of outposts covered the forward belt and the main defensive zone stretched for up to two miles behind the second belt.

German commanders had decided to intermingle German and Italian infantry battalions to prevent a British attack from punching an unmanageably large hole in the front by crushing an entire Italian division. Axis armoured divisions were held in reserve behind the front. There were almost 50,000 German and 54,000 Italian troops at El Alamein facing 195,000 men of the British Empire. Including *Luftwaffe* personnel and troops on the lines of communication, there were a total of 152,000 Axis troops in Egypt.[33] German staffs were able to accurately estimate the infantry, gun and tank strength of their opponent, but the exact timing and direction of the Eighth Army's upcoming thrust could only be guessed.

During the night of 22/23 October British assault troops moved up to their assembly areas to spend the tense daylight hours of the coming day in slit trenches camouflaged from aerial observation. The big attack finally began at 9.40 p.m. on the evening of 23 October when over 450 guns opened fire in support of XXX Corps' assault at the northern end of the El Alamein front. The night was cool and clear. The moon was full. Known Axis artillery positions were the target of an initial burst of shelling. The RAF had been steadily attacking *Luftwaffe* airfields over the past few days. RAF bombers supported the assault by striking targets close behind the front.

Zero hour for the infantry to move out was 10 p.m., at which time the artillery barrage began to creep forward into the enemy's defence zone at a pre-planned pace. The thunder and flashes of the barrage reminded older men of the First World War. It was the first really heavy barrage fired by British artillery since 1918. Axis artillery did not immediately reply to the barrage, which spared the Eighth Army's troops gathered for the attack from retaliatory shell fire. The 9th Australian, 51st Highland, 2nd New Zealand and 1st South African Divisions attacked from a six-mile start line. Two armoured brigades were in immediate support of the assault troops. The plan for that first night was to secure Kidney Ridge and Miteiriya Ridge.

Captain A. Grant Murray of the 5th Seaforth Highlanders watched events unfold from an outpost.

> Suddenly the whole horizon went pink and for a second or two there was perfect silence and then the noise of the Eighth Army's guns hit us in a solid wall of sound that made the whole earth shake. Through the din we made out other sounds – the whine of shells overhead, the clatter of the machine-guns … And eventually the pipes. Then we saw a sight, that will live for ever in our memories – line upon line of steel helmeted figures with rifles at the high port, bayonets catching in the moonlight and over all the wailing of the pipes.[34]

The infantry advanced behind the barrage in bright, silvery moonlight soon made hazy by the rising dust and smoke of bursting shells. The terrain ahead was mainly rising, undulating desert, broken in places by stunted bushes and swells in the ground. The Australians fired red tracer from Bofors guns to aid navigation as troops advanced behind the creeping barrage. Highlander pipers added their own noise to the tumult of battle. After the infantry had bitten a hole in the Axis front, two corridors through the minefields were to be cleared for the passage of X Corps' 1st and 10th Armoured Divisions into the open desert beyond.

The assault swiftly took the German-Italian outpost line. Several battalions of defenders were overrun and 1,000 prisoners taken. Casualties from the bombardment had not been heavy, but telephone communications had been badly disrupted. Second-wave attacking battalions leapfrogged through those that had opened the battle. In most places the Eighth Army's troops reached close to the planned final objective.

Mine clearance work was soon underway. Operators using detectors had to stand upright and carefully listen to the sounds in their ear-pieces amid the cacophony of a major battle. This kind of work, whether undertaken by detector or bayonet, imposed a terrible burden on the nerves of men. There was always the risk of an anti-tank mine connected to a booby trap. The two armoured divisions of X Corps began to move into the two corridors laboriously cleared through the minefields. By dawn there were long traffic jams leading to and beyond the old front line. At the southern end of the front, XIII Corps' infantry had attempted to penetrate the minefields during the night, but this diversionary thrust made little progress.

At daylight on 24 October, XXX Corps had broken into the Axis front, but the tanks of X Corps remained caught in traffic jams within the mined zone. During the day British infantry consolidated their captured positions as a tank battle developed around them. Tanks edged forward along the lanes cleared in the minefields. The ends to the lanes, however, were covered by Axis anti-tank guns and more mines. Burning tanks became 'Tommy cookers'. If the hatches of a stricken tank jammed shut a crew would be incinerated to leave shrunken, charred remains. An armour-piercing round that penetrated a tank might ricochet within the cabin to crush men and ignite fuel and ammunition. Oil and blood seeped into the sandy desert floor. British tanks and transport drew hostile artillery fire, much to the chagrin of infantry digging-in nearby. Burning vehicles only attracted further shell fire. In exposed locations the stretcher bearers of either side were sometimes left to their tasks without molestation. On such a flat battlefield it was difficult to evacuate wounded by daylight without the tacit cooperation of an enemy.

New Zealand and South African troops had captured most of Miteiriya ridge, and Montgomery ordered the 10th Armoured Division to advance beyond the ridge the following night of 24/25 October. The attack began at

10 p.m. but tanks were again stopped by mines and anti-tank gun fire on the exposed forward slope of the shallow ridge. The situation at the front line was confused and losses mounted. XXX and X Corps had become badly entangled. Axis armoured reserves had been brought forward to plug gaps in the line. In the southern part of the front, XIII Corps' operations again achieved little when the 7th Armoured Division tried to advance that night.

From the German viewpoint, the timing of the Eighth Army's attack had been a tactical surprise yet the opening period of the fighting had not required any dramatic redeployment. On the morning of 24 October General Stumme had driven forward to visit a subordinate commander as few reports had reached his headquarters during the night. Stumme was accompanied by his intelligence officer, Colonel Buechting, but he left behind the escort and radio truck Rommel typically brought with him on his personal forays across a battle zone. The vehicle strayed too close to the new front line and enemy fire killed Buechting. Stumme died of a heart attack in the ensuing chaos and his body was only found the following day. The veteran General von Thoma assumed command until Rommel arrived hurriedly back from Europe on the evening of the 25th. Hitler had rung Rommel to ask if he felt fit enough to resume command now that a crisis had erupted. Rommel later remarked: 'I knew that there were no more laurels to be earned in Africa.'[35]

After arrival in Egypt, Rommel reassessed the situation and began concentrating his forces against the northern salient pushing into his front. He ordered the 90th Light Division forward from general reserve to join the fighting. German and Italian armoured units were redeployed to block the growth of XXX Corps' bridgehead. The southern half of the front was stripped of German armour. The balance of human casualties in the battle thus far had favoured Rommel's forces, 3,600 killed, wounded and missing to the Eighth Army's casualties of 6,140. 300 British tanks had been knocked out or damaged. panzer losses were less severe.[36]

The initiative still lay with Montgomery, though a period of attrition would be needed before another major breakthrough attempt could be made. This new phase in the battle kicked off on the night of 25/26 October, when the 9th Australian Division attacked northwards towards the coastal railway. Meanwhile, Montgomery pulled the 10th Armoured and New Zealand Divisions into reserve to rest and refit. The 1st Armoured Division was ordered to keep pushing forward along the northern corridor pierced through the minefields. On the night of 26/27 October British motorised infantry made some progress westwards. In consequence, strong German counter-attacks were launched the following afternoon. The six-pounder anti-tank guns of the 2nd Rifle Brigade and a supporting battery destroyed and damaged numerous German tanks in what is generally acknowledged to be the stand-out unit action of the battle from the British viewpoint.

The fighting of this period took a toll on both the Eighth Army and the Afrika Korps. By 28 October there were only seventy-seven German tanks fit to fight. A diarist wrote of German counter-attacks against Point 29: 'Rivers of blood were split over miserable strips of land which, in normal times, even the poorest Arab would never have bothered his head about.'[37] RAF light bombers in neat formations encouraged British troops by pattern bombing Axis positions. Wellington medium bombers operated further to the rear during the hours of darkness. On the night of 28/29 October another attack northwards by the Australians made some more progress and polished off a pair of Axis battalions. Another Australian attack two nights later failed to reach the sea but got astride the coastal road and railway line, thereby drawing counter-attacks by units of the 21st Panzer Division.

By 29 October Rommel was worrying about the likelihood of retreat. His last reserves had been sucked into the battle around the northern salient in the Axis mine fields. The increasingly despondent Rommel immodestly recorded on that day: 'Sometimes it is disadvantageous to have a military reputation. One is aware of one's limits, but others go on expecting miracles.'[38] He was beginning to consider forming a new line to the rear of El Alamein at Fuka to prolong the campaign on Egyptian territory.

Operation Supercharge was Montgomery's next big push. He had started the battle with a two to one advantage over Rommel in manpower, and he had every intention of grinding onward to expand the northern breach in the front. Two British brigades were to attack towards the Rahman track, after which the New Zealand Division's 9th Armoured Brigade, followed by the 1st Armoured Division, was to push on into the open desert. The 7th Armoured Division had been brought up as an additional armoured reserve. The attack began at 1 a.m. on 2 November. The infantry, advancing behind a creeping barrage with a smoke screen on the flanks, made two and a half miles' progress into the Axis defensive zone as planned. The 9th Armoured Brigade, its 132 tanks already reduced to ninety-four by mines, shelling and breakdown during the night approach march, came into action around dawn. By evening seventy more tanks of the brigade had been put out of action. German tanks and anti-tank guns positioned behind a ridge to the west of the Rahman track had put up a fierce resistance. The confused day-long battle left the desert littered with burning vehicles. The sky was stained by columns of dark, acrid smoke.

On the evening of 2 November Thoma reported to Rommel that the front could not hold for much longer. He expected to have thirty-five tanks in action the next day, which was only one-twentieth of the Eighth Army's tank strength.[39] On 3 November Rommel's forces began to retreat, motorised rear echelon units leaving first whilst the combat units remained in contact. But at 1.30 p.m. Rommel received an order from Hitler that his forces were 'not to yield a step'. 'As for your men', signalled Hitler, 'you can offer them no path but to victory or death.' Rommel wrote in his memoirs of the stand-fast order: 'We were all dumbfounded, and for the first time during the African campaign I did not know what to do.'[40] Rommel prevaricated for a while but, with the support of the *Luftwaffe's* Field-Marshal Kesselring, he ordered a full retreat for nightfall of 4 November. He did not wait for Hitler to approve the decision, though the Führer grudgingly signalled his permission after the event. Before long RAF pilots were reporting that the coast road was a mass of motor transport stretching for miles. Relations between Hitler and Rommel were badly damaged by this defeat.

In the final round of fighting to cover the retreat General von Thoma was captured after his tank had been put out of action. Upon capture he was taken to see Montgomery and they discussed the battle over the dinner-table, prior to the British commander promptly heading off to bed at 9.30 p.m. According to Thoma: 'Instead of asking me for information, he said he would tell me the state of our forces, their supplies and their dispositions. I was staggered at the exactness of his knowledge, particularly of our deficiencies and shipping losses. He seemed to know as much about our position as I did myself.'[41] It would be many years before the secret of Ultra signals intelligence was finally revealed.

The start of the Eighth Army's pursuit was clumsy and marred by a lack of urgency and lost supply columns. After twelve days of battle there were no fresh British motorised formations for the pursuit. Montgomery did not intervene to take personal control and there was no wholesale entrapment of Rommel's mechanised divisions. The Afrika Korps's pre-eminent talent for manoeuvre was as applicable to a retreat as an advance. Supply shortages became less of a problem once Afrika Korps began to fall back along its lines of communication with a sharply reduced number of vehicles.

Heavy rains on 6 and 7 November hampered the movement of both armies and turned large parts of the desert into a bog. The non-motorised Italian infantry divisions were left behind on the battlefield to be rounded up. By the end of 11 November Axis forces had fled from Egypt. The Afrika Korps had been reduced to eleven tanks fit for mobile battle. All German divisions were crippled and had lost three-quarters of their combat manpower. Tobruk was re-captured by the Eighth Army on 13 November. Behind a screen of mines and booby-traps, the Afrika Korps continued to retreat across Libya, slowly rebuilding itself as stragglers were collected and armoured vehicles repaired.

A great and decisive victory had been won by the Eighth Army, a force that had been comprehensively routed only a few months before. The Eighth Army's losses for the battle were 2,350 killed, 8,950 wounded and 2,260 missing, for a total of 13,560. (About half the missing were POWs and the other half had been killed). The 51st Highland Division had lost 2,827 casualties. Nearly 500 British tanks had been put out of action, though the majority were repairable and still in British hands. On the other side of the line, Axis losses had been catastrophic. *The Rommel Papers* gave German casualties as 1,100 dead, 3,900 wounded and 7,900 prisoners. Italian losses had amounted to another 1,200 dead, 1,600 wounded and 20,000 prisoners.[42]

Rommel had lost the battle but he had got the very maximum out of his army. The interweaving of German and Italian infantry units had been inspired. Each and every German formation had fought effectively to the last gasp. That the Afrika Korps had been able to make an escape without being encircled was due to the damage they had inflicted on British formations during the course of a long, hard fought battle. Rommel has been criticised for committing his armour to the fight piecemeal, though to some extent that was an inevitable consequence of fighting a defensive battle. German infantry and tank units did have one notable tactical shortcoming and that was a lack of training for night attacks.[43] Local counter-attacks by night during the last days of October might have achieved more than daylight assaults into the teeth of the massed British artillery.

Church bells rang out in Britain to celebrate the victory at El Alamein. Churchill famously said of the battle: 'It marked in fact the turning of the "Hinge of Fate". It may almost be said, "Before Alamein we never had a victory. After Alamein we never had a defeat."' The 'Second Battle of El Alamein' (23 October to 4 November) had been attritional in nature, but that was a style of battle the Eighth Army could win. Mellenthin concluded:

> There can be no question that the fighting efficiency of the British improved vastly under the new leadership, and for the first time Eighth Army had a commander who really made his will felt throughout the whole force ... [Montgomery] illustrated once again the vital importance of personal leadership in war.[44]

At El Alamein the Eighth Army had enjoyed a commanding superiority in manpower and an even greater margin of superiority in tank reserves. But the Eighth Army had enjoyed material superiority for a year before Montgomery's arrival and still had been badly defeated at Gazala and Tobruk in the summer of 1942. Montgomery had managed to completely turn around the situation in the space of six months. In Burma, against Japanese forces, it would take General Slim's Anglo-Indian army two years to achieve a similar transition from defeat to victory. Montgomery's postwar boasting would subsequently damage his reputation. Fame went to Monty's head. Yet the British casualty list was similar for both the first July battle at El Alamein and the second October–November battle. Clearly so much more was achieved in Montgomery's engagement.

At the far end of northern Africa, on 8 November the landings of Operation Torch took place as planned on the coast of Morocco and Algeria. The descent on the coast of Morocco took place outside the Gibraltar strait. The landings to seize Oran and Algiers were on the Mediterranean coast of Algeria, but Tunisia was not directly assaulted from the sea, much to the relief of the Germans. Fears of French opposition had strongly influenced the choice of landing locations. The armada assembled for Torch might have landed forces much further into the Mediterranean. When British and United States troops began to push eastwards towards Tunis from ports of disembarkation far to the west, the Germans had enough time to airlift and ship men with equipment to Tunisia to build a new front. Rommel was decidedly bitter when large German reinforcements were found to fight for Tunisia that had previously been denied to the Afrika Korps. In hindsight, the twenty-nine German divisions in western Europe could have been more heavily drawn upon for Rommel's campaign in Libya and Egypt.

After the defeat at El Alamein, the Afrika Korps conducted a fighting retreat across Libya in the face of Montgomery's slow-moving pursuit to form the southern flank to the Axis army group that held out in Tunisia into 1943. When looked at from a cynical viewpoint, the Torch operation can make the battle at El Alamein seem redundant or somehow a tarnished achievement. But it is unlikely that the Torch landings would have compelled the Afrika Korps to retreat from Egypt without a fight. During this period Hitler was clinging to Stalingrad with great determination and he would not have permitted Rommel voluntarily to retreat from any position in Egypt or Libya. It would have greatly aided the Axis campaign in Tunisia if Rommel's forces could have held a front to the east of Tripoli. This would have created a more secure supply and reinforcement route for Axis forces in Africa, which was just what was needed to prolong Axis resistance in Tunisia.

Compared to Russia, the Middle East can seem a peripheral theatre of war. There was no vital Allied population or industrial base in the Middle East. Yet despite these qualifications, the Middle East was important to Allied fortunes in the war. A large British force in the Middle East and Mediterranean contained the Axis in southern Europe and Libya at a time when they might have ranged unstopped through large parts of Africa and western Asia. The Jewish community in Palestine would doubtless have shared the fate of Jews elsewhere in Europe if they had fallen under Nazi control for any length of time. The investment of three-quarters of a million heavily equipped British personnel had by 1942 given the Middle East a value it did not have in 1939. The Middle East was the arena in which the British Empire was willing to offer Hitler battle on land and able eventually to succeed in mastering that self-imposed challenge. El Alamein was the first irreversible victory for British forces on land. It was a much needed success for the British Army after the disappointments of 1940–42. During the first half of the Second World War Britain was Nazi Germany's most significant and enduring military opponent. Britain's survival and eventual success in any tenable theatre during the darkest period of the war was important to the forging of a Grand Alliance capable of beating the Axis.

9
Stalingrad

Operation Barbarossa had ended in disappointment for the *Wehrmacht* in the harsh Russian winter of 1941–42. The Soviet Union had not been collapsed by a single devastating campaign of invasion, and the Red Army remained a powerful force. Soviet industry in the unoccupied territories was undergoing a speedy reorganisation to fight a long war. The next round of fighting on the eastern front was destined to take place in the context of a global war. The Soviet Union, United States and Britain had formed a coalition against Germany. Berlin needed to cripple the Soviet war effort before the Anglo-Americans could open new theatres of war on the periphery of Axis Europe.

In the spring of 1942 Hitler was in a buoyant mood. He had never felt more confident of his own ability as a military commander, and he intended to trust his own judgement. He believed that his determination during the previous winter had halted the Soviet counter-offensive, thereby saving the *Wehrmacht* from the fate of Napoleon's Grand Armee in 1812. Hitler was to tell the *Reichstag*: 'We have mastered the destiny that broke another man 130 years ago.'[1] Hitler wanted another ambitious eastern campaign to establish a stranglehold over the Soviet Union. After a conversation with Hitler, Goebbels recorded in his diary on 20 March 1942: 'He does not want to overextend the war. His aims are the Caucasus, Leningrad and Moscow.' Once those places had been captured.

> He [Hitler] intends possibly to construct a gigantic line of defence and to let the eastern campaign rest there. A winter like the past can never again surprise us. Possibly this may mean a hundred years' war in the East, but that need not worry us. Our position toward what remains of Russia would then be like that of England toward India.[2]

The new campaign would not seek to destroy the Soviet state in a single blow. That had not worked the previous year.

In March planning discussions were held for the new campaign at OKW (Supreme High Command) and OKH (Army High Command). Hitler believed that Soviet strength was waning to a critical degree. The opportunity for a decisive campaign to cement a German domination of Europe was still present. General Halder, Chief of Staff at OKH, fell into line with Hitler's views, and army intelligence assessments of the situation in the east were often optimistic. OKH's Department of Foreign Armies East produced reports that cast doubt on whether the Soviets had sufficient manpower to create many new formations. Soviet tank production was also grossly underestimated. The war games the German General Staff had customarily used to test their plans were dispensed with. Hitler no longer had time for such things.

On 5 April 1942 Führer Directive No. 41 was issued. The directive asserted the belief that a defensive victory had been achieved in the winter's fighting. The Soviets were assumed to have expended the bulk of their reserves.

> As soon as the weather and the state of the terrain allows, we must seize the initiative again, and through the superiority of German leadership and the German soldier force our will upon the enemy. Our aim is to wipe out the entire defensive potential remaining to the Soviets, and to cut them off, as far as possible, from their most important centres of war industry ... All available forces, German and Allied, will be employed in this task. At the same time, the security of occupied territories in Western and Northern Europe, especially along the coast, will be ensured in all circumstances.

In the central section of the eastern front the German Army was to stand fast before Moscow. In the north, operations would continue to maintain pressure on Leningrad, where the civilian death toll continued to grow. But the main arena for operations in 1942 was to be southern Russia. The objective for Army Group South was to destroy Soviet forces 'before the Don, in order to secure the Caucasian oilfields and the possession of the Caucasian mountains themselves'. The German leadership had long coveted the oil reserves of the Soviet Union. The Baku oil fields accounted for over seventy per cent of the Soviet oil supply, and the overall Caucasus region eighty-five per cent. In 1940 the Soviet Union had produced over thirty-four million tons of crude oil. To win that objective would require an advance along the eastern shore of the Black Sea to the Caucasian Mountains, 500 miles beyond Rostov and the mouth of the River Don.

The city of Stalingrad on the River Volga was not a major objective in Führer Directive No. 41, though once the great bend in the River Don had been reached, a further advance to the line of the Volga would logically be needed, to shield the northern flank of the thrust aiming to seize the oil of the Caucasus. 'In any event, every effort will be made to reach Stalingrad itself, or at least to bring the city under fire from heavy artillery so that it may no longer be of any use as an industrial or communications centre.' An offensive in southern Russia would, at the outset, need the involvement of only one of the three *Wehrmacht* army groups in the east. This was a more realistic proposition than a broad front attack down the length of the eastern front, for which the reserves and transport no longer existed.

Oil had always been the Achilles heal in the German war effort. Upon the outbreak of war the Allied blockade by sea had cut Germany's oil supply by two-thirds. This was an under-acknowledged yet war-defining victory for Britain's Royal Navy. To paper over the shortfall, the Germans had invested heavily in expensively manufactured synthetic oil. Synthetic oil production had increased from 2.2 million tons in 1939 to 4.12 million tons in 1941. Synthetic oil was vital to the German war effort by the spring of 1942, but there were doubts as to how far that supply could be stretched. Synthetic oil refineries were highly vulnerable to aerial bombing.

The importation of oil from Romania was also vital to Germany. Hitler was concerned that the Soviets might use air bases in the Crimea to 'turn the Romanian oilfields into an expanse of smoking debris ... and the very life of the Axis depends on those fields'.[3] Twin-engine Soviet bombers flying from bases around Odessa had regularly attacked the Romanian oilfields in the early months of Barbarossa, though German flak and fighter defence at the oilfields had been strong and effective. Oil importation from Romania had peaked in August 1941, only to fall alarmingly across the winter of 1941–42. On 16 February 1942 the War Economy and Armaments Office had concluded: 'One thing is now clear: without Russian oil we cannot utilise fully the regions of Russia we now occupy. But above all, without Russian oil the German war machine must from now on become increasingly more impotent.'[4] Berlin had to supply German industry, Italy and a series of occupied countries from dwindling stocks. At the start of 1942 Germany had less than a million tons of oil in reserve.

By focusing on economic targets, Hitler ignored Clausewitz's dictum that the enemy's main field army should be an overriding objective in warfare. Hitler believed, however, that the notional rules of war had changed as mid-twentieth century militaries were so heavily dependent on an industrial economy. Besides, he was confident that the Red Army would defend their main oil supply, thus creating the opportunity for a decisive military campaign. Germany had driven Russia out of the First World War in 1917–18 without capturing Moscow, and had subsequently gone on to paralyse the new Bolshevik regime by overrunning Ukraine and parts of the Caucasus region. Hitler's plans and hopes for the 1942 campaign mirrored the successes of a generation before and were firmly rooted, for better or worse, in relatively recent historical precedent. In moments of high fancy Hitler dreamt of advancing beyond the Caucasus. Manstein later recalled 'the fantastic idea he disclosed to me ... of driving through the Caucasus to the Near East and India with a motorised army group'.[5] In a letter to Mussolini later in the year, Hitler made reference to Axis forces crossing the Caucasus to overrun the Middle East in cooperation with Rommel's army in North Africa.

The German ambition to fight a campaign in 1942 to cripple the Red Army appeared at first glance to have a reasonable expectation of success. By the spring of 1942 the Germans had conquered territory that had once held forty per cent of the Soviet population. In 1942 the Soviet supply of coal and steel would fall to half the level of the previous year. Yet the manpower and industrial circumstances of the Soviet Union had been less handicapped than those figures might imply.

The loss of so many people should have had a dramatic impact on the Red Army's influx of recruits, but that did not prove to be the case. There were several reasons for this. Firstly, the war had started with a Soviet population approximately double the Germanic populations of central Europe – 200 million against 100 million. Millions of Soviet citizens had fled the occupied regions ahead of the advancing Germans as refugees or as members of the retreating Red Army. Secondly, due to the trauma of the previous generation, seventy-eight per cent of the Soviet male population was under forty years of age, as against a corresponding figure of almost sixty-four per cent for Germany.[6] This consideration had created a vast number of additional recruits for the Red Army. Thirdly, the Soviet authorities did not hesitate ruthlessly to strip towns and the countryside of men for the army without regard for the civilian economy. In consequence, after the front had stabilised during the winter of 1941–42, the Soviets managed to retain a high level of their initial two-to-one manpower advantage over Germany. In 1942 the Red Army could expect at least two million recruits, which was sufficient to maintain a Soviet military six million strong.

At this stage of the war German intelligence assessments still showed little understanding of the extent to which Soviet war industries had recovered and developed during the winter and spring of 1941–42. Tank production would rise to over 24,000 in 1942. The corresponding figure for 1941 had been only 6,500.[7] Automotive and tractor factories had been hurriedly converted to the production of armoured vehicles and other categories of military equipment.[8] 1,500 factories had been relocated eastwards during the winter of 1941–42. Workers and industrial machinery had been entrained long distances and re-assembled under crude wooden sheds. The Soviets had decided to focus their economy on the production of munitions. The industrial work force, which included many women and elderly people, laboured long hours in appalling conditions.

On the economic front the Soviet Union was not entirely alone. Stalin had requested western military aid soon after the German invasion. The British had quickly accepted the need to help the Soviets, though Moscow had been an ally of Germany from 1939 to June 1941, at a time when Britain had been at its most vulnerable. In August 1941 convoys carrying military aid had begun to sail from Britain around the long coast of Norway to the northern Russian ports of Murmansk and Archangel. London and Washington were conscious that if they failed to aid Moscow, that would raise the possibility of another German-Russian agreement, as had occurred in 1917–18 and 1939–41.[9]

Allied shipping losses were light during the severe weather of the winter of 1941–42. German aircraft and submarines, however, took a rising toll of the monthly convoys during the spring of 1942. In summer there was perpetual daylight in the Arctic Circle and in early July convoy PQ 17 would be famously slaughtered to send almost 100,000 tons of cargo to the ocean's bottom, including 430 tanks. The convoys would only be resumed later in the year, despite Soviet protests.

The convoys to the Soviet Union also benefited the Allied cause by fuelling Hitler's anxiety that the Allies might be planning an invasion of Norway. Every time a convoy sailed it reminded the German leadership that an amphibious landing on coastal Scandinavia was very practical. Halder had noted on 28 March 1942: 'Major concern is for a landing in northern Norway and impact on Sweden.'[10] Large supplies of iron ore were mined in Sweden for export to Germany. Iron ore was as valuable a military raw material as oil. A strong German garrison remained in Norway for the entire war.

Western aid was also sent to the Soviet Union through Persia and the Pacific port of Vladivostok. Finished munitions were not sent across the north Pacific to Vladivostok for fear that might compel the Japanese to interfere. Raw materials and food was shipped instead under the Soviet flag. The Japanese did not want a breach with the Soviets as that could lead to American bombers obtaining bases in Siberia from which to bomb Japan. Almost half of all Allied aid to Russia was transported across the north Pacific.

By the war's end, the Americans and British would send to Russia large quantities of weaponry, vehicles, signals, railway equipment and industrial machinery. British aid to Russia included 5,200 tanks and 7,400 aircraft. Over half of those tanks had been dispatched by the end of 1942. American aid included 7,500 tanks and 14,800 aircraft. The Americans would dispatch 375,000 trucks, fifteen million pairs of boots, almost 2,000 locomotives and 11,000 railway flatcars and wagons. From 1942–44 the United States would supply three-quarters of the Soviet Union's new trucks.[11] A sizeable majority of the Red Army's motor vehicles came to be of American manufacture. Nikolai Khrushchev later said of the imported trucks: 'Just imagine how we would have advanced from Stalingrad to Berlin without them! Our losses would have been colossal because we would have had no manoeuvrability.'[12] In 1948 N.A. Voznesensky, Head of the Soviet State Planning Centre, would assert that western supplies had amounted to only four per cent of the Soviet Union's production from 1941–43. That was a piece of Cold War propaganda and more recent estimates have put western aid at ten to fifteen per cent of tanks and aircraft.[13] In November 1942 a quarter of Soviet tank brigades were partly or fully equipped with western tanks.

Above all else, Anglo-American efforts to send aid to the Soviet Union revealed that the anti-Axis coalition was a functioning alliance, in contrast to the failure of the Nazis and Japanese to cooperate. The effectiveness of Allied cooperation, and the ineffectiveness of Axis cooperation, were considerations that would lurk behind every battle of the later half of the Second World War, at some times more visibly than others, but always with a significant impact at a grand strategic level. Meetings between Allied leaders became a feature of the Grand Alliance. Churchill and a British delegation would visit Moscow from 12–17 August 1942 for discussions with the Soviet leadership.

The rains and thaw of the spring of 1942 had turned the ground and dirt roads of Russia to deep mud. The *rasputitsa* season typically stretched from mid-March to early May. But summer promised the return of good weather and firm ground for the panzer spearheads. Spring was spent re-equipping the German Army on the eastern front after the winter's fighting. On 30 March OKH reported that the sixteen Panzer divisions in Russia had only 140 operational tanks, compared to over 3,000 the previous June. The armies in the east needed over 600,000 men to replace losses. All categories of equipment were needed, especially motor vehicles and transport animals.

German armoured vehicle production would steadily increase during 1942 as it became belatedly clear that a desperate war of attrition was underway. In 1941, 3,245 tanks and 545 assault guns had been built. In 1942 this figure would rise to 4,137 tanks, 824 assault guns and 1,219 self-propelled guns.[14] Ninety per cent of new tanks were medium Mark IIIs and IVs. The building of light tanks had been largely discontinued. Assault and self-propelled guns were large anti-tank guns mounted on a tank chassis. An increased reliance on assault and SP guns was a short-cut alternative to building more tanks, but they were effective armoured weapons in the hands of skilled soldiers.

Führer Directive No. 41 had ordered the clearing of Soviet forces from the Crimea as a necessary prelude to the main operations planned for southern Russia. General von Manstein's Eleventh Army began an offensive in the Crimea on 8 May. After a heavy *Luftwaffe* bombardment, German forces crashed through the Soviet line defending the Kerch Peninsula. The Red Army was rapidly driven into the sea and 170,000 prisoners were captured. Soviet sources claimed that 120,000 troops escaped across the Kerch strait to safety.[15]

Sevastopol – previously made famous during a siege of the Crimean War – proved a tougher nut when it was assaulted on 7 June. The fortress had held out across the months of winter and spring. Stuka Ju 87 dive-bombers from General Wolfram von Richthofen's air corps pounded the city's fortifications and its garrison of over 100,000. The forts of Sevastopol's defences had to be reduced by costly attack. Flame-throwers were used to clear Fort Maxim Gorky. There was desperate fighting in tunnels and casements as the garrison's end neared. By 3 July resistance had ceased and the city had been reduced to rubble. The capture of Sevastopol had closely followed the fall of Tobruk. German arms seemed to be everywhere in the ascendancy. Unwisely, once the Crimea had been taken, the army of the newly promoted Field-Marshal von Manstein was dispersed across the eastern front and not held as a strategic reserve for southern Russia. Hitler had pencilled in the capture of Leningrad as Manstein's next task. Only one-sixth of Sevastopol's civilian population remained amid the rubble of their fallen city. Hitler declared that after the war Sevastopol was to be 'built up entirely as a German city'.[16]

To the chagrin of German commanders, the Soviets threatened to disrupt their plans by launching an offensive in Ukraine, south east of Kharkov. The Red Army's leadership believed that strong German forces were facing Moscow, and that success could be achieved by attacking in southern Russia. As it transpired, the Soviets advanced on 12 May into the teeth of alerted German forces gathering for Hitler's grand summer offensive. By 22 May the First Panzer Army and the Sixth Army had counter-attacked successfully to encircle a large Soviet force. The effectiveness of a mechanised pincer movement was reproved. The Soviets lost another 277,000 men and 1,200 tanks. Further successful mopping up operations were carried out by German forces in the weeks ahead. Soviet reserves in southern Russia were greatly diminished at a critical time.

Hitler flew to the headquarters of Army Group South for a conference on 1 June to discuss the upcoming main offensive. During the discussions he is reputed to have said: 'If we don't get [the oil of] Maikop and Grozny, I shall have to pack in this war.'[17] As a deception plan, preparations were made to give the impression that a renewed offensive on Moscow was imminent. Goebbels made indiscreet comments to the foreign press pointing in that direction.

The formations of Army Group South preparing for the offensive had been built up by stripping other forces on the eastern front of transport, armour and replacements. At the outset of Barbarossa, German Army strength had been 3,206,000 men in the east and 594,000 in other foreign theatres. Yet by the summer of 1942 the figures had changed to 2,847,000 in the east and 971,000 in other foreign theatres.[18] German manpower had become stretched at the margin. Local fighting on the fronts of Army Group North and Army Group Centre further dissipated German reserves in those regions. A growing partisan problem in occupied Russia, especially in wooded terrain, was another drain on manpower.

To make up for a lack of German troops, twenty-eight Axis satellite divisions were among the forces of Army Group South: twelve Romanian divisions, six Italian divisions and ten Hungarian divisions. To further augment the strength of the *Wehrmacht*, the Germans had come to rely on so-called *Hiwis* – *Hilfsfreiwillige* – for support tasks. *Hiwis* were Soviet prisoners, military or civilian. A German division might have 2,000 of these men. Hundreds of thousands of Russians were employed by the Germans across the front. Soviet citizens were willing to serve as voluntary auxiliaries in the *Wehrmacht* to avoid starvation.

The main German offensive in south Russia – Operation Blue – finally got underway on 28 June. The rolling offensive began on a frontage to the north of Kursk, with the aim of advancing to the River Don and Voronezh, about five miles beyond the river. Two days later, further south, the Sixth Army attacked from near Kharkov. Close to the Black Sea's coast, German forces allocated to capture the Caucasus region moved out a week later. When confronted by the big new German offensive, the Soviet High Command concluded that the offensive was most likely to push eastwards and then lunge to the north to get behind Moscow. Soviet reserves were deployed to block such a movement.

Halder wrote in his war diary on 6 July:

> The actual picture of the enemy situation is not yet clear to me. There are two possibilities: either we have overestimated the enemy's strength and the offensive has completely smashed him, or the enemy is conducting a planned disengagement or at least is trying to do so in order to forestall being inevitably beaten in 1942.[19]

By 7 July Voronezh on the upper Don had been reached to provide an anchor for the northern flank of the offensive, the main thrust of which now began to head south eastwards across the treeless, roadless steppe. The steppe country was a traditional home to Cossack horsemen. This was not what the Soviets had been expecting.

Army Group South was now split into two new army groups. Field-Marshal List's Army Group A headquarters came into operation on 9 July, and Army Group South headquarters were re-designated Army Group B. Army Group A was to press southwards into the Caucasus. Army Group B was to provide a flank guard along the Don. After securing the line of the Don, Army Group B was to keep advancing eastwards to clear territory beyond the 'great bend' of the Don leading across the steppe to the River Volga and the city of Stalingrad. The neutralisation of Stalingrad would cut the Volga as a supply route and help to shield the northern flank of German forces pressing southwards into the Caucasus. The decision to split the offensive into two diverging thrusts risked leaving one or both thrusts too weak to succeed.

Hitler moved elements of OKW (Supreme High Command) from Rastenburg in East Prussia to a pine forest near Vinnitsa in Ukraine to more closely monitor the blossoming offensive. On 16 July the SS's Heinrich Himmler visited Hitler at Vinnitsa. The following day Himmler went sightseeing at the concentration camp at Auschwitz in Poland and saw the gas chamber procedure in operation. He would shortly give the order for the 'total cleansing' of the Jewish population of Poland.[20] The *Wehrmacht* – and its operational excellence – was ultimately the servant of and assistant to a policy of monumental genocide.

As German forces pressed across southern Russia the length of the front line was dramatically increased. The front line in southern Russia was in the process of stretching from 500 to 1,300 miles. Satellite divisions were used to fill out the lengthening flank facing to the north east from behind the River Don. This appeared to be a secondary task at this stage of the offensive. The Don flank had been identified as a possible defence line for the coming winter. Perversely, the Hungarians had to be separated from the Romanians by the insertion of an Italian army between them. Local territorial disputes had long plagued Hungarian-Romanian relations.

The deployment of satellite divisions behind the Don was a consequence of a deliberate decision to retain a large German force in western Europe. Bizarrely, the risk of British raiding forces descending on the coast of Norway or France seemed to be a greater concern for Hitler than the Don flank facing Soviet forces gathered about Moscow. An Anglo-Canadian attack on the French port of Dieppe was massacred in August 1942. The assault had been ineptly planned, but Dieppe had also been strongly defended. There were many strongly defended places on the periphery of occupied Europe, whilst the long Don flank was naked of German troops and weaponry.

As the weeks of July passed, fast-moving German mechanised forces captured a lot of territory, but perceptive German commanders became concerned that they had not surrounded entire Soviet armies. Fuel shortages at critical times had aided the escape of Soviet forces, as had the wide open spaces of the steppe grasslands. Many German troops were still marching on foot and could not overtake the retiring Soviets. Bock was replaced as commander of Army Group B as Hitler became displeased at the pace of operations.

Unbeknownst to his opponents, Stalin had been persuaded to allow threatened units in the Don-Donetz region to retreat ahead of the Germans, rather than stand their ground and be destroyed by encirclement. Stalin was starting to value the guidance of his military advisors just at a time when Hitler was extending his control over his generals. Stalin may have been more willing to accept advice for retreat as the German offensive in southern Russia was not directly threatening Moscow and the security of his regime.

Nonetheless, Stalin soon tired of the principles of flexible defence. On 27 July Zhukov was ordered to report to Moscow from his post commanding an army group covering the western approaches to the capital. Zhukov was made Deputy Supreme Commander and dispatched to the Volga region. On 28 July the Soviet High Command issued Order 227, which was entitled 'Not a Step Back!'–'Each position, each metre of Soviet territory must be stubbornly defended, to the last drop of blood. We must cling to every inch of Soviet soil and defend it to the end!'[21] Dire punishment with 'penal battalions' was promised for the faint-hearted. The secret police .– NKVD – and 'blocking units' were deployed to ensure compliance with orders.[22]

On 23 July Rostov at the mouth of the Don was seized by Army Group A. Führer Directive No. 45 was issued that day.

After the destruction of enemy forces south of the Don, the most important task of Army Group A will be to occupy the entire eastern coastline of the Black Sea, thereby eliminating the Black Sea ports and the enemy Black Sea fleet ... At the same time a force composed chiefly of fast-moving formations will give flank cover in the east and capture the Groznyy area ... Thereafter the Baku area will be occupied by a thrust along the Caspian coast ... The task of Army Group B is, as previously laid down, to develop the Don defences and, by a thrust forward to Stalingrad, to smash the enemy forces concentrated there, to occupy the town, and to block the land communications between the Don and the Volga, as well as the Don itself. Closely connected with this, fast-moving forces will advance along the Volga with the task of thrusting through to Astrakhan and blocking the main course of the Volga in the same way.

The *Luftwaffe* was to ensure the destruction of Stalingrad by aerial bombardment. Once the next round of operations was successfully underway, Army Group North could begin operations to capture Leningrad.

Rostov was still 700 miles from Baku and there was no time to waste. Army Group A rapidly pushed across the Don onto plains of corn south of the river, and the dry steppe leading towards the Caucasian foothills. The Soviet front south of the Don rapidly collapsed. On 9 August the Maikop oilfield was reached, its wells and refineries already destroyed by the retreating Red Army. On 19 August the Nazi flag was raised on Mount Elbruz. Once German troops had reached the foothills of the Caucasian mountains, the advance slowed and eventually ground to a halt before steep, thickly forested mountain passes and defiles that strongly favoured the defending Soviets. The ever-paranoid Stalin had maintained strong forces in the Caucasus region to keep watch on the Turkish border.[23] These forces proved ideally located to parry the advance of the Germans into the Caucasus from the opposite direction. Fuel shortages plagued German formations. When supply columns ran short of fuel, animal transport – including camels – had to be used to haul forward what was needed. German forces were still over thirty miles from Grozny. Baku lay beyond a formidable mountain range. The Soviets were also successfully defending Army Group A's attempt to drive down the Black Sea shore line. An infuriated Hitler responded by dismissing Field-Marshal List, Army Group A's commander, and taking personal charge of the army group on 9 September. Army Group A did not make much further progress into the Caucasian mountains during September and October.

The advance of Army Group B began to threaten the Volga region and at Stalingrad, a city swollen by refugees to 850–900,000 inhabitants, civilian work parties were conscripted to build defences around the western perimeter. Most civilians were later evacuated as it became clear the city was about to become a battlefield. Stalingrad was a fifteen-mile strip of housing and modern factories built along the hilly west bank of the mile-wide River Volga. In places sand banks divided the giant Volga into separate channels to further widen the river. The Volga was unbridged and that was why there was little development on the eastern bank. The main railway from Astrakhan and the mouth of the Volga ran northwards to the upper Volga well to the east of Stalingrad. The city obviously sat alongside the region's main north–south river route, but was not astride the main north–south railway.

Stalingrad had great symbolic significance for Stalin and he ordered that it be strongly defended. The city had once been called Tsaritsyn, but had been renamed to commemorate Stalin's role in the region's civil war campaigns. The city had grown during the interwar period thanks to Soviet industrialisation projects. In particular, three huge factory complexes had been built along the river to the north of the city centre. The Stalingrad Tractor factory, the Red October steel plant and the Barricades ordnance factory were strongly built complexes and fine potential fortifications. The Tractor factory had been converted to produce tanks, and the Red October factory made shells and armour plating. The central residential and commercial district of Stalingrad was commanded by the low hill of Mamayev Kurgan, which was within two miles of the Volga. To the south of the city's centre, more housing stretched away beside the river.[24]

Whilst other German formations had advanced towards the Caucasus, the Sixth Army had pushed into the great bend of the Don, and then across the Don and onto the arid steppe land-bridge between the Don and the Volga. By 19 August the Sixth Army was outside Stalingrad. Four days later Richthofen's *Luftflotte* 4 heavily bombed the city. Hundreds of aircraft deluged Stalingrad with munitions. Wooden residential buildings burned fiercely to throw up a pall of smoke. Panzer forces reached the Volga to the north of Stalingrad to cut river traffic. The Germans, however, lacked the mechanised forces necessary to cross the river both north and south of Stalingrad to surround the city. An advance in strength across the mighty Volga had no place in German campaign planning. The Volga seemed to mark the frontier between European Russia and Asian Russia. When General von Weichs, Army Group B's commander, viewed Stalingrad from an aircraft, he described the city as 'a strange mixture of modern technology and an Asian type of landscape'.[25] The emptiness of the surrounding steppe gave Stalingrad a special significance.

The cutting of river traffic on the Volga was arguably enough to neuter Stalingrad's strategic value, but Hitler ordered that the city be captured. This meant that Stalingrad would have to be taken by frontal assault. On 31 August Halder recorded: 'The Führer has ordered that, upon penetration into the city, the entire male population be eliminated, since Stalingrad with its one million uniformly Communist inhabitants is extremely dangerous.' The female population 'must be shipped off'.[26] Fighting to enter the city soon began in earnest. The Fourth Panzer Army had crossed the Don to the south of the Sixth Army and had advanced on Stalingrad from a south westerly direction. To the south of the Fourth Panzer Army, a single motorised division watched the yawning gap stretching towards Army Group A in the Caucasus. Patrols briefly caught sight of the Caspian Sea but German troops were held 100 miles from Astrakhan, which had been strongly reinforced by the Soviets.

The commander of the Sixth Army, the main German force facing Stalingrad, was General Friedrich Paulus, a tall, handsome, modest man in his early 50s. Paulus haled from a Hessian middle-class background. He had married into the Romanian nobility. During the First World War and interwar period he had served mostly as a staff officer. Paulus had been Chief of Staff to an army in Poland and France, and Director of Operations at OKH during 1941. A careful man with limited command experience, Paulus had been appointed to the Sixth Army at the start of 1942. He would probably have been rotated back to a senior staff appointment at OKW or OKH if dramatic events had not intervened.

At Stalingrad the local Soviet defence was in the hands of the 62nd Army. The 64th Army prolonged the Soviet line to the south of the city. General V.I. Chuikov was made the 62nd Army's new commander. Chuikov's predecessor had begun to withdraw troops to the eastern shore of the Volga and had been promptly dismissed. An undoubtedly tough man, Chuikov had only recently returned from an advisory role to the Chinese Nationalists. A steady stream of reinforcements was ferried across the river by night to shore up the 62nd Army's front. The *Luftwaffe* was able to curtail the employment of Soviet shipping on the Volga by daylight but not by night.

The ground assault on Stalingrad had gathered pace in the early days of September. On 13 September a big German attack carried the fighting into the city's centre. During the night of 14/15 September the Soviet 13th Guards Division was brought across the Volga to counter-attack by daylight to recapture Mamayev Hill. Meantime the Fourth Panzer Army attacked into southern Stalingrad and reached the Volga to split the 62nd from the 64th Army. By this time fire had burnt out many wooden structures. Stone and iron commercial, residential and factory buildings attained great importance as they remained standing and were able to absorb shellfire. Advancing German troops compelled Chuikov to relocate his headquarters to the banks of the River Tsaritsa, near its junction with the Volga.

The fierce battle developing at Stalingrad sucked in more and more of the Sixth Army. The metre had replaced the kilometre as the most common unit of measurement on staff maps. In street fighting the Germans' skills at mechanised warfare were negated. It was hard to effectively deploy tanks and aircraft in dense urban terrain. The city had to be cleared street by street, and the buildings cleared floor by floor. Unusual structures like the Grain Elevator near No. 2 Station became part of the tactical battle. The tangled ruins broke up the Germans' assault formations and there was no clear front line. Soviet troops learnt to let tanks drive past to shoot up the following infantry. Snipers with telescopic sights stalked unwary and exhausted Germans. Burning buildings wreathed the city in a layer of ash which was gusted into clouds by the wind.

The Germans finally captured the Grain Elevator on the night of 20 September and had cleaned out the bed of the River Tsaritsa, to the south of Mamayev Kurgan, by the close of the following day. On 25 September the Germans began to attack into the factory districts to the north of the city's centre. By the end of September nine-tenths of Stalingrad was in German hands, though much of the streetscape had been reduced to rubble.

As German troops ground through Stalingrad, far to the rear big changes took place in the German High Command. On 24 September OKH's Chief of Staff, General Halder, was dismissed and sent into retirement. Hitler had become increasingly estranged from Halder and had made the latter the victim of ranting and unconcealed contempt. Halder was replaced by General Kurt Zeitzler, who was a blunter man, more able to deal with Hitler than the mild-mannered Halder. Zeitzler, born in 1895 and a lieutenant-colonel in the spring of 1939, had been Chief of Staff to the army group headquarters in western Europe prior to his elevation. Zeitzler had only been recently promoted to the rank of major-general. He was given a double promotion – thus skipping the rank of lieutenant-general – to become chief at OKH. His appointment was a mark of the growing importance of loyalty to National Socialism for promotion to the higher reaches of the German Army. Field-Marshal Keitel, OKW Chief of Staff, warned Zeitzler: 'Never contradict the Führer. Never remind him that once he may have thought differently of something. Never tell him that subsequent events have proved you right and him wrong. Never report on casualties to him – you have to spare the nerves of the man.' Zeitzler reputedly replied: 'If a man starts a war he must have the nerve to bear the consequences.' Once he was made responsible for the eastern front, Zeitzler began to push for the transfer of extra divisions to Russia, having only recently argued for the opposite course of action whilst Chief of Staff at Paris.[27]

Further attacks at Stalingrad took place in October. The clearance of the city had been made Army Group B's highest priority. Hitler wanted to secure the line of both the Don and Volga rivers as the launching pad for the following year's offensive. German bombing and artillery fire steadily turned larger pieces of rubble in the Soviet pocket of Stalingrad into smaller pieces of rubble. The novelist Konstantin Simonov wrote of the ruins: 'It seemed as though the houses had sunk into the ground and that grave mounds of bricks had been heaped over them.'[28] A German soldier wrote to his mother: 'Stalingrad is hell on earth. It is Verdun, bloody Verdun, with new weapons. We attack every day. If we capture twenty yards in the morning the Russians throw us back again in the evening.'[29] Another major German thrust was launched on 14 October and that night 3,500 Soviet wounded were ferried back over the Volga, the highest nightly tally of the battle.[30] German assault troops secured the Tractor factory, and soon gained a solid foothold in the Red October factory district.

On 18 October a Stuka pilot wrote in his diary: 'Yesterday we ploughed over the blazing field of ruins of the Stalingrad battlefield all day long. It is incomprehensible to me how people can continue to live in that hell, but the Russians are firmly established in the wreckage, in ravines, cellars, and in a chaos of twisted steel skeletons of the factories.'[31] Conditions within the built-up area wore down the resolve of the combatants. Some civilians remained trapped amid the two armies. Lieutenant Wiener of the 24th Panzer Division recorded in his diary that at one point his unit had fought over a single dwelling for fifteen days, storey to storey. Wiener had counted fifty-four dead Germans littering the cellars, landings and staircases.

> Stalingrad is no longer a town. By day it is an enormous cloud of burning, blinding smoke; it is a vast furnace lit by the reflection of the flames. And when night arrives, one of those scorching, howling, bleeding nights, the dogs plunge into the Volga and swim desperately to gain the other bank. The nights of Stalingrad are a terror for them. Animals flee this hell; the hardest storms cannot bear it for long; only men endure.[32]

Chuikov later wrote that 'the two armies were left gripping each other in a deadly clutch'.

After weeks of fierce fighting, the Sixth Army was running short of infantrymen and artillery ammunition. The Sixth Army's stores were running low as the logistical problems of maintaining a German force on the Volga had never been more than partly solved. Only one rail line was available for the Sixth Army. Motor transport was limited and horses were wasting away as steppe grass was of low nutritional value. By mid-October the Sixth Army's casualties since the beginning of the offensive had passed 40,000. The casualties of the 62nd Army were probably over twice that figure as German shells and bombs rained down into the contracting perimeter. Soviet reinforcements crossing the river and the landing stages on the west bank were subjected to steady attritional bombardment. There were Soviet divisions in the city that had been reduced to as few as 1,000–1,500 men, despite the continual replenishment of their ranks. The majority of the gun and searchlight crews of the Stalingrad anti-aircraft defence corps were manned by women, as were the signals units of the 62nd Army.[33]

By November the first ice had appeared on the Volga, which would be frozen in a few weeks. Soviet heavy artillery firing across the river became more effective as the Germans inched closer to the west bank. Multi-barrelled rocket-launchers added their support. Fighting in the factory complexes continued fiercely amid the sprawling warehouses. Both armies dug more deeply into the ground and the front line was within 1,000 yards of the Volga. The shared desire for survival gave the battle a subterranean character.

What proved to be the final German offensive in Stalingrad began on 11 November and caused another round of bitter fighting. Soviet troops were told to fight as if 'there is no land across the Volga'. The Germans pushed a corridor through the 62nd Army's front to capture a 500-yard stretch of the Volga's bank. Most of the Red October factory was taken, but the Sixth Army was spent and ebbing away in what was now a snow-covered cauldron. The will of local German commanders faltered as their once splendid formations lay shattered.

As the fighting in Stalingrad consumed German strength in south Russia, the long flanks stretching north west and south of the city had become more fragile. The greater the commitment of German troops to Stalingrad, the more the flanks had passed to the protection of Romanian, Italian and other Axis-satellite armies. Hitler's OKW headquarters had not done enough to find extra German divisions for southern Russia from other theatres of war. The Axis was paying a price for the extent to which the German operational war effort was run by two parallel headquarters staffs. OKH, Army High Command, was responsible for the eastern front but depended upon the agreement of the Supreme Commander's OKW staff to take reinforcements from other theatres such as France, Norway or south-east Europe.

Far from the ruins of Stalingrad, in Munich for the anniversary of the failed 1923 putsch, Hitler told an audience of dedicated National Socialists:

> I intended to reach the Volga, and at a specific place at a specific city. By chance it bears the name of Stalin himself. But don't think that I marched there because of that – it could be called anything – instead it's because it's a very important place. Namely we cut off thirty million tons of traffic there, including almost nine million tons of oil traffic. All the wheat from these vast areas of the Ukraine, the Kuban region, converges there for transport north.[34]

Hitler was clutching at straws. It had never been necessary to capture the entire city of Stalingrad to stop Soviet traffic on the Volga. Stalingrad could have been inexpensively blockaded. Yet Hitler had revealed an obsessive need to destroy the great cities of Russia over the past year. He had regularly spoken of his intention to destroy Leningrad and Moscow. Sevastopol had already received that treatment. As recently as 24 August Hitler had again issued instructions that Leningrad was to be levelled to the ground after it had been captured.[35] Hitler's desire to destroy the great cities of Russia was only partly motivated by military strategy. Their obliteration was also vital to the future domination of an agrarian Slavic society by a caste of Germanic settlers. The dream of a National Socialist future had fuelled the horrors of the Stalingrad battle.

As German assaults in Stalingrad had been gathering pace, the Soviet High Command had been considering how they might take advantage of the long, exposed flanks that lay either side of the city. The Soviet strategic reserve in the Moscow region was substantially intact and available for deployment to south Russia. First Deputy Defence Commissar Zhukov and General Aleksandr Vasilevsky, the Chief of the General Staff, had met Stalin on 13 September to explain a plan to encircle the German army at Stalingrad. Stalin had his doubts about this plan's practicability but he was persuaded after discussion. The generals had argued that the reserves existed for a major counter-offensive, and had successfully compelled Stalin to support an operation that aimed to encircle Stalingrad on a grand scale. Stalin had come to trust Zhukov's military judgement. In fact, the Soviet High Command had plans for two large offensives in the late autumn. Operation Uranus was intended to capture Stalingrad. Operation Mars was directed against Army Group Centre and the Rzhev salient. With a strength of six million, the Red Army could attempt more than one major task at the same time.

German divisions held the land bridge from the Volga to the Don, but in mid-November the flank north west of Stalingrad behind the River Don was guarded by the Third Romanian Army, backed by a slender reserve comprising a Romanian armoured division and a weak panzer division. The Romanians were heavily reliant on equipment captured from the French in 1940 and had few anti-tank guns and limited mechanised transport. On a front of seventy-five miles the Romanians had less than one heavy anti-tank gun per mile.[36] The Romanian front was not firmly against the Don either. The Soviets had a series of bridgeheads on the south bank up to ten miles deep. On the exposed, snow-covered, open steppe, Romanian divisions held sectors ten to twenty miles wide. Intelligence reports had been warning Axis commanders that the Soviets were building up their forces on the north-west flank of Stalingrad. There had always been a theoretical awareness in the German High Command that the Don flank was vulnerable, but German commanders doubted whether the Red Army was capable of launching a successful major offensive.

The Soviets gathered a million men and 1,500 tanks for Operation Uranus. Poor weather helped to shield this force from the preying eyes of *Luftwaffe* reconnaissance flights. Finally, on 19 November the Soviet Southwestern and Don Front army groups began an offensive north west of Stalingrad in snow and thick fog. The fronts were commanded by the forty-one year-old General N.F. Vatutin and General Rokossovsky respectively. The First Guards Army and the Fifth Tank Army tore through the surprised Romanians. The open steppe south of the Don was difficult terrain to defend once a front had been breached.

To the south of Stalingrad the flank was held by a force of Romanian and German infantry divisions. On 20 November the Soviet armies of General Yeremenko's Stalingrad Front army group crashed through Axis forces on that sector. Fugitives streamed rearwards. Parts of the front south of Stalingrad had only been guarded by patrols. The headquarters of the Fourth Romanian Army had been preparing to take over command of the line south of Stalingrad and did so under appalling circumstances on 21 November.

The Axis front had collapsed along a fifty mile stretch north west of Stalingrad. A thirty mile breach in the front had been made to the south, where the offensive had come as a greater surprise. On 23 November the Soviet pincers touched hands at Kalach on the Don, about fifty miles west of Stalingrad. The encirclement of the city had given Soviet commanders a specific objective, which had encouraged sensible planning. A quarter of a million Axis troops of the Sixth Army and a corps of the Fourth Panzer Army had been caught in a pocket. The pocket was thirty-five miles wide from east to west and over twenty miles across from north to south. The besieged Axis force included twenty German and two Romanian divisions, of which three were panzer divisions. A Croatian regiment and almost 20,000 Russian-auxiliaries were part of the Axis force. Most German divisions were non-motorised infantry formations. The average divisional ration strength was below 10,000. Two German divisions had fewer than 7,000 men.[37] The troops were supported by only 100 tanks, almost 2,000 guns, 10,000 motor vehicles and 40–50,000 horses. The Red Army had pressed onward to the south west to create a deep corridor separating the Stalingrad pocket from the rest of the *Wehrmacht*. Initially the Soviet General Staff thought they had only encircled 85–90,000 Germans.

The encirclement of Stalingrad confronted the German High Command with an exceptional crisis. Few reserves were locally available with which to plug gaps in the front in southern Russia. Hitler had been at Berchtesgaden in Bavaria when the crisis erupted. On the evening of 21 November he ordered the Sixth Army to maintain its position at Stalingrad and form a defensive perimeter. The Sixth Army was to adopt a 'hedgehog position'. On the evening of 22 November Paulus confirmed by radio that he would endeavour to hold his position, but he went on to say: 'Request freedom of action in case hedgehog does not succeed in the south. Situation might then compel abandonment of Stalingrad and northern front.'[38] The request was not granted, though Weichs, the commander of Army Group B, advised a retreat from the Volga the following day.

Hitler left southern Germany for East Prussia by train on the evening of 22 November. A twenty hour journey took him to Leipzig, from where he flew to his Rastenburg headquarters. General Zeitzler sensibly insisted to Hitler on 23 November that the Sixth Army should break out to the west before it was caught irrevocably in a trap. At first Hitler calmly rejected this advice. 'We have been in such positions often before, you know. In the end we always had the problem in hand again.'[39] By next day, though, Hitler was less confident and feeling the strain of the situation.

On 24 November Goering fatefully appeared in the situation room at Rastenburg, 'brisk and beaming like an operetta tenor who is supposed to portray a victorious Reich Marshal'. Hitler asked Goering about the possibility of supplying Stalingrad from the air. Smaller pockets had been supplied successfully earlier in the year. Goering declared that Stalingrad could indeed be supplied from the air. Zeitzler had strong doubts but Hitler accepted Goering's word without detailed explanation. 'Then Stalingrad can be held!' proclaimed Hitler, 'It is foolish to go on talking any more about a breakout of the Sixth Army. It would loose all its heavy weapons and have no fighting strength left. The Sixth Army remains in Stalingrad!'[40] Hitler still believed his refusal to authorise a general retreat in the eastern winter of 1941–42 had been the right decision. The stand fast order to Paulus mirrored the instruction only recently given to Rommel at El Alamein. The *Luftwaffe*'s general staff did not agree with Goering, yet he stood by his rash offer. On 24 November Hitler gave a firm order that the Sixth Army was to maintain its position and await re-supply from the air. Stalingrad was declared a fortress.

As the Soviet siege of Stalingrad commenced, Hitler already had a great deal to worry about given the recent defeat of the Afrika Korps at El Alamein and the Torch landings in French North Africa. German reserves in western Europe were in the process of heading to Tunisia to build up a new front in north-west Africa. New tanks would be needed to rebuild the Afrika Korps for the next inevitable round of fighting with Montgomery's Eighth Army. On top of that, it had proved necessary to occupy the forty per cent of France that had remained under the control of the Vichy regime. On 11 November German forces, including three valuable panzer divisions, had set out to swiftly overrun that zone. Petain ordered his troops not to offer any resistance. The French fleet at Toulon was scuttled on 27 November when Germans tried to storm the dockyard.

Events in Africa and France impacted upon Germany's ability to reinforce southern Russia, but to an even greater extent the new Soviet offensive on the central portion of the eastern front pinned down those panzer divisions that might best have been sent to help relieve Stalingrad. The opening of Operation Mars against Army Group Centre on 24/25 November imposed another commitment on the *Wehrmacht*. The Rzhev salient was a sharp chink in the eastern front to the north east of Smolensk, and an obvious potential launching pad for a renewed German advance on Moscow. Two Soviet army groups mounted pincer attacks against the eastern and western flanks of the salient. Plans for Mars may have begun development as a diversion, but over time the operation had become a major offensive in its own right. Mars proved to be a calamitous defeat for Zhukov as strong panzer reserves were close behind the Rzhev front. Zhukov recommended the cancellation of Operation Mars on 20 December, though not before Soviet casualties had mounted to over 335,000. Eight panzer-type divisions were involved in defeating Mars without serious loss of ground.[41]

Meanwhile, the command situation in southern Russia had been complicated by the arrival of Field-Marshal von Manstein to take charge of a new army group headquarters. Army Group B had been controlling seven armies and the creation of a new army group headquarters was needed to share the load. Manstein's Army Group Don was to take command of the Sixth Army, the Fourth Panzer Army and the Romanian armies. Manstein had been away from the southern part of the Russian front for the past ten weeks. His eldest son had been killed as a second lieutenant in a panzergrenadier regiment only a month previously.[42]

Manstein arrived at Army Group B headquarters on 24 November to be briefed on the situation. He was armed with orders from OKH to 'bring the enemy attacks to a standstill and recapture the positions previously occupied by us'.[43] At the outset Manstein was inclined to mount a relief effort of the Sixth Army. He sent a report to OKH on 24 November by telephone, which he later summed up in his memoirs:

> 'A break-out by Sixth Army to the south-west was probably still possible even now. To leave the army at Stalingrad any longer constituted an extreme risk, in view of the ammunition and fuel shortage. Nevertheless, since we considered that the best chance for an independent break-out had already been missed, it was preferable from the operational viewpoint at the present time to wait until the projected relief groups could come to the army's aid - always assuming that an adequate airlift could be counted upon.'[44]

This report may have bolstered Hitler's confidence in his decision to keep the Sixth Army against the Volga.

General von Seydlitz-Kurbach, a Sixth Army corps commander, urged Paulus to break out on 25 November in a written memorandum.

> Unless the Army High Command immediately rescinds its order to hold out in a hedgehog position, it becomes our inescapable duty before our own conscience, our duty to the army and to the German people to seize that freedom of action that we are being denied by the present order, and to take the opportunity which still exists at this moment to avert catastrophe by ourselves attacking. The complete annihilation of 200,000 fighting men and their entire equipment is at stake. There is no other choice.[45]

Paulus and his Chief of Staff, Major-General Arthur Schmidt, did not believe matters were so dire. Schmidt said of the memorandum: 'We don't have to rack the Führer's brain for him, nor does General von Seydlitz have to rack that of the army commander.'[46] Paulus was not the style of man to disobey Hitler's direct order, but he asked Manstein for freedom of action 'in the most extreme event' and attached Seydlitz's memorandum to the message.[47]

Left 1 Panzer: *Blitzkrieg* 1940

Below left 2 Hitler and Mussolini in Florence on the balcony of the Palazzo Vecchio

Below 3 General Gamelin, Commander-in-Chief of the French Army

4 RAF pilots, 1940

5 A Hurricane flight of No.73 Squadron over France during the 'Phoney War'

6 Dunkirk: A Hudson of Coastal Command patrolling during the evacuation

Above 7 Air Chief Marshal Sir Hugh Dowding, Air Officer Commander-in-Chief, Fighter Command, 1936–1940

Right 8 St Clement Danes, 10 May 1941

Below 9 Luftwaffe attack on a convoy in the English Channel, 14 July 1940

Left 10 A U–Boat
surrenders

Below 11 The sinking of
HMS *Ark Royal* in the
Mediterranean Sea, 14
November 1941

Above 12 A convoy on the western approaches to Britain

Below 13 HMS *Prince of Wales* at Singapore

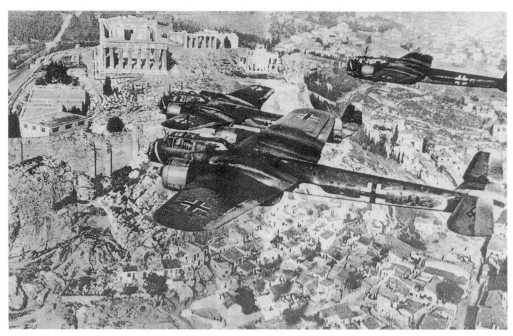

Above 14 *Luftwaffe* bombers over Athens and the Acropolis

Below 15 The *Wermacht* advancing in Russia

Left 16 German soldiers against a white-out snowscape

Above 17 Winter offensive

Below 18 Rommel strikes for Suez

Above 19 Tobruk, Libya

Below 20 Malta

Right 21 A Tanker burns in Malta's Grand Harbour

Right 22 Re-arming a Spitfire in the Mediterranean Theatre

Above 23 The Teheran Conference, December 1943. Front rwo: Stalin, Roosevelt and Churchill. Back row: Hopkins, Molotov, Harriman, Clark-Kerr and Eden

Left 24 Red Barricades: A view of a giant factory complex held by the Red Army at Stalingrad

Above 25, 26 & 27 Colonel-Generals Von Brauchitsch, Von Bock and Von Rundstedt

Below 28 General Guderian considers his next move

Left 29 Prime Minister Churchill visits General Montgomery's Headquarters

Below left 30 Air Chief Marshal Sir Charles Portal: The architect of the RAF's bombing offensive over occupied Europe

Below 31 Gliders in Normandy after the airborne landings

Top 32 A V.1 flying bomb

Above 33 The railway viaduct at Bielefeld after an air raid on 14 March 1945

Left 34 Oil refinery at Bremen under attack by Lancasters of Bomber Command, 21 March 1945

Left 35 The atomic bomb

Below & opposite 36 & 37 The aftermath at Hiroshima

Opposite below 38 Nagasaki

Manstein's reply to Paulus on 26 November strongly supported Hitler's current instructions to Paulus. 'The Führer's order relieves you of all responsibility other than the most appropriate and resolute execution of the Führer's order. What happens when, in execution of the Führer's order, the army has fired off its last bullet - for that you are not responsible!'[48] Paulus did not have sufficient information of events outside his perimeter to form an independent judgement strong enough to ignore the direct orders of his superiors.

Meanwhile, the Sixth Army's staff had radioed that they would need 750 tons of supplies a day merely to fight a defensive battle. The *Luftwaffe* would have struggled to fly in half that amount in optimum conditions. Troops were soon on half rations as supplies were short from the outset. Thick fog, ice and mounting Soviet aerial opposition badly interfered with the air lift. Transport aircraft were withdrawn from training units and Germany to build up the force under Richtofen's command. Bombers were pressed into service. A figure of around 300 transport-type aircraft was the peak total available in southern Russia. Half of the *Luftwaffe*'s transport aircraft were in the Mediterranean at this time, principally to meet the pressing transport needs of forces in Tunisia. Despite a great effort, and several airfields within the Stalingrad perimeter, the *Luftwaffe* averaged an air lift of not much more than 100 tons a day. During the siege almost 500 transport aircraft were lost to Soviet opposition, poor weather and accident.[49]

An expedition was hastily organised to mount an overland relief of Stalingrad. The Fourth Panzer Army's commander advised Manstein not to attack towards the Stalingrad pocket by the shortest route, which was a distance of about forty miles starting from near the junction of the Don and Chir rivers. The terrain was unfavourable and Soviet forces were massing in that sector. An attack starting from a more southerly location was chosen. Manstein's counter-offensive, Operation Winter Storm, began on 12 December. The relief force would need to cross eighty miles of frozen steppe. Winter Storm was spear-headed by a panzer corps that included a full strength panzer division recently railed to Russia from France. A single panzer corps contained only a fraction of German tank strength, but given the multiplicity of commitments facing the *Wehrmacht* in December 1942 that was all that was available. Manstein had asked for the transfer of Army Group A's panzer divisions but this had been refused for fear of weakening the front in the Caucasus. Nonetheless, in ten days half of the eighty miles across the steppe to the Sixth Army's perimeter had been covered. The gunfire of the beleaguered garrison could be heard in the distance.

To further complicate the German position in southern Russia, on 16 December the Soviets had launched Operation Little Saturn against Axis forces behind the middle Don. The blow crashed mostly against the Eighth Italian Army to tear another 100 mile gap in the front north-west of Stalingrad. German forces were frantically redeployed in a bid to patch up the situation.

The Stalingrad relief force reached a point thirty miles from the pocket but lacked sufficient infantry and artillery support to make further progress. On 19 December Manstein advised OKH that the Sixth Army would need to break out of the pocket as his forces could not break the Soviet ring. On that day Manstein also ordered Paulus to attack to link up with the relief force to permit a supply column to drive through into the pocket. Instead Paulus awaited instructions from OKH. By this time the bulk of the Sixth Army had been immobilised for lack of fuel and transport. The attempt to relieve Stalingrad had irrevocably failed by Christmas. The previous day the Soviets had overrun the main forward airfield outside Stalingrad used for the airlift. Hitler was advised that German forces must soon retreat from the Caucasus or risk a second Stalingrad-style encirclement. The Soviet press boasted that the Don Basin would become the sepulchre of the *Wehrmacht*.

In January 1942, as the cold worsened and the wind howled, the besieged soldiers of the Sixth Army were reduced to eating their transport horses. Oil and firewood became increasingly scarce. The first deaths from starvation were reported. Medical supplies were a constant source of anxiety. According to Colonel H.R. Dingler of the 3rd Motorised Division:

> The weather conditions were bearable during the first days of December. Later on heavy snowfalls occurred and it turned bitterly cold. Life became a misery. Digging was no longer possible as the ground was frozen hard and if we had to abandon our lines this meant that in the new lines we would have no dug-outs or trenches. The heavy snow diminished our small petrol supplies still further.[50]

Some of the beleaguered Germans were still inspired by National Socialist zeal. Captain Gebhardt wrote to his wife on 13 January:

> Many difficult weeks are now behind us, but the all-decisive hour is still ahead … Come what may, we shall never capitulate. Loyal to our military oath, we shall perform our duties believing in our beloved Führer, Adolf Hitler, and believing in the final victory of our glorious Fatherland … There is no human being who loves to die. However, if it has to be, then I have convinced myself that I want to be defeated in honest combat by superior enemy forces.

Not all were so idealistic. A soldier of the 94th Division recorded:

> The horses have already been eaten. I would eat a cat; they say its meat is also tasty. The soldiers look like corpses or lunatics, looking for something to put in their mouths. They no longer take cover from Russian shells; they haven't the strength to walk, run away and hide. A curse on this war![51]

An outbreak of typhus was another curse on the garrison.

On 8 January General Rokossovsky demanded the capitulation of Paulus's army. Two days later thousands of guns heralded a new Soviet offensive against the western end of the Stalingrad perimeter along a fifty mile front. Seven Soviet armies, including the 62nd Army, would be involved in the following battle. The cold, bitter wind and frozen ground added to the nightmare for all combatants. The main *Luftwaffe* aerodrome within the perimeter was soon overrun. *Luftwaffe* transports were reduced to parachuting a trickle of supplies into the contracting perimeter.

The Germans were pushed into the ruins of Stalingrad and on 26 January the garrison was broken into two pockets. The Sixth Army had almost completely run out of food, ammunition and fuel by the time of its surrender. All the transport animals had been eaten. By the end of January 20,000 wounded men had accumulated in makeshift hospitals beneath the ruins as the temperature outside fell to minus thirty degrees Celsius.[52] Another 20,000 frost-bite cases and stragglers without weaponry were also seeking shelter. Hitler promoted Paulus from colonel-general to field-marshal in the belief that would deter him from surrender. No German field-marshal had capitulated in the field since the creation of the German empire of 1871. But on 31 January the Sixth Army's headquarters in the basement of the Univermag department store was overrun and Paulus surrendered. The last German resistance at Stalingrad ceased on 2 February. The swastika flag no longer flew in sight of the Volga.

The sound of gunfire died away and the city was silent. Already weak from hunger, ill health and serious wounds, few of the 100–110,000 Axis prisoners, the bulk taken in the final capitulation, would survive captivity to tell the tale of their ordeal. The prisoners were marched and entrained to Tashkent, to the north of Afghanistan, by which time half had already perished.[53] (Paulus was not released until 1953). The most fortunate Germans of the Stalingrad force were the 30,000 wounded and specialists who had been flown out of the perimeter by the transport aircraft endeavouring to keep the garrison supplied. During the two and a half month siege of the pocket 100,000 German, Romanian and Russian auxiliaries had died. Albert Speer's younger brother Ernst was among the missing never to be heard of again. Many Axis servicemen had been killed in the fighting in the conventionally understood sense of combat-death, but just as many had probably been wounded or sick men who had died of exposure and exhaustion in the snow-covered waste. Red Army casualties at the hands of a desperate Sixth Army were also immense. The extreme cold took the lives of the wounded without discriminating between armies. Soviet losses in the three army groups involved in the campaign of Operation Uranus were almost half a million.

On 4 February the foreign press was flown to Stalingrad to inspect the ruins and wreckage. A fierce east wind blew across the snow-covered steppe. Alexander Werth was among the group taken to see the huddle of captured German generals, bedecked with medals, crosses and monocles. Lieutenant-General von Arnim was asked why the Sixth Army had been defeated. He replied: 'The question is badly put. You should ask how did we hold out so long against such overwhelming numerical superiority.'[54] Werth also observed the victorious General Chuikov: 'a tough, thickset type of Red Army officer, but with a good deal of bonhomie, a sense of humour, and a loud laugh. He had a golden smile: all his teeth were crowned in gold, and they glittered in the light of the electric lamp.' Chuikov promised his listeners that Stalingrad was merely the beginning, for the Germans 'their blackest day' was still to come.

The bells of the Kremlin rang out in triumph, whilst German state radio played Bruckner's Seventh Symphony as a commemoration of the lost army. Hitler ranted of Paulus's actions: 'In peacetime in Germany about 18,000 to 20,000 people a year choose to commit suicide although none of them is in a situation like this, and here's a man who has ... [many] of his soldiers die defending themselves bravely to the end – how can he give himself up to the Bolsheviks.' On 5 February Manstein was ordered to report at OKW. Hitler greeted the Field-Marshal upon his arrival by acknowledging: 'I alone bear the responsibility for Stalingrad! I could perhaps put some of the blame on Goering by saying that he gave me an incorrect picture of the *Luftwaffe's* potentialities. But he has been appointed by me as my successor, and as such I cannot charge him with the responsibility for Stalingrad.'[55] The sacrifice of the Sixth Army had arguably helped some divisions of the German army group in the Caucasus to retreat without being cut off. Hitler had finally authorised a full retreat from the region on 27 January. Part of Army Group A was ordered to withdraw into a bridgehead at Taman against the Black Sea, east of the Crimean peninsula, with a view to renewed operations after winter had passed.

The Sixth Army's fate at Stalingrad, and the collapse of the Axis offensive in southern Russia, was the result of a range of considerations. At the start of 1942 Hitler was still seeking the domination of Europe and world power status for Germany. Therefore the *Wehrmacht* needed to attack again in the east to win the war, or at least stalemate the war to Berlin's advantage. In hindsight, an offensive by Army Group South that wheeled north east behind Moscow to engage the mass of the Red Army – as the Soviets most feared – was probably the best alternative on offer. Instead Hitler made the decision to launch an offensive that aimed to seize the oil and raw materials of southern Russia and the Caucasus. He was probably trying to replicate the way in which the German Army had crippled Russia in 1917–18 by overrunning southern Russia without capturing Moscow. But by failing to focus on Moscow, the general push to the Volga and the Caucasus repeated the mistake of the Barbarossa campaign. The vast strength that the Soviets were able to mobilise in the lands east of Moscow was underestimated by Hitler for the second campaign in a row. The main sources of Soviet manpower and industry were not jeopardised by an offensive in southern Russia. The Germans gravely underestimated the resilience of Soviet industry and its ability to equip new mechanised formations. Superior lateral communications on the Soviet side of the front, particularly the great rail hub of Moscow, allowed the Red Army to make efficient use of its advantages.

Operation Blue began as an advance by a single army group on a restricted front, but it had bifurcated into offensives by two army groups pushing in divergent directions. It was fantastically ambitious to try to hold the line of the River Don, capture Stalingrad and scale the mountains of the Caucasus all at once. The oilfields were the primary objective of the campaign, yet how to transport the oil of the Caucasus back to the Third Reich was a question never answered. Even if the Sixth Army had quickly captured Stalingrad, or sensibly blockaded the city to cut traffic on the Volga, a heavy Soviet offensive against the long and brittle Don flank was bound to have eventuated late in the year. More sensible German decision-making might have avoided the Stalingrad cauldron, but a retreat from the Caucasus and Volga was probably inevitable once the Don flank started to collapse.

The defeat in southern Russia shattered the confidence of the Axis satellite states and their armed forces. The Romanians, Hungarians and Italians had loyally provided large armies for the campaign in southern Russia, only to be abandoned by the German Army. German military culture struggled to deal with the demands of coalition warfare, which was a terrible handicap given that their Anglo-American-Soviet opponents proved to have special gifts in that respect.

Stalingrad was certainly a personal defeat for Hitler, and a consequence of his firm control at both OKW and OKH. Paulus's conduct at Stalingrad had lacked heroic bravado but no German commander would have flatly disobeyed a direct and unambiguous order from higher authority at this stage of the war. Hitler had an immense talent for politics, ideology and propaganda, but his intuitive judgement, willingness to gamble and belief in the importance of will power was not enough to successfully solve complicated military problems that required careful technical analysis. Hitler had made use of modern radio and air communications to enforce his will on a distant battlefield. Two years later he told one of his doctors that his sleepless nights were marred by pictures of the campaign's battle map with its lost formations.

For a second winter the *Wehrmacht* had ended the campaigning season exhausted and overstretched in the great spaces of the east. The German Army in Russia had not been irrevocably beaten at Stalingrad, but the Soviets had regained the Donets basin and their main oil supply in the Caucasus was again secure. The Stalingrad defeat had badly shaken the German military's aura of invincibility. The Red Army now had its own version of the Cannae victory, Hannibal's double envelopment of the legions of Rome and perhaps the most famous battle of the ancient world.[56] Stalin made himself a Marshal of the Soviet Union, a mark of the dictator's prominent role in the Red Army's leadership.

Ironically, Germany did not suffer an oil crisis in 1943, as Hitler and other Nazi leaders had feared. Supplies would be short but a significantly expanded synthetic oil production, which was still beyond the effective reach of Anglo-American bombing, maintained German fuel supplies at an adequate minimum level.[57] The perceived desperate need for the oilfields of the Caucasus proved to be a mirage.

10

The Battle of Kursk: The Death of *Blitzkrieg*

The fall of Stalingrad did not bring the campaign in southern Russia to a sudden halt. The fighting seldom paused for long on the eastern front, and the Soviets were determined to press westwards to exploit their great victory. The immediate task for the German High Command was to rebuild and stabilise the front in southern Russia. The Germans had entered Russia with 3,350 tanks, but in late January 1943 tank strength had fallen to a dangerous low of 495 running panzers.[1]

On 6 February Manstein and Kluge met with Hitler in East Prussia. Hitler was aware that the situation had become dire in the east. The Rzhev salient on the front of Army Group Centre was to be evacuated at an early opportunity to shorten the front and free up reserves, in particular Model's Ninth Army. Further north, permission had already been given for Army Group North to evacuate the Demyansk salient. The Red Army's recent offensive to open a land route to Leningrad south of Lake Lagoda had secured a shell-devastated corridor five to eight miles wide. In southern Russia, Hitler conceded permission for a withdrawal from Rostov and the lower Don to the River Mius. The Soviets had also encircled a large Hungarian force west of the upper Don. In consequence, the Second Panzer Army in the neighbouring Voronezh sector had to fight its way to safety. Army Group B headquarters were closed down and Manstein's Army Group Don was renamed Army Group South.

On 16 February 1943 Kharkov – the fourth largest Soviet city – was evacuated by the *Wehrmacht*. The Red Army's advance soon created a salient in the German front to the south west of Kharkov. Hopes grew in Moscow that the Red Army might sever German supply lines in southern Russia leading rearwards to the mighty River Dnieper. As the crisis mounted Hitler ordered the transfer of a number of divisions from France and other subsidiary theatres. Over twenty German divisions were rapidly railed from western to eastern Europe.[2] The arrival of an SS panzer corps in southern Russia from France was a vital reinforcement.

Hitler visited Field-Marshal von Manstein's headquarters at Zaporozhe on 17 February accompanied by Generals Zeitzler and Jodl. Advancing Soviet troops were within fifty miles of Zaporozhe. Hitler had not come so near to the front during the Stalingrad crisis. A few days later General Guderian, following his appointment as Inspector-General of Panzer Troops, met with Hitler in the

Ukraine. Guderian was taken aback by the state of the Führer. 'His left hand trembled, his back was bent, his gaze was fixed, his eyes protruded but lacked his former lustre, his cheeks were flecked with red. He was more excitable, easily lost his composure and was prone to angry outbursts and ill-considered decisions.'[3]

The resourceful Manstein had plans for a counter-offensive. He launched the armoured divisions of Army Group South against the bulge in his front on 19 February. II SS Panzer Corps led the attack, and was joined by two more panzer corps in the days ahead. Over-extended and weakened Soviet formations were rapidly overrun. In open country fleeing columns could be spotted at ten miles' distance. There was little hope of escape. The Germans claimed to have destroyed or captured over 600 tanks and 1,000 guns. By mid-March Kharkov had been re-captured and the Soviets pushed eastwards across the River Donetz. The spring thaw in March – the *rasputitsa* – and strong Soviet reinforcements stalled operations before an improvised German attack could be launched on the salient at Kursk that had been created by the renewed German advance. 'Marshal Winter' had been succeeded by 'Marshal Mud'. The line had returned to about where the Germans had begun operations in the spring of 1942.

The strange lull that fell over the eastern front in the late spring of 1943 was the longest of the war. Soviet losses in the first three months of 1943 were 656,000 killed and 1.4 million wounded. During the year's second quarter from April to June this figure would fall dramatically to 125,000 killed and 471,000 wounded.[4]

At the end of April 1943 the initiative on the eastern front was again in German hands despite the severe defeat at Stalingrad. The German Army was still deep inside Soviet territory and had inflicted appalling losses on their opponent. In the spring of 1943 German commanders remained confident they could outlast the Red Army, and were immensely proud of their professional achievements in the war so far. The *Wehrmacht* clung to the belief that they were invincible in the summer months when the weather suited the rapid advance of armoured vehicles. The blame for the setbacks of the previous year was attributed to the collapse of Axis-satellite armies.

There was an argument that the *Wehrmacht* should rest on the defensive in the east for 1943 to save strength to deal with whatever offensive the Anglo-Americans were planning in the western and Mediterranean theatres. But Hitler and the Nazi leadership were waging a war of aggression in the east. The gains already made needed further extension and consolidation. As the Soviet leadership appeared resolute, the path towards German victory in the east required further offensive victories. When looking at their prospects for the year of 1943, German commanders were aware that an offensive on the scale of the previous two summers was no longer possible. The prospect of a great, annihilating success to drive the Soviet Union out of the war seemed remote. The Stalingrad defeat had been irreversible in that respect. According to Manstein: 'What did seem possible ... was that the Soviet Union could be worn down to such as extent that it would tire of its already excessive sacrifices and be ready to accept a stalemate.' Powerful local German offensives might sap the Soviets of the strength to launch their own offensives.[5] Manstein's initial preferred plan was to wait for the Soviets to again attack his Army Group South, and then launch a counter-attack to crush them. Manstein's headquarters submitted this plan but Hitler could not countenance a passive strategy that required even a temporary loss of the initiative. It was the will of the Führer that the *Wehrmacht* launch a fresh major offensive in the east.

The choice of location for the coming dry-weather offensive did not prove difficult for the German High Command. By the spring of 1943 the eastern front had been straightened out in many places, but the large Soviet salient around Kursk – 160 miles from north to south and 100 miles from east to west – was a prominent bulge in the line. The Kursk salient lay between two shallower German salients about Orel and Kharkov. Manstein suggested that Kursk was the most suitable place for an offensive.[6] After all, in June 1942 the *Wehrmacht* had smashed in the Red Army's front to the north and south of Kursk with relative ease to lunge forward to the River Don. Planning for another operation in that area was commenced. In the meantime the panzer divisions urgently needed deliveries of new tanks as they had lost heavily in the winter and spring fighting. For example, in April the 18th Panzer Division had only thirty-one tanks. On 15 April Hitler signed the order for an offensive at Kursk early in May if preparations could be completed.

The German offensive at Kursk would come up against a much-improved Red Army compared with the force the Germans had sliced through in 1941. This improvement had made itself evident in the Stalingrad campaign, though the Red Army had been unable to staunch the flow of their enormous losses. By the start of 1943 five Soviet tank armies had been formed in imitation of panzer formations. A tank army comprised several mechanised corps and tank corps. A Soviet tank corps possessed 168 tanks and was the equivalent of a strong panzer division. The days of dividing Soviet tank units into scattered penny packets had passed. New model T-34 tanks were fitted with radios and re-designed minor features. Thanks to the large number of United States trucks that had been shipped to the Soviet Union, the Red Army had become a more motorised force. Whether used on the lines of communications, or as transport for combat units, large numbers of sturdy, reliable trucks were vital for any army that aspired to advance across long distances. The stock of Soviet artillery had also become massive and would do a great deal of damage in a set-piece battle. Red Army formations that had distinguished themselves in battle had been renamed 'Guards' formations, a title with a decidedly Tsarist ring. The authority of officers had been enhanced, whilst political commissars lost parts of their powers over field commanders. Political commissars had even been abolished in some units, as had the NKVD blocking units previously deployed to shoot stragglers from the front line.[7] The massive casualties of 1941–42, however, had not been without impact. By the summer of 1943 Soviet rifle divisions had an average strength of 7,000, well below that of two years before.

The Red Army's leaders had learned much from past mistakes, and at the very top of the command chain Stalin had become more willing to accept their advice, especially in the wake of such a triumph as the capture of Stalingrad. Stalin was persuaded that the Red Army should await a renewed German attack. This was not an easy posture for Stalin to adopt. In Soviet political life a speedy attack to terrorise and vanquish opponents had long been Stalin's preferred and grimly effective method of operation. His instinct had been to apply the methods of domestic terror to external warfare. He was learning, though, to support a different style of strategic thought.

Zhukov recommended to Stalin in an 8 April strategic appreciation:

> An offensive on the part of our troops in the near future aimed at forestalling the enemy I consider to be pointless. It would be better if we grind down the enemy in our defences, break up his tank forces and then, introducing fresh reserves, go over to a general offensive to pulverise once and for all his main concentrations.[8]

In the winter of 1941–42 at Moscow, and at Stalingrad in the winter of 1942–43, the Red Army had counter-punched effectively after the German offensives of that year had become over-extended and exhausted. The Red Army would counter-punch again in 1943, but this time by design rather than expedient.

In his appreciation Zhukov went on to note that the Germans were concentrating the bulk of their armoured divisions about Orel and Kharkov, opposite the Kursk salient. It was likely that the Germans would attack on this sector so as to threaten Moscow from the city's southern flank. The enticing Kursk salient was an obvious target and it was standard German procedure to use a pincer movement with armoured forces whenever an opportunity was on offer. After the failed push into southern Russia of the previous year, Zhukov believed the Germans would next attack on a more central part of the eastern front. For once, unlike in 1941 and 1942, the Red Army's commanders had correctly divined the Germans' intentions for a summer campaign. By the spring of 1943 Soviet intelligence had greatly improved after two years of lacklustre performance. Aerial reconnaissance, radio intercepts, espionage and strategic common sense all pointed towards Kursk as the place of the next German offensive. The Germans and the Soviets chose to attack and defend the Kursk region at about the same time, so obvious was its vulnerability. Almost all Red Army commanders supported Zhukov's appreciation.

At a 12 April meeting of Stalin and his senior commanders at the Kremlin it was decided that the building of deep defences within and behind the Kursk salient should be a priority. The army groups to the north and south of Kursk were also to build defences in case of subsidiary German thrusts on those parts of the front. The local civilian population was mobilised to help dig successive lines of trenches and anti-tank obstacles. Vast mine fields were laid to cover the lines of earth works stretching rearwards for up to 100 miles. Half a dozen lines were built within the salient; a seventh line was dug across the base of the salient; an eighth line was laid out at the River Don.[9] The Soviets were turning Kursk into a giant Verdun, guarded by unprecedented depths of defence. The extent of Soviet preparations was a natural response to the battering the Red Army had taken during the previous two summers of the war. By May the Soviets were nearly certain that Kursk would be the arena for the predicted German offensive.

General Konstantin Rokossovsky's Central Front, in the northern half of the Kursk salient, comprised five armies, including the 2nd Tank Army. Rokossovky, a strong and decisive man, was the son of a train driver, and had been a cavalry sergeant during the First World War. He had joined the Red Army in 1918 and rose to be a corps commander by 1936, only to be imprisoned for three years during the purges on contrived charges of sabotage and 'impairing combat effectiveness'. He was tortured in prison only to be released in March 1940 to continue with his military career.[10] Such a bizarre outcome was typical of Russia during that period. Understandably, Rokossovsky regarded political officers with great bitterness. He had gone on to win enduring fame for his role in the capture of Stalingrad.

In the southern half of the Kursk salient, General Nikolai Vatutin's Voronzeh Front army group also comprised half a dozen armies, including a tank army. Vatutin was a proven general staff officer. He had been Zhukov's deputy in 1941 and had taken command of a key army group the following year. Rokossovsky's and Vatutin's army groups had been built up to include a million men, 3,200 armoured vehicles, 20,000 guns and mortars, 6,000 anti-tank guns and 920 *katyusha* rocket-batteries. Improvements in the equipment of the Red Air Force were also starting to reap dividends in the skies of the east. New aerodromes sprouted across the landscape to accommodate the Red Air Force's burgeoning strength.[11]

A large reserve force was built up to the rear of the Kursk salient. The Red Army's strategic reserve, the Steppe Front army group, would be close at hand. Briansk and South-Western Front army groups prolonged the line beyond the northern and southern shoulders of the bulge. Marshals Zhukov and Vasilevsky were dispatched by Stalin to play co-ordinating roles in the Kursk region. Once the German offensive had been halted, the Soviets planned to commence their own offensive against the Orel bulge and Kharkov, which were located to the north and south of the Kursk salient respectively.

Unaware of the extent to which the Soviets were planning to turn the Kursk salient into a field fortress, at Munich on 3–4 May a conference was held by the

German High Command. OKH Chief of Staff, General Zeitzler, was a strong supporter of the Kursk offensive. He was persuaded that the new Tiger and Panther tanks coming into service would make a decisive impact. Field-Marshal von Kluge of Army Group Centre was in agreement, but his subordinate, General Model of the Ninth Army, had reported that aerial reconnaissance had revealed that the Soviets were strongly fortifying the shoulders of the Kursk salient just where the Germans were planning to attack. Model wanted a delay so that his formations could build up their strength by absorbing replacements. Intelligence sources also indicated that the Red Army had withdrawn its mobile forces out of the front face of the salient, and were thus unlikely to be trapped by a successful pincer operation.

Hitler asked Manstein, commander of Army Group South, for his opinion. In the view of Guderian, Inspector-General of Panzer Troops, the tall, aloof, hook-nosed Manstein was 'a man of most distinguished military talents, a product of the German General Staff Corps, with a sensible, cool understanding ... our finest operational brain.'[12] Manstein told Hitler that the attack would have had a good chance of success back in April but was now problematic as time was slipping away. Kluge and Manstein were generally in favour of an offensive, but were keenly aware that delays had let the Red Army build up strength. Guderian, by his own account, did not mince words when he expressed his view. 'I ... declared that the attack was pointless ... if we attacked according to the plan of the Chief of the General Staff [Zeitzler] we were certain to suffer heavy tank casualties, which we would not be in a position to replace in 1943.' Guderian wanted to economise on tank losses in the east to build up strength for forces in western and southern Europe. He later met Hitler at the Chancellery in Berlin to discuss tank production. He asked Hitler why it was necessary to launch the planned offensive. Field-Marshal Keitel of OKW (Hitler's Supreme Headquarters) interjected, 'We must attack for political reasons.' Hitler replied that he was not yet fully committed to the project, and 'whenever I think of this attack my stomach turns over'.[13]

Operation Citadel – the codename for the Kursk offensive – was not ready by the first half of May, and was further delayed by Hitler to build up reserves of tanks. The aim of the operation was to seize the initiative by achieving a local victory, and thereby stabilise the entire front in a strategic sense. Citadel was intended to grind up Soviet formations, and in light of the deep advances achieved by the summer offensives of 1941 and 1942, German commanders at least assumed a successful local penetration of Soviet defences around Kursk.

There were further delays to the commencement of Citadel as the fall of Tunis in North Africa meant that the defence of Italy and southern Europe had to be buttressed. For instance, the 1st Panzer Division was ordered to Greece from France, where it had been rebuilding.[14] The prospect of an Allied invasion of southern Europe was starting to command a lot of Berlin's attention. By late spring of 1943 France, Italy, Norway and other subsidiary theatres were draining off a rising share of the German Army's strength, over 1.3 million troops.[15] The *Wehrmacht* was fighting in the east with one arm tied behind its back.

Great hopes had been invested in a new generation of German tanks. These new tanks might redress the balance. In late 1941 the German military had asked industry to design a tank able to outfight the T-34 and other heavy Soviet tanks. Across 1942 and into 1943 work on prototypes and new tank factories had moved steadily forward. The Panzer Mark VI Tiger, a heavily armoured vehicle of fifty-six tons, armed with an 88mm cannon, was designed to be the most powerful fighting tank in existence. A Tiger's frontal armour was especially thick. Small numbers of Tigers had already seen action in Tunisia against the Anglo-Americans and in local engagements in the east. The new forty-five ton Panzer Mark V Panther carried a 75mm gun. The Panther featured sloped armour to deflect shells, and was intended to become the medium-tank backbone of the *Wehrmacht*'s mechanised formations.

The delivery of new Tigers and Panthers was slow as manufacturers struggled to balance the desire to finely handcraft component parts with the need to produce vehicles in quantity. In general, however, 1943 saw an impressive expansion in the production of panzer vehicles, many of which were older-model Mark IV medium tanks. For 1942 a monthly average of 345 tanks had been driven out the factory gates. By May of 1943 this figure had risen to 689 tanks of a better overall quality. The production of assault guns and self-propelled guns had been expanded at an even faster rate. In 1942 over 4,100 German tanks had been built. Almost 6,000 would be built in 1943, together with a similar number of assault guns and self-propelled guns. Alas for the Germans, they still struggled to raise their tank strength in the east to anywhere near the more than 3,000 used at the commencement of Barbarossa. Rising loss rates were keeping pace with rising production rates. On 1 July 1943 the *Wehrmacht* in the east had 2,269 tanks and 997 assault guns. (The German Army had a grand total of 3,142 tanks and 1,422 assault guns across all theatres).[16]

In the spring of 1943 German infantry strength in Russia was dropping as a chronic manpower shortage began to plague the *Wehrmacht*. Most infantry divisions in Russia had been reduced from nine to six battalions, though this was counter-balanced by the extent to which the Red Army was experiencing much the same shortage. German divisions vital to the Kursk offensive were brought up to strength, but at the expense of other formations elsewhere in the east, which were starved of replacements. The divisions of Axis satellite armies shattered in the previous winter's campaign were either no longer in existence or too weak to be employed in a major operation.

The situation in Russia was becoming even more difficult for the *Luftwaffe* than for the German Army. The *Luftwaffe* had been forced to redeploy the majority of its strength to face the Anglo-Americans in western Europe and the Mediterranean. On the eastern front the *Luftwaffe* could only hope to establish local air superiority for limited periods, thus compromising one of the vital elements of *blitzkrieg* doctrine.

General Zeitzler and Field-Marshal Keitel played pivotal roles in ultimately persuading Hitler to go ahead with Operation Citadel. A date in May was postponed until June and then postponed again. On 16 June Hitler confirmed the operation would go ahead. Two days later General Jodl's OKW operations staff recommended cancelling Citadel so as to build up reserves, but Hitler was determined to go ahead with the operation.

At an operational level, the German plan took the form of a highly ambitious double envelopment of the Kursk salient. In autumn of 1941 the 200 mile-wide Kiev salient had been attacked and successfully closed off in about five days.[17] It was hoped to repeat that success at Kursk. The eastern front had been stripped of mechanised formations to build up the Citadel force, which comprised 2,500 tanks and assault guns. The Grossdeutschland Panzergrenadier Division had 170 tanks and assault guns.

Against the north face of the salient Model's Ninth Army of Army Group Centre was to attack with twenty-one divisions, of which seven would be panzer or panzergrenadier divisions. Against the southern face of the salient General Hoth's Fourth Panzer Army and Army Detachment Kempf had nine panzer or panzergrenadier divisions and a large force of infantry. Army Group South armoured formations included almost 1,000 tanks, of which ninety-four were Tigers and 200 Panthers. The southern assault force was the stronger of the German pincers. In the northern part of the Kursk front *Luftflotte* 6 deployed 750 aircraft. *Luftflotte* 4 had 1,100 aircraft to support the southern pincer.[18] Infantry divisions of the German Second Army faced the outer bulge of the salient between the two pincers.

At a 1 July conference Hitler addressed all senior commanders down to corps level. He spoke of how the Red Army was preparing for a winter offensive. Germany needed to seize the initiative and get a blow in first. This would help the *Wehrmacht* retain possession of conquered territory. The offensive would be a gamble but it would succeed. Hitler sent a message to his soldiers on the eve of Citadel: 'This day you are to take part in an offensive of such importance that the whole future of the war may depend on its outcome. More than anything else, your victory will show the whole world that resistance to the power of the German Army is hopeless.' The impending engagement that Hitler was setting in motion was to be one of the largest set piece battles in history, a Second World War engagement that in style approximated Napoleonic battles such as Borodino and Wagram.

On 2 July Soviet forces at Kursk went on full alert. There had been frequent false alarms of a German offensive, but field intelligence during May and June had consistently drawn the attention of Soviet commanders to Kursk. On 4 July there was little sign of German activity and the evening was clear and mild. Captured German prisoners brought to both Central Front and Voronezh Front headquarters had revealed that an attack was imminent. A Soviet spoiling barrage was fired in some sectors, particularly in the north, to disorganise German troops tensely waiting to move off their start lines.

On the northern flank of the salient Model's Ninth Army was to attack on a width of twenty-five miles, with the main thrust on a ten mile front. Three panzer corps comprising 1,000 tanks and assault guns formed the spearhead. Assault formations had to traverse a Soviet forward defensive zone up to three miles deep which was riddled with trenches, mines and interlocking screens of anti-tank guns. The minefields were sited to channel tanks towards batteries of anti-tank guns. There was a second defensive zone about seven miles to the rear of the first, and the next zone was twenty miles behind the second, with further lines to the rear. The countryside of the Kursk region was full of cornfields, villages, farms and the long slope of steppe hills. Valleys, copses and small rivers broke up the plains. Aerial reconnaissance had revealed much about Soviet defensive preparations to local German commanders, but camouflage had hidden the full complexity of those preparations.[19]

At the northern shoulder of the Kursk salient the Ninth Army's barrage opened at 4.30 a.m. on 5 July. It was met by a heavy counter-barrage. In the air a fierce battle was soon underway. On the opening day of Citadel the *Luftwaffe* flew thousands of sorties. Individual Ju 87 Stuka dive-bomber aircrew managed up to six sorties. On 5 July a five mile advance was made by German troops on a twenty mile front, but progress soon became more difficult as Soviet defences were particularly strong along the northern bulge of the salient. Slow-moving tanks proved vulnerable to anti-tank gun fire; woods and villages needed clearing of defenders; thick mine fields caused unexpected delays and heavy infantry casualties. German reserves that had been intended to exploit success had to be committed to battle at an early stage. The assault lost its momentum around the villages of Ponyri and Olkhovatka on 8 July and ground to a halt the following day. Model's infantry divisions had started Citadel badly understrength. This was a grave handicap when directly assaulting a strongly held enemy front.[20]

Against the southern flank of the Kursk salient, Hoth's Fourth Panzer Army possessed over 900 tanks, including 200 Panthers and fifty-seven Tigers. General Hoth, a Prussian general staff officer with an aristocratic profile, had successfully commanded panzer formations in Poland, France and Barbarossa. A neighbouring panzer corps of Army Detachment Kempf was to support Hoth's formations. The nine panzer-type divisions of Army Group South attacking en masse was a formidable concentration of armour.

Hoth's offensive began the afternoon before the main Citadel assault with a reconnaissance in force to discover more about the forward layer of Soviet defences. The day was hot and thunderstorms were not far off. German assault troops were confident, experienced and rigorously prepared for what lay ahead.

Covered by a short artillery and aerial bombardment, infantry and engineers had moved out to clear paths through the Soviet minefields. Probing attacks met limited resistance and plenty of thunder, lightning, rain and defensive artillery fire. Night operations by tanks were difficult unless the ground and weather were favourable.

Hoth's tanks advanced for the main attack the next morning of 5 July. Despite heavy overnight rain panzer troops carried the forward Soviet zone, though more rain in the morning turned streams into torrents, and movement for tanks and vehicles became increasingly compromised. Roads were often just sandy tracks and engineers struggled to bridge swampy ground. The Germans were coming under heavy artillery fire and had to wade through minefields of unexpected depth. Groups of German tanks advanced in wedge formations, with Tigers at the tip. By the end of the day German troops had penetrated the Soviet front in places to a maximum depth of six to seven miles.

The next day, 6 July, further progress was made by Army Group South towards Oboyan on the road leading to the town of Kursk, but again the standing corn and waterlogged ground gave Soviet infantry the chance to fight effectively against tanks. Voronezh Front headquarters began to feed the 1st Tank Army into its second defensive line to shore up its defences. Tanks were dug in alongside the infantry and artillery. New Russian anti-tank methods, referred to by the Germans as a 'Pakfront', involved batteries of up to ten anti-tank guns under a single commander firing at a single target on his order. Mines and ditches endeavoured to channel tanks towards those batteries. By the end of 6 July the Fourth Panzer Army and Group Kempf were deep within the second Soviet defensive belt but had lost more armoured vehicles than expected. Soviet resistance was stiffening as a steady stream of reserves began to arrive from the Steppe Front in reserve behind the salient. It had become apparent to Soviet commanders that Army Group South's offensive had more punch than that of Model's Ninth Army to the north.

Manstein's thrust included three panzer corps, the spearhead of which was II SS Panzer Corps comprising the elite *Leibstandarte Adolph Hitler, Das Reich* and *Totenkopf* ('Death's Head') SS panzergrenadier divisions. SS *Totenkopf* personnel were distinguished by a skull insignia on their cap and collar that might prove a death sentence if they fell into Soviet hands. The commander of II Panzer Corps was General Paul Hausser, a tough sixty-three year-old who had lost an eye to Soviet shrapnel. On 9 July tanks of the SS corps and XLVIII Panzer Corps pushed further into Soviet defences. The River Psel was crossed and Stukas dived out of the sky to bomb and strafe T-34s lurking in the vicinity. A fifteen mile penetration of Soviet lines was accomplished, but the southern pincer was still fifty-five miles from Kursk and ninety miles away from joining hands with the northern pincer.

In the face of Army Group South's offensive the Soviets had no alternative but to keep committing reserves from the Steppe Front army group. During the opening days of Citadel, General Pavel Rotmistrov's 5th Guards Tank Army had made a three day march by road to join Voronezh Front near the town of Prokhorovka. The journey was hot and dusty but mostly undisturbed by the *Luftwaffe*. Rotmistrov, born in 1901, had joined the Red Army in 1917 and was still a young man to be a senior general. This relative youth, though, was common to Soviet military leaders as so many of their elders had been murdered or dismissed by Stalin's regime. Rotmistrov wore black rimmed glasses, a large moustache and had a professorial appearance. When Rotmistrov arrived at Voronezh Front headquarters to see General Vatutin and Marshal Vasilevsky he was shown a map on which it was explained that the Germans had shifted their thrust eastwards to the railway corridor leading to Prokhorovka. The 5th Guards Tank Army was ordered to strike against that German movement. The plan was for Rotmistrov's forces to attack on 12 July to the south west of Prokhorovka.[21] On the other side of the lines, the SS panzer divisions had been held up on 11 July pushing towards Prokhorovka. SS troops readied themselves overnight in forested terrain to resume the fight the following day. Soviet scouts could hear the roar of massed German tank engines.

On 12 July a large tank battle developed around Prokhorovka, on a ten to fifteen mile arc to the south and west of the town. Formations of German tanks numbering in the hundreds engaged a Soviet force of similar strength. This was one of the biggest one-day tank engagements of the Second World War. The corridor between the River Psel and Belgorod-Kursk railway was the main field of battle. Rotmistrov's men and machines faced off against the National Socialist supermen of II SS Panzer Corps, which was advancing in a north easterly direction along the bank of the Psel.[22]

The weather on 12 July was warm, humid and cloudy. A head-on clash of German and Soviet armoured forces began mid-morning. Prokhorovka might best be described as a series of separate though linked engagements. Rotmistrov's headquarters was in an apple orchard above fields of corn and woodland. Sloping ground intersected by ravines and copses sub-divided the battlefield. Rain and thunderstorms dampened down the smoke and dust of the melee. Rotmistrov was to write of the fighting with a degree of literary license:

> I raised my binoculars and saw our famous T-34 tanks leaving cover and rushing ahead, gathering speed. At the same time, I caught sight of a host of enemy tanks. Apparently, both we and the Germans had launched our offensives simultaneously. I was surprised to see how close to each other both the German and our tanks had been moving. The two huge tank armadas were set for a head-on collision.[23]

The Tiger tank proved effective in close combat, such was the weight of its armour and the power of its gun. Most of the burning tanks littering the landscape were T-34s. Explosions hurled tank turrets into the air. T-34s were reduced to ramming the panzers when their ammunition ran out.

At nightfall on 12 July supply and repair vehicles drove out across the fields of charred crops and burning machines. Both forces were spent and it was time to gather up the surviving wounded. Losses totalled several hundred tanks destroyed or damaged. In terms of numbers of tanks destroyed the day had gone heavily in the Germans' favour, as was usually the case on the eastern front, but the panzer divisions had made little additional progress. On the following day German reconnaissance forces found the Red Army's front still strongly held around Prokhorovka. Zhukov, Rotmistrov and Nikita Khrushchev, a high Communist Party official, inspected part of the field of battle that remained in Soviet hands. In the summer heat Zhukov had the car stopped several times to inspect burnt-out tanks. He was visibly moved by the sight of the carnage and wreckage of combat.[24]

Whilst the tank battle had raged around Prokhorovka, beyond the northern flank of the Kursk salient events on 12 July had taken a dramatic turn. German troops had not made much additional progress into the northern shoulder of the salient, despite committing most available reserves. In six days the Ninth Army had managed a maximum advance of ten miles at a cost of 400 tanks destroyed and disabled.[25] Stalin had telephoned Zhukov to suggest that the time was right to launch a counter-offensive. As in the lead up to the offensive that had surrounded Stalingrad, the Soviets revealed themselves to be skilled at shielding their intentions from German observers. On 12 July the Soviet Bryansk Front and the northern wing of the Central Front launched Operation Kutuzov against the German line covering Orel and the rear of Model's northern pincer. The Soviet counter-offensive made progress, though the improvised German defence was conducted with considerable expertise. Nonetheless, the defensive battle for the weakly held Orel salient proved expensive for the *Wehrmacht*.

In the face of mounting disappointment, Manstein and Kluge were summoned by air to a conference with Hitler in East Prussia on 13 July. By that date Army Group South had taken 24,000 prisoners. This was not a significant haul by the standards of the eastern front. The new Tiger tanks had proved too few to make a difference. The Tigers lacked machine guns for close range fighting. Guderian lamented: 'Once they had broken into the enemy's infantry zone they literally had to go quail shooting with cannons.'[26] Panther tanks had also proved a disappointment as they were beset by mechanical problems and too easily set ablaze when hit to incinerate their crews. A Panther's oil and fuel system needed better protection.

Hitler ordered that Citadel be cancelled. His decision was influenced by the western Allies' 10 July landing on Sicily. An Italian collapse was likely and new armies would have to be formed in Italy and the Balkans, possibly drawing on forces from the east. Further Allied operations in southern Europe were likely to follow if Sicily was lost. Hitler was also rightly concerned by news of the

Orel counter-offensive to the north of Kursk. Citadel had not crippled the Red Army's offensive potential and did not seem to promise success as an attritional campaign. Kluge had reported that the Ninth Army's offensive had been halted by the diversion of forces to help contain the Soviet attack on Orel.

Manstein was still surprisingly optimistic. He told Hitler:

> Speaking for my own Army Group, I pointed out that the battle was now at its culminating point, and that to break it off at this moment would be tantamount to throwing a victory away. On no account should we let go of the enemy until the mobile reserves he had committed were completely beaten.[27]

Manstein believed that Soviet tank reserves were running low and Hitler grudgingly permitted Army Group South to prolong its offensive. Manstein's army group continued to probe the Prokhorovka area from 13–15 July, but without much success. On 16 July Army Group South began withdrawing to the positions they had held at the start of the Kursk offensive. The great German eastern offensive for the summer of 1943 had ended.

By mid-July the Kursk region had borne the brunt of a fortnight's battle. Most of the Steppe Front strategic reserve had been committed to soak up the German Army's assault. A western journalist who drove to the front observed:

> The area north of Belgorod had been turned into a hideous desert, in which every tree and bush had been smashed by shell-fire. Hundreds of burned-out tanks and wrecked planes were still littering the battlefield, and even several miles away from it the air was filled with the stench of thousands of only half-buried Russian and German corpses.[28]

Kursk has often been characterised as a great tank battle, but it also involved large numbers of infantry and artillerymen. Massed anti-tank guns were probably as important to the outcome as armoured vehicles. Soviet losses had certainly been heavy. During the 'Kursk defensive operation' from 5–23 July the Soviets suffered 70,330 killed and 107,517 wounded, for a total of 177,847. German casualties had been less severe. From 5–11 July the German Ninth Army lost 20,720 casualties, and from 5–20 July Army Group South had lost 29,102 casualties, for a combined total of 49,822.[29] The Soviets admitted they had lost 1,600 tanks and assault guns destroyed. This proved to be five times greater than for the *Wehrmacht*. The Germans had lost many vehicles damaged but were able to control the local battlefield sufficiently to recover damaged vehicles for repair.

The Kursk battle, nonetheless, had been a grave disappointment for the Germans. It had taken less than ten days for Hitler to acknowledge the reality of the *Wehrmacht's* defeat. 'By the failure of Citadel', wrote Guderian, 'we had suffered a decisive defeat. The armoured formations, reformed and re-equipped with so much effort, had lost heavily both in men and in equipment and would now be unemployable for a long time to come ... the Russians exploited their victory to the full.'[30] Colonel von Mellenthin, Chief of Staff of an Army Group South panzer corps, later put his views succinctly:

> The German Supreme Command ... [committed] exactly the same error as in the previous year. Then we attacked the city of Stalingrad, now we ... [attacked] the Fortress of Kursk. In both cases the German Army threw away its advantages in mobile tactics, and met the Russians on ground of their own choosing. Yet the campaigns of 1941 and 1942 had proved that our panzers were virtually invincible if they were allowed to manoeuvre freely across the great plains of Russia.[31]

Mellenthin termed Citadel a 'veritable death-ride' that had consumed the whole operational reserve.

At Kursk the German High Command had set out to bleed the Soviets white in a fashion that was reminiscent of the attempt to cripple the French Army at Verdun in 1916. The Germans were not seeking a war-winning victory; rather they sought to ward off future Soviet offensives by inflicting upon the Red Army a local defeat. The strategic concept behind Citadel had been relatively unambitious compared to previous campaigns, yet the *Wehrmacht* had been brought undone by an unprecedented level of tactical failure. An attacker usually struggles to win an attritional battle unless enjoying a commanding numerical and material superiority. At Kursk that advantage lay with the Red Army. Indeed, it was rare for a defender to be so strong at a point chosen by an attacker for a battle. The experience at Stalingrad should have made clear to the German High Command that it had become futile to attempt to storm a strongly defended Soviet position. Surprise had been a vital precondition for previous *blitzkrieg*-style victories, but that had not been a high priority for Citadel. The choice of Kursk as a battlefield had been too obvious; Hitler and the German General Staff had run out of ideas. The mounting of the Kursk offensive was fundamentally a failure of imagination. For the third year in a row the Red Army's strength had been underestimated.

If Kursk had revealed that the *Wehrmacht* was in relative decline, it had also proved that the Red Army was an improved institution. The reforms forced upon the Soviets since late 1941 in respect to equipment, organisation and training had started to bear fruit. New tank armies and artillery divisions had given the Soviets a mobility and punch that was bound to significantly attrite any opponent they engaged. The strategic posture of the Soviets could no longer be knocked off balance by the excellence of the *Wehrmacht*. German armour was no longer able to range deep into the rear of a Soviet force. Soviet anti-tank defences had achieved a new level of depth and hitting power. Henceforward the Germans had no option but to grimly defend on the eastern front. After the war German generals placed much of the blame for the disappointment of Kursk on Hitler's judgement. But they too, especially Manstein, had assumed that the Red Army only fought well in winter, and that in summer the *Wehrmacht* could break through any Soviet defensive system, even in the face of superior numbers.[32] By the autumn of 1943 the Red Army had proved it could succeed both in summer and winter. After Kursk the *Wehrmacht* became an anvil for the Red Army's hammer. Churchill, using once again the words with which he had described the meaning of El Alamein for Britain, wrote that 'for Russia, Stalingrad was the end of the beginning; but the Battle of Kursk was the beginning of the end'.[33]

Yet the summer campaign on the eastern front for 1943 was far from over, and in some respects was just beginning. The strategic initiative now lay in Soviet hands. The Kursk battle proved to be a giant ambush. The German High Command did not appreciate that the Soviets were ready to move onto the offensive, straight after parrying the blow at Kursk. According to Mellenthin, 'we were now in the position of a man who has seized a wolf by the ears and dare not let him go'.[34] The ability of the Soviets to move swiftly from defence to attack would make it clear that the Kursk fighting had not impaired the overall fighting power of the Red Army. This would be the greatest shock of all for the Germans, who had simply not understood that the Red Army was now capable of launching and sustaining a series of rolling counter-offensives. The Germans would have to face those offensives having recently bled white their own panzer divisions.

On 1 August Hitler ordered a withdrawal from the Orel salient to the north of Kursk. The need for troops in other theatres had become more urgent. German reinforcements to Italy mostly came from Germany or western Europe but that directly reduced the level of reinforcement that could be sent to restore a crumbling situation in the east. The eastern front would have to reinforce threatened sectors with its own minimal reserves.

On 3 August a major Soviet offensive was launched against Army Group South from Belgorod to Kharkov. From behind poor defences, 210,000 Germans and 250 tanks and assault guns faced a million Soviets and 2,400 armoured vehicles. On 5 August the German garrison of Belgorod was encircled and the Soviets claimed to have counted 3,000 enemy bodies in the ruins after the conclusion of bitter street fighting.[35] By late August steady combat had reduced the 11th Panzer Division to fifteen running tanks. The 19th Panzer Division had only seven tanks. Kharkov had fallen to the Soviets by the end of August, at which time Soviet forces were advancing on a front from Kursk southwards to the Black Sea.

Soviet offensives on the southern half of the eastern front would roll onward for the rest of 1943. The Germans of Army Groups Centre and South were pushed back to the line of the River Dnieper. Smolensk was recaptured late in September and by the start of October the Germans had retreated an average of 150 miles across a front of 650 miles.[36] Kiev, the capital of Ukraine, fell on 6 November. Before long German forces in the Crimea had been cut off from the mainland. Hitler refused to sanction a retreat from the Crimea so as to deny the Soviets bases from which they might bomb the oil fields of Romania. The Teheran conference of Allied leaders began on 28 November and Stalin was able to attend with Soviet fortunes in the ascendancy.

The costs of the driving Soviet offensives across the autumn and winter months of 1943 were very high. Mellenthin commented dismissively: 'The stoicism of the majority of Russian soldiers and their mental sluggishness makes them quite insensible to losses … To step on walls of dead, composed of the bodies of his former friends and companions, makes not the slightest impression on him [the Soviet soldier] and does not upset his equanimity at all.'[37] Nevertheless, the Red Army's ability to absorb losses was of immense military value in a bitter war. The demographic and industrial arithmetic of the eastern front had started to bear inexorably against the *Wehrmacht*. The Soviets would lose 23,500 tanks and self-propelled guns in 1943 but would produce a similar quantity to maintain the strength of their armoured formations. During 1943 the Soviet forces would expand from 5.9 million to 6.4 million men and women, despite loosing almost two million killed and missing and five and a half million wounded and sick. It defied previous human experience for an army to suffer so heavily and emerge in a numerically stronger position.[38] The Red Army was determined to avenge its losses. The *Wehrmacht* in the east would have to face that challenge without the divisions that would be despatched to Italy, the Mediterranean, Norway and western Europe to face the Anglo-Americans.

11
Strategic Bombing: Berlin, Winter 1943–44

As the great campaigns of the eastern front unfolded to set a new standard for land warfare, another style of warfare – strategic bombing – confronted Germany from the western skies. 'Total war' in the twentieth century involved entire national economies and their industrial work forces. Long-range bombing operations could attack those things. Air power enthusiasts believed that the traditional rules of war which forbade targeting non-combatants could be downplayed as war industries were a newly legitimate target.[1] Strategic bombing was conducted by Allied and Axis air forces according to a set of rules that evolved during the conflict.

RAF night bombing of Germany had begun during the battle of France. Daylight bombing had quickly been abandoned as the *Luftwaffe*'s day-fighters dominated the skies of occupied Europe. The *Luftwaffe*'s bombing of Britain in the winter of 1940–41 greatly stimulated the RAF's campaign to bomb Germany. Strategic bombing was a way for Britain to strike back at Germany when little else seemed possible. It enjoyed strong and enduring political and popular support. On 8 July 1941 Churchill wrote: 'There is one thing that will bring [Hitler] down, and that is an absolutely devastating exterminating attack by heavy bombers from this country upon the Nazi homeland.' When the Soviet Union entered the conflict, strategic bombing became a way for the British to support Moscow.

Across 1941 night raids by the RAF's Bomber Command took place against specific, military-industrial targets in Axis Europe. But investigations late in the year based on several thousand aerial photographs taken in the flash of bursting bombs concluded that bombing results had been very poor. Many bombers had dropped their bombs on open countryside. In consequence, during the winter of 1941–42 the fateful decision was made to adopt a policy of 'area bombing' or 'city busting'. In other words an entire city was to be the target for incendiaries. Success was to be adjudged according to how many urban acres were devastated. The idea that a bomb dropped anywhere on a city by night was never wasted had great allure. This type of bombing policy also seemed to replicate what the *Luftwaffe* had already done to London and other British cities.

The chief architect of the area bombing campaign was Air Chief Marshal Sir Charles Portal, Chief of the Air Staff from 1940–45. After a distinguished First World War flying career, Portal's rise in the RAF between the wars had been meteoric. He became head of Bomber Command in April 1940 and Chief of the Air Staff in October 1940. The reserved Portal had a prominent hooked nose, and considerable political and managerial ability. He had an effective working relationship with Churchill, though he seldom left London to visit an RAF station or headquarters.[2]

On 14 February 1942 an Air Staff directive was sent to Bomber Command stating that operations 'should now be focused on the morale of the enemy civilian population and in particular the industrial workers'.[3] The next day Portal asserted, 'I suppose it is clear that the new aiming points are to be the built-up areas, not, for instance, the dockyards or factories.' Key decision makers were well aware of the impact bombing would have upon civilians under the bombs. In a paper prepared for the Chiefs of Staff on 3 November 1942 Portal argued that by 1944 a British-American heavy bombing force of 4–6,000 aircraft should be created. If that force bombed Germany in accordance with the policy Portal desired, an estimate was given that by the end of 1944 six million German dwellings would be destroyed, twenty-five million people made homeless, 900,000 civilians killed and a million more seriously wounded.[4] British bombing policy intended to punish the German people for their nation's aggression.

Bombing operations continued to take place by night as the RAF lacked an effective long-range fighter able to contest the *Luftwaffe's* daylight aerial supremacy. At an early stage of the bombing campaign Portal had deflected the possibility of giving bombers fighter escorts able to fly long distances. When the inquisitive Churchill had asked Portal about the need for long-range fighter escorts the Chief of the Air Staff had rejected the concept. Portal believed it would only be possible to increase the range of fighters by retarding their speed and agility to a point where they could not compete against short-range *Luftwaffe* fighters. He had written to Churchill on 27 May 1941: 'The long-range fighter, whether built specifically as such, or whether given increased range by fitting extra tanks, will be at a disadvantage compared with the short-range high performance fighter.'[5] The RAF's commanders, who were mostly former aircrew, lacked the technical and engineering knowledge to see the potential for auxiliary drop tanks under the wings of fighters. The RAF turned its back on both day and night long-range fighters, though a twin-engine night-fighter would be especially well suited to carry the fuel load needed for long-range operations.

Shortly after the adoption of the area bombing policy, on 22 February 1942 Air-Marshal Sir Arthur Harris was appointed to direct Bomber Command. Harris had neither doubts nor scruples about the need to pulverise German cities. He was to comment: 'The Germans again and again missed their chance, as they did in the London blitz that I watched from the roof of the Air Ministry, of setting our cities ablaze by a concentrated attack.'[6] Harris was to provide Bomber Command with the driving operational leadership it genuinely needed at this stage of the war.

Harris had been born in Britain in 1892 and went out to Rhodesia aged sixteen to make his own way in life. At the outbreak of the First World War, Harris had joined the army and the Rhodesian Regiment. He saw service in a brief successful campaign in German South West Africa. He then went to England and joined the Royal Flying Corps late in 1915 to become a fighter pilot. From 1916–18 Harris had spells of combat based in France and Britain, though he did not record any confirmed victories in aerial combat.[7] Between the wars Harris held commands in India, Mesopotamia, Palestine and Transjordan. In 1939 he had taken charge of Bomber Command's No. 5 Group. The following year Harris was appointed Deputy Chief of the Air Staff. He had impressed Portal in that post.

Harris told a press interviewer at his High Wycombe headquarters the day he began his tenure at Bomber Command: 'There are a lot of people who say that bombing cannot win the war. My reply is that it has never been tried yet. We shall see.'[8] Harris rarely left his headquarters and spent much of his time with his loyal and thoroughly intimidated staff. Subordinate group commanders regularly visited High Wycombe and Harris spoke to them by telephone almost daily. In turn Portal would not visit Harris, and the latter would have to go to the Air Ministry to see his chief.

At a daily morning conference, Harris personally made decisions as to whether a raid should take place the following night and the target to be hit. The weather forecast over western Europe was carefully studied when operations were planned. Harris had to risk almost his entire front-line strength night after night. There is the story that when Harris was stopped by a motor-cycle policeman for speeding, and reminded that he might have killed someone, the Air-Marshal had retorted: 'Young man, I kill thousands of people every night!' A blunt, coarse, chain-smoking man, made bad-tempered by relentless stress, Harris believed that bombing would bring Germany to its knees. The Allied armies might then be re-introduced to western continental Europe as a mopping up force when the right moment had arrived.

Harris's misleading reputation for bluff honesty is a tribute to the effectiveness of his political cunning. He conducted a great deal of dining and lobbying for senior political and press figures. Harris liked to show visitors a room full of reconnaissance photographs of bombed-out urban districts. This was the evidence that mattered most to Harris. He had little interest in detailed analysis of the German war economy.[9]

The strong degree of governmental and Air Staff support for strategic bombing was not without its critics among army and navy leaders. Even within the RAF there was resentment. The Far East was desperately short of aircraft.

Coastal Command needed more aircraft for the war against the U-boats. That the Air Staff and Portal did not do more for Coastal Command from 1940–42 was a serious mistake and largely due to Bomber Command's priority.

By 1942 a strong industrial and manpower commitment to Bomber Command was firmly in place. Bomber Command's aircrew were drawn from all corners of the British Empire. About seventy per cent came from the United Kingdom. Canadians were the next largest contingent. One in ten aircrew were Australians and New Zealanders. Bomber crew flew a tour of thirty missions. After an interval, often as a training instructor, an airman returned for a second tour of twenty operations. During the middle war period only a third of aircrew survived their first tour of operations without being shot down, but the training system kept pumping out replacements to cover the losses and maintain the rate of Bomber Command's expansion. The morale of aircrew remained remarkably high in spite of the losses. This was partly due to the high quality of personnel who volunteered for flying, and the extent to which aircrew were shielded from the sights of war by returning to base after each mission. It was possible for aircrew to believe they were bombing military targets in urban areas. Operational missions were very much a 'military confrontation' for those airmen involved.[10] If a bomber was damaged, the pilot had to keep flying the aircraft long enough for the rest of the crew to bale out, or struggle with the controls all the way back to England. Once an airman had parachuted to the ground, after plunging down through the darkness, he was often treated surprisingly well by his captors.

During 1942 Bomber Command started to enjoy the benefits of improved navigational aids. The RAF began to use radio beams to assist night flying navigation over the Continent. The *Luftwaffe* had made effective use of such beams to attack Britain in 1940–41. An early system was jammed but an improved system called 'Oboe' came into service in late 1942. Oboe radio beams were transmitted from stations in England to intersect at a given point in enemy air space. A receiver in a bomber could pick up the radio signals to give the crew an accurate navigational fix on their position. When the beams were fixed to intersect over the target, Oboe became a blind-bombing system of considerable accuracy. The draw-back to Oboe was that the curvature of the earth restricted its range to western Germany.

New four-engine bombers, especially the famous Avro Lancaster, began to replace smaller, twin-engine aircraft. A Lancaster could carry a maximum bomb load of 14,000 pounds, which was three times the standard load of a German bomber during the Blitz. A four-engine Halifax could carry 13,000 pounds of high explosive and incendiary bombs. A heavy bomber typically carried a single 4,000-pound 'blockbuster', some smaller bombs and containers of incendiary sticks. RAF heavy bombers lacked armour and usually had no underside turret. At night bombers did not fly in a set formation, rather each bomber set out at a staggered interval from its home station. The bomber force flew towards its target in a long stream. In August 1942 the first 'Pathfinder' squadrons were formed. The Pathfinders were experienced aircrew who preceded the main bombing force to mark the target with brightly coloured flares. The rest of the bomber stream would then drop their bombs into the flares.[11]

After taking up his new post at Bomber Command, Harris quickly showed his resolve to follow Portal's and the Air Staff's orders to do the maximum possible damage to Germany's urban landscape. Raids on the historic towns of Lubeck and Rostock in March and April 1942 had set those places ablaze. It was easier to burn down a city than to blow it up. The first 1,000 bomber raid hit Cologne, the third largest city in Germany, on the night of 30/31 May 1942. The bomber force had included 600 twin-engine Wellingtons. The Cologne raid was a great success both in terms of the damage inflicted and the publicity and political support it generated for Bomber Command.

The size of the raid on Cologne caused the *Luftwaffe* to build up their night defences. In July 1940 a night-fighter division had been set up at Brussels under General Joseph Kammhueber. A chain of radar, command and air bases – the Kammhueber line – had been established to cover the Low Countries and northern France. 162 *Luftwaffe* aircraft were devoted to night air defence in January 1942, and this figure more than doubled by the year's end.

The twin-engine Messerschmitt Bf 110 had proved a poor day-fighter but was to become the backbone of the night-fighter force. It possessed a handy speed advantage over a heavy bomber, and was large enough to carry the fuel load, heavy armament, radar equipment and radar operator needed for effective hunting in the night skies. The twin-engine Dornier Do 217 and Junkers Ju 88 would play useful supporting roles in the night-fighter force.

After America's entry to the war, Bomber Command was joined in the skies over Europe by the United States Army Air Force's Eighth Air Force. The United States had never been bombed by the *Luftwaffe*, but that did not detract from America's determination to bomb Germany, especially as Japan was still out of reach. The first American raids over occupied Europe were flown in August 1942. American air force generals did not agree with Bomber Command's methods. The Americans attempted to bomb specific industrial targets by daylight. The modern industrial economy was believed to have delicate vital points, the destruction of which would do disproportionate damage to the overall economy. The backbone of the Eighth Air Force was the B-17 Flying Fortress. American commanders hoped that by flying bombers in tight box formations targets could be reached beyond the range of a fighter escort. In practise Germany was under cloud cover nearly half the time, and American bombers would often drop their loads through the clouds in a manner like a night-time area bombing raid.[12] Besides, it was institutionally convenient to divide the day and night between the two Allied air forces. Allied propaganda claimed that Germany was being attacked 'around the clock'.

In January 1943 Churchill, Roosevelt and the Combined Chiefs of Staff met at Casablanca in North Africa. Many important matters were discussed, including an agreement to postpone D-Day in north-west Europe until 1944. Fresh amphibious landings in the Mediterranean and increased strategic bombing would dominate Anglo-American operations in the interim. The Combined Chiefs ordered 'the progressive destruction and dislocation of the German military, industrial and economic system, and the undermining of the morale of the German people to a point where their capacity for armed resistance is fatally weakened'. Five priority targets were nominated: submarine yards, the aircraft industry, transportation, oil plant and 'miscellaneous' war industries. The directive went on to say, 'moreover other objects of great importance either from the political or military point of view must be attacked'. The second example of this to be cited was Berlin, 'which should be attacked when conditions are suitable for the attainment of specially valuable results unfavourable to the morale of the enemy or favourable to that of Russia'.[13] The Third Reich's capital had been marked out for attack. It was logical for a strategic bombing campaign to include the largest urban mass in Germany.

By the start of 1943 most Bomber Command squadrons had been re-equipped with four-engine aircraft. An average daily strength of 826 aircraft would be attained by May. Bombing accuracy at night had improved significantly over the previous two years. Whereas in 1941 only twenty per cent of Bomber Command sorties had bombed within five miles of a target, by 1943 sixty per cent of sorties were bombing within three miles of the aiming point.[14]

In the spring and early summer of 1943 a sustained campaign was waged by night against the towns of the Ruhr region. (The Ruhr river was a tributary of the lower Rhine). The Ruhr was western Germany's industrial heartland. Bomber Command was finally undertaking a task of true strategic consequence and the campaign lasted many weeks. 872 bombers were lost during the 'Battle of the Ruhr' at an uncomfortably high loss rate of 4.7 per cent. That is, for every 100-bomber sorties sent over occupied Europe, on average 4.7 bombers did not return.

On 16/17 May No. 617 Squadron destroyed the Mohne and Eder dams, which were important to the Ruhr's hydroelectricity supply. Almost 1,300 people died on the ground in the dams' raid, mostly from drowning. A puzzled Albert Speer, promoted to be Hitler's armaments minister, later pointed out that the RAF missed the opportunity to re-bomb the dam walls as they were rebuilt. By late September the breach in the Mohne dam would be closed in time to capture the rains due late in the year.[15]

The climax of the summer's bombing season was the series of raids against Hamburg. Operation Gomorrah was named after the Biblical city destroyed by God. Between 24/25 July and 2/3 August Hamburg was targeted by four RAF

night and two USAAF day attacks. Hamburg was situated near the coast of
north-west Germany and was highly vulnerable to bombing. It was one of the
largest cities in Germany and had a population of two million.

Hamburg was beyond the range of Oboe radio beams broadcast from England,
but earlier in the year an airborne radar called H2S had been introduced. H2S
was an adaptation of the radar set used to search for vessels on the surface of the
ocean. An image was produced on a cathode-ray tube as the radar scanned the
ground. The image might be blurred and required considerable interpretative
skill, but coast line, rivers and urban sprawl could be detected. Harris was
generally supportive of scientific advances that improved his bombers' ability
to plough up urban acreage. In addition, for the Hamburg raids RAF aircraft
dropped 'Window', bundles of strips a foot long with one side of aluminium
foil, to block the signals of ground-based radar stations. Window dropped on a
broad front hung in the air as it floated on the breeze to create the impression
on German radar screens that the sky was full of aircraft, thus disguising the
precise location and strength of the attacking bomber stream.

Hot weather and broken water mains helped to produce a firestorm after
a raid on the night of 27/28 July. The storm of concentrated fire generated
winds of over 300 mph. Bodies were incinerated by the intense heat or
melted to a charred, coagulated mess. 44,600 civilians died in the series of
raids on Hamburg, over sixty per cent of whom were women and children.
The great majority died in the firestorm of 27/28 July. Many thousands more
were injured and 900,000 lost their homes. Most of the surviving population
temporarily fled the smouldering ruins. Aerial photography revealed clearly the
level of destruction.

In the immediate wake of the devastation of Hamburg a shocked Speer
told Hitler that the similar destruction of another six cities could halt arms
production. Yet even in Hamburg industrial production was back to eighty per
cent of normal in five months. One of Hamburg's main war industries was
maritime construction. Over 400 submarines would be built in Hamburg's
shipyards during the war. But the main target area for Operation Gomorrah
had been the residential zone to the north of the River Elbe. The shipyards to
the south of the river were not seriously damaged.[16]

The Hamburg firestorm and the growing strength of the USAAF's Eighth
Air Force hastened efforts to strengthen Germany's air defences. In 1941 almost
1,000 heavy anti-aircraft batteries of 88mm calibre or above had been available
to defend the Nazi home front, but by 1943 that figure had more than doubled.
In the autumn of 1943 there would be over 1,600 day- and night-fighters in the
western theatre.[17] The eastern front had been stripped of aircraft. By daylight
that effort yielded fruit when unescorted B-17 bombers ranging deep into
southern Germany suffered fearsome losses in October.

The weight of the Ruhr and Hamburg raids had forced the adoption of a
new system of night-fighter defence. When a bomber force was located by

radar approaching the coast of occupied Europe, night-fighters were scrambled to orbit radio beacons, and then directed, often by a single controller, towards the bomber stream. Radar controllers might misread the course and target of the bombers, but with experience it became possible to bring a mass of night-fighters into the bomber stream. 250–300 night-fighter sorties could be flown each night. From mid-August 1943 Bf 110s, radar aerials protruding from the nose, started to mount twin upward-firing cannon to better destroy a bomber in an attack from beneath. Single-engine night-fighters without airborne radar were assembled over major cities to hunt for bombers in the glare of the search lights, flak and bomb blasts. Flak batteries were ordered not to fire beyond a designated height, above which the fighters operated.

At his headquarters in England, Bomber Harris had been hugely encouraged by the battles of the Ruhr and Hamburg. On 12 August he told Portal:

> It is my firm belief that we are on the verge of a final showdown in the bombing war, and that the next few months will be vital. Opportunities do not knock repeatedly and continuously. I am certain that given average weather and concentration on the main job, we can push Germany over by bombing this year.[18]

Portal agreed sufficiently to write on 19 August that 'attacks on Berlin on anything like the Hamburg scale must have an enormous effect on Germany as a whole'. Harris had long privately desired to launch a campaign against Berlin to crown his night offensive and further justify the concept of independent strategic bombing. The destruction of Hamburg seemed a portent of the annihilation Bomber Command could visit upon the cities and society of Nazi Germany.

Berlin was one of the largest cities in the world. It had been laid out across nearly 900 square miles and in 1939 had a population of over four million people. Berlin was the capital of both Germany and Prussia. Hitler and Speer had great plans to remodel the Third Reich's leading city, and the 1936 summer Olympic Games had brought Berlin to the attention of the world.

Berlin was a spacious city by the standards of Europe. Lakes, parkland and broad thoroughfares were plentiful. A chain of lakes were a feature of the western suburbs. Large blocks of solidly built flats up to six storeys high dominated the older residential areas. As had been the case with London, Berlin's outer residential and commercial districts had expanded rapidly during the 1920s and 1930s. New suburbs of low-rise flats, houses and factories had sprung out of the reclaimed countryside.

In the centre of the city was the imposing Wilhelmstrasse government district of ministerial buildings, the Chancellery and old Presidential palace.

Nearby was the famous Brandenburg Gate, topped by the four-horsed chariot of the goddess of victory. The Tiergarten was a large piece of heathland close to the city centre. Numerous military headquarters were based in the national capital, which was the hub for many major railway lines.

Industry was scattered across Berlin. Germany's largest tank factory at Alkett was in the west of the city. The Siemens electrical works and Borsig heavy engineering works were important contributors to the German war economy, as were the factories of German General Electric. One-tenth of Germany's aero-engines, one-third of electrical equipment, one-quarter of tanks and one-half of field artillery were produced in Berlin's many industrial plants. Hundreds of thousands of foreign workers had been brought to the Reich capital to labour in the armaments factories.

There had been air raids on Berlin during the early years of the war. A small RAF raid in August 1940 had been launched in retaliation for the bombing of London. Occasional raids across 1941 had culminated in a heavy attack on the night of 7/8 November. Early in 1943 another series of raids had killed 650 civilians. Stalin had given Churchill a clear indication that he viewed raids on Berlin with great favour.

As the war moved towards the close of its fourth year there had been more than enough time to prepare Berlin to face a major air offensive. By November 1943 790,000 women and children had been evacuated. Berlin's Jewish population had also been removed by this time. Berlin had contained a Jewish population of 160,000 when the Nazis came to power in 1933.[19] Ten years later the great majority of those Jews had either been forced to emigrate or taken off to concentration and death camps. Goebbels had declared Berlin '*Judenfrei*'.

Belts of search lights and flak batteries surrounded Berlin. Over a dozen decoy fire sites lay ready beyond the city's limits. Within central Berlin three large flak towers had been built in parkland and resembled medieval strongholds. The tower at the Zoological gardens was the height of a thirteen story building. Each tower mounted eight 128mm guns manned by regular soldiers. These guns could hurl a salvo upwards to 45,000 feet every ninety seconds. Lighter anti-aircraft weaponry could fire from lower levels of the towers, which also contained bomb-proof shelters. One tower was connected to an underground station and 21,000 people could be sheltered within the tower and station.[20]

Late in August 1943 another speculative series of RAF attacks was launched against Berlin. Harris was probing the defences of the capital. On the morning of 24 August the 14 year-old schoolboy Arno Abendroth went to visit his grandparents wearing his Hitler Youth uniform. A four-engine bomber had crashed nearby and police and flak soldiers were guarding the wreckage.

> I hung around and eventually saw the row of four bodies, only partly covered with canvas ... They told me they had identified the bodies as Canadians. They weren't

badly mangled but I do remember their deathly pale faces, chalk white. These were the first dead men of the war I had seen, but I must say that I had a deep satisfaction at the sight of those dead *Terrorflieger*. They were our enemies.[21]

The fifty-six aircraft that went missing on the night of 23/24 August was Bomber Command's greatest single-night loss of the war so far.

Another raid on Berlin on the night of 31 August was almost as costly and forty-seven bombers went missing. That night German aircraft dropped white flares on the final approach to the target to startle bomber crews. 'Creep-back' stretched for thirty miles as bombers dropped their loads at an early opportunity and turned for home. On the ground sixty-eight people died, which was fewer than the number of aircrew killed.[22] Berlin was far beyond the range of Oboe beams broadcast from England, and the H2S radar sets used by the Pathfinders had proved unhelpful given the sheer size of Berlin's urban area. The three raids to Berlin between 23 August and 4 September had comprised 1,669 sorties. 125 aircraft were lost at an unsustainable rate of seven and a half per cent of bomber sorties. Aerial photography revealed bombing accuracy to have been very poor. In the face of these heavy losses Harris decided to wait for longer nights and a more advanced H2S set due to come into service.

In the weeks to come a number of cities in southern and western Germany were targeted by Bomber Command. On 22/23 October the town of Kassel was struck with a severity that produced a firestorm of the Hamburg variety. At least 5,500 people were killed from a relatively small population. Harris wrote to the Under-Secretary of State at the Air Ministry on 25 October:

> The aim of the Combined Bomber Offensive, and the part which Bomber Command is required by agreed British-United States strategy to play in it, should be unambiguously and publicly stated. That aim is the destruction of German cities, the killing of German workers, and the disruption of civilised community life throughout Germany.[23]

Harris would not accept any sort of moral equivocation about his command's activities.

On 3 November Harris wrote to Churchill that aerial photographic reconnaissance had revealed nineteen German towns to have been 'virtually destroyed', another nineteen had been 'seriously damaged' and a further nine had been 'damaged'. Harris was 'certain that Germany must collapse before this programme, which is more than half completed already, has proceeded much further'. It was time to directly attack the capital of the Third Reich with a sustained campaign: 'We can wreck Berlin from end to end if the USAAF will come in on it. It will cost us between 400 and 500 aircraft. It will cost Germany the war.' The British leadership was aware that Harris was inclined to exaggerate his case, but there was not a lot of firm evidence available regarding German industrial production and morale upon which to base an independent judgement.

On 13 November the Air Staff informed Harris that he should attack Berlin when good opportunity arose. This was all the authorisation Harris required. Harris could count on strong support from Portal. The Chief of the Air Staff noted on 22 November that 'social disruption' threatened 'the structure of the entire home front' in Germany. Portal wrote on 3 December that he had 'no shadow of doubt' that German morale was very low and Bomber Command might be 'at least half-way along the road of industrial devastation towards the point where Germany will become unable to continue the war'.[24] As a rule the Air Staff only gave Bomber Command general instructions. Once a particular phase of the strategic bombing campaign was underway Harris had great latitude to develop a series of operations as he wished.

The first raid of the new campaign was conducted on the night of 18/19 November. Over 400 Lancasters set out on the long journey to Berlin. There was heavy cloud over the city, bombing was scattered, but only nine Lancasters were lost. That gave a loss rate of two per cent, which was an acceptable rate for a raid on a major target.

On the next major raid on Berlin, four nights later on 22/23 November, weather-bound German airfields restricted night-fighter activity. Berlin was again covered by cloud and bomber aircrew could only see the glow of orange explosions down through the haze. 764 aircraft took part in the raid; twenty-six or 3.4 per cent went missing. The bomber stream flew according to a plan that took them over the target in only twenty-two minutes, thereby reducing the threat of flak and fighters.

Speer, Hitler's armaments minister, was in Berlin that night. When the raid developed he drove to one of the flak towers to watch the skies from the observation platform.

> From the flak tower the air raids on Berlin were an unforgettable sight, and I had to constantly remind myself of the cruel reality in order not to be completely entranced by the scene: the illumination of parachute flares, which the Berliners called 'Christmas trees', followed by flashes of explosions which were caught by the clouds of smoke, the innumerable probing searchlights, the excitement when a plane was caught and tried to escape the cone of light, the brief flaming torch when it was hit. No doubt about it, this apocalypse provided a magnificent spectacle.[25]

The ferocity of the attack drove Speer to shelter. His ministry building was set ablaze and his private office was turned into 'a huge bomb crater'. Dry weather fanned the fires and the next day smoke was hanging high in the sky. From the centre of the city stretching westward, suburbs from Tiergarten to Spandau had been badly damaged.

A raid on Berlin by 383 aircraft attacked on the following night. Harris was keen to re-bomb the previous night's damage. RAF signallers tried to disrupt night-fighter operations by broadcasting a German speaking controller. Twenty bombers were lost, equivalent to 5.2 per cent. There was a price to be paid for doing the same thing two nights in a row. Cloud was again thick but bombs could be aimed at the glow of fires burning from earlier raids.

Berlin's Gauleiter, Dr Goebbels, also saw this set of raids at close quarters. In a deep bunker, Goebbels recorded in his diary:

> Hell itself seems to have broken loose over us. Mines and explosive bombs keep hurtling down upon the government quarter. One after another of the most important buildings begins to burn. As I look out on the Wilhelmplatz after the attack, the impression of the evening before becomes even more gruesome.

Goebbels concluded, 'This is one of the worst nights of my entire life', though he could console himself that the 'hatred of the English among the population of the Reich capital knows no bounds'.[26] Bombing had done serious damage to over thirty major industrial plants. Goebbels wrote on 25 November, 'This war must be seen through. It is better that our workers should crawl into cellars than that they should be sent to Siberia as slave labour. Every decent German realises this.' Goebbels went on an extended tour of the bombed districts. 'Berliners gather around my car. I was amazed at their excellent spirits. Nobody cries, nobody complains. People slapped me on the back familiarly, gave me good advice.'[27] The damage to gas, electricity, water and telephone services was severe, yet the clean up was progressing well. There were plans to bring 50,000 troops to the city to clear rubble from the streets.

Another raid by over 400 aircraft took place on 26/27 November. Twenty-eight Lancasters were lost (6.2 per cent) and a further fourteen crashed in poor weather upon return to England. The Berlin Zoo was badly hit and many exotic animals had to be destroyed or escaped into the surrounding district. Goebbels observed: 'The sky above Berlin is bloody, deep red, and awe-inspiringly beautiful. I just can't stand looking at it.' The next day he noted that the British were putting about false claims that a quarter of Berlin had been destroyed. 'I have every reason to want them to believe this and therefore forbid any denial. The sooner London is convinced that there is nothing left of Berlin, the sooner they will stop their air offensive against the Reich capital.'[28] The raids late in November killed 4,430 Berliners, bombed out over 400,000 people and badly damaged important industrial targets like the Rheinmetall Borsig heavy engineering plant and Alkett tank works. Throughout this period Hitler was at his military headquarters in East Prussia.

The next raid on Berlin on 2/3 December was not a success. Strong winds scattered the bomber stream and cleared fog from night-fighter aerodromes. More RAF aircrew were killed than people on the ground. 'The last twenty minutes to the target', recorded an airman, 'was one continual illumination of [German-dropped] fighter flares, with bombers blowing up every few minutes.'[29] A loss rate of 8.7 per cent was an unequivocal disaster. A heavy raid on Leipzig the following night, to the south of Berlin, lost 4.6 per cent of aircraft dispatched. Nonetheless, in a 7 December letter to the Air Ministry, Harris claimed that if production, sortie and loss rate projections were met, 'The Lancaster force alone should be sufficient but only just sufficient to produce in Germany by 1 April 1944 a state of devastation in which surrender is inevitable.'[30] This letter reveals that Harris was already thinking in terms of a campaign lasting into the coming spring.

The full moon period briefly halted operations as bombers were too visible to night-fighters in a brightly lit sky. This gave both RAF aircrew and German civilians some respite from early to mid-December. Harris, however, was determined to press on with his offensive, even though loss rates had steadily risen. Aircraft that crashed in England or near the coast were losses over and above those considered 'missing'. Bomber Command's intelligence staff reported in a fit of optimism that 'the administrative machine of the Nazis, their military and industrial organisation and above all their morale, have by these attacks suffered a deadly wound from which they cannot recover'.[31] Part of Berlin was clearly photographed by the RAF in mid-December for the first time. There had been numerous attempts but poor weather and cloud cover had plagued successive photo-reconnaissance missions. Aerial photographs revealed that the central Tiergarten and Wilhelmstrasse districts had been badly damaged by high explosive, but fire was the true destroyer of cities and Berlin, with its wide streets, well-built apartment blocks and parkland, was a difficult city to burn down.[32]

On the ground the bombardment had been terrifying for the populace, though there were plenty of old soldiers from the First World War familiar with the experience. Large basements served as effective air-raid shelters. Holes had been driven in basement walls to link up a whole street below pavement level. Attics had been cleaned out to take away fuel for incendiaries. Underground railway stations provided another chain of ready-made public shelters. Phosphorus in incendiaries was greatly feared as the burns were almost untreatable. Fires were left to blaze in some places, especially where water mains had been broken. During a raid, the engines of massed aircraft could be heard in the darkened sky. Bright flares would fall through the clouds, followed by shrieking bombs.

After eight nights of minor operations Bomber Command returned to Berlin on 16/17 December with 483 Lancasters and ten twin-engine Mosquitoes. Five per cent of aircraft went missing over the Continent and a further twenty-nine Lancasters crashed on return to England as the weather was so poor. A major raid on Frankfurt on the night of 20/21 December by 650 aircraft killed many more aircrew than people on the ground. Further raids to Berlin followed on 23/24 and 29/30 December. Foul weather disrupted the attacks and bombing results were poor.

Still more raids to Berlin followed on 1/2 and 2/3 January, after which the full moon period was due. On each of those raids more aircrew died than people on the ground beneath the bombs. Many bombs fell on open countryside and missed all of Berlin. On 1/2 January Hauptmann Heinrich Prinz zu Sayn-Wittgenstein shot down six Lancasters one after another. A seven per cent loss rate for a Berlin raid was starting to become the norm. Morale wilted as the average chance of a bomber aircrew surviving a thirty sortie tour of operations plunged below zero. Aircrew were well aware that the bulk of casualties were fatal. There were no stretcher bearers in the sky. Wing Commander Philip Patrick, then a flight commander in No. 7 Squadron, wrote of the briefing for the 2/3 January raid:

> That was the nearest thing I ever saw to mutiny in the RAF, when the guys walked in and saw the map showing Berlin again. There was a rumble of what I might call amazement, or horror, or disbelief. The Station Commander quietened the chaps down and there was no trouble, but you can imagine what it was like to be dead tired and then having to go again.[33]

Sixty of 383 bombers that flew that night turned back on the outward journey for various reasons, a rate well above usual. The incidence of aircrew dropping part of a bomb load over the North Sea to gain height for safety became too common to ignore, and one squadron's commanding officer even advised his men to jettison bombs.

The technical difficulties of flying to Berlin in the middle of winter proved immense. A round flight of 1,150 miles from England was needed. A heavy fuel load to fly such a great distance bit into the bomb load carried, unless aircraft were over-loaded, as was the case in some units. Rain, snow, and ice made the long hours of darkness a strain. It was hard to fool the defenders that Berlin was not the target once the bomber stream was deep over central Germany.

The Mark III H2S radar sets rushed into service did not turn out to be dramatically better than earlier sets. Over a target such as Berlin, radar screens showed a mass of undifferentiated urban sprawl, whereas the Pathfinders had been instructed to target a particular district. In fine conditions well-placed cascading and bursting target indicators were effective at achieving a good bombing concentration, but heavy 'ten-tenths' cloud meant that few RAF airmen saw much of Berlin. 'Skymarkers', floating flares, were used to mark the target on cloudy nights, but they could be blown around by the wind or disappear into the cloud to give off a vague glow. Cloud did at least obscure the beams of search lights, though search lights could illuminate the cloud base to silhouette the bombers above for night-fighters. Loss rates for Halifax and Stirling bombers had been a good deal higher than for Lancasters. The nimble twin-engine Mosquito squadrons lost fewer aircraft. The Lancaster, which most crews flew, had poorly sited escape hatches. Studies later indicated that of an average seven man crew, a destroyed Lancaster yielded 1.3 survivors, against 1.8 for the Stirling and 2.45 for the Halifax.

The Berlin campaign provided many opportunities for experienced *Luftwaffe* pilots to build upon already impressive victory scores. German ground stations became increasingly good at tracking a bomber stream by its radar transmissions. The new SN-2 airborne-radar set, introduced in the autumn of 1943, was a great success. The claims of night-fighter pilots were consistently accurate thanks to the need for supporting confirmation from crewmen, and the careful surveys of bomber wrecks across occupied Europe. It was not hard to tell if a fuel laden bomber had been fatally set ablaze in the night sky. Indeed, *Luftwaffe* night-fighter pilot victory claims are probably the most authenticated of the Second World War. Hauptmann Heinz-Wolfgang Schnaufer would achieve 121 bomber kills by the end of the war. There were other accomplished centurions, such as Oberstleutnant Helmut Lent who achieved 113 night and day victories.

Once the bomber stream had been found by the night-fighters, old-fashioned eyesight was often as important as airborne radar. On a dark night an experienced pilot might see one or two bombers, but up to twenty-five might be seen in bright moonlight. In contrast, an inexperienced *Luftwaffe* aircrew might struggle to even find the bomber stream. Ideally a night-fighter would attack a bomber from underneath as Lancasters and Halifaxes did not have an underside gun turret. The existence of upward firing machine guns mounted by night-fighters was not identified by RAF intelligence until mid 1944. Most bomber gunners never saw their attacker until it had opened fire at close range. If a night-fighter was spotted, or after the first cannon shells struck home, a Lancaster pilot's best bet was to desperately plunge his bomber into a corkscrew manoeuvre. Bombers could be surprisingly agile with a desperate pilot behind the controls. *Luftwaffe* night-fighter aircrew were seldom bothered by RAF night-fighters as they hunted the bomber stream. The number of RAF night-fighters dispatched on any given night was very small.

The first major raid after the January full moon period was to Brunswick on the night of the 14/15th. Thirty-eight Lancasters (7.6 per cent) were lost and only fourteen people were killed on the ground. A major raid on Berlin by 769 aircraft on 20/21 January achieved indifferent bombing results, and was followed by a disastrous raid on Magdeburg, sixty miles west of Berlin, the following night. Fifty-seven bombers were lost – 8.8 per cent – and the city was hardly touched by the bombing. Bomber Command, however, did get in a couple of useful blows that night. The night-fighter ace Prinz Wittgenstein was killed after bringing his tally to eight-seven enemy aircraft. His wireless operator and navigator baled out to survive. Hauptmann Manfred Meurer, an ace with sixty-five victories, was also killed when the bomber he was attacking exploded in a ball of fire.[34] The German night-fighter force suffered a slow but steady attritional toll. There was not the luxury of a defined tour of duty for *Luftwaffe* aircrew.

At the end of January Berlin was again attacked by Bomber Command with three raids in four nights. The raids were more effective bombing performances than the previous cluster of Berlin raids: on the ground 1,341 people were killed and another 1,090 were declared missing. Nonetheless, the Japanese Ambassador felt that the level of damage inflicted on the capital was bearable. 'Internal collapse will certainly not be brought about by means of air raids; the vicissitudes of the war situation as a whole will constitute spiritually, as well as otherwise, the most important factor.'[35] During January 1944 over 300 RAF heavy bombers were lost on night raids. German air controllers had become so expert that night-fighters were at times coming out to meet the incoming bomber stream over the North Sea.

After the next full moon period 891 aircraft flew to attack Berlin on 15/16 February with moderate success. On 19 February Flying Officer K.R. Holland flew a rare successful daylight photo-reconnaissance sortie over Berlin. Holland made four runs over the city amid heavy flak. Ten raids had taken place since the last set of photographs had been taken. Further damage had, of course, been inflicted but fire had not taken hold sufficiently to burn out a whole district. Earlier damage had acted as a firebreak.[36] This evidence was not encouraging for RAF commanders. Time was running out for Harris to prove his point that Germany could be laid low by independent strategic bombing.

The remainder of the campaign, however, proved catastrophic for Bomber Command. Raids scheduled for Berlin were cancelled on 16, 17 and 18 February, but a major raid set out for Leipzig on 19 February, deep inside central Germany. Seventy-eight bombers were lost from a force of over 800. Most of the missing bombers fell victim to night-fighters. Scant damage was caused to Leipzig and Bomber Command had suffered a record loss for a single night. Bomber Command went on to attack the ball bearing factories of Schweinfurt on 24/25 February, but this was months after the American daylight raids of the previous autumn and was an illustration of the extent of Harris's unwillingness to coordinate his plans with the USAAF. On 25/26 February Augsburg was bombed by almost 600 aircraft. The town was of cultural significance and 700 people were killed. German propaganda denounced the raid as a prime example of 'terror bombing'.[37]

After the early March full-moon period had passed, a raid on Stuttgart on 15/16 March saw few bombs fall near the city. Heavy raids attacked Frankfurt on

18/19 and 22/23 March. Severe damage was inflicted and losses on the ground from the pair of raids amounted to 1,400 dead. Another major raid headed to Berlin on the night of 24/25 March. It had been five weeks since the last big Berlin raid. The bomber stream of 800 aircraft flew into occupied Europe over Denmark but was broken up by an unexpectedly strong north wind. Scattered bombing inflicted limited casualties and damage. The raiders were savaged on the way home to England as they flew an obvious route over Holland to the north of the Ruhr. Seventy-three aircraft went missing, a loss rate of 9.1 per cent. Aircrew casualties included 392 killed and 131 POWs. Fourteen *Luftwaffe* night-fighters were also lost, a toll that included a number of accidents. Only six night-fighters were claimed destroyed by RAF gunners. Possibly bomber gunners who had the best opportunities to shoot down a night-fighter did not live to tell the tale. After studying this particular raid, Bomber Command's Operational Research Section concluded: 'Not less than forty-five aircraft are estimated to have been lost to Flak ... Fighters achieved comparatively little success, because the strong wind that scattered the bomber stream proved unfavourable to consistent interception by fighters.'[38] This assessment was false. Harris and his staff still did not understand the extent of the night-fighter menace.

On the night of 26/27 March a heavy raid hit Essen in western Germany. Only nine aircraft were lost, 1.3 per cent of the force. The *Luftwaffe* was caught out by an attack on a city far from those targeted over the previous few months. Essen was within Oboe-range of England and bombing accuracy was impressive.

Harris's campaign against Berlin and other long-range targets was now drawing to a close. There was only time left for one more big effort. A raid planned for Brunswick on the night of 29/30 March was cancelled, but on 30/31 March a raid on Nuremberg went ahead. The night of 30/31 March was dangerously close to the usual moon stand-down period. Initial weather reports for southern Germany had predicted cloud, but a weather reconnaissance aircraft reported on the day prior to the raid that Nuremberg would be cloud-covered and the approach route relatively clear of cloud. This was the opposite of what was desired but Harris went ahead with the operation. It was his last chance to send his Main Force deep into German skies before Bomber Command was diverted to attack French targets as part of the preparations for the planned Allied invasion of western Europe. Harris's deputy, Air Vice-Marshal Sir Robert Saundby, was to write,

> I can say that, in view of the met. report and other considerations, everyone, including myself, expected the C.-in-C. to cancel the raid. We were most surprised when he did not. I thought perhaps there was some top-secret political reason for the raid – something too top-secret for even me to know, but now I do not think that this was so.[39]

A running battle developed as the bombers headed eastwards towards Nuremberg and over half of missing aircraft were downed on the outward journey. The night-fighters had homed in on the stream of bombers even before their controllers could guess Nuremberg was the target. The moon did not set until 2 a.m. and the bombers left dense condensation trails. One RAF pilot noted thirty burning aircraft between Aachen and Nuremberg. Of 795 aircraft sent out, ninety-four went missing and seventy-one were damaged, which was a thirteen per cent rate of loss.[40] Bomber Command had suffered its worst defeat of the war. The *Luftwaffe's* Oberleutnant Martin Becker claimed seven Halifaxes. 'They seemed to be lining up to be shot down. I just had to stop after the seventh one, I was sick of the killing.'[41]

540 RAF aircrew were killed in the Nuremberg raid, another 25 wounded and 148 made POW. The number of aircrew killed on this single night was greater than the toll lost by Fighter Command in the many weeks of the Battle of Britain. Among the dead was Pilot Officer C.J. Barton, a Halifax pilot of No. 578 Squadron, to whom a posthumous Victoria Cross was awarded. On the way to the target Barton's bomber was damaged by a night-fighter. Three members of his crew baled out, but Barton had continued onward to drop his bomb-load and then head for home on three engines. Barton was killed when his Halifax crash-landed on the English coast. The remaining three crewmen survived with minor injuries.

A handful of RAF night-fighter sorties had been flown in support of the Nuremberg operation, but too few to make any difference. RAF night-fighter aircrew were trying to follow the transmissions of a German airborne radar no longer in use. Small diversionary operations had been mounted to distract attention from the force heading for Nuremberg, but German ground controllers had little trouble telling them apart. Needless to say, Nuremberg was hardly damaged by the attempt to bomb the city.

The Nuremberg raid brought the 'Battle of Berlin' to an end. In the thirty-five major raids mounted from late November to the end of March the missing rate had been 5.2 per cent. 1,047 bombers went missing and another 1,682 were damaged.[42] Those losses were not dramatically higher than during the spring and summer periods of 1943, but the damage dealt out to Berlin had not justified the effort. The capital was still a functioning industrial metropolis, though 10,305 Berliners had been killed on the ground.[43] Thousands more were killed in the other cities bombed during the campaign.

It is not hard to explain why the Berlin bombing campaign was a disappointment. Berlin was an extremely difficult target to bomb, and there had been no dramatic technological breakthrough to support the offensive. Berlin was beyond the range of the Oboe radio beams broadcast from England that had guided aircraft to the Ruhr in the spring of 1943. The H2S airborne radar sets that had worked well over coastal Hamburg proved to be of limited value over a large inland city like Berlin. Flares dropped by the Pathfinders had often been scattered and inaccurate. Bombing accuracy depended on the Pathfinders consistently fulfilling their role to a high standard. The commander of the Pathfinder's No. 8 Group, the Australian Air Vice-Marshal D.C.T. Bennett, was to report: 'There can be no doubt that a very large number of crews failed to carry out their attacks during the Battle of Berlin in their customary determined manner.' Reports of Pathfinder Force crews 'consistently showed that the amount of bombing on the markers which they dropped was negligible'. 'Fringe merchants' bombed only on the edge of a target city.[44] Commanders in England could not closely monitor bombing results as winter weather meant there had been little photographic evidence. On 7 April 1944 Harris wrote to the Air Ministry that long-range night-fighter protection was needed, but the horse had long since bolted.

In his final despatch, written post-war, an unrepentant Harris would remark that during 1942–43 he did not have enough bombers to 'saturate' Berlin's defences. In the winter campaign of 1943–44 the losses flying against Berlin 'could not be regarded as excessive in relation to the magnitude of the task ... By the summer of 1944, when the force had increased to a size which would have enabled me to tackle Berlin under reasonable conditions, the Command had been diverted to the support of the invasion of France.'[45] Harris's subordinates did not necessarily see things the same way. The Bomber Command senior officer with the most recent operational experience was the Pathfinders' Bennett. Earlier in the war Bennett had commanded squadrons. He had been shot down as a wing commander over Norway in a low level attack on the *Tirpitz* at Trondheim. He had escaped to Sweden and returned to Britain to be promoted by Harris to lead the Pathfinders. Bennett described the Berlin campaign as 'the worst thing that could have happened to the Command'.[46] He was also to comment that a great failing of Bomber Command's leadership was that he was the only senior officer to fly combat missions in the Second World War. Air Marshal Sir Ralph Cochrane of No. 5 Group recalled: 'Berlin won ... It was just too tough a nut.' Air Commodore Sidney Bufton, Director of Bombing Operations at the Air Ministry, said of Harris and the Berlin campaign: 'He [Harris] was a gambler doubling up on each losing throw.'[47] By late autumn of 1943 Harris had been at his post for eighteen months. He had become worn out and, in hindsight, was due for relief by the time he decided to embark on his campaign against Berlin. If Hamburg had proved that the night could not hide a German city from bombing, Berlin proved that the night could not hide RAF bombers from *Luftwaffe* night-fighters. The RAF's organisational philosophy that divided British-based fighters and heavy bombers into separate commands was deeply flawed.

The British official historians of the strategic air offensive, when reviewing the area bombing carried out from March 1943 to March 1944, concluded: 'Huge areas in many great towns all over Germany were severely stricken and some were devastated, but the will of the German people was not broken nor even significantly impaired and the effect on war production was remarkably small.'[48] German patriotism and discipline stood the civilian population beneath the bombs in good stead. Bombing damaged faith in the Nazi regime, but Hitler was to claim that 'the devastation actually works in our favour, because it is creating a body of people with nothing to lose – people who will therefore fight on with utter fanaticism'. Speer wrote of bombing:

> These air raids carried the war into our midst. In the burning and devastated cities we daily experienced the direct impact of the war. And it spurred us to do our utmost. Neither did the bombings and the hardships that resulted from them weaken the morale of the populace. On the contrary, from my visits to armaments plants and my contacts with the man in the street I carried away the impression of growing toughness. It may well be that the estimated loss of nine per cent of our production capacity was amply balanced out by increased effort.[49]

Strategic bombing certainly attrited German economic potential and civilian society in a tactical sense. Each raid exacted some sort of cost in damage and counter-measures. *Luftwaffe* aircraft, flak guns, flak ammunition, repair work, worker casualties and building damage were a drain on the German war effort, but only at the margin. The sum of the tactical consequences of bombing Germany never had a timely strategic impact. Berlin proved able to absorb a series of raids over a long period, as had been the case with London in the Blitz of 1940–41. German arms production would continue to rise to an all-time peak in mid-1944, and that was sufficient to support the boundless ambition of Hitler's strategic calculation. Nazi Germany developed its war economy by drawing on the raw materials, factories and labour force of all occupied and intimidated Europe.

The *Luftwaffe* had won an authentic victory over Bomber Command during the winter of 1943–44. Yet the German Air Force was on the cusp of its greatest defeat, primarily at the hands of United States Strategic Air Forces in Europe. The Americans had come to recognise the need to give their heavy bombers fighter escort on long-range daylight missions deep into German air space. The Americans had responded to the disasters of the autumn of 1943 with an innovative technological solution. Experiments with extra fuel tanks and drop tanks had been undertaken across the months of autumn and winter. *Luftwaffe* commanders were appalled when it became apparent that American fighters were pushing deeper and deeper to the east. Drop tanks pushed the range of the P-51 Mustang from 475 miles to 850 miles.

After a stretch of bad weather, on 20 February 1944 the Eighth and Fifteenth Air Forces commenced a major daylight offensive. Early in March the Eighth Air Force attacked Berlin as part of the campaign. The Eighth Air Force was a balanced command of heavy bombers and long-range fighters. Harris's night offensive was underway at the time and it was as if the RAF and the Americans inhabited parallel universes. But from the *Luftwaffe's* viewpoint, the raids of the Anglo-American air forces were a single threat, whether they came by day or night. On

4 March bad weather forced back most B-17 bombers but some reached Berlin accompanied by a P-51 fighter group. It was now possible to fill the skies over Berlin with American day-fighters.

On 6 March a large Eighth Air Force raid again headed for Berlin. 660 aircraft attacked in overcast conditions in the face of heavy *Luftwaffe* opposition. No less than sixty-nine bombers were shot down. The *Luftwaffe* fighter force – which included twin-engine night-fighters – also suffered heavy losses. Two days later another raid bombed Berlin against considerably lighter *Luftwaffe* opposition. 174 P-51s escorted the bombers over the target. Fierce air battles resulted in the loss of thirty-seven American bombers and seventeen escorting fighters.

Bad weather delayed an American return to Berlin by day until 22 March. In overcast conditions 669 bombers attacked. *Luftwaffe* opposition was weak and only a dozen bombers were lost, of which just one or two were downed by enemy aircraft. American fighters did not make any claims as German fighters deliberately avoided them.[50] Remarkably, the Eighth Air Force had managed to win daylight air supremacy over Berlin. The *Luftwaffe* had been shot out of the sky by day, even though it reined supreme at night. American bombing results, however, were a different matter. USAAF raids on Berlin showered bombs randomly without being more effective than Bomber Command.

The American raids against Berlin were only one part of the daylight offensive in the spring of 1944 that shattered the *Luftwaffe* by forcing it to come up and engage Allied fighter escorts. In January *Luftwaffe* fighter losses in western Europe and Germany had been 307. In February that figure rose to 456 (including sixty-five night-fighters). 567 fighters were destroyed in March (including ninety-four night-fighters).[51] The American bombing campaign was not cheap. From February to April over 1,000 heavy bombers were lost. The daylight bombers had often been no more than giant clay pigeons, but by directly contesting the *Luftwaffe's* aerial supremacy the United States Army Air Force had fumbled towards the correct solution. Allied bombers could not destroy German fighters in their factories but Allied fighters could shoot them down. In May the *Luftwaffe* wrote-off fifty per cent of single-engine fighters and twenty-five per cent of pilots.[52] This level of loss broke the back of the pilot training system.

By daylight the Americans managed to beat the *Luftwaffe*. American heavy bombers went on to exploit this success by carefully targeting German synthetic oil refineries, the destruction of which was the jewel in the crown of the Combined Bomber Offensive. The experimental strategy of bombing German cities by night had been overtaken by events. By the spring of 1944 it had become an obsolete method of war. The next great military operation to be launched from Britain – the invasion of France – needed a more direct support from Allied heavy bombers than the generalised bombing of urban Germany. The strategic bomber formations had to accept a role within a more balanced and coordinated war strategy.

12
Normandy

The Combined Bomber Offensive had been partly motivated by a desire to support the Soviets, and in the autumn of 1943 the Soviets had received some further assistance from their Anglo–American allies in the form of a land invasion of continental Europe. The invasion, however, took place in Italy and not France, for which Stalin had hoped. From the Soviet viewpoint, only a landing in France could truly be characterised as a 'Second Front', but the British were not in a hurry to revisit the scene of the blood-bath of 1914–18 and the defeats of 1940. There was great risk involved in putting ashore in France an army to face the likelihood of prompt counter-attack by massed panzer divisions. Churchill had once remarked to a colleague: 'Remember that on my breast there are medals of the Dardanelles, Antwerp, Dakar and Greece.' Churchill had a long record of backing high-risk amphibious operations in secondary theatres of war. He did that again by strongly advocating a landing at Anzio in Italy in January 1944. Yet the Prime Minister was not prepared to gamble with the main weight of the British war effort in the most vital theatre. Even if a landing force could secure a foothold on the coast of western France, stalemate might set in around a shallow bridgehead to create another Gallipoli-style disappointment on a grander scale. Across the grim middle period of the Second World War, Churchill and his Chief of the Imperial General Staff, General Sir Alan Brooke, were inclined to see an invasion of western Europe as a *coup de grace* to be administered once Germany had been sufficiently hammered on other fronts.[1]

The opening of a sustainable Second Front in France would depend more on the Americans than the British Empire. After the entry of the United States to the war, President Roosevelt had wanted to see American ground troops in action in the European theatre at an early opportunity. That was achieved with Operation Torch in French North Africa in November 1942. The next big strategic question for the Anglo-American coalition had been to decide what to do after North Africa had been cleared of Axis forces. At the Casablanca conference in January 1943 British and American leaders had met to decide that issue. General Marshall, the United States Army's Chief of Staff, was willing to consider an invasion of France in 1943, but the British, still licking their wounds after the Dieppe fiasco, had a strong preference for a Mediterranean strategy. Britain had a traditional Mediterranean presence stretching back to the eighteenth century, and a string of bases in the region such as Gibraltar,

Malta and Alexandria. It was agreed at Casablanca that Sicily should be invaded after the fall of Tunisia to secure sea communications in the Mediterranean. Allied control of the central Mediterranean would pose threats to southern France, Italy and the Balkans, the 'soft underbelly' of the Axis. The momentous 'unconditional surrender' terms had been made public after the Casablanca conference. There was to be no accommodation either with National Socialism or the German military.

As it turned out, stout German resistance in mountainous Tunisia – a natural redoubt – had delayed victory in Africa until May 1943. The following invasions of Sicily in August and the southern Italian mainland in September engaged German divisions desperately needed on the crumbling eastern front. Italy's departure from the war caused the deployment of additional German troops to the Balkans. By late 1943 a well-equipped German army group had been sent to southern Europe. The opening phase to the Allied campaign in Italy had seen Allied troops make steady progress northwards up the peninsula. But a sense of failure in Allied circles began to mount during the winter of 1943–44, when efforts were made to win decisive victories in terrain that was so helpful to the defending Germans. In terms of efficiency, the Italian campaign was unable to match the way the threat of Allied invasion held Axis forces in Norway to the end of the war. There were over 400,000 German troops in Norway midway through 1944.[2]

On 3 November 1943 Führer Directive No. 51 announced the decision to reinforce German forces in western Europe in the expectation of an invasion in the spring of 1944.

> The danger in the east remains, but a greater danger now appears in the west; an Anglo-Saxon landing. The vast extent of territory in the east makes it possible for us to lose ground, even on a large scale, without a fatal blow being struck to the nervous system of Germany. It is very different in the west. Should the enemy succeed in breaching our defences on a wide front here the immediate consequences would be unpredictable.

Hitler optimistically told his commanders at Berchtesgaden on 18 March 1944:

> Once defeated, the enemy will never try to invade again. Quite apart from their heavy losses they would need months to organise a fresh attempt. And an invasion failure would also deliver a crushing blow to British and American morale ... We shall then transfer [our divisions in the west] to the eastern front to revolutionise the situation there.[3]

The extent of the American build-up in the United Kingdom had made it obvious that an invasion of France would take place in 1944.

The Commander-in-Chief West, Field-Marshal von Rundstedt, controlled two army groups, Army Group G in the south of France, and Army Group B in northern France and the Low Countries. The elderly, aristocratic Rundstedt was a straightforward, orthodox soldier. He later summed up his dilemma as follows: 'I had over 3,000 miles of coastline to cover from the Italian frontier in the south to the German frontier in the north, and only sixty divisions with which to defend it. Most of them were low-grade divisions, and some of them were skeletons.'[4] There were 60,000 Russian turn-coats amongst Rundstedt's 850,000 men. Newly formed coastal divisions included many older men and invalids. Most divisions were dependent on the railways and horses for transport. German supply wagons were still drawn by teams of horses in 1944. From forty-one divisions in December 1943, German forces in western Europe would be built up to fifty-eight divisions by June 1944. This was all that could be managed given the severity of fighting in Russia and Italy.[5]

On 15 January 1944 Field-Marshal Rommel took charge of the vital Army Group B facing the English Channel. Army Group B's Fifteenth Army was deployed in Belgium, Holland and the coast of north-west France. General Dollmann's Seventh Army defended Normandy, Brittany and western France. Rommel urgently pushed ahead with the building of the so-called 'Atlantic Wall'. Mines and obstacles were laid on possible invasion beaches, and Rommel, as at El Alamein, displayed a talent for field engineering.

Disagreements soon developed between Rommel's and Rundstedt's headquarters regarding the employment of tanks. Rommel wanted to hold his panzer divisions as close to the coast as possible. He feared that Allied aircraft might prevent German formations from travelling swiftly to a threatened coastal point if they were located deep inland. In rivalry to Rommel, a Panzer Group West headquarters had been formed under General Freiherr Leo Geyr von Schweppenburg, who favoured meeting an invasion with a massed counter-attack by panzer divisions held in a central reserve. Hitler was compelled to intervene to arbitrate the dispute. OKW gave three panzer divisions to each army group in the west, and a further four panzer divisions were to be held as a general western reserve subject to OKW control. Of the three panzer divisions under Rommel's personal command, he placed one in Normandy and the other two north of the River Seine.[6]

At the start of June 1944, a clear majority of German infantry divisions were still in Russia, but over one-third were in other theatres. The German Army fielded 285 divisions, of which 164 were in the east (including Finland) and 111 were in the Balkans, Italy, France, Belgium, Holland, Norway and Denmark.[7] Of the fifty-eight divisions in the west, nine were panzer divisions and one was a panzergrenadier division.

German tank strength in the west had been 750 at the start of January but had grown to 1,400 by the end of April. By early in June there were almost

1,900 tanks and assault guns in the west. Most of the tanks were Mark IV medium tanks or Mark V Panthers.[8] Panzer production in 1944 was a good deal higher than the previous year. May to July 1944 saw the highest monthly tank production figures of the war. In July 840 tanks and 807 assault guns would be built. By late spring the *Wehrmacht* had almost as many panzer vehicles in the west and Italy as in the east. It should be noted, though, that the Germans were preparing to defend France in 1944 with fewer tanks than had been used to invade France in 1940.[9]

In the United Kingdom plans for an invasion of France – Operation Overlord – had been under development for many months. A military operation has seldom been less dependent on improvisation. A planning staff had been established in April 1943. At the Teheran meeting between Roosevelt, Churchill and Stalin at the end of November 1943 the President had outlined plans for Operation Overlord to an enthusiastic Stalin. A reluctant Churchill had been compelled to show his support. Stalin had demanded to know a firm date for the invasion and had been informed it would probably be 1 May. In return for the good news of a definite Second Front, Stalin promised that the Red Army would mount its own offensive to coincide with the landing. He also let it be known that the Soviets would enter the war against Japan once Germany had been defeated.[10]

Late in 1943 veteran Allied divisions began to transfer from the Mediterranean to Britain. A lot had been learnt about the conduct of combined operations and amphibious landings in Tunisia, Sicily and Italy. Big transports carried a horde of American troops directly across the Atlantic. It is sometimes forgotten that the greatest Lend Lease-type finished good sent to Britain by the United States was its own manpower. The Americans very likely had the resources to invade north-west Europe twice if the first attempt failed. The British, however, doubted they had that capacity and rightfully feared another Somme or Ypres. At a briefing in 1943 Churchill had shaken his head in dismay: 'I wake up at night and see the Channel floating with bodies of the cream of our youth.'[11] But by 1944 the balance of forces between the Allies and Axis had swung sufficiently to make an invasion a gamble worth the risk. The initial plan was to invade western and southern France more or less simultaneously, but the landing in southern France had to be postponed as it became clear there were insufficient landing craft in the European theatre to mount two major assaults on France and maintain the Anzio bridgehead in Italy all at the same time. Early in April the western Allies informed the Soviets that a new front in north-west Europe would be opened on a date soon after 31 May depending on the weather.[12]

The American General Dwight D. Eisenhower was designated Supreme Commander Allied Expeditionary Force. General Montgomery was appointed ground forces commander. 'Ike' was a fifty-four year-old Kansan of relatively humble origins. He had seen no overseas service in the First World War but his career had been advanced by a long period on General MacArthur's staff in Washington and Manila during the 1930s. Eisenhower had come to Marshall's attention and had been made chief of the War Plans Division. He left for Britain in mid 1942 to be the senior American commander in the European theatre, and had been intimately involved in the Tunisian, Sicilian and Italian campaigns.

The origin of Eisenhower's surname was the German word for 'iron hewer' or 'iron cutter', and is a reminder of the extent to which German immigrants had been harmoniously assimilated into the mainstream of the American population. Eisenhower's modesty and friendly personal restraint oiled the wheels of a complicated coalition command hierarchy. He was more concerned about the future of Anglo-American relations than self-publicity. Eisenhower had to bear great responsibility on behalf of often ungrateful subordinates who lacked his balanced personality. His temper was to be sorely strained by Montgomery's eccentric behaviour. Eisenhower was given a British deputy supreme commander and British naval and air force commanders for Operation Overlord. Anglo-American interests were merged for Overlord to an extent seldom seen in coalition warfare up to that point in time. This approach to coalition warfare had already been trialled with success in the recent Mediterranean campaigns.

It had been decided by planners that an invasion force should not be landed beyond the range of fighter aircraft stationed in Britain. The sacrifice of a Canadian division at Dieppe had also indicated that a French port was likely to be too strongly defended to seize by direct assault. The coasts of Holland and Belgium were easily flooded, leaving the Pas de Calais (north-west France) and Normandy as realistic options. Normandy was chosen ahead of the Pas de Calais as the less likely of the two alternatives.

The big risk for Operation Overlord was that German mechanised forces on land might move faster to counter-attack a bridgehead than amphibious forces could be put ashore. In September 1943 at Salerno, in the Bay of Naples, rapid panzer counter-attacks against narrow landing beaches had almost caused a disaster. Eisenhower and Montgomery agreed that a landing on a broad front would be needed to establish a bridgehead too wide to pinch out. The Allies intended to use their air superiority to delay the arrival of German reinforcements in Normandy. The invaders' initial objectives were to be the capture of the port of Cherbourg and Normandy's principal city of Caen. The exact date of the landing would be dictated by the combined need for a low tide at dawn for a sea landing and moonlight for airborne forces. Those factors only coincided a few days each month.[13]

The Germans could guess with near certainty that an invasion of France was approaching, but Allied planners worked hard to deceive the Germans regarding its time and location. To keep German eyes fixed on the Pas de Calais, Allied bombers dropped three times as many bombs north of the River Seine than to the south in the months leading up to the invasion. Reconnaissance missions, rail interdiction attacks, and the bombing of bridges were heavily weighted to targets in France away from Normandy. The shattering of the *Luftwaffe's* daylight fighter force earlier in the spring allowed Allied aircraft to range across France with reasonable freedom. By June rail traffic had been reduced to thirty per cent of the January figure. Bombing inflicted thousands of casualties on French civilians, but heavy bombers, whether flying by night or day, were able to achieve far better accuracy against short-range French targets than could be managed in more distant Germany.

The deception plan was enhanced by the use of false radio traffic and dummy camps to create a phantom United States army group based in Kent and Sussex under the command of General George S. Patton. Efforts were also made to mislead German intelligence into thinking that a diversionary invasion would be sent against Norway. This does not seem to have worked but Hitler had always feared a British descent upon Scandinavia. Twelve German divisions remained ready in Norway for that eventuality.[14]

It is difficult to say how well the deception plan worked, and exaggerated claims have often been made to its effectiveness. The *Luftwaffe* was unable to conduct effective aerial reconnaissance over southern England. Still, by May German intelligence believed it had identified seventy-nine Allied divisions in Britain, whereas there were only forty-seven present at that time. A seventy-nine division force could possibly mount landings in more than one location. The German belief that two different invasions of western Europe was a possibility was incorrect. German commanders' lack of experience of amphibious operations meant they did not appreciate that the shipping needed for two big invasions of western Europe was not available. The Germans were also accustomed by 1944 to fighting against heavy odds and did not appreciate that the Anglo-Americans were risk-averse.

An armada would be needed to land the assault force in Normandy, though it should be remembered that the landings in Sicily in 1943 and the landings in Saipan soon to take place in the Pacific were challenges of a similar magnitude during the opening phase. The unique aspect of the landings in Normandy was the extent and rapidity of the build-up ashore after the assault phase. This was an unprecedented challenge and would require chains of convoys on a daily basis. Allied navies had a great deal of experience in efficient convoy operations. To aid the unloading of cargo, two artificial floating harbours, code-named 'Mulberries', which included cement breakwaters and block-ships, were to be built off Normandy's open beaches. A fleet of warships would bombard the Normandy coast on the morning of the landing. Battleships such as HMS *Warspite* and USS *Nevada*, veterans of Jutland and Pearl Harbor respectively, were to be among the big ships lying off the assault beaches; 12,000 Allied aircraft were available to ensure that the already crippled *Luftwaffe* would struggle to make any sort of an appearance above an invasion bridgehead.

By May 1944 southern England had become a virtual armed camp. It was joked that only the many barrage balloons floating over the port towns of Britain was preventing the country from sinking into the sea under the weight of the forces concentrated for Overlord. On 15 May a final briefing was held for senior commanders with Churchill, King George VI and Prime Minister Smuts of South Africa in attendance. On the first day of Overlord five Allied divisions were to each disembark at separate beaches, which were code-named, *Utah*, Omaha, Gold, Juno and Sword. Three airborne divisions were to be dropped to help secure the flanks of the bridgehead. American forces were to land on the western beaches and Anglo–Canadian forces on the eastern beaches. This was partly because United States personnel had been assembling in camps in south-west England, and also because it was preferable for British forces to advance towards Germany through northern France and Belgium once the battle in Normandy had been won.[15]

With fifty-eight German divisions in France, the eight Allied divisions to be landed on D-Day might encounter disaster if German forces were deployed in the right places.[16] A stream of Allied reinforcement divisions stood ready in Britain to come ashore in support of the first day's assault troops. To give Allied operations and logistics planners a rough guide to the future, Montgomery's Twenty-First Army Group headquarters drew phase lines on planning maps. By D+20 the inland town of Falaise was scheduled for capture by the invaders. The distant Seine and Loire rivers were the target for D+90. This was not unlike the way a First World War general had nominated objective lines during an offensive, though, by 1944 a commander was far more liable to be held to account by his superiors for a rash prediction of future progress.

Anxiety mounted among Allied commanders as D-Day neared. In the distant Mediterranean, Rome fell to Allied forces on 4 June to achieve a brief flurry of publicity for the generals and troops involved. More importantly, the relief of the Anzio bridgehead released men and shipping for an invasion of southern France to go ahead after all, though not for another two to three months.

On 5 June General Brooke wrote in his diary that Overlord 'may well be the most ghastly disaster of the whole war'.[17] 5 June had been the original 'D-Day', but bad weather in the English Channel had caused a twenty-four hour postponement. Fortuitously for the Allies, the inclement weather of 5 June had given the Germans cause to believe that an invasion was not in the immediate offing. Allied forecasters were better able to study the weather rolling in from the west and advised that better conditions lay ahead. Eisenhower found the decision to postpone the long awaited invasion a great strain. On the evening prior to 6 June he visited American paratroopers of the 101st Airborne Division as they prepared to board their aircraft for the moonlight drop into France.

The Germans were taken by surprise by the place and timing of the invasion. Rommel had gone on leave to Germany for his wife Lucy's fiftieth birthday. (He had also been on leave when the Second Battle of El Alamein had begun). Rommel had concluded that a combination of forecast poor weather and the tide conditions would prevent an invasion for at least another fortnight.[18] Late on 5 June German intelligence intercepted and decoded a British radio message mobilising the French resistance movement. That message implied that an invasion was imminent, but did not indicate where and was not considered significant enough to act upon. Only three under-strength German divisions were on the beaches scheduled to be attacked. The 21st Panzer Division was quartered near Caen, the largest city in Normandy.

Three Allied airborne divisions were flown to Normandy in the early hours of the morning of 6 June. Twin-engine Douglas C-47 (DC-3) transports flew in tight, low-level formations at low speed. The paratroopers jumped from their aircraft or descended by glider. 2,600 heavy bombers attacked Normandy at dawn. United States, British and Canadian troops – some new to battle, others veterans from the Mediterranean and North Africa – came ashore on 6 June between 6 a.m. and 7.30 a.m. on a front of sixty miles. Seaborne assault troops took to their landing craft in heavy seas for the trip to the shore line. Underwater and beach obstacles proved a disappointment from the German viewpoint and did not greatly interfere with the overall operation.

At the western end of the invasion beaches, the two American divisions dropped overnight by parachute and glider, and another American division landed from the sea at *Utah* beach, all faced scattered resistance from a German division in the area. There were only 200 Allied casualties recorded at *Utah* beach. The flat country thereabouts made defence of that stretch of coast difficult.

At the eastern end of the landing front, British and Canadian troops, supported by commandos and 'swimming' Sherman tanks, made lodgements ashore against another dispersed German division. There was stiff fighting in places, especially for one British brigade at a fortified beach village that had not been badly damaged by the preliminary bombardment. D-Day cost the Canadians 1,000 casualties. Once ashore at Sword beach, the British 3rd Division's task was to push forward to the spires of the ancient Norman city of Caen, but inland strong points manned by coastal defence reserves and elements of the 21st Panzer Division were able to halt the advance. A panzer battle group drove forward into the gap between Juno and Sword beaches in the late afternoon of 6 June, but retired again shortly afterwards as its position became untenable. At the far eastern end of the landing zone a British airborne division successfully secured much of its allocated sector.

The greatest drama of D-Day was the United States 1st Division's landing at Omaha beach, to the east of *Utah* beach. Well-trained German troops of the 352nd Division were watching over the beach from a four mile stretch of cliffs, broken by narrow defiles. This difficult part of the Normandy coast had to be assaulted to cover the flanks of neighbouring assault beaches. Allied intelligence was of the belief that the 352nd Division was well inland from Omaha.[19]

When the troops came ashore, amid minefields and rows of obstacles on the water's edge, they were met by a withering fire from German infantry in concrete pillboxes and bunkers. Amphibious tanks intended to support the assault were launched too far from shore to be effective and many foundered in rough seas, their novel water-proofing and propeller system not up to the task. By design much of the naval and aerial bombardment at Omaha had fallen inland to avoid cratering the beach and impeding the logistical build up scheduled to follow the assault phase of the landing. The level of naval bombardment at Omaha was poor compared to what American commanders took for granted in the Pacific theatre by mid 1944.[20] German defenders had withstood the inadequate preliminary bombardment reasonably well, and had sufficient discipline to hold their fire until the first wave of troops reached the shore. American infantry who entered the planned killing zone and survived the initial hurricane of lead clung to the beach. Ironically, because the day's fight started so well for the Germans, local reserves at Omaha was sent to other sectors in Normandy, whereas American reinforcements kept coming ashore. Despite very heavy losses on the beaches, American infantry leaders were able to rally their men to fight their way forward to secure the high ground overlooking the beach.

Hitler had been asleep at the time of the invasion and he had given orders that he was not to be woken. This did not assist rapid German decision-making, but, after some delays, by the afternoon of 6 June Rommel's headquarters had been given permission to draw upon two of the panzer divisions held in reserve in France under OKW control. Field-Marshal von Rundstedt ordered the commander of the 1st SS Panzer Corps, General Joseph 'Sepp' Dietrich, to 'throw the enemy landed near Caen back into the sea'.[21] Yet it was already too late for German armour to push the Allies right out of Normandy. If more panzer units had been concentrated near the coast, as Rommel had wished, that would no doubt have jeopardised the landing in certain localities. But over 156,000 Allied troops were landed from the sea and air on D-Day. That force was too strong to be overwhelmed by counter-attack.

German reserve divisions faced difficult journeys to Normandy in the face of Allied air superiority. On 7 June the 12th SS (Hitler Youth) Panzer Division arrived to counter-attack the Canadian enclave and block the path inland from that beach. Panzer Lehr Division left for Normandy from the Chateaudun area, south-west of Paris, late on the afternoon of 6 June. Not until early on 8 June did the division arrive between Bayeaux and Caen. Camouflage precautions had ensured that only five of 140 tanks and ten to fifteen per cent of soft vehicles were knocked out by air attack en route, but the delays in transit were what mattered most.[22] The German Seventh Army in Normandy and

Brittany was principally responsible for fighting the battle that was underway. The Fifteenth Army was ordered to keep watching the Pas de Calais coast for another invasion force.

By 13 June four panzer divisions were in the Caen sector. This blocked an Allied advance across some of the most open terrain in Normandy. The 17th SS Panzergrenadier Division had entered the battle at the American end of the bridgehead. A shortage of infantry divisions meant that the panzer divisions had to take their place in the front line and could not be assembled into a mass for a coordinated counter-attack. Panzer Group West headquarters, located south of Caen, were devastated by a signals intelligence-directed air attack to further reduce the likelihood of a solid panzer counter-punch. Hitler ordered the 9th and 10th SS Panzer Divisions to start a trek from the eastern front to Normandy. The 1st and 2nd SS Panzer Divisions were also on the road from different parts of France. It would take the 2nd SS Panzer Division almost two weeks to reach Normandy from Limoges in the face of air attack and the activities of the French resistance. As a reprisal, at Oradour-sur-Glane nearly 600 hostages were killed by SS troops.[23]

The first priority for Allied ground forces in Normandy was to link up the beaches to form a continuous front. That had been achieved by 12 June as shipping poured men, equipment and supplies into the bridgehead. As the German cordon around the swelling bridgehead was starting to harden, the British 7th Armoured Division made an ambitious thrust towards the central Norman town of Villers-Bocage. The town, from which roads lead south to Mont Pincon and east to Caen, was entered on the morning of 13 June. British tanks emerging from Villers-Bocage were roughly dealt with by a small number of German tanks led by the 'ace' SS Obersturmfuehrer Michael Wittmann in a formidable Tiger tank. The Desert Rats were forced onto the defensive and a ruined Villers-Bocage was back in German hands two days later.[24]

Gales badly damaged the Mulberry harbours during a three day storm from 19–21 June. Local French civilians believed that storm to be the worst along the Normandy coast in forty years. The American Mulberry was badly wrecked. The build-up of Allied forces and supplies was held up at a vital time, and the poor weather allowed German troops on the road to Normandy a temporary respite from air attack. If the 'great gale' had coincided with the period immediately after the initial invasion, a desperate situation might have ensued. Eisenhower later commented: 'Thank the gods of war we went when we did!'[25] By 26 June twenty-five Allied divisions were ashore, whereas only fourteen German divisions were facing the bridgehead. Eight of those fourteen divisions were panzer divisions. Panzer troops had the motor transport to reach Normandy faster than infantry. By early July French rail traffic had been brought to a halt by air attack and striking workers.

Strategically, the Allies seemed to be winning the race to build up an overwhelming force in Normandy, but tactically the task of the Germans was more practical in the short term as the 'bocage' country of inland Normandy was very good defensive terrain. By no means all, but a large part of the front comprised bocage. Across a fifty mile stretch in western Normandy, mostly confronting the Americans, small fields were separated by hedgerows on thick banks and winding, sunken roads. Unobserved movement, even by vehicles, was often possible along sunken roads and tracks. In central Normandy, twenty miles south of Bayeux, Mont Pincon was in a region of forest country even more difficult than bocage. To the east of Bayeux was a mixture of bocage, farm land, small villages and woods. In the British and Canadian sector, the Orne and Odon rivers retarded progress to the south west of Caen. East of the Orne wooded ridges and the flooded Dives valley formed a natural barrier to the eastern end of the bridgehead.[26]

The German front line in Normandy typically comprised a thin line of posts. Main positions were sited by preference on reverse slopes. This was a nasty surprise to Allied troops trained to attach great importance to the capture of high ground, only to find Germans dug in behind the crest of a hill. The German general purpose MG-42 machine gun could fire belts or drums of ammunition at a rate of 1,200 rounds a minute, which gave small groups of men a great deal of direct or suppressive firepower. Mines and snipers were complemented by pre-ranged mortar and artillery fire. The bocage was ideal mortar country. Mortars, in the hands of experienced troops, used ammunition efficiently and accurately. This was important as shells were always in short supply. During the June–July fighting seventy per cent of Allied infantry casualties were caused by mortar fire.[27] Dead horses and cows with stiff legs added to the foulness of the battlefield.

Normandy had been chosen by Allied headquarters staff as the best place for a coastal assault landing, and not because it was a good place to fight a battle inland. A senior staff officer later acknowledged: 'We simply did not expect to remain in the bocage long enough to justify studying it as a major tactical problem.'[28] The cramped country made it hard for the Allies to deploy their tanks and artillery. The standard medium battle tank for United States, British and Canadian forces was the Sherman, a good tank by the standards of 1942–43 but too vulnerable to heavy calibre anti-tank guns by 1944–45. The Sherman was almost a match for the older Panzer Mark IV but had otherwise fallen behind German tank development. High percentages of Allied tanks were knocked out by a single hit and brewed up, whereas Allied guns struggled to penetrate the armour of Panther and Tiger tanks. The superior range of German tank and anti-tank guns meant that Allied tanks could be stopped well short of the German firing line, forcing Allied infantry accompanying the tanks to go to ground far from their objectives.

Still, sheer weight of firepower and numbers was a major trump card for the Allies. Air superiority allowed Allied ground forces to assemble and manoeuvre behind their own lines with a great deal of freedom. Dramatic improvements in radio communications allowed Allied artillery to be quickly directed against otherwise fleeting targets. In North Africa Rommel had written: 'In static warfare, victory goes to the side which can fire the most ammunition.'[29] German artillery in Normandy was badly outgunned in numbers of guns and especially in numbers of shells.

With the Allies firmly ashore, on 17 June Rommel drove to meet with Hitler at an underground headquarters near Soissons in French Champagne. Field-Marshal von Rundstedt and General Jodl, OKW's operations chief, were in attendance. Hitler told his commanders: 'Don't call it a beach-head, but the last piece of French soil held by the enemy.'[30] Hitler perceptively noted that many of Britain's more experienced divisions had been identified in Normandy. That suggested that Normandy was the main Allied landing, though another diversionary landing in the Pas de Calais could not be ruled out. Rommel also had an eye on that possibility.[31] The coastal divisions of the German Fifteenth Army remained north of the Seine watching the Pas de Calais shore line.

Late in June Rommel and Rundstedt again set out to meet with Hitler, this time at Berchtesgaden in southern Germany. Hitler was in a bitterer mood on this occasion and greeted his generals with a harangue about holding onto ground. Rundstedt would soon be relieved of his command due to the pessimistic nature of his reports and recommendations. On the night of 1 July Rundstedt went so far as to advise Field-Marshal Keitel at OKW that making peace was the best option for Germany. Field-Marshal von Kluge, a veteran of the eastern front, was appointed CIC West.

During the closing weeks of June the Americans pushed north westwards into the Cherbourg peninsula, much of which was reclaimed marshland and poor terrain for tanks. The German commander at Cherbourg surrendered on 26 June. Resistance ended in the peninsula four days later, by which time demolitions had destroyed the port's facilities. The United States 4th Division, the original division to land at *Utah* beach, had endured 6,000 casualties by this time.[32] The German Seventh Army suffered an important casualty in the closing days of June when its commander died. It was rumoured that General Friedrich Dollmann had been killed in action or had died from a heart attack, but a despairing suicide by poison seems more likely.[33]

At the British end of the bridgehead, a renewed effort was made to take Caen. The Epsom offensive by VIII Corps took place to the south west of Caen from 25–30 June, and was spearheaded by the Scots of the 15th Division. Infantry followed an artillery barrage across rolling fields of corn in a manner that would have been familiar to soldiers of 1918. Epsom aimed to envelop Caen from the west, but counter-attacks by SS panzer troops helped to seal off the new bulge pushed into the German line after heavy fighting about Hill 112. Montgomery's original campaign plan had been to break out beyond Caen at an early opportunity.[34]

Meantime V-1 flying bombs, which were unmanned jet rockets, had first landed in Britain mid-June. The V-1 flew at 375 mph and carried a one-ton explosive warhead. It would be followed by the much faster V-2 in the months ahead, the forerunner to the intercontinental ballistic missiles of another era. At a time when the Allies were taking the war to German-occupied France, the Germans were bringing the war back to the British people, and London especially, in the most sustained series of aerial attacks since the spring of 1941.

At the eastern end of the European continent Nazi Germany faced another major threat in the summer of 1944 – the growing strength of the Red Army. At the Teheran conference of Allied leaders in November 1943 Stalin had promised Roosevelt and Churchill that he would endeavour to coordinate his main offensive for 1944 with Allied landings in France. Across the early months of 1944 there had been continual fighting in the Ukraine as Soviet forces had pushed beyond the River Dnieper towards Romania, the Carpathian Mountains and southern Poland. Large German forces had been encircled in the campaign, including the Seventeenth Army in the Crimean peninsula.[35] At the northern end of the eastern front, Leningrad's siege had finally been lifted.

In Belorussia Field-Marshal Ernst von Busch's Army Group Centre had held its ground in the late winter and spring of 1944. Army Group Centre's front formed a large salient around Minsk. The Soviet High Command adjudged that to be the best place for their next major offensive. The Germans, however, were expecting the Red Army to continue with its attacks at the southern end of the front. Army Group Centre had three panzer divisions, whereas Army Groups North Ukraine and South Ukraine had eight apiece. Stalin decided to codename the offensive against Army Group Centre Operation Bagration, after a Russian general who had been mortally wounded at the battle of Borodino in the 1812 war against Napoleon. On paper there were more panzer divisions deployed in the east in the summer of 1944 than in the western theatre, but the panzer divisions in the west had higher tank strengths, sometimes double that of the eastern average. The bulk of SS panzer troops had been deployed in the west.

On 22 June, the third anniversary of the start of Operation Barbarossa, the main Red Army offensive against Army Group Centre got underway. 166 Soviet divisions fell upon thirty-seven German divisions. Soviet tanks and mechanised forces pushed open gaps in the shallow German front, which rapidly collapsed. Hitler frantically called for his forces to stand their ground, but in two weeks the Red Army penetrated a hundred miles on a 250 mile front. The bulk of the Fourth Army was trapped in a pocket east of Minsk. Twenty-five divisions of Army Group Centre were destroyed and over 300,000 German prisoners were taken. On 17 July 57,000 German prisoners were paraded through the streets of Moscow. The roadway behind them was scrubbed clean with disinfectant to erase the poison of National Socialism. The Soviet offensive rolled on into eastern Poland and the River Vistula.

Astride the Vistula sat the Polish capital of Warsaw. On 1 August the Polish Home Army rose up to liberate the city before the Soviets could arrive and impose a Communist leadership on the country. In two months of fighting the insurgency in Warsaw was crushed and the city destroyed by SS formations. It has been argued that the Soviets stopped their advance to allow the Germans to put down the revolt ahead of their arrival, but Soviet exhaustion and the building of a new German defensive line along the Vistula were the main reasons why the Red Army came to a halt after an advance of over 200 miles.

An attempt to assassinate Hitler took place on 20 July to further disrupt the German High Command at a crucial moment of the war. Hitler was injured by a bomb in a briefcase placed under a conference table at Rastenburg by the disabled Colonel Count Claus von Stauffenberg. The conspiracy was quickly crushed by Nazi loyalists, and the officer corps was purged of those involved or under suspicion. The main consequence of the assassination attempt was that the grip of Hitler and the Nazi security services on the German armed forces and civilian population was further tightened. There were several plots against Hitler's life during the war years but they had consistently amounted to little in practice. The Germans were not the sort of people who assassinated their leaders.

In Normandy the build-up of men and equipment in the slowly expanding bridgehead gathered pace in July. Allied casualties to the end of June had been over 60,000, but that was less than had been expected. 850,000 Allied troops had been landed to the end of June. Nonetheless, unlike the Americans, the British and Canadian authorities were starting to have problems finding infantry replacements. On 30 June the British Second Army comprised only 108,000 infantry, as against 114,000 artillerymen and 84,000 engineers. The low infantry strength of British and Canadian divisions was hidden by the overall numerical superiority of Allied forces. The British government had not allocated the British Army enough recruits during 1942–43. On top of that, inexplicably, the British Army had based casualty replacement calculations for Normandy on the experience of North Africa, instead of France in 1914–18.[36] The British Army was 2.7 million strong in 1944, but a creeping paralysis was threatening the entire institution due to a lack of all-important infantrymen.

By early July British and Canadian troops had reached the outskirts of Caen, a city already devastated by bombing. Eisenhower and Churchill were becoming increasingly impatient with the slow progress of Montgomery's army in Normandy. The Allied air forces wanted more space in the bridgehead for new aerodromes. On the night of 7/8 July Caen was reduced to rubble by aerial bombing and again attacked. The northern half of the city was taken but the Germans retained possession of the ruins south of the River Orne, which bisected Caen.

On 15 July Rommel gloomily told Kluge, his new commander as CIC West:

The position in Normandy is becoming daily more difficult and is approaching a serious crisis. Owing to the intensity of the fighting, the exceptionally strong material supplies of the enemy, especially in artillery and armoured vehicles, and the operations of their air force, which commands the battlefield unchecked, our own losses are so high that the fighting strength of the divisions is rapidly sinking.[37]

Rommel was badly wounded in an air attack on 17 July. During the afternoon he had been returning from visiting a panzer corps headquarters when low flying aircraft struck. Rommel was thrown from his car as it turned over out of control. His skull was fractured.

Meanwhile a new offensive had been prepared for the Caen sector. This time armour was to lead the way. Lieutenant-General Sir Miles Dempsey, the commander of the Second Army, later observed: 'Our strength in tanks was increasing all the time – tank reinforcements were pouring into Normandy faster than the rate of tank casualties. So we could well afford, and it was desirable, to plan an operation in which we could utilise that surplus of tanks and economise infantry.'[38] Three British armoured divisions were to advance one behind the other, around the eastern side of Caen and across the River Orne and Caen Canal. The terrain to the immediate south and south east of Caen was farmland of corn and small woods, broken by hedges and streams. Rural hamlets and stone farm buildings dotted the landscape. The ridge of Bourguebus was the most important feature south of Caen.

On 18 July Operation Goodwood was launched after an intensive carpet bombardment by over 2,000 British and American heavy bombers at dawn on a fine summer's day. 800 British tanks moved to the attack on a narrow front. Under blue sky and in clear visibility, the massed tanks passed through gaps in the British defensive minefields east of Caen and pushed on past standing crops and plough land. An artillery barrage was fired in support and motorised infantry followed behind to mop up villages bypassed by the leading armoured regiments. The British were relying on their Sherman tanks, a high-profiled vehicle that used petrol instead of diesel to increase the risk of fire if struck by an anti-tank projectile. On balance, though, tank crewmen were better off than the infantrymen following behind in thin-skinned transport. As a Royal Tank Regiment sergeant recalled: 'You could hear them squealing like rabbits when the machine-guns caught them round our tanks.'[39]

The 16th *Luftwaffe* Field Division and elements of the 21st Panzer Division were awaiting the assault. After the devastating aerial bombardment, German soldiers emerged stunned to be taken prisoner. Panzers had been turned upside down by the blasts. Yet the Germans managed to improvise a screen of anti-tank guns and tanks on the approaches to Bourguebus ridge. At the village of Cagny, to the north of a railway line running towards Caen, Colonel Hans von Luck, a panzer battle group commander positioned a surviving Mark IV tank, an army 88mm anti-tank gun and four *Luftwaffe* 88mm anti-aircraft guns that had survived the bombardment. To encourage the commander of the *Luftwaffe* guns, Luck had placed a pistol to that officer's head as a reminder that the guns had a dual role against both aircraft and tanks. Luck told his junior colleague that he could 'either die now on my responsibility or win a decoration on his own'.[40] From an orchard the 88mm guns quickly knocked out a dozen tanks of the Fife and Forfar Yeomanry as they passed westwards across their front towards Bourguebus ridge. To the north east of Cagny the Guards Armoured Division was starting to fan out from behind the leading 11th Armoured Division, only to run up against a company of Tiger tanks near the village of Emieville with predictably disastrous results.

The assault of the 11th Armoured Division broke down on the approaches to Bourguebus ridge in the face of an improvised defence. The ridge's crest was occupied by men of the 21st Panzer Division's engineer battalion and reconnaissance battalion. The division's assault gun battalion was equipped with 105mm guns mounted on French Hotchkiss tank chassis. SS Panther tanks intervened from the west to batter the leading British armoured regiments. The Germans had received advance warning that something was about to take place on the Caen front. It had been hard to hide the massing of so much armour. *Luftwaffe* flare-light reconnaissance photographs had been helpful.[41] Further attempts by Montgomery's forces to advance on 19 July did not achieve much, though Canadian infantry managed to clear southern Caen of Germans.

Another disappointing battle in the Caen sector had come to a close. Several hundred British tanks had been destroyed or damaged during Operation Goodwood. The Germans had lost almost 100 precious tanks in the bombardment and the fighting that had followed. Heavy British tank losses had at least reduced the severity of infantry casualties. Goodwood was an illustration of how effective anti-tank screens had become in the few short years since 1940.

Montgomery was to claim postwar that fighting on the British and Canadian front drew German armoured forces away from the American sector. Late in July two panzer divisions and 190 tanks were facing the Americans, whereas six panzer divisions and 645 tanks were facing the British and Canadians.[42] The main problem for the Germans in Normandy was the sheer size of the Allied force building up in the bridgehead. By 25 July the Allies had landed thirty-six divisions and 1,450,000 men. Allied tank strength had topped 4,000. The casualty toll for the Germans in Normandy was also steadily rising. Rommel had reported in a 15 July memorandum that he had lost 97,000 men but had received only 6,000 replacements.[43]

The Americans, and not the British, launched the offensive that cracked open the German front in Normandy. Across the opening weeks of July, at the western end of the bridgehead, heavy fighting had raged in the bocage country south of Cotentin. By this stage of the campaign, hundreds of Shermans had been fitted with hedge cutters to help cross-country manoeuvre. With the front under pressure on both flanks, on 22 July Kluge advised Hitler that 'the moment is fast approaching when this overtaxed front line is bound to break. And when the enemy once reaches the open country a properly co-ordinated command will be almost impossible, because of the insufficient mobility of our troops.'[44] A twenty mile advance to the St Lo-Periers road cost 40,000 American casualties. The severity of that fighting was overshadowed by the dramatic armoured confrontations simultaneously underway around Caen.

An attack by the United States Army's VII Corps on 25 July – Operation Cobra – was a big set piece affair. The worst of the bocage had been passed and intention was to use three divisions to punch a 7,000 yard hole in the German front. 1,500 heavy bombers supported the attack and the countryside was turned into a moonscape. The assaulting troops, however, were also heavily hit by the preliminary bombardment. This was largely because the bombers had flown across rather than parallel to the American front line. It became apparent in Normandy that heavy bombers were best used against an enemy's reserve positions, rather than the front line zone.[45] Lieutenant-General L.J. McNair was among those killed by the 'friendly' bombardment. Nonetheless, the opening to the offensive was a great success and American troops made fifteen miles' progress in the first two days of Cobra.

Lieutenant-General George Patton's Third Army started to deploy in Normandy to add weight to the offensive. The flamboyant and bold Patton had been a cavalryman for much of his career. He had made a name for himself as a corps commander in Tunisia and as an army commander in Sicily. In Normandy, by 30 July American troops and armour had captured Avranches and were preparing to fan out into Brittany. The German front had finally broken after almost two months of steady fighting. On 3 August Patton was ordered to swing his tanks eastwards behind the German army group in Normandy.

Instead of ordering a retreat, at the start of August Hitler ordered a massive counter-attack against the Americans at Mortain to seal the corridor cut though the broken German front. Common sense, by this stage, should have made it clear that a German withdrawal out of Normandy towards the River Seine was urgently needed. But in light of the purge that had followed the bomb plot, Kluge could not dispute a direct order from the Führer. The newly created Fifth Panzer Army was to mount the attack with several panzer divisions. The long-delayed arrival of fresh German infantry divisions in Normandy from the Pas de Calais had allowed the panzer divisions on the British and Canadian front to be withdrawn and massed against the Americans. The planned operation, though, had been detected by Ultra signals intercepts. On 7 August the Mortain offensive began but the fog cleared from 11 a.m. to expose German tanks to aerial attack by low-flying rocket-firing Hawker Typhoons and

P-47 Thunderbolts. The rockets were hard for the pilots to aim accurately and destroyed few tanks, but low-level rocket attack was more effective against men and soft vehicles. At the vital Hill 317 in front of Mortain American infantry held off the German assault.[46]

From 8 August British, Canadian and Polish forces began to push southwards as the strength of the panzer forces on their front had fallen. As the Mortain offensive petered out, Patton's armour swung eastwards behind the bulk of the Germans in Normandy. By 11 August only twenty miles lay between Patton's spearhead and Anglo-Canadian troops advancing from the north. The entire German army group was in danger of encirclement. At first Hitler refused to address the threat. He had been considering new attacks in Normandy despite the Mortain disaster. Local German commanders, however, were adamant an immediate retreat was needed. An irate Hitler responded by replacing Field-Marshal von Kluge with Field-Marshal Model as CIC West on the evening of 15 August. Though his relief was underway, the next day Kluge ordered a retreat from the shrinking pocket in anticipation that OKW would agree.[47] Kluge later took poison as he was being transported to Germany. There was suspicion that he was peripherally involved in the recent bomb plot.

Operation Dragoon, the invasion of southern France from the Mediterranean, got underway on 15 August. The United States Seventh Army comprised American and French divisions, and soon compelled a voluntary German withdrawal from south-western France, and a rapid fighting retreat from the south eastern part of the country. Marseilles was captured to give the Allies possession of a major French port.

In Normandy opportunities were missed to close more quickly the Allied pincers upon trapped German forces. Montgomery and his American colleagues did not cooperate particularly well. When Patton's forces reached Argentan they were halted by General Omar Bradley, the US army group commander, to avoid colliding with Canadians advancing from the north towards Falaise. Patton had mischievously reported to Bradley: 'We now have elements in Argentan. Shall we continue and drive the British into the sea for another Dunkirk?'[48]

Hitler had belatedly come to see that the situation in Normandy was untenable. Model took over his new command with instructions to rebuild a front at the Seine. German forces retreated eastwards through the neck of the Falaise pocket as fast as their transport would allow. Heavy air attacks blocked roads with burning vehicles and dead horses and men. The SS Hitler Youth Panzer Division played a feature role in the battle to keep the escape route open as long as possible. An Allied interrogation report of the captured Hitler Youth's commander, SS Major-General Kurt Mayer, later concluded: 'To him the battle of Caen-Falaise was magnificent in the best Wagnerian tradition. As he described his actions and those of his men, it seemed as though he liked to consider himself as Siegfried leading his warriors to their death.'[49] On 19 August the neck of the pocket was closed. The Polish Armoured Division played a big part in the last phase of fighting. The thin cordon around the pocket leaked *Wehrmacht* escapees during the next day, including a wounded General Hausser, commander of the Seventh Army.

In the Falaise pocket thousands of Germans were killed and another 50,000 prisoners were taken, of whom many were wounded. The carnage and wreckage within the captured pocket shocked Allied observers. General Eisenhower toured the field and wrote: 'Forty-eight hours after the closing of the gap I was conducted through it on foot, to encounter scenes that could be described only by Dante. It was literally possible to walk for hundreds of yards at a time, stepping on nothing but dead and decaying flesh.'[50] A rapid retreat from most of France was the only option for the defeated *Wehrmacht*. Within days French armoured units had entered Paris to liberate the great city. The Vichy French leaders Petain and Laval left France for Germany, in contrast to their refusal to leave France for North Africa or Britain when the boot was on the other foot in 1940.[51]

During the early autumn of 1944 German troops retreated to the border of Germany and the Rhine tributaries in Holland. Brussels was entered by British troops on 3 September. The Allied force advancing from southern France linked up with Allied troops from Normandy in Alsace. German garrisons, on Hitler's orders, stayed behind in the port towns of Le Harve, Boulogne and Calais, which had to be captured in battle. The garrisons at Dunkirk and the Channel Islands were bypassed and withered on the vine until the end of the war.

To the end of August, Allied losses in Normandy had been 210,000 killed, wounded and missing, to which thousands more air force and naval casualties should be added. English language literature generally claims that the Germans lost 200,000 killed and wounded, and another 200,000 prisoners in Normandy.[52] The figure for prisoners is probably accurate, thousands of whom would also be wounded. But the 200,000 killed and wounded figure far too conveniently matches the official figure for Allied land casualties. About half of the German loss figure of 117,000 to 25 July had been prisoners, many of whom had been taken in the Cherbourg peninsula. A figure of 120–140,000 German killed and wounded in Normandy is a better estimate.

German equipment losses in Normandy were 1,300 tanks, 500 assault guns and 5,500 guns.[53] German tanks losses had been modest until the end of July, but had been heavy in the Falaise pocket. Many tanks were abandoned in the retreat towards the Seine due to a lack of fuel. The 21st Panzer Division had started the campaign with 127 tanks and forty assault guns but lost the lot. Fewer than 120 German armoured vehicles escaped across the Seine.

Surprisingly, much of the equipment lost by the *Wehrmacht* in Normandy, Poland and Belorussia in the summer and autumn of 1944 was quickly replaced. Speer's arms industries reached peak production midway through 1944. The material revival of the German Army late in the year for another desperate series of campaigns was a personal triumph for the man who had devotedly followed

Hitler since the early days of the Third Reich. The Allied strategic bombing campaign against German industry had not made more than a marginal overall difference to weapons production, though the American daylight bombing of the synthetic oil industry was starting to have a dramatic impact.

The liberation of a large part of occupied Europe from June to August 1944 was a genuine achievement for Allied forces. The *Wehrmacht* had made possible the execution of Nazi policies outside German territory. Now that the *Wehrmacht* had been pushed much of the way back to the borders of Germany, a variety of genocidal activities, and more common place atrocities, could only be practised against those still trapped within the Third Reich and its shrinking empire.

In some respects, the reconquest of France in 1944 was similar to the events of 1940. Both campaigns were relatively brief and resulted in a decisive victory. The novel achievement of *blitzkrieg* in 1940 was matched by the distinctive military accomplishment of a vast amphibious landing in 1944. Where the outcomes of the campaigns in France of 1940 and 1944 so greatly differ was in their overall impact on the fate of their respective victors. Victory in France in 1940 did not win the war for Germany, whereas the Allied reconquest of France in 1944 would play a vital role in their eventual triumph in the Second World War in Europe.

13

The Battle of Leyte Gulf:
Philippines, October 1944

1943 had been a year of transition in the war between Imperial Japan and the Allies. The defeats at Midway and Guadalcanal had cost the Japanese the initiative in the Pacific, though Tokyo's position on the east Asian mainland remained formidable. Japanese forces continued to occupy large parts of China and South-East Asia.

General MacArthur's United States and Australian forces in the south-west Pacific had spent 1943 steadily pushing back the Japanese in the Solomons and New Guinea. Rabaul, at the top of the Solomons chain, had been hammered by air attack and its large garrison blockaded and neutralised.

In the central Pacific, Admiral Nimitz's fleet had been strongly reinforced during 1943. The new American aircraft carriers that came into service from the later half of the year would transform the naval war. Essex-class fleet carriers and Independence-class light fleet carriers embarked Hellcat fighters, a faster and hardier aircraft than the legendary Zero. Nimitz began a campaign against the Japanese-occupied Gilbert Islands in November 1943. Bitter fighting at Tarawa in the Gilberts was followed by less costly operations in the Marshalls early the following year. In the Caroline Islands the Japanese fleet base at Truk was bypassed, its installations devastated by United States carrier aircraft. Japanese plans to turn island bases into an interlocking network of unsinkable aircraft carriers failed as the Pacific Ocean was too vast to make the theory match reality.

In Tokyo Prime Minister General Tojo had responded to the setbacks of 1943 by making himself War Minister. The Japanese leadership resolved to adopt a more offensive posture in 1944. On the Asian mainland new offensives would be launched against Allied forces in eastern India and south-west China. At sea the main Japanese fleet had not contested American operations since the ending of the campaign at Guadalcanal early in 1943. The next round of American amphibious operations was likely to attempt to win bases from which heavy bombers could directly strike at Japan. The Imperial Japanese Navy would have to contest that threat. New Japanese aircraft carriers had been built to make up for the ships lost at Midway. The First Mobile Fleet was formed in a bid to prepare for a decisive naval campaign against the Americans.

In the spring of 1944 an American invasion force was prepared to tackle the Marianas, a series of islands forming an arc of which Saipan, Tinian, Rota and Guam were the most important. 32,000 Japanese troops had been deployed to defend Saipan under the command of Admiral Nagumo, who had been relegated from command of aircraft carriers to a shore role. Admirals Nimitz and Spruance were unsure if the Japanese navy would strongly oppose landings in the Marianas.[1] The commanders of the First Mobile Fleet, however, fully intended to attack the powerful USN task forces protecting an invasion force. The First Mobile Fleet was counting on assistance from aircraft based on land in the Marianas.

Spruance, the cool and remote victor at Midway, was in overall command of the USN's Fifth Fleet and the Marianas invasion force. Spruance had the tasks of covering the Saipan landing and engaging any Japanese relieving force. The main component of the Fifth Fleet was the carrier and battleship groups of Task Force 58. Vice-Admiral M.A. Mitscher's eight fleet carriers and seven light carriers embarked 900 aircraft.[2] Vice-Admiral R.K. Turner commanded Task Force 51, the amphibious expeditionary force destined for Saipan. Turner's task force included squadrons of older battleships and escort aircraft carriers. The Fifth Fleet's long logistical tail stretched back to Pearl Harbor and the west coast of the United States.

American landings commenced on Saipan on the morning of 15 June, and had been preceded by several days of carrier air strikes to win local air superiority. In Japan Admiral Soemu Toyoda, the commander of the Combined Fleet, ordered the First Mobile Fleet into action to contest the invasion. American submarines spied the Japanese fleet entering the Philippines Sea.

Unlike in previous Pacific battles, such as Midway, Japanese commanders had concentrated their carrier forces in the Philippines Sea for a single powerful blow. Vice-Admiral Jisaburo Ozawa had replaced Nagumo as Japan's principal commander of carriers. Ozawa's First Mobile Fleet included five fleet carriers, four light carriers, five battleships and eleven heavy cruisers. The fleet had embarked 430 carrier aircraft. The battleships and cruisers carried another forty-three float planes. Nevertheless, in terms of numbers of naval aircraft, the odds in the Philippines Sea engagement were not in the Imperial Japanese Navy's favour.

In addition, whereas American naval pilots had been given two years' training, and pre-war IJN pilots had over three year's training, by mid-1944 the training period for Japanese naval pilots had dropped to an average of six months and far less in many cases. The typical Japanese naval pilot of 1944 knew few of the skills needed for successful aerial combat. At times navigational training had been reduced to following a leader. Light-weight Japanese aircraft were manoeuvrable and could fly long distances, but lacked armour and self-sealing fuel tanks.[3]

Late on 18 June Japanese aircraft sighted Spruance's and Mitscher's carriers 200 miles west of Saipan. Admiral Ozawa decided against a late afternoon attack in preference to a strike the following morning. The Japanese fleet was divided into three groups. Force C – commanded by Vice-Admiral Kurita – comprised three light carriers and four battleships. Force C was 100 miles ahead of Forces A and B, which included a combined total of five fleet carriers, one light carrier and one battleship.

At 7.30 a.m. on 19 June, a clear day with few clouds, a blue ocean and forty mile visibility at ship level, Japanese scouts found the American carrier force. The first of a series of air strikes was launched within the hour. The first blow of the day, however, was struck against the Japanese fleet by an American submarine. Ozawa had too few destroyers to effectively screen his big ships, and Japanese seaplanes were busy scouting for American carriers rather than watching for submarines. At about 9.20 a.m. *Taiho*, Ozawa's flagship, took one hit from the submarine USS *Albacore*. Later in the day *Taiho* would be devastated by an explosion in the upper hanger. An elevator had jammed and the ventilation system became filled with gasoline fumes. An electrical pump was started and a spark is believed to have ignited the fumes. The carrier capsized with heavy loss of life. The 33,000 ton *Taiho* had been the largest and newest IJN fleet carrier. To make matters worse for Ozawa, at 12.20 p.m. the submarine *Cavalla* torpedoed the fleet carrier *Shokaku*, which was stricken by fire and explosions. *Shokaku* had been one of the half dozen fleet carriers that had raided Pearl Harbor.

Meanwhile the radar of American carriers had given timely and efficient warning of approaching Japanese aircraft. Japanese torpedo-bombers and dive-bombers were overwhelmed by American fighters. The first ragged wave of Japanese raiders lost two-thirds of its strength to Hellcat fighters and scored just a single hit on the battleship *South Dakota*. The second wave of Japanese aircraft lost an even greater proportion of its strength without inflicting much damage. Ozawa's third and fourth air strikes were no more successful and many aircraft failed to even find the American carriers. Some Japanese aircraft flew on to Guam to crash-land or be destroyed on the ground by marauding American fighters. By the end of 19 June the Japanese had lost 346 carrier- and ground-based aircraft. Only 100 Japanese carrier aircraft remained ready for action. An American airman remarked that the aim of Japanese pilots had been so poor they 'couldn't hit an elephant if it was tied down'.[4] The Americans had lost only thirty aircraft and the day became known as the 'Great Marianas Turkey Shoot'.

Nonetheless, Ozawa was told by returning aircrew that heavy damage had been inflicted on the enemy. The Japanese admiral planned to resume battle on 21 June, after refuelling on the 20th. On 20 June, however, Japanese scouts informed Ozawa that American carrier strength was undiminished. Ozawa sensibly revised his plans and turned his fleet to the north west to break off the battle.

Due to a poorly organized pattern of reconnaissance flights, the Americans did not locate the First Mobile Fleet until 3.40 p.m. on the afternoon of 20

June.[5] The Japanese were 275 miles away, which was at extreme range for an air strike. Spruance accepted the risk of an evening strike and the likely problems of recovering aircraft after nightfall. Over 200 American fighters, dive-bombers and torpedo-bombers were launched. A two hour flight brought them to an attack position by 6.40 p.m. Against the backdrop of a beautiful Pacific sunset; the weak screen of defending fighters was shot apart. Serious damage was inflicted on the fleet carrier *Zuikaku*. The order was given to abandon ship but the fires were brought under control and the great ship reached Japan. American aircraft inflicted heavy damage on other carriers. The fleet carrier *Hiyo* sank after a series of explosions. The remaining six surviving carriers of the First Mobile Fleet retired to safety with only thirty-five serviceable aircraft left of the 430 available at the start of the battle. Seventeen American aircraft were downed in the attacks, but another eighty-two failed to return to their carriers in the darkness. The pilots were forced to ditch and wait for rescue the next day.[6]

Spruance was subjected to a good deal of post-battle criticism – 'Monday morning quarterbacking' in American parlance – for not sinking more of the Japanese carriers. For most of the battle Spruance had elected to stay close to Saipan to protect the invasion fleet and bridgehead in case unlocated Japanese forces were moving around his flank. There was disappointment within the Fifth Fleet that the battle of the Philippines Sea had not been a truly decisive battle.[7] It was true that many of the Japanese carriers had escaped, but the strength of Japanese naval aviation had been shattered in the engagement. In Japan desperate attempts were made to train new air groups for the carriers.

Ashore in the Marianas, fighting at Saipan dragged onward. When defeat was imminent for Japanese forces, Admiral Nagumo, the man who had raided Pearl Harbor and lost his carriers at Midway, committed suicide rather than be captured alive. On 18 July 1944 General Tojo resigned from the government as a consequence of the latest round of defeats.

In the south-west Pacific there had been further landings along the coast of north-west New Guinea in mid-1944. The island of Morotai in the Moluccas was assaulted on 15 September only 300 miles from the southern Philippines.[8] The Japanese worked frantically to build up their army in the Philippines. General Yamashita, the 'Tiger of Malaya', was put in command of Japanese ground forces. A steady stream of reinforcements was sent to the archipelago from the Asian mainland.

Admiral King, the USN's Chief of Naval Operations, had initially favoured an invasion of Formosa ahead of an invasion of the Philippines. General MacArthur, on the other hand, was strongly and passionately committed to retaking the Philippines at an early opportunity. He had an undeniable personal commitment to the invasion. His father had been military governor of the Philippines, and MacArthur was the commander who had lost the territory in

1942. The Philippines was still a United States colony, but MacArthur believed that 'purely military considerations demand the reoccupation of the Philippines in order to cut the enemy's communications to the south and to secure a base for our further advance'.[9] Early in September the Joint Chiefs of Staff, with President Roosevelt's approval, ordered an invasion of the island of Mindanao in the southern Philippines on 15 November. This was to be followed by landings on the island of Leyte in the central Philippines on 20 December. Whether Luzon, the largest Philippines island, or Formosa would be invaded after that remained an open question, but either way it was desirable to take Leyte to establish air and sea bases in the region.

For the next round of operations the Pacific Fleet's principal force would be commanded by Admiral William F. 'Bull' Halsey, a man who had earned his wings at the age of fifty-two to qualify for command of an aircraft carrier. Nimitz swapped Spruance's Fifth Fleet headquarters with Halsey's Third Fleet headquarters. Halsey would command more or less the same fleet of ships. Spruance and his staff were scheduled to return to the forefront of operations after the Philippines campaign was completed. Nimitz alternated his fleet commanders to allow them a period of rest, though if he had possessed more confidence in either man he might possibly have left one or the other continually in place.

Halsey commanded the Third Fleet from the fast battleship *New Jersey*. He had distinguished himself as a commander in the Doolittle raid, the Guadalcanal campaign and subsequent operations in the Solomons. His aggressive spirit had been important during the early days of the Pacific war. Halsey had missed the Coral Sea, Midway and Philippines Sea battles. He was very keen to win the next great victory over the Imperial Japanese Navy. A strong, pugnacious, outspoken man, Halsey's speeches to units featured lines such as, 'Kill Japs, kill Japs, kill more Japs!' He gave press correspondents plenty of quotable material, once characterising the Japanese as 'lousy yellow rat monkey bastards'.[10]

The Third Fleet's main strike group was Task Force 38, an armada of sixteen aircraft carriers and over 1,000 aircraft. Six battleships and a host of smaller warships completed the fleet. After preliminary air strikes on the Philippines from early to mid-September, the invasion date for Leyte, on Halsey's recommendation, was brought forward from 20 December to 20 October. A rescued United States Navy pilot shot down over Leyte had reported that the island was not strongly garrisoned. Aerial reconnaissance seemed to corroborate that opinion. Nimitz and MacArthur quickly agreed to Halsey's suggestion and successfully sought Washington's approval. There was little remaining desire in Washington to invade Formosa as a recent Japanese offensive in central and southern China had badly defeated the Chinese Nationalists.[11]

Carrier raids on Formosa, Okinawa and Luzon in mid-October further damaged Japanese air power. Formosa (Taiwan) was over 200 miles north of the Philippines. Japanese air reinforcements had been sent from Japan to help defend Formosa. Ozawa's depleted carrier air groups were stripped of available aircraft. In three days fighting over and around Formosa, Japanese aircraft losses on the ground and in the air tallied up to 500. According to Vice-Admiral Shigeru Fukudome: 'Our fighters were nothing but so many eggs thrown at the stone wall of the indomitable enemy formation.'[12] Japanese pilots claimed to have inflicted heavy losses on American shipping lying off Formosa to give their commanders some cause for relief and celebration. In reality none of Halsey's ships had been sunk, though an aircraft carrier and several cruisers had been damaged. Seventy-nine USN aircraft were destroyed in the operations.

The amphibious assault on Leyte was to be conducted by General MacArthur's South-West Pacific Command. MacArthur's troops were to be transported and given close support by the Seventh Fleet of Vice-Admiral Thomas C. Kinkaid. Halsey's Third Fleet was to protect the invasion from the possible intervention of the Japanese Combined Fleet. Overall naval command for the campaign was not unified as Halsey took his orders from Nimitz at Hawaii, and Kinkaid's fleet was part of MacArthur's command. Washington had found it difficult to reconcile the claims of MacArthur and Nimitz for overall command. The obvious solution would have been to place all naval forces under Nimitz, but that would have involved taking Kinkaid's Seventh Fleet away from MacArthur. The administration in Washington did not wish to anger MacArthur given his standing in American political life.

Nimitz believed that landings at Leyte would probably force the Japanese fleet to come out to fight. He instructed Halsey to protect the invasion force and destroy Japanese shipping in the area, though he added the conflicting rider: 'In case opportunity for destruction of major portion of the enemy fleet offered or can be created, such destruction becomes the primary task.'[13] In light of the Japanese fleet's perceived escape in the Philippines Sea, Nimitz considered it necessary to issue more explicitly aggressive instructions.

The first American landings were made at Leyte on 20 October 1944, thereby triggering a series of naval actions that comprise one of the largest naval battles in history. After a heavy shore bombardment, the initial landing on the north-east coast of Leyte was successfully accomplished against modest Japanese ground and aerial opposition. An armada of American warships protected transports carrying four army divisions and 160,000 troops.[14] All amphibious landing craft and transports were commanded by Kinkaid's Seventh Fleet, which included six battleships, eight cruisers and eighteen escort aircraft carriers. General MacArthur waded ashore from a landing craft to announce into a microphone: 'People of the Philippines, I have returned.' It had taken him slightly over two years and seven months, less than might have been predicted in May 1942.

In October 1944 the IJN's aircraft carriers were based in home waters, but Japanese battleships had been based in the East Indies to be near the oil fields of the region. The super-battleships *Yamato* and *Musashi* of Admiral Matome

Ugaki's Battleship Division One were among the warships at Lingga Roads near Singapore. At 70,000 tons loaded, these battleships carried very heavy steel plate armour. *North Carolina*-class battleships displaced only 40,000 tons and the famous German battleship *Bismarck* had displaced 45,000 tons. Ugaki looked to the future with confidence: 'We are not afraid of a million enemies or a thousand carriers because our whole force shares the same spirit.' Apart from *Musashi* and *Yamato*, all other Japanese battleships had been launched around the time of the First World War. *Kongo* had been built in a British shipyard and launched in 1912. The older battleships, however, had been extensively modernised in the 1930s and carried fourteen-inch gun batteries. A high bridge and pagoda-like masts gave Japanese battleships a distinctive silhouette.

The Japanese had a number of contingency plans drawn up to deal with any future American offensive. Late in July Imperial Headquarters in Tokyo had issued a 'Plan for the Conduct of Future Operations'. This plan was called *Sho* – Victory – and comprised four variations. *Sho* 1 was the Philippines defence plan. *Sho* 2, 3 and 4 were plans to combat assaults on Formosa, the Ryukyus or the home islands. As the necessary planning conferences had already been held, there was no need for the Japanese to flood the air waves with radio messages to activate an operation. Allied signals intelligence was unable to make any major breakthroughs during this period.[15]

Admiral Toyoda, commander of the Combined Fleet, knew that a major battle would have to be fought to defend the Philippines. If the Americans captured the Philippines that would largely cut the supply route between Japan and South-East Asia, meaning that no oil could be sent to warships at Japan and no ammunition could be sent from Japan to those warships based near Singapore. The Imperial Japanese Navy could either fight to defend the Philippines and the route to South-East Asia, or become steadily paralysed as a fighting force. Toyoda logically commented: 'In the end even if you had a fleet, it would have been a white elephant.'[16] According to the *Sho* 1 plan, Vice-Admiral Ozawa's carrier force was to sail from Japanese waters to act as a decoy to draw American warships away from a Philippines invasion bridgehead. Ozawa's force comprised the fleet carrier *Zuikaku*, three light carriers, two hybrid battleship-carriers and a mix of cruisers and destroyers. These carriers, however, had only 116 aircraft aboard, crewed by inexperienced pilots. There had been little time to train new aircrew after the debacles of the Marianas and Formosa. The hybrid battleship-carriers *Ise* and *Hyuga* had been rebuilt by replacing some gun batteries with a short after flight deck. In theory seaplanes could be launched off the flight deck and recovered again by landing alongside to be winched aboard by a crane. In practice neither the seaplanes nor the aircrew needed were available at this stage of the war.

As Ozawa's carriers approached the Philippines from the north, Vice-Admiral Takeo Kurita's heavy units at Lingga Roads were to sail from South-East Asia to close on the Philippines to devastate the invasion bridgehead with gunfire.

Kurita was the principal Japanese sea-going commander for the upcoming operation, and he was undoubtedly a highly experienced combatant. He had commanded the heavy cruiser *Mikuma* at Midway, and had bombarded Henderson Field at Guadalcanal with the battleship *Kongo*, before going on to hold further major commands in the Solomons and Marianas campaigns.[17]

Kurita's task force was to sail from Lingga roads, refuel at Brunei, and then cross the Sibuyan Sea to the San Bernardino Strait and Leyte Gulf. As Kurita's force entered Leyte Gulf from the north through the San Bernardino Strait, another force was to enter Leyte Gulf from the south through Surigao Strait. The force bound for the Surigao Strait was to comprise two groups, the first sailing from Lingga Roads under Vice-Admiral Shoji Nishimura, the second sailing from Japan under Vice-Admiral Kiyohide Shima. Nishimura commanded two battleships, one heavy cruiser and four destroyers. Shima commanded two heavy cruisers, one light cruiser and four destroyers. It was hoped that the complexity of the Japanese plan would confuse American commanders and allow one or both pincers to enter Leyte Gulf. If the Japanese could destroy American shipping supporting the invasion bridgehead that would assist the Imperial Japanese Army's defence of Leyte. The plan hinged on all the different task forces keeping to a tight schedule, and Ozawa's carrier decoy force had to do its job effectively. To some extent, the dispersed location of Japanese naval bases and the geography of the Philippines imposed complexity upon Japanese planning. The straightforward concentration of naval forces adopted for the Marianas fighting had not proved a success.

Kurita's and Nishimura's ships had left Lingga roads early on 18 October as an invasion of the Philippines seemed imminent.[18] Kurita left Brunei Bay, Borneo, after fuelling, at 8 a.m. on 22 October, two days after the Leyte landings had commenced. Nishimura left Brunei that afternoon to sail a separate route. The previous evening Kurita had explained the audacious plan to his gathered subordinates. His concluding remarks included: 'Would it not be shameful to have our fleet remain intact while our nation perishes? ...You must remember that there are such things as miracles. What man can say that there is no chance for our fleet to turn the tide of war in a decisive battle?'[19] Ozawa's carriers had sailed from Japan's Inland Sea unseen by nearby American submarines.

Kurita's battle began at dawn on 23 October when two United States submarines found his fleet of five battleships, ten heavy and two light cruisers and thirteen destroyers on the western side of Palawan Island, to the west of the Philippines. The fleet had not been deployed by Kurita with the danger of submarine attack in mind. There was no destroyer screen in the van as the fleet traversed the narrow Palawan Passage.

USS *Darter* lay in ambush ahead of the approaching columns of Japanese warships. She fired her bow tubes at one ship and then swung around to fire the stern tubes at another ship. The heavy cruiser *Atago*, Kurita's flagship, was crippled and soon sank with heavy loss of life. Kurita, a recent dengue fever sufferer, was forced to jump into the sea to be rescued by a destroyer from the oily water.[20] The heavy cruiser *Takao* was also badly damaged by *Darter's* torpedoes. The Japanese formation then ran into the waiting USS *Dace*, which torpedoed and sank the heavy cruiser *Maya* with over 300 of her crew. Kurita and his staff transferred to *Yamato*, and *Takao* limped back towards Brunei with two escorting destroyers. The submarines made their escape but one of them – *Darter* – later ran firmly aground and had to be abandoned, the crew rescued by *Dace*. USN submarines achieved great things in the war against Japan but twenty-two per cent of American submariners who made war patrols went missing.[21]

The following morning of 24 October, whilst Ozawa's carriers approached the Philippines from the north, Kurita's five battleships, nine remaining cruisers and thirteen destroyers started their run through the Sibuyan Sea amid the Philippines archipelago. To the south, Nishimura's force was crossing the Sulu Sea towards the Surigao Strait, with Shima's cruisers and destroyers some distance to the rear.

As the Japanese approached, the United States Seventh Fleet continued with its duties in respect to the invasion of Leyte. The battleships of the Seventh Fleet were inside Leyte Gulf supporting the troops ashore. The eighteen escort carriers of Rear-Admiral Thomas L. Sprague's Task Force 77.4 hovered just outside the gulf. To the east and north east of Leyte Gulf the carrier groups of the Third Fleet provided more distant cover. The Third Fleet included eight fleet carriers and eight light carriers, though Halsey had detached Vice-Admiral John S. McCain's TG 38.1 to resupply at Ulithi. McCain's carrier group was the strongest of the Third Fleet's four carrier groups. The strange timing of its detachment indicates that Halsey and his staff had a low estimation of the Japanese navy's offensive potential.

On the morning of 24 October American aerial reconnaissance found Kurita's force in the Sibuyan Sea. Halsey lost no opportunity to strike. He was spoiling for a fight and recalled McCain's carrier group, by now a day's distance away. Heavy and sustained air attacks on Kurita's force began soon after 10.25 a.m., when Japanese lookouts saw masses of approaching American aircraft. It is noteworthy how often in this campaign important sightings of the enemy were made by Japanese lookouts. Eyesight was a method of observation as old as mankind. The Japanese did not have the number or the range of radar equipment available to the Americans, even aboard the most important warships.[22]

As American carrier aircraft were swarming towards Kurita's fleet, the opening blow of the day had already been struck against Halsey's carriers by Japanese aircraft based on nearby Philippines airfields. Kurita would have welcomed air cover and later commented: 'I requested that they send fighters from land bases, but they did not send any ... leaving [my] fleet without the expected cover.'[23] The training of Japanese pilots was so poor that their commanders intended only to use them to attack American shipping. They were hopelessly unprepared for air-to-air combat. Rear-Admiral Sherman's TG 38.3, the northernmost Third Fleet carrier group was lying off central Luzon. Incoming Japanese raiders were massacred by more skilled American aviators, but a little after 9.30 a.m. a single Yokosuka D4Y Suisei (Judy) broke through the defensive screen by following returning American aircraft and hiding in low cloud. A 550-pound bomb hit the 11,000 ton light carrier *Princeton*. The bomb penetrated deep into the ship and exploded to cause fires that ignited munitions and fuel. The raging fires that followed were brought under control but mid-afternoon a magazine exploded. The blast on *Princeton* wrought terrible carnage on the crowded decks of the light cruiser *Birmingham* drawn alongside. The decks literally ran red with blood. Over 300 men were killed on the two warships and *Princeton* sank.[24]

From late morning into the afternoon the Third Fleet launched five strikes against Kurita's fleet in the Sibuyan Sea. Kurita's battleships and cruisers threw up a formidable anti-aircraft barrage. In the initial round of attacks, a bomb hit was scored on *Yamato* and another bomb and torpedo struck her sister behemoth *Musashi*. Damage was minimal. The super-battleships could absorb a great deal of punishment. The heavy cruiser *Myoko* was damaged by a torpedo, lost speed and had to limp back for Brunei.

As the day wore on *Musashi* attracted a great deal of punishment from each wave of attackers. A succession of bomb and torpedo hits slowed the giant, which began to flood and list once both the outer and inner hulls had been shattered by torpedoes. In desperation, special anti-aircraft rounds were fired by the main eighteen-inch batteries. *Musashi* reported her plight to the flagship *Yamato* by flag. As *Musashi* was starting to fall out of formation, Kurita ordered her to turn about. Kurita did not see his mission as a form of suicide and clearly intended to save damaged ships. On the outward journey he had adopted a cruising speed to conserve fuel for the return journey. By 1.30 p.m. *Musashi* was twenty miles behind the rest of the force.[25] She would roll over in the evening, taking almost half of her crew of 2,200 with her. She had taken an estimated nineteen torpedoes and seventeen bomb hits.

About 3.00 p.m. Kurita retired his whole force westwards. At 4 p.m. he signalled Admiral Toyoda in Japan that he was temporarily retiring to avoid air attacks. Once the air attacks had stopped, Kurita decided to turn eastwards again at 5.15 p.m. for a night passage of the San Bernadino Strait. An hour later a signal arrived from a concerned Toyoda: 'All forces will dash to the attack, trusting in divine guidance.' Kurita had lost a number of hours endeavouring to evade the air strikes. The battleships *Yamato* and *Nagato* and the heavy cruiser *Tone* had suffered bomb hits during the day but only limited damage had been inflicted.[26] Of 259 attacking American aircraft, eighteen had been shot down.

During 24 October Nishimura's force had been sighted and attacked by American aircraft as it headed towards the Surigao Strait. Some damage was inflicted to Nishimura's warships. Curiously, Nishimura did not contact or wait for Shima's force sailing behind him.

Ozawa's carrier force, now off northern Luzon, had still not been located by the Americans. By this stage of the operation, Ozawa wanted his decoy force to be discovered, and his own reconnaissance had located the carriers of the Third Fleet. At 11.45 a.m. on 24 October Ozawa ordered an air strike by seventy-six aircraft, the bulk of the slender force his carriers had embarked. An hour later these aircraft appeared on the radar screens of Halsey's carriers. Controllers sent out fighters to shoot down many of the poorly trained Japanese aviators, leaving the survivors to fly on to shore airfields in the Philippines.

With the battle entering a critical period, the lack of direct and efficient communications between the commanders of the Third and Seventh Fleets started to cause confusion. As Halsey's messages were directly copied to Nimitz at Pearl Harbor and King in Washington, both those admirals were better able to track Halsey's actions than Kinkaid and the staff of the Seventh Fleet. At 3.12 p.m., whilst his aircraft were hammering Kurita in the Sibuyan Sea, Halsey had sent out a contingency message about forming a new Task Force 34 within the Third Fleet comprising four battleships under Vice-Admiral Willis A. Lee. This message had been copied as per routine to Nimitz and King, but had not been officially copied to Kinkaid. Yet Kinkaid's Seventh Fleet communications staff had overheard the message. To those outside the Third Fleet the wording of Halsey's message was open to misinterpretation, and Kinkaid, Nimitz and King all assumed that Halsey's contingency plan would actually be executed. An additional assumption was that the TF 34 battleships would be deployed to cover the northern flank of the Leyte Gulf bridgehead. These assumptions suited Kinkaid's own plans to use his battleships to cover the southern flank and deal with Nishimura's approaching fleet. Arguably, Kinkaid believed what he wanted to hear. The eavesdroppers of the Seventh Fleet did not overhear messages subsequently sent by short-range radio within Halsey's fleet that might have clarified the status of the yet-to-be-formed TF 34.[27]

Ozawa's fleet was finally sighted by Halsey's aircraft 190 miles to the north just before 5 p.m. on 24 October. Halsey believed that Kurita's force had been smashed by the day-long air attacks and was no longer a threat. He enthusiastically headed north towards Ozawa with the whole of the Third Fleet in the early evening. Halsey was well aware of the criticism of Spruance's decision not to chase the Japanese fleet more aggressively in the Marianas campaign. Halsey told his staff: 'We will run north at top speed and put those carriers out for keeps.' Sixty-five warships of the Third Fleet were setting out to run down the seventeen warships of Ozawa's force. A little after 8 p.m. Halsey retired to his cabin having had little rest or sleep during the previous forty-eight hours. At 8.24 p.m. Kinkaid finally received an official message from Halsey: 'Strike reports indicate enemy heavily damaged. Am proceeding north with three groups to attack enemy carrier force at dawn.'[28] Kinkaid and Nimitz assumed this message referred to the carrier groups of the Third Fleet and that the battleships of TF 34 would remain behind to watch the San Bernadino Strait. Night reconnaissance missions to the Sibuyan Sea were flown from the Third Fleet's light carrier *Independence*. Pilots found Kurita's force heading for the San Bernadino Strait but their reports do not seem to have registered with the Third Fleet's staff. By the time Kurita passed the strait at thirty-five minutes past midnight American night-fliers had lost contact.

During daylight hours of 24 October Kinkaid's and the Seventh Fleet's attention had been devoted mostly to Nishimura's force known to be approaching Leyte Gulf from the south. Those Japanese ships would likely enter the Surigao Strait in the early hours of the morning. During the afternoon Kinkaid prepared by deploying his battleship group at the northern end of the strait to fight a night action with gunfire. Kinkaid was able to mass his battleships in the Surigao Strait as he falsely believed Halsey was covering the San Bernadino Strait further north. Four heavy cruisers (including HMAS *Shropshire*), four light cruisers and numerous destroyers (including HMAS *Arunta*) and patrol-torpedo (PT) boats completed the force sent to block the Surigao Strait. Five out of six of Rear-Admiral Jesse Oldendorf's battleships had been present at the Pearl Harbor raid. *California* and *West Virginia* had been sunk in shallow water on 7 December 1941, only to be raised and extensively repaired. The chance for revenge was finally at hand.

Nishimura did not want to risk missing a night passage of Surigao Strait, and he pressed ahead into the evening gloom. After night fall, on a smooth and glassy sea, American destroyers and PT boats were sent forward of Oldendorf's battle line to harass the flanks of Nishimura's approaching column, which comprised four destroyers, the battleships *Yamashiro* and *Fuso* and the heavy cruiser *Mogami*. Under an overcast night sky, lookouts on the PT boats first sighted the Japanese warships at 10.50 p.m. The PT boats attacked with torpedoes without scoring any hits, but their reports were able to keep American commanders well informed as to the approaching Japanese force's location.

As the Japanese warships neared, groups of American destroyers set off down the flanks of the strait to join the fray. The Japanese sighted hostile destroyers at 2.56 a.m. Star-shells and the pencils of search lights lit up the darkness. The first wave of American destroyer torpedoes was launched at almost 10,000 yards' range and would need eight minutes to reach the intended targets. A scissor attack that launched torpedoes at a target from more than one direction was the preferred form of destroyer attack. Gunfire was avoided as the flash could give away a ship's position. About 3.09 a.m. American destroyer crewmen heard detonations in the distance. The battleship *Fuso* had been struck by torpedoes. She slowed and fell out of formation. More American destroyers launched their torpedoes and big explosions about 3.20 a.m. marked fatal hits on two Japanese destroyers. A third Japanese destroyer had her bow blown off.

Hits were also scored on the battleship *Yamashiro*, Nishimura's flagship, but she sailed onward. Admiral Oldendorf ordered his destroyers to retire as the ragged Japanese column pushed on to be within range of the guns of his battleships and cruisers.[29]

Six battleships, four heavy cruisers and four light cruisers were waiting for the Japanese. Only the battleship *Yamashiro*, heavy cruiser *Mogami* and a single destroyer continued to steam up the strait towards the Allied force. The destroyer attacks had accounted for the majority of Nishimura's ships. Still, the Americans were about to achieve the War College fantasy of capping the T of their opponent's formation, as the Japanese had done to the Russians at Tsushima Strait in 1905. Oldendorf ordered his cruisers to open fire at 3.51 a.m. at 15,600 yards' range. Two minutes later the battleships, lying further to the north, opened fire at a range of 22,800 yards. Salvoes made crimson streaks of light as the shells arced through the sky. An American destroyer captain thought the shells looked like 'the tail-lights of automobiles going across Brooklyn Bridge'.[30] Great columns of water rose around the Japanese ships as shells from six- to sixteen-inch calibre rained down. By now *Yamashiro* had slowed to twelve knots and she and *Mogami* fired some salvoes at targets sighted ahead spitting fire. American battleship salvoes were fired at roughly forty second intervals and before long the radar pips of the Japanese warships had faded from the screens of American operators. Three of the American battleships were equipped with up to date fire-control radar and their gunfire had been highly accurate. The other three battleships had struggled to see their targets and one did not open fire.

Yamashiro was set ablaze and Admiral Nishimura was dead. The surviving destroyer *Shigure* turned about and headed south to safety, as did the battered heavy cruiser *Mogami*. Oldendorf ordered ceasefire. The crippled *Yamashira* capsized and sank at 4.19 a.m. with few survivors. By now *Fuso* had blown up. The burning halves of the ship drifted on the strait.

Nishimura had not radioed a report back to Shima's force sailing behind, which was left to discover for itself evidence of the fierce battle that had taken place in the strait. Surigao Strait was full of smoke from destroyer screens and wrecked ships. At 3.25 a.m. Shima's light cruiser *Abukuma* took a torpedo hit from a PT boat, and at 4.10 a.m. the burning pieces of *Fuso* were encountered. All questions were answered when the battered *Mogami* was passed retiring southwards. Shima's force took flight to narrowly avoid destruction.

Daylight next morning found the strait full of oil and wreckage. Japanese survivors swam away to refuse American rescue. Those who made it to shore were dealt with harshly by local Filipinos. The destroyer *Asagumo* was finished off by American gunfire and the limping *Mogami* was scuttled after suffering further damage from air attack. Only the destroyer *Shigure* survived of Nishimura's force.

Whilst the fighting in Surigao Strait had been underway, Halsey's five fleet carriers and six light carriers steamed north. At 2.08 a.m. Ozawa's force was located and Halsey sent his battleships ahead of the carrier groups as a vanguard. The elaborate Japanese decoy plan was working. Halsey's staff ignored air reconnaissance reports that the San Bernadino Strait's navigation lights were lit. A number of Halsey's subordinates felt that the Third Fleet's battleships should have been covering that strait. Admiral Mitscher's staff believed they were chasing a decoy but the leathery featured commander of the Third Fleet's carrier groups was reluctant to give Halsey advice without being asked. Halsey later explained in his after-action report that he 'was convinced that the Centre Force [Kurita] was so heavily damaged that it could not win a decision, while the possible maximum strength of the Northern Force [Ozawa] ... constituted a fresh and powerful threat'.[31] The Japanese, however, had fooled Halsey into leaving the San Bernadino Strait unguarded. The Japanese had used carriers as bait. That was a heresy in 1944. Tiredness and thirst for a personal victory had played a role in Halsey's decision-making. The battle in the Surigao Strait had been a big distraction for Kinkaid, but about 4 a.m. he finally directly asked Halsey if he was guarding the San Bernadino Strait.

Admiral Kurita's powerful battleship task force had come through the San Bernadino Strait to find open, empty sea. This was an enormous relief to those Japanese commanders and staffs who had feared that an American force would be waiting on the far side of the strait. In the days of wooden sailing ships an admiral might have left at least a frigate to watch a stretch of water as important as the San Bernadino Strait.[32] Neither Kinkaid nor Halsey had bothered to do so much. Kurita turned his ships southwards towards Leyte Gulf. For another six and a half hours Kurita's force sailed onwards, amid occasional rain squalls, in accordance with the *Sho* 1 plan. Kurita received the news at 5.30 a.m. that Nishimura's force had been smashed in the Surigao Strait.

When Japanese lookouts spotted the masts of shipping ahead, Kurita's Chief of Staff thought to himself, 'God has come to our assistance'.[33] Lookouts in the crow's-nest of *Yamato* sighted American ships at 6.44 a.m. An extraordinary opportunity lay before the Japanese, as the sighted ships were escort carriers of the Seventh Fleet. Only the escort carriers and their attendant destroyers lay between the invasion bridgehead on Leyte and the big guns of Kurita's battleships.

Kurita ordered a general attack by divisions of ships, rather than forming his fleet into a single battle line. This proved to be a bad and elementary mistake as the attacking force soon became ragged and uncoordinated. But four battleships, six heavy cruisers, two light cruisers and eleven destroyers comprised a formidable force, especially from the viewpoint of those American observers soon to watch it approach. The Japanese pressed forward in two columns of heavy cruisers, with two pairs of battleships behind, and two destroyer columns on the flanks. During the opening phase of the battle, Kurita ordered his destroyers and light cruisers to follow to the rear of the battleships and heavy cruisers. The destroyers should have been sent racing ahead for torpedo attacks from the flanks, as Oldendorf had initiated in the Surigao Strait the previous night.

Rear-Admiral Clifton A.F. 'Ziggy' Sprague's Task Force 77.4.3 (Taffy 3) was the northernmost of the Seventh Fleet's three escort carrier groups. Taffy 3 was off southern Samar. The six escort carriers of Taffy 3 had 165 aircraft between them, a mixture of Wildcat fighters and Avenger torpedo-bombers.[34] Escort carriers were sometimes referred to as 'baby flattops' or 'jeep' carriers. They were usually built on the hulls of merchant ships and were a little shorter in length than a cruiser. The primary tasks of escort carriers were to support the troops ashore and anti-submarine duties. Taffy 2 was about fifty miles to the south of Taffy 3. Taffy 1 was a similar distance to the south of Taffy 2.

At 6.46 a.m. Taffy 3 made radar contact with an unidentified force to the north. A pilot on an anti-submarine patrol soon reported a force of Japanese warships twenty miles away. American lookouts sighted the masts of big Japanese fighting ships to remove any doubt that something had gone terribly wrong. At 6.58 a.m. the Japanese opened fire. Huge geysers from near misses revealed they were heavy shells. The yellow, red, green, blue or purple dye in the shells helped the gunnery directors of each Japanese ship track the fall of their ship's salvoes.

The six escort carriers of Taffy 3 turned away from the Japanese as fast as their engines would allow, which was only about eighteen knots. Admiral Sprague sent out plain-language radio cries for help. The sea was calm and the humid climate kept smoke hanging low in the air. Taffy 3's carriers headed east and launched their aircraft as quickly as possible. The Japanese pursued them from the west. Further south, Taffy 1 and Taffy 2 also began to launch their available aircraft in response to news of the sudden crisis. The first wave of escort carrier aircraft carried only fragmentation bombs and depth charges. For a time a rain squall shielded Taffy 3. Sprague turned south under the cover of the squall, whilst Kurita kept heading east. This opened the range. The Japanese needed steady visual conditions for effective gunnery.

At 7.16 a.m. Sprague ordered his three destroyers – *Heermann*, *Johnston* and *Hoel* – into the attack. Constantly making smoke screens, the little ships attacked the Japanese battleships despite the great odds stacked against them. Scrambled smoke screens gave the destroyers the cover they needed to dart in and launch their torpedoes. *Johnston* managed to score a torpedo hit on the heavy cruiser *Kumano*, which fell away.[35] *Johnston* closed to within 5,000 yards of the battleship *Kongo*, which could not depress her main armament sufficiently to open fire. The five-inch shells of the destroyers, however, bounced off the armour of the larger Japanese warships. *Heermann* joined the fray to fire torpedoes at the battleship *Haruna* from 4,400 yards. *Yamato* was forced to turn back north for almost ten minutes to avoid torpedo tracks, carrying Kurita away from the action.

Before long Japanese gunfire began to hit the American destroyers. *Hoel* received several dozen hits before her crew was ordered to abandon ship. The destroyer escorts *Samuel B. Roberts*, *Raymond*, *Dennis* and *John C. Butler* joined the action to fire their torpedoes. After all torpedoes had been expended, the surviving small ships, trailing smoke screens, headed back towards the escort carriers. *Johnston* and *Samuel B. Roberts* were left behind to sink with heavy loss of life. The attacks by the small ships had delayed and disorganised the Japanese fleet's progress. As the chaotic fight between the American destroyers and Japanese heavy units was underway, flight deck and anti-aircraft personnel on the escort carriers could only watch the battle unfolding in the distance as spectators. A single five-inch gun was all that an escort carrier possessed.

Some Japanese warships had fired on the carriers whilst the battle with the American destroyers was underway. The escort carrier *Kalinin Bay* took a direct hit at 7.50 a.m. Japanese shooting was generally poor but *Fanshaw Bay* and *Whites Plains* suffered a number of hits and *Kitkun Bay* was splashed by near misses. Some armour piercing rounds punched straight through the unarmoured carriers without detonating. The escort carrier *Gambier Bay* received the heaviest punishment. By 8.10 a.m. the range had closed to 10,000 yards. *Gambier Bay* lost speed and more damage was suffered from a near miss that ruptured hull plating at the waterline. The listing and doomed escort carrier was dead in the water by 8.45 a.m. and capsized within half an hour. A large majority of the crew survived but it would be two days and two nights before they were rescued. The battleship *Kongo* reported to Kurita's flagship that they had sunk an *Enterprise*-class carrier. Other Japanese reports also spoke of engaging *Enterprise*-class carriers.[36] Shortly after 9 a.m. the Japanese destroyers made their only organised attack of the action, but launched their torpedoes at too great a range to matter.

Whilst all this was taking place, Taffy carrier aircraft and American shore-based aircraft had been attacking Kurita's warships. American aviators heavily damaged three Japanese heavy cruisers. *Chokai* blew up and had to be scuttled. *Chikuma* fell out of line crippled and sank just before 9 a.m. *Suzuya* was also slowed by damage.

To his amazement, at 9.25 a.m. Sprague became aware that the Japanese force in hot pursuit was now in retreat.[37] Kurita had broken off the action just when Taffy 3's defences had been largely broken down. In his after-action report Sprague included 'the definite partiality of Almighty God' among the reasons for the escape of Taffy 3.

Kurita's force headed north till 10.55 a.m. and then circled around, at times heading south west, until turning north again at 12.36 p.m. to head for the San Bernadino Strait. Kurita's ships were not short of ammunition. He had signalled Tokyo that he had abandoned the Leyte Gulf operation to search north for enemy forces. The Japanese passed back through the San Bernadino Strait that evening. Kurita was never entirely clear as to why he retreated when he did.

After the war he refused requests to discuss the battle. Admiral Ugaki on *Yamato* wrote in his diary: 'I felt irritated on the same bridge seeing that they [Kurita and his staff] lacked fighting spirit and promptitude.'[38]

Kurita, his staff and subordinates were weary men after the tension of the previous two days. Naval commanders at sea have to make rapid decisions under fire. Kurita may have believed he was pushing further and further into a trap. It seems likely that Kurita and his staff did not entirely appreciate that they were facing slow escort carriers. They seem to have believed that they were fighting Halsey's fleet carriers. Kurita's Chief of Staff, Rear-Admiral Koyanagi, later said that he had not been aware that the leading Japanese cruisers had been less than 10,000 yards from the American carriers when the action was called off.[39] Communications within the Japanese force had been poor and the gunnery had also been of a low standard. From the outset, Kurita may have harboured doubts about the wisdom of the operation he had been ordered to carry out. He can perhaps be criticised for breaking off the action at the moment he did, but his instinct to turn for safety was understandable. The original Japanese plan had lost much of its validity after Nishimura's force was destroyed in the Surigao Strait. Kurita had good reason to believe that his force would be annihilated if he lingered for too long east of the San Bernadino Strait.

At 6.48 a.m., as Kurita's fight with Taffy 3 had been getting underway, a surprised Halsey had received Kinkaid's message asking if Task Force 34 was guarding the San Bernardino Strait. Halsey replied in the negative and it had taken over two and a half hours for Kinkaid's message to reach its recipient. Halsey later wrote that, 'it was not my job to protect the Seventh Fleet. My job was offensive, to strike with the Third Fleet, and we were even then rushing to intercept a force which gravely threatened not only Kinkaid and myself, but the whole Pacific strategy.'[40] Kinkaid again appealed to Halsey for help when he was made aware that Taffy 3 was under attack.

At Pacific Fleet headquarters, far from the Philippines, Nimitz had monitored the messages sent by Kinkaid and Halsey. He was also perplexed as to the location of Halsey's Task Force 34. Nimitz decided directly to ask Halsey for the answer to that question. Nimitz's staff transmitted: 'Where is repeat where is Task Force thirty-four.' At Pacific Fleet headquarters padding was routinely added to the front and end of radio messages to thwart decoding. But the end padding 'the world wonders' was not deleted before the message was handed to Halsey at 10 a.m. Halsey was enraged by what he felt to be Nimitz's sarcasm in a message that was also copied to Admirals King and Kinkaid. Halsey recalled:

> I was stunned as if I had been struck in the face. The paper rattled in my hands. I snatched off my cap, threw it on the deck, and shouted something that I am ashamed to remember … I was so mad I couldn't talk. It was utterly impossible for me to believe that Chester Nimitz would send me such an insult.[41]

In response to these messages, Halsey divided his forces just before 11 a.m. He ordered south the battleships of Task Force 34, accompanied by one of his carrier groups. At this time, the Japanese carriers of Ozawa's force were only forty-two miles distant and already under American air attack. 'I turned my back', said Halsey, 'on the opportunity I had dreamed of since my days as a cadet.'[42] Halsey refused to admit he had made a mistake heading north to attack Ozawa but, 'I am in agreement that I made a mistake in bowing to pressure and turning south. I consider this the gravest error I committed during the Battle of Leyte Gulf.'[43] The leading ships of Halsey's Task Force 34 reached the San Bernadino Strait after midnight on 26 October and sank a Japanese destroyer from Kurita's force that had stayed behind to rescue survivors from the ships sunk in battle with Taffy 3. Kurita's fleet was subjected to long-range air strikes on 26 October and a light cruiser was sunk. Kurita's battleships and surviving smaller warships reached Brunei Bay and later sailed for Japan.

As Halsey and Task Force 34 had headed south, the rest of the Third Fleet under the command of Admiral Mitscher had continued with attacks on Ozawa's force, which comprised a fleet carrier, three light carriers, two battleships, three light cruisers and some destroyers. A small Japanese fighter screen over the carriers was quickly destroyed. Japanese warships twisted and turned wildly to avoid the succession of strikes involving hundreds of American aircraft that lasted well into the afternoon. The light carrier *Chitose* sank mid-morning. The light carrier *Chiyoda* was crippled and abandoned to be sunk later by the gunfire of American cruisers. *Chitose* and *Chiyoda* were converted seaplane tenders. *Zuikaku*, the last survivor of the six fleet carriers that had raided Pearl Harbor, sank in the afternoon, as did the light carrier *Zuiho*, a veteran of the Aleutians phase of the Midway operation. In total, four carriers, a cruiser and two destroyers were sunk of Ozawa's decoy force, the remainder of which returned to Japan.

Halsey struggled to accept that he had fallen into a trap laid for him by the Japanese, though he later conceded that it might have been better if the more cautious Spruance had commanded at Leyte. Halsey would add to his reputation for recklessness when he sailed his task groups through major typhoons in December 1944 and July 1945. Kinkaid was not without blame either. Halsey wrote in his autobiography: 'I wondered how Kinkaid had let Ziggy Sprague get caught like this.'[44] Kinkaid made assumptions about Halsey's actions that suited his own convenience and made little effort to confirm those assumptions. Kinkaid chose not to guard the San Bernadino Strait so as to mass his forces to fight the Surigao Strait battle. That was a similar type of decision to Halsey's choice to mass his forces to chase Ozawa. Both admirals decided to deal with one particular threat and left Kurita for their colleague to repel. Nimitz and King did not think much of Halsey's decision-making. Nimitz wrote to King: 'It never occurred to me that Halsey, knowing the composition of the ships in the Sibuyan Sea, would leave San Bernadino Strait unguarded.'[45]

A flawed command structure for the Philippines invasion was the root cause of the confusion between Kinkaid and Halsey, but, despite that, the American fleets commanded by the two admirals had won a great victory.

The destruction of Ozawa's force was not the end of the Leyte Gulf battles. A new military phenomenon was about to get fully underway. Vice-Admiral Takijiro Onishi, commander of the First Air Fleet in the Philippines, had formed a new special attack corps. These were the kamikaze, the 'divine wind'. They were named after the great storms of 1274 and 1281 that had destroyed the fleets and armies of the Mongol emperor to save Japan from invasion. Kamikaze aircrew volunteered for one-way suicide missions to crash their aircraft into warships. The ancient warrior code of Bushido and its fanatical spirit of self-sacrifice was a source of inspiration for naval airmen. Kamikazes prepared for their impending doom in a ritual of prayers, farewells and the donning of the *hachimaki*, a white cloth tied around the forehead adorned with poetic calligraphy and the rising sun symbol. Onishi told the first of the kamikaze: 'You are already gods without earthly desires.'[46] It is worth bearing in mind that by this stage of the war Japanese aircraft loss rates had become so high that any mission carried a high chance of death.

On the morning of 25 October, in the immediate aftermath of the crisis caused by Kurita's foray towards Leyte Gulf, two escort carriers of Taffy 1 were deliberately struck by Japanese aircraft that crashed through the flight decks into the hanger bays, where the bombs carried by the aircraft exploded. The fires were brought under control and the ships survived. Later that morning Taffy 3, still licking its wounds from the surface action with Kurita's fleet, came under renewed attack when aircraft were spotted at 10.53 a.m. The escort carriers *Kitkun Bay* and *White Plains* were struck by kamikazes that inflicted minor damage. *St Lo* was not so lucky. A kamikaze broke up on her deck. The bomb carried by the aircraft penetrated beneath to explode and cause a huge ball of fire. A large part of the flight deck was blown off. Aircraft were hurled high into the air and *St Lo* sank with heavy loss of life. More carriers were damaged in the days ahead. American anti-aircraft gunners discovered that it was not enough to shoot down a kamikaze; they had to be blown out of the sky.

Fierce fighting on land in the Philippines would continue for the rest of the war, but the American victory at sea from 23–26 October 1944 had doomed the Japanese ashore to eventual defeat. Nearly 200,000 sailors had been carried by the 218 Allied and 64 Japanese warships involved in the series of engagements. 1,500 American and 10,500 Japanese lives were forfeited.[47] The Imperial Japanese Navy lost three battleships, four carriers, ten cruisers and nine destroyers. The United States Navy lost one light carrier, two escort carriers, two destroyers and one destroyer escort.[48] The Leyte Gulf battles proved to be the last battleship-versus-battleship confrontation in naval history. The Japanese plan had hinged on the ability of the big guns of battleships and heavy cruisers to win victory without the direct support of air power. This was a dramatic step backwards from the visionary manner in which carrier air power had been utilised in the Pearl Harbor raid.

After the Leyte Gulf battles the Imperial Japanese Navy was ruined as a serious fighting force, and would – with a few exceptions – spend the rest of the war sheltering from American air attack in Japanese home waters. Japanese Navy Minister, Admiral Yonai, later acknowledged: 'Our defeat at Leyte was tantamount to the loss of the Philippines. When you took the Philippines, that was the end of our resources.'[49] The raw materials of South-East Asia could no longer be shipped to Japan. Japanese merchant ships had been struggling to reach Japan anyway in the face of an increasingly effective American submarine force. The Leyte campaign went a long way towards giving the United States Navy possession of the Pacific Ocean, the world's greatest ocean. The Americans could now project their national power to the far western shores of the Pacific.

14
The Final Battle for Berlin

The strategic situation for Germany at the close of 1944, in the wake of the failed Ardennes offensive, was unequivocally desperate. An SS colonel was overheard to comment that before long a street car ride from one side of Berlin to the other side would be the distance from the eastern to the western front.[1] Still, the fragmented nature of the Nazi state helped Hitler to maintain his control over Germany, with the increasing assistance of the security services. There was no government cabinet or Nazi Party council in which dissidents could unite to topple the Führer. Only the army's General Staff remained a distinctly separate group in German society, and many key senior officers were devoted to the Nazi cause. Limited army involvement in the July 1944 bomb plot had cast suspicion on some officers, but these men had been swiftly eliminated. Field-Marshal Rommel had been compelled to take poison when faced by the accusation he had prior knowledge of the plot.[2]

Hitler was master of German strategy but he was a physical wreck from the strain of watching his plans and dreams unravel. He had no intention of ending the war unless he could negotiate from a position of strength. There would be no repeat of November 1918. So long as Hitler lived, the war effort of Nazi Germany would continue with the intention of outlasting the Allied coalition.

In London, Washington and Moscow there was an equal determination to fight on. Victory was in sight. The Allied powers had publicly made it clear that the only terms on offer were unconditional surrender. The Allies did not intend to repeat November 1918 either. Germany was to be thoroughly defeated and the unconditional surrender demand was important to maintaining unity between the Soviets and Anglo-Americans. It was intended to continue the war until final victory for the Allies was achieved on the battlefield.

General Guderian had been made OKH Chief of Staff in the aftermath of the bomb plot. On 9 January 1945 Guderian frankly told Hitler: 'The Eastern Front is like a house of cards. If the front is broken through at one point all the rest will collapse.'[3] The range of strategic problems confronting the German High Command was daunting. By the start of 1945 the Red Army had overrun much of south-east Europe and large parts of Poland. Finland had agreed to an armistice with Moscow. Anglo-American forces in western Europe were fighting their way forward to the Rhine.

The German Army had 260 divisions to meet its many commitments. Seventy-five divisions were on the eastern front between the Carpathians and the Baltic; seventy-six divisions were in the west; twenty-four divisions were in Italy; seventeen divisions were in Norway and Denmark; ten divisions were in Yugoslavia; twenty-eight divisions were in Hungary; thirty divisions were in the Baltic states.[4] Guderian wanted Army Group North withdrawn from Courland in western Latvia to create a new general reserve, but Hitler's OKW headquarters believed that force shielded the navy's U-boat training activities in the Baltic.[5]

Surprisingly, military manpower was not an overriding problem for the Third Reich. From a peak strength of nine and a half million in mid 1943, at the start of 1945 the German armed forces still comprised over nine million people, despite the massive losses of the previous twelve months. A remarkably thorough mobilisation of German manpower had helped the *Wehrmacht* to fight on through the winter of 1944–45.[6] The millions of foreign workers forced into the German economy was an important reason for the high proportion of German males available for service in the armed forces. The efforts of German industry, despite the loss of so much occupied territory, were also formidable during the months of winter. Despite enormous losses in 1944, the stockpile of army weaponry was about the same at the start of 1945 as at the start of 1944. Industrial production was maintained by eating into stockpiled components and raw materials, though deliveries of these were no longer arriving at factories in large quantities.

The next task for the Red Army was the launching of a huge new offensive in Poland. In 1813 Russian armies had entered central Europe to help overthrow Napoleon, and the Russians were again poised to enter central Europe in a bid to end the reign of another hegemonic tyrant. The long Soviet delay on the Vistula until the winter of 1944–45 had been necessary to build up supplies. The Soviet military's lines of communication operated slowly compared to the armies of the Anglo-Americans. The mid-December to mid-January Ardennes offensive in the west consumed a large part of the *Wehrmacht*'s strategic panzer reserves. This would greatly benefit the Red Army in the early months of 1945.

The Soviet offensive in Poland began on 12 January with attacks by Konev's First Ukrainian Front. Other Soviet army groups joined the offensive in the following days and Zhukov's First Belorussian Front made swift progress westwards. The de-populated ruins of Warsaw were quickly cleared. Krakow fell on 19 January. The Soviet vanguard raced ahead to reach the River Oder, within striking distance of Berlin. East Prussian military officers were appalled when Soviet troops reached German soil to threaten their home districts. The Tannenberg Memorial for the great victory of 1914 was blown up by German troops and the remains of Field-Marshal von Hindenburg removed to safety.

Many German prisoners were taken as the front crumbled. A large pocket of German troops at Poznan was surrounded and by-passed. As the crisis unfolded, common sense should have dictated that German reinforcements be deployed on the Warsaw-Berlin axis. The Soviet advance from the Vistula was the greatest immediate threat to the Third Reich. Yet in mid-January the Sixth SS Panzer Army was withdrawn from the western front and sent by Hitler's orders to Hungary rather than Poland.[7]

Long columns of German refugees tramped westwards away from the Red Army. The German population and many Poles falling into Soviet hands were subjected to rape and murder by troops determined on revenge and brutalised by combat. On 27 January Soviet troops entered the Auschwitz-Birkenau complex in southern Poland, where so many Jewish people had died in gas chambers. There were few emaciated survivors compared to the numbers who had entered the camps. The sites of death camps such as Treblinka, Maidanek and Belzek had already been overrun in eastern Poland.

At the end of January shattered formations of the German Ninth Army and Fourth Panzer Army hastily and wearily regrouped behind the snow-covered banks of the Oder. German units lacked equipment and included many older men and boys. Zhukov ordered his subordinates to establish bridgeheads across the river. 'If we succeed in capturing the west bank of the Oder the operation to take Berlin will be fully guaranteed.'[8] The Oder was 300 yards wide and covered by thin ice. On 31 January Soviet troops crossed the ice north of Kustrin fortress, which was at the junction of the Oder and Warta rivers. The citadel of the fortress was on an island in the river.

Ferocious German resistance behind the Oder exacted a heavy toll on the Soviets, and the Red Army's offensive finally stalled. The late winter thaw had flooded roads in Poland upon which the Red Army depended for transport. The *Wehrmacht* had lined the Oder with flak guns, an ideal tank killer. 300 heavy anti-aircraft batteries had been redeployed to the eastern front specifically for artillery and anti-tank duties.[9] In the final months of the war, 88mm flak guns often bolstered the army's anti-tank defences. The initiative of local commanders sucked many flak guns into a ground role on top of the redeployments ordered by the High Command.

To the disgust of Guderian, Hitler made Reichfuehrer Heinrich Himmler the commander of the newly formed Army Group Vistula, which was the force responsible for holding the line of the Oder. This army group was the northernmost of the three German army groups endeavouring to stem the tide on the eastern front. Himmler, the SS's chieftain, was no stranger to the supervision of organised violence, but he had little experience of warfare against an armed opponent who might strike back. Himmler wrote to Guderian: 'In the present state of war the thawing water [in Poland] is for us a gift of fate. God has not forgotten the courageous German people.'[10] This respite could only be temporary.

The Soviet advance to the Oder had bypassed strong German forces posted along the Baltic coast of East Prussia. The German front against the Baltic stretched eastwards to Danzig and Konigsberg. The *Wehrmacht's* well-deserved reputation for counter-attack discouraged the Red Army from attacking across the Oder without first clearing its flanks. A series of Soviet operations got underway to conquer the remainder of East Prussia.

To the south of the Soviet wedge at the Oder facing Berlin, the Red Army had pushed into Silesia to reach the southern arm of the Oder and city of Breslau, which had been encircled by 15 February. The industrial region of German Upper Silesia was overrun. Speer sent Hitler a memorandum pointing out that the loss of Upper Silesia would do irreversible damage to armaments production. Further to the south, strong German forces continued to contest the Red Army's progress in Hungary and Austria.

The leaders of the principal Allied governments – Roosevelt, Churchill and Stalin – met at Yalta from 4–11 February 1945 to discuss the last phase of the war in Europe. Yalta was in the Crimea; Stalin had a strong preference for meetings to be held within his own territories. It had already been tentatively decided to divide Germany into separate and roughly equal zones of occupation, one each for the Americans, British and Soviets. Berlin would be 100 miles within the planned Soviet occupation zone, though the city would then be sub-divided into local zones for each Allied power. Churchill pressed for the French to be given a separate occupation zone to assist the Allies' hold-down Germany. He had no great love for the French but was worried what would happen if the Americans withdrew from Europe, as they had done after the First World War. The future frontiers of Poland and eastern Germany were also discussed. The decisions confirmed at Yalta had a definite impact on Allied military decision-making in the final period of the war. The Anglo-American leaders were relieved to reach an agreement with Stalin that seemed to keep the Red Army out of much of central Europe. Moscow, however, had secret ambitions for eastern Europe.[11]

On 28 March Supreme Commander Eisenhower sent a telegram to the United States military mission in Moscow to be forwarded to Stalin. Eisenhower asked for an indication of Stalin's intentions and revealed that his own main line of advance would likely be to the south of Berlin towards Dresden.[12] The occupation zones were to apply postwar. There was no agreed line at which Anglo-American and Soviet forces should meet whilst hostilities were still underway. The situation was too fluid to predict ahead of time exactly where that line might be placed. Eisenhower was keen to avoid any sort of accidental fighting with the Soviets. 'It didn't seem to be good sense to try, both of us, to throw our forces toward Berlin and get mixed up – two armies that couldn't talk the same language, couldn't even communicate with each other. It would have been a terrible mess.'[13] Stalin certainly did not want the Anglo-Americans to reach Berlin first, and the Red Army at the Oder was already on the city's doorstep. Propaganda was immensely important for a totalitarian state. The glory of capturing the capital of the Third Reich had the potential to resound to Stalin's benefit among his suffering peoples for years to come.

Churchill, however, felt that Eisenhower had gone beyond the limits of his authority. Whether or not to take Berlin was a political decision. Berlin in Allied hands might prove a useful bargaining chip once the war was concluded. If the Soviets liberated both Berlin and Vienna, Churchill was worried that they might gain too much credit for the Allied victory, which could have unforeseen consequences in the postwar world. Churchill was willing to support a western drive to take Berlin.

> Why should we not cross the Elbe and advance as far eastward as possible? This has an important political bearing as the Russian armies of the South seem certain to enter Vienna and overrun Austria. If we deliberately leave Berlin to them, even if it should be in our grasp, the double event may strengthen their conviction already apparent, that they have done everything ... I do not consider myself that Berlin has yet lost its military and certainly not its political significance. The fall of Berlin would have a powerful psychological effect on German resistance in every part of the Reich.[14]

Britain's bargaining power with the Americans, though, had dwindled by the spring of 1945. What the Americans wanted would generally prevail now that the bulk of troops in western Europe were from the United States.

After German forces had been cleared from the heavily defended western bank of the Rhine, Eisenhower's army was ready for its own major offensive into central Germany. By late March both Montgomery's and Bradley's army groups had crossed the mighty river and were advancing rapidly eastwards. Field-Marshal Model and 325,000 German troops were encircled by American forces in the Ruhr. In western Germany there was a degree of relief among the civilian population that they were not passing under Soviet occupation. On 31 March Eisenhower told Montgomery, 'that place [Berlin] has become, so far as I am concerned, nothing but a geographical location, and I have never been interested in these. My purpose is to destroy the enemy's force and his powers to resist.'[15] When General Bradley was asked his opinion, he speculated that it would cost 100,000 additional American casualties to capture Berlin. That was 'a pretty stiff price for a prestige objective, especially when we've got to fall back and let the other fellows take over'.[16] At this time, United States commanders had become concerned that German forces were readying themselves for a last ditch defence in the mountains of southern Bavaria. If this was the case that would be a specifically American problem as Bavaria was to be in the future American occupation zone. It made sense for American forces to overrun and clear of guerrilla activity those parts of Germany destined to be under western administration. According to Bradley, 'The national Redoubt [in southern Bavaria] existed largely in the imaginations of a few fanatical Nazis. It grew into so exaggerated a scheme that I am astonished we could have believed it as innocently as we did. But while it persisted this legend ... shaped our tactical thinking.'[17] Eisenhower's plan, as his army's vanguard thrust eastwards, was to push American forces deep into southern Germany, whilst the British made for Denmark. If the Soviets could be kept from entering Denmark that would simplify postwar negotiations and secure the British occupation zone in north-west Germany.

On 7 April Eisenhower informed the Combined Chiefs of Staff that once the River Elbe had been reached, he intended to order his forces to clear the flanks of that line to the north and south.

> I regard it as militarily unsound at this stage of the proceedings to make Berlin a major objective, particularly in view of the fact that it is only thirty-five miles from the Russian lines ... I am the first to admit that a war is waged in pursuance of political aims, and if the Combined Chiefs of Staff should decide that the Allied effort to take Berlin outweighs purely military considerations in the theater, I would cheerfully readjust my plans and my thinking so as to carry out such an operation.[18]

The Combined Chiefs of Staff were content to back Eisenhower's judgement.

As Eisenhower intended, American forces were ordered to halt at the Elbe on 14 April. The United States Ninth Army had reached the Elbe to the south of Magdeburg, sixty-five miles from Berlin. The British successfully reached the Baltic coast of Germany near the Danish frontier before the arrival of the Soviets, and German troops in the Ruhr pocket surrendered on 18 April. The Ninth Army's General W.H. Simpson had asked permission to keep moving beyond the Elbe but Eisenhower had refused to give that authorisation. After a 200 mile advance in two weeks American forces were undoubtedly stretched. A corps commander of the Ninth Army later speculated that his formation could have pushed patrols to the fringe of Berlin's western suburbs. On 21 April Eisenhower told the Soviets via the Allied military missions in Moscow that he would be halting his forces on the line of the Elbe-Mulde. The Anglo-American armies would then clear German forces from territory behind the line of those rivers.

By April a coherent German front had no longer existed to face the advancing Anglo-Americans, but there were many local engagements that often commenced with an Allied column driving into an ambush. Almost as many American soldiers died in Europe in April 1945 as in June 1944.[19] The ideological commitment of some youthful soldiers of the Third Reich was immense. The last six weeks of the war for American, British and Canadian infantrymen and tank crews was a strange mixture of rounding up relieved prisoners and sharp, bloody fights against small groups of recalcitrant and fanatical foes.

Hitler had returned to Berlin in the aftermath of the failed Ardennes offensive. Given the risk of assassination, he did not trust the military sufficiently to reside in an army headquarters. Instead he chose to spend his time in a bunker complex beneath central Berlin's ministerial district. The Führer bunker beneath the cratered garden of the bomb-damaged Reich Chancellery comprised eighteen rooms clustered along a central corridor. The walls were bare concrete, but a portrait of the Prussian monarch Frederick the Great adorned the wall of Hitler's living room. An iron spiral staircase led down from a basement above. A diesel generator supplied electricity and powered the water pump. This subterranean world was reminiscent of a First World War soldier's life in the trenches. Those residing in the bunker saw little daylight and Hitler did not emerge very often. He dealt with disappointment by leading an increasingly isolated existence. His misanthropic estrangement from the rest of the human race matched the gloomy, tomb-like setting of the bunker. SS guards and a thick concrete roof were the guarantee of the Führer's personal safety from local assassins and Allied bombers.[20]

Hitler placed his waning hopes on the divergent natures of the Allied powers. Surely the common front between the ultra-capitalist west and ultra-Marxist Soviets would fall apart under the weight of the Grand Alliance's internal contradictions? On 6 February Hitler had told Martin Bormann, his private secretary, 'There is no such thing as a desperate situation! Think how many examples of a turn of fortune the history of the German people affords. During the Seven Years War, Frederick found himself reduced to desperate straits, then behold – the Czarina died unexpectedly and the whole situation was miraculously reversed.'[21] Hitler undoubtedly drew inspiration from the life and trials of the Prussian soldier-king Frederick the Great (1740–80). In 1762 Prussia had been facing defeat at the hands of a coalition of France, Austria and Russia, but the death of the Czarina had caused the coalition to fall apart, the so-called 'miracle of the House of Brandenburg'. The rise of eighteenth-century Prussia had hinged upon wars of survival and expansion in the face of great odds. Frederick had grimly triumphed in a long series of bloody campaigns. Guderian believed that Hitler admired Frederick more than any other historical or living person. On the other hand, Churchill was demonised by Hitler as an 'alcoholic demagogue' and Roosevelt suffered from 'syphilitic paralysis'.

Heavy American daylight air raids pounded Berlin regularly from February to April. At night the RAF's Bomber Command struck other east German cities, including Dresden. Hitler was last filmed in the Chancellery gardens on

17 March receiving and decorating members of the Hitler Youth. Hitler was pale, seemingly shrunken and had a noticeable tremor on his left side. The following day an especially large daylight raid on Berlin took place. 1,250 heavy bombers and a large P-51 Mustang fighter escort filled the skies. Twenty-four American bombers and five fighters were downed by *Luftwaffe* jet-fighters and Berlin's flak defences. The Messerschmitt Me 262 jet fighter had a maximum speed of 540 mph and was an impressive technical breakthrough, but there were too few available to be more than a nuisance to the Allied aerial armada. Nonetheless, the development of the Me 262 jet-fighters is a reminder that Nazi Germany was capable of dramatic technical achievement even in the last phase of the war.

OKW's conduct of grand strategy collapsed as Hitler lost his grip on reality and was reduced to rambling about new super weapons. On 20 March Guderian managed to have Himmler replaced as commander of Army Group Vistula, but Guderian was himself sent on sick leave by Hitler on 28 March. Relations between the two men had been faltering for months as the Führer became less and less rational in his approach to strategy.

Speer remained closely involved in the Nazi government as armaments minister. He advised that the final collapse of the German economy was only four to eight weeks away. Speer was uneasy that a scorched earth policy that destroyed everything ahead of the advancing Allies would endanger the German people in the postwar period. Hitler remarked dismissively: 'If the war is lost, the nation will also perish ... Besides, those who remain after the battle are only the inferior ones, for good ones will have been killed.'[22]

Hitler and his entourage remained enveloped in a world of fantasy and flickering electric light as the days of spring lengthened. Berlin had been declared a fortress. Hitler continued to believe that the leaders of Germany had surrendered too soon in 1918. But the ideology of National Socialism did not leave room for negotiation. Victory or death were the only alternatives. Hitler's fifty-sixth birthday was in the offing and he had never expected to live a long life. He saw a strong political dimension to war and it was his personal task to give the regime its willpower. However bad the military situation, a change in the political position might bring about unexpected military success.

The Soviets spent most of March consolidating their position against the Oder. Kustrin was assaulted on 28 March by Chuikov's 8th Guards Army after a heavy bombardment by aircraft and artillery. The reduction of Kustrin was needed to clear the way for the final offensive on Berlin. Meanwhile, to the north, the Second and Third Belorussian Fronts pushed through East Prussia towards the Baltic coast. Konigsberg was isolated and heavy fighting around that fortress continued into April. Konigsberg surrendered on 10 April though German troops in the swamps at the mouth of the Vistula fought on.

The Red Army that was poised to drive on Berlin in April 1945 was a formidable force, despite the losses of the past few years. Over six million men and women were organised into an army that included 529 rifle divisions, twenty-seven tank corps and almost 400 independent tank brigades and regiments.[23] A mass call up had taken place in reoccupied Soviet territories. Three million recruits had been absorbed by the Soviet armed forces in the year of 1944. Despite that steady influx of manpower, the Red Army was exhibiting severe signs of war weariness. The authorised strength of a Soviet rifle division had fallen from 10,500 in July 1942 to an average of 4,000 by early 1945. The numbers of artillery and tank formations supporting the infantry had risen considerably, yet tactical problems were created when an offensive battle had to be fought with weak infantry divisions. It was up to the humble infantryman to occupy and hold captured ground.

On the eve of the final push on Berlin, Zhukov and Konev were ordered to report to Moscow. The two commanders arrived on 1 April and met Stalin and his staff at the Kremlin. Stalin was determined to capture the German capital and had little intention of keeping the western powers abreast of his plans. Zhukov's First Belorussian Front and Konev's First Ukrainian Front were to bear the brunt of the upcoming offensive. Further north, close to the Baltic coast, Rokossovsky's Second Belorussian Front was to fulfil a supporting role. The three Soviet army groups comprised 2,500,000 soldiers, 41,000 guns and mortars, 6,200 tanks and assault guns and 7,500 aircraft.[24] Zhukov's front would attack from the Oder valley directly towards Berlin. To the south, Konev's front was to initially drive at Leipzig and Dresden and then turn north westwards towards Berlin. Planning for the offensive did not lay down inter-front boundaries for Zhukov's or Konev's troops on the approaches to Berlin. Stalin is alleged to have told his commanders, 'whoever breaks in first, let him take Berlin'. Fuel and ammunition had been laboriously hauled forward from the Vistula to the Oder in preparation for the final offensive.

German civilian refugees from East Prussia and the Baltic 'balcony' fled westwards by land so long as the roads remained open. Shipping successfully evacuated many civilians from Baltic ports over a period of weeks. As many as two million civilians and soldiers were evacuated by sea. The crowded evacuation ships that were sunk number among the greatest maritime tragedies in recorded history. The sinking of the transport *Goya* on the night of 15/16 April cost over 6,000 lives.[25] *Goya* was torpedoed by a Russian submarine and rapidly sank in icy water after breaking in two.

In the bunker the steady arrival of bad news was punctuated by the announcement of Roosevelt's death. This sparked a brief spurt of optimism. Goebbels saw propaganda possibilities in the death of a United States president. Disastrous news, though, soon followed. On 13 April Hitler was informed that Vienna had fallen to the Red Army. The German front had crumbled in south-east Europe, and the loss of the historic capital of the Habsburgs put that in a clear perspective. On 15 April Hitler ordered that if the Reich was split into two by Allied incursions, Doenitz was to command the northern zone and Field-Marshal Kesselring the southern zone. Hitler told a senior general about this time: 'If the German people lose the war, it will have shown itself as not worthy of me.'[26] Wagner's *Gotterdammerung* was played on the gramophone in the bunker.

The Berlin that awaited the final phase of the war in Europe was in a sorry state compared to the great metropolis that had hosted the 1936 summer Olympics. Refugees poured through the city with stories of rape, murder and looting by Soviet troops. In July 1943 Berlin had 3,665,000 registered inhabitants. In January 1945 that figure had declined to 2,846,000 and had fallen by another half a million by April.[27] There were nominally three defence lines around Berlin. The outer line was beyond the suburbs; the second line ran mainly around the S-Bahn railway lines encircling the inner city; and a final defensive zone lay between the River Spree and Landwehr Canal. Within Berlin, canals and the cuttings and embankments of railways were defensible barriers. The *Volkssturm* – a people's militia – had been mobilised and the population was bombarded by propaganda warning of the barbarism of the approaching Russians. Trapped amid entire suburbs of damaged housing, civilians had acquired a fatalistic attitude, not unlike passengers on a sinking ocean liner. People struggled with the routine of life amid the mounting rubble as food, gas and electricity supplies dwindled. Special passes were needed to leave the city. SS and other security detachments enthusiastically hanged deserters and stragglers from street posts, with sign boards around their necks warning others they would share that fate if they did not do their duty to the end.

Hitler's last order of the day for the eastern front on 15 April spoke of destroying the Red Army before Berlin in a bath of blood.

> For the last time, the Jewish-Bolshevik mortal enemy has set out with its masses on the attack. He is attempting to demolish Germany and to exterminate our people. You soldiers from the East know yourselves in large measure what fate threatens above all German women, girls, and children. While old men and children are murdered, women and girls are denigrated to barrack-whores. The rest are marched off to Siberia.[28]

Hitler – suffering as he was from ill-health, stress and drug addiction – could offer the defenders of Berlin little more than rhetoric. Large German forces were out of reach in Norway, Latvia and Italy, vainly endeavouring to hold onto the last shreds of Nazi Germany's empire. Hitler and his commanders were not shoring up the eastern front at the expense of the western front. At a critical moment, when reserves were desperately needed to cover eastern Berlin, the newly formed Twelfth Army of General Wenck had been dispatched to try to relieve the Ruhr pocket in the west. The attempt had been a dismal failure and the Twelfth Army was bundled back to the line of the Elbe.

General Gotthard Heinrici's Army Group Vistula held the eastern front from the Baltic to the junction of the Neisse and Oder rivers, which lay to the south east of Berlin. At the northern end of the line, General Hasso von Manteuffel's Third Panzer Army opposed the Second Belorussian Front. General Theodor Busse's Ninth Army faced Zhukov's First Belorussian Front, thereby directly blocking the road to Berlin from Kustrin. Further south, the left-flank army of Army Group Centre – the Fourth Panzer Army – opposed Konov's First Ukrainian Front. These three German armies comprised thirty-nine divisions. Army Group Vistula's reserve was General Helmuth Weidling's LVI Panzer Corps.[29] German units had filled up their depleted ranks with sixteen and seventeen year-olds and elderly men. Ad hoc units based around training schools and headquarters had been formed, as had many new Volkssturm battalions. Police units and Hitler Youth detachments had also been mobilised to support the army. Nonetheless, Army Group Vistula was short of artillery, aircraft and reserves. To oppose the three Soviet fronts (army groups) directly involved in the Berlin operation, it is difficult to say exactly how many German troops were present. By one estimate, one million German troops were backed by 1,500 tanks and over 9,000 guns.[30] Inexplicably, Hitler believed that the next Soviet offensive would be launched against Czechoslovakia. Early in April three panzergrenadier divisions had been removed from Army Group Vistula to reinforce that region.

For Zhukov's front, the offensive was to begin before dawn on 16 April. He had decided to attack under the cover of darkness. Two days before the offensive was due to begin, a series of battalion-strength reconnaissance probes had been sent out by Zhukov's and Konev's forces. These probes indicated to the Germans the likelihood of imminent attack, but also revealed to the Soviets the German intention to step back from the Oder to a secondary defensive line to avoid the worst of the Soviet preliminary bombardment.

Zhukov had a large bridgehead west of the Oder at Kustrin. Soviet forces either side of the bridgehead would have to make an assault crossing of the river. The ground on the west bank of the Oder was low-lying and marshy. Flooded ditches, ploughland and streams made the going difficult in many places, especially for mechanised transport and armoured vehicles. There were few roads leading westwards from the Oder. The Seelow Heights, rising to 200 feet, were the main geographic barrier standing between the Soviets and Berlin. From that long escarpment, German defenders had a good view down into the Oder valley.

Zhukov's plan was for a short, half-hour bombardment, after which 140 search lights positioned at 200-yard intervals were to be switched on in the pre-dawn darkness to blind the Germans in their forward posts. The search lights were crewed by female soldiers. Chuikov's 8th Guards Army was to play a spearhead role, and the Kustrin bridgehead had been crammed with Soviet troops. Chuikov's command post was on a sandy hill on the banks of the Oder. Zhukov and his staff arrived at the post before dawn to observe the opening phase of the operation.

The attack began at 3 a.m. with a massive bombardment by artillery and *katyusha* rocket launchers sited wheel to wheel. The search lights, however, merely silhouetted Soviet assault troops against the smoke and dust of battle. The German front line was found to be mostly deserted. Daylight gave German artillerymen the visibility needed accurately to shell their enemies crowded into the valley before them. It took three hours' fighting for the Soviets to reach the second German line at the foot of the heights. Rising ground, steep in places, and ditches in front of the heights covered by 88mm anti-tank guns, brought the advance to a halt. The defenders of the Seelow Heights included the 9th Parachute Division, the 20th Panzergrenadier Division and the Muencheberg Panzer Division. German resistance was fierce and one German prisoner pointed out to his captors that he and his comrades would have been shot if they had retreated without order. Shoulder-fired *panzerfaust* missiles proved effective against Soviet armoured vehicles.

Around midday an impatient Zhukov decided to introduce his tank armies to the offensive. The 1st and 2nd Guards Tank Armies comprised over 1,350 tanks and self-propelled guns. The few roads and passable tracks leading beyond the Oder to Seelow were soon jammed with mechanised vehicles. During the coming night Soviet armour and artillery regrouped and aircraft bombed the exhausted German defenders. At 8 a.m. on 17 April a fresh bombardment began amid light rain and low cloud. Soviet tanks moved out with infantry following behind. German machine gun, 88mm and panzerfaust fire tore holes in the Soviet ranks. Seelow town was only captured after another bloody day's fighting and part of the heights remained in German hands. The Seelow defence line was finally breached the following day. Zhukov's tank formations reached open country beyond Seelow. A short stretch of forest and hamlets lay ahead leading to the eastern suburbs of Berlin. The capture of the heights had cost Zhukov's army group tens of thousands of casualties.[31] The German defenders had fought well but could not hold out indefinitely in the face of massive Soviet firepower. There was no German strategic reserve covering the capital.

Whilst Zhukov's troops had attacked directly towards Berlin, to the south east of the Third Reich's capital Konev's First Ukrainian Front had conducted an assault crossing of the River Neisse. The attack was launched on a narrow front and had made better early progress than Zhukov's assault. A dense smoke screen had been laid by Konev's artillery and aircraft to cover the crossing. By the end of the day ferries, pontoons and fixed bridges had been put in place to rush troops and equipment across the Neisse.

On 17 April the 3rd and 4th Guards Tank Armies had crossed the river into the bridgehead. Advancing Soviet troops bypassed pockets of resistance and had little trouble repelling local counter-attacks. The ground ahead of Konev's forces was less waterlogged than the approaches to the Seelow Heights. Mechanised units were able to make rapid progress, though frequent forests and lakes gave desperate defenders places around which to regroup. On the evening of 17 April Stalin spoke to Konev by radio and instructed him to turn his tank formations north west towards Berlin. Konev, not surprisingly, turned down the suggestion that Zhukov's armour might share the use of his bridgehead. Stalin made sure that Zhukov knew that Konev's tanks were bound for Berlin.

On the Baltic flank, Rokossovsky's Second Belorussian Front joined the offensive on 18 April. The lower Oder was divided into two branches, with two miles of flooded marshland in between the branches. This made the Oder a formidable obstacle and it took two days for the Soviets to get across both branches of the river. Mantauffel's Third Panzer Army was pinned in position by the Soviet attacks and could offer no help to Berlin to the south.

Large parts of the German Ninth Army had been bypassed on both flanks once Zhukov's and Konev's thrusts had broken their front open. Soviet troops threatened to sever the Ninth Army's lines of communication, but Hitler ordered German units against the Oder to remain in position. As Soviet troops closed on Berlin, the first Red Army artillery shells were fired into the eastern suburbs from long range. The 128mm flak guns mounted on Berlin's flak towers returned fire.

20 April was Hitler's birthday. Around midday a two hour bombing raid on Berlin took place. In sunshine the Allied bombers flew in tight formations to pattern bomb the city yet again. The water mains received further damage. On the afternoon of his birthday Hitler left the bunker for the garden above to meet some Hitler Youth and SS troops who had distinguished themselves in battle.

That afternoon of 20 April the Third Reich's principal leaders gathered for the last time, at least until their trial after the war at Nuremberg. Goering, Doenitz, Keitel, Ribbentrop, Speer, Jodl and Himmler were all present. There was little to discuss as Nazi Germany had no obvious future. Goering left the beleaguered city that night and most of the other senior Nazis wasted no time in doing likewise. Hitler had already determined on suicide as a way out of his personal dilemma. This knowledge had probably informed his strategic decision-making for an unknowable length of time beforehand. According to Speer, Hitler 'was shrivelling up like an old man. His limbs trembled; he walked stooped, with dragging footsteps. Even his voice became quavering and lost its old masterfulness.'[32]

Apart from those *Wehrmacht* formations falling back into Berlin from the Oder, the capital's garrison comprised the 1st Flak Division, some naval and SS troops, the civil police, thirty Volkssturm battalions, headquarters detachments and Berlin's Hitler Youth. The security services continued to hunt down and hang or shoot stragglers and deserters. The military command of Berlin's garrison passed through several pairs of hands until on 24 April Hitler appointed General Weidling, the commander of LVI Panzer Corps. Weidling's corps had lost touch with its parent Ninth Army, but had successfully withdrawn many troops into the capital's suburbs. Weidling's corps comprised the battered units of several panzer and panzergrenadier divisions. The SS Nordland formation included French and Scandinavian Nazis. It is likely that fewer than 100,000 German troops were defending Berlin, possibly only 60,000, even after all miscellaneous military detachments are counted. The garrison was supported by only fifty to sixty tanks.[33]

On the afternoon of 22 April, after a conference in the bunker, Hitler told Keitel, his faithful OKW chief, that he had no intention of accepting advice that he should leave for a new headquarters in southern Germany. 'I already have taken a decision: I will never leave Berlin again; I will defend the city with my dying breath.'[34] Hitler believed that his continued presence in the capital would calm civilian opinion and provide inspiration for the fighting men. OKW ordered Wenck's Twelfth Army, which was facing to the west at the Elbe, to retire eastwards to Potsdam. Mantauffel's army on the Baltic flank was instructed to attack southwards towards Berlin. Keitel visited Wenck's headquarters early on 23 April to see how matters were progressing.

It soon became clear, however, that no German force outside Berlin could hope to reinforce the city and Hitler was reduced to a renewed bout of fury. He ranted of the Russians suffering the 'bloodiest defeat in their history before the gates of the city of Berlin'. Hitler told Speer on 23 April:

> I shall not fight personally. There is always the danger that I would only be wounded and fall into the hands of the Russians alive. I don't want my enemies to disgrace my body either. I've given orders that I be cremated. Fraulein Braun wants to depart this life with me, and I'll shoot Blondi [Hitler's Alsatian dog] beforehand. Believe me, Speer, it is easy for me to end my life. A brief moment and I'm freed of everything, liberated from this painful existence.

In the early hours of the following morning Speer departed the bunker for the last time after a weak handshake from Hitler.[35]

The troops of Zhukov and Konev fought a ferocious battle for their enemy's capital. Chuikov's army and the 1st Tank Army faced determined German resistance on the eastern side of Berlin. Street fighting took a steady toll of men and tanks. German defenders fired from top floor windows and strong points leading down to fortified basements. Chuikov's men were considered to be especially expert at urban warfare. Some soldiers wore Medals For the Defence of Stalingrad. A great many of the recipients of that medal, though, fell in battle long before Berlin was reached.

Konev's mechanised formations had advanced to Berlin from a south-easterly direction, leaving behind infantry to deal with bypassed pockets of resistance. By midday of 24 April Zhukov's and Konev's troops had joined hands to the south east of Berlin to cut off those formations of the German Ninth Army still falling back from the Oder. Meanwhile Zhukov's right wing crossed the Havel to the north west of Berlin and turned south towards Potsdam. On 25 April Soviet forces encircled Berlin to the west. Also that day, Soviet and United States patrols joined hands at Torgau near the Elbe to the south west of Berlin.

The attempt by Wenck's Twelfth Army to pull back from the Elbe towards Berlin took the Soviets by surprise at the outset, but the German thrust ran out of steam near the Potsdam lakes. The Ninth Army, joined by other troops and long refugee columns, made an effort to fight a passage westwards towards the Americans. Some of these troops and civilians managed to reach Wenck's force but the Ninth Army was mostly destroyed. North of Berlin, Mantauffel's front near the Baltic was crumbling and he had no reserves to send south to Berlin. Command arrangements were plunged into further confusion when Heinrici was dismissed from the command of Army Group Vistula on the night of 28/29 April. He was replaced by a general located in Holland, which meant that a third general had to take over in the interim.

Konev's troops made steady progress through the southern suburbs of Berlin. Soviet artillery shelled barricades and road blocks at close range to help infantry capture the city block by block. Konev later acknowledged that his army group lost 800 tanks destroyed or badly damaged in the final Berlin operation, many within the city's suburbs.[36] Columns of tanks were vulnerable if the lead vehicle was knocked out to trap the tanks behind and expose them to concentrated fire. Zhukov's army group had pushed five armies into Berlin in an arc from the eastern suburbs of the city stretching to the north-western suburbs. By 28 April Soviet troops had captured the district of Old Moabit on the Tiergarten's northern edge. Fighting was underway in the subway system. Chuikov's men reached within 1,000 yards of the Chancellery as other Soviet troops closed in from the north.

Reports reached the Führer bunker that Red Army tanks were nearby. The telegraph wires connecting the bunker to the outside world still allowed interrupted communication. With the end obviously not far off, Hitler signed his last will and testament at 4 a.m. on 29 April. Earlier that night Hitler and Eva Braun had married. Now that Hitler had decided to die he was willing to grant her marriage. According to Hitler's dictated political testament, Doenitz was to become the next Reich President and Goebbels was to be the Chancellor. Goebbels and his family had taken up residence in the bunker. He seems to have wanted his own place in the pantheon of Teutonic heroes, and had dreams of a future in which the last days of National Socialism would acquire a mythical status.[37] On the afternoon of 29 April a prussic acid capsule was tested on Hitler's dog.

On the morning of 30 April it was clear that Soviet troops would soon overrun the Chancellery. Hitler ordered that his body be burnt after his death. He did not want his corpse displayed in a waxworks in Moscow.[38] In the bunker Hitler shot himself in the temple in the afternoon and Eva Braun took prussic acid. The bodies of the couple were taken from the bunker to the garden above, doused with petrol and set alight.

The *Reichstag*, a tall, burnt-out, domed building, and not the Chancellery, had been picked out by the Soviets as an objective of great propagandistic value. Fighting around the *Reichstag* and the nearby Brandenburg Gate had begun on 29 April. Late on the following morning a red banner was raised over the ruined building. On the evening of 30 April a German officer was sent with a white flag to seek permission for General Hans Krebs, the army's Chief of the General Staff, to cross Zhukov's lines for ceasefire discussions. Prior to 4 a.m. on 1 May Krebs, accompanied by a senior staff officer and an interpreter, crossed the lines and travelled onwards to Chuikov's headquarters. Krebs had been military attaché in Moscow and spoke some Russian. He had been authorised by Bormann and Goebbels to seek a truce and reported to the Soviets that Hitler was dead. Chuikov telephoned Zhukov's headquarters and in turn Moscow was given the welcome news. After midday Krebs returned with the message that an unconditional surrender was the only acceptable outcome. There was to be no quibbling about ceasefires or truces. In the interim, the Red Army's attacks on the central government district continued.

The Third Reich's Berlin leadership finally disintegrated. Bormann went missing whilst trying to escape, Goebbels committed suicide in the coming night and Krebs also shot himself. Tragically, the Goebbels family's six young children aged from four to twelve were also murdered under the supervision of their parents. The already drugged children were fed prussic acid capsules before their parents took the same poisonous medicine.

The German surrender in Berlin came at 6 a.m. on 2 May when General Weidling called the hopeless battle off after another anxious night. Fighting had ended by the afternoon. One of the last recorded engagements involved a group of Germans holding out in an air-raid shelter in the Tiergarten. The noise of gunfire died away and the smoke hanging over the city began to clear.

From his headquarters in northern Germany, Doenitz broadcast news of Hitler's death but delayed surrendering the Third Reich's government and *Wehrmacht* to help German troops and civilians flee westwards to evade the Soviets. Army Group Vistula and the Twelfth Army joined the columns moving westwards towards the Elbe. In Berlin, Hitler's burnt and charred corpse was recovered by the Soviets and disposed of after adequate identification.

A formal surrender of all German forces was signed at Eisenhower's headquarters at Rheims on 7 May. The surrender was to come into force by the close of the 8th. Jodl signed the surrender on the authority of Doenitz. The western Allies overran at least a third of the future Soviet zone of occupation before the fighting had finished, despite efforts not to push too far eastwards. Another surrender was signed by Field-Marshal Keitel at Zhukov's headquarters outside Berlin just after midnight on 9 May.

At the time of the Third Reich's final surrender large pockets of German forces remained in Norway, Denmark, northern Holland, Czechoslovakia and Austria. In Norway the British would take the surrender of 365,000 German servicemen.[39] Fighting in Czechoslovakia lasted until 11 May. Of ten million German prisoners taken during the war, less than a third fell into Soviet hands. *Wehrmacht* personnel interned by the Soviets faced a grim period of captivity from which many would not return.

After the fall of Stalingrad a Soviet colonel had pointed to a pile of rubble and shouted at some nearby German prisoners: 'That's how Berlin is going to look!'[40] It had been a long way from the banks of the Volga to Berlin, but the end to the war in Europe in the ruins of Berlin was the only way the era of National Socialism could be brought to an end. The Soviet offensive for Berlin had cost the Red Army 80,000 killed and missing and 280,000 wounded. The German capitulation was followed by a celebratory orgy of rape and murder amid the civilian population. Almost half of Soviet losses – 179,490 – had been suffered by Zhukov's First Belorussian Front. The advance from the Oder to the *Reichstag* had been contested by desperate German resistance. Soviet losses in the second quarter of 1945 (April to May) were over three-quarters of a million, which was as enormous a rate of loss as had been the case throughout the 'Great Patriotic War'.[41] The Berlin operation had only accounted for half that figure, and a great deal of fighting had simultaneously taken place to the south in Czechoslovakia and Hungary. The ability of the Soviets to accept losses had been extraordinary.

German civilian and military losses in the battle for Berlin are unknown. During the Berlin operation the Soviets claimed 480,000 military prisoners, of whom 70,000 were taken in the capital.[42] A figure of 100,000 German military and civilian dead in Berlin is a commonly cited but unsubstantiated estimate. Berlin had been reduced to rubble and the city's more than two million remaining citizens had to survive the coming weeks with little food and without the infrastructure of civilised urban life. Still, by the end of May many street cars were operating again and the main roads had been cleared. Soviet soldiers were gradually re-subjected to the restraint of military discipline. Preparations were underway for the western Allies to take over a large part of the city won at great cost by the Red Army.

15
The Capitulation of Japan

In mid-June 1944 the first B-29 Superfortress raid attacked southern Japan from bases in China. More raids would follow. The world war had finally reached the Japanese home islands. The B-29 was the most advanced mass-produced heavy bomber of the Second World War. Its long range and high altitude was ideal for a strategic bombing campaign. As had been the case in Germany, the concluding period to the war in Asia and the Pacific would be traumatic for the defeated, and the manner in which Japan was forced to capitulate wrote a new chapter in military history.

On 24 November 1944 a B-29 raid was launched against Japan from the Marianas in the Pacific. New air bases at Saipan, Tinian and Guam had been specifically built for raids against Japan. This next phase of the bombing campaign would devastate urban Japan. The Americans had commenced bombing Japan with the intention of hitting military targets with accurate, high-level air strikes by daylight. That intention had been undermined from the outset by the precedent of the carpet-bombing of Germany's cities. American air force planners also believed that Japanese industry relied on numerous small workshops, which were often in residential areas.[1] More importantly, poor weather and heavy cloud cover over Japan proved to be a serious problem for effective high-level, precision bombing. In Europe inclement weather had often forced American daylight bombing forces to jettison their bombs through cloud at targets indistinctly plotted on radar screens. What made matters more difficult over Japan was the existence of the 'jetstream', a hitherto under-appreciated atmospheric phenomenon. The jetstream caused fierce currents at high altitudes as it flowed out of Siberia and across the northern hemisphere. Winds blew at 200 mph at 30,000 feet. On a more positive note for the Americans, B-29 combat losses over Japan proved to be modest compared to operations in Europe. In January 1945 the Marianas-based XXI Bomber Command lost almost six per cent of its aircraft, a loss-rate that the Eighth Air Force might have suffered in a day or two at the height of its campaign against Germany.[2]

The answer to the jetstream for the XXI Bomber Command's chief, Major-General Curtis E. Le May, was low-level bombing by night. Winds were less severe closer to the ground and there were few Japanese night-fighters. In addition, during February experiments were made with a new type of incendiary projectile, which could be dropped in place of high-explosive bombs. The M-69 projectile was filled with napalm, a slow-burning gasoline substance. Japanese cities of wood and paper buildings were highly vulnerable to fire.

Le May decided to hit Tokyo, the Japanese capital, as hard as he could. The incendiary raid of Tokyo flown from the Marianas on the night of 9/10 March involved 325 B-29 Superfortresses. The bombers flew at a low level through the darkness to take the Japanese by surprise. The fuel and equipment loads carried by the B-29s were kept to a minimum to increase bomb loads. Downtown Tokyo was either side of the Sumida River. There were some specific industrial and military sites in the general target area, but the city was mostly a jungle of closely packed two-storey buildings of wood and paper. The grounds of the Imperial Palace were one of the few large open spaces in central Tokyo. With 135,000 people per square mile, downtown Asakusa ward was one of the most densely populated places on earth.

The raid achieved enormous destruction. The bombing was accurate. The weather that night was clear, and high winds fanned the flames caused by incendiaries into a firestorm that raced through the night. Water boiled in the city's canals. Dr Kuboto Shigenori was at Ryogoku Bridge before dawn:

> In the black Sumida River countless bodies were floating, clothed bodies, naked bodies, all as black as charcoal. It was unreal. These were dead people, but you couldn't tell whether they were men or women. You couldn't even tell if the objects floating by were arms and legs or pieces of burnt wood.[3]

Almost sixteen square miles of central Tokyo and a quarter of a million buildings were destroyed. In the burnt out areas wooden structures were destroyed down to the ground. Fire-fighters were overwhelmed. Officially, 83,000 people were thought to have been killed and over one million made homeless. In terms of scale, the firestorm in Tokyo was among the worst one-day disasters – natural or man-made – to befall urbanised human society up to that time. The main contender was the 1923 earthquake that had also devastated Tokyo and Yokohama. That Tokyo had seen a similar catastrophe within the past generation helped both the populace and government to accept the crisis. The firestorm raid did not have much discernible impact on the national will to fight on.[4]

Further air attacks on Tokyo followed. By the end of May 1945 over fifty-six square miles of the city had been destroyed. The Superfortresses went on to steadily plough up urban Japan. Sixty-six of the largest Japanese cities and towns would be devastated. Millions of people fled urban Japan for refuge in the countryside. General Ira C. Eaker, deputy commander of the United States Army Air Forces, later said that, 'It made a lot of sense to kill skilled workers by burning whole areas.'[5] The destruction wrought to Tokyo, Nagoya and Osaka was greater than the acreage devastated by all strategic bombing of Germany. In total, Tokyo recorded 97,031 deaths from air raids. In Osaka, Nagoya, Yokohama and Kobe almost 30,000 people died in air raids.[6] By the summer of 1945 the Americans would start to run out of undamaged Japanese targets to bomb with a force of almost 600 B-29s. The air staffs began searching for alternative targets. After the incineration of Japan's cities had been completed, the strategic bombing campaign intended to move on to the destruction of the Japanese rail system. This had the potential to cause famine affecting millions, as food would become difficult to distribute in a land without the fuel or vehicles for a comprehensive system of road transport.

As the strategic bombing campaign was gathering pace, American ground forces closed in by sea to defeat Imperial Japan. In October 1944 the Philippines had been invaded to shut off the shipping lanes between Japan and South-East Asia. Heavy fighting had followed on land lasting for many months. Washington decided to by-pass Formosa, northern China and Korea to invade Japan directly, but as a next step a further series of amphibious operations were needed to establish sea and air bases closer to Japan than the Philippines and Marianas. The bulk of the islands on the southern approaches to Japan were part of two separate island groups. American commanders intended to establish a new base in each of the two island groups.

The volcanic island of Iwo Jima was the target of the next major American assault landing. Iwo Jima was midway between Saipan and Japan. It was a small, pear-shaped, volcanic rock, four and a half miles long and two and a half miles wide. Mount Suribachi dominated the southern end of the island. The rugged topography of Iwo Jima was only too apparent from the air. What aerial reconnaissance could not detect, though, was the extent of the subterranean world the Japanese garrison had built within the rock of the island. Over a period of months, underground fortifications had been tunnelled into the earth and rock. The bombs of sporadic American air raids had only encouraged the Japanese to redouble their efforts.[7]

A force of three United States Marine Corps divisions began landing on 19 February after a three day naval bombardment. The marines' commanders had wanted a ten day bombardment. Lieutenant-General Tadamichi Kuribayashi was determined to fight a drawn-out battle of attrition without any wasteful counter-attacks. There was not the space on Iwo Jima to fight any other sort of battle. From tunnels and blockhouses the Japanese poured artillery, mortar and machine gun fire upon the marines, who had to fight their way forward yard by yard. American armoured vehicles became bogged in the volcanic ash. The raising of the stars and stripes on Mount Suribachi has achieved enduring fame but a great deal of fighting was needed after that to clear the main Japanese defences in the northern part of the island. By the end of March 6,821

American marines had been killed and almost 20,000 had been wounded. Very few prisoners were taken from the 21,000-man Japanese garrison, almost all of whom died in the desperate campaign. The airfields of an American-occupied Iwo Jima subsequently proved a useful emergency landing ground for B-29s returning from missions to Japan, but few of those landings were urgently necessary.

The final piece of territory the Allies needed as a base for an assault on the Japanese home islands was Okinawa, 350 miles south west of Japan. Okinawa had been part of the Japanese empire since 1879 and the mountainous parts of the island had been heavily fortified. The invasion began on 1 April using an armada of Allied shipping that rivalled the Normandy assault. The initial landing phase went smoothly but henceforward waves of kamikaze aircraft caused unprecedented United States Navy losses. Sixty-four ships were sunk or crippled and another sixty ships were damaged by suicide-piloted aircraft.[8] So long as the campaign lasted ashore, American warships and transports had to remain in waters off Okinawa. A Royal Navy carrier task force took its share of kamikaze hits.

The largest kamikaze of all was the super-battleship *Yamato*, which sailed for Okinawa with only enough fuel for a one-way trip. By this stage of the war Japan had consumed all but a small fraction of the oil supply held in storage. The intention was for *Yamato* to attack American warships off Okinawa and then beach herself to support the troops ashore. Massed American carrier aircraft sank the super-battleship and several smaller escorting warships on 7 April.

The Okinawa campaign ground steadily forward during May. Ruthless mopping-up operations lasted into the later half of June. The Japanese fought tenaciously from steep ridge lines in the south-central part of the island. American casualties on land, sea and air in the weeks of fighting needed to secure the territory were 12,520 killed and missing and 36,631 wounded. Japanese dead at Okinawa – both military and civilian – has been estimated to be as high as 150,000. There were terrible losses among the civilian population as the defenders' perimeter shrank. Prisoners were taken at a higher rate than at Iwo Jima but they were still only a small percentage of total Japanese losses.

In the summer of 1945 United States warships finally reached the doorstep of Japan, ninety-three years after Americans had first forced Japan to open its doors to western trade. As recently as 1940 the Japanese people had celebrated their 2,600 year anniversary. A belief that they had never been invaded was central to the collective Japanese identity.[9] During July American aircraft carrier task groups were able to directly raid targets in coastal Japan. On 14 July a force of American battleships and heavy cruisers bombarded the ironworks at Kamaishi on Honshu. The next day another battleship force bombarded steel and ironworks in a coastal town of the northern home island of Hokkaido. Both bombardments drew no Japanese opposition. More Allied carrier and warship raids on coastal Japan followed. The battleships *Haruna, Ise* and *Hyuga*, survivors of the Leyte campaign, were wrecked by air raids whilst sheltering in port.

American commanders prepared for an invasion of Japan, fearful of the massive losses that were bound to involve given the extreme nature of Japanese resistance in all the phases of the Pacific war from Guadalcanal to Okinawa. At an 18 June 1945 White House meeting with the Joint Chiefs of Staff and Secretaries for War and Navy, President Truman was presented with plans for a November invasion of the southern Japanese island of Kyushu. Truman expressed the hope that it would be possible to defeat Japan without 'an Okinawa from one end of Japan to the other'.[10] Admiral William Leahy, Chairman of the Joint Chiefs of Staff, told Truman that army and marine casualties on Okinawa had been thirty-five per cent of troops landed. If 767,000 troops were committed to invade Kyushu that would mean 268,000 casualties. American estimates of the total cost of an invasion of Japan ranged from several hundreds of thousands of casualties to upwards of a million, depending on the date and inclinations of the official making the estimate. Despite the likely cost, it was agreed that the Kyushu operation should go ahead. Preparations were also to be commenced for landings on the main Japanese island of Honshu. Kyushu D-Day – Operation Olympic – was set for 1 November. Honshu landings to clear the Tokyo region – Operation Coronet – would follow if needed in March 1946.

The Kyushu invasion was deemed necessary as no progress had been made towards ending the war by diplomatic negotiation. After General Tojo's resignation in July 1944, the retired General Koiso had headed a Cabinet. He was succeeded as prime minister by the retired Admiral Kantaro Suzuki in April 1945. The defeat of Germany, Japan's principal Axis partner, did not appear to dampen Tokyo's resolve. It was likely that the Americans would insist on Japan accepting similar terms to those that had been forced upon Germany. At an Imperial Conference on 8 June the Japanese government agreed to 'prosecute the war to the bitter end', though privately several senior ministers had their doubts as to the wisdom of that decision. On 22 June the Emperor also revealed an equivocal attitude at an Imperial Conference.[11] Nonetheless, a desire by some key individuals for an end to the war on reasonable terms was not the same as accepting defeat and unconditional surrender. To give up Japanese territory outside the home islands would mean letting go of all achievements made during the past two to three generations. Korea, Formosa and parts of Manchuria had been acquired prior to 1914. In a police state like Japan there could be no public discussion of ending the war. To some extent, the propaganda of the military was the only source of information even for senior civilian officials.

Foreign Minister Togo embarked on an attempt to win the support of the neutral Soviets as intermediaries for peace negotiations with the Allies. Given that Moscow had announced the end of their neutrality pact with Tokyo in April, the Soviets were a curious choice as an intermediary. American intercepts of communications by telegraph between Togo and his ambassador in Moscow suggested there was no agreement about peace terms within the Japanese government. This correctly raised questions as to whether the Japanese military was willing to accept an unconditional surrender. Japanese peace feelers to the Soviets were interpreted by Washington as an attempt to avoid the consequences of defeat.

Die-hards in the Japanese military welcomed the prospect of an American invasion of Japan as they wanted to inflict defeat and massive casualties on an invasion force, prior to making a more favourable peace than might previously have been available. So long as the Japanese could resist conquest by invasion, unconditional terms like those given to Germany in May 1945 seemed inappropriate. The Imperial Japanese Navy had been smashed by mid 1945, but the Imperial Japanese Army was substantially intact and successfully occupying large swaths of territory across eastern Asia and the western Pacific. After offensives in southern and south-west China in 1944, the Japanese army held more Chinese territory than ever in 1945. A large army of unbeaten troops remained in the field. The army's leaders did not feel they had been defeated. Although the army and naval air forces had been crippled by fuel shortages and a lack of skilled pilots, over 5,000 aircraft of all types were still available in Japan for suicide missions. In some respects Japan's position in mid 1945 was reminiscent of Germany in November 1918, when German territory had yet to be invaded and considerable tracts of foreign territory had still been occupied by German forces.

An invasion of Japan would be a difficult task. The southern Japanese island of Kyushu featured mountainous terrain. There would be abundant opportunities for Japanese troops to build tunnelled coastal defences as at Iwo Jima and Okinawa. Indeed, topographically Kyushu was a giant Okinawa, sprinkled with Iwo Jima-sized rock-formations. Japanese commanders had been encouraged by the effective performance of relatively small garrisons in the various Pacific island campaigns. There was reason to view a prospective campaign on Kyushu with a degree of optimism. The Imperial Japanese Army had based its Pacific defences on the sacrifice of its riflemen, machine gunners, mortar teams and field artillery. The general collapse of Japanese industry, transport and urban life was not likely to disrupt that military system. The problems of supply were expected to become easier in the Japanese home islands. Japan was in the process of mobilising the entire male population to resist invasion or die in the attempt.

American commanders did not intend to capture all of Kyushu, just enough of the southern part of the island to secure the sea and air bases needed to support further landings on Honshu. In April 1945 American estimates of Japanese troop strength on Kyushu had been 230,000. By August that estimate would reach 680,000, and the actual figure was 735,000.[12] Three divisions and numerous smaller units had defended Okinawa, but fourteen divisions and five independent brigades were preparing to defend Kyushu. The build up of Japanese forces on Kyushu meant that the Americans would struggle to land enough troops to raise the odds much higher than one to one. Heavy losses were a certainty under those circumstances. The rapid military build-up underway in Kyushu, and detected by the Americans, made it apparent that the Japanese intended to continue the war with vigour. Events in the summer of 1945 reminded some American officials of the lead-up to Pearl Harbor, when the Japanese had pursued feeble and vague efforts for peace whilst undertaking the most energetic of war preparations.[13]

Despite the fall of Nazi Germany, the United States Army's draft intake rose as 1945 wore onwards in preparation for heavy expected casualties in Japan. Kyushu would be invaded by forces already in the Pacific, but to land on the main island of Honshu would require the redeployment of troops from Germany. There were tentative plans for a corps-sized British Commonwealth force to take part in the 1946 landings, though American commanders both in Washington and the Pacific were not well-disposed towards that as it would complicate their plans. In USN circles there were doubts about the wisdom of invading Japan. Some admirals wanted to give the naval blockade more time to bring Japan to terms. Naval blockade, however, was a blunt and incremental instrument. By mid 1945 Japanese trade had been so effectively throttled there was little more that naval blockade could achieve in the short term.[14]

American preparations to invade Japan were abruptly intruded upon by a new technical development. The progress of the Asia-Pacific war, and warfare in general, was dramatically changed forever by the advent of the atomic bomb, the world's first nuclear weapon. Science and technology had played an enormous role during both world wars, but the development of the atomic bomb was a frightening leap forward into the unknown.

Early in the twentieth century scientists had learned that the atom was composed of smaller particles, and that it was possible to split an atom into neutrons, electrons and other matter. A German chemist discovered in 1938 that if uranium was bombarded by neutrons it could be split – a process called fission – in a manner that potentially caused a self-sustaining chain reaction. This chain reaction might release enough energy for a great explosion if the chain reaction became uncontrolled. If the process was controlled electricity might be generated.[15] The best material for the fission process was an isotope known as uranium 235, of which only small quantities could be found in natural uranium.

In October 1939 Albert Einstein, the celebrity scientist and emigrant to the United States, had written to President Roosevelt on behalf of two younger physicists warning that great scientific advances had recently been made in

Europe. In consequence of that, Germany might seek to build an atomic bomb. It was feared that the Germans might be a long way ahead of Allied scientists. An American government commission was established that reported that a new bomb of immense power was feasible. Research into nuclear physics had required only limited funding up to that point, but henceforward a huge effort would be needed to develop the atomic bomb.

Meanwhile in Europe, German efforts to develop an atomic bomb had not progressed far. Too many Jewish German scientists had fled the country by the 1939. Berlin had not been willing to invest sufficient resources in the necessary research. The Americans later concluded that the Germans got no closer to developing a bomb beyond the point they had reached by 1940.

The Manhattan Project to develop an atomic bomb had been run by the army as a military operation. General Leslie Groves was in overall command and J. Robert Oppenheimer headed the team of scientists and engineers at the Los Alamos Laboratory in New Mexico. The material for a bomb had to be manufactured, especially sufficient quantities of U-235 and the synthetic element plutonium. The Americans had been rightly concerned about British security in respect to atomic secrets, but information was shared between the two English-speaking powers. Some useful work on nuclear physics was underway in Britain. The Americans did not reveal anything to the Soviets, but Communist spies were among the scientists working on atomic-related projects to keep the Kremlin roughly in touch with developments.

When Truman had become President on 12 April 1945, he had been informed about the Manhattan Project and its progress to build a new super weapon. The war had featured all sorts of rumours about secret weapons, but this was different. On 16 July the first atomic bomb was tested in the desert of New Mexico. The blast was an awe-inspiring success and was measured as the equivalent of 17,000 tons of TNT. A blinding flash of light was generated and the blast of the bomb crushed the air. The world's first mushroom cloud sped up into the atmosphere from the desert floor. Oppenheimer watched the test from as close as was safe. He recalled to mind the Sanskrit lines of poetry: 'If the radiance of a thousand suns were to burst at once into the sky, that would be like the splendour of the Mighty One ... I am become Death, Shatterer of Worlds.' Prior to the test it had been theoretically understood that an atomic bomb had immense power, but the test had been needed to prove the magnitude of that power.[16]

What the test did not reveal was the likely lethality of radiation exposure. There had been illness caused by radiation poisoning as the bomb had been developed. It was generally understood that radiation was a terrible thing, but the New Mexico test blast had not involved human guinea pigs. If the bomb was detonated in the air it was speculated that the explosion might not greatly contaminate the ground below. Oppenheimer wrote on 23 July: 'With such high firing heights, it is not expected that radioactive contamination will reach the ground.'[17] It was hoped that a radioactive cloud might rapidly disperse. During the bomb's development it had not been clear if the device would be light enough to be carried by a heavy bomber, but that issue had been satisfactorily resolved by mid 1945. The B-29 was the ideal vehicle to deliver an atomic bomb.

As the dust was re-settling in the desert of New Mexico, the Potsdam conference of Allied leaders got underway on 17 July on the outskirts of a ruined Berlin. As well as reaching important agreements concerning the future of Europe, there was much to be discussed about Japan, the Axis power yet to be defeated. At the Teheran conference of November 1943 Stalin had agreed to enter the war against Japan, but only after Germany had been defeated. At Potsdam the Soviets finally agreed to enter the war against Japan by mid-August. Stalin told this to Truman on 17 July and the President wrote to his wife the next day. 'I've gotten what I came for – Stalin goes to war August 15 ... I'll say that we'll end the war a year sooner now, and think of the kids who won't be killed! That is the important thing.'[18] Truman welcomed Soviet intervention as it promised to tie down Japanese forces on the Asian mainland.

The Allied Potsdam Declaration of 26 July was intended to be a final warning to Japan to immediately surrender or be severely punished in the next round of fighting. It was issued jointly by the United States, Chinese Nationalist and British governments. The Soviet Union was still technically neutral. The Japanese were advised not to indulge in 'futile and senseless' resistance like Germany. The terms of surrender had many things in common with what the Allies were starting to implement in Germany. The Allies intended to remove Japanese militarists from 'authority and influence'; the armed forces were to surrender unconditionally; the country would be occupied; Japanese sovereignty would be confined to the home islands; war criminals were to be tried and punished. Japan, however, would not be 'enslaved as a race nor destroyed as a nation'. The Allies would establish a new Japanese government 'in accordance with the freely expressed will of the Japanese people'. There were no threats to divide Japan, though the stripping away of all territory outside the home islands acquired over the previous fifty years would be a form of permanent division. The final paragraph to the declaration stated: 'We call upon the Government of Japan to proclaim now the unconditional surrender of all the Japanese armed forces, and to provide proper and adequate assurances of their good faith in such action. The alternative for Japan is complete and utter destruction.' The declaration has been consistently criticised over the decades for not giving positive reassurances as to the position of the Emperor. Nothing was said to directly threaten Hirohito, but equally was he to be one of the war criminals put on trial? The Emperor was arguably the closest Japanese equivalent to Hitler, who had ended the war as a charred corpse. The failure to mention the Emperor was to some extent a capitulation to public opinion by America's leaders.[19] Behind the scenes in Washington, the balance of official opinion was in favour of the Emperor's retention. Washington, though, was not going to enter into any sort of deal with Imperial Japan's military cliché. Truman told Churchill at Potsdam 'that he did not think the Japanese had any military honour after Pearl Harbor'.[20] The Potsdam Declaration was an order to lay down arms and not a polite offer to open negotiations. The Japanese government ignored the Potsdam Declaration. The Allies were not surprised and interpreted the silence as a rejection.

Whilst preparations to invade Japan continued to grind forward, it was quickly decided to use the atomic bomb. The bomb had been developed to be used in combat. It had not been developed as a deterrent. In his 1947 memoir, Secretary of War Henry L. Stimson wrote: 'I felt that to extract a genuine surrender from the Emperor and his military advisers, they must be administered a tremendous shock which would carry convincing proof of our own power to destroy the Emperor.'[21] The atomic bomb was a psychological weapon as well as a weapon of great destructive power. The potential shock of an atomic bomb would be diluted if the Japanese government was given advance warning. The blasting of a relatively undamaged target would add to the psychological shock. A technical demonstration of the atomic bomb's power in an isolated place might merely convince the Japanese that Washington lacked the resolve to use the bomb against a city. A demonstration bomb might be argued away by Tokyo as an earthquake or meteor.[22]

The day before the Potsdam declaration was issued, and in anticipation of its rejection, the order was given to the Twentieth Air Force to drop the first atomic bomb on the first visual bombing day after 3 August. Additional atomic bombs were to be dropped when more bombs were ready. There were two bombs ready to be dropped in August. Another bomb was nearing completion but it would be some time before more were available. On 3 July the Joint Chiefs of Staff had banned further conventional air attacks on the list of target cities to be set aside for a possible atomic bomb. The slate of target cities was Hiroshima, Kokura, Niigata and Nagasaki. Stimson and Truman had decided to remove the old Japanese capital of Kyoto from the list. In addition to Kyoto's cultural significance, the city contained one million inhabitants.

Given the level of damage inflicted on Japanese cities by B-29 raids, the extent of destruction and death an atomic bomb might cause was not expected to be unprecedented. There was also no guarantee that the Japanese would surrender as a result of atomic attack. The fire-bombing of Tokyo had apparently made no impact on the determination of the Japanese government. American codebreakers had decrypted a Japanese message estimating the death toll from the Tokyo firestorm as 100,000.[23] The knowledge that so many people had been killed by conventional bombing in a single night on a previous occasion made the decision to drop the bomb more palatable. The army air force's General Arnold believed that dropping an atomic bomb would be a more efficient alternative to redeploying B-17 bombers from the European theatre. General

Marshall, the army's Chief of Staff, was considering using atomic bombs to soften up the beaches of Kyushu if an invasion of Japan went ahead.

B–29 aircraft and aircrew of the 509th Composite Group had been deployed to the Marianas in July with the Manhattan Project in mind. The 509th's commander was the twenty-nine year-old Colonel Paul W. Tibbets, a B–29 test pilot and combat veteran from the European theatre. Tibbets's crews refined their bombing technique on conventional missions over Japan in late July and early August. They practised dropping a single bomb on a run into the wind, after which the B–29s were turned away by at least 150 degrees to use the wind to speed away from the target as fast as possible.

At Tinian in the Marianas on the afternoon of 4 August a briefing was held for the B–29 aircrew taking part in the 'Little Boy' mission. By this time Niigata had been taken off the target list, leaving Hiroshima, Kokura and Nagasaki marked out for possible destruction. Hiroshima was to be the primary target for the first atomic mission. The airmen were to be shown a cinema film of the test bomb explosion in New Mexico but the projector chewed up the newsreel. A verbal account was given instead. The USN's Captain William Parsons, Director of Ordnance Development at Los Alamos, told the airmen that the bomb was the most destructive weapon in history and could potentially lay waste to a three mile stretch. Tibbets, the mission commander, said the dropping of the bomb might shorten the war by six months.

The Little Boy uranium bomb, which looked like 'an elongated trash can with fins', was winched aboard a B–29 named *Enola Gay*. The bomb was only ten feet long, thirty inches in diameter and weighed 9,700 pounds. The weapon's fuses would be set in flight so as to detonate the bomb at 1,800 feet after it had been dropped from the aircraft. The atomic bomb was intended to blow a city down rather than blow it up.

Hiroshima's peak wartime population was 380,000, but by August 1945 evacuation had reduced that to a little under a quarter of a million. The city, at the southern end of Honshu Island, contained some military installations and war-related industry, as was inevitably the case in virtually any Japanese town or city given the depth of military mobilisation by 1945. The Second Army's headquarters at Hiroshima commanded army forces in the southern half of Japan and there were thousands of servicemen in the city. Hiroshima was sited on the flat delta of the River Ota. Seven riverlets flowed through the urban landscape into Hiroshima Bay. The city was twenty-six square miles in extent, but only seven square miles were built up and contained seventy-five per cent of the population. There had been small air attacks on Hiroshima earlier in the war that had caused relatively few casualties.

In the early hours of 6 August six B–29s took off, each loaded with 7,000 gallons of fuel. The first three bombers were for weather reconnaissance purposes. The second flight of three bombers carried the bomb and observation teams. At 7.15 a.m. the reconnaissance B-29s reported from over Hiroshima that the weather was fine.

Just after 8.09 a.m. on a clear summer's day, another three Superfortresses approached Hiroshima, the eighth largest city in Japan. Earlier in the morning there had been an air raid alert caused by the reconnaissance B-29s, but the all-clear had been given and no further alert was signalled when more B-29s came into view. Susumu Kimura, a schoolgirl, later speculated, 'You could say that it was the sound of this siren [the all-clear] that killed the great majority of citizens of Hiroshima.'[24]

The atomic bomb carried by Tibbets's B-29 was dropped at 8.15 a.m. from 31,600 feet. The drop time was fifty seconds. The aiming point was the Aioi Bridge in the centre of the city. If dropped on the centre of the city, there was a good prospect that the bomb would destroy just about the entire built up area. The bomb exploded almost 2,000 feet above ground, 550 feet from the aiming point, in a fireball of brilliant light with a temperature of 5,400 degrees Fahrenheit at its most intense. From a quickly formed sea of swirling dust a rising mushroom-shaped column of cloud crowned the occasion. An observer in *Enola Gay* thought Hiroshima below had become a 'pot of boiling black'. The shock wave of the blast rocked the fleeing B-29s.[25]

The population of Hiroshima had been caught going about their day-to-day lives when the bomb detonated. Many were caught in the open travelling to their places of work. An intense wave of light and heat demolished and vaporised wood and paper buildings and human beings. The ruined skeletons of reinforced concrete and stone buildings remained standing but there were not many of those structures in a Japanese city. Shadows of people were later found cast on granite or stone surfaces by the flash of the blast. A fire storm caused by the blast swept through the city. The river channels did little to retard the conflagration, and became full of debris and corpses. A pall of darkness was cast over the ruins by dust and smoke.

It was later estimated that sixty-nine per cent of the city's built-up area had been destroyed and hospitals and medical services had vanished with so much else. The day after the blast a German priest wrote of the scene: 'Where the city stood everything, as far as the eye could reach, is a waste of ashes and ruins. Only several skeletons of buildings completely burned out in the interior remain. The banks of the river are covered with dead and wounded, and the rising waters have here and there covered some of the corpses.'[26] 4.7 square miles had been destroyed by a twelve and a half kiloton blast. Japanese authorities put the toll at Hiroshima from the blast and immediate aftermath as 71,379 killed and missing. A further 68,023 had been wounded, of whom 19,691 were seriously injured. The United States Strategic Bombing Survey's postwar estimate was a death toll of 70–80,000.

Nearby Kure Naval Station promptly reported to the Navy Ministry in Tokyo that Hiroshima had been raided by three B-29s and a new type of bomb had been detonated.

> A terrific explosion accompanied by flame and smoke occurred at an altitude of
> 500 to 600 metres. The concussion was beyond imagination and demolished prac-
> tically every house in the city ... About eighty per cent of the city was wiped out,
> destroyed, or burned ... Casualties have been estimated at 100,000 persons.[27]

Kure Naval Station was twelve miles south of central Hiroshima and from that
vantage point the terrible rising cloud over the city was an awesome sight.
Further reports from Kure spoke of raging fires and collapsed buildings. 'It is
as though a great steel fist had suddenly descended on Hiroshima.'[28] The War
Ministry in Tokyo also received reports from army bases in the region that had
survived the blast.

Military teams were sent from Tokyo to assess the situation. After sunset on
7 August a naval officer with a party of investigators flew over Hiroshima in
a transport aircraft towards the nearby naval air base. 'A ghastly and terrible
light flared from the stricken city. The still-burning Hiroshima cast a deep-red,
flickering glow which reflected from the black smoke which billowed upward
from the earth.' The following morning the military investigators entered the
city, one of whom later recalled the scene:

> Hiroshima's debacle is a familiar tale, but all the thousands of stories do not repro-
> duce the shuddering and screaming cries of the victims who already were beyond
> all possible help; they do not show you the dust and ash swirling about the burned
> bodies which grovelled and writhed in indescribable agony; the twitching and
> spasmodic jerking of fingers which were the only expressions of agony; the seek-
> ing of water by things which only a short while before had been human beings.
> Words do not convey the overwhelming, choking, nauseating stench, not from the
> dead, but from the searing living-dead.[29]

The city had become a brown scar on the face of the earth.

On 7 August the Army General Staff in Tokyo received news of President
Truman's announcement that an atomic bomb with a potential power of
20,000 tons of TNT had been used against Japan. 'It is a harnessing of the basic
power of the universe. The source from which the sun draws its power ... It
was to spare the Japanese from utter destruction that the ultimatum of 26 July
was issued at Potsdam. Their leaders promptly rejected that ultimatum. If they
do not accept our terms they may expect a rain of ruin from the air, the like of
which has never been seen on this earth.' An emergency meeting of Japanese
cabinet ministers began on the afternoon of 7 August to consider the news of
the President's broadcast.

The strategic bombing of Japan resumed on the day after the Hiroshima blast.
On 7 August 131 B-29s raided the Toyokawa naval ammunition works. 1,400

people were killed by the bombing. The next day Yawata was bombed in clear weather; 245 B-29s hit the industrial city of a quarter of a million inhabitants and twenty-two per cent of the urban area was burnt out by the raid. A small raid was also sent against an aircraft plant in Tokyo.[30] It was business as usual for the Superfortresses.

The situation was transformed again at dawn on 9 August when news was received in Tokyo of a Soviet declaration of war. Any hopes of securing Soviet mediation had obviously gone. The timing of Stalin's declaration was a surprise but Soviet intervention was not unexpected. The non-aggression pact between Japan and the Soviet Union had been due for renewal in April, but had instead been denounced by Stalin. The Soviet build-up in the Far East had been detected without difficulty. Japanese diplomatic couriers could plainly see troops and equipment streaming eastwards along the Trans-Siberian railway during the summer months of 1945.[31] Tokyo had hoped that the Soviets' likely entry to the war would be later in the year, or even as far away as the spring of 1946. Three Soviet army groups were poised to invade Manchuria, 1,500,000 troops under Marshal Vasilevsky, backed by a powerful array of tanks, artillery and mechanised transport. In August 1945 the Manchurian-based Kwangtung Army comprised 713,000 men and was poorly equipped compared to the mechanised juggernaut poised to hit them.

The Soviet offensive would prove to be a rapid success, but it is important to bear in mind that on 9 August little more than the fact of a Soviet attack was known in Tokyo. The collapse of the Kwangtung Army would only become apparent in the days ahead. The Japanese defeat in Manchuria in August 1945 would largely repeat the circumstances of the Red Army's victory at Nomonhan in 1939, albeit on a much larger scale. Japanese light infantry were no match for Soviet tank formations on an open plain. Two giant Soviet mechanised pincers crashed through the Japanese front and raced onwards. Huge pockets of Japanese troops were bypassed by the Soviet *blitzkrieg* and cordoned off for reduction. Soviet intervention made it clear that Japan had little future prospect of maintaining a position on the Asian mainland in any shape or form.

The Japanese Supreme War Council met at 10.30 a.m. on 9 August to consider the war situation, only to receive further dramatic news just before 1 p.m. A second atomic bomb had been dropped to remove any doubts as to whether the Americans possessed more than a single bomb. The second bomb proved that the Americans were willing to keep attacking urban targets. The dropping of the Fat Man plutonium bomb had been scheduled for 11 August, but had been brought forward to 9 August as a period of unsuitable weather was expected after that date. Local American commanders in the Pacific had been instructed to use additional atomic bombs against Japan as they became available. It had been well understood in Washington at the start of August that two atomic bombs were available in the Marianas to be used at short notice. Thus there was no separate decision to drop a second bomb.

The B-29s carrying the second bomb had left their base in the early hours of 9 August for the long flight to Japan. Kokura, in northern Kyushu, was to have been the target for the second atomic bomb. Kokura had a population of 168,000 in 1940 and possibly 110,000 by 1945. Kokura, however, was covered by smoke and haze when the American heavy bombers arrived over their intended target. The mission commander, Major Charles Sweeney, had been ordered to only drop his bomb under visual conditions. Three bombing runs were made over Kokura with bomb bay doors open, but the city below could not be seen. Fuel was running low and Japanese fighters were beginning to climb upwards in the distance. The poor weather caused Sweeney to turn away to strike the nominated secondary target, which was Nagasaki. This city lay to the south west of Kokura and was also in Kyushu.

Since the opening of Japan to western influence, Nagasaki had been a port for foreign trade, and a centre for Christian missionary activity. Nagasaki's port was at the top of a long bay and the city was laid out in two converging valleys separated by a mountain spur. Nagasaki was a home to the Mitsubishi industrial combine, which included shipyards, munitions factories and steelworks. Mitsubishi works and yards had received some bombing in the past, though Nagasaki was a difficult city to attack in poor weather, or by night, as the surrounding hilly terrain interfered with the standard radar used by the heavy bombers of 1945. There were few uniformed servicemen based in Nagasaki, far fewer than had been the case in Hiroshima.[32]

When Sweeney's B-29 reached Nagasaki, the city was covered by heavy cloud – eight-tenths cloud-cover– but Commander Fred Ashworth, the mission's weapons officer, decided to authorise a non-visual bomb drop through the clouds guided by radar. With fuel running low due to a faulty fuel pump, only one bombing run was to be made by the B-29 named *Bock's Car*. At the last minute, a break in the clouds meant it was possible to drop the bomb visually, though a long way from the planned aiming point. A blinding flash spread over Nagasaki just after 11.00 a.m. Of the city's quarter of a million inhabitants, 35–45,000 were killed by the blast. Perhaps half of Nagasaki's 14,000 Christians were among the dead.[33] The bomb's blast killed hundreds in the Cathedral of Our Lady of the Immaculate Conception. One and a half square miles of urban terrain was destroyed, representing forty-four per cent of the built-up area. The Nagasaki atomic bomb had the power of 22,000 tons of TNT (twenty-two kilotons). The hilly terrain around the city had confined the explosion to some extent, though the bowl shape in which some districts were located ensured massive destruction in those areas.

The issue of radiation sickness only fully emerged in the wake of the atomic blasts. Reports were soon in circulation that people in Hiroshima and Nagasaki were continuing to die in mysterious circumstances. In the years ahead malignant tumours and disfigurement plagued survivors. If radiation deaths after the event are included, a total figure of 160–200,000 dead for the pair of atomic bombs is credible.[34]

High-level meetings in Tokyo during 9 August revealed that a deadlock within the Japanese government still existed, despite the twin doses of additional bad news received that day. When the Supreme Council met, the Army Minister and the Chiefs of the Army and Navy General Staff opposed unconditional surrender. The Prime Minister, Foreign Minister and Navy Minister were in favour of quickly ending the war on whatever terms were available, providing the Emperor's position could be secured. Those holding out wanted to qualify the nature of surrender by limiting an Allied occupation and retaining the Japanese military's autonomy to the extent of conducting their own demobilisation and trying their own war criminals. The War Minister, General Korechika Anami, led the push to continue the war. Anami believed that war was a contest of spirit and will. Great suffering in war was to be expected. The Army Minister believed that Japan could still win a battle against an invasion of the home islands. Cabinet meetings lasting from 2.30 p.m. into the evening did not see any change in the situation.[35]

During the day Foreign Minister Togo pressed Prime Minister Suzuki to seek new ways to end the war. The previous day, on the afternoon of 8 August, Togo had discussed the Hiroshima bomb with the Emperor. Hirohito had told Togo: 'Now that this kind of weapon had been used in the war, it was even more impossible for Japan to continue the war ... Japan could no longer afford to talk about the conditions of her surrender terms. She must aim for a speedy resolution of the war.'[36] Emperor Hirohito had also told Marquis Koichi Kido, Lord Keeper of the Privy Seal, 'now that the Soviets have entered the war with Japan, there was urgent need to resolve the problem of a cease-fire'.[37] Kido had been instructed to communicate the Emperor's views to the Prime Minister.

Prime Minster Suzuki called another high-level meeting for the evening of 9 August. This meeting was to be held in the presence of the Emperor. The Imperial Conference – which was a Supreme Council meeting conducted in the presence of the Emperor – assembled in the underground air-raid shelter of the Imperial Palace. Those who had pushed for the conference were hoping the Emperor could be provoked into breaking the deadlock in the government in favour of a rapid surrender. The Imperial Conference began at ten minutes to midnight. After another round of the arguments that had been made at other meetings, Hirohito finally sided with his civilian ministers against his military chiefs to end the war on the Potsdam terms, subject to the Imperial house retaining its status. Hirohito spoke of the need for peace and expressed scepticism as to the state of preparations to repel an invasion. 'There are those who say that the key to national survival lies in a decisive battle in the homeland. The experience of the past, however, shows that there has always been a discrepancy between plans and performance.'[38] The Emperor had belatedly realised that the claims of the military over the previous couple of years had been exaggerated. There was little chance of repelling an Allied invasion.

The Emperor's intervention was made in the early hours of 10 August, and was confirmed by a Cabinet meeting soon afterwards. Later that day the Japanese government signalled to the Allies a willingness to accept the Potsdam terms so long as the Imperial institution was retained. The signal was sent via the Japanese embassies in Sweden and Switzerland. The possibility of communicating with the Allies via those embassies had always existed and had always hitherto been rejected. A brief round of discussions was held in Washington regarding the position of Hirohito. Clearly the Emperor could play a useful role in ordering Japanese forces outside the home islands to lay down their arms. Secretary of War Stimson believed that the Emperor's retention could save 'us from a score of bloody Iwo Jimas and Okinawas' that might otherwise be needed to clear Japanese forces from the Asia-Pacific region.[39] Stimson also saw advantages in bringing the war to a rapid conclusion to minimise the Soviet impact on affairs in east Asia. The Americans replied to Tokyo that the Emperor 'shall be subject to' an Allied Supreme Commander.

The final conclusion to the Pacific war was a savage contest of wills between the leaders of Japan and America (on behalf of the Allies). The atomic bombs had created the psychological conditions needed for the Japanese to surrender and acknowledge the accumulated defeats of the past several years. Marquis Kido commented: 'It is not correct to say that we were driven by the atomic bomb to end the war. Rather it might be said that we of the peace party were assisted by the atomic bomb in our endeavour to end the war.'[40] In December 1945 Suzuki summed up the decision-making process of his government:

> The Supreme War Council, up to the time the atomic bomb was dropped, did not believe that Japan could be beaten by air attack alone ... [the Supreme War Council] had proceeded with one plan of fighting a decisive battle at the landing point and was making every possible preparation to meet such a landing. They proceeded with that plan until the Atomic bomb was dropped, after which they believed the United States ... need not land when it had such a weapon; so at that point they decided that it would be best to sue for peace.[41]

The advanced technology of the atomic bomb helped the Japanese military save face as their moral resolution was not the aspect of Japanese national life that had been defeated.

The atomic bombs and Soviet intervention were all catalysts for Japan's surrender. It is difficult to disentangle the events of 6–9 August but the atomic bombs were a direct, unexpected attack on the Japanese home islands, whereas the Soviet attack on Manchuria was generally expected and still far from Japan. It is unlikely that the Soviet declaration of war in isolation would have compelled a Japanese surrender. The Japanese leadership did not want to involve a regicidal Communist regime in their capitulation. If Japan had to surrender, Tokyo preferred to surrender to the Americans and undergo an American occupation.

After the 10 August decision to surrender there were still elements in the Japanese leadership unwilling to accept that outcome. At a conference on the evening of 13 August Vice-Chief of the Naval General Staff, Vice-Admiral Onishi, expressed the apocalyptic opinion, 'Let us formulate a plan for certain victory, obtain the Emperor's sanction, and throw ourselves into bringing the plan to realisation. If we are prepared to sacrifice 20,000,000 Japanese lives in a special attack effort, victory will be ours!'[42] This point of view, however, was exceptional and the decision to surrender was confirmed within the Japanese government on 14 August. By that time reliable news of the collapsing front in Manchuria had reached Tokyo, Emperor Hirohito prepared a speech to be broadcast by radio to let the nation know the result of the war. On the evening of 14 August a half-hearted attempt at a military coup was made by mostly junior officers with little support from their seniors. War Minister Anami committed suicide to remove from the earthly scene one of those most opposed to surrender. A new government was installed on 15 August to oversee the country during the uneasy period before the agreed arrival of an Allied occupation force.

The Emperor's broadcast was made at noon on 15 August. He announced in very formal Japanese 'that Our Empire accepts the provisions of their Joint Declaration'. Despite the service and devotion of the Japanese military and people:

> The war situation has developed not necessarily to Japan's advantage, while the general trends of the world have all turned against her interest. Moreover, the enemy has begun to employ a new and most cruel bomb, the power of which to do damage is indeed incalculable, taking the toll of many innocent lives. Should We continue to fight, it would not only result in an ultimate collapse and obliteration of the Japanese nation, but it would lead to the total extinction of human civilisation.[43]

A number of senior Japanese military men would commit suicide in the days ahead, including Admiral Onishi. If Japan had not surrendered after the two atomic bombings it is difficult to say how other bombs might have been used as they became operational. At the very least, a review of policy in Washington would have been needed before a third bomb could have been dropped. The use of the atomic bombs are an illustration of the way a long, harsh war leads to an escalation of violence and a relaxation of the conventions governing the use of violence.

The advance party of the occupation force destined for Japan landed by air at a base near Tokyo on 28 August. On 2 September General MacArthur accepted the formal Japanese surrender aboard the battleship *Missouri* in Tokyo Bay. President Truman had turned down Soviet requests for an occupation zone for the Red Army in the northern Japanese island of Hokkaido. The Russians had to content themselves with overturning the outcome of the 1904–5 war in Manchuria. The British Commonwealth received an occupation zone in southern Japan under the umbrella of the American Supreme Commander. 5.4 million Japanese army and 1.8 million naval prisoners were demobilised by the Allies. Seven million Japanese were repatriated to the home islands, about half of whom were civilians.

The atomic bombs helped to determine the timing of the war's ending in mid-August 1945. This mattered greatly to many people. Across the Asia-Pacific region there was enormous relief among servicemen from many nations in many places. Churchill described the abrupt ending of the war as a 'miracle of deliverance', which it certainly was for the Allied soldier marked out by fate to take the next bullet. At the time of the surrender, fighting was still underway in China, Manchuria and numerous other points across eastern Asia and the western Pacific. The next major Allied operation in the war against Japan was scheduled to be the British-Indian invasion of Malaya on 9 September 1945, which had the aim of retaking Singapore.

Aside from combat, war conditions had imposed a ceaseless attrition on the populations of east Asia, the cost of which was worsening as the period of the Japanese occupation lengthened. Famine in Indo-China in 1944–45 had caused at least half a million deaths. A great many unknown civilians across eastern Asia also benefited from the war concluding suddenly on 15 August 1945, to put an end to the horrors of Japan's Greater East Asia Co-Prosperity Sphere.

16
The Defeat of the Axis

The scale of destruction wrought by the Second World War was one of the greatest man-made calamities in human history. Fifty to sixty million people died as combatants and civilians from causes directly brought about by war conditions. The enormous toll of the Second World War was caused by the conduct of military operations on a greater scale than ever before. From 1939–45 mechanisation gave warfare an expanded geographic scope. It was the breadth of that geographic scope that consumed a larger civilian population than ever before. Perhaps two-thirds of those who died were civilians. The bulk of these died from pestilence and starvation. A proportion, however, were exterminated by the deliberate policies and technology of a centralised nation-state.

The Second World War had a decisive conclusion and did not drag on unduly. For a large portion of the human race to resolve its differences through warfare in only six years was remarkable. But at certain points of the conflict things might have turned out differently. The outcome was not preordained. At the very least, victory or defeat in particular campaigns had the power to alter the trajectory of the conflict to the benefit or doom of millions.[1] Part of the fascination with battle is the 'fear and awe' it evokes.[2] A state can expand into an empire if successful in warfare, whereas a defeated state may suffer occupation, division or permanent destruction.[3]

The study of a particular battle or campaign helps to restore the significance of dramatic human action to war. In events of finite duration the actions of participants are especially important. There can be no dogmatic definition of a 'decisive battle' or campaign. Rather, an intimate knowledge of a particular conflict will indicate to a keen student of history where the points of military significance might lie. A war between two poorly matched protagonists – such as the 1870–71 Franco-Prussian War – can be resolved relatively quickly by means of decisive victories in a short, sharp series of battles. But wars conducted between coalitions across large territories – such as the Second World War – have always needed a long series of battles to reach a conclusion. Even a well-conducted military campaign will struggle to achieve decisive results beyond a particular theatre of war. This was characteristic of large wars in the days of Rome, Louis XIV and Napoleon, as well as the twentieth century.

In the First World War, fighting on the Western Front, the most important theatre of the conflict, was often a static form of combat waged by men, munitions and industrially produced machine guns and artillery. By 1914 the one-day land battle had become a relic of a bygone age. A battle might last days, weeks or several months. Armies had become too large to fight their way to a decisive conclusion any more quickly. The suddenness of the armistice of November 1918, after Germany had enjoyed success on both the eastern and western fronts earlier that year, made it hard for the Germans to accept defeat. German territory had not been entered and only a little over one-tenth of the country was occupied after the armistice. In November and December 1918 the German Army marched home to demobilise itself in a manner not so different from the way a genuinely victorious war might have ended. The conclusion to the First World War was to a substantial extent an act of diplomacy. Germany had lost the war, but the Germans did not feel sufficiently defeated in a strictly military sense to accept fully the terms imposed by diplomatic negotiations conducted far from the battlefield at Versailles.

During the interwar period German professional military officers sought to learn lessons from the recently concluded war. The armistice had not significantly disrupted the social and political influence of the military in German culture. The advent of a new political leadership determined to revise or overturn the result of 1918–19 gave those efforts greatly added impetus. It is an open question as to the extent to which new forms of offensive warfare drew inspiration from the undoubted dynamism and aggressiveness of fascism and Nazism. A belief in the importance of effective war-fighting was vital to the Nazi vision of Germany's future. A decisive style of battle was a way for a weaker force to achieve victory over a stronger force they might struggle to beat in a war of attrition. In the mid to late 1930s the Nazi government of Germany made plans for war from a position of perceived weakness. Yet the unprecedented pace of technological change in the twentieth century had meant that a stream of new inventions were readily at hand for military innovators to exploit. Aircraft, armoured vehicles and new forms of motorised transport had become available to make possible a fresh style of offensive warfare. In hindsight this was labelled the *blitzkrieg* or lightning war.

The Polish state had been revived by the manner in which the First World War had ended. That state's destruction at the start of the next great conflict was a clear sign that the Second World War was a delayed continuation of the previous conflict. The rapidity of Poland's defeat has caused the campaign to be lightly skimmed over in many English-language books about the Second World War. But the fighting was severe and taught the Germans a great deal about the practice of mechanised warfare. Mechanisation offered the possibility of rapid victory as a vigorous pursuit of a defeated foe could transform a local battlefield victory into a campaign victory.[4]

The destruction of Poland highlights the significance of the Berlin-Moscow alliance, one of the pivotal events of its generation. The dominant position achieved by the Germans from 1939–41 owed much to the cooperation of Communist Russia. Stalin was more than just the greatest appeaser of Hitler; he wanted an alliance with Nazi Germany so as actively to share in the spoils on offer in eastern Europe. In contrast, Britain and France declared war on Germany in support of Poland but dared not attack Germany. Britain, France and Poland failed to function as meaningful military allies. Hitler and Stalin had no such problems.

In Poland the genocidal policies of Nazi Germany came out of the shadows. This was not entirely new to twentieth-century warfare, as the 'ethnic cleansing' and death marches that had consumed so many of the Ottoman Empire's Armenian population during the First World War, over one million people, had also been the result of deliberate state policy. In August 1939, when he had been discussing with his commanders his intention to clear living space in Poland mercilessly, Hitler allegedly said: 'Who, after all, speaks today of the annihilation of the Armenians?'[5] In Poland, a large civilian population fell under the control of a predatory enemy drunk with the elation of success and a sense that their triumph was irreversible. The leadership of Nazi Germany, at least at the outset, was convinced it would not be called to account for its excesses. Stalin's Soviet Union had much the same outlook. The mass killing and internment policies of Hitler and Stalin joined hands in Poland. The predatory nature of the destruction of Poland set the scene for a desperate total war that plunged large parts of the world into a new dark age.

After the winter lull of 1939–40, a German offensive was launched in the Low Countries and France, one of Western warfare's traditional arenas of conflict. A *blitzkrieg*-style offensive, its mechanised techniques refined in Poland, defeated France in weeks. French military thinking in 1940 still relied on the methods of 1918. The main shortcoming of the methods of 1918 was that they had not been good enough to place a single soldier on German soil before the armistice of that year. Military methods that had been barely sufficient in 1918 had even less hope of achieving success a generation later. By 1940 the speed of warfare had dramatically increased. Warfare had again become a high stakes, winner-takes-all pursuit in which the rewards of victory were well worth the cost. The fall of France overturned the result of the First World War and destroyed France as a great power. It created a German-dominated Europe. Most of what followed in the next phase of the war flowed as a consequence of the opportunities presented to the Axis by the fall of France.

It is possible, though, to be too harsh in judgements of France in 1940. After all, in the First World War France had needed an enormous sacrifice from its army, and those of Russia and Britain, to stave off defeat at the hands of Germany. It had then needed the intervention of the United States in 1917–18 to gain a favourable armistice at Germany's expense. In 1940 France did not have the strong and effective support of allies on the field of battle. Thus the odds had been heavily stacked against France in a war with Germany. When France had stood alone against Germany in 1870 it had also been rapidly defeated. The inability of the 1919–39 Third Republic to form timely and effective international alliances merely reflected its never-ending internal upheavals. The fall of France in 1940 was followed by the accession of Italy, Japan and several other eastern European nations to the Axis. At the time, these all seemed major steps towards creating a sustainable and stable Axis superpower.

That France fell and Britain survived revealed that the British Empire was a good deal stronger than the French Empire, if only because of geography and governmental unity. In 1939 it had been claimed in Allied propaganda that France had the strongest army in the world and Britain the strongest navy. The former claim proved to be wholly an illusion, but the later was at least sufficiently true to save Britain from an invasion. Whether or not the Dunkirk evacuation took place probably made no difference to London's decision to fight on. Dunkirk only involved a small fraction of the British Empire's armed forces. In June 1940 Britain lost its bridgehead in western Europe, but otherwise the bulk of its armed forces were undefeated. It was impossible for the British government to trust the German leadership in light of the events not merely of 1938–40, but in light of everything that had happened from 1914 down to 1940.

The Battle of Britain that was fought between the RAF and *Luftwaffe* was less bloody than some other battles of the Second World War. But death does not have equivalence of impact in warfare. Sometimes the death of a handful of people matters a great deal to the overall course of immense wars. In the autumn of 1940 the Germans had to be defeated somewhere and somehow to bring an extraordinary run of success to a halt. The Battle of Britain was fought seemingly without the involvement of land and sea forces. Yet the unsung hero of the campaign was the English Channel, with the significance of geography in warfare proven again. The Channel and adequate naval strength had saved Britain from Napoleon early in the nineteenth century and from the Spanish Armada of 1588. As an empire created by sea power, the geographic logic of the British Empire was different from that of a continental land power like Germany. British naval power did not just preserve the United Kingdom from invasion; it also permitted trade, troop movements and communication with the rest of the British Empire and the United States. As in the First World War, Germany was facing an enemy that could use the seas of the world to great advantage. In hindsight, the destruction of the German surface fleet at the conclusion of the First World War had helped to secure Britain for the next generation.

The air attack on Britain was followed by an even greater effort to damage Britain by means of a submarine campaign against sea trade. U-boat warfare had been a major part of the 1914–18 war. A renewed U-boat campaign had begun in 1939 as Germany's geographic relationship with Britain had not changed. The conquest of France and the possession of Atlantic ports gave Germany further encouragement to build submarines, as the opportunity to damage British merchant shipping was greater than in the previous conflict.

A massive construction programme kept the U-boat campaign going for the entire Second World War, but it was clear by the end of 1941 that submarines were an attritional and not a decisive weapon against Britain's trade. U-boats were unable to interfere with the movement of troops by fast liner. During the years 1939–41, the vital period that shaped the destiny of Nazi Germany, in terms of equipment, the industrial investment in submarines was appreciably greater than the industrial investment in armoured vehicles, the weapon upon which the *Wehrmacht* depended for victory in land warfare. The Germans had wasted a lot of resources on a fleet in the First World War and they did it again from 1939–45. Hitler did not understand that seapower required a massive commitment, something that Napoleon and the Kaiser had not grasped either. The Germans invaded Russia in 1941 with only marginally more tanks than used in France a year before. At a critical time, scarce industrial resources were ploughed into building U-boats for Doenitz rather than building tanks. The panzer arm, despite its enduring fame, lacked a champion in the German High Command and Nazi Party hierarchy of Doenitz's stature. Doenitz had no interest in how naval strategy might hurt Germany's prospects in the east.

Based on the experience of the First World War, the defeat of both France and Russia seemed to hold the key to overall German victory. Given Hitler's personal ambitions for eastern Europe, it is difficult to see any scenario in which Nazi Germany would not have turned to a war against the Soviets once France had been defeated. An invasion of Russia was the key to turning domination of Europe into domination of Eurasia and a lasting hegemony for Nazi Germany and the Axis. Operation Barbarossa, the invasion of Russia, was more than just an ideological crusade: it was vital for turning Germany into a world power.

Barbarossa did not aim for a strictly military outcome, insofar as Hitler hoped to collapse the Soviet state as a political entity, much as had happened to the Tsarist regime in the First World War. The Nazi invasion of Russia had a definite political strategy and that strategy was terror, an approach that was consistent with the intended nature of postwar occupation. If the Soviet state and armed forces collapsed, that would make victory in the east possible without literally overrunning Siberia and central Asia. Transport and supply over long distances had never been the German military's speciality and the *Wehrmacht* was still not a fully motorised force in 1941.

In the early weeks and months of Barbarossa German armoured columns crashed through the Red Army. The numbers of Soviet troops killed and captured and the territory overrun exceeded what had been achieved in the campaign in France of May–June 1940. But that was not enough, as the Soviets had a far greater population and geographic size. The Soviet state did not crumble under the assault. In the years preceding Barbarossa, Stalin had been a dedicated militarist and that was a good preparation for total war against Germany. The iron grip of Stalin's dictatorship cannot be compared to the limp body politic of the Third Republic, or the tepid authoritarianism of Tsar Nicholas II.

The twin failures to knock Britain and Russia out of the war exposed Nazi Germany to a dire future. Each time the Germans attacked and failed to defeat an opponent they augmented the strength of the opposing coalition. This ran the risk of turning the war into an attritional conflict, like the war of 1914–18. Hitler had intended to attack and defeat his victims one at a time to avoid that eventuality. Ultimately, Hitler had the same problems subduing Britain and Russia as Napoleon had experienced in the early period of the nineteenth century.[6] Napoleon was a French dictator who had overrun Germany; Hitler was a German dictator who had conquered France. That did not prove to be enough in either case. The basic facts of geography and the European system of states had not changed fundamentally in less than 150 years. Situated at either end of Europe, Britain and Russia had sufficient geographic and demographic security to oppose an enemy with hegemonic ambitions.

Japan, like Germany, had emerged as a great power in the late nineteenth century. A triumphant sense of rapid emergence had given momentum to the aggressive ambitions of both countries. Unlike Germany, Japan had managed to be on the winning side in the First World War, at almost no cost to itself. That success had further fuelled Tokyo's long-term pursuit of policies of military expansion on the Asian mainland, where Japan already possessed Korea and a stake in Manchuria. Full-scale war between Japan and China began in 1937. The stalemate in China that followed the Japanese capture of Shanghai and Nanking was important to the deterioration of Japanese-American relations. The fate of China under Japanese occupation steadily made it clear that Washington and Tokyo had irreconcilable differences. United States trade with Japan was too central to the Japanese war effort in China for Washington to allow it to continue. Yet Japan could not maintain its war machine on the Asian mainland without alternative sources of raw materials. Japan needed to seize the raw materials of South-East Asia, and embark on a war with the United States, to prolong its occupation of China.

The Pearl Harbor raid was a one-day engagement. Even in the Second World War a great deal could happen in a day, and naval warfare often provides the best examples. The Japanese deployment of massed aircraft carriers and high-performance naval aircraft was the sea warfare equivalent of tanks and the *blitzkrieg*. This was a new method of war never before seen in such a concentrated form. Japanese expertise in naval aviation did not develop in a vacuum. The Imperial Japanese Navy had four years' experience of air warfare in China. Japanese methods at Pearl Harbor had been refined beforehand in other places, just as the Germans had used Spain and Poland to build up the experience of the panzer arm.

Given that war had not been declared, the Japanese blow at Pearl Harbor was always likely to have inflicted a great deal of damage on the United States Navy's Pacific Fleet. American commanders at Hawaii would have looked more capable, however, if they had detected the approach of the Japanese. There was nothing revolutionary about effective reconnaissance. Pearl Harbor was another turning point, like the fall of France, after which the Second World War became a dramatically different conflict from the First World War.

Above all else, the Pearl Harbor raid brought the United States into the war against both Japan and Germany. The United States was not part of Europe or Asia. In both world wars it took great provocation to haul the Americans into the conflict. Hitler's declaration of war on the United States was one of his worst mistakes. He did not fear the United States sufficiently in light of the Great Depression and Washington's retreat to isolation during the 1920s.

Berlin and Tokyo made matters worse by failing to wage war in accordance with an agreed global strategy. The Japanese could not be tempted to attack the Soviets in Siberia to support Nazi Germany. Likewise, there would be scant opportunity for U-boats based at North Atlantic ports to cooperate with a Japanese surface fleet based in east Asia. The Indian Ocean was a place where German and Japanese forces might have potentially joined hands, but the region lacked objectives sufficiently compelling to draw the Axis together from their separate halves of the world.

The United States Navy soon regained the initiative from the Japanese at the battle of Midway in June 1942. Signals intelligence played a major role in the Midway and Coral Sea campaigns. Naval radio signals were far more vulnerable to interception than the signals of land forces, the most important of which were generally sent by telephone land line or short-range radio. The effectiveness of signals intelligence at Midway should not blind us to the fact that intelligence coups were far and few between in the Second World War. Most of the really important operational initiatives went relatively undetected even in the face of an alerted opponent straining to uncover information.

At Midway American aircraft carriers proved to be as good as Japanese aircraft carriers, ship for ship. The investment the Americans had made in carrier aviation across the interwar period paid handsome dividends. The manner in which the Japanese split their forces between the Coral Sea and central Pacific, and again subdivided the forces used at Midway into several fleets, was a clear-cut display of ineptitude. As an operational commander, Admiral Yamamoto was a flop. The American victory at Midway caused a reversal of the war situation in the Pacific. Only two months later the Americans moved onto the offensive to land troops at Guadalcanal in the Solomon Islands. The American grand strategic intention to give a greater priority to the war against Germany was able to roll forward smoothly in the wake of the Midway triumph. The period during which the Japanese were able dramatically to interfere with Allied plans was brief, though undoubtedly calamitous for the colonial empires and peoples of South-East Asia.

For much of the Second World War Britain confronted a diverse array of enemies whilst seeking to protect territorial commitments across the globe. This caused the unavoidable dispersion of an otherwise substantial war effort. It was hard for the British Empire to achieve a decisive outcome alone in any given theatre. The Middle East theatre, however, was an important exception. It was a place to which a large British army could be safely deployed when Britain's fortunes in the war were running low. The Nile delta was also a place to which India, Australia, New Zealand and South Africa could send forces to play a constructive role in a global war that would otherwise have left them as marginal players. The British presence in the Middle East helped to hem the Axis powers into southern Europe and Italian Libya. If that had not happened, Axis forces would have ranged across Africa and western Asia at will. The Jews of Palestine would have been exterminated. Given the enormous challenges Nazi Germany undertook during 1941–42, any diversion of Axis forces to a subsidiary theatre had an impact on the overall war situation. What might the Afrika Korps have achieved in Russia if they had not been in North Africa?

El Alamein was a smaller battle than those simultaneously underway on the eastern front. It was about the scale of many of the larger battles of the Napoleonic period and American Civil War. The personalities of the rival commanders – Rommel and Montgomery – loom large for that reason. Britain's land war in North Africa had been marred by disappointments prior to Montgomery's victory at El Alamein. It took the British Army overwhelming resources finally to overturn past failures. The victory at El Alamein and the Eighth Army's subsequent advance to the west of Tripoli helped to trap Axis forces in Tunisia, with the cooperation of Allied forces landed in Morocco and Algeria.

Hitler could not lose the war in Africa, but the *Wehrmacht* could only win the war by knocking the Soviet Union to its knees. For Moscow the failed attempt to form an alliance with Germany from 1939–41 made it virtually impossible to reach any agreement that left Hitler and the Nazis in power. Hitler's offensive in southern Russia from June 1942 aimed at economic objectives, especially the oil of the Caucasus. This strategy showed a definite disregard for the Red Army, which had administered the Germans a heavy defeat before Moscow the previous winter. After impressive initial success, the German offensive could not make headway in the Caucasus Mountains. The simultaneous attempt to capture all of Stalingrad, instead of blockading the city like Leningrad, was a failure that drew German forces into an unnecessary urban battle. One of the themes of the Second World War is the rise of the urbanised battlefield. Remarkable little of the First World War had been fought within the great cities of Europe and the Middle East. The growing incidence of urban warfare reflected the headlong urbanisation of human society in the twentieth century.

Paulus's army was trapped in Stalingrad by a Soviet counter-offensive of unexpected strength. The final fall of the Stalingrad pocket was a military epic and a comprehensive German defeat. The failure of the 1942 eastern campaign proved Hitler wrong in his opinion that economic considerations were of overriding importance in the era of industrialised warfare. An enemy's army remained a more important immediate objective than the industry and raw materials supporting that army.

After the failure of the Stalingrad campaign, the Germans attempted to regain the initiative by undertaking another great offensive in the summer of 1943. The Kursk battle proved to be a ponderous and unimaginative attack by massed panzer formations. The Soviets were expecting the assault. The element of surprise that had been so important to successful *blitzkrieg*-style offensives was missing. Kursk made it clear that the Red Army had successfully redefined itself as an effective rival of the *Wehrmacht*.

The failed Kursk offensive had been preceded by the Axis capitulation in Tunisia and was interrupted by the Allied invasion of Sicily. The war in the Mediterranean had entered a new phase. German reserves would be needed to contain threats in that theatre and western Europe. Such reserves would no longer be available to shore up the eastern front at times of crisis.

With no land front in western Europe, in 1942–43 the British and Americans had supported the Soviets with a strategic bombing campaign over Germany and occupied Europe. The strategic bombing of an enemy's civilian society flew in the face of the Clausewitzian principle that an enemy's armed forces should be the main objective. But with the British driven off the Continent, bombing was the only way directly to hit back at Germany from bases in the United Kingdom. The Axis bombing of Warsaw, Rotterdam, London and the cities of China had set a precedent for the indiscriminate bombing of urban populations. Nonetheless, there was an experimental dimension to the strategic bombing of Germany. It was difficult to know ahead of time how civilian society and industry would cope with massive air bombardment on an unprecedented scale.

During 1943 the levels of damage inflicted by the RAF's Bomber Command on the Ruhr towns and Hamburg provided genuine cause for optimism that the technical challenges of night bombing could be mastered. The decision to attempt the devastation of Berlin across the winter of 1943–44 was intimately linked with the ambition of RAF commanders to prove that strategic bombing was a decisive weapon of war. The story of the bombing of Berlin highlighted the perils of flying deep into Germany, but bombing results against the Third Reich's capital and nearby cities were generally poor.

Bomber Command continued the saturation bombing of German cities during the last winter of the war. In a bid to bomb supply and communications centres behind the eastern front, Dresden was struck on the night of 13/14 February 1945. 50,000 civilians died in the raid. The Dresden attack was a fluke in its effectiveness, but it was what Bomber Harris had hoped to achieve on many occasions over the previous three years, especially in relation to Berlin. The failures of the winter bombing campaign of 1943–44 are important to understanding why Harris was so determined to resume 'city-busting' in the following winter of 1944–45. He still wanted to prove that Bomber Command could achieve decisive results. It is difficult to say to what extent saturation bombing mobilised and energised German society behind an apocalyptic Nazi war effort. German boys and old men under the bombs of 1942–43 became the soldiers of 1944–45. The Bolshevik threat was still distant when bombing was real. For Germans on the home front, without direct experience or even knowledge of the excesses of the Nazi regime, total war was something that came to them from the skies.

An Anglo-American invasion of western Europe was necessary to defeat Germany. Before landings in France could be undertaken the Allies had to win long and difficult campaigns at sea in the Atlantic and in the skies of France. The assault on the beaches of Normandy on 6 June 1944 was a hazardous *enterprise*, but once ashore it was a matter of the Allies piling men and equipment into their bridgehead until the pressure of numerical superiority burst the dam of the German defensive front. The Anglo-American armies in Normandy were heavily equipped. To counter that a large panzer force had to be committed to the defence of France. This split German armoured forces between east and west at a time when the *Wehrmacht* could least afford that.

Operation Bagration, the Soviet summer offensive in Russia for 1944, is the lesser known twin to the famous Normandy landings. The swift collapse of the *Wehrmacht's* Army Group Centre, and its flight to Poland, left Nazi grand strategy in ruins. Hitler's refusal to permit retreat in Normandy meant that the German army in the west was also hammered to pieces, though not before the Germans gave a fine fighting performance in the face of massive Allied firepower and the best troops the western Allies could muster. France was liberated in 1944 almost as rapidly as it had been conquered in 1940.

By early 1945 disaster was facing Nazi Germany. In the spring Hitler retreated to a bunker beneath central Berlin. In April the final Soviet offensive broke the German defensive front along the River Oder. The Red Army swiftly went on to surround Berlin, as there was no German strategic reserve covering the capital. There were fewer than 100,000 defenders in Berlin, a small fraction of the *Wehrmacht's* strength. The personal drama of the deaths of Hitler, Eva Braun and the Goebbels family mirrored and obscured the unrecorded similar fate of many Germans during this period. Hitler would not be spending his last years on St Helena like Napoleon Bonaparte. The ruins of Berlin were the only permissible shrine to National Socialism. Hitler received no triumphal monuments like those of Napoleon in Paris, though the Führer's psychological presence for Germans after 1945 has proved to be immense.

Germany's struggle for a dominating position on the world stage had ended. The Soviet handover of much of Berlin to the western allies, and Soviet cooperation regarding the occupation zones of Germany, should serve as a reminder that the Cold War lay in the future in 1945. The Soviets and the Anglo-Americans kept to many of the main agreements confirmed at high-level meetings at Yalta and Potsdam. The Anglo-American alliance with the Soviets was one of the more unlikely of history's coalitions. But, as Churchill was to say, 'There is only one thing worse than fighting with allies, and that is fighting without them!' The Grand Alliance had come together out of a need for survival, and its ongoing unity had owed much to a shared desire to inflict severe punishment upon Germany. Allied leaders were determined there would be no third war fought over the question of Germany's place in the world. After the Yalta meeting Roosevelt had said that the Germans needed to 'begin to re-establish themselves as people whom the world might accept as decent neighbours'.[7] After 1918 the victorious powers had made an effort to reabsorb Germany into a stable international order. That effort had failed and matters would be approached differently after the Second World War.

In 1945 Germany was divided into four occupation zones, one each for the Soviets, Americans, British and French. The occupation was projected to last as long as necessary to remove all vestiges of Nazism and militarism from the German people. In addition to partition, Germany permanently lost a great deal of its eastern territories. This was because the Soviets had wanted to move Poland's 1939 eastern frontier westwards, as eastern Poland was largely inhabited by Soviet nationalities. In compensation the Soviets proposed to the Anglo-Americans that the western frontier of Poland be pushed, at Germany's expense, as far west as the River Oder and the western arm of the Neisse river. East Prussia was to disappear from the map, half going to Poland and half to the Soviets. The Poles also received Silesia and Pomerania. Stalin had pointed out at the Yalta conference that German civilians were fleeing from the Third Reich's eastern territories anyway. Churchill agreed there would be room for a certain number of repatriated Germans in other parts of the country, as millions of Germans would be dead by the war's end.[8] The 1945 settlement simplified eastern European geography. This was a reaction against the way the 1919 settlement had created so many complications in that region.

The land redistribution in eastern Europe caused over nine million Germans east of the Oder–Neisse line, three and a half million Sudeten Germans in Czechoslovakia and hundreds of thousands of Germans in south-east Europe to flee or be relocated to the remainder of occupied Germany.[9] Hitler had used the presence of German minorities in Czechoslovakia and Poland as pretexts for invasion. Therefore no eastern European state was willing to run the risk of

Germans continuing to reside on their soil. German lands lost to Poland and other lost lands in the east were comparable in size to the future East Germany. Over two million Germans died in the chaos of the expulsions and deportations. Cities such as Konigsberg, Danzig and Breslau were emptied of their remaining German inhabitants. Slavic colonists took over German territory, rather than the other way around, as had been intended by the Nazis.

The ethnic cleansing of German lands east of the Oder–Neisse line was in keeping with an Allied desire to destroy Prussia, which was the largest state within Germany. This was a central part of the programme to erase militarism from Germany. Prussia, and the eastern Prussian lands stretching from Berlin to the Baltic coast in particular, was viewed in Allied capitals as the core of the professional German Army, and the cradle of a military tradition stretching back to the eighteenth century. The Prussian state had unified and created a centralised German state on the Prussian model that had waged two world wars. A state created by the sword had gone on to live by the sword. The professional military officers of the Prussian tradition had been willing and effective agents of Nazism. The two camps had become irrevocably intertwined. When the Allied Control Council formally abolished the Prussian state in February 1947 it was denounced as 'the bearer of militarism and reaction in Germany'.

The Allies had treated the eastern Prussian lands as the Romans had treated Carthage. After over a century of bitter warfare, Rome had destroyed Carthage after the city's capture in 146 BC. Carthage, in the north of modern Tunis, had been levelled to the ground by the victorious legions and the surviving population cast into slavery. The Carthaginian state had been annihilated and the Phoenicians of Carthage lost their identity as they were assimilated into neighbouring populations.[10] The fate of eastern Prussia was not very different. Prussian provinces west of the Elbe were given autonomy or made part of other administrative units. The Prussian soldier-philosopher Clausewitz had written that in war the result is never final, but there has never been another war over Germany, Prussia or Carthage.

The partitioned, postwar Germany was remade alone the lines of western-liberal and eastern-Communist ideologies. West Germany – the unified American, British and French occupation zones – was integrated with the western powers economically, politically and militarily. West Germany was given a federal constitution that was in keeping with the 'federative' character of the German states prior to the 1860s.[11] East Germany – the Soviet occupation zone – became part of the Soviet bloc. The need for vigilance against the Communists of eastern Europe gave Nazi Germany and West Germany an important common philosophical thread. The dictatorship that governed East Germany also had obvious links to a totalitarian past, though the regime claimed the opposite.

The Nazi period was a unique period in German history, but it was not disconnectedly unique. Rather the Nazi period was the extreme third act in a three act play about the place of a unified and centralised German state in Europe and the world. In the wars of 1864–71, the First World War and the Second World War, Germany's Prussian or Prussified-Nazi leadership had chosen warfare to secure it a glorious future. The irreversible defeat of 1945 changed the nature of the German state and leadership cadre to bring about the realisation that if the German people chose to live in harmony with their neighbours there was an excellent chance of that happening. As it transpired, the German anxiety to project power globally, some of which had been caused by unflattering comparisons to the British and French, was solved in part by the fact that the British and French empires crumbled away post-1945. All the former European 'great powers' came to share a legacy of decline. Increasingly the West Germans would come to share the English language with the Americans and British, which has led to a high degree of cultural convergence.

The war in Europe had ended with great finality, but meanwhile the war in Asia and the Pacific had taken a different course. Washington had possessed sufficient industrial strength to build a fleet of new aircraft carriers for Pacific service by 1944. In the Philippines Sea a much larger American carrier force had been able to shatter Japanese naval aviation. The Americans had quickly moved on to invade the Philippines. At the Battle of Leyte Gulf in October 1944 the United States Navy won command of the Pacific, the world's greatest ocean.

The American military began to prepare for an invasion of Japan, but the extraordinary invention of the atomic bomb cut across events in July 1945. The appearance of the atomic bomb was the most sudden increase in the power of weaponry in recorded history. Gunpowder had taken several generations to transform western warfare. Even powered flight had taken a single generation to become an important part of modern warfare. The hypothetical question as to whether the atomic bomb would have been used against Nazi Germany has little meaning, as the atomic bomb had not been available at the start of 1945.

The atomic bomb had been built to be dropped and the destruction of Hiroshima and Nagasaki brought about the rapid surrender of Japan. Since the war the Japanese people have felt aggrieved to have been subjected to atomic warfare. But the mushroom clouds over Hiroshima and Nagasaki were needed to make the Japanese government release its grip on China, Korea and South-East Asia, a region containing a significant portion of the human race. There was nothing diplomatic about the extreme violence of an atomic bombing, but, ironically, it soon brought about the resumption of diplomatic relations between bitter enemies. In the decades since 1945 the possibility of the use of nuclear weapons has continued to be the cause of a great deal of diplomatic discussion. The introduction of nuclear technology into human warfare was bound to be a fraught period. The hammering into submission of the Axis, to destroy those regimes just in time for the dawn of nuclear warfare, was a great stroke of good fortune for the international system of states.

That Japan was not invaded made the Japanese capitulation quite different from that of Germany. Japanese forces were still occupying large parts of eastern Asia at the time of their surrender. The American victory over Japan was primarily dependent on naval power. Victory in the Pacific war did not give Washington its way inland from the coast of east Asia. Indeed the spoils of the Asian mainland after the defeat of Japan fell largely to the Communists, who were soon to be America's enemy. The failure of American forces to secure a land victory in Asia during the Second World War meant that the United States was unable to remake the Asian mainland. The American-led defeat of Japan merely secured the Japanese evacuation of eastern Asia, important though that was. Millions of Japanese troops returned from the Asia-Pacific region in Allied transports to be demobilised in the occupied home islands. The United States of the 1940s is sometimes seen as a nation so powerful that all plans could be fulfilled simultaneously. The saving of Nationalist China, however, was beyond the scope of American resources and political will. American involvement in future wars in Korea and Vietnam followed on from the Western failure to win a dominating influence over the east Asian mainland in 1945.

The need for victory in the Second World War was immensely important to both the Allies and Axis. Germany and Japan are today among the largest economies in the world, which suggests that the dreams of their wartime leaderships for an enduring world power status had plenty of foundation. Early twentieth-century German and Japanese governments had a strong sense that their nations were on an upward trajectory. That sense of destiny was shared by a large part of the population. The economic power of Germany and Japan was such that if an Axis bloc could have been established, in a stalemated Second World War, there was no likelihood of an internal economic collapse, such as would one day overtake the Soviet Union. The Anglo-Americans and the Soviet Union had to win the war against the Axis by military means to secure the survival of their respective systems.

The international system of states has functioned more smoothly since 1945 precisely because a severe and paralysing defeat was inflicted upon Germany and Japan. That the German and Japanese peoples have cooperated in the transformation of their societies since 1945 is largely due to the depth of their military defeat. The removal of an unstable and uncooperative France from the front rank of international decision-makers has also been vital for the harmony of the international system. For Washington, the Second World War brought about the full realisation that there cannot be a stable global order without the strongest nation in the world playing a major role in most facets of international affairs. The collapse of Britain as an empire in the postwar period was managed without a general cataclysm, though great trauma was suffered in northern India and other places. To an appreciable extent Britain and parts of the former empire have found a useful new role supporting the American imperium.

The Allied victory of 1945 brought partly to a close the 'era of tyrannies' unleashed by the chaotic aftermath to the First World War. Nazism and fascism had been defeated in Europe, though it would take another two generations before Communism was sufficiently discredited to give the constitutional state an ascendant position in the international system.[12] The Cold War necessary to purge the world of Communism would be waged more by economic than by military means. This was fortuitous but certainly not accidental. The costs of a full-scale nuclear war between east and west were a definite and sufficient deterrent. Another reason the Cold War never became hot was that fundamentally east and west were satisfied by the deal they had struck to pacify Germany and expel Japan from the Asian mainland. Anglo-American and Soviet forces garrisoned in divided Germany until the 1980s had a shared legacy of the victory won in 1945. The decisive nature of the Grand Alliance's victory in the Second World War settled many important disputes – past, present and future – with great finality.

39 Germany and Poland, 1 September 1939
(See Chapter 1)

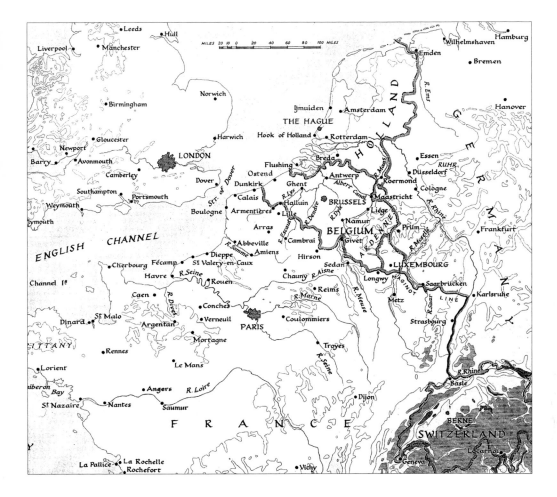

40 Western Europe in 1940.
(See Chapter 2)

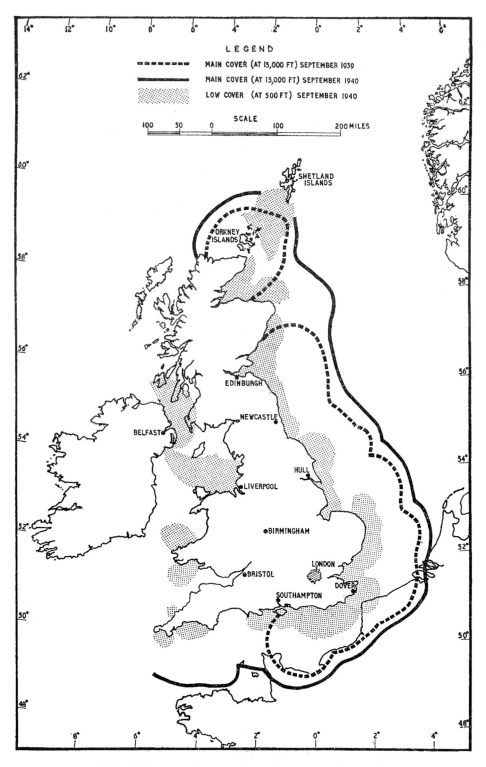

41 United Kingdom radar cover, September 1939 and September 1940
(See Chapter 3)

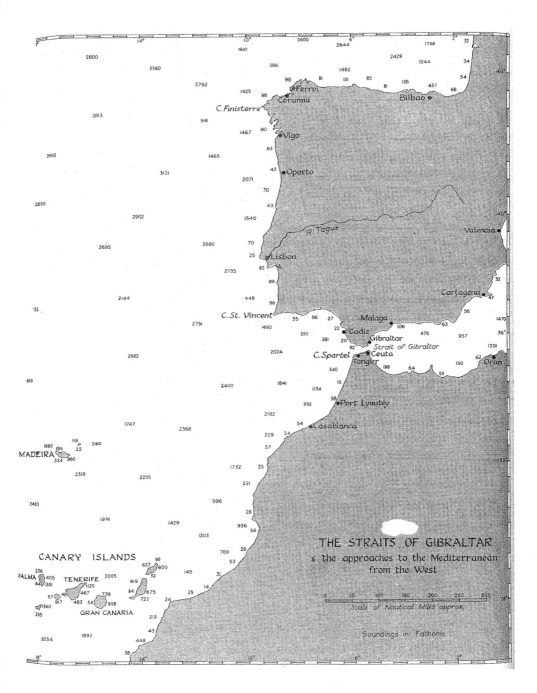

42 The Straits of Gibraltar
(See Chapter 4)

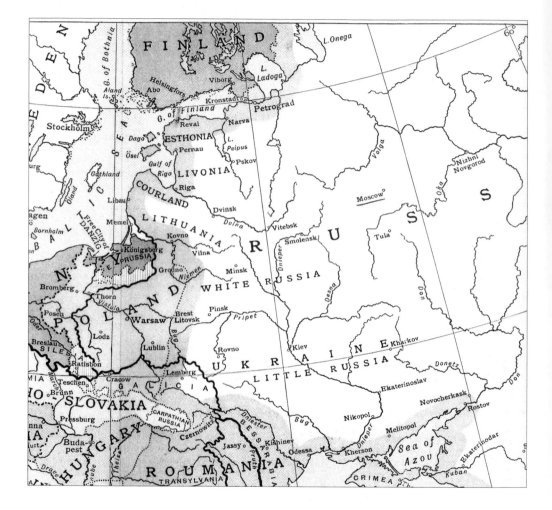

43 Barbarossa, 1941
(See Chapter 5)

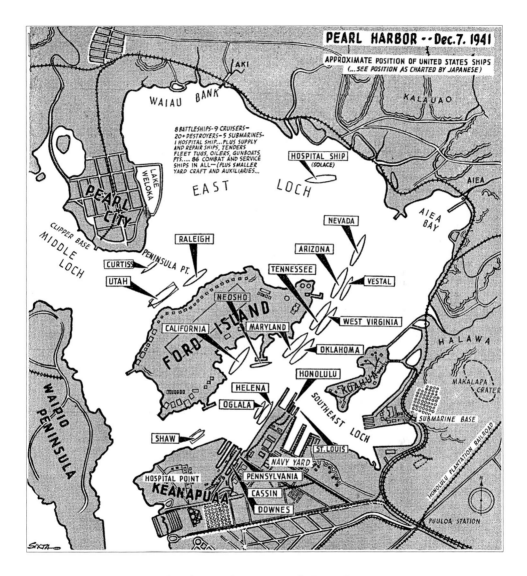

44 Pearl Harbor on the morning of 7 December 1941
(See Chapter 6)

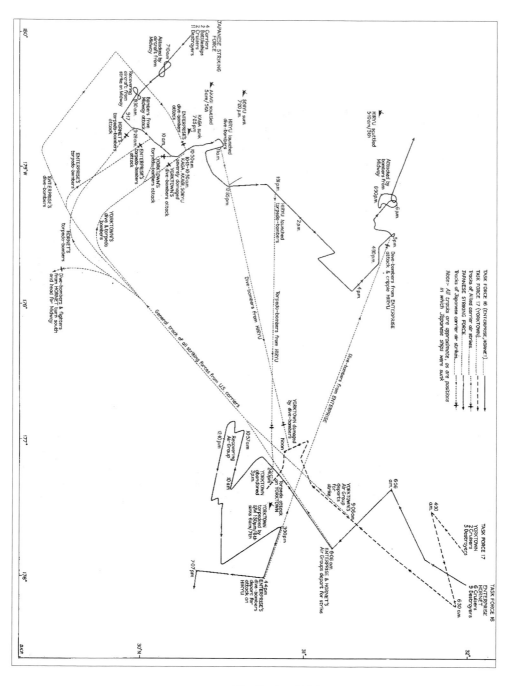

45 The Battle of Midway
(See Chapter 7)

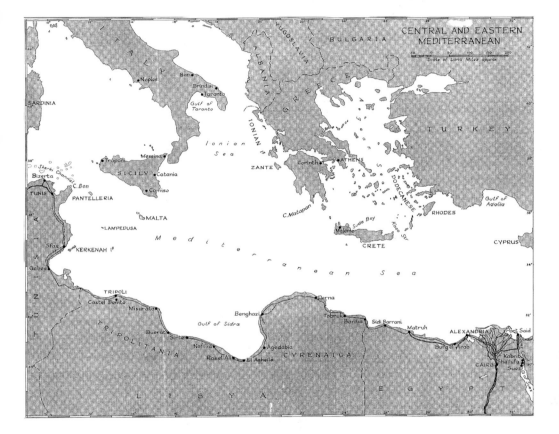

46 The Mediterranean Theatre
(See Chapter 8)

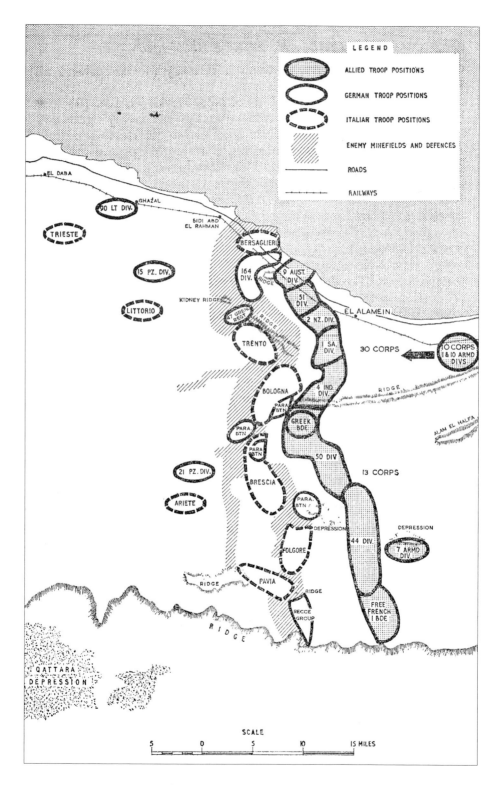

47 The position at El Alamein, 23 October 1942
(See Chapter 8)

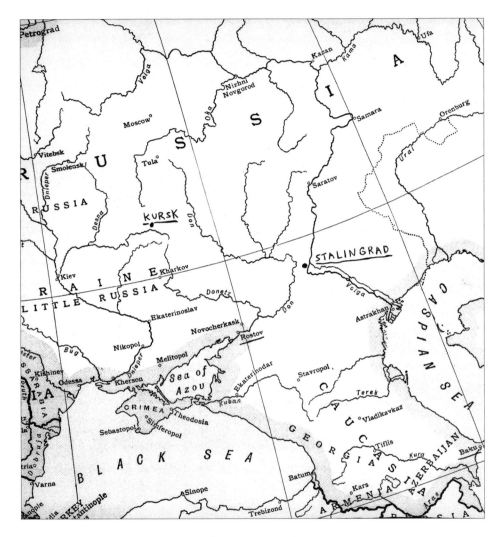

48 Stalingrad and Kursk
(See Chapters 9 and 10)

49 Strategic bombing
(See Chapter 11)

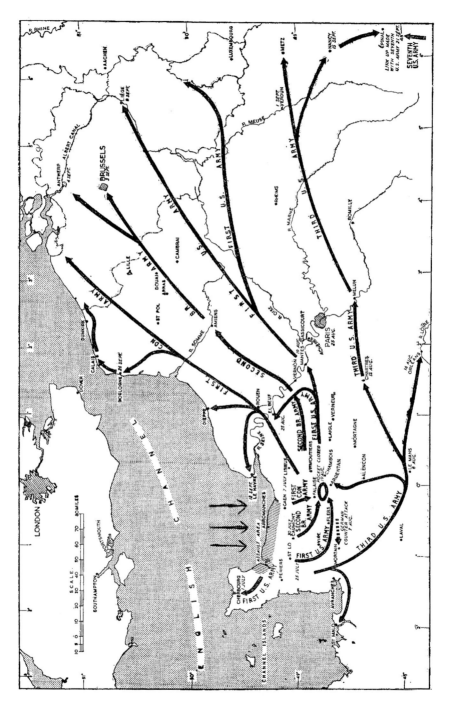

50 Battle for France, 1944
(See Chapter 12)

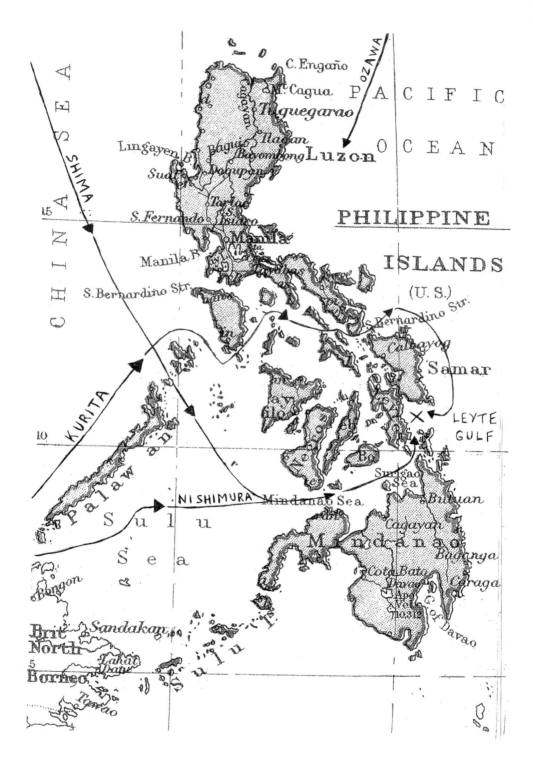

51 Battle of Leyte Gulf: Philippines, October 1944
(See Chapter 13)

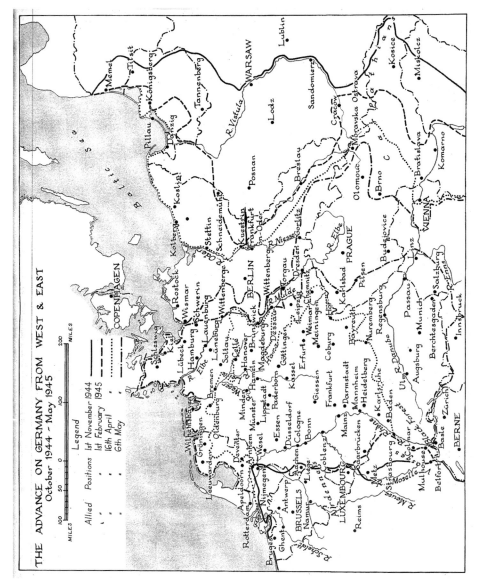

52 The advance on Berlin, 1945
(See Chapter 14)

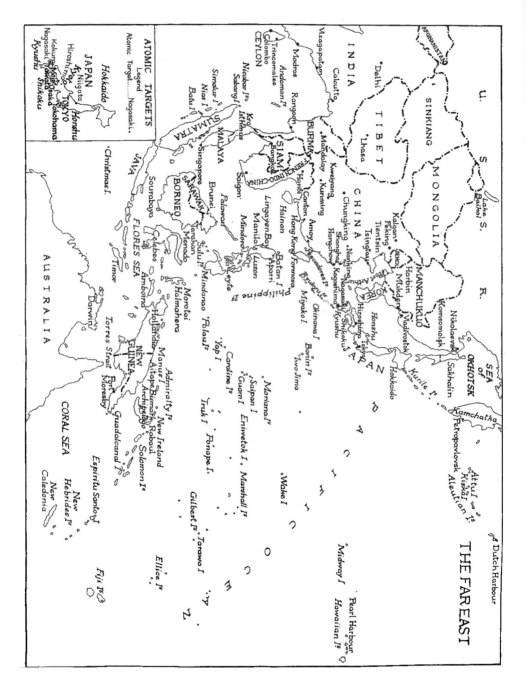

53 The Far East
(See Chapter 15)

Notes

Preface

1. A. Speer, *Inside the Third Reich* (New York, 1970), p. 132.
2. H.R. Trevor-Roper, *Hitler's Table Talk, 1941–44* (London, 1973), p. 99.
3. Speer, *Inside the Third Reich*, p. 171.
4. Ibid., p. 172.
5. Telfold Taylor, *The March of Conquest* (London, 1959), p. 323.
6. G.E. Rothenberg, *The Napoleonic Wars* (London, 1999), p. 20.
7. H.W. Koch (ed.), *The Origins of the First World War* (London, 1984), p. 10.
8. Katharine A. Lerman, 'Wilhelmine Germany', in M. Fulbrook (ed.), *German History since 1870* (London, 1997), pp. 221–22.

Chapter 1: The Invasion of Poland

1. A. Seaton, *The German Army, 1933–45* (London, 1982), pp. 4–5.
2. Ibid., p. 8; W. Murray, 'Armoured Warfare: The British, French, and German Experiences', in W. Murray and A.R. Millett (eds), *Military Innovation in the Interwar Period* (Cambridge, 1996), p. 39; W. Murray, *The Change in the European Balance of Power, 1938–39* (Princeton, 1984), p. 31.
3. H. Guderian, *Achtung Panzer* (London, 1995), p. 24.
4. Robin Prior and Trevor Wilson, *The First World War* (London, 2000), p. 181.
5. Murray, 'Armoured Warfare', pp. 26, 38–41; H. Guderian, *Panzer Leader* (Washington, 1952), p. 45.
6. B. Bond, *Liddell Hart: A Study of his Military Thought* (New Brunswick, New Jersey, 1977), pp. 220–27.
7. Adolf Hitler, *Mein Kampf* (London, 1939), p. 363; Murray, 'Armoured Warfare', p. 17.
8. F.K. Mason, *Battle Over Britain* (London, 1969), pp. 55–57; W. Murray, *Luftwaffe: Strategy for Defeat, 1933–45* (London, 1985), pp. 21–24.
9. Murray, *Luftwaffe*, pp. 37–39.
10. Hugh Thomas, *The Spanish Civil War* (London, 1988), p. 829.
11. Ibid., pp. 370, 463, 624, 977, 984.
12. Murray, *European Balance of Power*, pp. 41–43.
13. Jan Karski, *The Great Powers and Poland, 1919–1945* (London, 1985), p. 279.
14. Murray, *European Balance of Power*, p. 48.
15. Karski, *The Great Powers and Poland*, p. 281.
16. Ibid., p. 355.
17. Seaton, *The German Army*, p. 113.
18. F.W. von Mellenthin, *Panzer Battles, 1939–1945* (London, 1955), p. 4.
19. J.B. Cynk, *History of the Polish Air Force, 1918–1968* (Reading, 1972), p. 122.
20. R.M. Kennedy, *The German Campaign in Poland* (Washington, 1956), p. 48.
21. S. Zaloga and V. Madej, *The Polish Campaign, 1939* (New York, 1985), pp. 7–9.
22. Ibid., p. 18.
23. Cynk, *Polish Air Force*, p. 122.

24 Zaloga and Madej, *The Polish Campaign*, pp. 50, 82, 88–89.

25 R.M.Watt, *Bitter Glory: Poland and its Fate, 1918 to 1939* (New York, 1979), p. 417.

26 Zaloga and Madej, *The Polish Campaign*, p. 29.

27 Ibid., pp. 44, 76.

28 Ibid., p. 119; Kennedy, *The German Campaign in Poland*, pp. 81–82; B.Watts and W. Murray, 'Military Innovation in Peacetime', in Murray and Millett, *Military Innovation in the Interwar Period*, p. 374.

29 Watt, *Bitter Glory: Poland and its Fate*, p. 423.

30 W.Anders, *An Army in Exile* (London, 1949), p. 3.

31 Kennedy, *The German Campaign in Poland*, pp. 102–8.

32 M. Gilbert, *Second World War* (London, 1989), p. 9.

33 J. Erickson, 'The Red Army's March into Poland, September 1939', and R. Szawlowski, 'The Polish-Soviet War of 1939', in K. Sword (ed.), *The Soviet Take-Over of the Polish Eastern Provinces, 1939–41* (London, 1991), pp. 12, 1718, 31–32.

34 Karski, *The Great Powers and Poland,* p. 288; Szawlowski, 'The Polish-Soviet War', p. 32; Zaloga and Madej, *The Polish Campaign*, p. 157.

35 Karski, *The Great Powers and Poland*, p. 392.

36 Kennedy, *The German Campaign in Poland*, p. 113.

37 Karski, *The Great Powers and Poland*, pp. 212–18, 236.

38 Ibid., pp. 329, 331; G.L.Weinberg, *A World at Arms* (Cambridge, 1994), p. 50.

39 N. Bethell, *The War Hitler Won* (London, 1972), p. 91.

40 Ibid., p. 35.

41 Karski, *The Great Powers and Poland*, pp. 329–31.

42 A. Horne, *To Lose a Battle: France, 1940* (London, 1969), pp. 127–29.

43 Bethell, *The War Hitler Won*, p. 119.

44 Watt, *Bitter Glory: Poland and its Fate*, p. 431.

45 Mellenthin, *Panzer Battles*, p. 9.

46 W.S. Churchill, *The Second World War*, ii (London, 1949), p. 49.

47 W.L. Shirer, *Berlin Diary* (London, 1941), pp. 160–62.

48 Gilbert, *Second World War*, p. 18.

49 S.W. Roskill, *The War at Sea, 1939–1945*, i (London, 1954), p. 106; W.S. Churchill, *The Second World War*, i (London, 1948), p. 354; Correlli Barnett, *Engage the Enemy More Closely: The Royal Navy in the Second World War* (New York, 1991), p. 66.

50 Roskill, *The War at Sea*, i, pp. 73–74, 105–6.

51 K.A. Maier, H. Rohde, B. Stegemann, H. Umbreit, *Germany and the Second World War*, ii (Oxford, 1991), p. 214.

52 E. von Manstein, *Lost Victories* (Chicago, 1958), p. 61.

53 Maier, Rohde, Stegemann, Umbreit, *Germany and the Second World War*, ii, p. 214.

54 Guderian, *Panzer Leader*, p. 73.

55 Erickson, 'The Red Army's March into Poland', p. 22; B.R. Kroener, R. Muller, H. Umbreit, *Germany and the Second World War*, v, part 1 (Oxford, 2000), p. 730.

56 Cynk, *History of the Polish Air Force*, p. 149; Zaloga and Madej, *The Polish Campaign*, p. 148.

57 Gilbert, *Second World War*, p. 19.

58 C. Burdick and H. Jacobsen (eds), *The Halder War Diaries, 1939–1942* (Novato, California, 1988), p. 52.

59 A.B. Rossino, *Hitler Strikes Poland* (Lawrence, Kansas, 2003), pp. 22, 120, 163–64.

60 Ibid., pp. xiii, 1.

61 Szawlowski, 'The Polish-Soviet War', p. 31.

62 Gilbert, *Second World War*, p. 11; Weinberg, *A World at Arms*, p. 96.

63 Rossino, *Hitler Strikes Poland*, p. 234.

64 Murray, 'Armoured Warfare', p. 40.

65 Kennedy, *The German Campaign in Poland*, p. 134.

Chapter 2: The Fall of France

1 R. Boyce (ed.), *French Foreign and Defence Policy, 1918–1940* (London, 1998), p. 183.

2 W. Murray, 'Armoured Warfare: The British, French and German Experiences', in W. Murray and A.R. Millett (eds), *Military Innovation in the Interwar Period* (Cambridge, 1996), p. 14.

3 A. Horne, *To Lose a Battle: France 1940* (London, 1969), pp. 52, 121.

4 Telford Taylor, *The March of Conquest* (London, 1959), p. 158.

5 M. Gilbert, *Second World War* (London, 1989), p. 30.

6 Taylor, *The March of Conquest*, pp. 170–72.

7 Ibid., p. 175.

8 W.D. Irvine, 'Domestic Politics and the Fall of France in 1940', in *Historical Reflections*, 22 (1996), pp. 79, 87.

9 J.A. Gunsburg, *Divided and Conquered: The French High Command and the Defeat of the West, 1940* (London, 1979), p. 103.

10 Ibid., p. 88; J. Jackson, *The Fall of France* (Oxford, 2003), p. 158; E.C. Kiesling, *Arming Against Hitler: France and the Limits of Military Planning* (Lawrence, Kansas, 1996), p. 39.

11 A. Bryant, *The Turn of the Tide, 1939–1943* (London, 1957), p. 71.

12 E. Kier, *Imagining War: French and British Military Doctrine between the Wars* (Princeton, 1997), p. 73; C.A. Kupchan, *The Vulnerability of Empire* (Ithaca, New York, 1994), p. 231.

13 Horne, *To Lose a Battle*, p. 134; Kiesling, *Arming Against Hitler*, p. 82.

14 Horne, *To Lose a Battle*, p. 150.

15 Ibid., p. 152; Kiesling, *Arming Against Hitler*, p. 235.

16 M.S. Alexander, 'Prophet Without Honour?: The French High Command and Pierre Taittinger's Report on the Ardennes Defences, March 1940', *War and Society*, May 1986, p. 55.

17 W. Murray, *The Change in the European Balance of Power, 1938–1939* (Princeton, 1984), p. 20. In 1935 the figures for Germany, France and Britain were 8, 5.7 and 3.3 per cent respectively. Kiesling, *Arming Against Hitler*, p. 149.

18 French tank production had risen from 403 in 1938 to 1059 in 1939 and to 854 in the first half of 1940. Murray, 'Armoured Warfare', pp. 13–14; J. Jackson, '1940 and the Crisis of Interwar Democracy in France', in M.S. Alexander (ed.), *French History since Napoleon* (London, 1999), pp. 234–35.

19 K.A. Maier, H. Rohde, B. Stegemann, H. Umbreit, *Germany and the Second World War*, ii (Oxford, 1991), pp. 274, 279.

20 E.A. Cohen and J. Gooch, *Military Misfortunes: The Anatomy of Failure in War* (New York, 1990), p. 211.

21 Jackson, *The Fall of France*, pp. 15–16; J.A. Gunsburg, 'The Battle of the Belgian Plain, 12–14 May 1940: The First Great Tank Battle', *The Journal of Military History*, April 1992, p. 213.

22 Horne, *To Lose a Battle*, p. 218.

23 L.F. Ellis, *The War in France and Flanders, 1939–1940* (London, 1953), p. 19.

24 J.P. Harris, 'British Armour and Rearmament in the 1930s', *The Journal of Strategic Studies*, June 1988, pp. 220–22.

25 Murray, 'Armoured Warfare', p. 28; B. Bond, *British Military Policy between the Two World Wars* (Oxford, 1980), pp. 159, 170–75; Ellis, *The War in France and Flanders*, p. 322.

26 B. Bond, *France and Belgium, 1939-1940* (London, 1975), p. 40.

27 B. Collier, *The Defence of the United Kingdom* (London, 1957), p. 78.

28 A.S. Milward, *The New Order and the French Economy* (Oxford, 1970), p. 37; Murray, *European Balance of Power*, pp. 106–7.

29 Maier, Rohde, Stegemann, Umbreit, *Germany and the Second World War*, ii, pp. 269, 279; Jackson, *The Fall of France*, p. 15.

30 Bond, *France and Belgium*, p. 77; Taylor, *The March of Conquest*, pp. 60–61.

31 Cohen and Gooch, *Military Misfortunes*, p. 202; Horne, *To Lose a Battle*, p. 164.

32 Horne, *To Lose a Battle*, pp. 233–34; F.H. Hinsley, *British Intelligence in the Second World War*, i (London, 1979), pp. 62, 134.

33 Hinsley, *British Intelligence*, i, p. 134.

34 Horne, *To Lose a Battle*, pp. 215–16.

35 B.A. Lee, 'Strategy, Arms and the Collapse of France, 1930–40', in R. Langhorne (ed.), *Diplomacy and Intelligence during the Second World War* (Cambridge, 1985), p. 52.

36 A. Seaton, *The German Army, 1933–45* (London, 1982), pp. 127, 138; Horne, *To Lose a Battle*, p. 217.

37 Seaton, *The German Army*, p. 128.

38 Remy, *The Eighteenth Day: The Tragedy of King Leopold III of Belgium* (New York, 1978), pp. 23–29.

39 Horne, *To Lose a Battle*, p. 256; Gilbert, *Second World War*, p. 62.

40 J. Keegan, *The Second World War* (London, 1989), p. 67.

41 Horne, *To Lose a Battle*, p. 223.

42 Ibid., pp. 311–12.

43 H. Guderian, *Panzer Leader* (Washington, 1952), p. 90.

44 W. Murray and A.R. Millett, *A War to Be Won* (Cambridge, Mass., 2000), p. 70; Horne, *To Lose a Battle*, p. 301.

45 Horne, *To Lose a Battle*, p. 329.

4 B.H. Liddell Hart, *History of the Second World War* (London, 1970), p. 79.

47 Horne, *To Lose a Battle*, p. 362.

48 B.H. Liddell Hart (ed.), *The Rommel Papers* (London, 1953), pp. xiii-xix.

49 Horne, *To Lose a Battle*, p. 374.

50 D. Richards, *Royal Air Force, 1939–1945*, i (London, 1953), p. 120.

51 A. Beaufre, *1940: The Fall of France* (London, 1967), p. 183.

52 Gunsburg, 'The Battle of the Belgian Plain', pp. 210–12.

53 Ibid., pp. 213, 230–32.

54 Ibid., pp. 241–42.

55 Horne, *To Lose a Battle*, p. 406.

56 Gilbert, *Second World War*, p. 64.

57 W.S. Churchill, *The Second World War*, ii (London, 1949), p. 52.

58 C. Burdick and H. Jacobsen (eds), *The Halder War Diary, 1939–1942* (Novato, California, 1988), p. 149; B.H. Liddell Hart, *The German Generals Talk* (New York, 1948), p. 128.

59 B. Watts and W. Murray, 'Military Innovation in Peacetime', in Murray and Millett, *Military Innovation in the Interwar Period*, p. 382.

60 Horne, *To Lose a Battle*, p. 542.

61 R. Macleod (ed.), *The Ironside Diaries, 1937–1940* (London, 1962), p. 321.

62 Horne, *To Lose a Battle*, p. 611.

63 Seaton, *The German Army*, p. 142.

64 Burdick and Jacobsen, *The Halder War Diary*, p. 167.

65 Taylor, *The March of Conquest*, p. 264.

66 Ellis, *The War in France and Flanders*, p. 214.

67 Churchill, *The Second World War*, ii, p. 94.

68 Gilbert, *Second World War*, pp. 76–78; Murray and Millett, *A War to be Won*, p. 80; Ellis, *The War in France and Flanders*, p. 244; Taylor, *The March of Conquest*, pp. 266–73.

69 Bond, *France and Belgium*, p. 152.

70 Ellis, *The War in France and Flanders*, p. 220; A. Kesselring, *The Memoirs of Field-Marshal Kesselring* (London, 1953), p. 59; Richards, *Royal Air Force*, i, p. 140.

71 Ellis, *The War in France and Flanders*, p. 321; Taylor, *The March of Conquest*, p. 266.

72 Marc Bloch, *Strange Defeat* (New York, 1999), p. 20.

73 Ellis, *The War in France and Flanders*, pp. 246–48; S.W. Roskill, *The War at Sea, 1939–1945*, i (London, 1954), pp. 228, 603.

74 Churchill, *Second World War*, ii, p. 108.

75 K. Gerbert (ed.), *Generalfeldmarschall Fedor von Bock: The War Diary, 1939–1945* (Atglen, *Pennsylvania*, 1996), p. 162.

76 Beaufre, *1940: The Fall of France*, p. 200; Liddell Hart, *Second World War*, p. 90.

77 Ellis, *The War in France and Flanders*, pp. 304–5.

78 Gilbert, *Second World War*, p. 89.

79 R.J.Young, *In Command of France* (Cambridge, Massachuetts, 1978), p. 252.

80 W.L. Shirer, *Berlin Diary* (London, 1941), p. 323.

81 Boyce, *French Foreign and Defence Policy*, p. 1.

82 Horne, *To Lose a Battle*, pp. 649–50; Ellis, *The War in France and Flanders*, p. 326.

83 M.S.Alexander,'"No Taste for the Fight"?: French Combat Performance in 1940 and the Politics of the Fall of France', in P.Addison and A. Calder (eds), *Time to Kill* (London, 1997), p. 174. In 1968 Belgium's Historical Services of the Army estimated that the 1940 campaign had caused 5481 military deaths and another 6,552 civilian deaths.W.Warmbrunn, *The German Occupation of Belgium, 1940–1944* (New York, 1993), p. 47.

84 Ellis, *The War in France and Flanders*, pp. 326–27; Horne, *To Lose a Battle*, p. 650.

85 Maier, Rohde, Stegemann, Umbreit, *Germany and the Second World War*, ii, p. 290; Liddell Hart, *The Rommel Papers*, p. 84.

86 Murray, *European Balance of Power*, pp. 24, 36.

87 Richards, *Royal Air Force*, i, pp. 149–50.

88 Murray and Millett, *A War to be Won*, p. 52.

89 Milward, *New Order and the French Economy*, pp. 1–21.

90 Murray, *European Balance of Power*, pp. 15–16.

91 Ibid., p. 13.

92 Milward, *New Order and the French Economy*, p. 39.

93 Ibid., pp. 76, 111–12. In the summer of 1943 the number of Belgian workers in Germany was 250–300,000.Warmbrunn, *The German Occupation of Belgium*, p. 237.

94 M.S.Alexander,'The Fall of France, 1940', *The Journal of Strategic Studies*

Chapter 3: The Battle of Britain

1 L. Deighton, *Fighter* (London, 1977), p. 15.

2 J.R.M. Butler, *Grand Strategy*, ii (London, 1957), p. 271.

3 W. Deist, M. Messerschmidt, H.E.Volkmann,W.Wette, *Germany and the Second World War*, i (Oxford, 1990), p. 480.

4 K.A. Maier, H. Rohde, B. Stegemann, H. Umbreit, *Germany and the Second World War*, ii (Oxford, 1991), pp. 61, 156.

5 C. Bekker, *Hitler's Naval War* (London, 1974), p. 169.

6 Ibid., p. 174.

7 B. Collier, *The Defence of the United Kingdom* (London, 1957), pp. 175–76; B.H. Liddell Hart, *The German Generals Talk* (New York, 1948), p. 148.

8 Collier, *The Defence of the United Kingdom*, p. 182.

9 C. Burdick and H. Jacobsen (eds), *The Halder War Diary, 1939–1942* (Novato, California, 1988), pp. 235, 238.

10 Ibid., p. 240.

11 W.S. Churchill, *The Second World War*, ii (London, 1949), p. 226; N. Longmate, *Island Fortress* (London, 1991), p. 474; Collier, *The Defence of the United Kingdom*, pp. 124–30.

12 G.L.Weinberg, *A World at Arms* (Cambridge, 1994), pp. 143–44, 146.

13 Butler, *Grand Strategy*, ii, p. 227; A.J. Marder, *From Dardanelles to Oran* (London, 1974), p. 200.

14 Churchill, *The Second World War*, ii, p. 203.

15 R. Overy, *The Battle of Britain* (London, 2000), p. 29.

16 Asher Lee, *Goering: Air Leader* (London, 1972), p. 91.

17 Ibid., p. 92.

18 W. Murray, *The Change in the European Balance of Power, 1938–1939* (Princeton, 1984), p. 381.

19 Overy, *The Battle of Britain*, p. 30; S. Bungay, *The Most Dangerous Enemy* (London, 2000), p. 37 Deighton, *Fighter*, pp. 28–31.

20 W. Murray and A.R. Millett, *A War to be Won* (Cambridge, Massachusetts, 2000), p. 45.

21 W. Murray, *Luftwaffe: Strategy for Defeat,* 1933–45 (London, 1985), p. 77.

22 Overy, *The Battle of Britain*, p. 54.

23 Lee, *Goering*, pp. 92–94.

24 R. Overy, *The Air War,* 1939–1945 (London, 1980), pp. 15–25.

25 W. Murray, 'Innovation: Past and Future', in W. Murray and A.R. Millett, *Military Innovation in the Interwar Period* (Cambridge, 1996), pp. 306–7.

26 Overy, *The Battle of Britain*, p. 43; Deighton, *Fighter*, p. 117; A. Beyerchen, 'From Radio to Radar: Interwar Military Adaptation to Technological Change in Germany, the United Kingdom, and the United States', in Murray and Millett, *Military Innovation in the Interwar Period*, p. 269.

27 F.K. Mason, *Battle Over Britain* (London, 1969), pp. 61–64.

28 Ibid., p. 125; Overy, *The Battle of Britain*, p. 34; Lee, *Goering*, p. 101; Maier, Rohde, Stegemann, Umbreit, *Germany and the Second World War*, ii, pp. 381–82.

29 Murray, *Luftwaffe*, p. 84.

30 Deighton, *Fighter*, p. 128.

31 Ibid., p. 163.

32 Ibid., pp. 198, 203, 215, 250; D. Richards, *Royal Air Force,* 1939–1945, i (London, 1953), p. 165.

33 Lee, *Goering*, p. 107.

34 Maier, Rohde, Stegemann, Umbreit, *Germany and the Second World War*, ii, p. 385; Deighton, *Fighter*, p. 215; J. Terraine, *The Right of the Line* (London, 1985), p. 187.

35 Adolf Galland, *The First and the Last* (London, 1955), p. 68; Murray, *Luftwaffe*, p. 87.

36 V. Orange, *Air Chief Marshal Sir Keith Park* (London, 1984), p. 96.

37 Lee, *Goering*, p. 108; Burdick and Jacobsen, *The Halder War Diary*, p. 253.

38 Deighton, *Fighter*, p. 204.

39 Overy, *The Battle of Britain*, p. 87.

40 Deighton, *Fighter*, p. 253.

41 Overy, *The Air War*, pp. 32–34.

42 Bungay, *The Most Dangerous Enemy*, p. 239.

43 Mason, *Battle Over Britain*, p. 311; Orange, *Keith Park*, p. 103.

44 Bungay, *The Most Dangerous Enemy*, p. 191; Deighton, *Fighter*, p. 278; Terraine, *The Right of the Line*, p. 187.

45 Overy, *The Battle of Britain*, p. 88.

46 Deighton, *Fighter*, pp. 258–59; Orange, *Keith Park*, p. 107.

47 Collier, *The Defence of the United Kingdom*, p. 216.

48 Orange, *Keith Park*, p. 109.

49 Overy, *The Battle of Britain*, pp. 95–96.

50 Murray, *Luftwaffe*, p. 88.

51 Orange, *Keith Park*, p. 105.

52 Overy, *The Battle of Britain*, p. 127.

53 Collier, *The Defence of the United Kingdom*, pp. 179, 221.

54 Correlli Barnett, *Engage the Enemy More Closely: The Royal Navy in the Second World War* (New York, 1991), p. 189.

55 Collier, *The Defence of the United Kingdom*, pp. 222, 227.

56 Ibid., pp. 225–26.

57 M. Gilbert, *Second World War* (London, 1989), p. 125; F.H. Hinsley, *British Intelligence in the Second World War*, i (London, 1979), pp. 185–86; Collier, *The Defence of the United Kingdom*, p. 227.

58 J. Keegan, *The Second World War* (London, 1989), p. 102.

59 Gilbert, *Second World War*, p. 115; Hinsley, *British Intelligence*, i, p. 190.

60 Weinberg, *A World at Arms*, p. 171; Mason, *Battle Over Britain*, p. 17.

61 Collier, *The Defence of the United Kingdom*, p. 504; Richards, *Royal Air Force*, i, p. 217.

62 Maier, Rohde, Stegemann, Umbreit, *Germany and the Second World War*, ii, p. 387; Collier, *The Defence of the United Kingdom*, p. 528.

63 Overy, *The Battle of Britain*, p. 104.

64 Overy, *The Air War*, p. 33; Overy, *The Battle of Britain*, p. 162; Mason, *Battle Over Britain*, p. 481.

65 Richards, *Royal Air Force*, i, p. 190; Bungay, *The Most Dangerous Enemy*, p. 368.

66 Bungay, *The Most Dangerous Enemy*, p. 368; Deighton, *Fighter*, p. 276.

67 Orange, *Keith Park*, p. 136.

68 Overy, *The Battle of Britain*, p. xi.

Chapter 4: The Battle of the Atlantic

1 C. Blair, *Hitler's U-boat War: The Hunters, 1939–1942* (New York, 1996), p. 20.

2 H.H. Herwig, 'Innovation Ignored: The Submarine Problem', in W. Murray and A.R. Millett, *Military Innovation in the Interwar Period* (Cambridge, 1996), pp. 244–45, 250–51.

3 Ibid., p. 232.

4 Karl Doenitz, *Memoirs: Ten Years and Twenty Days* (London, 1990), p. 41.

5 Blair, *Hitler's U-boat War: The Hunters*, p. 52; J. Keegan, *The Price of Admiralty* (London, 1988), p. 222.

6 H. Boog, W. Rahn, R. Stumpf, B. Wegner, *Germany and the Second World War*, vi (Oxford, 2001), p. 328.

7 J.A. Maiolo, 'Deception and Intelligence Failure: Anglo-German Preparations for U-boat Warfare in the 1930s', in *The Journal of Strategic Studies*, December 1999, p. 69.

8 Keegan, *The Price of Admiralty*, p. 224.

9 C.B.A. Behrens, *Merchant Shipping and the Demands of War* (London, 1955), pp. 2, 34, 157.

10 M. Middlebrook, *Convoy* (London, 1976), p. 2.

11 Doenitz, *Memoirs*, pp. 93–94.

12 Ibid., pp. 124–25.

13 R. Hough, *The Longest Battle* (London, 1986), p. 37.

14 J.M. Packard, *Neither Friend Nor Foe* (New York, 1992), pp. 38–40.

15 Keegan, *The Price of Admiralty*, p. 227.

16 Doenitz, *Memoirs*, pp. 124–25.

17 W. Murray and A.R. Millett, *A War to be Won* (Cambridge, Mass., 2000), p. 244.

18 D. van der Vat, *The Atlantic Campaign* (London, 1988), p. 165; J.P.M. Showell, *German Naval Code Breakers* (Annapolis, 2003), pp. 21–22; Correlli Barnett, *Engage the Enemy More Closely: The Royal Navy in the Second World War* (New York, 1991), p. 194.

19 J. Terraine, *The Right of the Line* (London, 1985), p. 233.

20 Ibid., p. 241.

21 Behrens, *Merchant Shipping*, p. 178; P. Kaplan and J. Currie, *Convoy: Merchant Sailors at War, 1939–1945* (London, 1998), p. 29.

22 S.W. Roskill, *The War at Sea, 1939–1945*, i (London, 1954), pp. 615–18.

23 Blair, *Hitler's U-boat War: The Hunters*, p. 114; Boog, Rahn, Stumpf, Wegner, *Germany and the Second World War*, vi, p. 353.

24 Barnett, *Engage the Enemy More Closely*, p. 262.

25 Murray and Millett, *A War to be Won*, pp. 244–45; van der Vat, *The Atlantic Campaign*, p. 108; F.H. Hinsley, *British Intelligence in the Second World War*, i (London, 1979), pp. 487–91.

26 Boog, Rahn, Stumpf, Wegner, *Germany and the Second World War*, vi, pp. 346–47.

27 J. Buckley, 'Atlantic Airpower Co-operation, 1941–1945', in *The Journal of Strategic Studies*, March 1995, p. 175; Roskill, *The War at Sea*, i, p. 614; S.W. Roskill, *The War at Sea, 1939–1945*, iii, part ii (London, 1961), p. 472; Boog, Rahn, Stumpf, Wegner, *Germany and the Second World War*, vi, p. 361.

28 J. Rohwer, 'The Wireless War', in S. Howarth and D. Law, *The Battle of the Atlantic, 1939–1945* (London, 1994), pp. 411, 416.

29 J. Gardner, 'The Battle of the Atlantic, 1941 – The First Turning Point?', in *The Journal of Strategic Studies*, March 1994, pp. 118–120; Boog, Rahn, Stumpf, Wegner, *Germany and the Second World War*, vi, p. 355.

30 Boog, Rahn, Stumpf, Wegner, *Germany and the Second World War*, vi, pp. 311–12; Rohwer, 'The Wireless War', p. 411.

31 J. Ellis, *Brute Force* (New York, 1990), p. 145.

32 Terraine, *The Right of the Line*, p. 735; United States Strategic Bombing Survey, *The Effects of Strategic Bombing on the German War Economy* (Washington, 1945), p. 2.

33 D. Richards and H. St G. Saunders, *Royal Air Force, 1939–1945*, ii (London, 1954), p. 105; Middlebrook, *Convoy*, p. 50.

34 Boog, Rahn, Stumpf, Wegner, *Germany and the Second World War*, vi, pp. 348, 362; Blair, *Hitler's U-boat War: The Hunters*, p. 403; Doenitz, *Memoirs*, p. 159.

35 Blair, *Hitler's U-boat War: The Hunters*, p. 399.

36 Barnett, *Engage the Enemy More Closely*, p. 275; Blair, *Hitler's U-boat War: The Hunters*, pp. 392–93; H. T. Lenton, *Britain and Empire Warships of the Second World War* (London, 1998), p. 114.

37 T. Robinson, *Walker, R.N.* (London, 1956), p. 29.

38 Blair, *Hitler's U-boat War: The Hunters*, pp. 410–11.

39 Richards, *Royal Air Force*, i, p. 351; Blair, *Hitler's U-boat War: The Hunters*, p. 413; Robinson, *Walker*, pp. 44–48.

40 Robinson, *Walker*, pp. 49–50; Blair, *Hitler's U-boat War: The Hunters*, p. 413.

41 Robinson, *Walker*, pp. 52–53.

42 Ibid., p. 53; Blair, *Hitler's U-boat War: The Hunters*, p. 414.

43 Blair, *Hitler's U-boat War: The Hunters*, pp. 414–15; Robinson, *Walker*, pp. 54–55.

44 Blair, *Hitler's U-boat War: The Hunters*, p. 415.

45 Robinson, *Walker*, p. 57.

46 van der Vat, *The Atlantic Campaign*, p. 218; Blair, *Hitler's U-boat War: The Hunters*, pp. 416–17; P. Kemp, *The Admiralty Regrets: British Warship Losses of the Twentieth Century* (London, 1999), p. 163.

47 Blair, *Hitler's U-boat War: The Hunters*, pp. 416–17; Robinson, *Walker*, p. 58.

48 Richards, *Royal Air Force*, i, p. 351; Robinson, *Walker*, p. 60.

49 Roskill, *The War at Sea*, i, pp. 599–600, 615–18.

50 Doenitz, *Memoirs*, p. 181.

51 Roskill, *The War at Sea*, i, pp. 599–600, 615–18.

52 Blair, *Hitler's U-boat War: The Hunters*, p. 418; Murray and Millett, *A War to be Won*, p. 255; S W. Roskill, *The War at Sea, 1939–1945*, ii (London, 1956), p. 475.

53 Boog, Rahn, Stumpf, Wegner, *Germany and the Second World War*, vi, p. 337.

54 Ellis, *Brute Force*, p. 160.

55 R. H. Kohn (ed.), 'The Scholarship on World War II: Its Present Condition and Future Possibilities', in *The Journal of Military History*, July 1991, p. 381; G. Till, 'The Battle of the Atlantic as History', in Howarth and Law, *The Battle of the Atlantic*, p. 588.

56 United States Strategic Bombing Survey, *The Effects of Strategic Bombing*, p. 144.

57 Boog, Rahn, Stumpf, Wegner, *Germany and the Second World War*, vi, p. 323.

58 G. C. Wynne, *If Germany Attacks: The Battle in Depth in the West* (London, 1939), p. 321.

Chapter 5: Operation Barbarossa: The Invasion of Russia

1 A. Speer, *Inside the Third Reich* (New York, 1970), p. 173.

2 C. Burdick and H. Jacobsen (eds), *The Halder War Diary, 1939–1942* (Novato, California, 1988), p. 245.

3 Adolf Hitler, *Mein Kampf* (London, 1939), p. 354.

4 Ibid., pp. 360–61, 371.

5 B. A. Leach, *German Strategy Against Russia, 1939–1941* (Oxford, 1973), p. 11.

6 G. L. Weinberg, *A World at Arms* (Cambridge, 1994), pp. 179–82.

7 Ibid., p. 200; Leach, *German Strategy Against Russia*, p. 63.

8 Leach, *German Strategy Against Russia*, p. 94.

9 J. Ellis, *Brute Force* (New York, 1990), p. 40.

10 M. Gilbert, *Second World War* (London, 1989), p. 167.

11 Burdick and Jacobsen, *The Halder War Diary*, p. 297.

12 Leach, *German Strategy Against Russia*, p. 126.

13 B. Wegner, 'The Road to Defeat: The German Campaigns in Russia, 1941–43', in *The Journal of Strategic Studies*, March 1990, p. 108.

14 Weinberg, *A World at Arms*, pp. 229–30; Leach, *German Strategy Against Russia*, p. 167.

15 Leach, *German Strategy Against Russia*, p. 91.

16 Burdick and Jacobsen, *The Halder War Diary*, p. 339.

17 H.R. Trevor-Roper (ed.), *Hitler's War Directives, 193–-1945* (London, 1964), pp. 79–80.

18 R. Overy, *Russia's War* (London, 1997), p. 17.

19 Ibid., p. 19.

20 Ibid., p. 23.

21 H. Boog, *Germany and the Second World War*, iv (Oxford, 1998), p. 66.

22 J. Erickson, *The Road to Stalingrad* (London, 1975), p. 13; D.M. Glantz and J.M. House, *When Titans Clashed* (Lawrence, Kansas, 1995), p. 23.

23 Boog, *Germany and the Second World War*, iv, p. 78.

24 A. Seaton, *The Russo-German War, 1941–45* (London, 1971), p. 92; W. Murray, *The Change in the European Balance of Power, 1938–1939* (Princeton, 1984), p. 126; Leach, *German Strategy Against Russia*, p. 130; W.S. Dunn, *Hitler's Nemesis: The Red Army, 1930–1945* (Westport, 1994), pp. 175, 201.

25 Weinberg, *A World at Arms*, p. 204.

26 D.M. Glantz, *Barbarossa* (Charleston, 2001), p. 14.

27 Seaton, *The Russo-German War*, p. 62. In 1940 1,459 tanks had been manufactured. 3,245 were built in 1941. United States Strategic Bombing Survey, *The Effects of Strategic Bombing on the German War Economy*, (Washington, 1945), pp. 278–79.

28 Leach, *German Strategy Against Russia*, p. 94; Asher Lee, *Goering: Air Leader* (London, 1972), p. 118.

29 M. van Creveld, *Supplying War* (Cambridge, 1977), p. 176.

30 W. Richardson and S. Freidin (eds), *The Fatal Decisions* (London, 1956), p. 42.

31 Dunn, *Hitler's Nemesis*, p. 162.

32 Glantz, *Barbarossa*, p. 39.

33 Burdick and Jacobsen, *The Halder War Diary*, pp. 443, 453.

34 Leach, *German Strategy Against Russia*, p. 213; P. Calvocoressi, G. Wint, J. Pritchard, *The Penguin History of the Second World War* (London, 1972), p. 196.

35 Burdick and Jacobsen, *The Halder War Diary*, pp. 446–47.

36 Calvocoressi, Wint, Pritchard, *Second World War*, p. 193; Wegner, 'The Road to Defeat', p. 111; Weinberg, *A World at Arms*, p. 268.

37 Leach, *German Strategy Against Russia*, p. 166.

38 Burdick and Jacobsen, *The Halder War Diary*, pp. 478, 521; Seaton, *The Russo-German War*, p. 58.

39 Dunn, *Hitler's Nemesis*, pp. 35, 56–57; Glantz, *Barbarossa*, p. 68.

40 Burdick and Jacobsen, *The Halder War Diary*, p. 506.

41 H. Guderian, *Panzer Leader* (London, 1952), p. 200.

42 W. Murray and A.R. Millett, *A War to be Won* (Cambridge, Mass., 2000), p. 126; Leach, *German Strategy Against Russia*, p. 212.

43 H.E. Salisbury (ed.), *Marshall Zhukov's Greatest Battles* (London, 1969), p. 13; Overy, *Russia's War*, p. 100.

44 Glantz, *Barbarossa*, p. 114; Overy, *Russia's War*, pp. 104, 107.

45 A.W. Turney, *Disaster at Moscow: von Bock's Campaign, 1941–42* (Albuquerque, New Mexico, 1970), pp. 87–88.

46 Gilbert, *Second World War*, p. 242; Glantz, *Barbarossa*, p. 153.

47 Glantz, *Barbarossa*, p. 161; Turney, *Disaster at Moscow*, p. 135; W. Murray, *Luftwaffe: Strategy for Defeat, 1933–45* (London, 1985), p. 147.

48 J. Keegan, *Second World War* (London, 1989), p. 201.

49 Richardson and Freidin, *The Fatal Decisions*, p. 50; Burdick and Jacobsen, *The Halder War Diary*, p. 571; E. Raus, *Panzer Operations: The Eastern Front Memoir of General Raus, 1941–1945* (Cambridge, Mass., 2003), p. 89.

50 K. Gerbet (ed.), *Generalfeldmarschall Fedor von Bock: The War Diary, 1939–1945* (Atglen, Pennsylvania, 1996), p. 376; Ellis, *Brute Force*, p. 72.

51 Glantz, *Barbarossa*, p. 186.

52 Turney, *Disaster at Moscow*, pp. 153–55.

53 Glantz, *Barbarossa*, p. 210.

54 Weinberg, *A World at Arms*, p. 300; W. Deist, M. Messerschmidt, H.E. Volkmann, W. Wette, *Germany and the Second World War*, i (Oxford, 1990), p. 1177.

55 Burdick and Jacobsen, *The Halder War Diary*, p. 599; Deist, Messerschmidt, Volkmann, Wette, *Germany and the Second World War*, i, p. 1181.

56 van Creveld, *Supplying War*, p. 157; Murray, *Luftwaffe*, p. 12.

57 Leach, *German Strategy Against Russia*, p. 180; A. Coox, *Nomonhan: Japan Against Russia, 1939*, ii (Stanford, 1985), p. 1036.

58 Boog, *Germany and the Second World War*, iv, p. 4.

59 Keegan, *Second World War*, p. 179.

60 A. Speer, *Inside the Third Reich* (London, 1970), p. 165.

Chapter 6: Pearl Harbor

1 S.E. Morison, *History of United States Naval Operations in World War II*, iii (Boston, 1948), p. 15; W. Murray and A.R. Millett, *A War to be Won* (Cambridge, Massachuetts., 2000), p. 151.

2 A.D. Coox, *Nomonhan: Japan Against Russia, 1939*, ii (Stanford, 1985), p. 1036.

3 G.W. Prange, *December 7, 1941: The Day the Japanese Attacked Pearl Harbor* (New York, 1988), p. 9; Morison, *United States Naval Operations*, iii, p. 82; R. Pineau, 'Admiral Isoroku Yamamoto', in M. Carver (ed.), *The War Lords* (London, 1976), p. 393; G. Till, 'Adopting the Aircraft Carrier', in W. Murray and A.R. Millett (eds), *Military Innovation in the Interwar Period* (Cambridge, 1996), p. 203.

4 M.R. Peattie, *Sunburst: The Rise of Japanese Naval Air Power, 1909–1941* (Annapolis, Maryland, 2001), p. 123.

5 H.P. Willmott, *Pearl Harbor* (London, 2001), p. 53.

6 Morison, *United States Naval Operations*, iii, p. 46.

7 J.D. Potter, *Admiral of the Pacific: The Life of Yamamoto* (London, 1965), p. 53; S. Roskill, *The War at Sea, 1939–1945*, i (London, 1954), pp. 300–1; J. Greene and A. Massignari, *The Naval War in the Mediterranean, 1940–1943* (London, 1998), p. 104.

8 M. Gannon, *Pearl Harbor Betrayed* (New York, 2002), p. 41.

9 Potter, *Admiral of the Pacific*, p. 68.

10 Morison, *United States Naval Operations*, iii, p. 43; R.H. Spector, *Eagle Against the Sun: The American War with Japan* (New York, 1985), p. 1.

11 Gannon, *Pearl Harbor Betrayed*, p. 15.

12 G.W. Prange, *Pearl Harbor: The Verdict of History* (New York, 1986), p. 119.

13 Spector, *Eagle Against the Sun*, pp. 16, 75.

14 Gannon, *Pearl Harbor Betrayed*, p. 191.

15 Ibid., pp. 192, 195.

16 Morison, *United States Naval Operations*, iii, p. 77.

17 Gannon, *Pearl Harbor Betrayed*, p. 165.

18 Ibid., p. 97.

19 Ibid., pp. 162, 166–67.

20 Prange, *December 7, 1941*, pp. 20–22.

21 Ibid., pp. 26, 36.

22 Gannon, *Pearl Harbor Betrayed*, pp. 195–96.

23 Ibid., pp. 196-97.

24 Prange, *December 7, 1941*, p. 41.

25 D. van der Vat, *The Pacific Campaign* (New York, 1991), p. 19.

26 Gannon, *Pearl Harbor Betrayed*, p. 186.

27 Willmott, *Pearl Harbor*, p. 60.

28 Peattie, *Sunburst*, pp. 139–40.

29 Willmott, *Pearl Harbor*, pp. 100–2.

30 Gannon, *Pearl Harbor Betrayed*, pp. 233–34.

31 Spector, *Eagle Against the Sun*, p. 3; Willmott, *Pearl Harbor*, p. 97.

32 Spector, *Eagle Against the Sun*, p. 4; Morison, *United States Naval Operations*, iii, p. 97; Gannon, *Pearl Harbor Betrayed*, pp. 225–29.

33 Potter, *Admiral of the Pacific*, p. 98.

34 Morison, *United States Naval Operations*, iii, p. 94; Prange, *December 7, 1941*, p. 115.

35 Gannon, *Pearl Harbor Betrayed*, p. 4.

36 Ibid., pp. 4–5.

37 Peattie, *Sunburst*, p. 140.

38 Gannon, *Pearl Harbor Betrayed*, p. 6.

39 Prange, *December 7, 1941*, pp. 119, 204.

40 Willmott, *Pearl Harbor*, p. 123.

41 Prange, *December 7, 1941*, p. 269.

42 W.F. Craven and J.L. Cate, *The American Air Forces in World War II*, i (Chicago, 1948), p. 197.

43 Gannon, *Pearl Harbor Betrayed*, pp. 242, 244, 317; Prange, *December 7, 1941*, p. 327.

44 Willmott, *Pearl Harbor*, pp. 116, 127.

45 Ibid., p. 156.

46 Potter, *Admiral of the Pacific*, pp. 109, 123.

47 Gannon, *Pearl Harbor Betrayed*, p. 264.

48 Prange, *December 7, 1941*, p. 156.

49 Willmott, *Pearl Harbor*, p. 132.

50 Prange, *Verdict of History*, p. 348; Gannon, *Pearl Harbor Betrayed*, pp. 277–79.

51 Prange, *December 7, 1941*, p. 335.

52 G.W. Prange, *Miracle at Midway* (New York, 1982), p. 9.

53 H.H. Herwig, 'Innovation Ignored: The Submarine Problem, Germany, Britain and the United States, 1919–1939', in Murray and Millett, *Military Innovation in the Interwar Period*, p. 264.

54 Prange, *December 7, 1941*, p. 372.

55 G.L. Weinberg, *Germany, Hitler and World War II* (Cambridge, 1995), p. 202.

56 Murray and Millett, *A War to be Won*, p. 136.

57 R. Overy, *Why the Allies Won* (New York, 1996), p. 205.

58 A. Speer, *Inside the Third Reich* (London, 1970), p. 121.

Chapter 7: The Battle of Midway

1 D.M. Horner, *High Command* (Sydney, 1982), p. 181.

2 G.W. Prange, *Miracle at Midway* (New York, 1982), pp. 23–25.

3 J. Keegan, *The Price of Admiralty* (New York, 1989), p. 160.

4 S.E. Morison, *History of United States Naval Operations in World War II*, iv (Boston, 1949), p. 18.

5 H.P. Willmott, *The Barrier and the Javelin* (Annapolis, 1983), p. 198.

6 H. Bicheno, *Midway* (London, 2000), p. 49.

7 Prange, *Miracle at Midway*, pp. 32–33.

8 Ibid., pp. 56-57.

9 B. Tillman, 'The Battle of Midway', in J. Sweetman (ed.), *Great American Naval Battles* (Annapolis, 1998), p. 265.

10 E.P. Hoyt, *How They Won the War in the Pacific: Nimitz and his Admirals* (New York, 2000), p. 88.

11 D.C. Fuquea, 'Task Force One: The Wasted Assets of the United States Pacific Battleships Fleet, 1942', *The Journal of Military History*, October 1997, pp. 710-18.

12 Willmott, *The Barrier and the Javelin*, p. 309.

13 Keegan, *The Price of Admiralty*, p. 189.

14 T.B. Buell, *The Quiet Warrior: A Biography of Admiral Raymond A. Spruance* (Annapolis, 1988), pp. 136, 143.

15 Willmott, *The Barrier and the Javelin*, pp. 97, 102, 104–9.

16 Tillman, 'The Battle of Midway', p. 270.

17 Mitsuo Fuchida and Masatake Okumiya, *Midway* (Annapolis, 1955), p. 182.

18 Prange, *Miracle at Midway*, pp. 154, 165.

19 J.B. Lundstrom, 'Raymond A. Spruance: The Thinking Man's Admiral (1886–1969)', in J. Sweetman (ed.), *The Great Admirals* (Annapolis, 1997), p. 467.

20 Hiroyuki Agawa, *Reluctant Admiral: Yamamoto and the Imperial Navy* (New York, 1979), p. 314.

21 Lundstrom, 'Raymond A. Spruance', p. 467; Prange, *Miracle at Midway*, p. 239; Buell, *The Quiet Warrior*, p. 146.

22 Prange, *Miracle at Midway*, p. 214.

23 Ibid., pp. 216–17; Keegan, *The Price of Admiralty*, pp. 197–98; Agawa, *Reluctant Admiral*, p. 315.

24 Fuchida and Okumiya, *Midway*, p. 201.

25 Prange, *Miracle at Midway*, pp. 233–35.

26 Buell, *The Quiet Warrior*, pp. xii-xiv.

27 Ibid., p. 147; Prange, *Miracle at Midway*, pp. 241–42.

28 R.H. Spector, *Eagle Against the Sun: The American War with Japan* (New York, 1985), p. 174.

29 Fuchida and Okumiya, *Midway*, p. 213.

30 Agawa, *Reluctant Admiral*, p. 317; M.R. Peattie, *Sunburst: The Rise of Japanese Naval Air Power, 1909–1941* (Annapolis, 2001), p. 159.

31 C.G. Reynolds, *The Carrier War* (Chicago, 1982), p. 94; Keegan, *The Price of Admiralty*, p. 206; Fuchida and Okumiya, *Midway*, p. 223; Tillman, 'The Battle of Midway', p. 279.

32 Agawa, *Reluctant Admiral*, pp. 317–18; Reynolds, *The Carrier War*, p. 96; Masatake Okumiya and Jiro Horikoshi, *Zero! The Story of the Japanese Navy Air Force, 1937–1945* (New York, 1956), pp. 124–25.

33 Fuchida and Okumiya, *Midway*, p. 252.

34 Keegan, *The Price of Admiralty*, p. 210; Bicheno, *Midway*, p. 9.

35 Buell, *The Quiet Warrior*, p. xv.

36 Bicheno, *Midway*, p. 9.

37 Prange, *Miracle at Midway*, p. 396.

38 Ibid., p. 381.

39 Willmott, *The Barrier and the Javelin*, p. 200.

40 Matome Ugaki, *Fading Victory* (Pittsburgh, 1991), pp. 138, 140.

41 J.D. Potter, *Admiral of the Pacific: The Life of Yamamoto* (London, 1965), p. 260; Agawa, *Reluctant Admiral*, p. 322.

42 Fuquea, 'Task Force One', p. 718.

43 Potter, *Admiral of the Pacific*, p. 300.

Chapter 8: El Alamein

1 D. Porch, *The Path to Victory* (New York, 2004), p. xi.

2 Ibid., p. x; M. van Creveld, *Supplying War* (Cambridge, 1977), p. 182.

3 van Creveld, *Supplying War*, p. 185.

4 F.W. von Mellenthin, *Panzer Battles, 1939–1945* (London, 1955), p. 43.

5 B.H. Liddell Hart, *The German Generals Talk* (New York, 1948), p. 162.

6 J. Latimer, *Alamein* (London, 2002), p. 150.

7 I.S.O. Playfair, *The Mediterranean and Middle East*, iii (London, 1960), p. 274; R. Bennett, *Ultra and Mediterranean Strategy* (New York, 1989), p. 128.

8 W.S. Churchill, *Second World War*, iv (London, 1951), p. 343.

9 Playfair, *The Mediterranean and Middle East*, iii, pp. 314, 327, 330.

10 A. Chalfont, *Montgomery of Alamein* (London, 1976), p. 150; Porch, *The Path to Victory*, p. 278; R. Neillands, *Eighth Army* (New York, 2004), p. 208.

11 Mellenthin, *Panzer Battles*, p. 127.

12 Playfair, *The Mediterranean and Middle East*, iii, p. 343.

13 H. Kippenberger, *Infantry Brigadier* (London, 1949), p. 180.

14 B.H. Liddell Hart (ed.), *The Rommel Papers* (London, 1953), p. 262.

15 Chalfont, *Montgomery of Alamein*, p. 171.

16 Ibid., p. 153.

17 C. Barnett, *The Desert Generals* (London, 1983), p. 199.

18 Playfair, *The Mediterranean and Middle East*, iii, p. 371.

19 Liddell Hart, *The Rommel Papers*, p. 269.

20 Mellenthin, *Panzer Battles*, p. 140.

21 Playfair, *The Mediterranean and Middle East*, iii, p. 391.

22 I.S.O. Playfair and C.J.C. Moloney, *The Mediterranean and Middle East*, iv (London, 1966), p. 2; M. Carver, *El Alamein* (London, 1962), p. 14.

23 N. Hamilton, *The Full Monty: Montgomery of Alamein, 1887–1942* (London, 2001), p. 685.

24 J. Ellis, *Brute Force* (New York, 1990), p. 262.

25 B.H. Liddell Hart, *The Tanks*, ii (London, 1959), p. 227.

26 V. Orange, *Tedder: Quietly in Command* (London, 2004), pp. 187–88.

27 Playfair and Moloney, *The Mediterranean and Middle East*, iv, pp. 9–10; R. Lewin, *The Life and Death of the Afrika Korps* (London, 1977), p. 164.

28 D. Petracarro, 'Italian Army in North Africa, 1940-1943: An Attempt at Historical Perspective', *War and Society*, October 1991, pp. 104–17.

29 Mellenthin, *Panzer Battles*, p. 141.

30 Playfair and Moloney, *The Mediterranean and Middle East*, iv, p. 25; Porch, *The Path to Victory*, p. 715; T. Spooner, *Supreme Gallantry: Malta's Role in the Allied Victory, 1939–1945* (London, 1996), pp. 326–27.

31 D. Fraser, *Knight's Cross: A Life of Field-Marshal Erwin Rommel* (London, 1993), p. 361; Liddell Hart, *The Rommel Papers*, p. 232.

32 Playfair and Moloney, *The Mediterranean and Middle East*, iv, pp. 28–29.

33 Ibid., p. 30; Porch, *The Path to Victory*, p. 718.

34 P. Delaforce, *Monty's Highlanders* (London, 2000), p. 44.

35 J. Pimlott (ed.), *Rommel in His Own Words* (London, 1994), p. 135; H. Boog, W. Rahn, R. Stumpf, B. Wegner, *Germany and the Second World War*, vi (Oxford, 2001), p. 778.

36 Playfair and Moloney, *The Mediterranean and Middle East*, iv, pp. 51–52.

37 M. Parsons, *Gunfire!: A History of the 2/12th Australian Field Regiment, 1940–1946* (Melbourne, 1991), p. 128.

38 Pimlott, *Rommel in His Own Words*, p. 139.

39 Playfair and Moloney, *The Mediterranean and Middle East*, iv, pp. 66–67, 69; Carver, *Alamein*, p. 179; Pimlott, *Rommel in His Own Words*, p. 142.

40 Boog, Rahn, Stumpf, Wegner, *Germany and the Second World War*, vi, p. 784.

41 Liddell Hart, *The German Generals Talk*, p. 165.

42 Playfair and Moloney, *The Mediterranean and Middle East*, iv, pp. 78–79; Liddell Hart, *The Rommel Papers*, p. 358.

43 Porch, *The Path to Victory*, p. 322.

44 A. Stewart, *Eighth Army's Greatest Victories* (London, 1999), p. 46.

Chapter 9: Stalingrad

1 A. Seaton, *The Russo-German War, 1941–45* (London, 1971), p. 256; J. Hayward, 'Hitler's Quest for Oil: The Impact of Economic Considerations on Military Strategy, 1941–42', *The Journal of Strategic Studies*, December 1995, p. 124.

2 L.P. Lochner, *The Goebbels Diaries* (London, 1948), p. 92.

3 Hayward, 'Hitler's Quest for Oil', p. 99.

4 Hayward, 'Hitler's Quest for Oil', pp. 115, 117–21, 127; H.R. Trevor-Roper (ed.), *Hitler's War Directives,*

1939–1945 (London, 1964), pp. 116–18.

5 E. von Manstein, *Lost Victories* (Chicago, 1958), p. 275; Seaton, *The Russo-German War*, p. 266.

6 T.N. Dupuy and P. Martell, *Great Battles of the Eastern Front* (New York, 1982), pp. 2–3; W.S. Dunn, *Nemesis: The Red Army,* 1930-1945 (Westport, 1994), p. 54.

7 D.M. Glantz and J.M. House, *When Titans Clashed* (Lawrence, Kansas, 1995), pp. 101–2.

8 R. Overy, *Russia's War* (London, 1997), p. 155.

9 G.L. Weinberg, *A World at Arms* (Cambridge, 1994), p. 287.

10 C. Burdick and H. Jacobsen (eds), *The Halder War Diary,* 1939–1942 (Novato, California, 1988), p. 611.

11 J. Beaumont, *Comrades in Arms: British Aid to Russia,* 1941–1945 (London, 1980), pp. 204, 208, 215.

12 Ibid., p. 212.

13 Ibid.; Dunn, *Nemesis*, p. 160.

14 United States Strategic Bombing Survey, *The Effects of Strategic Bombing of the German War Economy* (Washington, 1945), pp. 278–79.

15 H. Boog, W. Rahn, R. Stumpf, B. Wegner, *Germany and the Second World War*, vi (Oxford, 2001), p. 932.

16 Ibid., p. 939.

17 Seaton, *The Russo-German War*, p. 262.

18 Ibid., p. 270.

19 Burdick and Jacobsen, *The Halder War Diary*, p. 635.

20 M. Gilbert, *Second World War* (London, 1989), p. 343.

21 Overy, *Russia's War*, p. 156.

22 Boog, Rahn, Stumpf, Wegner, *Germany and the Second World War*, vi, p. 1029.

23 Weinberg, *A World at Arms*, p. 417; B.H. Liddell Hart, *The German Generals Talk* (London, 1948), p. 203.

24 R. Overy, *Why the Allies Won* (London, 1995), p. 72; E.P. Hoyt, 199 *Days: The Battle for Stalingrad* (New York, 1993), p. 105.

25 Boog, Rahn, Stumpf, Wegner, *Germany and the Second World War*, vi, p. 1078.

26 Gilbert, *Second World War*, p. 358; Seaton, *The Russo-German War*, p. 293.

27 G.P. Megargee, *Inside Hitler's High Command* (Lawrence, Kansas, 2000), p. 191.

28 Overy, *Russia's War*, p. 172.

29 Overy, *Why the Allies Won*, p. 75.

30 J. Erickson, *The Road to Stalingrad* (London, 1975), p. 436; Boog, Rahn, Stumpf, Wegner, *Germany and the Second World War*, vi, p. 851; Hoyt, 199 *Days*, pp. 150–54.

31 Boog, Rahn, Stumpf, Wegner, *Germany and the Second World War*, vi, p. 1097.

32 G. Roberts, *Victory at Stalingrad* (London, 2002), p. 103.

33 V.I. Chuikov, *The Battle for Stalingrad* (New York, 1964), pp. 223–24.

34 P. Carell, *Stalingrad: The Defeat of the German Sixth Army* (Atglen, Pennsylvania, 1993), p. 155.

35 Boog, Rahn, Stumpf, Wegner, *Germany and the Second World War*, vi, p. 995.

36 R.L. DiNardo, 'The Dysfunctional Coalition: The Axis Powers and the Eastern Front in World War II', *The Journal of Military History*, October 1996, p. 721.

37 Boog, Rahn, Stumpf, Wegner, *Germany and the Second World War*, vi, p. 1106.

38 Ibid., p. 1129.

39 A. Speer, *Inside the Third Reich* (New York, 1970), p. 248.

40 Ibid., p. 249.

41 D.M. Glantz, *Zhukov's Greatest Defeat: The Red Army's Epic Disaster in Operation Mars,* 1942 (Lawrence, Kansas, 1999), pp. 283, 319; Boog, Rahn, Stumpf, Wegner, *Germany and the Second World War*, vi, p. 1102.

42 Manstein, *Lost Victories*, p. 269.

43 Ibid., p. 294.

44 Ibid., p. 306.

45 F.W. von Mellenthin, *German Generals of World War II* (Norman, Oklahoma, 1977), p. 116; Boog, Rahn, Stumpf, Wegner, *Germany and the Second World War*, vi, p. 1171.

46 Boog, Rahn, Stumpf, Wegner, *Germany and the Second World War*, vi, p. 1134.

47 Ibid., p. 1137.

48 Ibid., p. 1139.

49 W. Murray, *Luftwaffe: Strategy for Defeat,* 1933–45 (London, 1988), p. 214.

50 F.W. von Mellenthin, *Panzer Battles, 1939–1945* (London, 1955), p. 185.

51 Chuikov, *The Battle for Stalingrad*, p. 254.

52 Overy, *Russia's War*, p. 223; Boog, Rahn, Stumpf, Wegner, *Germany and the Second World War*, vi, p. 1164.

53 Seaton, *The Russo-German War*, p. 336.

54 A. Werth, *The Year of Stalingrad* (London, 1946), p. 444.

55 Manstein, *Lost Victories*, p. 365.

56 Overy, *Why the Allies Won*, p. 84.

57 Hayward, 'Hitler's Quest for Oil', p. 127.

Chapter 10: The Battle of Kursk & The Death of *Blitzkrieg*

1 A. Seaton, *The Russo-German War, 1941–45* (London, 1971), p. 352.

2 W.S. Dunn, *Kursk: Hitler's Gamble, 1943* (London, 1997), p. xiv.

3 J. Keegan, *The Second World War* (London, 1989), p. 458.

4 Dunn, *Kursk*, p. 21.

5 E. von Manstein, *Lost Victories* (Chicago, 1958), p. 443.

6 W. Murray, *Luftwaffe: Strategy for Defeat, 1933–45* (London, 1988), p. 221; Dunn, *Kursk*, p. 94.

7 D.M. Glantz and J.M. House, *When Titans Clashed* (Lawrence, Kansas, 1995), p. 157; R. Overy, *Russia's War* (New York, 1997), p. 256.

8 J. Erickson, *The Road to Berlin* (London, 1983), p. 68; H.E. Salisbury (ed.), *Marshall Zhukov's Greatest Battles* (London, 1969), p. 198.

9 C. Bellamy, 'Kursk – Sixty Years On', *The Royal United Services Institute Journal*, October 2003, p. 85; Erickson, *The Road to Berlin*, p. 66.

10 D.M. Glantz and J.M. House, *The Battle of Kursk* (Lawrence, Kansas, 1999), p. 45.

11 Erickson, *The Road to Berlin*, p. 71; Glantz and House, *When Titans Clashed*, p. 163.

12 H. Guderian, *Panzer Leader* (London, 1952), p. 302.

13 Ibid., pp. 307, 309.

14 S.W. Mitcham, *The Panzer Legions* (Westport, 2001), p. 39.

15 Seaton, *The Russo-German War*, p. 353.

16 United States Strategic Bombing Survey, *The Effects of Strategic Bombing of the German War Economy* (Washington, 1945), pp. 278–79; Seaton, *The Russo-German War*, p. 353.

17 Dunn, *Kursk*, p. 108.

18 Murray, *Luftwaffe*, p. 223; Seaton, *The Russo-German War*, pp. 357–58.

19 Murray, *Luftwaffe*, p. 223.

20 Overy, *Russia's War*, p. 204; S.H. Newton, *Hitler's Commander: Field-Marshal Walther Model* (Cambridge, Mass., 2006), p. 243.

21 R.N. Armstrong, *Red Army Tank Commanders* (Atglen, Pennsylvania, 1994), pp. 303, 347; J. Erickson (ed.), *Main Front: Soviet Leaders Look Back on World War II* (London, 1987), pp. 108, 112.

22 Glantz and House, *Kursk*, p. 152.

23 Erickson, *Main Front*, p. 113.

24 Overy, *Russia's War*, p. 208.

25 Glantz and House, *Kursk*, p. 121; Salisbury, *Marshall Zhukov's Greatest Battles*, pp. 237–38; Seaton, *The Russo-German War*, p. 366.

26 Guderian, *Panzer Leader*, p. 311.

27 Manstein, *Lost Victories*, p. 449.

28 A. Werth, *Russia at War, 1941-1945* (London, 1964), p. 684.

29 J. Erickson, 'Soviet War Losses', in J. Erickson and D. Dilks (eds), *Barbarossa: The Axis and the Allies* (Edinburgh, 1994), pp. 264–65; Glantz and House, *Kursk*, pp. 275–76.

30 Guderian, *Panzer Leader*, p. 312.

31 F.W. von Mellenthin, *Panzer Battles, 1939–1945* (London, 1955), p. 213.

32 Glantz and House, *Kursk*, p. 255.

33 J. Lucas, *Panzer Elite: The Story of Nazi Germany's Crack Grossdeutschland Corps* (London, 2000), p. 81.

34 Mellenthin, *Panzer Battles*, p. 225.

35 Glantz and House, *Kursk*, pp. 245, 252; Erickson, *The Road to Berlin*, p. 120.

36 Erickson, *The Road to Berlin*, p. 137; Seaton, *The Russo-German War*, p. 379; A. Clark, *Barbarossa* (London, 1965), p. 402.

37 Mellenthin, *Panzer Battles*, p. 228.

38 Glantz and House, *When Titans Clashed*, pp. 292, 306.

Chapter 11: Strategic Bombing: Berlin, Winter 1943–44

1 R. Overy, *Why the Allies Won* (London, 1995), p. 106; G.P. Gentile, *How Effective is Strategic Bombing?* (New York, 2001), p. 31; Malcolm Smith, 'The Allied Air Offensive', *The Journal of Strategic Studies*, March 1990, pp. 68–69; T.D. Biddle, 'British and American Approaches to Strategic Bombing: Their Origins and Implementation in the World War II Combined Bomber Offensive', *The Journal of Strategic Studies*, March 1995, p. 101.

2 D. Richards, *Portal of Hungerford* (London, 1977), pp. 69, 175.

3 C. Webster and N. Frankland, *The Strategic Air Offensive Against Germany, 1939–1945*, i (London, 1961), p. 323.

4 C. Webster and N. Frankland, *The Strategic Air Offensive Against Germany, 1939–1945*, iv (London, 1961), pp. 258–60.

5 Webster and Frankland, *The Strategic Air Offensive*, i, p. 323; W. Murray, 'Armoured Warfare: The British, French and German Experiences', in W. Murray and A.R. Millett (eds), *Military Innovation in the Interwar Period* (Cambridge, 1996), p. 19.

6 A. Harris, *Bomber Offensive* (London, 1990), p. 83.

7 M. Middlebrook, 'Marshal of the Royal Air Force Sir Arthur Harris', in M. Carver (ed.), *The War Lords* (London, 1976), p. 317.

8 M. Middlebrook, *The Battle of Hamburg* (London, 1980), p. 32.

9 United States Strategic Bombing Survey, *The Effects of Strategic Bombing of the German War Economy* (Washington, 1945), p. 2.

10 Middlebrook, *The Battle of Hamburg*, p. 36; Overy, *Why the Allies Won*, p. 118.

11 M. Middlebrook, *The Nuremberg Raid* (London, 1973), pp. 17–20, 31; Webster and Frankland, *The Strategic Air Offensive*, i, p. 316.

12 T.R. Searle, '"It Made a Lot of Sense to Kill Skilled Workers": The Firebombing of Tokyo in March 1945', *The Journal of Military History*, January 2002, pp. 108–9; W.H. Park, '"Precision" and "Area" Bombing: Who Did Which, and When?', *The Journal of Strategic Studies*, March 1995, pp. 148–54.

13 Webster and Frankland, *The Strategic Air Offensive*, iv, p. 153.

14 Middlebrook, *The Battle of Hamburg*, p. 34.

15 Middlebrook, *The Nuremberg Raid*, p. 21; Middlebrook, *The Battle of Hamburg*, p. 30; M. Middlebrook and C. Everitt, *The Bomber Command War Diaries* (London, 1985), p. 388; A. Speer, *Inside the Third Reich* (London, 1970), p. 281.

16 Speer, *Inside the Third Reich*, p. 284; Middlebrook, *The Battle of Hamburg*, pp. 82, 101, 331–32.

17 W. Murray, *Luftwaffe: Strategy for Defeat, 1933-45* (London, 1985), p. 262; C. Webster and N. Frankland, *The Strategic Air Offensive Against Germany, 1939-1945*, ii (London, 1961), p. 46.

18 M. Hastings, *Bomber Command* (London, 1979), p. 256; F.H. Hinsley, *British Intelligence in the Second World War*, iii, part 1 (London, 1984), p. 293.

19 A. Read and D. Fisher, *The Fall of Berlin* (London, 1992), p. 27; A. Ritchie, *Faust's Metropolis: A History of Berlin* (London, 1998), p. 517.

20 M. Middlebrook, *The Berlin Raids* (London, 1988), pp. 24, 27; Read and Fisher, *The Fall of Berlin*, p. 53; Speer, *Inside the Third Reich*, p. 289; A.W. Cooper, *Bombers Over Berlin* (London, 1989), pp. 12–13.

21 Middlebrook and Everitt, *The Bomber Command War Diaries*, p. 417; Middlebrook, *The Berlin Raids*, p. 338.

22 Middlebrook and Everitt, *The Bomber Command War Diaries*, pp. 427, 440.

23 Biddle, 'British and American Approaches to Strategic Bombing', p. 124.

24 Webster and Frankland, *The Strategic Air Offensive*, ii, pp. 47–48; D. Richards, *RAF Bomber Command in the Second World War* (London, 2001), p. 208; Hinsley, *British Intelligence*, iii, part 1, p. 301.

25 Speer, *Inside the Third Reich*, p. 288.

26 L.P. Lochner (ed.), *The Goebbels Diaries* (London, 1948), pp. 425, 427–30.

27 Ibid., p. 435.

28 Ibid., p. 438; Richards, *RAF Bomber Command*, p. 210.

29 Middlebrook and Everitt, *The Bomber Command War Diaries*, pp. 456–57; Middlebrook, *The Berlin Raids*, p. 134; J. Herington, *Air War Against Germany and Italy, 1939–1943* (Canberra, 1954), p. 641.

30 Webster and Frankland, *The Strategic Air Offensive*, ii, pp. 54–57; Middlebrook, *The Nuremberg Raid*, p. 25.

31 Hastings, *Bomber Command*, p. 262.

32 Middlebrook, *The Berlin Raids*, p. 139; Hinsley, *British Intelligence*, iii, part 1, p. 301.

33 Middlebrook, *The Berlin Raids*, pp. 211–12, 214.

34 Ibid., p. 378; J. Foreman, J. Matthews, S. Parry, *Luftwaffe Night-Fighter Victory Claims* (Walton, Surrey, 2004), p. 189; D.C. Isby (ed.), *Fighting the Bombers* (London, 2003), p. 224; K. Delve, *Nightfighter: The Battle for the Night Skies* (London, 1995), p. 158; Middlebrook, *The Berlin Raids*, pp. 231–32.

35 Herington, *Air War Against Germany and Italy*, p. 642; Middlebrook, *The Berlin Raids*, p. 257; Webster and Frankland, *The Strategic Air Offensive*, iv, p. 432; Hinsley, *British Intelligence*, iii, part 1, p. 304.

36 Herington, *Air War Against Germany and Italy*, p. 647.

37 Middlebrook, *The Berlin Raids*, p. 270; Murray, *Luftwaffe*, p. 292; Middlebrook and Everitt, *The Bomber Command War Diaries*, p. 476.

38 Middlebrook, *The Berlin Raids*, p. 303.

39 Ibid., p. 305.

40 Herington, *Air War Against Germany and Italy*, p. 662; Webster and Frankland, *The Strategic Air Offensive*, ii, p. 192; Richards, *RAF Bomber Command*, p. 219; Middlebrook, *The Berlin Raids*, p. 305.

41 Foreman, Matthews, Parry, *Luftwaffe Night-Fighter Victory Claims*, p. 243.

42 Webster and Frankland, *The Strategic Air Offensive*, ii, p. 197.

43 Middlebrook, *The Berlin Raids*, p. 321.

44 Webster and Frankland, *The Strategic Air Offensive*, ii, p. 196.

45 A.T. Harris, *Despatch on War Operations, 23rd February, 1942, to 8th May, 1945* (London, 1995), p. 20; Hastings, *Bomber Command*, p. 241.

46 W. Murray, *War in the Air, 1914–45* (London, 1999), p. 152.

47 Hastings, *Bomber Command*, p. 268.

48 Webster and Frankland, *The Strategic Air Offensive*, iii, p. 288.

49 R. Overy, *The Air War, 1939-1945* (London, 1980), p. 119; Speer, *Inside the Third Reich*, p. 278.

50 W.F. Craven and J.L. Cate, *The Army Air Forces in World War II*, iii (Chicago, 1951), pp. 48-53.

51 Ibid., p. 46.

52 Murray, *Luftwaffe*, p. 370.

Chapter 12: Normandy

1 C. D'Este, *Decision in Normandy* (New York, 1983), p. 29.

2 W. Murray and A.R. Millett, *A War to be Won* (Cambridge, Mass., 2000), p. 66.

3 J. Keegan, *Six Armies in Normandy* (London, 1982), p. 65.

4 B.H. Liddell Hart, *The German Generals Talk* (New York, 1948), p. 228.

5 Keegan, *Six Armies in Normandy*, p. 61.

6 D'Este, *Decision in Normandy*, p. 115; A.F. Wilt, *War From the Top* (Bloomington, 1990), p. 265; D. Fraser, *Knight's Cross: A Life of Field-Marshal Erwin Rommel* (London, 1993), p. 466.

7 L. F. Ellis, *Victory in the West*, i (London, 1962), pp. 58–59.

8 Ibid., p. 117; G. Bernage, *The Panzer and the Battle of Normandy* (Bayeux, 2000), p. v.

9 United States Strategic Bombing Survey, *The Effects of Strategic Bombing of the German War Economy*

(Washington, 1945), pp. 163, 278-79; R. Overy, *Why the Allies Won* (London, 1995), p. 154.

10 Overy, *Why the Allies Won*, pp. 142–43; J. Ehrman, *Grand Strategy*, v (London, 1956), p. 173.

11 D'Este, *Decision in Normandy*, p. 89; Overy, *Why the Allies Won*, p. 141.

12 Wilt, *War From the Top*, p. 260; G.L. Weinberg, *A World at Arms* (Cambridge, 1994), p. 676.

13 Murray and Millett, *A War to be Won*, p. 412; D'Este, *Decision in Normandy*, p. 109.

14 Overy, *Why the Allies Won*, pp. 151–52.

15 D'Este, *Decision in Normandy*, pp. 72, 90–91.

16 M. van Creveld, *Supplying War* (Cambridge, 1977), p. 206.

17 S. Hart, 'Montgomery, Morale, Casualty Conservation and "Colossal Cracks": 21st Army Group's Operational Technique in North-West Europe, 1944-45', *The Journal of Strategic Studies*, December 1996, p. 135.

18 Keegan, *Six Armies in Normandy*, p. 65; W. Richardson and S. Freidin (eds), *The Fatal Decisions* (London, 1956), p. 185.

19 A.R. Lewis, 'The Failure of Allied Planning and Doctrine for Operation Overlord: The Case of Minefield and Obstacle Clearance', *The Journal of Military History*, October 1998, p. 797.

20 Murray and Millett, *A War to be Won*, p. 419.

21 D'Este, *Decision in Normandy*, p. 141.

22 I. Gooderson, 'Allied Fighter-Bombers Versus German Armour in North-West Europe, 1944-1945: Myths and Realities', *The Journal of Strategic Studies*, June 1991, p. 216.

23 Ellis, *Victory in the West*, i, p. 294.

24 D'Este, *Decision in Normandy*, pp. 188–89.

25 Overy, *Why the Allies Won*, p. 178.

26 D'Este, *Decision in Normandy*, p. 154.

27 R.A. Hart, *Clash of Arms* (London, 2001), p. 398; J.J. Carafano, *After D-Day: Operation Cobra and the Normandy Breakout* (Boulder, Colorado, 2000), p. 27.

28 M. Hastings, *Overlord: D-Day and the Battle for Normandy* (London, 1984), p. 36.

29 D. Graham, *Against Odds* (London, 1999), p. 133; T. Ripley, *The Wehrmacht* (New York, 2003), p. 307; J. Ellis, *Brute Force* (London, 1990), p. 275.

30 Keegan, *Six Armies in Normandy*, p. 164.

31 Fraser, *Knight's Cross*, pp. 497-500.

32 D'Este, *Decision in Normandy*, p. 248.

33 Ibid., p. 242; R.F. Weigley, *Eisenhower's Lieutenants* (Bloomington, 1981), p. 124; S.W. Mitcham, *The Desert Fox in Normandy* (Westport, 1997), p. 122.

34 A. Horne, *The Lonely Leader: Monty, 1944-1945* (London, 1994), pp. 151, 158.

35 D.M. Glantz and J.M. House, *When Titans Clashed* (Lawrence, Kansas, 1995), pp. 184, 191; R. Overy, *Russia's War* (London, 1997), p. 236.

36 R.A. Hart, *Clash of Arms*, p. 310; S. Hart, 'Montgomery, Morale, Casualty Conservation', p. 136; D'Este, *Decision in Normandy*, p. 255; D. French, *Raising Churchill's Army* (Oxford, 2000), p. 244.

37 W. Murray, *Luftwaffe: Strategy for Defeat, 1933–45* (London, 1988), p. 379.

38 D'Este, *Decision in Normandy*, p. 355.

39 Keegan, *Six Armies in Normandy*, p. 198; D. Fraser, *War and Shadows* (London, 2002), pp. 196–98.

40 Keegan, *Six Armies in Normandy*, p. 206.

41 Ibid., p. 212.

42 Overy, *Why the Allies Won*, p. 167; Horne, *The Lonely Leader*, p. 215.

43. Wilt, *War From The Top*, p. 270; H. Speidel, *We Defended Normandy* (London, 1951), pp. 125-26.

44 Keegan, *Six Armies in Normandy*, p. 219; S.T. Powers, 'The Battle of Normandy: The Lingering Controversy', *The Journal of Military History*, July 1992, p. 456.

45 Murray and Millett, *A War to be Won*, p. 429; Carafano, *Operation Cobra*, p. 260.

46 D'Este, *Decision in Normandy*, p. 419; Gooderson, 'Allied Fighter-Bombers Versus German Armour', p. 220.

47 Keegan, *Six Armies in Normandy*, p. 259.

48 D'Este, *Decision in Normandy*, p. 430; Keegan, *Six Armies in Normandy*, p. 274.

49 D'Este, *Decision in Normandy*, p. 142.

50 Ibid., p. 432.

51 Weinberg, *A World at Arms*, p. 695.

52 D'Este, *Decision in Normandy*, pp. 517–18; Hart, *Clash of Arms*, p. 373; Weigley, *Eisenhower's Lieutenants*, p. 106; N. Zetterling, *Normandy, 1944* (Manitoba, 2000), p. 77.

53 D'Este, *Decision in Normandy*, pp. 434, 456, 518.

Chapter 13: Battle of Leyte Gulf: Philippines, October 1944

1 T.J. Cutler, *The Battle of Leyte Gulf, 23–26 October 1944* (New York, 1994), p. 14.

2 H.P. Willmott, 'The Battle of the Philippine Sea', in J. Sweetman (ed.), *Great American Naval Battles* (Annapolis, 1998), p. 329.

3 S.E. Morison, *The Two-Ocean War* (Boston, 1963), pp. 330, 333; M.R. Peattie, *Sunburst: The Rise of Japanese Naval Air Power, 1909-1941* (Annapolis, 2001), p. 187.

4 Cutler, *Leyte Gulf*, p. 17; Morison, *The Two-Ocean War*, p. 343; Peattie, *Sunburst*, p. 188.

5 Morison, *The Two-Ocean War*, p. 343.

6 Ibid., pp. 344–45; Willmott, 'The Battle of the Philippine Sea', p. 339.

7 Morison, *The Two-Ocean War*, p. 345; Cutler, *Leyte Gulf*, p. 20.

8 R.H. Spector, *Eagle Against the Sun: The American War with Japan* (New York, 1985), p. 294.

9 Cutler, *Leyte Gulf*, p. 23.

10 T.J. Cutler, 'The Battle of Leyte Gulf', in Sweetman, *Great American Naval Battles*, p. 344; C.G. Reynolds, 'William F. Halsey, Jr. The Bull (1882–1959)', in J. Sweetman (ed.), *The Great Admirals* (Annapolis, 1997), pp. 483–85, 487.

11 R. Steinberg, *Return to the Philippines* (New York, 1979), p. 49; G.L. Weinberg, *A World at Arms* (Cambridge, 1994), p. 842.

12 Cutler, *Leyte Gulf*, pp. 70–71; Morison, *The Two-Ocean War*, p. 429.

13 Cutler, *Leyte Gulf*, p. 347.

14 E.J. Drea, *In the Service of the Emperor* (Lincoln, Nebraska, 1998), p. 127.

15 Ibid., pp. 131–32.

16 Steinberg, *Return to the Philippines*, p. 52.

17 J.D. Hornfischer, *The Last Stand of the Tin Can Sailors* (New York, 2004), pp. 12-13.

18 S.E. Morison, *History of United States Naval Operations*, xii (Boston, 1958), p. 167; Morison, *The Two-Ocean War*, p. 439; P.S. Dull, *A Battle History of the Imperial Japanese Navy, 1941-1945* (Annapolis, 1978), p. 319.

19 Cutler, *Leyte Gulf*, p. 93.

20 Dull, *A Battle History of the Imperial Japanese Navy*, p. 316.

21 Spector, *Eagle Against the Sun*, p. 487.

22 D.C. Evans and M.R. Peattie, *Kaigun: Strategy, Tactics and Technology in the Imperial Japanese Navy, 1887-1941* (Annapolis, 1997), p. 508.

23 Cutler, *Leyte Gulf*, p. 117.

24 Ibid., p. 131.

25 Morison, *United States Naval Operations*, xii, p. 186; E.B. Potter, *Bull Halsey* (Annapolis, 1985), p. 291; Cutler, *Leyte Gulf*, p. 150.

26 Cutler, *Leyte Gulf*, pp. 151-53; Morison, *United States Naval Operations*, xii, pp. 184, 187-89.

27 Cutler, *Leyte Gulf*, pp. 159-61; Potter, *Bull Halsey*, p. 293.

28 Cutler, *Leyte Gulf*, p. 170; Potter, *Bull Halsey*, p. 296; Morison, *United States Naval Operations*, xii, pp. 189-90.

29 Morison, *United States Naval Operations*, xii, pp. 215–16.

30 Cutler, *Leyte Gulf*, p. 195.

31 Ibid., p. 214.

32 Morison, *United States Naval Operations*, xii, p. 247.

33 Ibid., p. 248; Cutler, *Leyte Gulf*, p. 222.

34 Hornfischer, *Tin Can Sailors*, p. 70.

35 Morison, *United States Naval Operations*, xii, p. 256.

36 Cutler, *Leyte Gulf*, p. 256.

37 Morison, *United States Naval Operations*, xii, p. 288.

38 Cutler, *Leyte Gulf*, p. 264.

39 Morison, *United States Naval Operations*, xii, p. 298.

40 Cutler, *Leyte Gulf*, p. 237.

41 E.B. Potter, *Nimitz* (Annapolis, 1976), p. 340.

42 Potter, *Bull Halsey*, p. 304.

43 Cutler, *Leyte Gulf*, p. 261.

44 Hornfischer, *Tin Can Sailors*, p. 417.

45 Ibid.

46 Steinberg, *Return to the Philippines*, p. 96.

47 Cutler, *Leyte Gulf*, pp. 361–62.

48 Potter, *Bull Halsey*, p. 306.

49 Morison, *United States Naval Operations*, xii, p. 338.

Chapter 14: The Final Battle for Berlin

1 A. Ritchie, *Faust's Metropolis: A History of Berlin* (London, 1998), p. 551.

2 N. Stone, *Hitler* (London, 1980), p. 203; H. Trevor-Roper, *The Last Days of Hitler* (Chicago, 1992), p. 53.

3 H. Guderian, *Panzer Leader* (London, 1953), p. 387.

4 I. Kershaw, *Hitler, 1936-45: Nemesis* (London, 2000), p. 1018.

5 Guderian, *Panzer Leader*, p. 372.

6 A.S. Milward, *The German Economy at War* (London, 1965), p. 113.

7 D.M. Glantz and J.M. House, *When Titans Clashed* (Lawrence, Kansas, 1995), p. 236.

8 A. Read and D. Fisher, *The Fall of Berlin* (London, 1992), p. 217.

9 United States Strategic Bombing Survey, *The Effects of Strategic Bombing of the German War Economy* (Washington, 1945), pp. 187-88.

10 C. Duffy, *Red Storm on the Reich* (London, 1991), p. 180.

11 W.S. Churchill, *The Second World War*, vi (London, 1953), p. 291.

12 D.E. Shepardson, 'The Fall of Berlin and the Rise of a Myth', *The Journal of Military History*, January 1998, pp. 139–40.

13 Ibid., p. 141.

14 Ritchie, *Faust's Metropolis*, p. 553.

15 S.E. Ambrose, *Eisenhower and Berlin* (New York, 1986), p. 60.

16 D.C. Large, *Berlin* (London, 2000), p. 356.

17 Ritchie, *Faust's Metropolis*, p. 553.

18 Ambrose, *Eisenhower and Berlin*, p. 65; Shepardson, 'The Fall of Berlin', p. 144.

19 W. Murray and A.R. Millett, *A War to be Won* (Cambridge, Mass., 2000), pp. 480, 483.

20 A. Speer, *Inside the Third Reich* (New York, 1970), p. 302.

21 Ibid., p. 307; Read and Fisher, *The Fall of Berlin*, p. 250; G.P. Megargee, *Inside Hitler's High Command* (Lawrence, Kansas, 2000), p. 181.

22 Kershaw, *Hitler, 1936-45: Nemesis*, p. 785; Read and Fisher, *The Fall of Berlin*, p. 260.

23 W.S. Dunn, *Nemesis: The Red Army, 1930-1945* (Westport, 1994), pp. 48, 61.

24 A. Seaton, *The Russo-German War, 1941-45* (London, 1971), p. 566.

25 Duffy, *Red Storm on the Reich*, p. 290.

26 Kershaw, *Hitler, 1936-45: Nemesis*, pp. 791, 1018.

27 Large, *Berlin*, p. 347.

28 Kershaw, *Hitler, 1936-45: Nemesis*, p. 792; Seaton, *The Russo-German War*, p. 571.

29 Seaton, *The Russo-German War*, p. 570.

30 R. Overy, *Russia's War* (London, 1997), p. 266; Glantz and House, *When Titans Clashed*, p. 260.
31 M. Hastings, *Armageddon: The Battle for Germany, 1944–1945* (New York, 2004), p. 466; T. Le Tissier, *Race for the Reichstag* (London, 1999), pp. 5-7.
32 Speer, *Inside the Third Reich*, p. 472.
33 Le Tissier, *Race for the Reichstag*, p. 72; Read and Fisher, *The Fall of Berlin*, p. 387.
34 W. Gorlitz (ed.), *The Memoirs of Field-Marshal Keitel* (London, 1965), p. 201.
35 Speer, *Inside the Third Reich*, p. 479; Kershaw, *Hitler, 1936-45: Nemesis*, p. 808.
36 Seaton, *The Russo-German War*, p. 582; Kershaw, *Hitler, 1936–45: Nemesis*, p. 803.
37 Kershaw, *Hitler, 1936-45: Nemesis*, pp. 811, 821, 824.
38 Ibid., p. 827.
39 S. Weintraub, *The Last Great Victory* (New York, 1995), p. 318.
40 A. Beevor, *Berlin: The Downfall, 1945* (London, 2002), p. xxxiii.
41 Glantz and House, *When Titans Clashed*, p. 292.
42 Le Tissier, *Race for the Reichstag*, p. 195.

Chapter 15: The Capitulation of Japan

1 E.B. Kerr, *Flames Over Tokyo* (New York, 1991), p. 72.
2 R.H. Spector, *Eagle Against the Sun: The American War with Japan* (New York, 1985), p. 493.
3 R. Schaffer, *Wings of Judgment* (New York, 1985), p. 135.
4 W.F. Craven and J.L. Cate, *The Army Air Forces in World War II*, v (Chicago, 1953), p. 617.
5 T.R. Searle, "'It Made a Lot of Sense to Kill Skilled Workers': The Firebombing of Tokyo in March 1945', *The Journal of Military History*, January 2002, p. 118.
6 R.B. Frank, *Downfall: The End of the Imperial Japanese Empire* (New York, 1999), pp. 77, 350.
7 Spector, *Eagle Against the Sun*, p. 497.
8 W. Murray and A.R. Millett, *A War to be Won* (Cambridge, Mass., 2000), p. 515.
9 J.W. Dower, *Embracing Defeat* (London, 1999), pp. 19, 43.
10 A.D. Coox, 'Needless Fear: The Compromise of United States Plans to Invade Japan in 1945', *The Journal of Military History*, April 2000, p. 414.
11 Spector, *Eagle Against the Sun*, p. 548.
12 Coox, 'Needless Fear', p. 415; Spector, *Eagle Against the Sun*, pp. 543-44; Frank, *Downfall*, p. 340; D.M. Giangreco, 'Casualty Projections for the United States Invasions of Japan, 1945-46: Planning and Policy Implications', *The Journal of Military History*, July 1997, p. 581.
13 E.J. Drea, *In the Service of the Emperor* (Lincoln, Nebraska, 1998), p. 210.
14 R.J. Maddox, *Weapons for Victory* (Columbia, Missouri, 1995), pp. 146–47; Frank, *Downfall*, p. 276.
15 G.L. Weinberg, *A World at Arms* (Cambridge, 1994), pp. 568–69.
16 L. Freedman and S. Dockrill, 'Hiroshima: A Strategy of Shock', in G. Martel (ed.), *The World War Two Reader* (New York, 2004), pp. 66-67.
17 Maddox, *Weapons for Victory*, p. 152.
18 Weinberg, *A World at Arms*, p. 837.
19 Spector, *Eagle Against the Sun*, p. 546.
20 W.S. Churchill, *The Second World War*, vi (London, 1953), p. 511.
21 Frank, *Downfall*, p. 70.
22 Ibid., p. 73; Maddox, *Weapons for Victory*, p. 148.
23 Drea, *In the Service of the Emperor*, p. 248.
24 Frank, *Downfall*, p. 264; D. Rees, *The Defeat of Japan* (Westport, 1997), p. 155.
25 Craven and Cate, *The Army Air Forces*, v, p. 720; S. Weintraub, *The Last Great Victory* (New York, 1995), p. 424.
26 K.P. Werrell, *Blankets of Fire* (Washington, 1996), p. 217; Craven and Cate, *The Army Air Forces*, v, p. 722.
27 Sadao Asada, 'The Shock of the Atomic Bomb and Japan's Decision to Surrender - A Reconsideration', *Pacific Historical Review*, November 1998, p. 477.

28 Masatake Okumiya and Jiro Horikoshi, *Zero! The Story of the Japanese Navy Air Force, 1937–1945* (New York, 1956), p. 322.

29 Ibid., p. 323.

30 Frank, *Downfall*, pp. 271, 277.

31. Ibid., p. 281; E.J. Drea, 'Missing Intentions: Japanese Intelligence and the Soviet Invasion of Manchuria, 1945', *Military Affairs*, April 1984, pp. 68–69.

32 Craven and Cate, *The Army Air Forces*, v, p. 719; F.W. Chinnock, *Nagasaki: The Forgotten Bomb* (London, 1970), p. 145; Frank, *Downfall*, p. 263.

33 Craven and Cate, *The Army Air Forces*, v, p. 720; Frank, *Downfall*, pp. 284–85; D.M. Goldstein, K.V. Dillon, J.M. Wenger, *Rain of Ruin* (London, 1995), p. 106.

34 Frank, *Downfall*, p. 287.

35 Drea, *In the Service of the Emperor*, p. 204; Rees, *The Defeat of Japan*, p. 163.

36 Frank, *Downfall*, p. 77.

37 Freedman and Dockrill, 'Hiroshima: A Strategy of Shock', p. 76.

38 Rees, *The Defeat of Japan*, p. 166; Drea, *In the Service of the Emperor*, p. 208.

39 Spector, *Eagle Against the Sun*, p. 556.

40 Asada, 'The Shock of the Atomic Bomb', p. 497.

41 Frank, *Downfall*, p. 347.

42 Ibid., p. 311.

43 Rees, *The Defeat of Japan*, p. 183.

Chapter 16: The Defeat of the Axis

1 J.M. McPherson, *Battle Cry of Freedom* (London, 1990), p. 858.

2 B. Bond, *The Pursuit of Victory* (Oxford, 1996), p. 4.

3 Ibid., pp. 1–2.

4 R.M. Citino, *Quest for Decisive Victory* (Lawrence, Kansas, 2002), p. xii.

5 L.P. Lochner, *What About Germany?* (New York, 1942), p. 2.

6 R. Overy, *Why the Allies Won* (New York, 1996), p. 21.

7 R.B. Frank, *Downfall: The End of the Imperial Japanese Empire* (New York, 1999), p. 337.

8 W.S. Churchill, *The Second World War*, vi (London, 1953), pp. 308–9.

9 G.L. Weinberg, *A World at Arms* (Cambridge, 1994), p. 791.

10 N. Bagnall, *The Punic Wars* (London, 1990), p. 320; A. Goldsworthy, *The Punic Wars* (London, 2000), p. 354.

11 W. Ropke, *The German Question* (London, 1946), p. 154.

12 Ibid., p. 35.

Bibliography

Addison, P. and Calder, A. (eds), *Time to Kill* (London, 1997).

Agawa, Hiroyuki, *Reluctant Admiral: Yamamoto and the Imperial Navy* (New York, 1979).

Alexander, M.S., 'The Fall of France, 1940', *The Journal of Strategic Studies*, March 1990, pp. 10–44.

Ambrose, S.E., *Eisenhower and Berlin* (New York, 1986).

Asada, Sadao, 'The Shock of the Atomic Bomb and Japan's Decision to Surrender – A Reconsideration', *Pacific Historical Review*, November 1998, pp. 477–512.

Barnett, C., *Engage the Enemy More Closely: The Royal Navy in the Second World War* (New York, 1991).

Barnett, C., *The Desert Generals* (London, 1983).

Beaufre, A., *1940: The Fall of France* (London, 1967).

Beaumont, J., *Comrades in Arms: British Aid to Russia, 1941–1945* (London, 1980).

Beevor, A., *Berlin: The Downfall, 1945* (London, 2002).

Behrens, C.B.A., *Merchant Shipping and the Demands of War* (London, 1955).

Bekker, C., *Hitler's Naval War* (London, 1974).

Bethell, N., *The War Hitler Won* (London, 1972).

Biddle, T.D., 'British and American Approaches to Strategic Bombing', *The Journal of Strategic Studies*, March 1995, pp. 91–144.

Blair, C., *Hitler's U-boat War: The Hunters, 1939–1942* (New York, 1996).

Bloch, Marc, *Strange Defeat* (New York, 1999).

Bond, B., *British Military Policy Between the Two World Wars* (Oxford, 1980).

Bond, B., *France and Belgium, 1939–1940* (London, 1975).

Bond, B., *Liddell Hart: A Study of his Military Thought* (New Brunswick, New Jersey, 1977).

Boyce, R. (ed.), *French Foreign and Defence Policy, 1918-1940* (London, 1998).

Brice, M.H., *The Royal Navy and the Sino-Japanese Incident, 1937–41* (London, 1973).

Bryant, A., *The Turn of the Tide, 1939–1943* (London, 1957).

Buckley, J., 'Atlantic Airpower Co-operation, 1941–1945', *The Journal of Strategic Studies*, March 1995, pp. 175–97.

Buell, T.B., *The Quiet Warrior: A Biography of Admiral Raymond A. Spruance* (Annapolis, 1988).

Bungay, S., *The Most Dangerous Enemy* (London, 2000).

Burdick, C. and Jacobsen, H. (eds), *The Halder War Diaries, 1939–1942* (Novato, California, 1988).

Calvocoressi, P., Wint, G., Pritchard, J., *The Penguin History of the Second World War* (London, 1999).

Carafano, J.J., *After D-Day: Operation Cobra and the Normandy Breakout* (Boulder, Colorado, 2000).

Carell, P., *Stalingrad: The Defeat of the German Sixth Army* (Atglen, Pennsylvania, 1993).

Carlson, E.F., *The Chinese Army* (Westport, 1940).

Carver, M., *El Alamein* (London, 1962).

Chalfont, A., *Montgomery of Alamein* (London, 1976).

Chang, Iris, *The Rape of Nanking* (New York, 1997).

Chuikov, V.I., *The Battle for Stalingrad* (New York, 1964).

Churchill, W.S., *The Second World War*, i-vi (London, 1948–54).

Cohen, E.A. and Gooch, J., *Military Misfortunes: The Anatomy of Failure in War* (New York, 1990).

Collier, B., *The Defence of the United Kingdom* (London, 1957).

Cooper, A.W., *Bombers Over Berlin* (London, 1989).

Coox, A.D., 'Needless Fear: The Compromise of United States Plans to Invade Japan in 1945', *The Journal of Military History*, April 2000, pp. 411–37.

Coox, A.D., *Nomonhan: Japan Against Russia,* 1939 (Stanford, 1985).

Craven, W.F. and Cate, J.L., *The American Air Forces in World War II,* i-v (Chicago, 1948–53).

Cutler, T.J., *The Battle of Leyte Gulf, 23–26 October 1944* (New York, 1994).

Cynk, J.B., *History of the Polish Air Force, 1918–1968* (Reading, 1972).

Deighton, L., *Fighter* (London, 1977).

Deist, W. et al, *Germany and the Second World War,* i-vi (Oxford, 1990–2001).

D'Este, C., *Decision in Normandy* (New York, 1983).

DiNardo, R.L., 'The Dysfunctional Coalition: The Axis Powers and the Eastern Front in World War II', *The Journal of Military History,* October 1996, pp. 711–30.

Doenitz, Karl, *Memoirs: Ten Years and Twenty Days* (London, 1990).

Dower, J.W., *Embracing Defeat* (London, 1999).

Drea, E.J., *In the Service of the Emperor* (Lincoln, Nebraska, 1998).

Dreyer, E.L., *China at War, 1901–1949* (London, 1995).

Duffy, C., *Red Storm on the Reich* (London, 1991).

Dunn, W.S., *Hitler's Nemesis: The Red Army, 1930–1945* (Westport, 1994).

Dunn, W.S., *Kursk: Hitler's Gamble, 1943* (London, 1997).

Ellis, J., *Brute Force* (New York, 1990).

Ellis, L.F., *The War in France and Flanders, 1939–40* (London, 1953).

Erickson, J. and Dilks, D. (eds), *Barbarossa: The Axis and the Allies* (Edinburgh, 1994).

Erickson, J. (ed.), *Main Front: Soviet Leaders Look Back on World War II* (London, 1987).

Erickson, J., *The Road to Berlin* (London, 1983).

Erickson, J., *The Road to Stalingrad* (London, 1975).

Evans, D.C. and Peattie, M.R., *Kaigun: Strategy, Tactics and Technology in the Imperial Japanese Navy, 1887–1941* (Annapolis, 1997).

Farmer, R., *Shanghai Harvest* (London, 1945).

Frank, R.B., *Downfall: The End of the Imperial Japanese Empire* (New York, 1999).

Fraser, D., *Knight's Cross: A Life of Field-Marshal Erwin Rommel* (London, 1993).

Fuchida, Mitsuo and Okumiya, Masatake, *Midway* (Annapolis, 1955).

Fulbrook, M., (ed.), *German History Since 1870* (London, 1997).

Fuquea, D.C., 'Task Force One: The Wasted Assets of the United States Pacific Battleships Fleet, 1942', *The Journal of Military History,* October 1997, pp. 707–34.

Galland, Adolf, *The First and the Last* (London, 1955).

Gannon, M., *Pearl Harbor Betrayed* (New York, 2002).

Gardner, J., 'The Battle of the Atlantic, 1941 – The First Turning Point?', *The Journal of Strategic Studies,* March 1994, pp. 109–23.

Gerbert, K. (ed.), *Generalfeldmarschall Fedor von Bock: The War Diary, 1939-1945* (Atglen, Pennsylvania, 1996).

Giangreco, D.M., 'Casualty Projections for the United States Invasions of Japan, 1945–46: Planning and Policy Implications', *The Journal of Military History,* July 1997, pp. 521–81.

Gilbert, M., *Second World War* (London, 1989).

Glantz, D.M., *Barbarossa* (Charleston, 2001).

Glantz, D.M. and House, J.M., *The Battle of Kursk* (Lawrence, Kansas, 1999).

Glantz, D.M. and House, J.M., *When Titans Clashed* (Lawrence, Kansas, 1995).

Glantz, D.M., *Zhukov's Greatest Defeat: The Red Army's Epic Disaster in Operation Mars, 1942* (Lawrence, Kansas, 1999).

Gooderson, I., 'Allied Fighter-Bombers Versus German Armour in North-West Europe, 1944–1945: Myths and Realities', *The Journal of Strategic Studies,* June 1991, pp. 210–31.

Gordon, D.M., 'The China-Japan War, 1931-1945', *The Journal of Military History,* January 2006, pp. 137–82.

Graham, D., *Against Odds* (London, 1999).

Greene, J. and Massignari, A., *The Naval War in the Mediterranean, 1940–1943* (London, 1998).

Guderian, H., *Achtung Panzer* (London, 1995).

Guderian, H., *Panzer Leader* (Washington, 1952).

Gunsburg, J.A., *Divided and Conquered: The French High Command and the Defeat of the West, 1940* (London, 1979).

Gunsburg, J.A., 'The Battle of the Belgian Plain, 12-14 May 1940: The First Great Tank Battle', *The Journal of Military History*, April 1992, pp. 207–44.

Harries, M. and S., *Soldiers of the Sun: The Rise and Fall of the Imperial Japanese Army, 1868– 1945* (London, 1991).

Harris, J.P., 'British Armour and Rearmament in the 1930s', *The Journal of Strategic Studies*, June 1988, pp. 220–44.

Hart, R.A., *Clash of Arms* (London, 2001).

Hastings, M., *Armageddon: The Battle for Germany, 1944–1945* (New York, 2004).

Hastings, M., *Bomber Command* (London, 1979).

Hastings, M., *Overlord: D-Day and the Battle for Normandy* (London, 1984).

Hayward, J., 'Hitler's Quest for Oil: The Impact of Economic Considerations on Military Strategy, 1941– 42', *The Journal of Strategic Studies*, December 1995, pp. 94–135.

Hayward, J., 'Too Little, Too Late: An Analysis of Hitler's Failure in August 1942 to Damage Soviet Oil Production', *The Journal of Military History*, July 2000, pp. 769–94.

Hinsley, F.H., *British Intelligence in the Second World War*, i–iii (London, 1979–88).

Hitler, Adolf, *Mein Kampf* (London, 1939).

Horne, A., *The Lonely Leader: Monty, 1944–1945* (London, 1994).

Horne, A., *To Lose a Battle: France, 1940* (London, 1969).

Hornfischer, J.D., *The Last Stand of the Tin Can Sailors* (New York, 2004).

Howarth, S. and Law, D., *The Battle of the Atlantic, 1939-1945* (London, 1994).

Hsiung, J.C. and Levine, S.I. (eds), *China's Bitter Victory* (New York, 1992).

Irvine, W.D., 'Domestic Politics and the Fall of France in 1940', *Historical Reflections*, vol. 22, no. 1, 1996, pp. 77–90.

Jackson, J., *The Fall of France* (Oxford, 2003).

Jones, F.C., *Shanghai and Tientsin* (New York, 1940).

Jordan, D.A., *China's Trial by Fire* (Ann Arbor, Michigan, 2001).

Karski, Jan, *The Great Powers and Poland, 1919–1945* (London, 1985).

Katsuichi, Honda, *The Nanking Massacre* (New York, 1999).

Keegan, J., *Six Armies in Normandy* (London, 1982).

Keegan, J., *The Price of Admiralty* (London, 1988).

Keegan, J., *The Second World War* (London, 1989).

Kennedy, R.M., *The German Campaign in Poland* (Washington, 1956).

Kerr, E.B., *Flames Over Tokyo* (New York, 1991).

Kershaw, I., *Hitler, 1936–45: Nemesis* (London, 2000).

Kier, E., *Imagining War: French and British Military Doctrine Between the Wars* (Princeton, 1997).

Kiesling, E.C., *Arming Against Hitler: France and the Limits of Military Planning* (Lawrence, Kansas, 1996).

Kohn, R.H. (ed.), 'The Scholarship on World War II: Its Present Condition and Future Possibilities', *The Journal of Military History*, July 1991, pp. 365–93.

Kupchan, C.A., *The Vulnerability of Empire* (Ithaca, 1994).

Langhorne, R. (ed.), *Diplomacy and Intelligence During the Second World War* (Cambridge, 1985).

Latimer, J., *Alamein* (London, 2002).

Leach, B.A., *German Strategy Against Russia, 1939–1941* (Oxford, 1973).

Lee, Asher, *Goering: Air Leader* (London, 1972).

Le Tissier, T., *Race for the Reichstag* (London, 1999).

Lewin, R., *The Life and Death of the Afrika Korps* (London, 1977).

Lewis, A.R., 'The Failure of Allied Planning and Doctrine for Operation Overlord: The Case of Minefield and Obstacle Clearance', *The Journal of Military History*, October 1998, pp. 787–807.

Liddell Hart, B.H., *German Generals Talk* (New York, 1948).

Liddell Hart, B.H., *History of the Second World War* (London, 1970).

Liddell Hart, B.H. (ed.), *The Rommel Papers* (London, 1953).

Liu, F.F., *A Military History of Modern China, 1924–1949* (Princeton, 1956).

Lochner, L.P. (ed.), *The Goebbels Diaries* (London, 1948).

Maiolo, J.A., 'Deception and Intelligence Failure: Anglo-German Preparations for U-boat Warfare in the

1930s', *The Journal of Strategic Studies*, December 1999, pp. 55–76.

Manstein, E. von, *Lost Victories* (Chicago, 1958).

Marder, A.J., *From Dardanelles to Oran* (London, 1974).

Martel, G. (ed.), *The World War Two Reader* (New York, 2004).

Mason, F.K., *Battle Over Britain* (London, 1969).

Megargee, G.P., *Inside Hitler's High Command* (Lawrence, Kansas, 2000).

Mellenthin, F.W. von, *German Generals of World War II* (Norman, Oklahoma, 1977).

Mellenthin, F.W. von, *Panzer Battles, 1939–1945* (London, 1955).

Middlebrook, M., *Convoy* (London, 1976).

Middlebrook, M., *The Battle of Hamburg* (London, 1980).

Middlebrook, M., *The Berlin Raids* (London, 1988).

Middlebrook, M. and Everitt, C., *The Bomber Command War Diaries* (London, 1985).

Middlebrook, M., *The Nuremberg Raid* (London, 1973).

Milward, A.S., *The New Order and the French Economy* (Oxford, 1970).

Mitcham, S.W., *The Panzer Legions* (Westport, 2001).

Morison, S.E., *History of United States Naval Operations in World War II*, i–xv (Boston, 1947–61).

Morison, S.E., *The Two-Ocean War* (Boston, 1963).

Murray, W. and Millett, A.R., *A War to be Won* (Cambridge, Mass., 2000).

Murray, W., *Luftwaffe: Strategy for Defeat, 1933–45* (London, 1985).

Murray, W. and Millett, A.R. (eds), *Military Innovation in the Interwar Period* (Cambridge, 1996).

Murray, W., *The Change in the European Balance of Power, 1938–39* (Princeton, 1984).

Murray, W., *War in the Air, 1914–45* (London, 1999).

Okumiya, Masatake and Horikoshi, Jiro, *Zero! The Story of the Japanese Navy Air Force, 1937–1945* (New York, 1956).

Orange, V., *Air Chief Marshal Sir Keith Park* (London, 1984).

Overy, R., *Russia's War* (London, 1997).

Overy, R., *The Air War, 1939–1945* (London, 1980).

Overy, R., *The Battle of Britain* (London, 2000).

Overy, R., *Why the Allies Won* (New York, 1996).

Park, W.H., '"Precision" and "Area" Bombing: Who Did Which and When?', *The Journal of Strategic Studies*, March 1995, pp. 145–74.

Peattie, M.R., *Sunburst: The Rise of Japanese Naval Air Power, 1909–1941* (Annapolis, 2001).

Petracarro, D., 'Italian Army in North Africa, 1940–1943: An Attempt at Historical Perspective', *War and Society*, October 1991, pp. 103–27.

Playfair, I.S.O. and Moloney, C.J.C., *The Mediterranean and Middle East*, i–iv (London, 1954–73).

Porch, D., *The Path to Victory* (New York, 2004).

Potter, E.B., *Bull Halsey* (Annapolis, 1985).

Potter, E.B., *Nimitz* (Annapolis, 1976).

Potter, J.D., *Admiral of the Pacific: The Life of Yamamoto* (London, 1965).

Powers, S.T., 'The Battle of Normandy: The Lingering Controversy', *The Journal of Military History*, July 1992, pp. 455–71.

Prados, J., *Combined Fleet Decoded* (New York, 1995).

Prange, G.W., *December 7, 1941: The Day the Japanese Attacked Pearl Harbor* (New York, 1988).

Prange, G.W., *Miracle at Midway* (New York, 1982).

Prange, G.W., *Pearl Harbor: The Verdict of History* (New York, 1986).

Prior, R. and Wlison, T., *The First World War* (London, 2000).

Raus, E., *Panzer Operations: The Eastern Front Memoir of General Raus, 1941–1945* (Cambridge, Mass., 2003).

Read, A. and Fisher, D., *The Fall of Berlin* (London, 1992).

Rees, D., *The Defeat of Japan* (Westport, 1997).

Remy, *The Eighteenth Day: The Tragedy of King Leopold III of Belgium* (New York, 1978).

Richards, D., *Portal of Hungerford* (London, 1977).

Richards, D., *RAF Bomber Command in the Second World War* (London, 2001).

Richards, D. and Saunders, H. St. G., *Royal Air Force,* 1939–1945, i-iii (London, 1953–54).

Ritchie, A., *Faust's Metropolis: A History of Berlin* (London, 1998).

Robinson, T., *Walker, R.N.* (London, 1956).

Roskill, S.W., *The War at Sea,* 1939–1945, i-iii (London, 1954–61).

Rossino, A.B., *Hitler Strikes Poland* (Lawrence, Kansas, 2003).

Rothenberg, G.E., *The Napoleonic Wars* (London, 1999).

Schaffer, R., *Wings of Judgment* (New York, 1985).

Searle, T.R., '"It Made a Lot of Sense to Kill Skilled Workers": The Firebombing of Tokyo in March 1945', *The Journal of Military History*, January 2002, pp. 103–33.

Seaton, A., *The German Army,* 1933–45 (London, 1982).

Seaton, A., *The Russo-German War,* 1941–45 (London, 1971).

Shepardson, D.E., 'The Fall of Berlin and the Rise of a Myth', *The Journal of Military History*, January 1998, pp. 135–53.

Shirer, W.L., *Berlin Diary* (London, 1941).

Showell, J.P.M., *German Naval Code Breakers* (Annapolis, 2003).

Smith, Malcolm, 'The Allied Air Offensive', *The Journal of Strategic Studies*, March 1990, pp. 67–83.

Snow, Edgar, *Scorched Earth* (London, 1941).

Spector, R.H., *Eagle Against the Sun: The American War with Japan* (New York, 1985).

Speer, A., *Inside the Third Reich* (New York, 1970).

Sweetman, J. (ed.), *Great American Naval Battles* (Annapolis, 1998).

Sweetman, J. (ed.), *The Great Admirals* (Annapolis, 1997).

Sword, K. (ed.), *The Soviet Take-Over of the Polish Eastern Provinces,* 1939–41 (London, 1991).

Taylor, Telford, *The March of Conquest* (London, 1959).

Terraine, J., *The Right of the Line* (London, 1985).

Thomas, Hugh, *The Spanish Civil War* (London, 1988).

Trevor-Roper, H.R., *Hitler's Table Talk,* 1941–44 (London, 1973).

Trevor-Roper, H.R. (ed.), *Hitler's War Directives,* 1939–1945 (London, 1964).

Tuchman, B., *Sand Against the Wind: Stilwell and the American Experience in China,* 1911–45 (New York, 1970).

Turney, A.W., *Disaster at Moscow: von Bock's Campaign,* 1941–42 (Albuquerque, New Mexico, 1970).

Ugaki, Matome, *Fading Victory* (Pittsburgh, 1991).

United States Strategic Bombing Survey, *The Effects of Strategic Bombing on the German War Economy* (Washington, 1945).

van Creveld, M., *Supplying War* (Cambridge, 1977).

Wasserstein, B., *Secret War in Shanghai* (London, 1999).

Watt, R.M., *Bitter Glory: Poland and its Fate,* 1918 to 1939 (New York, 1979).

Webster, C. and Frankland, N., *The Strategic Air Offensive Against Germany,* i-iv (London, 1961).

Wegner, B., 'The Road to Defeat: The German Campaigns in Russia, 1941–43', *The Journal of Strategic Studies*, March 1990, pp. 105–27.

Weigley, R.F., *Eisenhower's Lieutenants* (Bloomington, 1981).

Weinberg, G.L., *A World at Arms* (Cambridge, 1994).

Weinberg, G.L., *Germany, Hitler and World War II* (Cambridge, 1995).

Weintraub, S., *The Last Great Victory* (New York, 1995).

Werrell, K.P., *Blankets of Fire* (Washington, 1996).

Willmott, H.P., *Pearl Harbor* (London, 2001).

Willmott, H.P., *The Barrier and the Javelin* (Annapolis, 1983).

Wilson, D., *When Tigers Fight: The Story of the Sino-Japanese War,* 1937–1945 (New York, 1982).

Wilt, A.F., *War From the Top* (Bloomington, 1990).

Yamamoto, Masahiro, *Nanking: Anatomy of an Atrocity* (Westport, 2000).

Young, R.J., *In Command of France* (Cambridge, Mass., 1978).

Zaloga, S. and Madej, V., *The Polish Campaign,* 1939 (New York, 1985).

Zetterling, N., *Normandy,* 1944 (Manitoba, 2000).

List of Illustrations

All illustrations are from the author's collection.

Index

TEMPUS – REVEALING HISTORY

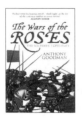
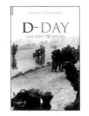

The Wars of the Roses
The Soldiers' Experience
ANTHONY GOODMAN
'Sheds light on the lot of the common soldier as never before' **Alison Weir**
'A meticulous work'
The Times Literary Supplement

£12.99   0 7524 3731 3

D-Day
The First 72 Hours
WILLIAM F. BUCKINGHAM
'A compelling narrative' **The Observer**
A **BBC History Magazine** Book of the Year 2004

£9.99   0 7524 2842 2

English Battlefields
500 Battlefields that Shaped English History
MICHAEL RAYNER
'A painstaking survey of English battlefields… a first-rate book' **Richard Holmes**
'A fascinating and, for all its factual tone, an atmospheric volume' **The Sunday Telegraph**

£18.99   978 07524 4307 2

Trafalgar Captain Durham of the Defiance: The Man who refused to Miss Trafalgar
HILARY RUBINSTEIN
'A sparkling biography of Nelson's luckiest captain' **Andrew Lambert**

£17.99   0 7524 3435 7

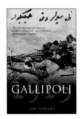
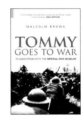

Battle of the Atlantic
MARC MILNER
'The most comprehensive short survey of the U-boat battles' **Sir John Keegan**
'Some events are fortunate in their historian, none more so than the Battle of the Atlantic. Marc Milner is *the* historian of the Atlantic Campaign… a compelling narrative'
Andrew Lambert

£12.99   0 7524 3332 6

Okinawa 1945 The Stalingrad of the Pacific
GEORGE FEIFER
'A great book… Feifer's account of the three sides and their experiences far surpasses most books about war' **Stephen Ambrose**

£17.99   0 7524 3324 5

Gallipoli 1915
TIM TRAVERS
'The most important new history of Gallipoli for forty years… groundbreaking' **Hew Strachan**
'A book of the highest importance to all who would seek to understand the tragedy of the Gallipoli campaign' **The Journal of Military History**

£13.99   0 7524 2972 8

Tommy Goes To War
MALCOLM BROWN
'A remarkably vivid and frank account of the British soldier in the trenches' **Max Arthur**
'The fury, fear, mud, blood, boredom and bravery that made up life on the Western Front are vividly presented and illustrated' **The Sunday Telegraph**

£12.99   0 7524 2980 9

If you are interested in purchasing other books published by Tempus, or in case you have difficulty finding any Tempus books in your local bookshop, you can also place orders directly through our website

www.tempus-publishing.com

Private 12768 Memoir of a Tommy
JOHN JACKSON

'Unique... a beautifully written, strikingly honest account of a young man's experience of combat' *Saul David*

'At last we have John Jackson's intensely personal and heartfelt little book to remind us there was a view of the Great War other than Wilfred Owen's' *The Daily Mail*

£9.99   0 7524 3531 0

The German Offensives of 1918
MARTIN KITCHEN

'A lucid, powerfully driven narrative' *Malcolm Brown*

'Comprehensive and authoritative... first class' *Holger H. Herwig*

£13.99   0 7524 3527 2

Verdun 1916
MALCOLM BROWN

'A haunting book which gets closer than any other to that wasteland marked by death'
Richard Holmes

£9.99   0 7524 2599 4

The Forgotten Front
The East African Campaign 1914–1918
ROSS ANDERSON

'Excellent... fills a yawning gap in the historical record'
The Times Literary Supplement

'Compelling and authoritative'
Hew Strachan

£12.99   978 07524 4126 9

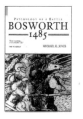

Agincourt
A New History
ANNE CURRY

'A highly distinguished and convincing account'
Christopher Hibbert

'A *tour de force*' *Alison Weir*

'The book on the battle' *Richard Holmes*

A *BBC History Magazine* Book of the Year 2005

£12.99   0 7524 3813 1

The Welsh Wars of Independence
DAVID MOORE

'Beautifully written, subtle and remarkably perceptive'
John Davies

£12.99   978 07524 4128 3

Bosworth 1485 Psychology of a Battle
MICHAEL K. JONES

'Most exciting... a remarkable tale' *The Guardian*

'Insightful and rich study of the Battle of Bosworth... no longer need Richard play the villain' *The Times Literary Supplement*

£12.99   0 7524 2594 3

The Battle of Hastings 1066
M.K. LAWSON

'Blows away many fundamental assumptions about the battle of Hastings... an exciting and indispensable read' *David Bates*

A *BBC History Magazine* Book of the Year 2003

£12.99   978 07524 4177 1

TEMPUS – REVEALING HISTORY

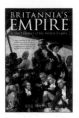

Britannia's Empire
A Short History of the British Empire
BILL NASSON

'Crisp, economical and witty' *TLS*
'An excellent introduction the subject' *THES*

£12.99   0 7524 3808 5

Madmen
A Social History of Madhouses,
Mad-Doctors & Lunatics
ROY PORTER

'Fascinating'
The Observer

£12.99   0 7524 3730 5

Born to be Gay
A History of Homosexuality
WILLIAM NAPHY

'Fascinating' *The Financial Times*
'Excellent' *Gay Times*

£9.99   0 7524 3694 5

William II
Rufus, the Red King
EMMA MASON

'A thoroughly new reappraisal of a much maligned king.
The dramatic story of his life is told with great pace and
insight'
John Gillingham

£25   0 7524 3528 0

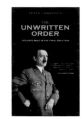

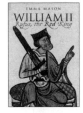

To Kill Rasputin
The Life and Death of Grigori Rasputin
ANDREW COOK

'Andrew Cook is a brilliant investigative historian'
Andrew Roberts
'Astonishing' *The Daily Mail*

£9.99   0 7524 3906 5

The Unwritten Order
Hitler's Role in the Final Solution
PETER LONGERICH

'Compelling' *Richard Evans*
'The finest account to date of the many twists and turns in
Adolf Hitler's anti-semitic obsession' *Richard Overy*

£12.99   0 7524 3328 8

Private 12768
Memoir of a Tommy
JOHN JACKSON
FOREWORD BY HEW STRACHAN

'A refreshing new perspective' *The Sunday Times*
'At last we have John Jackson's intensely personal and
heartfelt little book to remind us there was a view of the
Great War other than Wilfred Owen's' *The Daily Mail*

£9.99   0 7524 3531 0

The Vikings
MAGNUS MAGNUSSON

'Serious, engaging history'
BBC History Magazine

£9.99   0 7524 2699 0

If you are interested in purchasing other books published by Tempus, or in case you have difficulty finding any
Tempus books in your local bookshop, you can also place orders directly through our website
www.tempus-publishing.com

TEMPUS – REVEALING HISTORY

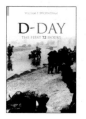

D-Day The First 72 Hours
WILLIAM F. BUCKINGHAM

'A compelling narrative' *The Observer*
A **BBC History Magazine** Book of the Year 2004

£9.99   0 7524 2842 X

The London Monster
Terror on the Streets in 1790
JAN BONDESON

'Gripping' *The Guardian*
'Excellent... monster-mania brought a reign of terror to the ill-lit streets of the capital'
The Independent

£9.99   0 7524 3327 X

London
A Historical Companion
KENNETH PANTON

'A readable and reliable work of reference that deserves a place on every Londoner's bookshelf'
Stephen Inwood

£20   0 7524 3434 9

M: MI5's First Spymaster
ANDREW COOK

'Serious spook history' *Andrew Roberts*
'Groundbreaking' *The Sunday Telegraph*
'Brilliantly researched' *Dame Stella Rimington*

£9.99   978 07524 3949 9

Agincourt
A New History
ANNE CURRY

'A highly distinguished and convincing account'
Christopher Hibbert
'A *tour de force*' *Alison Weir*
'*The* book on the battle' *Richard Holmes*
A **BBC History Magazine** Book of the Year 2005

£12.99   0 7524 3813 1

Battle of the Atlantic
MARC MILNER

'The most comprehensive short survey of the U-boat battles' *Sir John Keegan*
'Some events are fortunate in their historian, none more so than the Battle of the Atlantic. Marc Milner is *the* historian of the Atlantic campaign... a compelling narrative' *Andrew Lambert*

£12.99   0 7524 3332 6

The English Resistance
The Underground War Against the Normans
PETER REX

'An invaluable rehabilitation of an ignored resistance movement' *The Sunday Times*
'Peter Rex's scholarship is remarkable'
The Sunday Express

£12.99   0 7524 3733 X

Elizabeth Wydeville: England's Slandered Queen
ARLENE OKERLUND

'A penetrating, thorough and wholly convincing vindication of this unlucky queen'
Sarah Gristwood
'A gripping tale of lust, loss and tragedy'
Alison Weir
A **BBC History Magazine** Book of the Year 2005

£9.99   978 07524 3807 8

If you are interested in purchasing other books published by Tempus, or in case you have difficulty finding any Tempus books in your local bookshop, you can also place orders directly through our website

www.tempus-publishing.com

TEMPUS – REVEALING HISTORY

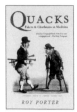

Quacks Fakers and Charlatans in Medicine
ROY PORTER

'A delightful book' *The Daily Telegraph*
'Hugely entertaining' *BBC History Magazine*

£12.99   0 7524 2590 0

The Tudors
RICHARD REX

'Up-to-date, readable and reliable. The best
introduction to England's most important
dynasty' *David Starkey*
'Vivid, entertaining... quite simply the best short
introduction' *Eamon Duffy*
'Told with enviable narrative skill... a delight for
any reader' *THES*

£9.99   0 7524 3333 4

The Kings & Queens of England
MARK ORMROD

'Of the numerous books on the kings and
queens of England, this is the best'
Alison Weir

£9.99   0 7524 2598 6

The Covent Garden Ladies
Pimp General Jack & the Extraordinary Story of Harris's List
HALLIE RUBENHOLD

'Sex toys, porn... forget Ann Summers, Miss
Love was at it 250 years ago' *The Times*
'Compelling' *The Independent on Sunday*
'Marvellous' *Leonie Frieda*
'Filthy' *The Guardian*

£9.99   0 7524 3739 9

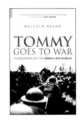

Okinawa 1945
GEORGE FEIFER

'A great book... Feifer's account of the three
sides and their experiences far surpasses most
books about war'
Stephen Ambrose

£17.99   0 7524 3324 5

Tommy Goes To War
MALCOLM BROWN

'A remarkably vivid and frank account of the
British soldier in the trenches'
Max Arthur
'The fury, fear, mud, blood, boredom and
bravery that made up life on the Western Front
are vividly presented and illustrated'
The Sunday Telegraph

£12.99   0 7524 2980 4

Ace of Spies The True Story of Sidney Reilly
ANDREW COOK

'The most definitive biography of the spying
ace yet written... both a compelling narrative
and a myth-shattering *tour de force*'
Simon Sebag Montefiore
'The absolute last word on the subject' *Nigel West*
'Makes poor 007 look like a bit of a wuss'
The Mail on Sunday

£12.99   0 7524 2959 0

Sex Crimes
From Renaissance to Enlightenment
W.M. NAPHY

'Wonderfully scandalous' *Diarmaid MacCulloch*
'A model of pin-sharp scholarship' *The Guardian*

£10.99   0 7524 2977 9

If you are interested in purchasing other books published by Tempus, or in case you have difficulty finding any
Tempus books in your local bookshop, you can also place orders directly through our website

www.tempus-publishing.com